Learn Computer Game Programming with DirectX 7.0

D1557900

Ian Parberry, Ph.D.

Wordware Publishing, Inc.

Library of Congress Cataloging-in-Publication Data

Parberry, Ian
    Learn computer game programming with DirectX 7.0 / by Ian Parberry.
      p.   cm.
    Includes index.
    ISBN 1-55622-741-8 (pbk.)
    1. Computer games--Programming.   2. DirectX.   I. Title.

    QA76.76.C672 P37   2000
    794.8'15268--dc21   00-043491
                                                CIP

ISBN 1-55622-741-8
10 9 8 7 6 5 4 3 2
0007

Product names mentioned are used for identification purposes only and may be trademarks of their respective companies.

All inquiries for volume purchases of this book should be addressed to Wordware Publishing, Inc., at the above address. Telephone inquiries may be made by calling:

(972) 423-0090

Contents

Contents

Contents

Foreword

So, you want to be a game programmer? But how do you get that first gig?

First, you will need a concise and relevant resume listing, along with education and experience, any (repeat any) and all computer skills that are not from the Land That Time Forgot. Next, code samples are an absolute must; approximately three pages of very clean, well-commented code. Finally, you'll need a game demo. Game companies want to know that not only can you cut code, but that you have a passion for games. So dedicated are you to the making of games, that you would program your own game just out of sheer love for the industry. It doesn't matter if the game is a pixelated mess; just show that you made the effort and you have the passion. This goes a long way. Ask around. You'll find that most folks in this biz are not here for the money.

It is essential that you know the right tools for the job, but even more important that you learn those tools by doing a real-world application. To get a programming job in this burgeoning industry, you'll need to know the most common programming tools utilized by the industry. Enter DirectX. Enter *Learn Computer Game Programming with DirectX 7.0* by Dr. Ian Parberry.

There are plenty of programming courses out there, but rare is the one that actually prepares budding software engineers for what it takes to land a job in the gaming industry. Dr. Parberry's smart and innovative program at the University of North Texas is that rare course. Wisely teaming computer science students with computer graphic art students to create a real game demo, Dr. Parberry's unique program provides the skills necessary for a future job.

Now, Dr. Parberry brings his teaching style and expertise out of the classroom and directly to you. If you are serious about doing all that you can to gain entrance into the wonderful world of game programming, then Ian Parberry's *Learn Computer Game Programming with DirectX 7.0* is a must read.

Melanie Cambron, Game Recruiting Goddess
Virtual Search
www.vsearch.com

Preface

I am constantly amazed by the politeness of students in Texas. Not one of the students in my game programming classes has ever, in seven years, asked me the obvious question, which is, "Who are you, and what makes you think that you know anything about game programming?" with its equally obvious corollary, "If you're so good, why aren't you out in the game industry earning the Big Bucks?" The answers to those questions apply to you, the reader, too. Why should you buy a book on game programming from just anybody?

Before I answer, let me digress and tell you how I got into game programming. In 1993 I was going through what in academic circles passes for a midlife crisis. In the business world, the recognized panacea for men who go through midlife crises usually involves a red sports car and a young trophy wife. In academia we rarely have enough money or panache for the red sports car and the trophy wife, but we have coping strategies of our own.

Part of the typical midlife crisis involves questioning who we are and what we are doing in life. The academic midlife crisis sometimes involves questioning the validity of the typical academic lifestyle, which for a computer scientist like myself involves doing research, publishing the results of that research in scientific journals, and getting grants from federal funding agencies to do more research. Oh, and we teach too.

I had a lot of experience doing all of the above. But that "Oh, and we teach too" attitude was beginning to bother me. And the rising pace of the computer industry, the way it was beginning to transform the economy, and *everything* about modern life was beginning to bother me. Actually, it was more the fact that computer science as taught at universities just *didn't get it*, and our students *knew* that it didn't get it. We were beginning to see entering college the crest of what was once called the *Nintendo generation*, the generation of kids for whom computers were a normal fixture of everyday life, as much as a microwave oven or a CD player was to the previous generation. This generation thinks nothing of reformatting their hard

hard drive and installing a new operating system, a process that is *still* beyond the reach of many Ph.D.-bearing professors of computer science. And yet computer science in college was—and mostly still is—being taught much the way it was taught in the 1970s. The excuse that most academics give is that we are teaching "fundamentals," and leave the cutting-edge aspects of computer science to on-the-job training. "Give them a firm foundation of fundamentals," they say, "And the students will be able to learn the tools they need to get a job."

During my midlife crisis, I underwent what is euphemistically called a *paradigm shift*. I changed from being a card-carrying theoretician who always quoted the party line on college education to holding the following belief: While I agree that students need a firm grasp of the fundamentals of computer science, I believe that it is *now no longer enough*. The tools of the trade that they will be using on the job have become too large and too sophisticated, and there are just too many of them to leave it all to "on-the-job-training" (making it Somebody Else's Problem) after college. Students have the right to training in fundamentals, and to have those fundamentals illustrated on at least one real-world application using the same tools and techniques that they will be using in their first job, weeks or days after they graduate.

This poses a challenge for academia. The tools that programmers use change too quickly. Academics don't like to change what they teach, and for good reason. State legislators seem to believe that the average academic is basically lazy, so we are allowed very little time for the preparation of new material. Developing new classes takes time. Computer science professors are typically burned by this already, as they must revamp most of their classes every few years. The prospect of doing this *every semester* is frightening.

Nonetheless, I was coming to the conclusion that *some* of us need to do it. We owe it to our students. I was (and still am) under no illusion that I can change academia by talking and writing papers about the phenomenon. Instead, I chose to lead by example—I would just go ahead and do it. After all, I have tenure, and the concept of *academic freedom*, the freedom of a professor to develop his or her own vision of education, is strong at the University of North Texas.

The question was, what area of computer science should I apply my grandiose scheme to? There are just too many areas to choose from. It should be something new and different, something that captures the imagination of students, territory that is largely untrodden by academic feet. One evening, with these kinds of thoughts on my mind I walked by the General Access Computer Lab on my way out of the building and noticed that the usual group of students playing games was absent. Instead, there was a sign on the wall saying something like "The Playing of Games in the General Access Lab is Banned." This kind of "Dilbert Decision" is one that always annoys me—a rule made by administrators to make their lives easy. The desired result is to make sure that students don't play games when other students are waiting in line for computers to finish their homework assignments, but it is so much easier to ban games altogether than to constantly have to confront students who either by accident or design continue playing into busy periods.

This dislike of arbitrary rules and a general feeling of restlessness drove me to talk to some of these students who seemed addicted to games. After a few minutes' conversation, I quickly learned that, more than playing games, these students wanted to *write their own games*. The problem was, in 1993 there was almost no published material on game programming—almost no books, and no information on the fledgling World Wide Web. That was a *"Eureka!"* moment for me. I had found my niche. With hubris typical of a theoretician, I signed up to teach an experimental course on game programming, with the idea that the students would help me research the area and we would learn together. The course was a wild success, and the rest, as they say, is history. The class became more formal and got its own course code, and now my game laboratory is recognized as one of the premier places in the country to learn game programming.

Since then, I have written and published several games and trained hundreds of students in game programming, the very best of whom have gone on to become successful game programmers in major corporations. I have over 16 years of experience as a professor and seven years of experience in teaching game programming. I know how to teach a class, and I know how to structure a book so that people can actually learn from it. That's who I am, and what makes me think I can write a book on game programming.

As for making Big Bucks, I am doing okay without becoming a full-time member of the computer game industry. The salary for a full professor of computer science at the University of North Texas is pretty good for a non-flagship state university; my salary for the 2000-2001 academic year is projected to be within 8% of the national average for my rank. Still, with the money I make writing games and other cool Windows apps in the three-month summer break, I make a salary that is every bit as good as most of my colleagues in industry. And it would take a great deal of money to replace the buzz I get from what I do.

Acknowledgments

I would like to take this opportunity to thank the talented team of people who worked on this book with me. Although I wrote the text and the code, I had a *lot* of help.

I owe a great debt to Keith Smiley, who designed and created the incredible artwork in *Ned's Turkey Farm*. Good artwork can make the difference between a lame game and a cool one, and Keith's artwork is *excellent*. I would also like to thank Steve Wilson and his wife, Mikayla, for the voice-overs that you will hear once you get to Demo 8 (Chapter 10). Steve also acted as sound engineer on that project, a service he has performed for me on many occasions. (No, they don't normally sound like that.)

My thanks go to Paul Bleisch, a graphics developer who has worked with graphics hardware vendors and game development companies, for checking the manuscript of this book for technical accuracy. His diligence saved me from several *faux pas* and improved the quality of my material substantially. Thanks also to Virginia Holt, a technical writer who read the manuscript for pedagogical soundness. Her suggestions helped make the manuscript a lot more readable than it otherwise would have been.

I am very grateful to Melanie Cambron, the Game Recruiting Goddess from Virtual Search, for writing the foreword to this book. I have been fortunate to have Melanie as a regular guest speaker in my game programming class at the University of North Texas for several years. For some reason, my students will accept what she says about getting a job in the game industry more readily than they will accept what I say. (Go figure.)

I also need to thank a select group of administrators at the University of North Texas: president and chancellor Dr. Albert Hurley; former provost, Blaine Brownell; the former and current dean of the College of Arts and Sciences, Nora Bell and Warren Burggren, respectively; and the former and current chair of the Computer Sciences Department, Paul Fisher and Tom Jacob, respectively. Their support has enabled me to establish and operate my game laboratory and my game programming classes in the face of vocal opposition from many of my colleagues, some of which continues today. Although my activities have generated more than their fair share of controversy, I am privileged to work in an institution of higher education whose administrators are visionary and tolerant of intellectual diversity, and are more protective of academic freedom than many of its faculty. Without the time and facilities to develop my laboratory and my courses, this book would never have been written.

Finally, I should thank generations of my students for poking and prodding at my code until it was halfway decent enough to publish.

To everybody, thank you.

Learn Computer Game Programming with DirectX 7.0

Chapter 1

Here's what you'll learn:

- What this book is all about

- What background knowledge you need

- What DirectX is all about

- How to take best advantage of this book

- How to install the stuff on the CD

- How to set up the Visual C++ 6.0 compiler so you can begin

Read This First

Have I got your attention yet? "Read this First" reminds me of the purchase of my first home computer in the 1980s. It came with no less than seven documents that said "Read This First" in big bold letters at the top of the page and they all threatened dire consequences if I failed to do the things listed on that particular piece of paper *first*. I did my best to follow the instructions, but bad things happened anyway. I suspect that bad things would have happened no matter *what* I did.

Such is *not* the case for this book. Browsing this chapter will, however, help you to get started on the right foot. Feel free to skip it if you are feeling macho enough. I presume that you paid for it to be printed, so it's no skin off my nose.

Are You Reading This in the Bookstore?

Are you reading this while standing in the bookstore trying to decide whether to buy this book? If you are, then this section is written just for you. Sit on the floor for a few minutes while I explain what it's all about and how purchasing this book can help you get your start in the computer game industry. If you are in one of those wonderful bookstores that have plush chairs and actually *encourage* you to sit and browse through the books, you may as well make yourself comfortable instead of skulking in the aisles getting in the way of other customers. A cup of coffee might go down well too. My writing style is highly caffeinated. Just don't spill any on the pages.

I assume that you picked up this book and opened the cover because you are an aspiring game programmer and the title looked appealing, not because you are male and "Melanie Cambron, Game Recruiting Goddess" sounded attractive. Well, maybe a little of both. Let me tell you right now that she is intelligent and very good at what she does, which is find employees for game companies. If you haven't read her foreword already, I recommend that you do it *right now*. It contains sensible advice about getting started in the game industry, *and* a picture of Melanie. Have you done it yet? Good. Now that we've satisfied our curiosity, let's take a more serious look at what this book has to offer.

But first, let me tell you what this book is *not*.

Most DirectX books fall into two categories. Some attempt an encyclopedic coverage of the DirectX API, describing all of the possible permutations of all of the awesome and confusing choices of parameters of almost every DirectX function. You can spot those books by their huge tables listing functions and parameters—tables that often look as though they were cut and pasted directly from the DirectX documentation. This book is *not* like that. It assumes that you are smart enough to look up parameters yourself using the DirectX online help.

The second category of DirectX books gives you a monolithic game engine, essentially a wrapper for the DirectX API that you can use to make a game of your own. They plunk this huge piece of code (thunk) on the table, and then explain how to go about making it work for *you*. It is usually a piece of code that attempts to be all things to all people, and even though it contains more than you need to know to get started, it may not end up being exactly what you need. This book is *not* like that. It assumes that you want to write your own code from the ground up, not customize somebody else's engine.

There is nothing wrong with either of these approaches. I have both kinds of books on my bookshelf. The approach that I take in this book, however, is different. It is the product of seven years of teaching game programming to students of computer science at the University of North Texas. Typically, those students are smart enough to read the documentation that comes with the DirectX SDK, and smart enough to experiment with the code samples. The problem is, all that information is fragmentary and overwhelming in its complexity. There's just so much information that it's hard to know where to begin.

That's where my class comes in. I teach using a series of game demos for a side-scroller called *Ned's Turkey Farm*. Each demo adds a new feature or set of features onto the previous one, much as a real game is developed. Thus, the class is as much about the *process* of coding a game as it is about DirectX.

This book is designed to give you a taste of the same experience without having to come to Texas. Admittedly, you lose out on the other things that my class would give you—including the experience of hanging out in my lab and the opportunity to work on a game demo in a group with other programming and art students, but there's not much I can do about that. I will go through the code function by function, line by line, explaining what I am doing and why I am doing it. There's nothing cut and pasted from the DirectX documentation, and I won't ever assume that you are a dummy or an idiot. If this sounds good to you, then go ahead and buy this book.

What You Need to Know

There are a few things that you need to know before using this book. First, you need to be a competent C++ programmer. If you know C but not C++ yet, you will need to brush up on a few C++ tricks, including the following:

- Classes, with private and public member variables and functions
- Derived classes, protected members
- Function overloading
- Virtual functions
- The operators `new` and `delete`
- Call-by-reference parameters
- Default values for parameters in functions
- Conditional assignment using the `?` operator.

You should be familiar with elementary data structures such as arrays, lists, structures, and pointers. You also need to be familiar with at least one C++ compiler under Windows. The code in this book was developed under Visual C++ 5.0 and 6.0, and I'll be giving instructions for how to compile *Ned's Turkey Farm* using Visual C++ 6.0 later in this chapter.

You don't need to learn Windows API programming to be able to use this book. I will give you enough insight into it to get started. However, it wouldn't hurt to get more information about it from other sources.

DirectX: Who, What, Where, When, How, and Why?

Before we get down to business, let's take a quick look at the who, what, where, when, how, and why of DirectX.

The Who

Who developed DirectX? Microsoft, of course. And who is using it? Almost every company in the business of producing PC games.

The What

What is this thing called DirectX? DirectX is what Microsoft calls an API, an *application programming interface*. It consists of a collection of libraries that you compile into your game. Developers use what is called the DirectX SDK, an acronym that stands for *software developer's kit*. DirectX is an API that allows the programmer direct access to the computer's hardware instead of going through the many layers of slow and clunky Windows API. It consists of many parts. We will be using two of them in this book: DirectDraw (which allows direct access to the graphics hardware) and DirectSound (which allows direct access to the sound hardware). Also of interest to the game developer but beyond the scope of this book are DirectInput (which allows direct access to the input hardware) and DirectPlay (which allows direct access to the networking hardware).

The Where

Where do you get it? Microsoft has always distributed the DirectX SDK free of charge so that game developers will be encouraged to use it. Sometimes it can be downloaded from Microsoft's web page, although Microsoft has been known to disable downloading when traffic gets too high (the DirectX 7.0a SDK download is 125 MB in size). If you don't have access to a fast connection to the Internet, you can purchase a CD from Microsoft's web site for about the price of the media and shipping. Fortunately for you, the DirectX 7.0a SDK is included on the companion CD at the end of this book.

The When

When was it created? The DirectX SDK has a long history, but the most powerful thing about it is that it is constantly updated and improved. The updates often come out several times per year, so odds are that version 7.0a of the SDK will be out of date by the time you read this. However, the two parts of DirectX that we need for this book, DirectDraw and DirectSound, are relatively stable. I don't expect them to change much in the next few years. To forestall any fears that you may have about compiling the code from this book under later versions of DirectX, I will maintain a web site containing updates and supplements to this book, including exactly this type of information. A link to this web site is included in the pdf version of this book, which will be installed with the software from the CD.

The How

How do you use DirectX? Well, that's a large enough subject for a book—or several of them. Funny about that. Read on, MacDuff. (And damn'd be him that first cries, "Hold, enough!")

The Why

Why use DirectX? Because it's important to know about it if you want a job in the game industry, since it's the API that most game companies use. There are other graphics APIs in use, such as Glide and OpenGL, but DirectX is currently the most popular.

Why develop games for Windows? Because it is a large market, and one that is cheap and easy to get into. The Mac and Linux markets are smaller, and the console market usually requires proprietary and expensive hardware and software —and DirectX is now moving into consoles too.

How to Use This Book

Each chapter of this book describes the code to a game demo that was built out of the code from the previous chapter. Here's how to get the most out of this experience. Every chapter begins with a section called "Experiment with Demo xx." It invites you to play with the demo for that chapter, and directs you to experiment with and observe the relevant features. You should go to the Experiment folder in the *Ned's Turkey Farm* software installed from the CD and run the demo by double-clicking on the appropriate icon, for example, `Demo00.exe` for Demo 0.

In the middle of each chapter, you will find a section that lists the code files for the chapter's demo, describing which files are reused from the previous demo, which files have been updated, and which files are new. Play close attention to the list of required library files. If you don't list these in the list of library files that the compiler keeps for your project, you will get linker errors when you try to compile. See the section titled "The Linker Settings" later in this chapter for instructions on how to do this with Visual C++ 6.0.

The last section of each chapter consists of a series of code listings for the new and modified files, although a long file may not be listed if the changes involve only a few lines of code. The body of the chapter proceeds methodically through the code, describing the changes and the new code in detail. The descriptions in the body of the chapter proceed in a logical order, whereas the file listings are in alphabetical order so that you can navigate among them more easily (in the one departure from strict alphabetical ordering, each header file has been printed before the corresponding code file to aid comprehension).

Code is written in a `Courier` font, in contrast to the Roman font used here and elsewhere in the text. Code that has not changed since the previous demo will look like this example, the `CInputManager` constructor from Demo 9.

```
CInputManager::CInputManager(){ //constructor
  InputDevice=KEYBOARD_INPUT; //current input device
  ButtonManager=NULL; //for managing menu buttons
}
```

Code that has changed or been added since the previous demo will be highlighted like this example from Demo 10, in which the last two lines of the `CInput-Manager` constructor are new. (The method of highlighting may look different in the printed version than in the pdf version of this book.)

```
CInputManager::CInputManager(){ //constructor
  InputDevice=KEYBOARD_INPUT; //current input device
```

```
ButtonManager=NULL; //for managing menu buttons
JoystickManager.initialize(); //set up joystick
JoystickManager.autorepeat(FALSE); //disable autorepeat
}
```

It is important that you refer back to the code frequently as you read through the chapter text so that you can see the changes *in the context of the existing code*. I suggest that you do this by reading this book in front of your computer while referring to the code listings at the end of the chapter on the pdf version of this book, which can be installed from the CD. (See the following section for instructions on how to install the CD contents and how to access the pdf version of the text.)

Using the Companion CD

When you install *Ned's Turkey Farm* from the companion CD, it will by default create a folder named Ned's Turkey Farm on the root of your primary drive. You may, during the setup process, direct it to install *Ned's Turkey Farm* into a different folder. However, we will assume in the rest of this chapter that you used the default location. Inside the Ned's Turkey Farm folder you will find the following folders, as depicted in Figure 1.1.

- Demo00 to Demo13: Each of these folders contains one of the demos described in this book. It consists of the complete code, header, image, and sound files for the demo. Each demo corresponds to a chapter. Demo 0 is described in Chapter 2, Demo 1 is described in Chapter 3, etc.

- Experiment: This folder contains the executables for Demos 0 through 13 and a copy of all of the image and sound files. This is where you should come to experiment with each of the demos to see what it does (you are asked to do this at the start of each chapter).

- Pdf: This folder contains an electronic version of this book in Adobe pdf file format. To view it, open the Pdf folder and double-click on Index.html. This will open the index file using your default web browser. There, you will find instructions on how to obtain a free pdf file viewer from the web, links to each of the chapters in pdf format, and some useful web links for more information relating to this book. The page numbering and the page breaks on the pdf version may, however, look different from the print version.

- Sound Test: This folder contains some extra sound samples that will be used to illustrate some of the sound quality issues discussed in Chapter 10.

The *Ned's Turkey Farm* setup program will also place some new entries into your Start menu. To access them, click on the Start button, then select Programs, then Ned's Turkey Farm (see Figure 1.2). You will then see the following options.

- Code: Selecting this will pop up a submenu with fourteen items, named Demo 00 through Demo 13. Selecting Demo 00, for example, will open an Explorer window on the `C:\Ned's Turkey Farm\Demo00` folder so that you can browse the Demo 0 code files.

- Demos: Selecting this will pop up a submenu with 14 items, named Demo 00 through Demo 13. Selecting Demo 00, for example, will run Demo 0.

- Electronic Book: Selecting this will open the electronic version of this book.

- Sound Test: Selecting this will open an Explorer window on the `C:\Ned's Turkey Farm\Sound Test` folder, which is used in Chapter 10.

- Uninstall: Selecting this will open a maintenance window that will allow you to install or uninstall selected components of *Ned's Turkey Farm*, reinstall it, or uninstall it completely. You can also uninstall *Ned's Turkey Farm* using the Add/Remove Programs control in the Control Panel.

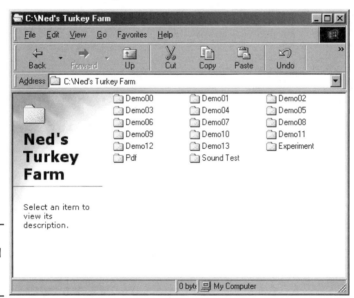

Figure 1.1
Folders installed from the companion CD

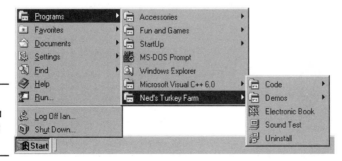

Figure 1.2
The Start menu items for Ned's Turkey Farm

Installing Ned's Turkey Farm

If Autorun is enabled on your computer, simply inserting the CD from this book into your CD-ROM drive will start the *Ned's Turkey Farm* setup. Otherwise, open the CD-ROM drive with Explorer and double-click on the `Setup.exe` icon and follow the instructions that appear. During the installation, you will be asked to choose from three different setup types.

◎ Typical: This setup type will install everything, as shown in Figure 1.1.

◎ Compact: This setup type installs only the executables and media files. You will get only the `Experiment` and `Sound Test` folders shown in Figure 1.1, but neither the code files nor the electronic book. Use this setup type if you plan to run the demos and the sound test in later chapters but do not wish to compile the code or use the electronic version of this book.

◎ Custom: This setup lets you pick exactly which components you want installed. You can install all of the code or just a few demos. You can also choose whether or not to install the executables and the electronic book. If you change your mind later, you can adjust your installation by selecting Uninstall from the Start menu.

Installing the DirectX 7.0a SDK

The last dialog box of the *Ned's Turkey Farm* setup has a check box for installing the DirectX 7.0a SDK (see Figure 1.3). Clicking on the Finish button with that check box checked will begin the installation of the DirectX 7.0a SDK. Should you choose not to install it at this time, you can install it later by opening the `Dx7asdk` folder on the CD-ROM and double-clicking on the `Setup.exe` icon.

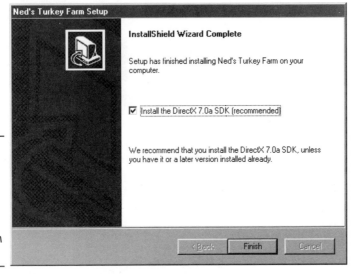

Figure 1.3
Installing the DirectX 7.0a SDK from the Ned's Turkey Farm setup

The rest of this chapter assumes that the DirectX 7.0a SDK has been installed to the default location `C:\mssdk`. If Microsoft changes this default location in later versions of the SDK or you chose to install it in a different location, then you'll just have to wing it.

Some important folders that you'll want to explore after installing the DirectX 7.0a SDK include:

- `C:\mssdk\doc\DirectX7\Word` contains the DirectX documentation in the form of nine MS Word files. This is a very thorough and complete reference set. Although it is not organized in a way that would make it a useful learning tool for beginners, you will find it invaluable once you have absorbed the basics of DirectX programming.

- `C:\mssdk\doc\DirectX7` contains the help file `Directx.chm`. To view this, you will need Explorer 5.0 or higher. I use this so often that I have a shortcut to it on my desktop. You should use it rather than the help file that comes with your compiler because it contains more up-to-date information.

- `C:\mssdk\samples\Multimedia` contains some sample DirectX programs.

Setting up Visual C++ 6.0

Although I assume that you are familiar with using the Visual C++ 6.0 compiler, let me take a few moments to describe how to set it up for use with the code for *Ned's Turkey Farm*. If you are using a different compiler, the details of the setup process will be different, but the issues will be the same. Setup for Visual C++ 5.0 is almost identical, but the exact sequence of dialog boxes will be slightly different. You may also see slightly different menus and dialog boxes depending on which edition of Visual C++ 6.0 you have installed.

Setting the Include and Library Directories

When you install Visual C++ it will come with an old version of the header and library files for DirectX. Naturally, you will want to use the latest version of DirectX, not the one that shipped with your compiler. The following description assumes that you have installed the latest version of the DirectX SDK, which at the time of this writing is 7.0a. If you haven't already done so, refer to the previous section for instructions on installing the SDK from the companion CD. I do recommend, however, that you use the latest version of the SDK that you can find. Information about updates can be found on a web page maintained by the author—see the links at the end of the `Index.html` file in the electronic version of this book.

The first thing that you will need to do is to add the folders from the new SDK to the list of folders from which the compiler gets headers and library files. Select Options from the Tools menu of Visual C++ 6.0. This will display the Options dialog box, from which you should select the Directories tab. Select Include Files from the drop-down menu at upper right. Enter the new folder c:\mssdk\ include in the large pane and make sure that it is listed *before* the default folders as shown in Figure 1.4. Then, select Library Files from the drop-down menu and enter c:\mssdk\lib in the large pane as shown in Figure 1.5. Click OK when you are finished.

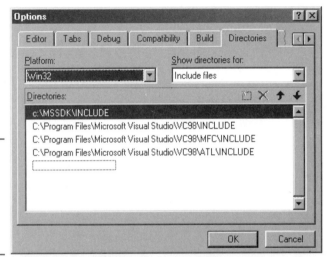

Figure 1.4
Setting the Include directory for the DirectX 7.0 SDK

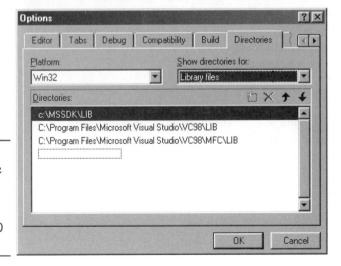

Figure 1.5
Setting the Library directory for the DirectX 7.0 SDK

Creating a Project

The next thing you need to do if you want to modify the code for any of the demo versions of *Ned's Turkey Farm* using Visual C++ 6.0 is create a project. Start by selecting New from the File menu.

Select the Projects tab from the New dialog box that pops up (see Figure 1.6). Select Win32 Application from the large pane on the left. Type a name for the project in the upper of the two edit boxes on the right—we'll use "Demo 0" for this example. Select a location for the project in the Location edit box. We will use `C:\Ned's Turkey Farm\Demo00`, which is the default installation location for the companion CD. (If you opted to have the software installed in a different location, you will just have to browse for it.) Be careful though—Visual C++ thinks it is smarter than you are, and while you are not looking it may try to make the location `C:\Ned's Turkey Farm\Demo00\Demo00`. You should double-check that the location is correct before hitting the OK button.

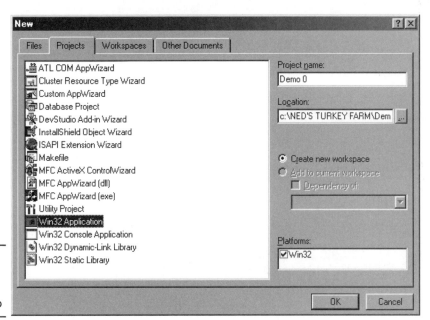

Figure 1.6
Filling out
the New
Projects tab

After clicking OK on the New dialog box, you will see a dialog box with the title Win32 Application—Step 1 of 1. (Nice job, Microsoft.) You should select the radio button for an empty project as shown in Figure 1.7, and then click on the Finish button.

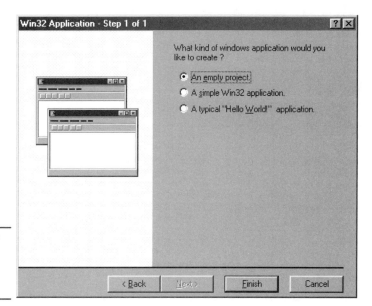

Figure 1.7
Specifying
an empty
project

Next, you will see the New Project Information dialog box (Figure 1.8), in which you should click OK. Now you have a new project with nothing in it.

Figure 1.8
The New
Project
Information
dialog box

Your next step is to add the Demo 0 files to the project. Select Add To Project, then Files from the Project menu as shown in Figure 1.9. You will see the Insert Files into Project dialog box. Select all of the code and header files by clicking on the icons with the left mouse button while holding down the Ctrl key. Once they are all highlighted, as shown in Figure 1.10, click on OK to add them to the project. Now, you are *almost* ready to roll. (If you don't see the code files as depicted in Figure 1.10, it probably means that, as I tried to warn you, Visual C++ 6.0 sneakily created the project in `C:\Ned's Turkey Farm\Demo00\Demo00`. You can either scrap the project and begin again, or copy the code files down from the folder above.)

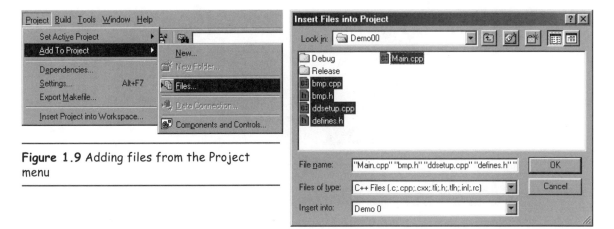

Figure 1.9 Adding files from the Project menu

Figure 1.10 Selecting files to insert into the project

The Linker Settings

In the middle of each chapter there is a section that lists the library files that must be used by the compiler in compiling the corresponding demo. Failure to notify the compiler of this will result in linker errors. Here's how to add Ddraw.lib, the library file for DirectDraw, to the default libraries for your project. Start by selecting Settings from the Project menu.

Next, you will see the Project Settings dialog box. Type Ddraw.lib in the pane for Object/library modules on the Linker tab, as shown in Figure 1.11. (Be sure that the pull-down menu has the General Category selected.) Click on the OK button when this is done. Now you are ready to roll.

Figure 1.11 Inserting Ddraw.lib under the Link tab

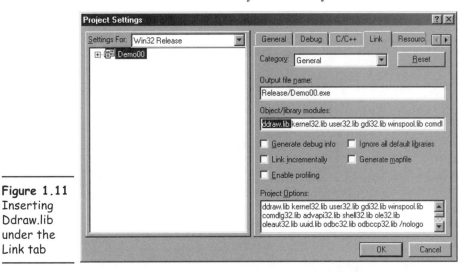

Chapter 2

Here's what you'll learn:

- What's involved in choosing a screen format
- How to write your first Windows API program
- How to implement WinMain and the message pump
- How to handle Windows messages with a window procedure
- How to set up DirectDraw and create a primary surface
- How to set screen resolution
- How to read in and display a background image
- How to exit the program correctly

Displaying the Background

In Demo 0, we learn how to read in an image created by an artist and display it on the screen. Of course, there are many different image file formats, such as gif, jpeg, tiff, bmp, postscript, etc. We are going to use bmp format, for a simple reason: It is native to the Windows API, meaning that the API is set up to make reading bmp files very easy for you. Well... relatively easy compared to the other options.

Demo 0 does something that at first glance looks very simple. It reads in a bmp file called Bckgnd.bmp from disk and displays it on the screen. Then it just sits there until you hit the Escape key (Esc) to exit. The Escape key is the programmer's friend. It is a good idea to make sure that wherever you are in your program—in the middle of a game, in the third level of a series of nested menus, or wherever—you can exit the game by repeatedly hitting the Escape key. You will be running your program thousands of times during development, testing, and debugging, and even a seemingly innocent series of keystrokes and mouse moves can become irritating over time. There is something satisfying about being able to exit your program by closing your eyes and mashing on the Escape key repeatedly to get out safely after your code failed again—for the hundredth time—while debugging, especially at 4 a.m.

There's a lot going on in such a seemingly simple program. It registers a default display window with the operating system, creates the window, initializes DirectDraw, sets the screen resolution to 640x480x8, reads in an image from a file, converts it to an internal format, loads the image to video memory where it will be displayed on your screen, then waits patiently for you to hit the Escape key. When you do, it shuts down DirectDraw, cleans up, resets the display resolution to whatever it was before you ran the program, and shuts down gracefully.

Experiment with Demo 0

Take a moment now to run Demo 0.

- You should see the picture shown in Figure 2.1. Notice that it is displayed in 640x480 resolution, no matter what resolution your desktop is set to by default.

- Hit the Escape key to exit the program. Notice that your desktop is set back to the original resolution.

- Double-click on `Bckgnd.bmp` to fire up the default paint program on your computer (usually Microsoft Paint) to verify to yourself that when you ran Demo 0 you were seeing the image that is stored in that file.

Figure 2.1
Screen shot of
Demo 0

Choosing the Screen Format

Before you even begin coding, you should choose the screen format for your game, specifically, the screen resolution and the number of colors (called the *color depth*). Ideally, your game should run in a number of different formats—high-resolution, high-color formats for people with expensive computers and graphics cards, and low-resolution, low-color formats for people with the bargain basement PCs that you get almost for free when you sign up with an Internet service provider. This is a very important point—there are more people with low-end PCs than high-end ones, and their money is the same color as everybody else's (green). I know that you probably want to make the coolest game possible, and that means you will want to use the latest hardware and display devices to make it look as cool as possible—and there is nothing wrong with that. I am just suggesting that you have some low-power settings for everybody else. Although they have cheap computers, they will have paid as much for your game as people with high-end computers, and so they have a right to expect your game to run. Sure, it may not look as cool, but it ought to look as cool as everything else that they run on their computer, assuming you have done your job correctly.

Here are some of your choices for screen resolution, from low end to high end:

- 640x480, meaning 640 pixels wide, 480 pixels high
- 800x600
- 1024x768
- 1280x960

Here are some of your choices for color depth, from low end to high end:

- 8-bit color, in which each pixel is stored as an 8-bit index into a color table (called a *palette*) of 256 potentially (though not necessarily) distinct 24-bit color values
- 16-bit color, in which each pixel is stored as a 16-bit color value (65,536 colors)
- 24-bit color, in which each pixel is stored as a 24-bit color value (16,777,216 colors)
- 32-bit color, which is really 24-bit color with an unused 8-bit field (actually, it is used in 3D programming for the alpha value, but that is out of the scope of this book)

Although I am not much of an artist, I will say this: For your average picture, 16-bit color is dramatically better than 8-bit color, while 24-bit color is a little better. This is for an *average* picture—I have seen 8-bit color pictures that look every bit as good as a 16-bit color version, and I have seen 24-bit color pictures that are dramatically better than 16-bit color. It depends on the individual picture, and of course, the quality of your artist and his or her art tools.

I have chosen the lowest acceptable screen format for the code demos in this book, 640x480, 8-bit color. Why? Because it saves on disk space, and because 8-bit color is arguably the hardest to program for. The Windows API has some wonderful functions for loading images and displaying them on the user's screen. They will automatically stretch or shrink the image and remap the colors to fit the user's screen resolution and color depth. You would find that converting the code demos in this book to 24-bit color, for example, would be a breeze using these functions. You might even be tempted to let them take care of everything, converting your artwork to 8-bit color if the player has his or her desktop set to 8-bit color. Why not—it is a breeze to the programmer.

Unfortunately, there are two serious drawbacks to doing this. The first is that the Windows API is heartbreakingly slow at remapping colors. This speed problem is particularly bad on a slow machine, and you can be pretty sure that the user who has his desktop set at 256 colors is doing it because he has an old computer with a low-end graphics card and a slow processor. The second problem is that the Windows API is notoriously bad at producing a 256-color image. If left alone to map your 24-bit color file into an 8-bit color image, it will do a commendable job—for a machine. However, to the human eye it will often look terrible. What do you expect? It is only a machine—it knows nothing about art, aesthetics, or even what you wanted it to look like. Worse still, it will have a hankering to meddle with your palette even if you provide your images in 8-bit format. What I will do in this chapter is explain how to deal with 8-bit artwork while telling Windows to keep its hairy hands away from your palette.

I have also chosen to go full screen, that is, to take over the Windows desktop completely. You may also want to run your game inside a normal Windows window if it is appropriate for your style of game. That is more complicated, since it means cooperating with Windows, and we will not be covering that in this book.

It is a good idea to decide on what screen resolutions and color depths you are going to be using *before* you start coding. Make sure your artists have some input into this and understand what is at stake here. You can do some conversions on-the-fly in your code, but it is a good idea to have several versions of the artwork shipped with your program—at least a version in 8-bit color and a version in 24-bit color (Note: there is no 16-bit bmp file format). You might want to consider having a low-resolution and a high-resolution version of the artwork too, since the tools available to the artist will most likely be more sophisticated than the code that you will write, and artists typically will have a better eye for color and detail than you do. To simplify things in this book, we will stick with the one screen resolution and color depth.

Getting Started

We begin by looking at the code in the Demo00 folder. The main source code file is Main.cpp. This file begins with some system includes. The first two includes get us access to the Windows API functions that we need for this program. The third include is the header file for DirectDraw, Ddraw.h.

```
#include <windows.h>
#include <windowsx.h>
#include <ddraw.h>
```

If you forget to include Ddraw.h, the compiler will complain that the DirectDraw functions used in your project have not been declared.

Next, we have a system define that gets us the smallest, fastest version of the API:

```
#define WIN32_LEAN_AND_MEAN
```

Now we are ready for some global declarations. First, there are some DirectDraw things that we will skip over now and come back to later.

```
LPDIRECTDRAW lpDirectDrawObject; //direct draw object
LPDIRECTDRAWSURFACE lpPrimary; //primary surface
LPDIRECTDRAWPALETTE lpPrimaryPalette; //its palette
```

The next declaration is a Boolean variable that we will ensure is set to TRUE whenever our game is the active application (as opposed to it being minimized on the Windows taskbar, for example):

```
BOOL ActiveApp; //is this application active?
```

Finally, the last declaration is our bmp file reader class CBmpFileReader, which we will meet later in Bmp.cpp and Bmp.h. Its job is to read in an image from a bmp file and hold it in memory until it is delivered to DirectDraw to be drawn on the screen.

```
CBmpFileReader background; //background image
```

Next, we have prototypes for two very important functions, WinMain, and the window procedure WindowProc:

```
int WINAPI WinMain(HINSTANCE hInstance,
  HINSTANCE hPrevInstance,LPSTR lpCmdLine,int nCmdShow);
long CALLBACK WindowProc(HWND hwnd,UINT message,
  WPARAM wParam,LPARAM lParam);
```

WinMain is the Windows equivalent of the function main that you may be used to if you are familiar with old-style text processing. This is the operating system's main entry point into your program, that is, where it starts execution when the user runs it. We are interested in only two of WinMain's parameters. The first parameter, hInstance, gives us an instance handle, which is an operating system bookkeeping thing we will need to pass on to other Windows API functions. The last parameter, nCmdShow, will be nonzero if Windows thinks that the window associated with our program should be visible to the user.

The *window procedure* is the operating system's second entry point into your program. Windows is a *message passing* operating system. This means that the operating system will communicate with your program by passing it messages. These messages contain useful information such as user keystrokes, mouse motion, that your program has been minimized, etc. It passes this information to your program by calling your window procedure. I have called it WindowProc in this code, but you are free (within the normal C++ function naming rules) to call it what you like. The first parameter in the window procedure is hwnd, a handle to the window that is to receive the message. This is useful in programs that open several windows on the desktop. For example, it helps you decide which of your

windows received a mouse click, but it is less useful to us because we will open
only one window that will cover the whole screen. The second parameter, `mes-
sage`, tells us what message is being delivered, and the last two parameters,
`wParam` and `lParam`, convey any parameters that the message has. For example,
if the message is a mouse move message, then `lParam` will contain the new
mouse cursor screen coordinates.

WinMain

Skip over the functions in `Demo0.cpp` until you come to `WinMain`. `WinMain`'s
job is to open a window on the desktop, but before it can do that it must register
the window with the operating system and maintain a message pump to deal with
Windows messages. It has these local variables:

```
MSG msg; //current message
HWND hwnd; //handle to fullscreen window
```

Local variable `msg` is used to store the current Windows message in the message
pump. The next local variable, `hwnd`, is used to store a handle to the display window, which the operating system will provide us when we create the window. The
window handle can be passed to various Windows API functions to perform useful
operations on the display window.

The first thing we do is create a default window for our game, which we have
wrapped up in the function `CreateDefaultWindow`, found in `Ddsetup.cpp`.
We pass it a name for our application and the instance handle for our program,
which is given to us by the operating system as parameter `hInstance` to
`WinMain`. It returns a window handle, which we store in `hwnd`.

```
hwnd=CreateDefaultWindow("directX Demo 0",hInstance);
```

The call to `CreateDefaultWindow` actually returns a handle to the created
window only if it was successful. If it fails, it returns `NULL`. In the unlikely event of
this happening, we should bail out of `WinMain`.

```
if(!hwnd)return FALSE;
```

Having created a window, we can go ahead and do some initialization. The next
three function calls use the window handle `hwnd` returned by `CreateDefault-
Window`. We show the window and draw it.

```
ShowWindow(hwnd,nCmdShow); UpdateWindow(hwnd);
```

Next, we set up the input devices, specifically the keyboard and the mouse, using
Windows API function calls. We allow keyboard input.

```
SetFocus(hwnd); //allow input from keyboard
```

We hide the mouse cursor:

```
ShowCursor(FALSE); //hide the cursor
```

Setting the parameter of ShowCursor to TRUE will show the mouse again. Actually, ShowCursor is implemented with a counter, which means that you have to call ShowCursor with parameter TRUE as many times as you called it with FALSE in order to get the mouse cursor to reappear—remember this later when your mouse cursor doesn't reappear when you think it should.

Having cleared everything with the operating system, we are now ready to get down to business. A call to my function InitDirectDraw, which is found in Ddsetup.cpp, attempts to initialize DirectDraw and returns TRUE if it succeeds. We store the return value in a Boolean variable called OK.

```
BOOL OK=InitDirectDraw(hwnd);//initialize DirectDraw
```

If the call to InitDirectDraw succeeded, we attempt to load the image from disk with a call to my function LoadImages, which we will also describe in more detail later. In addition to loading the image from disk, LoadImages also displays the background image to the screen. It returns TRUE if it succeeds, so again we store the return result in OK.

```
if(OK)OK=LoadImages(); //load images from disk
```

If either the InitDirectDraw or LoadImages fails, OK will be FALSE. If this happens, we call the API function DestroyWindow to clean up the window we created, and bail out.

```
if(!OK){ //bail out if initialization failed
  DestroyWindow(hwnd); return FALSE;
}
```

The last thing we have to do in WinMain is to start a message pump:

```
while(TRUE)
  if(PeekMessage(&msg,NULL,0,0,PM_NOREMOVE)){
    if(!GetMessage(&msg,NULL,0,0))return msg.wParam;
    TranslateMessage(&msg); DispatchMessage(&msg);
  }
  else if(!ActiveApp)WaitMessage();
```

The message pump handles the Windows message passing process. If our application is not the active app (the one that Windows is currently focusing on), then ActiveApp will have been set to FALSE elsewhere in the program, and our app will simply wait for messages (most importantly, for the message that makes our app active again). Otherwise it does the Windows default message processing action, which is beyond the scope of this book.

Creating a Full-screen Window

You will recall that `WinMain` uses the function `CreateDefaultWindow`, found in `Ddsetup.cpp`, to set up a default display window. `CreateDefaultWindow` has two parameters, `name`, a string name for our app, and `hInstance`, the instance handle for our program. It begins with the declaration of a local variable `wc`, a structure of type `WNDCLASS`, which we will load with information about the kind of window we want to open. We will pass this structure to the operating system when we open the window.

```
WNDCLASS wc; //window registration info
```

The first thing we do in `WinMain` is fill in various fields in local variable `wc` to describe what kind of window we want to open. The style field is an example of something we will see a lot of: a Windows flag. This is essentially an unsigned integer with a single bit reserved for each property. Here we want to set two of these bits, corresponding to "redraw the screen on horizontal movement or width change," and "redraw the screen on vertical movement or width change." Luckily for us, we don't have to remember which bits to set. The Windows API gives us predefined constants, `CS_HREDRAW` and `CS_VREDRAW`, which are powers of two corresponding to these bit positions. To set both of these bits, simply OR together both of these values using the bitwise-OR operator "|" (not the Boolean OR operator "||").

```
wc.style=CS_HREDRAW|CS_VREDRAW; //style
```

The `lpfnWndProc` field is a pointer to the window procedure, which is `WindowProc` in this example:

```
wc.lpfnWndProc=WindowProc; //window message handler
```

The next two fields are not used in our program and can safely be set to zero:

```
wc.cbClsExtra=wc.cbWndExtra=0;
```

The `hInstance` field must be set to the instance handle for our program, which is given to us as a parameter to `CreateDefaultWindow`:

```
wc.hInstance=hInstance;
```

We can create a custom icon for our program. This is the icon that will show up on the desktop, among other places. But here we will satisfy ourselves with the default application icon.

```
wc.hIcon=LoadIcon(hInstance,IDI_APPLICATION);
```

Similarly, we will use the default arrow mouse cursor:

```
wc.hCursor=LoadCursor(NULL,IDC_ARROW);
```

We can direct the operating system to color the background of the window, but here we will tell it not to bother. We will take care of all drawing ourselves.

```
wc.hbrBackground=NULL;
```

We are not going to be using a menu in this program, so set the menu name field to NULL:

```
wc.lpszMenuName=NULL;
```

Set the class name to the name parameter:

```
wc.lpszClassName=name;
```

Now we register our window with the operating system:

```
RegisterClass(&wc);
```

Having described our window, we can now request that the operating system go ahead and create it using the `CreateWindowEx` API function:

```
hwnd=CreateWindowEx(WS_EX_TOPMOST,name,name,
    WS_POPUP,0,0,GetSystemMetrics(SM_CXSCREEN),
    GetSystemMetrics(SM_CYSCREEN),NULL,NULL,hInstance,NULL);
```

`CreateWindowEx` has 12 parameters. The first parameter to this function is the extended window style, and we use it to specify that the window is a topmost window, that is, it should stay above all nontopmost windows. The second parameter is the class name, which should be the same as that provided in the earlier call to `RegisterClass`. The third parameter is a window name; it really does not matter what we use here. The fourth parameter is the window style, for which we choose a popup window style `WS_POPUP`; again it really does not matter what we use here, since we are going to be running full screen. The fifth and sixth parameters, which are set to zero, are the screen coordinates of the top left corner of the window. The seventh and eighth parameters are the width and height of the window, which we set to the screen height and width, ascertained by calls to the API function `GetSystemMetrics`. The ninth parameter is a handle to the parent window, which can be NULL since we specified the `WS_POPUP` style. The 10th parameter is a handle to the menu, which is NULL again since we are not using a menu. The 11th parameter is the instance handle, and we are not using the 12th and last parameter, so we can set it to NULL.

Setting Up DirectDraw

Setting up DirectDraw takes several steps. We will declare a set of global variables to give easy access to the various parts of DirectDraw that we will be using. Then, we need to set up a DirectDraw object, a primary surface, and a palette.

Declarations

Now we can get back to those global variables that we promised we would return to later. First, we need a *DirectDraw object*, which is an object that will manage the video hardware for us. We reserve space for a pointer to the DirectDraw object, and will create it later.

```
LPDIRECTDRAW lpDirectDrawObject; //direct draw object
```

Second, we will need a *primary surface*. A *surface* is the DirectDraw term for an object used to store an image. Modern video cards carry large amounts of memory that allow us to store several images in video memory, but only one of these—the primary surface—will be displayed at any given time. The primary surface, then, is a surface that is stored in video memory on the video card and contains the image that is currently displayed on the monitor. Again, we reserve space for a pointer to the primary surface, which is to be created later.

```
LPDIRECTDRAWSURFACE lpPrimary; //primary surface
```

Third, since we are going to be in 8-bit color, we are going to need a palette for the primary surface:

```
LPDIRECTDRAWPALETTE lpPrimaryPalette; //its palette
```

The DirectDraw Object

I have encapsulated the DirectDraw initialization into a function called InitDirectDraw, found in Ddsetup.cpp. This function takes a window handle as a parameter, and returns TRUE if it succeeds.

```
BOOL InitDirectDraw(HWND hwnd){ //direct draw initialization
```

The first thing it does is create a DirectDraw object and place a pointer to it in the global variable lpDirectDrawObject. We need to save a pointer to it because the DirectDraw object is a video hardware manager—once created it takes control of the video hardware from the operating system, and we will then be able to ask it to perform various video hardware oriented tasks for us; we ask it by calling the relevant member function of the DirectDraw object. The DirectDraw object is created by calling the DirectDraw function DirectDrawCreate. This function takes three parameters, the first of which should be NULL, and the last of which *must* be NULL. The second parameter is the address where you would like

DirectDraw to put a pointer to the DirectDraw object after it is created. `DirectDrawCreate` will return `DD_OK` if it succeeds; if it fails we will bail out and return `FALSE`. Rather than checking the return value of `DirectDraw-Create` against `DD_OK`, it is slightly more readable to make use of the Windows API macros `SUCCEEDED` and `FAILED`.

```
if(FAILED(DirectDrawCreate(NULL,&lpDirectDrawObject,NULL)))
  return FALSE;
```

The DirectDraw object is a powerful tool, so powerful that we can take control of the video hardware away from the operating system. The next thing we have to do is specify how much of this power we will use, that is, to what extent we will share the video hardware with the operating system, and through it, with other applications. This is done with the DirectDraw object's `SetCooperativeLevel` member function. The first parameter to this function is a window handle, and the second parameter is a flag word that contains one bit for each of several properties. Simply set the corresponding bits by performing a logical OR of the predefined constants for each property. We will be asking for exclusive mode, meaning that we will not share the video hardware, and fullscreen mode, meaning we will take over the whole desktop. We get this set of properties by ORing together the two values `DDSCL_EXCLUSIVE` and `DDSCL_FULLSCREEN`. `SetCooperativeLevel` returns `DD_OK` if it succeeds, and we bail if it fails. (For that matter, all of the DirectDraw functions used in the rest of this section return `DD_OK` if they succeed, and we bail out if any one of them fails—so I won't mention it again.)

```
if(FAILED(lpDirectDrawObject->SetCooperativeLevel(hwnd,
DDSCL_EXCLUSIVE|DDSCL_FULLSCREEN)))
    return FALSE;
```

Now we have complete control of the screen. The first thing we do with this control is change screen resolution using the `SetDisplayMode` member function of the DirectDraw object. This function takes three parameters, from left to right, the screen width, screen height, and color depth. We will use constants `SCREEN_WIDTH`, `SCREEN_HEIGHT`, and `COLOR_DEPTH` defined in `Defines.h`. Note that the parameters have to correspond to some sensible values corresponding to some hardware supported video mode, such as 640x480, 800x600, 1024x768, etc., with 8-, 16-, 24-, or 32-bit color.

```
if(FAILED(lpDirectDrawObject->
SetDisplayMode(SCREEN_WIDTH,SCREEN_HEIGHT,COLOR_DEPTH)))
    return FALSE;
```

The Primary Surface

Now we create the primary surface. We should do this only after the display mode has been set, since the primary surface will automatically be created to be the same size and color depth as the display mode. DirectDraw will let you create surfaces of many different sizes and flavors. This is done using the DirectDraw object's `CreateSurface` member function, the first parameter of which is a *DirectDraw surface descriptor*, which is a structure that describes the type of surface to be created. First, we declare a local DirectDraw surface descriptor.

```
DDSURFACEDESC ddsd; //direct draw surface descriptor
```

Then we fill in the relevant fields. Like many Windows structures, it has a size field that *must* be set to the size of the structure:

```
ddsd.dwSize=sizeof(ddsd);
```

A second feature common to this type of structure is the flags field. Since the structure has many fields that may or may not be used, for speed we can specify exactly which of the fields contain sensible values; the rest can be skipped over and ignored by `CreateSurface`. As always, this is performed by doing a logical OR of the relevant predefined constants, which can be found in the DirectX help files. In this instance it is easy, as we will be using only one field, the capabilities field. We set the `dwFlags` field of `ddsd` accordingly.

```
ddsd.dwFlags=DDSD_CAPS;
```

Now, we set the capabilities field to indicate that this will be the primary surface:

```
ddsd.ddsCaps.dwCaps=DDSCAPS_PRIMARYSURFACE;
```

Now we can pass the DirectDraw surface descriptor containing the specifications for the primary surface as the first parameter to the `CreateSurface` member function of the DirectDraw object. The second parameter is the address of a pointer that we will use later to access the primary surface; after all, we will need to draw an image there so it can be displayed on the video screen. The third parameter must be set to `NULL`.

```
if(FAILED(lpDirectDrawObject->
CreateSurface(&ddsd,&lpPrimary,NULL)))
   return FALSE;
```

The Palette

Having created the primary surface, we attach a palette to it using my `Create-Palette` function (to be described in more detail in a moment), and save a pointer to it so that we can load color values later:

```
lpPrimaryPalette=CreatePalette(lpPrimary);
```

If we get to this point in the code we can assume that DirectDraw initialization has succeeded, and so we

```
return TRUE;
```

My `CreatePalette` function, also found in `Ddsetup.cpp`, will create a DirectDraw palette, set every color entry in the palette to black, attach that palette to the surface given to it as a parameter, and return a pointer to the palette:

```
LPDIRECTDRAWPALETTE CreatePalette(LPDIRECTDRAWSURFACE surface){
```

The function has two local variables: a `PALETTEENTRY` array `pe` that we will use to set the initial colors in the DirectDraw palette, and a pointer that we will use to point to the DirectDraw palette that we create. The `PALETTEENTRY` array has 256 entries, which is specified using the constant `COLORS` defined in `Defines.h`.

```
PALETTEENTRY pe[COLORS]; //new palette
LPDIRECTDRAWPALETTE lpDDPalette; //direct draw palette
```

We start by setting each color in `pe` to black:

```
for(int i=0; i<COLORS; i++)
  pe[i].peRed=pe[i].peGreen=pe[i].peBlue=0;
```

Then we use the `CreatePalette` member function of the DirectDraw object to create the palette. The first parameter specifies that we want 8-bit color, and the second is the address of a pointer to the new palette. The third parameter must be `NULL`.

```
if(FAILED(lpDirectDrawObject->
CreatePalette(DDPCAPS_8BIT,pe,&lpDDPalette,NULL)))
  return NULL;
```

Having created the DirectDraw palette and gotten a pointer to it in the local variable `lpDDPalette`, we now attach the palette to the surface that was specified as the parameter to my `CreatePalette` function, using the surface's `SetPalette` member function:

```
surface->SetPalette(lpDDPalette);
```

Finally, we return a pointer to the newly created DirectDraw palette:

```
return lpDDPalette;
```

Loading Graphics

The graphics images are loaded by my `LoadImages` function. All of the real work is going to be done by a global `CBmpFileReader` class object, which we will describe in more detail later. For now, let's just look at how the object is used. There is only one image to be loaded, a file named `Bckgnd.bmp`. We load it from disk into the global `CBmpFileReader` class object `background`, and bail out if the load fails.

```
if(!background.load("bckgnd.bmp")) //read from file
  return FALSE; //read failed
```

The load operation got us the image data and the palette. We first load the palette to the primary surface palette. Recall that we kept a pointer to that palette in the global variable `lpPrimaryPalette`.

```
if(!background.setpalette(lpPrimaryPalette)) //set palette
   return FALSE; //set palette failed
```

Having done that, we load the image to the primary surface. Note that we load the palette, then load the image to the primary surface in that order. Note that if we already had an image that uses a different palette drawn to the primary surface (we didn't—all we had was black, but just suppose for a moment that we did), then there would have been a small amount of time during which we had the old image drawn with the new palette, which would make it look pretty awful, depending on how different the palettes were. Doing it the other way would display the new image in the old palette, which would look just as bad. However, loading a palette means moving 256 color entries of 3 bytes each, for a total of 768 bytes. Loading a 640x480 image means moving 307,968 bytes—more than 400 times as much data. Which would be faster? Doesn't it make more sense to have things looking bad while we are loading a small palette than have things looking bad for longer while we draw a large image? That is why we load the palette first, then draw the image.

```
if(!background.draw(lpPrimary)) //draw to surface
   return FALSE; //draw failed
```

If all is well, we should now see the image displayed on the screen using the correct palette, so we can

```
return TRUE; //all steps succeeded
```

The Window Procedure

The window procedure `WindowProc` is the function that is called by the operating system whenever a message is to be passed to your program. You'll find it in `Main.cpp`. It has four parameters, which are set by the operating system. The first is the handle of the window to which the message is being sent, which is important if your application has more than one window; ours does not, so we will pretty much ignore it. The second is an unsigned integer encoding of the message. Fortunately for us, the Windows API has predefined constants for these messages, including, for example, `WM_KEYDOWN` for the message sent when the player hits a key on the keyboard. The last two function parameters carry the parameters of the message, which differ from message to message. For example, for the `WM_KEYDOWN` message, the third parameter to `WindowProc` is set to a value that encodes the actual key that was hit.

```
long CALLBACK WindowProc(HWND hwnd,UINT message,
                    WPARAM wParam,LPARAM lParam){
```

The body of `WindowProc` is a simple switch statement that specifies the action to be taken for each message. We begin with five simple cases. The first is `WM_ACTIVATEAPP`, which is sent whenever our application becomes the active application or becomes inactive; `wParam` will be `TRUE` in the first case, and `FALSE` in the latter. We will record this in the global variable `ActiveApp`.

```
case WM_ACTIVATEAPP: ActiveApp=wParam; break;
```

The second case is `WM_CREATE`, which is sent when the `CreateWindowEx` function called from our function `CreateDefaultWindow` (found in `Ddsetup.cpp`) creates the window for our application. This is where we can do initialization that should take place immediately after the window has actually been created. We will do nothing, but it is good practice to include this for later.

```
case WM_CREATE: break;
```

The third case is `WM_KEYDOWN`, which is sent when a keyboard key goes down. We notify a keyboard handler function to take care of it (we'll come back to this at the end of this section).

```
case WM_KEYDOWN: //keyboard hit
  if(keyboard_handler(wParam))DestroyWindow(hwnd);
  break;
```

The fourth case is `WM_DESTROY`, which is our signal to shut down the game. The DirectDraw object and the DirectDraw surfaces are Windows COM objects, which for the purposes of this book means that they are just like C++ classes except for the fact that they don't have constructors and destructors. Instead of a destructor, they have a function `Release` which we must call explicitly on shutdown. Every surface we create must be released, and it must be released *before* we release the DirectDraw object. So, when exiting the game, we release the primary surface, then release the DirectDraw object. After the DirectDraw object has been released, we show the mouse cursor. The last thing that we must do when shutting down is call the Windows API function `PostQuitMessage` to indicate to the operating system that our program is ready to quit.

```
case WM_DESTROY: //end of game
  if(lpDirectDrawObject!=NULL){ //if DD object exists
    if(lpPrimary!=NULL) //if primary surface exists
      lpPrimary->Release(); //release primary surface
    lpDirectDrawObject->Release(); //release DD object
  }
  ShowCursor(TRUE); //show the mouse cursor
  PostQuitMessage(0); //and exit
  break;
```

Finally, we have a handler for all of the other messages; we just pass them back to the operating system using the Windows API function `DefWindowProc`:

```
default: //default window procedure
  return DefWindowProc(hwnd,message,wParam,lParam);
} //switch(message)
```

Finally, we return zero and exit from the window procedure.

For convenience, we moved the keyboard handler into a separate function in Main.cpp rather than just put the code in the switch statement in the window procedure. As you might image, this function will become *much* more complicated as our game develops. We pass the keyboard handler the wParam parameter that was given to the window procedure as an argument to the WM_KEYDOWN message. If an alphabetic or numeric key went down, wParam contains the ASCII code of that key. For example, if it was the "A" key, then wParam contains 'A'. There is a set of predefined constants called *virtual key codes* for the rest of the keys. We will check to see whether wParam is the Esc key by comparing wParam to VK_ESCAPE. We'll have the keyboard handler return TRUE if this happens.

```
BOOL keyboard_handler(WPARAM keystroke){ //keyboard handler
  BOOL result=FALSE; //return TRUE if game is to end
  switch(keystroke){
    case VK_ESCAPE: result=TRUE; break; //exit game
  }
  return result;
} //keyboard_handler
```

The Bmp File Reader

The bmp file reader class CBmpFileReader will input bmp files and store them in an internal format ready to be drawn to a DirectDraw surface. We will keep this internal format image around even after it has been drawn to a surface because all surfaces are prone to *surface loss*, which is as catastrophic as it sounds. It means that the memory that has been allocated to your surface, along with the image in that memory, has been taken away from you by the operating system or the video hardware. After surface loss, we will need to restore all of the surfaces and redraw what was on them. Why not reload the images from disk when surfaces need to be restored? Well we could, but that would take longer than keeping them in memory. But won't that waste memory? Well, the Windows memory manager will swap them out of real memory onto virtual memory on disk if real memory is low, because it automatically pages out memory that is not being accessed often. But isn't reloading paged-out memory on disk just as slow as reloading the image? At worst it is no slower, and at best the image won't be on disk at all, and we will have a real speed win. So, it is to our advantage to just leave a copy of each image in a CBmpFileReader class instance and just let Windows manage resources for us.

Palettized Art

As you may recall, we're going to be using fixed-palette, 256-color artwork. That means that we can use up to 256 different colors, with each color described using 24 bits. The palette is specified as a color table with 256 entries, each entry being 3 bytes long, for a total of 768 bytes. The 3 bytes for each color is used as follows: one byte for the intensity of red, one byte for green, and one byte for blue, in that order. Black has zero intensity in all three colors, which we will express as having an *RGB value* of (0,0,0). White has full intensity in all three colors, that is, an RGB value of (255,255,255).

The best way of thinking of palettized art is to think of it as a paint-by-numbers set. Once the 256 colors in the palette have been specified, we can list the pixels in the image in row-major order using one byte for each pixel to specify which of the 256 palette positions is used to paint that pixel. The image in file Bckgnd.bmp is shown in Figure 2.2 next to its palette of 256 colors arranged in 16 rows of 16 colors. Palette position 0, which is filled with a shade of dark red, is at the top-left corner of the palette as it is drawn in that figure. Palette position 255, which is filled with an obnoxious shade of pink (technically called magenta) with an RGB value of (255,0,255), is at the lower-right corner. The palette entries in between are drawn in row-major order in Figure 2.2.

Figure 2.2
Bckgnd.bmp
(left) and its
palette
(right).

While each palette entry can potentially hold a different color, it doesn't have to; we could have several palette entries containing the same 24-bit color. If we change the color in one of the palette entries, then all of the pixels that are drawn using that palette index are changed too. For example, Figure 2.3 shows Bckgnd.bmp with color number 73 changed from off-white with an RGB value of (244,243,254) in Figure 2.2 to black. We can see that palette position 73 (indicated by the large arrow in Figure 2.3) was used to draw many of the pixels in the clouds, the ones that have turned black.

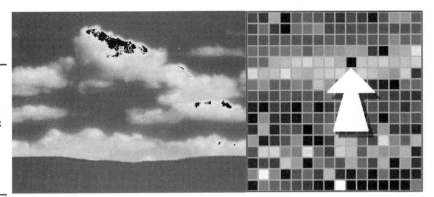

Figure 2.3
Bckgnd.bmp
from Figure
2.2 with one
palette
entry
changed to
black

The Bmp File Format

The bmp file format that we will be using is as follows (see Figure 2.4). First, there is a file header, then an info header. The info header contains useful information such as the width, height, and color depth of the image. Then there are 768 bytes of palette, listed as 256 24-bit RGB values. Lastly, the image data is listed, one byte for each pixel, using 640x480=307,200 bytes of image data in `Bckgnd.bmp`. Although this is not important in Demo 0, there's a subtlety that you should remember if you want to read bmp files of nonstandard sizes—the rows of the image are rounded up in size to the next multiple of 4, so that, for example, an image that is 21 pixels wide and 10 pixels high will use 24x10=240 bytes of image data, not 21x10=210 bytes as you might expect.

There is one other subtlety about bmp files—they are stored upside-down. That is, the order of the rows is reversed. The first row of the image is actually where you would expect the *last* row to be stored (see Figure 2.5).

File Header
File Info
Palette (256 entries each 3 bytes long)
Image (Indices into palette, one byte per pixel)

Figure 2.4
The bmp file
format

Figure 2.5
How the
image is
stored in a
bmp file

Last row	Filler
. . .	Filler
Second row	Filler
First row	Filler

Bmp File Reader Overview

The header file for CBmpFileReader is Bmp.h. It starts with a small set of includes for the Windows API and DirectDraw, and our defines file Defines.h.

```
#include <windows.h>
#include <windowsx.h>
#include <ddraw.h>

#include "defines.h"
```

Notice that the entire file is bracketed by an ifndef. This is just to keep the compiler happy. We will be including our header files in many different code files, which will cause the compiler to complain the second time it sees the definition of CBmpFileReader. To prevent this, we define a unique symbol __bmp_h__ the first time the compiler sees Bmp.h, and prevent the compiler from seeing it again by placing an #ifndef of the same symbol in front of everything. I usually use the name of the file with the period replaced by an underscore, with two underscores in front of and two underscores behind the name, just to make sure it is unique. If you let Visual C++ create the file for you, it will do the same thing using a very long, very obscure string that it creates automatically.

```
#ifndef __bmp_h__
#define __bmp_h__
   . . .
#endif
```

CBmpFileReader has four protected member variables—they could be private, but I have chosen to make them protected because we will be deriving a new class from CBmpFileReader in Chapter 5. They are, respectively, the file header, the file info, the palette, and the image data. Note that we know ahead of time that the palette will be 768 bytes long, whereas the size of image data will depend on the file width and height. The bmp file reader class is designed to read in files of any size, not just 640x480, so we will declare the image data to simply be a pointer to BYTE data, and we will allocate enough memory later when we know the image resolution.

```
BITMAPFILEHEADER m_BMPFileHead; //bmp header
BITMAPINFOHEADER m_BMPFileInfo; //bmp file information
RGBQUAD m_rgbPalette[COLORS]; //the palette
BYTE *m_cImage; //the image
```

CBmpFileReader has five public member functions, starting with a constructor and a destructor:

```
CBmpFileReader(); //constructor
~CBmpFileReader(); //destructor
```

Function `load` is given a filename, and loads the bmp file with that name into the protected member variables, returning TRUE if it succeeds:

```
BOOL load(char *filename); //load from file
```

Function `draw` will draw the image pointed to by private member variable `m_cImage` to a DirectDraw surface:

```
BOOL draw(LPDIRECTDRAWSURFACE surface); //draw image
```

Function `setpalette` will load a palette from private member variable `m_rgbPalette` to a DirectDraw palette:

```
BOOL setpalette(LPDIRECTDRAWPALETTE palette); //set palette
```

The code file for `CBmpFileReader` is `Bmp.cpp`. The constructor sets the image pointer `m_cImage` to zero. The destructor deletes the memory pointed to by `m_cImage`. Note that if no memory has been allocated for the image, the destructor still does not crash, since the C++ `delete` operation will do nothing to a zero pointer. If, however, we had failed to initialize `m_cImage` in the constructor, and accidentally deleted it before assigning any memory to it, we might find ourselves garbage-collecting part of our program (or even the operating system) code, leading to a messy crash. We assume, however, that in the normal course of events memory has been allocated to `m_cImage`, which then is garbage-collected by the destructor. Note also the use of `delete[]`, which deletes a whole array of BYTEs, instead of plain `delete`, which would delete only the first BYTE pointed to by `m_cImage`.

```
CBmpFileReader::CBmpFileReader(){ //constructor
m_cImage=0; //memory not yet allocated
}

CBmpFileReader::~CBmpFileReader(){ //destructor
  delete[]m_cImage; //reclaim memory from image data
}
```

Loading Bmp Files

The `CBmpFileReader` `load` function begins with four local variables: a handle `hfile` to the input file, two counters `actualRead` (the number of bytes actually read) and `image_size` (the size of the image part of the bmp file, that is, the image width times the image height), and a helper Boolean called `OK` that we will use for the return value of the function, keeping set to TRUE as long as no error has yet occurred:

```
HANDLE hfile; //input file handle
DWORD actualRead; //number of bytes actually read
int image_size; //size of image (width*height)
BOOL OK=TRUE; //no error has occurred yet
```

We open the file for reading using the Windows API function `CreateFile`, bailing out if the open failed:

```
hfile=CreateFile(filename,GENERIC_READ,FILE_SHARE_READ,
  (LPSECURITY_ATTRIBUTES)NULL,OPEN_EXISTING,
  FILE_ATTRIBUTE_NORMAL,(HANDLE)NULL);
if(hfile==INVALID_HANDLE_VALUE)return FALSE;
```

We then read the file header and the file info. You will notice that I carefully have not said how large the file info and the file header are. That's because we don't really need to know. The Windows structures `BITMAPFILEHEADER` and `BITMAPINFOHEADER` are exactly the right size, so we'll just read in `sizeof(m_BMFileHead)` and `sizeof(m_BMPFileInfo)` bytes, respectively, using the Windows API function `ReadFile`.

```
OK=ReadFile(hfile,&m_BMPFileHead,sizeof(m_BMPFileHead),
  &actualRead,NULL);
if(OK)OK=ReadFile(hfile,&m_BMPFileInfo,
  sizeof(m_BMPFileInfo),&actualRead,NULL);
```

We immediately put the file info to good use by verifying that the file is a 256-color (8-bit color) file:

```
if(OK)OK=m_BMPFileInfo.biBitCount==COLOR_DEPTH;
```

We read the palette:

```
if(OK)OK=ReadFile(hfile,m_rgbPalette,sizeof(m_rgbPalette),
  &actualRead,NULL);
```

At this point, we bail out if something went wrong, before we allocate any memory for the image:

```
if(!OK){CloseHandle(hfile); return FALSE;}
```

We calculate the image size from information in the file info structure:

```
image_size=m_BMPFileInfo.biWidth*m_BMPFileInfo.biHeight;
```

We allocate memory for the image, carefully deleting any that has already been allocated, thinking ahead that someday someone may want to reuse a `CBmpFileReader` class instance to read in several bmp files. We bail out if the memory allocation fails.

```
if(m_cImage)delete[]m_cImage; //dispose of any old space
m_cImage=new BYTE[image_size]; //allocate new space
if(!m_cImage){ //bail if alloc failed
  CloseHandle(hfile); return FALSE;
}
```

Recall that I mentioned that rows of a bmp image are rounded up in size to the next multiple of 4. The width that we read from the file into m_BMPFileInfo.

`biWidth` is the expected width of the image (which may not be a multiple of 4), not the padded width found in the image data in the file (which *is* a multiple of 4). We can round it up to the next multiple of 4 using the following slightly obscure line of C++ code.

```
int width=(m_BMPFileInfo.biWidth+3)&~3;
```

Here's how it works: ~3 is the bitwise complement of 3, that is, a word with all ones except for the least significant 2 bits, which are zero. (OK, so I'm forgetting the sign bit... so don't use this code to read in huge bmp files.) So, performing a bitwise & of any number with ~3 will set its least significant 2 bits to zeros, which is the same as rounding it down to the next lower multiple of 4. Therefore, taking `m_BMPFileInfo.biWidth`, adding 3, then performing a bitwise & of it with ~3 will round it up to the next multiple of 4. To convince yourself of this last step of my reasoning, consider the four possible remainders when `m_BMPFile-Info.biWidth` is divided by 4, and recall that &~3 rounds down to the next lowest multiple of 4, which implies that:

```
4i&~3=(4i+1)&~3=(4i+2)&~3=(4i+3)&~3=4i.
```

Case 1: `m_BMPFileInfo.biWidth=4i`. Then, `width=(4i+3)&~3=4i`.

Case 2: `m_BMPFileInfo.biWidth=4i+1`. Then, `width=(4i+4)&~3=(4(i+1))&~3=4(i+1)`.

Case 3: `m_BMPFileInfo.biWidth=4i+2`. Then, `width=(4i+5)&~3=(4(i+1)+1)&~3=4(i+1)`.

Case 4: `m_BMPFileInfo.biWidth=4i+3`. Then `width=(4i+6)&~3=(4(i+1)+2)&~3=4(i+1)`.

In all four cases, `width` gets set to the smallest multiple of 4 that is greater than or equal to `m_BMPFileInfo.biWidth`, as required.

We declare a line counter, and 4 bytes in which to hold the (at most) 4 bytes of filler at the end of each row of pixels in the image data:

```
int i=0; //counter
BYTE trash[4]; //to hold the trash at the end of each line
```

Then, we compute the number of filler bytes at the end of each row, which will be a number between 0 and 3, inclusive:

```
int remainder=width-m_BMPFileInfo.biWidth; //width of trash
```

We use `i` to count the number of rows, reading one row per iteration of a `while` loop, bailing out of the loop if any of the reads fail. We use two calls to the API function `ReadFile`, first reading the real data, then the filler (if any) at the end of the row.

```
while(OK&&i<m_BMPFileInfo.biHeight){
  //read data
  OK=OK&&ReadFile(hfile,
    (BYTE*)(m_cImage+i*m_BMPFileInfo.biWidth),
    m_BMPFileInfo.biWidth,&actualRead,NULL);
  //read trash at end of line
  OK=OK&&ReadFile(hfile,trash,remainder,&actualRead,NULL);
  i++; //next line
}
```

If the read failed, we clean up, close the file handle, and exit:

```
if(!OK)delete[]m_cImage; //clean up if failed
//close up and exit
CloseHandle(hfile);
return OK;
```

Drawing to a Surface

The `CBmpFileReader draw` function draws the image from the member variable m_cImage to a DirectDraw surface. It has a single parameter, a pointer to a DirectDraw surface called `surface`. It begins with four local variables, first a DirectDraw surface descriptor that we will use to get information about the surface pointed to by `surface`.

```
DDSURFACEDESC ddsd; //direct draw surface descriptor
```

Next, we declare a pair of source and destination pointers that we will use to move byte data from m_cImage to `surface`:

```
BYTE *dest,*src; //destination and source pointers
```

Finally, we declare a variable to hold the width of the image in m_cImage:

```
int src_width; //width of source
```

We prepare the surface descriptor by filling it with zeros, and setting its size field to its size:

```
memset(&ddsd,0,sizeof(DDSURFACEDESC));
ddsd.dwSize=sizeof(ddsd);
```

We need to get access to the portion of the DirectDraw surface that contains the byte data for the image. While we load our image to that location, we have to ensure that nothing else accesses that memory. This is done by *locking down* the surface. Locking down a surface is potentially time-consuming, so we lock it only when we need to and unlock it as soon as we are able. Surfaces are locked and unlocked using their `Lock` and `Unlock` member functions. The call to `Lock` has four parameters. The first parameter can be set to a pointer to a rectangle within the surface that we wish to lock down; setting it to `NULL` will lock down the entire surface. The second parameter is a pointer to our DirectDraw surface descriptor, which will receive useful information about surface. The third parameter is a flag word, which we will set to DDLOCK_WAIT, which instructs DirectDraw to only return when either a lock has been achieved or an error has occurred. Conceivably, we could instead allow the Lock to fail and go off to do some other work instead, but there's no need to get that complicated here. The fourth parameter must be set to NULL. If the Lock fails, we will bail out of the draw function.

```
if(FAILED(surface->Lock(NULL,&ddsd,DDLOCK_WAIT,NULL)))
  return FALSE;
```

Now we start using the information stored in the DirectDraw surface descriptor ddsd by the Lock function. We set dest to point to the place in the surface where we want to store the byte data for the image.

```
dest=(BYTE*)ddsd.lpSurface; //destination
```

Similarly, we set src to point to the place within m_cImage that we want to start moving bytes from. Recall that bmp files are stored upside-down and so the first row of the image is actually where you would expect the last row to be stored (see Figure 2.5).

```
src=m_cImage+
  ((m_BMPFileInfo.biHeight-1)*m_BMPFileInfo.biWidth);
```

The width in bytes of the surface is stored in ddsd.lPitch; if the image is too wide for the surface, we clip it, which may look strange but is better than crashing.

```
if(m_BMPFileInfo.biWidth>ddsd.lPitch)src_width=ddsd.lPitch;
else src_width=m_BMPFileInfo.biWidth;
```

Now we move data to the surface. Note the careful way that we do it. We move one row at a time, subtracting src_width from src each time (to get to the start of the previous row of the source) and adding ddsd.lPitch to dest (to get to the start of the next row of the destination). Don't make the mistake of assuming that each row of the image in the surface is adjacent to the previous one. In reality, there is space left at the end of each row, which is used by DirectDraw for various purposes (see Figure 2.6). By using dest+=ddsd.lPitch, we make sure that we skip over it.

```
for(int i=0; i<m_BMPFileInfo.biHeight; i++){
  memcpy(dest,src,src_width);
  dest+=ddsd.lPitch; src-=src_width;
}
```

Now we are done, so we can unlock the surface and exit:

```
surface->Unlock(NULL);
return TRUE;
```

First row	Used by DirectDraw
Second row	Used by DirectDraw
. . .	Used by DirectDraw
Last row	Used by DirectDraw

Figure 2.6 How the image is stored in a DirectDraw surface.

Setting the Palette

The CBmpFileReader setpalette function loads the palette from the member variable m_rgbPalette to a DirectDraw palette. It has a single parameter, a pointer to a DirectDraw palette called palette. It begins with a local variable, an array of PALETTEENTRYs called pe.

```
PALETTEENTRY pe[COLORS]; //intermediate palette
```

We load pe from m_rgbPalette:

```
for(int i=0; i<COLORS; i++){ //for each palette entry
  pe[i].peRed=m_rgbPalette[i].rgbRed; //set red
  pe[i].peGreen=m_rgbPalette[i].rgbGreen; //set green
  pe[i].peBlue=m_rgbPalette[i].rgbBlue; //set blue
}
```

Then, we load the palette from pe to palette using the DirectDraw palette's member function SetEntries. SetEntries has four parameters. The first must be NULL. The second and third allow us to load only part of the palette by specifying the lower and upper indices of the entries to be loaded; we will load the entire palette, from index 0 to index COLORS (which, you will recall, is set to 256 in Defines.h). The last parameter is a pointer to the PALETTEENTRY array pe.

```
palette->SetEntries(NULL,0,COLORS,pe);
```

Demo 0 Files
Code Files

The following files are used in Demo 0:

- Bmp.h
- Bmp.cpp
- Ddsetup.cpp
- Defines.h
- Main.cpp

Media Files

The following image files are used in Demo 0:

◎ Bckgnd.bmp

Required Libraries

◎ Ddraw.lib

Code Listings

Bmp.h

```
//bmp.h: header file for the bmp file reader

//Copyright Ian Parberry, 1999
//Last updated September 2, 1999

#include <windows.h>
#include <windowsx.h>
#include <ddraw.h>

#include "defines.h"

#ifndef __bmp_h__
#define __bmp_h__

class CBmpFileReader{ //bmp file input class
  protected:
    BITMAPFILEHEADER m_BMPFileHead; //bmp header
    BITMAPINFOHEADER m_BMPFileInfo; //bmp file information
    RGBQUAD m_rgbPalette[COLORS]; //the palette
    BYTE *m_cImage; //the image
  public:
    CBmpFileReader(); //constructor
    ~CBmpFileReader(); //destructor
    BOOL load(char *filename); //load from file
    BOOL draw(LPDIRECTDRAWSURFACE surface); //draw image
    BOOL setpalette(LPDIRECTDRAWPALETTE palette); //set palette
};

#endif
```

Bmp.cpp

```cpp
//bmp.cpp: member functions for the bmp file reader

//Copyright Ian Parberry, 1999
//Last updated May 22, 2000

#include "bmp.h" //header file

//constructors and destructors

CBmpFileReader::CBmpFileReader(){ //constructor
  m_cImage=0; //memory not yet allocated
}

CBmpFileReader::~CBmpFileReader(){ //destructor
  delete[]m_cImage; //reclaim memory from image data
}

//member functions

BOOL CBmpFileReader::load(char *filename){ //load bmp from file
  HANDLE hfile; //input file handle
  DWORD actualRead; //number of bytes actually read
  int image_size; //size of image (width*height)
  BOOL OK=TRUE; //no error has occurred yet
  //open input file for reading
  hfile=CreateFile(filename,GENERIC_READ,FILE_SHARE_READ,
    (LPSECURITY_ATTRIBUTES)NULL,OPEN_EXISTING,
    FILE_ATTRIBUTE_NORMAL,(HANDLE)NULL);
  //bail if file could not be opened
  if(hfile==INVALID_HANDLE_VALUE)return FALSE;
  //read the header and info structures
  OK=ReadFile(hfile,&m_BMPFileHead,sizeof(m_BMPFileHead),
    &actualRead,NULL);
  if(OK)OK=ReadFile(hfile,&m_BMPFileInfo,
    sizeof(m_BMPFileInfo),&actualRead,NULL);
  //make sure the bmp is 8-bit color
  if(OK)OK=m_BMPFileInfo.biBitCount==COLOR_DEPTH;
  //get the bmp palette
  if(OK)OK=ReadFile(hfile,m_rgbPalette,sizeof(m_rgbPalette),
    &actualRead,NULL);
  //bail out if something went wrong
  if(!OK){CloseHandle(hfile); return FALSE;}
  //allocate memory for image data
  image_size=m_BMPFileInfo.biWidth*m_BMPFileInfo.biHeight;
  if(m_cImage)delete[]m_cImage; //dispose of any old space
  m_cImage=new BYTE[image_size]; //allocate new space
  if(!m_cImage){ //bail if alloc failed
    CloseHandle(hfile); return FALSE;
```

```
    }
    //round up line width to next multiple of 4
    int width=(m_BMPFileInfo.biWidth+3)&~3;
    //read bmp image
    int i=0; //counter
    BYTE trash[4]; //to hold the trash at the end of each line
    int remainder=width-m_BMPFileInfo.biWidth; //width of trash
    while(OK&&i<m_BMPFileInfo.biHeight){
      //read data
      OK=OK&&ReadFile(hfile,
        (BYTE*)(m_cImage+i*m_BMPFileInfo.biWidth),
        m_BMPFileInfo.biWidth,&actualRead,NULL);
      //read trash at end of line
      OK=OK&&ReadFile(hfile,trash,remainder,&actualRead,NULL);
      i++; //next line
    }
    if(!OK)delete[]m_cImage; //clean up if failed
    //close up and exit
    CloseHandle(hfile);
    return OK;
} //load

BOOL CBmpFileReader::draw(LPDIRECTDRAWSURFACE surface){
    DDSURFACEDESC ddsd; //direct draw surface descriptor
    BYTE *dest,*src; //destination and source pointers
    int src_width; //width of source
    //init surface descriptor
    memset(&ddsd,0,sizeof(DDSURFACEDESC));
    ddsd.dwSize=sizeof(ddsd);
    //lock down surface
    if(FAILED(surface->Lock(NULL,&ddsd,DDLOCK_WAIT,NULL)))
      return FALSE;
    //calculate addresses and width
    dest=(BYTE*)ddsd.lpSurface; //destination
    src=m_cImage+
      ((m_BMPFileInfo.biHeight-1)*m_BMPFileInfo.biWidth);
    //trim bmp if too wide
    if(m_BMPFileInfo.biWidth>ddsd.lPitch)src_width=ddsd.lPitch;
    else src_width=m_BMPFileInfo.biWidth;
    //move data to surface
    for(int i=0; i<m_BMPFileInfo.biHeight; i++){
      memcpy(dest,src,src_width);
      dest+=ddsd.lPitch; src-=src_width;
    }
    //clean up and return
    surface->Unlock(NULL);
    return TRUE;
} //draw

BOOL CBmpFileReader::setpalette(LPDIRECTDRAWPALETTE palette){
```

```
      PALETTEENTRY pe[COLORS]; //intermediate palette
      //construct pe[]
      for(int i=0; i<COLORS; i++){ //for each palette entry
        pe[i].peRed=m_rgbPalette[i].rgbRed; //set red
        pe[i].peGreen=m_rgbPalette[i].rgbGreen; //set green
        pe[i].peBlue=m_rgbPalette[i].rgbBlue; //set blue
      }
      //load direct draw palette to surface
      palette->SetEntries(NULL,0,COLORS,pe);
      return TRUE;
    }
```

Ddsetup.cpp

```
      //ddsetup.cpp: directDraw setup and release
      //Copyright Ian Parberry, 1999
      //Last updated May 22, 2000

      //system includes
      #include <windows.h>
      #include <windowsx.h>
      #include <ddraw.h>

      //custom includes
      #include "defines.h"

      //globals
      extern LPDIRECTDRAW lpDirectDrawObject; //direct draw object
      extern LPDIRECTDRAWSURFACE lpPrimary; //primary surface
      extern LPDIRECTDRAWPALETTE lpPrimaryPalette; //its palette

      //helper functions

      LPDIRECTDRAWPALETTE CreatePalette(LPDIRECTDRAWSURFACE surface){
      //create surface palette
        PALETTEENTRY pe[COLORS]; //new palette
        LPDIRECTDRAWPALETTE lpDDPalette; //direct draw palette
        //construct pe[], set to black
        for(int i=0; i<COLORS; i++)
          pe[i].peRed=pe[i].peGreen=pe[i].peBlue=0;
        //create direct draw palette
        if(FAILED(lpDirectDrawObject->
        CreatePalette(DDPCAPS_8BIT,pe,&lpDDPalette,NULL)))
          return NULL;
        //load direct draw palette to surface
        surface->SetPalette(lpDDPalette);
        return lpDDPalette;
      } //CreatePalette

      BOOL InitDirectDraw(HWND hwnd){ //direct draw initialization
```

```
    //create and set up direct draw object
    if(FAILED(DirectDrawCreate(NULL,&lpDirectDrawObject,NULL)))
      return FALSE;
    //set cooperative level
    if(FAILED(lpDirectDrawObject->SetCooperativeLevel(hwnd,
    DDSCL_EXCLUSIVE|DDSCL_FULLSCREEN)))
      return FALSE;
    //change screen resolution
    if(FAILED(lpDirectDrawObject->
    SetDisplayMode(SCREEN_WIDTH,SCREEN_HEIGHT,COLOR_DEPTH)))
      return FALSE;
    //create the primary surface
    DDSURFACEDESC ddsd; //direct draw surface descriptor
    ddsd.dwSize=sizeof(ddsd);
    ddsd.dwFlags=DDSD_CAPS;
    ddsd.ddsCaps.dwCaps=DDSCAPS_PRIMARYSURFACE;
    if(FAILED(lpDirectDrawObject->
    CreateSurface(&ddsd,&lpPrimary,NULL)))
      return FALSE;
    //create its palette
    lpPrimaryPalette=CreatePalette(lpPrimary);
    return TRUE;
  } //InitDirectDraw

long CALLBACK WindowProc(HWND hwnd,UINT message,
  WPARAM wParam,LPARAM lParam);

//windows system functions
HWND CreateDefaultWindow(char* name,HINSTANCE hInstance){
  WNDCLASS wc; //window registration info
  //register display window
  wc.style=CS_HREDRAW|CS_VREDRAW; //style
  wc.lpfnWndProc=WindowProc; //window message handler
  wc.cbClsExtra=wc.cbWndExtra=0;
  wc.hInstance=hInstance;
  wc.hIcon=LoadIcon(hInstance,IDI_APPLICATION);
  wc.hCursor=LoadCursor(NULL,IDC_ARROW);
  wc.hbrBackground=NULL;
  wc.lpszMenuName=NULL;
  wc.lpszClassName=name;
  RegisterClass(&wc);
  //create and set up fullscreen window
  return CreateWindowEx(WS_EX_TOPMOST,name,name,
    WS_POPUP,0,0,GetSystemMetrics(SM_CXSCREEN),
    GetSystemMetrics(SM_CYSCREEN),NULL,NULL,hInstance,NULL);
}
```

Defines.h

```
//defines.h: essential defines
//Copyright Ian Parberry, 1999
//Last updated September 2, 1999

#define SCREEN_WIDTH 640 //pixels wide
#define SCREEN_HEIGHT 480 //pixels high
#define COLORS 256 //number of colors
#define COLOR_DEPTH 8 //number of bits to store colors
```

Main.cpp

```
//main.cpp

//Read 640x480x256 bmp & display full screen (ESC to exit)

//Copyright Ian Parberry, 1999
//Last updated May 22, 2000

//system includes
#include <windows.h>
#include <windowsx.h>
#include <ddraw.h>
#include <stdio.h>

//system defines
#define WIN32_LEAN_AND_MEAN

//custom includes
#include "defines.h"
#include "bmp.h"

//globals
LPDIRECTDRAW lpDirectDrawObject=NULL; //direct draw object
LPDIRECTDRAWSURFACE lpPrimary=NULL; //primary surface
LPDIRECTDRAWPALETTE lpPrimaryPalette; //its palette
BOOL ActiveApp; //is this application active?
CBmpFileReader background; //background image

//helper functions

LPDIRECTDRAWPALETTE CreatePalette(LPDIRECTDRAWSURFACE surface);
BOOL InitDirectDraw(HWND hwnd);
HWND CreateDefaultWindow(char* name,HINSTANCE hInstance);

BOOL LoadImages(){ //load pictures from disk
  //draw the first image to the primary surface
  if(!background.load("bckgnd.bmp")) //read from file
    return FALSE; //read failed
```

```
    if(!background.setpalette(lpPrimaryPalette)) //set palette
      return FALSE; //set palette failed
    if(!background.draw(lpPrimary)) //draw to surface
      return FALSE; //draw failed
    return TRUE; //all steps succeeded
} //LoadImages

BOOL keyboard_handler(WPARAM keystroke){ //keyboard handler
  BOOL result=FALSE; //return TRUE if game is to end
  switch(keystroke){
    case VK_ESCAPE: result=TRUE; break; //exit game
  }
  return result;
} //keyboard_handler

//message handler (window procedure)
long CALLBACK WindowProc(HWND hwnd,UINT message,
                         WPARAM wParam,LPARAM lParam){
  switch(message){
    case WM_ACTIVATEAPP: ActiveApp=wParam; break;
    case WM_CREATE: break;
    case WM_KEYDOWN: //keyboard hit
      if(keyboard_handler(wParam))DestroyWindow(hwnd);
      break;
    case WM_DESTROY: //end of game
      if(lpDirectDrawObject!=NULL){ //if DD object exists
        if(lpPrimary!=NULL) //if primary surface exists
          lpPrimary->Release(); //release primary surface
        lpDirectDrawObject->Release(); //release DD object
      }
      ShowCursor(TRUE); //show the mouse cursor
      PostQuitMessage(0); //and exit
      break;
    default: //default window procedure
      return DefWindowProc(hwnd,message,wParam,lParam);
  } //switch(message)
  return 0L;
} //WindowProc

int WINAPI WinMain(HINSTANCE hInstance,HINSTANCE hPrevInstance,
                   LPSTR lpCmdLine,int nCmdShow){
  MSG msg; //current message
  HWND hwnd; //handle to fullscreen window
  hwnd=CreateDefaultWindow("directX Demo 0",hInstance);
  if(!hwnd)return FALSE;
  //set up window
  ShowWindow(hwnd,nCmdShow); UpdateWindow(hwnd);
  SetFocus(hwnd); //allow input from keyboard
  ShowCursor(FALSE); //hide the cursor
  //init graphics
```

```
BOOL OK=InitDirectDraw(hwnd);//initialize DirectDraw
if(OK)OK=LoadImages(); //load images from disk
if(!OK){ //bail out if initialization failed
  DestroyWindow(hwnd); return FALSE;
}
//message loop
while(TRUE)
  if(PeekMessage(&msg,NULL,0,0,PM_NOREMOVE)){
    if(!GetMessage(&msg,NULL,0,0))return msg.wParam;
    TranslateMessage(&msg); DispatchMessage(&msg);
  }
  else if(!ActiveApp)WaitMessage();
} //WinMain
```

Chapter 3

Here's what you'll learn:

- How the video serializer works

- What tearing is and how to avoid it

- How to implement page flipping in DirectDraw

- How to create a secondary surface in DirectDraw

- What surface loss is, and how to deal with it by restoring and reloading

Page Flipping

In Demo 1, we learn how to do page flipping in video memory to avoid the animation flaw known as tearing. Along the way, we'll learn a little about how the video hardware inside your computer works. Demo 1 reads in a bmp file called Up.bmp from disk and displays it on the screen. The image in Up.bmp looks very similar to the one in Bckgnd.bmp from Demo 0 (see Chapter 2), with the addition of a crow with its wings up in the center of the screen (see Figure 3.1). When you hit the Spacebar, this image is replaced by the one in Down.bmp, which has the crow with its wings down (see Figure 3.2). Each time you hit the Spacebar, the image on the screen flips between the two images in a process called *page flipping*. The transition between the two images is clean, clear, and crisp.

Figure 3.1
Single frame of crow with wings up

Figure 3.2
Single frame
of crow with
wings down

Experiment with Demo 1

Take a moment now to run Demo 1.

- You should see the picture shown in Figure 3.1.
- Hit the Spacebar; you should see Figure 3.2.
- Each time you hit the Spacebar, it should flip between the two images.
- After reading this chapter, hold down the Spacebar and let autorepeat make the crow look like it is flapping its wings. Look for tearing.
- Hit the Esc key to exit the program.
- Double-click on Up.bmp and Down.bmp to fire up the default paint program on your computer (usually Microsoft Paint) to verify to yourself that when you ran Demo 1 you were seeing the images that are stored in those files.

Why Flip Pages?

Before we get to the programming part of this chapter, let's take a quick look at how the graphics hardware on your PC works.

The Video Serializer

Think about your game as an interactive movie. You will be composing frames of this movie on-the-fly in response to the player's actions, and displaying them on the monitor. Obviously, each frame is composed by the CPU using system memory. So how does it get from system memory to the monitor? Your video card has two important pieces of hardware on it: *video memory* and the *video serializer*. The video memory contains the image to be displayed on the monitor, and it is the video serializer's job to display it. The video serializer takes the image from the video memory and sends it to the monitor at a constant rate, usually somewhere between 60 and 80 times per second. It does this even if the image doesn't change, because your monitor can only display an image for a fraction of a second before it begins to fade from the screen. While it is doing this, the CPU is attempting to send the next frame of animation to video memory. The process is shown in Figure 3.3. We can see from this description that both the CPU and the video serializer need access to video memory.

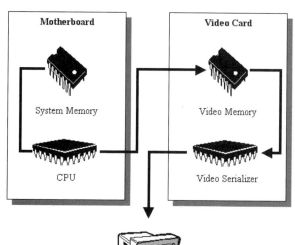

Figure 3.3
How the image gets to your monitor

Here's how the typical CRT computer monitor works, described in broad terms (the details are actually more complicated, but not important here). The surface of the screen is divided into rows and columns of pixels. Each pixel is coated with a special phosphor, which glows when it is hit with electrons, and will continue to glow for a fraction of a second afterwards. An electron beam scans the pixels from left to right, top to bottom, firing the right amount of electrons at each pixel in response to information provided by the video serializer. The video serializer has preferential access to video memory so that it can keep to a regular clock-like refresh schedule, thus ensuring that the image on your monitor stays clear and bright at all times. In order to do this, the video serializer takes the majority of available access cycles to the video memory, while the CPU often has to wait. As a result, the video serializer can read from video memory faster than the CPU can write to it. This leads to a problem known as tearing, which results from having a new frame only partially replace the frame before it.

Tearing

Consider the two frames of animation shown in Figures 3.4 and 3.5. Frame 1 (Figure 3.4) shows an outhouse, a silo, and a barn. In Frame 2 (Figure 3.5), the camera has panned 6 pixels to the left, and so everything in the image has shifted 6 pixels to the right. Ideally, we would like to show Frame 1, then Frame 2, and then move on to Frame 3, etc.

Figure 3.4
Frame 1 of animation

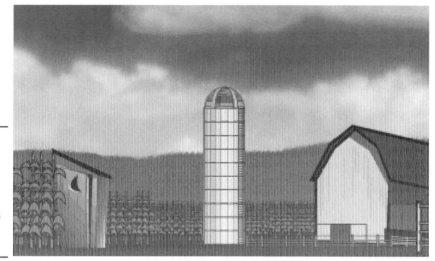

Figure 3.5
Frame 2 of animation: the camera pans left from Frame 1 (Figure 3.4)

Suppose that Frame 1 has already been loaded to video memory, and that the video serializer has already drawn it to the monitor, perhaps several times. When the video serializer is drawing from the bottom of Frame 1 in video memory, we quickly start to draw Frame 2 over it, starting at the top. However, since the video serializer has preferential access to video memory, it will read faster than the CPU can write. After a while we get the situation shown in Figure 3.6, where the CPU is still drawing Frame 2 on top of Frame 1, but the video serializer is catching up. Eventually it will pass the point at which the CPU is writing Frame 2 into video memory and start reading from Frame 1 again. We will see displayed on the monitor a frame that consists of the top of Frame 2 pasted on the bottom of Frame 1, as shown in Figure 3.7. It looks like the bottom of the frame has been torn off and shifted slightly to the left, hence the term *tearing*.

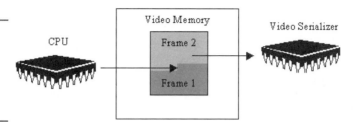

Figure 3.6
Animation with one page of video memory

Figure 3.7
What is actually drawn in one-page animation (see Figure 3.6): the top of Frame 2 (Figure 3.5) and the bottom of Frame 1 (Figure 3.4), leaving a tear

This is a very simplified account of what is going on; in reality you will probably see many tears, not just one. The tears occur very quickly, in the blink of an eye. They can be in different places on each frame, and there can be a different number of tears on each frame. It takes a fast eye to see them, and unless you are aware of what is going on and are really watching for them, you probably won't notice them consciously. Subconsciously, however, you will be aware that the animation looks *bad* without being able to put your finger on exactly what the problem is. You will see this behavior exhibited by many old DOS games, Mac games, and games that you play in a web browser. Now that you know what to look for, go look carefully at one of these types of games and look for tearing.

How to Avoid Tearing

The only way to avoid tearing is to grab control of the video hardware, and take advantage of the large amounts of video memory that are now available on even quite low-end video cards. Unfortunately, Windows, like any sensible operating system, will not let you take control of the video hardware when other applications are likely to be using it. Fortunately, DirectX gives you the power to do so when your game is running in full-screen mode. That's why we are running full screen in this book.

When the CPU is writing to video memory, it simply takes a pointer to video memory and moves that pointer down the memory while writing bytes of data. Likewise, the video serializer reads data from a pointer. Our solution to the tearing problem is to use two frames' worth of video memory, and allow the video serializer to draw from a completed frame while the CPU is drawing the next frame someplace else in video memory (see Figure 3.8). These frames in video memory are called *pages*. When the CPU has finished writing its frame, we do what

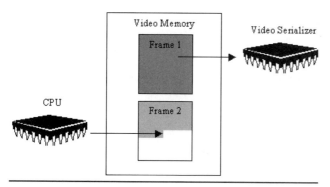

Figure 3.8 Two-page animation: the video serializer refreshes from a complete frame (Frame 1) in one page while the CPU loads the next frame (Frame 2) to the other page

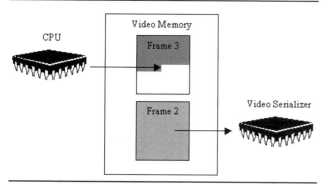

Figure 3.9 Two-page animation after page flipping: when Frame 2 is complete, the video serializer refreshes from it while the CPU loads Frame 3 to the other page

is called *page flipping*, which puts the video serializer's pointer at the top of the new frame, and puts the CPU's pointer at the top of the old frame that the serializer just finished with (see Figure 3.9). In this way, the video serializer always has a complete frame to draw from except for a brief period while the pointers are being moved, which is so small that it can usually be done in the *vertical retrace interval*, which is the time period during which your monitor's electron beam moves from the lower-right pixel on the screen to the top-left pixel.

The page that the CPU is writing to is called the *front buffer*, while the page that the video serializer is reading from is called the *back buffer*. Page flipping is the process of swapping the front buffer and the back buffer, but keep in mind that this does not involve moving the image data in the pages, just moving two pointers.

The Secondary Surface

The back buffer is a secondary surface that we request from the DirectDraw object. We declare in Main.cpp a pointer for the back buffer, which we will call lpSecondary, and one for its palette, lpSecondaryPalette.

```
LPDIRECTDRAWSURFACE lpSecondary=NULL; //back buffer
LPDIRECTDRAWPALETTE lpSecondaryPalette; //its palette
```

These are externed at the top of Ddsetup.cpp. In InitDirectDraw, we change the flags slightly in ddsd to show that we will be requesting a number of back buffers, in our case only one, but DirectDraw will let us attempt to use more than one back buffer if we wish. This is done by ORing in DDSD_BACKBUFFER-COUNT to ddsd.dwFlags.

```
ddsd.dwFlags=DDSD_CAPS|DDSD_BACKBUFFERCOUNT;
```

In order to get DirectDraw to let us page flip, we modify the dwCaps field to allow a flippable, complex surface by ORing in the appropriate two flags. A complex surface means one that has other surfaces attached to it, the secondary surface will be attached to the primary surface.

```
ddsd.ddsCaps.dwCaps=DDSCAPS_PRIMARYSURFACE|DDSCAPS_FLIP
    |DDSCAPS_COMPLEX;
```

We specify that there will be one back buffer:

```
ddsd.dwBackBufferCount=1;
```

We add code at the end of InitDirectDraw to attach a secondary surface to the primary surface (while we asked the DirectDraw object to create the primary surface, we must ask the primary surface to attach a secondary surface). This is done using a call to the primary surface's GetAttachedSurface member function and specifying that we need a back buffer using a DDSCAPS structure.

```
DDSCAPS ddscaps;
ddscaps.dwCaps=DDSCAPS_BACKBUFFER;
```

We attach the secondary surface to the primary surface, and create a palette for it:

```
if(FAILED(lpPrimary->
GetAttachedSurface(&ddscaps,&lpSecondary)))
    return FALSE;
lpSecondaryPalette=CreatePalette(lpSecondary);
```

Returning to Main.cpp, we declare two CBmpFileReader class instances frame0 and frame1, to hold the two frames of animation.

```
CBmpFileReader frame0; //first frame
CBmpFileReader frame1; //second frame
```

Function LoadImages loads Up.bmp, draws it to the primary surface, and sets the palette using the CBmpFileReader class instance frame0:

```
if(!frame0.load("up.bmp"))return FALSE; //read from file
if(!frame0.setpalette(lpPrimaryPalette)) //set palette
    return FALSE;
if(!frame0.draw(lpPrimary))return FALSE; //draw
```

Then it loads Down.bmp, draws it to the secondary surface, and sets the palette using the CBmpFileReader class instance frame1:

```
if(!frame1.load("down.bmp"))return FALSE; //read from file
if(!frame1.setpalette(lpSecondaryPalette)) //set palette
```

```
      return FALSE;
    if(!frame1.draw(lpSecondary))return FALSE; //draw
```

Page flipping is done using the primary surface's `Flip` member function. Unfortunately, DirectDraw surfaces are not just set-and-forget structures. They can be lost at awkward times that are out of the programmer's control (for example, if the user hits Alt+Tab to select another running application as the active app, it has the unpleasant side effect of causing all surfaces in our game to become lost). In particular, we may find out that surfaces have been lost when we attempt to page flip. If so, the surfaces must be restored. We will write a function `RestoreSurfaces` to take care of this detail. The page flipping operation, then, consists of calling the primary surface's `Flip` member function and restoring the surfaces if it reports surface loss by returning `DDERR_SURFACELOST`.

```
BOOL PageFlip(){ //return TRUE if page flip succeeds
  if(lpPrimary->Flip(NULL,DDFLIP_WAIT)==DDERR_SURFACELOST)
    return RestoreSurfaces();
  return TRUE;
} //PageFlip
```

The primary and secondary surfaces are restored by calling their `Restore` member functions. This reallocates the memory but does not redraw the image; we have to that ourselves using the appropriate `CBmpFileReader` class instances.

```
BOOL RestoreSurfaces(){ //restore all surfaces
  BOOL result=TRUE;
  if(SUCCEEDED(lpPrimary->Restore()))
    result=result&&frame0.draw(lpPrimary)&& //redraw image
      frame0.setpalette(lpPrimaryPalette); //set palette
  else return FALSE;
  if(SUCCEEDED(lpSecondary->Restore()))
    result=result&&frame1.draw(lpSecondary)&& //redraw image
      frame1.setpalette(lpSecondaryPalette); //set palette
  else return FALSE;
  return result;
} //RestoreSurfaces
```

To make the page flip happen in response to the Spacebar, we need to add the following case to the switch statement in function `keyboard_handler`:

```
  case VK_SPACE: result=!PageFlip(); break;
```

Lastly, in response to the `WM_DESTROY` message case in `WindowProc`, we need to release the secondary surface. Since it is attached to the primary surface, we make sure that we release the secondary surface first, then the primary surface.

```
  if(lpSecondary!=NULL) //if secondary surface exists
    lpSecondary->Release(); //release secondary surface
```

We will be adding a lot more surfaces to our game as we move from demo to demo. The process will be same for each new surface; they will each need to be:

- Created by the DirectDraw object.
- Drawn to (when initializing and when restoring) from a `CBmpFileReader` object.
- Restored (and redrawn to) in function `RestoreSurfaces` when surfaces are lost.
- Released in `WindowProc` in response to the `WM_DESTROY` message. Take care though; the `Release` function of each surface must be called only once. Calling it more often is a common cause of crashes.

Demo 1 Files

Code Files

The following files in Demo 1 are used without change from Demo 0:

- `Bmp.h`
- `Bmp.cpp`
- `Defines.h`

The following files in Demo 1 have been modified from Demo 0:

- `Ddsetup.cpp`
- `Main.cpp`

Media Files

The following image files are new in Demo 1:

- `Down.bmp` (to be used only in Demos 1 and 2)
- `Up.bmp` (to be used only in Demos 1 and 2)

Required Libraries

- `Ddraw.lib`

Code Listings

Ddsetup.cpp

```cpp
//ddsetup.cpp: directDraw setup and release
//Copyright Ian Parberry, 1999
//Last updated May 22, 2000

//system includes
#include <windows.h>
#include <windowsx.h>
#include <ddraw.h>

//custom includes
#include "defines.h"

//globals
extern LPDIRECTDRAW lpDirectDrawObject; //direct draw object
extern LPDIRECTDRAWSURFACE lpPrimary; //primary surface
extern LPDIRECTDRAWPALETTE lpPrimaryPalette; //its palette
extern LPDIRECTDRAWSURFACE lpSecondary; //back buffer
extern LPDIRECTDRAWPALETTE lpSecondaryPalette; //its palette

//helper functions

LPDIRECTDRAWPALETTE CreatePalette(LPDIRECTDRAWSURFACE surface){
//create surface palette
  PALETTEENTRY pe[COLORS]; //new palette
  LPDIRECTDRAWPALETTE lpDDPalette; //direct draw palette
  //construct pe[], set to black
  for(int i=0; i<COLORS; i++)
    pe[i].peRed=pe[i].peGreen=pe[i].peBlue=0;
  //create direct draw palette
  if(FAILED(lpDirectDrawObject->
  CreatePalette(DDPCAPS_8BIT,pe,&lpDDPalette,NULL)))
    return NULL;
  //load direct draw palette to surface
  surface->SetPalette(lpDDPalette);
  return lpDDPalette;
} //CreatePalette

BOOL InitDirectDraw(HWND hwnd){ //direct draw initialization
  //create and set up direct draw object
  if(FAILED(DirectDrawCreate(NULL,&lpDirectDrawObject,NULL)))
    return FALSE;
  //set cooperative level
  if(FAILED(lpDirectDrawObject->SetCooperativeLevel(hwnd,
  DDSCL_EXCLUSIVE|DDSCL_FULLSCREEN)))
    return FALSE;
```

```
    //change screen resolution
    if(FAILED(lpDirectDrawObject->
    SetDisplayMode(SCREEN_WIDTH,SCREEN_HEIGHT,COLOR_DEPTH)))
      return FALSE;
    //create the surfaces
    DDSURFACEDESC ddsd; //direct draw surface descriptor
    ddsd.dwSize=sizeof(ddsd);
    ddsd.dwFlags=DDSD_CAPS|DDSD_BACKBUFFERCOUNT;
    ddsd.ddsCaps.dwCaps=DDSCAPS_PRIMARYSURFACE|DDSCAPS_FLIP
      |DDSCAPS_COMPLEX;
    ddsd.dwBackBufferCount=1;
    if(FAILED(lpDirectDrawObject->
    CreateSurface(&ddsd,&lpPrimary,NULL)))
      return FALSE;
    //create its palette
    lpPrimaryPalette=CreatePalette(lpPrimary);
    //get pointer to the secondary surface
    DDSCAPS ddscaps;
    ddscaps.dwCaps=DDSCAPS_BACKBUFFER;
    if(FAILED(lpPrimary->
    GetAttachedSurface(&ddscaps,&lpSecondary)))
      return FALSE;
    //create its palette
    lpSecondaryPalette=CreatePalette(lpSecondary);
    return TRUE;
} //InitDirectDraw

long CALLBACK WindowProc(HWND hwnd,UINT message,
    WPARAM wParam,LPARAM lParam);

//windows system functions
HWND CreateDefaultWindow(char* name,HINSTANCE hInstance){
    WNDCLASS wc; //window registration info
    //register display window
    wc.style=CS_HREDRAW|CS_VREDRAW; //style
    wc.lpfnWndProc=WindowProc; //window message handler
    wc.cbClsExtra=wc.cbWndExtra=0;
    wc.hInstance=hInstance;
    wc.hIcon=LoadIcon(hInstance,IDI_APPLICATION);
    wc.hCursor=LoadCursor(NULL,IDC_ARROW);
    wc.hbrBackground=NULL;
    wc.lpszMenuName=NULL;
    wc.lpszClassName=name;
    RegisterClass(&wc);
    //create and set up fullscreen window
    return CreateWindowEx(WS_EX_TOPMOST,name,name,
      WS_POPUP,0,0,GetSystemMetrics(SM_CXSCREEN),
      GetSystemMetrics(SM_CYSCREEN),NULL,NULL,hInstance,NULL);
}
```

Main.cpp

```cpp
//main.cpp

//Experiment with back buffer and page flipping - hit Spacebar
//to flip page.

//Copyright Ian Parberry, 1999
//Last updated May 22, 2000

//system includes
#include <windows.h>
#include <windowsx.h>
#include <ddraw.h>
#include <stdio.h>

//system defines
#define WIN32_LEAN_AND_MEAN

//custom includes
#include "defines.h"
#include "bmp.h"

//globals
LPDIRECTDRAW lpDirectDrawObject=NULL; //direct draw object
LPDIRECTDRAWSURFACE lpPrimary=NULL; //primary surface
LPDIRECTDRAWPALETTE lpPrimaryPalette; //its palette
LPDIRECTDRAWSURFACE lpSecondary=NULL; //back buffer
LPDIRECTDRAWPALETTE lpSecondaryPalette; //its palette
BOOL ActiveApp; //is this application active?
CBmpFileReader frame0; //first frame
CBmpFileReader frame1; //second frame

//helper functions

LPDIRECTDRAWPALETTE CreatePalette(LPDIRECTDRAWSURFACE surface);
BOOL InitDirectDraw(HWND hwnd);
HWND CreateDefaultWindow(char* name,HINSTANCE hInstance);

BOOL LoadImages(){
  //draw the first image to the primary surface
  if(!frame0.load("up.bmp"))return FALSE; //read from file
  if(!frame0.setpalette(lpPrimaryPalette)) //set palette
    return FALSE;
  if(!frame0.draw(lpPrimary))return FALSE; //draw
  //draw the second image to the secondary surface
  if(!frame1.load("down.bmp"))return FALSE; //read from file
  if(!frame1.setpalette(lpSecondaryPalette)) //set palette
    return FALSE;
  if(!frame1.draw(lpSecondary))return FALSE; //draw
```

```
      //success exit
      return TRUE;
  } //LoadImages

  BOOL RestoreSurfaces(){ //restore all surfaces
    BOOL result=TRUE;
    if(SUCCEEDED(lpPrimary->Restore()))
      result=result&&frame0.draw(lpPrimary)&& //redraw image
        frame0.setpalette(lpPrimaryPalette); //set palette
    else return FALSE;
    if(SUCCEEDED(lpSecondary->Restore()))
      result=result&&frame1.draw(lpSecondary)&& //redraw image
        frame1.setpalette(lpSecondaryPalette); //set palette
    else return FALSE;
    return result;
  } //RestoreSurfaces

  BOOL PageFlip(){ //return TRUE if page flip succeeds
    if(lpPrimary->Flip(NULL,DDFLIP_WAIT)==DDERR_SURFACELOST)
      return RestoreSurfaces();
    return TRUE;
  } //PageFlip

BOOL keyboard_handler(WPARAM keystroke){ //keyboard handler
  BOOL result=FALSE; //return TRUE if game is to end
  switch(keystroke){
    case VK_ESCAPE: result=TRUE; break; //exit game
    case VK_SPACE: result=!PageFlip(); break;
  }
  return result;
} //keyboard_handler

//message handler (window procedure)
long CALLBACK WindowProc(HWND hwnd,UINT message,
                         WPARAM wParam,LPARAM lParam){
  switch(message){
    case WM_ACTIVATEAPP: ActiveApp=wParam; break;
    case WM_CREATE: break;
    case WM_KEYDOWN: //keyboard hit
      if(keyboard_handler(wParam))DestroyWindow(hwnd);
      break;
    case WM_DESTROY: //end of game
      if(lpDirectDrawObject!=NULL){ //if DD object exists
        if(lpSecondary!=NULL) //if secondary surface exists
          lpSecondary->Release(); //release secondary surface
        if(lpPrimary!=NULL) //if primary surface exists
          lpPrimary->Release(); //release primary surface
        lpDirectDrawObject->Release(); //release DD object
      }
      ShowCursor(TRUE); //show the mouse cursor
```

```
        PostQuitMessage(0); //and exit
        break;
      default: //default window procedure
        return DefWindowProc(hwnd,message,wParam,lParam);
    } //switch(message)
    return 0L;
} //WindowProc

int WINAPI WinMain(HINSTANCE hInstance,HINSTANCE hPrevInstance,
                   LPSTR lpCmdLine,int nCmdShow){
  MSG msg; //current message
  HWND hwnd; //handle to fullscreen window
  hwnd=CreateDefaultWindow("directX demo 1",hInstance);
  if(!hwnd)return FALSE;
  //set up window
  ShowWindow(hwnd,nCmdShow); UpdateWindow(hwnd);
  SetFocus(hwnd); //allow input from keyboard
  ShowCursor(FALSE); //hide the cursor
  //init graphics
  BOOL OK=InitDirectDraw(hwnd);//initialize DirectDraw
  if(OK)OK=LoadImages(); //load images from disk
  if(!OK){ //bail out if initialization failed
    DestroyWindow(hwnd); return FALSE;
  }
  //message loop
  while(TRUE)
    if(PeekMessage(&msg,NULL,0,0,PM_NOREMOVE)){
      if(!GetMessage(&msg,NULL,0,0))return msg.wParam;
      TranslateMessage(&msg); DispatchMessage(&msg);
    }
    else if(!ActiveApp)WaitMessage();
} //WinMain
```

Chapter 4

Here's what you'll learn:

- How to implement a game timer using the Windows API function timeGetTime

- How to use the timer to regulate animation speed

- How to modify the message loop to allow full-screen animation

Full-screen Animation

In Demo 2, we learn how to perform full-screen animation using three frames of animation to make the crow from Demo 1 look like it is flying (well, flying against a headwind—it flaps like crazy but never gets anywhere). The trick is to make the crow's wings beat at about the same speed whether you have an antique 90 MHz Pentium I or one of the new gigahertz Pentium IIIs that are the hottest thing on the market at the time of this writing (but won't be by the time this book reaches the stores). We will achieve this by using a *timer* to control the rate at which the frames are displayed. The timer is a simple class that we will use a lot. In a game, everything must be time-based to ensure that it is playable on a range of available hardware. The advantage to making it a class is that we can reuse it in multiple projects, and if we wish, we can change the implementation of the timer midway through the project with a minimum of recoding and recompilation.

Experiment with Demo 2

Take a moment now to run Demo 2.

- You should see the crow from Demo 1 flapping its wings.
- Hit Alt+Tab to make the game inactive. All the surfaces have just been lost. Reactivate it from the Windows taskbar; the surfaces will be restored and reloaded.
- If you can, try it on several computers of different speeds. Note that the crow flaps its wings at about the same speed on all of them.
- Hit the Esc key to exit the program.

The Timer

The header file for the timer class `CTimer` is `Timer.h`. The timer acts like a stopwatch, counting the time that has elapsed in milliseconds since it was started. `CTimer` has a single protected member variable that records the time at which the timer was started.

```
int m_nStartTime; //time that timer was started
```

The public member functions include a constructor and a `start` function. The `start` function is made virtual because we will be deriving a new timer class from `CTimer` in Demo 13 (see Chapter 15) that will override the `start` function.

```
CTimer(); //constructor
virtual void start(); //start the timer
```

The `time` function, also virtual, will return the number of milliseconds since the `start` function was called:

```
virtual int time(); //return the time in ms
```

Finally, the `elapsed` function takes two parameters, `start` and `interval`. If `interval` milliseconds have elapsed since `start`, the function returns `TRUE` and sets `start` to the current time. Otherwise, it returns `FALSE`. Notice that `start` is declared as a call-by-reference parameter, `int &start`. This function will be used extensively for events that must repeat after a certain amount of time. We will keep a variable for each repeating event and use it to record the last time that the event occurred. This variable will be passed to the timer's `elapsed` function as the first parameter.

```
BOOL elapsed(int &start,int interval);
```

The `CTimer` functions are all very simple. Their implementation can be found in `Timer.cpp`. The constructor sets the member variable to a sensible value.

```
CTimer::CTimer(){ //constructor
  m_nStartTime=0;
}
```

The `start` function sets the start time using the Windows API function `timeGetTime`, which returns the number of milliseconds since Windows was rebooted. The value returned by `timeGetTime` wraps around to zero every 2^{32} milliseconds, which is about 49.71 days. If you think that your game will be running when Windows has been up for that long, then you will need to take further action. Personally, I can't keep Windows from crashing for more than a few hours, so I'm going to be lazy and assume that the same is true of my customers. The `timeGetTime` function is not a very good timer on some hardware. In general, it is accurate only down to about 5 milliseconds—but this is accurate enough for *Ned's Turkey Farm*.

```
void CTimer::start(){ //start the timer
  m_nStartTime=timeGetTime();
}
```

The `CTimer time` function simply subtracts the start time from the current time returned by the API function `timeGetTime`:

```
int CTimer::time(){ //return the time
  return timeGetTime()-m_nStartTime;
}
```

Finally, the `elapsed` function checks to see whether the current time is later than (or equal to) `start+interval`, sets `start` to the current time, and returns TRUE if so and FALSE if not:

```
int CTimer::elapsed(int &start,int interval){
  //has interval elapsed from start?
  int current_time=time();
  if(current_time>=start+interval){
    start=current_time; return TRUE;
  }
  else return FALSE;
}
```

Using the Timer

In `Main.cpp` we must, of course, include the header for the timer class:

```
#include "timer.h" //game timer
```

Then, we have some new declarations. We add a `CBmpFileReader` object for frame 2 of the animation.

```
CBmpFileReader frame0,frame1,frame2;
```

A frame counter is used to keep track of which frame is currently being displayed:

```
int current_frame=0; //current frame of animation
```

A `CTimer` object is declared for the game timer:

```
CTimer Timer; //game timer
```

The body of `LoadImages` is changed to load the three frames of animation from `Down.bmp`, `Middle.bmp`, and `Up.bmp`. All three of the images will use the same palette, which we will load from `frame0`. The artist must, of course, be aware that all artwork used in the body of the game will use the same palette. We won't bother to check that the artist has done this; if the palettes don't match, you will notice it pretty quickly during play testing.

```
BOOL LoadImages(){ //load graphics from files to surfaces
  //load the first frame
  if(!frame0.load("down.bmp"))return FALSE; //read from file
  frame0.draw(lpPrimary); //draw to primary surface
  //set palettes in all surfaces
  if(!frame0.setpalette(lpPrimaryPalette))return FALSE;
  if(!frame0.setpalette(lpSecondaryPalette))return FALSE;
  //load the other frames
  if(!frame1.load("middle.bmp"))return FALSE; //read from file
  if(!frame2.load("up.bmp"))return FALSE; //read from file
  return TRUE;
} //LoadImages
```

Recall the movie analogy that we used for game animation in Chapter 3. Our aim is to compose and display movie frames as fast as we possibly can. In Windows API programming, this can be done in the message loop—when your application isn't processing messages, it should be processing frames. The message loop from Demos 0 and 1 looked like this:

```
while(TRUE)
  if(PeekMessage(&msg,NULL,0,0,PM_NOREMOVE)){
    if(!GetMessage(&msg,NULL,0,0))return msg.wParam;
    TranslateMessage(&msg); DispatchMessage(&msg);
  }
  else if(!ActiveApp)WaitMessage();
```

We modify the last line of this code to say that if the app is active, then we process a frame, otherwise we do the `WaitMessage()`:

```
while(TRUE)
  if(PeekMessage(&msg,NULL,0,0,PM_NOREMOVE)){
    if(!GetMessage(&msg,NULL,0,0))return msg.wParam;
    TranslateMessage(&msg); DispatchMessage(&msg);
  }
  else if(ActiveApp)ProcessFrame(); else WaitMessage();
```

Function `ProcessFrame` processes a frame—that is, it composes it in the secondary surface, then flips it to the primary surface:

```
BOOL ProcessFrame(){ //process a frame of animation
  ComposeFrame(); //compose a frame in secondary surface
  return PageFlip(); //flip video memory surfaces
} //ProcessFrame
```

Function `ComposeFrame` composes a frame of animation to the secondary surface. We will change frames 10 times per second. (It is not a good idea in general to constrain your frame rate this way—we are just doing this as an example. Later, we will let the frame rate get as high as it can, and use similar techniques to govern the animation of objects within the game instead.) We start with a static local variable (that is, one that persists after the function has been called) `last_time` to record the last time the frame was changed.

```
static int last_time=Timer.time();
```

Recall that we are using a global variable `current_frame` to keep track of which frame is to be displayed. Sensibly, we first make sure that this value is in range. We allow it to take one of four possible values, from 0 to 3 inclusive so we can draw the frames in this order—frame 0 (wings down), frame 1 (wings middle), frame 2 (wings up), frame 1 (wings middle), then repeat.

```
if(current_frame<0)current_frame=0;
if(current_frame>3)current_frame=3;
```

The `CBmpFileReader draw` function is used to draw the current frame to the secondary surface:

```
switch(current_frame){
  case 0: frame0.draw(lpSecondary); break;
  case 1: frame1.draw(lpSecondary); break;
  case 2: frame2.draw(lpSecondary); break;
  case 3: frame1.draw(lpSecondary); break;
}
```

Finally, we increment `current_frame`, wrapping around to zero again when it exceeds three. Note the use of the `CTimer elapsed` function: If 100 milliseconds (one tenth of a second) has elapsed, then we increment `current_frame`. Remember that the `CTimer elapsed` function has a side effect of setting `last_time` to "now" when it returns TRUE, so that the frame is changed on a regular schedule, ten times per second.

```
if(Timer.elapsed(last_time,100))
  if(++current_frame>=4)current_frame=0;
```

But wait a second, we compose a frame to the secondary surface and then page flip. Doesn't that mean that the next frame—and every second frame thereafter—should be composed to the primary surface? The answer is no. DirectDraw takes care of swapping `lpPrimary` and `lpSecondary` for us every time we page flip. So the rule is, the primary surface is the one that the video serializer displays on the monitor, and the secondary surface is the one that we compose frames on.

The last thing we must remember to do is to start the timer during the initialization period, before we enter the message loop:

```
Timer.start();
```

Demo 2 Files

Code Files

The following files in Demo 2 are used without change from Demo 1:

- Bmp.h
- Bmp.cpp
- Ddsetup.cpp
- Defines.h

The following files in Demo 2 have been modified from Demo 1:

- Main.cpp

The following files are new in Demo 2:

- Timer.h
- Timer.cpp

Media Files

The following image files are new in Demo 2:

- Middle.bmp (to be used only in Demo 2)

Required Libraries

- Ddraw.lib
- Winmm.lib

Code Listings

Main.cpp

```cpp
//main.cpp

//Full-screen animation. One of three full-screen frames is
//written to the secondary buffer at regular intervals
//using a timer.  Hit Alt+Tab to test surface loss and
//recovery.

//Copyright Ian Parberry, 1999
//Last updated September 28, 1999

//system includes
#include <windows.h>
#include <windowsx.h>
#include <ddraw.h>
#include <stdio.h>

//system defines
#define WIN32_LEAN_AND_MEAN

//custom includes
#include "defines.h" //global definitions
#include "bmp.h" //bmp file reader
#include "timer.h" //game timer

//globals

BOOL ActiveApp; //is this application active?

LPDIRECTDRAW lpDirectDrawObject=NULL; //direct draw object
LPDIRECTDRAWSURFACE lpPrimary=NULL; //primary surface
LPDIRECTDRAWPALETTE lpPrimaryPalette; //its palette
LPDIRECTDRAWSURFACE lpSecondary=NULL; //back buffer
LPDIRECTDRAWPALETTE lpSecondaryPalette; //its palette

//animation frames (full screen)
CBmpFileReader frame0,frame1,frame2;
int current_frame=0; //current frame of animation

CTimer Timer; //game timer

//helper functions

LPDIRECTDRAWPALETTE CreatePalette(LPDIRECTDRAWSURFACE surface);
BOOL InitDirectDraw(HWND hwnd);
HWND CreateDefaultWindow(char* name,HINSTANCE hInstance);
```

```
BOOL LoadImages(){ //load graphics from files to surfaces
  //load the first frame
  if(!frame0.load("down.bmp"))return FALSE; //read from file
  frame0.draw(lpPrimary); //draw to primary surface
  //set palettes in all surfaces
  if(!frame0.setpalette(lpPrimaryPalette))return FALSE;
  if(!frame0.setpalette(lpSecondaryPalette))return FALSE;
  //load the other frames
  if(!frame1.load("middle.bmp"))return FALSE; //read from file
  if(!frame2.load("up.bmp"))return FALSE; //read from file
  return TRUE;
} //LoadImages

BOOL RestoreSurfaces(){ //restore all surfaces
  BOOL result=TRUE;
  if(SUCCEEDED(lpPrimary->Restore()))
    result=result&&frame0.draw(lpPrimary)&& //redraw image
      frame0.setpalette(lpPrimaryPalette); //set palette
  else return FALSE;
  if(SUCCEEDED(lpSecondary->Restore()))
    result=result&&frame1.draw(lpSecondary)&& //redraw image
      frame1.setpalette(lpSecondaryPalette); //set palette
  else return FALSE;
  return result;
} //RestoreSurfaces

BOOL PageFlip(){ //return TRUE if page flip succeeds
  if(lpPrimary->Flip(NULL,DDFLIP_WAIT)==DDERR_SURFACELOST)
    return RestoreSurfaces();
  return TRUE;
} //PageFlip

BOOL ComposeFrame(){ //compose a frame of animation
  static int last_time=Timer.time();
  //paranoia
  if(current_frame<0)current_frame=0;
  if(current_frame>3)current_frame=3;
  //show a frame
  switch(current_frame){
    case 0: frame0.draw(lpSecondary); break;
    case 1: frame1.draw(lpSecondary); break;
    case 2: frame2.draw(lpSecondary); break;
    case 3: frame1.draw(lpSecondary); break;
  }
  //go to next frame
  if(Timer.elapsed(last_time,100))
    if(++current_frame>=4)current_frame=0;
  return TRUE;
} //ComposeFrame
```

```
BOOL ProcessFrame(){ //process a frame of animation
  ComposeFrame(); //compose a frame in secondary surface
  return PageFlip(); //flip video memory surfaces
} //ProcessFrame

BOOL keyboard_handler(WPARAM keystroke){ //keyboard handler
  BOOL result=FALSE; //return TRUE if game is to end
  switch(keystroke){
    case VK_ESCAPE: result=TRUE; break; //exit game
    default: break;
  }
  return result;
} //keyboard_handler

//message handler (window procedure)
long CALLBACK WindowProc(HWND hwnd,UINT message,
                         WPARAM wParam,LPARAM lParam){
  switch(message){
    case WM_ACTIVATEAPP: ActiveApp=wParam; break;
    case WM_CREATE: break;
    case WM_KEYDOWN: //keyboard hit
      if(keyboard_handler(wParam))DestroyWindow(hwnd);
      break;
    case WM_DESTROY: //end of game
      if(lpDirectDrawObject!=NULL){ //if DD object exists
        if(lpSecondary!=NULL) //if secondary surface exists
          lpSecondary->Release(); //release secondary surface
        if(lpPrimary!=NULL) //if primary surface exists
          lpPrimary->Release(); //release primary surface
        lpDirectDrawObject->Release(); //release DD object
      }
      ShowCursor(TRUE); //show the mouse cursor
      PostQuitMessage(0); //and exit
      break;
    default: //default window procedure
      return DefWindowProc(hwnd,message,wParam,lParam);
  } //switch(message)
  return 0L;
} //WindowProc

int WINAPI WinMain(HINSTANCE hInstance,HINSTANCE hPrevInstance,
                   LPSTR lpCmdLine,int nCmdShow){
  MSG msg; //current message
  HWND hwnd; //handle to fullscreen window
  hwnd=CreateDefaultWindow("directX demo 2",hInstance);
  if(!hwnd)return FALSE;
  //set up window
  ShowWindow(hwnd,nCmdShow); UpdateWindow(hwnd);
  SetFocus(hwnd); //allow input from keyboard
```

```
    ShowCursor(FALSE); //hide the cursor
    //init graphics
    BOOL OK=InitDirectDraw(hwnd);//initialize DirectDraw
    if(OK)OK=LoadImages(); //load images from disk
    if(!OK){ //bail out if initialization failed
      DestroyWindow(hwnd); return FALSE;
    }
    //start game timer
    Timer.start();
    //message loop
    while(TRUE)
      if(PeekMessage(&msg,NULL,0,0,PM_NOREMOVE)){
        if(!GetMessage(&msg,NULL,0,0))return msg.wParam;
        TranslateMessage(&msg); DispatchMessage(&msg);
      }
      else if(ActiveApp)ProcessFrame(); else WaitMessage();
} //WinMain
```

Timer.h

```
//timer.h, header file for timer.cpp
//Copyright Ian Parberry, 1999
//Last updated September 20, 1999

//system includes
#include <windows.h> //needed for BOOL

#ifndef __timer_h__
#define __timer_h__

class CTimer{ //game timer class
  protected:
    int m_nStartTime; //time that timer was started
  public:
    CTimer(); //constructor
    virtual void start(); //start the timer
    virtual int time(); //return the time in ms
    //has interval ms elapsed since start?
    BOOL elapsed(int &start,int interval);
};

#endif
```

Timer.cpp

```
//timer.cpp, the timer class
//Copyright Ian Parberry, 1999
//Last updated September 20, 1999

#include "timer.h"
```

```
CTimer::CTimer(){ //constructor
  m_nStartTime=0;
}

void CTimer::start(){ //start the timer
  m_nStartTime=timeGetTime();
}

int CTimer::time(){ //return the time
  return timeGetTime()-m_nStartTime;
}

int CTimer::elapsed(int &start,int interval){
  //has interval elapsed from start?
  int current_time=time();
  if(current_time>=start+interval){
    start=current_time; return TRUE;
  }
  else return FALSE;
}
```

Chapter 5

Here's what you'll learn:

- What a sprite is and how to set up a sprite file

- What blitting is

- How to do transparent blitting in DirectDraw

- Why you should separate an object's image from its other physical properties

- How to load and draw multi-framed sprites to the screen

- What happens if you try to draw outside the screen

Sprite Animation

In Demo 3, we learn how to do sprite animation. A *sprite* is a small piece of artwork that moves across the screen. *Sprite animation*, then, is the process of animating a sprite. Sprites may have several frames of animation, but in this example, we simply move a single-frame sprite depicting a plane across the background (see Figure 5.1). The process of drawing a sprite on top of the background is called *blitting*. DirectDraw allows us to blit from one surface to another with *transparency*, which means that we can designate one or more palette positions as transparent, that is, undrawn. This allows us to draw sprites with holes in them through which we can see the background.

Figure 5.1
A plane
sprite flying
across the
background

Experiment with Demo 3

Take a moment now to run Demo 3.

- You should see a plane flying from right to left across the background.

- Notice that the plane disappears as soon as its leftmost pixel leaves the screen. DirectDraw refuses to draw anything that goes outside the target surface. This is for a simple reason—if it didn't, you could accidentally end up drawing the plane anywhere in memory, for example, in the middle of the executable code for your game, or in the middle of the operating system. This would be a Bad Thing. So, remember this: If you try to draw a sprite but see nothing, it may mean that you have missed the surface completely.

- If you wait long enough, the plane will reappear on the right—as soon as its rightmost pixel is on the screen, that is.

- Hit the Esc key to exit the program.

The Sprite File

The sprites for our game were drawn by the artist in the file `Sprites.bmp` (see Figure 5.2). Notice that there are many sprites included in that file. Many artists prefer to put multiple sprites into a single file so that they can easily compare frames of animation to make sure they are consistent with each other. `Sprites.bmp` uses the same palette as `Bckgnd.bmp`. You must make sure that the artist realizes that all of the artwork to be used in the game must be drawn with the same palette.

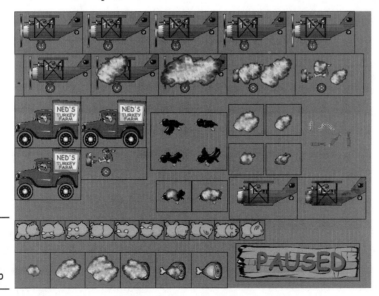

Figure 5.2
The sprite file
Sprites.bmp

The background color used in Sprites.bmp is magenta, with an RGB value of (255,0,255). The important thing is not the color that is used, but its palette position. You and the artist must agree on a palette position that will be used for the background so that you can use that palette position to indicate transparent pixels—if the artwork is inconsistent with your program, the plane will be drawn with a rectangular block around it (see Figure 5.3). Although in principle any palette position can be used, it is normal to use either the first or last palette position (that is, either palette position 0 or palette position 255). This helps the artist to locate it in the palette. However, many art tools do not give any indication to the artist which end of the palette is which, so don't blow a fuse if the artist gets it wrong initially. In addition, you should know that the same art tool on two different platforms (such as PC and Mac) has been known to reverse the palettes on their images.

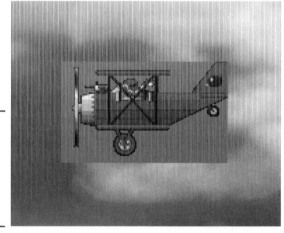

Figure 5.3
What you will see if you mess up the transparent color

It doesn't matter to the game what color you put in the transparent palette position, since pixels in that palette position aren't ever drawn. However, it is best that you put some color that isn't used elsewhere in the game so that the artist (or more accurately, the automated art tools that the artist may use) isn't tempted to use that palette position expecting it to actually be drawn. You can use the same color in another palette position if you have to, but the artist must be sure that the transparent palette position is used only for transparent pixels, otherwise your sprites will get holes in them where you don't necessarily want them.

You must also tell your artist not to antialias the sprites to the background. *Antialiasing* is the process of blurring the outer pixels of the sprites into the background. It is used to reduce the jaggedness of edges where the pixelation makes it look rough. Antialiasing our sprites onto the background will just give a pink haze around them when they are drawn onto the blue sky, which is an effect that we can live without. Tell the artist that the sprite will be drawn onto a variety of colored backgrounds, so there is nothing that we can antialias to. Be forewarned that it is normal for an artist, particularly a novice, to forget to turn off antialiasing occasionally. This is why I like to put magenta into the transparent palette position—when the artist forgets, it is immediately obvious to the naked eye, whereas antialiasing to black or white (which is a popular choice among artists) may go undetected for a long time.

You will notice if you take another look at Figure 5.2 that most of the sprites have a black rectangle around them. This is called the *bounding rectangle*. The bounding rectangle should be the smallest rectangle that will fit around the object. I have chosen in this game to have all of the frames in a multi-frame sprite have the same height and width, even though some frames may be smaller than others. Wasting transparent pixels around an image will slow your game slightly, so it should be avoided, but it is not a major issue.

Somebody—either you or the artist—must measure each of the sprite frames, recording the height and width of the sprite, and the position of the top left pixel of each frame (the top left pixel of the image is pixel (0,0), and the bottom right pixel is pixel (639,479) in our 640x480 resolution images). Explicitly drawing a bounding rectangle around each sprite frame will help you to identify the top left pixel easily even when the top left portion of the image is transparent, and it will have another positive effect: You will undoubtedly mess up your measurements at least once—I almost never manage to get them all right the first time. If you make the frame too small, the sprite image will be clipped along at least one edge. If you make it too big, it may infringe on the neighboring sprite by as little as one pixel, which will give you a floating pixel off to one side of your sprite. A single floating pixel is easy to miss. Using a bounding rectangle will ensure that if you make your sprite too large, one edge of the bounding box will appear on the screen. This is easy to spot (see Figure 5.4, for example) and the problem can then be quickly corrected.

Figure 5.4
Drawing part of the bounding box by accident

The Bmp Sprite File Reader

Since sprite files may contain multiple frames of sprite images within a single file, we need a way to read rectangles from a bmp file. The bmp sprite file reader class `CBmpSpriteFileReader` is derived from `CBmpFileReader` and adds to it a new public member `draw` function that draws to a surface, from the image stored in the `CBmpFileReader` member variable `m_cImage`, a rectangle of a given width and height with the top left pixel at a given pair of coordinates. The header file for `CBmpSpriteFileReader` is `Sbmp.h`, in which we find the following declaration:

```
class CBmpSpriteFileReader:
public CBmpFileReader{ //bmp sprite file input class
  public:
    BOOL draw(LPDIRECTDRAWSURFACE surface,
      int width,int ht,int x,int y); //draw sprite
};
```

Naturally, the code for `CBmpSpriteFileReader::draw`, found in `Sbmp.cpp`, is very similar to the code for `CBmpFileReader::draw`. The first difference is that the source pointer `src` is now initially set to point `y` rows up from the bottom of the image (recall from Chapter 2 that bmp files are stored upside-down) and `x` pixels across, where `x` and `y` are parameters to the `draw` function:.

```
src=m_cImage+ //source pointer
  ((m_BMPFileInfo.biHeight-1-y)*m_BMPFileInfo.biWidth+x);
```

The second difference is that the for-loop that moves data from the image to the surface now only move `ht` rows of data, and each row has width `width`, where `ht` and `width` are also parameters to the draw function:

```
for(int i=0; i<ht; i++){ //for each row
  memcpy(dest,src,width); //copy
  dest+=ddsd.lPitch; src-=m_BMPFileInfo.biWidth; //next row
}
```

The Base Sprite

A sprite is our abstraction of the image of an object. I find that it helps to abstract out the concept of the image of an object from its other features. That way, if we have multiple objects in the game that have the same image (for example, we will have multiple crows), we can share the image data and not waste memory on multiple copies of the same image. Our base sprite class is called `CBaseSprite`.

Base Sprite Overview

The header file for `CBaseSprite` is `Bsprite.h`. `CBaseSprite` has four private member variables and a private member function. The first private member variable is an array of pointers to DirectDraw surfaces. We will use one surface for each frame of the sprite. Because we have no way of knowing at compile time how many surfaces there will be, we declare it as a pointer to pointers to a DirectDraw surface and will `new` ourselves enough space in the `CBaseSprite` constructor.

```
LPDIRECTDRAWSURFACE *m_lpDDImage; //sprite image
```

The next three private member variables record how many frames of animation the sprite has, and the width and height of those frames. Recall that in this simple game, we will insist that all frames of animation in a given sprite have the same width and height (although they may be different for different sprites). This means that they must be as large as the largest frame, which is usually not too wasteful of space unless the sprite is *much* larger in some frames than others. I wouldn't use this technique, for example, in a maritime game in which the sprite frames record how a ship looks from different angles, since the face-on view of a ship can be very narrow compared to the side-on view.

```
int m_nFrameCount; //how many frames used in sprite
int m_nWidth,m_nHeight; //dimensions of sprite images
```

The private member function `CreateSurfaces` creates the surfaces for the sprite frames, assuming that the three private member variables `m_nFrameCount`, `m_nWidth`, and `m_nHeight` have been set:

```
void CreateSurfaces(); //create surfaces
```

`CBaseSprite` has, in addition to a constructor and a destructor, seven public member functions. The constructor has three parameters, the number of frames, and the frame width and height.

```
CBaseSprite(int frames,int w,int h); //constructor
~CBaseSprite(); //destructor
```

The `CBaseSprite` `load` function loads a frame from a `CBmpSpriteFileReader` image. It has four parameters, a pointer to the `CBmpSpriteFileReader` class instance containing the sprite frame, the number of the frame to be loaded, and the x and y coordinates from which the frame is to be loaded.

```
BOOL load(CBmpSpriteFileReader *image,int frame,
    int x,int y); //load sprite image
```

The `CBaseSprite` `draw` function is a virtual function because we will derive a more general sprite class from `CBaseSprite` in the next chapter. It takes four parameters, the number of the frame to be drawn, the x and y coordinates that the lower center pixel of the sprite is to be drawn to, and a pointer to the surface on which to draw it at those coordinates.

```
virtual void draw(int frame,int x,int y,
    LPDIRECTDRAWSURFACE destination); //draw sprite
```

Recall from Chapter 4 that every surface must be restored when surfaces are lost, and released when the game is over. Therefore, every class that contains member surfaces should have a restore and a release function.

```
void Release(); //release direct draw surfaces
BOOL Restore(); //restore surfaces
```

Finally, CBaseSprite has three public *reader functions*, which are used to provide read-only access to private member variables:

```
int frame_count(); //return number of frames
int height(); //return height
int width(); //return width
```

Creation and Destruction

The code for CBaseSprite can be found in Bsprite.cpp. The CBaseSprite constructor first records the number of frames, width, and height of the sprite.

```
CBaseSprite::CBaseSprite(int frames,int width,int height){
  //settings
  m_nWidth=width; m_nHeight=height; //width and height
  m_nFrameCount=frames; //assign number of frames
```

Then, it allocates space for the array of frame pointers, m_lpDDImage, and sets all of the pointers in the array to NULL:

```
m_lpDDImage=new LPDIRECTDRAWSURFACE[frames];
for(int i=0; i<frames; i++)m_lpDDImage[i]=NULL;
```

Finally, it calls private member function CreateSurfaces to create the surfaces in the frame array lpDDImage, and returns:

```
CreateSurfaces();
}
```

The CBaseSprite destructor merely deletes the memory allocated in the constructor:

```
CBaseSprite::~CBaseSprite(){ //destructor
  //deallocate memory allocated in constructor
  delete[]m_lpDDImage;
}
```

The CBaseSprite private member function CreateSurfaces has the task of creating and initializing one surface for each frame of the sprite:

```
void CBaseSprite::CreateSurfaces(){ //create surfaces
```

It has a single local variable, a DirectDraw surface descriptor:

```
DDSURFACEDESC ddsd; //direct draw surface descriptor
```

As we did the last time we used a DirectDraw surface descriptor, we set the size field of ddsd to the structure's size:

```
ddsd.dwSize=sizeof(ddsd); //required field
```

We indicate in the flags field that we're going to set the surface capabilities, height, and width:

```
ddsd.dwFlags=DDSD_CAPS|DDSD_HEIGHT|DDSD_WIDTH; //attributes
```

In the capabilities field, we ask for a plain offscreen surface, that is, one that will reside in system memory as opposed to video memory. Then, we set the width and height of the surface to be the sprite frame height and width.

```
ddsd.ddsCaps.dwCaps=DDSCAPS_OFFSCREENPLAIN; //offscreen
ddsd.dwHeight=m_nHeight; //sprite height
ddsd.dwWidth=m_nWidth; //sprite width
```

In order to set the transparent palette position, we declare a local variable ddck of type DDCOLORKEY. Actually, we can set a range of palette positions to use for the transparent color, so we set both the lower value for the range and the upper value equal to TRANSPARENT_COLOR, which is defined to be 255 in Defines.h.

```
DDCOLORKEY ddck; //direct draw color descriptor
ddck.dwColorSpaceLowValue=
  ddck.dwColorSpaceHighValue=
    TRANSPARENT_COLOR; //one color
```

Finally, we create the surfaces in a "for each frame" style for-loop. Each surface is created with a call to the DirectDraw object's CreateSurface member function, and then we set the transparent color in the new surface using its SetColorKey member function. SetColorKey has two parameters. We set the first to DDCKEY_SRCBLT to indicate that when a sprite surface is blitted the color key is in the source surface. The second parameter is a pointer to the DDCOLORKEY local variable that we loaded with the transparent color for our game.

```
for(int i=0; i<m_nFrameCount; i++){ //for each frame
  //create surface
  if(FAILED(lpDirectDrawObject->
  CreateSurface(&ddsd,&(m_lpDDImage[i]),NULL)))
    m_lpDDImage[i]=NULL;
  //set the transparent color
  m_lpDDImage[i]->SetColorKey(DDCKEY_SRCBLT,&ddck);
  }
}
```

The CBaseSprite Release function calls the Release member function of each surface in the m_lpDDImage array:

```
void CBaseSprite::Release(){ //release all sprite surfaces
  for(int i=0; i<m_nFrameCount; i++) //for each frame
    if(m_lpDDImage[i]!=NULL) //if it is really there
      m_lpDDImage[i]->Release(); //release it
}
```

Loading and Drawing

The CBaseSprite load function loads a sprite frame from a CBmpSpriteFileReader class instance. It simply calls the CBmpSpriteFileReader draw function to draw from the appropriate rectangle in its stored image into the correct frame in its m_lpDDImage array.

```
BOOL CBaseSprite::load(CBmpSpriteFileReader *buffer,
                       int frame,int x,int y){
//grab sprite image from (x,y) in *buffer
//and store in m_lpDDImage[frame]
  return buffer->draw(m_lpDDImage[frame],
    m_nWidth,m_nHeight,x,y);
}
```

The CBaseSprite draw function uses the destination surface's BltFast member function to blit the image from the correct frame in its lpDDImage array. The flags field is set to DDBLTFAST_SRCCOLORKEY|DDBLTFAST_WAIT, indicating respectively that the source surface has a transparency palette range set, and that if the blitter is busy the blit function is to wait and return only after the blitter has responded. The DirectDraw BltFast function takes as its first two parameters the x and y coordinates at which the *top left* pixel of the sprite is to appear. We will find it more convenient for the CBaseSprite draw function to take instead the x and y coordinates at which the *lower center* pixel of the sprite is to appear. Hence, the CBaseSprite draw function must subtract half of the sprite width from the x coordinate, and the sprite height from the y coordinate to get the target coordinates of the top left pixel. The third parameter to BltFast is a pointer to the source surface, and the fourth parameter is a pointer to a rectangle from which to blit from within the source surface. Leaving the rectangle pointer NULL will draw the whole surface.

```
void CBaseSprite::draw(int frame,int x,int y,
                       LPDIRECTDRAWSURFACE dest){
  dest->BltFast(x-m_nWidth/2,y-m_nHeight,m_lpDDImage[frame],
    NULL,DDBLTFAST_SRCCOLORKEY|DDBLTFAST_WAIT);
}
```

Other Member Functions

The CBaseSprite Restore function calls the Restore member function of each surface in the m_lpDDImage array:

```
BOOL CBaseSprite::Restore(){ //restore surfaces
  BOOL result=TRUE; //return TRUE if all surfaces restored OK
  for(int i=0; i<m_nFrameCount; i++) //for each frame
    if(m_lpDDImage[i]) //if it exists
      result=result&&
        SUCCEEDED(m_lpDDImage[i]->Restore()); //restore it
  return result;
}
```

The remaining three CBaseSprite reader functions frame_count, height, and width return the values in the respective private member variables. Rather than list these simple functions here, we will leave it for you to read them in the listing of Bsprite.cpp later in this chapter.

The Object Class

Each of the objects in our game will be described using a class called CObject. CObject will encapsulate everything about an object, including its physical characteristics and its image.

Object Overview

The header file for CObject is Objects.h. CObject has six private member variables that together comprise the internal state of an object—its location in the virtual universe (which in this game is two-dimensional), its speed, the last time it moved, and a pointer to a sprite that represents its image. For memory efficiency we use a *pointer to a sprite* instead of a sprite, so that multiple objects can share the same sprite.

```
int m_nX,m_nY; //current location
int m_nXspeed,m_nYspeed; //current speed
int m_nLastXMoveTime; //last time the object moved
CBaseSprite *m_pSprite; //pointer to sprite
```

In addition to a constructor, CObject has four public member functions. The CObject draw function takes a pointer to a DirectDraw surface, and draws the object on that surface. Notice that the draw function has no other parameters, which implies that the object is responsible for determining where it should be drawn on the screen from its location in the virtual universe.

```
void draw(LPDIRECTDRAWSURFACE surface); //draw
```

The `CObject create` function sets the initial state of the object. The parameters to that function list the object's initial position, speed, and a pointer to its shared sprite.

```
void create(int x,int y,int xspeed,int yspeed,
  CBaseSprite *sprite); //create instance
```

The `CObject accelerate` function changes the x and y components of the object's speed, and takes as parameters the amounts by which those components must change:

```
void accelerate(int xdelta,int ydelta=0); //change speed
```

The `CObject move` function makes the object move. Notice that this function has no parameters, which implies that the object is responsible for determining how far it should move from its internal state. It does this by modifying its location in the virtual universe depending on its speed and the time since the last move was made. This dependence on time is crucial if our game is to run at the same apparent speed on a variety of hardware. Neglecting the dependence on time—one of the most common mistakes that I have seen novice game programmers make—will make objects that travel at a fixed speed move a fixed distance on every frame. However, a faster computer will have a higher frame rate, which means that objects should move less on each frame if they are to achieve the same apparent motion across the screen as on a slow computer. We must also consider the fact that the frame rate of your game will not remain constant, because Windows is a multitasking operating system, meaning that other applications may be running simultaneously, making demands on the CPU's processing power at random times. We overcome both of these problems by measuring the time since the object last moved (which should have been during the previous frame), and then moving it a distance proportional to that time.

```
void move(); //make a move depending on time and speed
```

Object Code

The code for `CObject` can be found in `Objects.cpp`. The `CObject` constructor puts some reasonable initial values into the private member variables.

```
CObject::CObject(){ //constructor
  m_nX=m_nY=m_nXspeed=m_nYspeed=0;
  m_pSprite=NULL; m_nLastXMoveTime=0;
}
```

Next, we have the `CObject draw` function, which draws the object to a given surface. It calls the object's sprite's `draw` function to draw frame 0 to position (`m_nX,m_nY`) on `surface`, where `m_nX` and `m_nY` are the `CObject` private member variables that record the object's location in the virtual universe.

```
void CObject::draw(LPDIRECTDRAWSURFACE surface){ //draw
  m_pSprite->draw(0,m_nX,m_nY,surface);
}
```

The CObject create function initializes the object's private member functions, setting m_nLastXMoveTime to zero, and the rest of them to values provided as parameters:

```
void CObject::create(int x,int y,int xspeed,int yspeed,
                     CBaseSprite *sprite){
  m_nLastXMoveTime=0; //time
  m_nX=x; m_nY=y; //location
  m_nXspeed=xspeed; m_nYspeed=yspeed; //speed
  m_pSprite=sprite; //image
}
```

The CObject accelerate function accelerates the object by adding a delta to its speed in the x and y directions:

```
void CObject::accelerate(int xdelta,int ydelta){
  //change speed
  m_nXspeed+=xdelta; m_nYspeed+=ydelta;
}
```

The Move Function

The CObject move function moves the object a distance that depends on its speed and the time since it last moved. We begin the function with the declaration of two constants. XSCALE is a constant whose value we set by experiment—more about that in a moment. MARGIN is a width of a guard band that extends to the left and the right of the screen by 100 pixels; that is, the virtual universe for this demo consists of the background plus a 100-pixel wide strip to the left of the screen and another to the right of the screen.

```
void CObject::move(){ //move object
  const int XSCALE=8; //to scale back horizontal motion
  const int MARGIN=100; //margin on outside of page
```

We next declare two local variables, xdelta, which will record the distance moved in the x direction (in this demo all motion will be in the x direction), and time which records the current time, obtained from the global game timer Timer, which is externed at the top of Objects.cpp:

```
int xdelta; //change in position
int time=Timer.time(); //current time
```

We then set a local variable tfactor to the amount of time since the object last moved, which is recorded in private member variable m_nLastXMoveTime:

```
int tfactor=time-m_nLastXMoveTime; //time since last move
```

The distance that the object moves in the x direction is equal to its speed multiplied by the time factor. This value needs to be scaled back slightly. For example, at 30 frames per second (33.33 milliseconds between frames), `tfactor` will be approximately 33, which means that at a speed of 1 the object will move 33 pixels per frame, which comes out to be approximately 1000 pixels—more than the width of the virtual universe—per second. We scale back the distance moved by dividing it by `XSCALE`, and experimenting with the value of `XSCALE` until it looks right. (Remember the First Law of Graphics Programming: If it looks right, it *is* right.) The distance moved in the x direction, `xdelta`, is added into the object's x location.

```
xdelta=(m_nXspeed*tfactor)/XSCALE; //x distance moved
m_nX+=xdelta; //x motion
```

The object in this demo (the plane) will move left across the screen, and so its x coordinate will eventually become negative. When it reaches the edge of the guard band, we move it to the other guard band at the right-hand side of the screen.

```
if(m_nX<-MARGIN)m_nX=SCREEN_WIDTH+MARGIN; //wrap left
```

Next, we record the time of the current move. It is tempting to just write "m_nLastXMoveTime=time" here, and leave it at that. However, the situation is slightly more subtle than it first appears. The object could move so slowly that it moves only one pixel on every second frame. For example, suppose that the game runs at 60 frames per second, the object has an m_nXspeed of 1, and we set XSCALE to 32. On the first frame, the time-since-last-move will be 16 milliseconds, and `xdelta` will be 16/32, which will be rounded down to zero. On the next frame we want the time-since-last-move to be 32 milliseconds, so that `xdelta` will be 32/32=1 pixel. Therefore, we *don't* want to set m_nLastXMoveTime to time unless `xdelta` is nonzero. Unless, of course, `xdelta` is zero because m_nXspeed is zero—we don't want our object to take off at light speed after sitting still for a few minutes!

```
if(xdelta||m_nXspeed==0) //record time of move
  m_nLastXMoveTime=time;
```

Although we don't use it in this demo, I have also added code for wrapping an object moving rightwards across the screen:

```
if(m_nX>SCREEN_WIDTH+MARGIN)m_nX=-MARGIN; //wrap right
}
```

Changes to Ddsetup.cpp and Main.cpp

The changes to `Ddsetup.cpp` in Demo 3 are all related to the background surface:

```
extern LPDIRECTDRAWSURFACE lpBackground; //background image
```

At the end of `InitDirectDraw`, we add code to set up the background surface as a plain offscreen surface of the same height and width as the screen. This code is almost identical to that used for setting up the surfaces for the sprite frames in `CBaseSprite` earlier in this chapter.

```
ddsd.dwSize=sizeof(ddsd);
ddsd.dwFlags=DDSD_CAPS|DDSD_HEIGHT|DDSD_WIDTH;
ddsd.ddsCaps.dwCaps=DDSCAPS_OFFSCREENPLAIN;
ddsd.dwHeight=SCREEN_HEIGHT; ddsd.dwWidth=SCREEN_WIDTH;
if(FAILED(lpDirectDrawObject->
CreateSurface(&ddsd,&lpBackground,NULL)))
  return FALSE;
```

The changes to `Main.cpp` involve initializing, using, and cleaning up the objects and their sprites. After the declarations of the pointers for the primary and secondary surfaces that we use from Demo 2, we insert a declaration for a pointer for a surface to hold the background image ready for blitting to the secondary surface during animation.

```
LPDIRECTDRAWSURFACE lpBackground=NULL; //background image
```

Next, we declare a `CBmpFileReader` class instance to load the background file, and a `CBmpSpriteFileReader` class instance to load the sprite file:

```
CBmpFileReader background; //background image
CBmpSpriteFileReader g_cSpriteImages; //sprite images
```

Demo 3 has just one object, Ned's trusty old biplane:

```
CObject plane; //plane object
```

The plane sprite is a different entity from the plane object:

```
CBaseSprite *planesprite=NULL; //plane sprite
```

The LoadPlaneSprite and LoadImages Functions

The first piece of code is the function `LoadPlaneSprite`, which loads the plane sprite by calling the `planesprite load` function. The `load` function has four parameters, the first of which is a pointer to the `CBmpSpriteFileReader` class instance `g_cSpriteImages` that holds the sprite image. The next parameter is 0, indicating that we are loading frame 0 of the sprite (which only has one frame). The next two parameters are 1, 1, which are the coordinates of the top left pixel of the rectangle containing the plane sprite image (the plane sprite is at the top left corner of Sprites.bmp, inside a bounding box of width 1—see Figure 5.2).

```
BOOL LoadPlaneSprite(){ //load plane image
  return planesprite->load(&g_cSpriteImages,0,1,1);
} //LoadPlaneSprite
```

The body of function LoadImages is replaced completely by the following code. First, we load the background image from the file Bckgnd.bmp into the CBmpFileReader class instance background, then draw it to the background surface pointed to by lpBackground.

```
if(!background.load("bckgnd.bmp"))return FALSE; //read file
background.draw(lpBackground); //draw to background surface
```

We then set the palettes of the primary and secondary surfaces:

```
if(!background.setpalette(lpPrimaryPalette))return FALSE;
if(!background.setpalette(lpSecondaryPalette))return FALSE;
```

Next, we load the sprite image file Sprites.bmp into the CBmpSpriteFile-Reader class instance g_cSpriteImages:

```
if(!g_cSpriteImages.load("sprites.bmp"))return FALSE;
```

We then new ourselves a planesprite of type CBaseSprite, a base sprite with one frame, 121 pixels wide and 72 pixels high. How do we figure out the height and width of the plane sprite? We open up the sprite file Sprites.bmp with an art tool, such as Microsoft Paint, and measure the coordinates of the top left pixel and the bottom right pixel of the plane sprite in the top left corner of the file, just inside the bounding box. In general, if the top left pixel is at (x_1,y_1) and the bottom right pixel is at (x_2,y_2), then the sprite is x_2-x_1+1 pixels wide, and y_2-y_1+1 pixels high.

```
planesprite=new CBaseSprite(1,121,72);
if(!LoadPlaneSprite())return FALSE; //load plane images
```

The CreateObjects Function

The function CreateObjects creates the objects in the game. At this stage of development we have just the plane, of course. It calls the CObject plane create function with five parameters. The first two are the initial coordinates of the bottom center pixel of the plane sprite, (320,271), which puts it approximately at the center of the screen. The next two are the x and y components of its speed, -1,0, which makes it move left at speed 1. The last parameter is a pointer to its sprite, planesprite.

```
void CreateObjects(){
  plane.create(320,271,-1,0,planesprite); //create plane
} //CreateObjects
```

The RestoreSurfaces Function

In function `RestoreSurfaces`, after some minor changes to how the primary and secondary surfaces are redrawn after they are restored (in Demo 2 they were redrawn from `frame0` and `frame1`, while here in Demo 3 they are redrawn from `background`), we add code to restore and redraw the `lpBackground` surface (using the DirectDraw surface `Restore` function) and the `planesprite` sprite frame surface (using our `CBaseSprite Restore` member function):

```
if(SUCCEEDED(lpBackground->Restore())) //if background restored
   result=result&&background.draw(lpBackground); //redraw image
else return FALSE;
if(planesprite->Restore()) //if plane sprite restored
   result=result&&LoadPlaneSprite(); //redraw image
else return FALSE;
```

The ComposeFrame Function

The body of `ComposeFrame` gets totally rewritten. Now it is beginning to look like a *real* sprite animation engine, except for the fact that Demo 3 has only one object. First, we draw the background to the secondary surface. Setting the `DDBLTFAST_NOCOLORKEY` flag in `BltFast` ensures that no transparencies are used. It is a little inefficient at this point to redraw the whole background on each frame since most of it doesn't change, but later in the development we will add a moving background that will change on almost every frame. If this weren't so, we could just redraw the background behind the plane instead of redrawing the whole thing—such a process is called *dirty rectangle animation*.

```
lpSecondary->BltFast(0,0,lpBackground,NULL,
   DDBLTFAST_NOCOLORKEY|DDBLTFAST_WAIT);
```

Then we move the objects:

```
plane.move();
```

Then, we draw them on top of the secondary surface:

```
plane.draw(lpSecondary);
```

The Window Procedure and WinMain

The final thing we need to do to the new surfaces in `Main.cpp` is to release them when we are finished with them. In the switch statement in `WindowProc`, under the `WM_DESTROY` case, we must add the following code after the primary and secondary surfaces have been released. (And we can delete the `planesprite` while we are cleaning up.) The background surface is released using its DirectDraw surface `Release` function, and `planesprite` is released using our `CBaseSprite Release` member function.

```
if(lpBackground!=NULL) //if background exists
  lpBackground->Release(); //release background
if(planesprite!=NULL) //if plane sprite exists
  planesprite->Release(); //release plane sprite
delete planesprite; //delete plane sprite
```

Finally, a call to CreateObjects in WinMain just before we enter the message loop will create our objects for us:

```
CreateObjects();
```

Demo 3 Files

Code Files

The following files in Demo 3 are used without change from Demo 2:

- Bmp.h
- Bmp.cpp
- Timer.h
- Timer.cpp

The following files in Demo 3 have been modified from Demo 2:

- Ddsetup.cpp
- Defines.h
- Main.cpp

The following files are new in Demo 3:

- Bsprite.h
- Bsprite.cpp
- Objects.h
- Objects.cpp
- Sbmp.h
- Sbmp.cpp

Media Files

The following image files are new in Demo 3:

- Bckgnd.bmp (previously used in Demo 0 but not Demos 1 and 2)
- Sprites.bmp

Required Libraries

- Ddraw.lib
- Winmm.lib

Code Listings

Bsprite.h

```
//bsprite.h
//header file for base sprite class

//Copyright Ian Parberry, 1999
//Last updated September 28, 1999

#include <windows.h>
#include <windowsx.h>
#include <ddraw.h>
#include "sbmp.h"

#ifndef __BSPRITE__
#define __BSPRITE__

class CBaseSprite{ //simplest sprite
  protected:
    LPDIRECTDRAWSURFACE *m_lpDDImage; //sprite image
    int m_nFrameCount; //how many frames used in sprite
    int m_nWidth,m_nHeight; //dimensions of sprite images
    void CreateSurfaces(); //create surfaces
  public:
    CBaseSprite(int frames,int w,int h); //constructor
    ~CBaseSprite(); //destructor
    BOOL load(CBmpSpriteFileReader *image,int frame,
      int x,int y); //load sprite image
    virtual void draw(int frame,int x,int y,
      LPDIRECTDRAWSURFACE destination); //draw sprite
    void Release(); //release direct draw surfaces
    BOOL Restore(); //restore surfaces
    int frame_count(); //return number of frames
    int height(); //return height
    int width(); //return width
};

#endif
```

Bsprite.cpp

```cpp
//bsprite.cpp: base sprite class functions

//Copyright Ian Parberry, 1999
//Last updated May 22, 2000

#include <string.h> //for memcpy
#include "defines.h"
#include "bsprite.h"

extern LPDIRECTDRAW lpDirectDrawObject; //direct draw object

CBaseSprite::CBaseSprite(int frames,int width,int height){
  //settings
  m_nWidth=width; m_nHeight=height; //width and height
  m_nFrameCount=frames; //assign number of frames
  //create space for sprite surface pointers
  m_lpDDImage=new LPDIRECTDRAWSURFACE[frames];
  for(int i=0; i<frames; i++)m_lpDDImage[i]=NULL;
  //create surfaces for sprite images
  CreateSurfaces();
}

CBaseSprite::~CBaseSprite(){ //destructor
  //deallocate memory allocated in constructor
  delete[]m_lpDDImage;
}

void CBaseSprite::CreateSurfaces(){ //create surfaces
  //set parameters of surface to be created
  DDSURFACEDESC ddsd; //direct draw surface descriptor
  ddsd.dwSize=sizeof(ddsd); //required field
  ddsd.dwFlags=DDSD_CAPS|DDSD_HEIGHT|DDSD_WIDTH; //attributes
  ddsd.ddsCaps.dwCaps=DDSCAPS_OFFSCREENPLAIN; //offscreen
  ddsd.dwHeight=m_nHeight; //sprite height
  ddsd.dwWidth=m_nWidth; //sprite width
  //color key for transparent color
  DDCOLORKEY ddck; //direct draw color descriptor
  ddck.dwColorSpaceLowValue=
    ddck.dwColorSpaceHighValue=
      TRANSPARENT_COLOR; //one color
  //create surfaces
  for(int i=0; i<m_nFrameCount; i++){ //for each frame
    //create surface
    if(FAILED(lpDirectDrawObject->
    CreateSurface(&ddsd,&(m_lpDDImage[i]),NULL)))
      m_lpDDImage[i]=NULL;
    //set the transparent color
    m_lpDDImage[i]->SetColorKey(DDCKEY_SRCBLT,&ddck);
```

```
    }
  }

  void CBaseSprite::Release(){ //release all sprite surfaces
    for(int i=0; i<m_nFrameCount; i++) //for each frame
      if(m_lpDDImage[i]!=NULL) //if it is really there
        m_lpDDImage[i]->Release(); //release it
  }

  BOOL CBaseSprite::load(CBmpSpriteFileReader *buffer,
                         int frame,int x,int y){
  //grab sprite image from (x,y) in *buffer
  //and store in m_lpDDImage[frame]
    return buffer->draw(m_lpDDImage[frame],
      m_nWidth,m_nHeight,x,y);
  }

  void CBaseSprite::draw(int frame,int x,int y,
                         LPDIRECTDRAWSURFACE dest){
    dest->BltFast(x-m_nWidth/2,y-m_nHeight,m_lpDDImage[frame],
      NULL,DDBLTFAST_SRCCOLORKEY|DDBLTFAST_WAIT);
  }

  BOOL CBaseSprite::Restore(){ //restore surfaces
    BOOL result=TRUE; //return TRUE if all surfaces restored OK
    for(int i=0; i<m_nFrameCount; i++) //for each frame
      if(m_lpDDImage[i]) //if it exists
        result=result&&
          SUCCEEDED(m_lpDDImage[i]->Restore()); //restore it
    return result;
  }

  //reader functions

  int CBaseSprite::frame_count(){ //return number of frames
    return m_nFrameCount;
  }

  int CBaseSprite::height(){ //return height
    return m_nHeight;
  }

  int CBaseSprite::width(){ //return width
    return m_nWidth;
  }
```

Ddsetup.cpp

```
//ddsetup.cpp: directDraw setup and release
//Copyright Ian Parberry, 1999
//Last updated May 22, 2000

//system includes
#include <windows.h>
#include <windowsx.h>
#include <ddraw.h>

//custom includes
#include "defines.h"

//globals
extern LPDIRECTDRAW lpDirectDrawObject; //direct draw object
extern LPDIRECTDRAWSURFACE lpPrimary; //primary surface
extern LPDIRECTDRAWPALETTE lpPrimaryPalette; //its palette
extern LPDIRECTDRAWSURFACE lpSecondary; //back buffer
extern LPDIRECTDRAWPALETTE lpSecondaryPalette; //its palette
extern LPDIRECTDRAWSURFACE lpBackground; //background image

//helper functions

LPDIRECTDRAWPALETTE CreatePalette(LPDIRECTDRAWSURFACE surface){
//create surface palette
  PALETTEENTRY pe[COLORS]; //new palette
  LPDIRECTDRAWPALETTE lpDDPalette; //direct draw palette
  //construct pe[], set to black
  for(int i=0; i<COLORS; i++)
    pe[i].peRed=pe[i].peGreen=pe[i].peBlue=0;
  //create direct draw palette
  if(FAILED(lpDirectDrawObject->
  CreatePalette(DDPCAPS_8BIT,pe,&lpDDPalette,NULL)))
    return NULL;
  //load direct draw palette to surface
  surface->SetPalette(lpDDPalette);
  return lpDDPalette;
} //CreatePalette

BOOL InitDirectDraw(HWND hwnd){ //direct draw initialization
  //create and set up direct draw object
  if(FAILED(DirectDrawCreate(NULL,&lpDirectDrawObject,NULL)))
    return FALSE;
  //set cooperative level
  if(FAILED(lpDirectDrawObject->SetCooperativeLevel(hwnd,
  DDSCL_EXCLUSIVE|DDSCL_FULLSCREEN)))
    return FALSE;
  //change screen resolution
  if(FAILED(lpDirectDrawObject->
```

```
    SetDisplayMode(SCREEN_WIDTH,SCREEN_HEIGHT,COLOR_DEPTH)))
      return FALSE;
    //create the surfaces
    DDSURFACEDESC ddsd; //direct draw surface descriptor
    ddsd.dwSize=sizeof(ddsd);
    ddsd.dwFlags=DDSD_CAPS|DDSD_BACKBUFFERCOUNT;
    ddsd.ddsCaps.dwCaps=DDSCAPS_PRIMARYSURFACE|DDSCAPS_FLIP
      |DDSCAPS_COMPLEX;
    ddsd.dwBackBufferCount=1;
    if(FAILED(lpDirectDrawObject->
    CreateSurface(&ddsd,&lpPrimary,NULL))
      return FALSE;
    //create its palette
    lpPrimaryPalette=CreatePalette(lpPrimary);
    //get pointer to the secondary surface
    DDSCAPS ddscaps;
    ddscaps.dwCaps=DDSCAPS_BACKBUFFER;
    if(FAILED(lpPrimary->
    GetAttachedSurface(&ddscaps,&lpSecondary)))
      return FALSE;
    //create its palette
    lpSecondaryPalette=CreatePalette(lpSecondary);
    //background surface
    ddsd.dwSize=sizeof(ddsd);
    ddsd.dwFlags=DDSD_CAPS|DDSD_HEIGHT|DDSD_WIDTH;
    ddsd.ddsCaps.dwCaps=DDSCAPS_OFFSCREENPLAIN;
    ddsd.dwHeight=SCREEN_HEIGHT; ddsd.dwWidth=SCREEN_WIDTH;
    if(FAILED(lpDirectDrawObject->
    CreateSurface(&ddsd,&lpBackground,NULL)))
      return FALSE;
    return TRUE;
  } //InitDirectDraw

long CALLBACK WindowProc(HWND hwnd,UINT message,
  WPARAM wParam,LPARAM lParam);

//windows system functions
HWND CreateDefaultWindow(char* name,HINSTANCE hInstance){
  WNDCLASS wc; //window registration info
  //register display window
  wc.style=CS_HREDRAW|CS_VREDRAW; //style
  wc.lpfnWndProc=WindowProc; //window message handler
  wc.cbClsExtra=wc.cbWndExtra=0;
  wc.hInstance=hInstance;
  wc.hIcon=LoadIcon(hInstance,IDI_APPLICATION);
  wc.hCursor=LoadCursor(NULL,IDC_ARROW);
  wc.hbrBackground=NULL;
  wc.lpszMenuName=NULL;
  wc.lpszClassName=name;
  RegisterClass(&wc);
```

```
    //create and set up fullscreen window
    return CreateWindowEx(WS_EX_TOPMOST,name,name,
      WS_POPUP,0,0,GetSystemMetrics(SM_CXSCREEN),
      GetSystemMetrics(SM_CYSCREEN),NULL,NULL,hInstance,NULL);
}
```

Defines.h

```
//defines.h: essential defines
//Copyright Ian Parberry, 1999
//Last updated September 28, 1999

#ifndef __DEFINES_H__
#define __DEFINES_H__

#define SCREEN_WIDTH 640 //pixels wide
#define SCREEN_HEIGHT 480 //pixels high
#define COLORS 256 //number of colors
#define COLOR_DEPTH 8 //number of bits to store colors
#define TRANSPARENT_COLOR 255 //transparent palette position

#endif
```

Main.cpp

```
//main.cpp

//A plane sprite moves from right to left across the
//background.  Notice how it disappears and reappears -
//DirectDraw is protecting you from GPFs.

//Copyright Ian Parberry, 1999
//Last updated May 22, 2000

//system includes
#include <windows.h>
#include <windowsx.h>
#include <ddraw.h>
#include <stdio.h>

//system defines
#define WIN32_LEAN_AND_MEAN

//custom includes
#include "defines.h" //global definitions
#include "bmp.h" //bmp file reader
#include "timer.h" //game timer
#include "bsprite.h" //for base sprite class
#include "objects.h" //for object class
```

```
//globals

BOOL ActiveApp; //is this application active?

LPDIRECTDRAW lpDirectDrawObject=NULL; //direct draw object
LPDIRECTDRAWSURFACE lpPrimary=NULL; //primary surface
LPDIRECTDRAWPALETTE lpPrimaryPalette; //its palette
LPDIRECTDRAWSURFACE lpSecondary=NULL; //back buffer
LPDIRECTDRAWPALETTE lpSecondaryPalette; //its palette
LPDIRECTDRAWSURFACE lpBackground=NULL; //background image

CTimer Timer; //game timer

CBmpFileReader background; //background image
CBmpSpriteFileReader g_cSpriteImages; //sprite images

CObject plane; //plane object
CBaseSprite *planesprite=NULL; //plane sprite

//helper functions

LPDIRECTDRAWPALETTE CreatePalette(LPDIRECTDRAWSURFACE surface);
BOOL InitDirectDraw(HWND hwnd);
HWND CreateDefaultWindow(char* name,HINSTANCE hInstance);

BOOL LoadPlaneSprite(){ //load plane image
  return planesprite->load(&g_cSpriteImages,0,1,1);
} //LoadPlaneSprite

BOOL LoadImages(){ //load graphics from files to surfaces
  //get the background image
  if(!background.load("bckgnd.bmp"))return FALSE; //read file
  background.draw(lpBackground); //draw to background surface
  //set palettes in all surfaces
  if(!background.setpalette(lpPrimaryPalette))return FALSE;
  if(!background.setpalette(lpSecondaryPalette))return FALSE;
  //load the plane sprite
  if(!g_cSpriteImages.load("sprites.bmp"))return FALSE;
  planesprite=new CBaseSprite(1,121,72);
  if(!LoadPlaneSprite())return FALSE; //load plane images
  return TRUE;
} //LoadImages

void CreateObjects(){
  plane.create(320,271,-1,0,planesprite); //create plane
} //CreateObjects

BOOL RestoreSurfaces(){ //restore all surfaces
  BOOL result=TRUE;
  if(SUCCEEDED(lpPrimary->Restore())) //if primary restored
```

```
      result=result&&background.draw(lpPrimary)&& //redraw image
        background.setpalette(lpPrimaryPalette); //set palette
    else return FALSE;
    if(SUCCEEDED(lpSecondary->Restore())) //if secondary restored
      result=result&&background.draw(lpSecondary)&& //redraw image
        background.setpalette(lpSecondaryPalette); //set palette
    else return FALSE;
    if(SUCCEEDED(lpBackground->Restore())) //if background restored
      result=result&&background.draw(lpBackground); //redraw image
    else return FALSE;
    if(planesprite->Restore()) //if plane sprite restored
      result=result&&LoadPlaneSprite(); //redraw image
    else return FALSE;
    return result;
} //RestoreSurfaces

BOOL PageFlip(){ //return TRUE if page flip succeeds
  if(lpPrimary->Flip(NULL,DDFLIP_WAIT)==DDERR_SURFACELOST)
    return RestoreSurfaces();
  return TRUE;
} //PageFlip

BOOL ComposeFrame(){ //compose a frame of animation
  //draw background
  lpSecondary->BltFast(0,0,lpBackground,NULL,
    DDBLTFAST_NOCOLORKEY|DDBLTFAST_WAIT);
  //move objects
  plane.move();
  //draw objects
  plane.draw(lpSecondary);
  return TRUE;
} //ComposeFrame

BOOL ProcessFrame(){ //process a frame of animation
  ComposeFrame(); //compose a frame in secondary surface
  return PageFlip(); //flip video memory surfaces
} //ProcessFrame

BOOL keyboard_handler(WPARAM keystroke){ //keyboard handler
  BOOL result=FALSE; //return TRUE if game is to end
  switch(keystroke){
    case VK_ESCAPE: result=TRUE; break; //exit game
    default: break;
  }
  return result;
} //keyboard_handler

//message handler (window procedure)
long CALLBACK WindowProc(HWND hwnd,UINT message,
                         WPARAM wParam,LPARAM lParam){
```

```
      switch(message){
        case WM_ACTIVATEAPP: ActiveApp=wParam; break;
        case WM_CREATE: break;
        case WM_KEYDOWN: //keyboard hit
          if(keyboard_handler(wParam))DestroyWindow(hwnd);
          break;
        case WM_DESTROY: //end of game
          if(lpDirectDrawObject!=NULL){ //if DD object exists
            if(lpSecondary!=NULL) //if secondary surface exists
              lpSecondary->Release(); //release secondary surface
            if(lpPrimary!=NULL) //if primary surface exists
              lpPrimary->Release(); //release primary surface
            if(lpBackground!=NULL) //if background exists
              lpBackground->Release(); //release background
            if(planesprite!=NULL) //if plane sprite exists
              planesprite->Release(); //release plane sprite
            delete planesprite; //delete plane sprite
            lpDirectDrawObject->Release(); //release DD object
          }
          ShowCursor(TRUE); //show the mouse cursor
          PostQuitMessage(0); //and exit
          break;
        default: //default window procedure
          return DefWindowProc(hwnd,message,wParam,lParam);
      } //switch(message)
      return 0L;
    } //WindowProc

    int WINAPI WinMain(HINSTANCE hInstance,HINSTANCE hPrevInstance,
    LPSTR lpCmdLine,int nCmdShow){
      MSG msg; //current message
      HWND hwnd; //handle to fullscreen window
      hwnd=CreateDefaultWindow("directX demo 3",hInstance);
      if(!hwnd)return FALSE;
      //set up window
      ShowWindow(hwnd,nCmdShow); UpdateWindow(hwnd);
      SetFocus(hwnd); //allow input from keyboard
      ShowCursor(FALSE); //hide the cursor
      //init graphics
      BOOL OK=InitDirectDraw(hwnd);//initialize DirectDraw
      if(OK)OK=LoadImages(); //load images from disk
      if(!OK){ //bail out if initialization failed
        DestroyWindow(hwnd); return FALSE;
      }
      //start game timer
      Timer.start();
      //create objects
      CreateObjects();
      //message loop
      while(TRUE)
```

```
        if(PeekMessage(&msg,NULL,0,0,PM_NOREMOVE)){
          if(!GetMessage(&msg,NULL,0,0))return msg.wParam;
          TranslateMessage(&msg); DispatchMessage(&msg);
        }
        else if(ActiveApp)ProcessFrame(); else WaitMessage();
} //WinMain
```

Objects.h

```
//objects.h: header file for CObject class

//Copyright Ian Parberry, 1999
//Last updated September 28, 1999

#ifndef __OBJECTS__
#define __OBJECTS__

#include "bsprite.h"

class CObject{ //class for a moving object
  private:
    int m_nX,m_nY; //current location
    int m_nXspeed,m_nYspeed; //current speed
    int m_nLastXMoveTime; //last time the object moved
    CBaseSprite *m_pSprite; //pointer to sprite
  public:
    CObject(); //constructor
    void draw(LPDIRECTDRAWSURFACE surface); //draw
    void create(int x,int y,int xspeed,int yspeed,
      CBaseSprite *sprite); //create instance
    void accelerate(int xdelta,int ydelta=0); //change speed
    void move(); //make a move depending on time and speed
};

#endif
```

Objects.cpp

```
//objects.cpp

//Copyright Ian Parberry, 1999
//Last updated September 28, 1999

#include "objects.h"
#include "timer.h" //game timer

extern CTimer Timer;

CObject::CObject(){ //constructor
  m_nX=m_nY=m_nXspeed=m_nYspeed=0;
```

```
    m_pSprite=NULL; m_nLastXMoveTime=0;
}

void CObject::draw(LPDIRECTDRAWSURFACE surface){ //draw
  m_pSprite->draw(0,m_nX,m_nY,surface);
}

void CObject::create(int x,int y,int xspeed,int yspeed,
                     CBaseSprite *sprite){
  m_nLastXMoveTime=0; //time
  m_nX=x; m_nY=y; //location
  m_nXspeed=xspeed; m_nYspeed=yspeed; //speed
  m_pSprite=sprite; //image
}

void CObject::accelerate(int xdelta,int ydelta){
  //change speed
  m_nXspeed+=xdelta; m_nYspeed+=ydelta;
}

void CObject::move(){ //move object
  const int XSCALE=8; //to scale back horizontal motion
  const int MARGIN=100; //margin on outside of page
  int xdelta; //change in position
  int time=Timer.time(); //current time
  //horizontal motion
  int tfactor=time-m_nLastXMoveTime; //time since last move
  xdelta=(m_nXspeed*tfactor)/XSCALE; //x distance moved
  m_nX+=xdelta; //x motion
  if(m_nX<-MARGIN)m_nX=SCREEN_WIDTH+MARGIN; //wrap left
  if(xdelta||m_nXspeed==0) //record time of move
    m_nLastXMoveTime=time;
  if(m_nX>SCREEN_WIDTH+MARGIN)m_nX=-MARGIN; //wrap right
}
```

Sbmp.h

```
//sbmp.h: header file for sprite file reader
//Copyright Ian Parberry, 1999
//Last updated September 28, 1999

#include <windows.h>
#include <windowsx.h>
#include <ddraw.h>

#include "bmp.h" //for base class
#include "defines.h"

#ifndef __sbmp_h__
#define __sbmp_h__
```

```
class CBmpSpriteFileReader:
public CBmpFileReader{ //bmp sprite file input class
  public:
    BOOL draw(LPDIRECTDRAWSURFACE surface,
      int width,int ht,int x,int y); //draw sprite
};

#endif
```

Sbmp.cpp

```
//sbmp.cpp: member functions for sprite file reader
//Copyright Ian Parberry, 1999
//Last updated May 22, 2000

#include "sbmp.h"

BOOL CBmpSpriteFileReader::draw(LPDIRECTDRAWSURFACE surface,
                                int width,int ht,int x,int y){
  DDSURFACEDESC ddsd; //direct draw surface descriptor
  BYTE *dest,*src; //destination and source pointers
  //init surface descriptor
  memset(&ddsd,0,sizeof(DDSURFACEDESC));
  ddsd.dwSize=sizeof(ddsd);
  //lock down surface
  if(FAILED(surface->Lock(NULL,&ddsd,DDLOCK_WAIT,NULL)))
    return FALSE;
  //calculate addresses and width
  dest=(BYTE*)ddsd.lpSurface; //destination pointer
  src=m_cImage+ //source pointer
    ((m_BMPFileInfo.biHeight-1-y)*m_BMPFileInfo.biWidth+x);
  //move data to surface
  for(int i=0; i<ht; i++){ //for each row
    memcpy(dest,src,width); //copy
    dest+=ddsd.lPitch; src-=m_BMPFileInfo.biWidth; //next row
  }
  //clean up and return
  surface->Unlock(NULL);
  return TRUE;
} //draw
```

Chapter 6

Here's what you'll learn:

- What sprite clipping is

- How to create and use a DirectDraw clipper

- How to add more objects to the game

Sprite Clipping

In Demo 4, we learn how to clip sprites so that they don't disappear prematurely at the edge of the screen. Fortunately, DirectDraw provides us with a mechanism that can quickly and easily clip sprites for us. So that you can test clipping at the top and bottom of the screen, we have added code to the keyboard handler to allow you to steer the plane using the arrow keys on the keyboard. There are also more objects than there were in Demo 3—we have added two crows who flap their wings as they move across the screen. One moves faster than the other, and flaps its wings faster too. One crow is behind the plane, and the other is in front of it.

Figure 6.1
Screen shot of Demo 4 showing clipped plane sprite

Experiment with Demo 4

Take a moment now to run Demo 4.

- You should see a plane and two crows flying from right to left across the background.

- Notice that the plane no longer disappears as soon its leftmost pixel leaves the screen. The plane is clipped, that is, if only part of it is on the screen, only that part is drawn.

- If you wait long enough, the plane will reappear on the right.

- Use the left and right arrow keys to accelerate and decelerate the plane.

- Use the up and down arrow keys to move the plane up and down. Notice how it clips correctly on all four sides of the screen.

- Hit the Esc key to exit the program.

Creating a DirectDraw Clipper

Sprite clipping is done with an object called a *DirectDraw clipper*. The code for creating the clipper goes into the `InitDirectDraw` function in `Ddsetup.cpp`. First, we create a local variable `lpClipper` to point to the clipper.

```
LPDIRECTDRAWCLIPPER lpClipper; //pointer to the clipper
```

Next, we ask the DirectDraw object to create the clipper for us, returning a pointer to it in `lpClipper`. If this fails, we bail out of `InitDirectDraw`.

```
if(FAILED(lpDirectDrawObject-> //create the clipper
CreateClipper(NULL,&lpClipper,NULL)))
  return FALSE;
```

The clipper can be set to clip to any rectangle or to the entire window. Since we are running fullscreen, we will use the clipper's `SetHWnd` member function to achieve the latter effect. The `SetHWnd` function gives the clipper a window handle, and says, in effect, "Hey, clip to this window." This is actually a very powerful operation that can be used in windowed mode to clip objects correctly even when other windows partially obscure your game.

```
if(FAILED(lpClipper->SetHWnd(NULL,hwnd)))
  return FALSE;
```

Finally, we attach the clipper to the secondary surface so that every sprite that gets drawn to the secondary surface gets clipped. This is done by calling the secondary surface's `SetClipper` member function with a pointer to the clipper; this is why we need the local variable `lpClipper` in the first place.

```
if(FAILED(lpSecondary->SetClipper(lpClipper)))
  return FALSE;
```

The Clipped Sprite

DirectDraw clippers are set-and-forget objects. We've created it; now it will do its job without any further prompting from us… except for one small detail. In Demo 3 we used the `BltFast` member function to draw sprites to the secondary surface. `BltFast` is actually a scaled-down version of a function called `Blt`, which can do much more than `BltFast` can but, as the name suggests, the smaller stripped-down `BltFast` is much faster than `Blt` at doing the things that it can do. Well, you've probably guessed it by now—`BltFast` is fast but it cannot clip. Because it is sometimes useful to have sprites that aren't clipped (for example, for things like buttons that don't go anywhere near the edge of the screen), we will leave our `CBaseSprite` class the way it is, and derive a new class from it called `CClippedSprite`. `CClippedSprite` essentially looks the same as `CBaseSprite` except for the fact that sprite frames are drawn with `Blt` instead of `BltFast`.

Clipped Sprite Overview

The header file for `CClippedSprite` is `Csprite.h`. `CClippedSprite` is derived from `CBaseSprite`:

```
class CClippedSprite: public CBaseSprite{
```

It has one private variable, a bounding rectangle; `Blt` requires you to specify a rectangle from which to blit in the source surface. We use the Windows API structure `RECT`, which has four fields, `left`, `right`, `top`, and `bottom`. The rectangles specified by `RECT` structures are reminiscent of C arrays, in that the horizontal extent is `left` to `right-1`, and the horizontal extent is `top` to `bottom-1`. Notice that the rectangle has width `right-left` and height `bottom-top`.

```
private:
  RECT m_rectSource; //bounding rectangle
```

It has its own constructor, and of course a virtual override for the `draw` function.

```
public:
  CClippedSprite(int frames,int w,int h); //constructor
  virtual void draw(int frame,int x,int y,
    LPDIRECTDRAWSURFACE destination); //draw sprite
};
```

Clipped Sprite Code

The code file for `CClippedSprite` is `Csprite.cpp`. It begins with the `CClippedSprite` constructor, which calls the `CBaseSprite` constructor, then sets the source bounding rectangle to be the same as the sprite frames. Notice that setting `m_rectSource.left` to 0 and `m_rectSource.right` to w makes the horizontal extent of the rectangle span from pixel 0 to pixel w−1, that is, a rectangle of width exactly w.

```
CClippedSprite::CClippedSprite(int frames,int w,int h):
CBaseSprite(frames,w,h){ //constructor
  //set bounding rectangle for use with Blt()
  m_rectSource.left=0; m_rectSource.right=w;
  m_rectSource.top=0; m_rectSource.bottom=h;
}
```

Recall from Chapter 5 that the `BltFast` function required the coordinates at which to draw the top left pixel of the source surface within the destination surface. The `Blt` function requires a destination *rectangle* instead of the x-y coordinates. The source image will be scaled to fit in the destination rectangle, which is a cool effect if you need it, but if you *don't* need it, make sure that the source rectangle is *exactly* the same size as the destination rectangle. If you are off by one pixel, your rendering speed will take a small hit as the sprite is scaled unnecessarily, and more importantly, the quality of your artwork will take a perceptible hit because one row or column of pixels of your sprite never gets drawn. The `CClippedSprite draw` function is an override of the `CBaseSprite draw` function.

```
void CClippedSprite::draw(int frame,int x,int y,
                    LPDIRECTDRAWSURFACE dest){ //draw
```

It has a local variable holding the destination rectangle. (The source rectangle is kept in the private member variable `m_rectSource` since its value never changes, whereas the destination rectangle is potentially different each time the sprite is drawn.)

```
RECT rectDest; //destination rectangle
```

We compute the horizontal extent of the destination rectangle, remembering that the coordinates of a sprite in our game are defined to be the coordinates of its bottom center pixel:

```
rectDest.left=x-m_nWidth/2;
rectDest.right=rectDest.left+m_nWidth;
```

It's a good idea to verify with pencil and paper that the destination rectangle is the right width. In this case it is easy to see that `rectDest.right-rect-Dest.left` is `m_nWidth` as required. Coding it the way we did has made it bulletproof whether `m_nWidth` is odd or even. It may be tempting to you to set `rectDest.right` to `x+m_nWidth/2` to make it symmetrical with `rectDest.left`. However, that would be wrong when `m_nWidth` is odd, because halving an odd integer will round it down. For example, if `m_nWidth` is 21, then `m_nWidth/2=10`, and so `rectDest.left` is set to `x-10` and `rectDest.right` would erroneously be set to `x+10`, resulting in a rectangle of width

```
rectDest.right-rectDest.left=(x+10)-(x+10)=20
```

instead of 21. Next, we set the vertical extent of the destination rectangle. Since the bottom row of pixels of the sprite must be drawn at row y of the destination, we set `rectDest.bottom` to y+1. Then, we set `rectDest.top` to whatever it will take to give the rectangle height `m_nHeight`.

```
rectDest.top=y-m_nHeight+1;
rectDest.bottom=y+1;
```

Did we get it right?

```
rectDest.bottom-rectDest.top=(y+1)-(y-m_nHeight+1)=m_nHeight,
```

as required. Now we can blit the image using the destination surface's `Blt` function. The first four parameters of this function are the destination rectangle, the source surface, the source rectangle, and a flags word (set the same—although the names of the flags have changed slightly—as for the `BltFast` function in Chapter 5). The last parameter, which we will leave `NULL`, would allow us to set some special blit effects if we used it.

```
dest->Blt(&rectDest,m_lpDDImage[frame],&m_rectSource,
  DDBLT_KEYSRC|DDBLT_WAIT,NULL);
}
```

Changes to the Object Class

Since Demo 4 has more sophisticated objects than Demo 3 did, we need to add some functionality to the object class `CObject`.

Declarations

The first change to `Objects.h` involves the declaration of an enumerated type for the different kinds of object in our game:

```
enum ObjectType{CROW_OBJECT=0,PLANE_OBJECT,NUM_SPRITES};
```

Enumerated types are very useful; we use them here to give human-readable names to things like crows and planes while at the same time allowing us to index them easily. We could do the same thing with a collection of `#define`s or `const ints`, but enumerated types are easier because the compiler takes care of assigning numbers to the names. Notice that the last declaration is `NUM_SPRITES`. We'll leave that at the end when we insert new object names into the list, giving us a handy way of knowing how many object types there are without the overhead of having to increment a counter by hand whenever a new object type is introduced.

    `CObject` needs some new private member variables. Now our objects can move both horizontally and vertically, so we add a new member variable `m_nLastYMoveTime` to go along with the `m_nLastXMoveTime` declared in Demo 3.

```
int m_nLastYMoveTime; //last time moved vertically
```

Our objects need a minimum and maximum allowed speed to prevent the user (or any new code) from making them move faster or slower than they are allowed to:

```
int m_nMinXSpeed,m_nMaxXSpeed; //min, max horizontal speeds
int m_nMinYSpeed,m_nMaxYSpeed; //min,max vertical speeds
```

The crows have multiple frames of animation (wings flapping), so we'll record the current frame index, the total number of frames, the last time the frame was changed, and the *frame interval*, that is, the number of milliseconds between frame changes. We'll make the crows' wings flap faster by decreasing the frame interval when they fly faster.

```
int m_nCurrentFrame; //frame to be displayed
int m_nFrameCount; //number of frames in animation
int m_nLastFrameTime; //last time the frame was changed
int m_nFrameInterval; //interval between frames
```

Some of our animations will repeat in cyclic order. For example, if there are four frames of animation, they will be displayed in the following order: 0, 1, 2, 3, 0, 1, 2, 3,… Others, for example the crow wing beats, will repeat forward to the last frame, then repeat backward, as follows: 0, 1, 2, 3, 2, 1, 0, 1, 2,… We will keep a Boolean variable m_bForwardAnimation, which is TRUE when the animation sequence is going forward and FALSE when it is going backward.

```
BOOL m_bForwardAnimation; //is animation going forwards?
```

The CObject public member function create gets its parameters changed from Demo 3. Instead of getting a pointer to the sprite image for the object, it gets a parameter of type ObjectType and must locate the sprite corresponding to that object type itself.

```
void create(ObjectType object,int x,int y,
    int xspeed,int yspeed); //create object
```

Some Code Changes

The first noteworthy change to the CObject code in Objects.cpp is the extern declaration of an array of sprite pointers. This array will be declared and initialized in Main.cpp, and will be indexed using an index of type ObjectType. This will let us easily locate a pointer to the shared sprite for any object.

```
extern CClippedSprite *g_pSprite[]; //sprites
```

The CObject constructor gets some new code to set the new private member variables to sensible initial values. Notice that a frame interval of 30 milliseconds gets us a frame rate of about 33 frames a second.

```
m_nLastXMoveTime=m_nLastYMoveTime=0;
m_nCurrentFrame=m_nFrameCount=m_nLastFrameTime=0;
m_bForwardAnimation=TRUE;
m_nFrameInterval=30;
```

The Draw Function

The CObject draw function first draws the current frame, using the frame number recorded in the private member variable m_nCurrentFrame:

```
void CObject::draw(LPDIRECTDRAWSURFACE surface){ //draw
    //draw the current frame
    m_pSprite->draw(m_nCurrentFrame,m_nX,m_nY,surface);
```

After having drawn the current frame, we have to figure out which frame is next. We want the crows wings to beat faster when it flies faster in the x direction, so we compute a frame interval `t` that is inversely proportional to `m-nXspeed`. As `m_nXspeed` increases, the frame interval gets smaller, which makes the animation move faster. Notice the use of the C standard library function `abs` to ensure that the frame interval is always positive, and the addition of `1` to the denominator to prevent a divide-by-zero error.

```
int t=m_nFrameInterval/(1+abs(m_nXspeed)); //frame interval
```

We use the timer to make sure that the frame number is only updated when sufficient time has passed, and we make use of the way that Boolean expressions are evaluated in C and C++ to ensure that the question never even arises unless the sprite has more than one frame:

```
if(m_nFrameCount>1&&Timer.elapsed(m_nLastFrameTime,t))
```

We check that the animation is going forward:

```
if(m_bForwardAnimation){ //forward animation
```

If it is going forward, we increment the frame number and check to see whether we have just displayed the last frame. Notice that we use pre-incrementing so that the value is tested after it has been incremented.

```
if(++m_nCurrentFrame>=m_nFrameCount){ //wrap
```

If we have just displayed the last frame, `m_nCurrentFrame` needs to be wound back to the second-from-last frame, which is frame `m_nFrameCount-2` (the last frame is frame `m_nFrameCount-1`). We then set `m_bForwardAnimation` to `FALSE` so that the animation now goes backward.

```
      m_nCurrentFrame=m_nFrameCount-2;
      m_bForwardAnimation=FALSE;
    }
  }
```

Otherwise, the animation is already going backward:

```
else{ //backward animation
```

We decrement the current frame and check to see whether we just displayed the first frame, frame 0. If so, we set the current frame to the second frame, frame 1, and set `m_bForwardAnimation` to `TRUE` so the animation now goes forward.

```
  if(--m_nCurrentFrame<0){ //wrap
    m_nCurrentFrame=1;
    m_bForwardAnimation=TRUE;
  }
 }
}
```

The Create Function

The `CObject create` function has some small changes; it now initializes `m_nLastYMoveTime` along with `m_nLastXMoveTime` to the current time so that the first move will be a reasonable one:

```
m_nLastXMoveTime=m_nLastYMoveTime=Timer.time(); //time
```

Instead of being given a pointer to the shared sprite that stores the image of this object, the `create` function was given an `ObjectType` parameter called `object`. We use this to index into the global sprite array `g_pSprite` to get that pointer.

```
m_pSprite=g_pSprite[object]; //sprite
```

Next, we interrogate the sprite object for its frame count so that we can manage the animation of this particular object. Note that although many objects will share the same sprite, they each have their own frame counter, and can therefore potentially be at different points in the sprite animation.

```
m_nFrameCount=m_pSprite->frame_count(); //frame count
```

Finally, the `create` function has a block of code that sets the object properties that are common for all objects of a given type, but are different from one type to another. Ideally, we should place this information into a text file and read it into our game at the appropriate point so that play-testers can tune the values to improve gameplay without the need to recompile the code. However, hard-coding the values like this works fine for a simple game in which the programmer most likely *is* the primary play-tester.

```
//customize properties of each object type
switch(object){
  case PLANE_OBJECT:
    m_nMinXSpeed=-3; m_nMaxXSpeed=-1;
    m_nMinYSpeed=-4; m_nMaxYSpeed=4;
    break;
  case CROW_OBJECT:
    m_nMinXSpeed=-2; m_nMaxXSpeed=-1;
    m_nMinYSpeed=-1; m_nMaxYSpeed=1;
    m_nFrameInterval=250;
    break;
}
```

The Accelerate and Move Functions

The CObject accelerate function gets some simple code to enforce maximum and minimum speed limits. After m_nXspeed is increased by xdelta we enforce the horizontal speed limits.

```
if(m_nXspeed<m_nMinXSpeed)m_nXspeed=m_nMinXSpeed;
if(m_nXspeed>m_nMaxXSpeed)m_nXspeed=m_nMaxXSpeed;
```

After m_nYspeed is increased by ydelta we enforce the vertical speed limits:

```
if(m_nYspeed<m_nMinYSpeed)m_nYspeed=m_nMinYSpeed;
if(m_nYspeed>m_nMaxYSpeed)m_nYspeed=m_nMaxYSpeed;
}
```

The last change to CObject code in Objects.cpp involves modifying the move function to manage vertical movement as in addition to the horizontal movement, which was all that was allowed in Demo 3. We change XSCALE to 16 (because it looks better) and declare a corresponding constant YSCALE for vertical motion.

```
const int XSCALE=16; //to scale back horizontal motion
const int YSCALE=32; //to scale back vertical motion
```

Then, we declare an integer ydelta for the change in vertical position, to match the corresponding xdelta for change in horizontal position from Demo 3:

```
int xdelta,ydelta; //change in position
```

Finally, we add code to manage vertical motion. This code looks almost identical to the code for horizontal motion from Demo 3 with all the x's changed to y's.

```
tfactor=time-m_nLastYMoveTime; //time since last move
ydelta=(m_nYspeed*tfactor)/YSCALE; //y distance moved
m_nY+=ydelta; //y motion
if(m_nY<-MARGIN)m_nY=-MARGIN; //wrap top
if(m_nY>SCREEN_HEIGHT+MARGIN)
  m_nY=SCREEN_HEIGHT+MARGIN; //wrap bottom
if(ydelta||m_nYspeed==0) //record time of move
  m_nLastYMoveTime=time;
```

Changes to Main.cpp

The first significant change to `Main.cpp` is the declaration of two crow objects and the sprite array alluded to in the last section. Notice that the sprite array has `NUM_SPRITES` slots, which is the last entry in the `ObjectType` declaration in `Objects.h`, and will therefore (assuming we remember to keep it the last entry) be the number of different object types in the game.

```
CObject crow1,crow2; //crow objects
CClippedSprite *g_pSprite[NUM_SPRITES]; //sprites
```

The LoadCrowSprite Function

Like the `LoadPlaneSprite` function that we've met already, we create a `LoadCrowSprite` function to load the crow sprite images. The crow sprite has four frames, the top left pixels of which can be found at coodinates `(256,183)`, `(320,183)`, `(256,237)`, and `(323,237)` respectively, in the sprite file `Sprites.bmp`.

```
BOOL LoadCrowSprite(){
  BOOL result=TRUE;
  result=result&&g_pSprite[CROW_OBJECT]->
    load(&g_cSpriteImages,0,256,183); //frame 0
  result=result&&g_pSprite[CROW_OBJECT]->
    load(&g_cSpriteImages,1,320,183); //frame 1
  result=result&&g_pSprite[CROW_OBJECT]->
    load(&g_cSpriteImages,2,256,237); //frame 2
  result=result&&g_pSprite[CROW_OBJECT]->
    load(&g_cSpriteImages,3,323,237); //frame 3
  return result;
} //LoadCrowSprite
```

The LoadImages Function

The code to load the sprites in function `LoadImages` gets updated as follows, after the background has been loaded and the palette set. The sprite file is loaded into the bmp sprite file reader `g_cSpriteImages`.

```
if(!g_cSpriteImages.load("sprites.bmp"))return FALSE;
```

A new one-frame, 121x72 clipped sprite object is created and attached to the appropriate place in the global sprite array `g_pSprite[PLANE_OBJECT]`:

```
g_pSprite[PLANE_OBJECT]=new CClippedSprite(1,121,72);
```

The plane sprite image is loaded to the sprite from the bmp sprite file reader:

```
if(!LoadPlaneSprite())return FALSE; //load plane images
```

A new four-frame, 58x37 clipped sprite object is created and attached to the appropriate place in the global sprite array g_pSprite[CROW_OBJECT]:

```
g_pSprite[CROW_OBJECT]=new CClippedSprite(4,58,37);
```

The crow sprite images are loaded to the sprite from the bmp sprite file reader:

```
if(!LoadCrowSprite())return FALSE; //load crow images
```

The CreateObjects Function

The body of function CreateObjects is replaced by code to create the plane and two crows with the appropriate initial values:

```
void CreateObjects(){
  plane.create(PLANE_OBJECT,320,271,-1,0); //create plane
  crow1.create(CROW_OBJECT,400,100,-2,0); //create a crow
  crow2.create(CROW_OBJECT,300,100,-1,0); //another crow
} //CreateObjects
```

The RestoreSurfaces Function

In the RestoreSurfaces function, in addition to the minor replacement of the now defunct plane sprite pointer planesprite with g_pSprite[PLANE_OBJECT], we need to add code to restore the crow sprite. The code for this looks very similar to the code used to restore the plane sprite; we call the crow sprite's Restore member function, and if the restoration succeeds, we reload the sprite image from the bmp sprite file reader by calling the LoadCrowSprite function described above.

```
if(g_pSprite[CROW_OBJECT]->Restore()) //if crow restored
  result=result&&LoadCrowSprite(); //redraw image
else return FALSE;
```

The ComposeFrame Function

The body of ComposeFrame needs to be modified to handle the new objects. First, we use Blt instead of BltFast to draw the background. In order to do this, we need a local variable rect to store the destination rectangle, which we set to the whole screen. Then, we blit the background surface to that rectangle using the secondary surface's Blt member function, in much the same way that we blitted the clipped sprites.

```
RECT rect; //drawing rectangle
rect.left=0; rect.right=SCREEN_WIDTH;
rect.top=0; rect.bottom=SCREEN_HEIGHT;
lpSecondary->Blt(&rect,lpBackground,&rect,DDBLT_WAIT,NULL);
```

Then, we move the objects. They can be moved in any order.

```
plane.move();
crow1.move();
crow2.move();
```

Having moved the objects, we draw them. They must be drawn back-to-front, since the more recently drawn objects will overwrite objects previously drawn to the same pixels. We draw one crow first (behind the plane), then the plane, then the other crow (in front of the plane).

```
crow1.draw(lpSecondary);
plane.draw(lpSecondary);
crow2.draw(lpSecondary);
```

The Keyboard Handler

The keyboard_handler function has four new cases added to its switch statement to handle responses to the arrow keys, which are used to accelerate the plane either up, down, left, or right. The virtual key codes for the arrow keys are VK_UP, VK_DOWN, VK_LEFT, and VK_RIGHT.

```
case VK_UP: plane.accelerate(0,-1); break;
case VK_DOWN: plane.accelerate(0,1); break;
case VK_LEFT: plane.accelerate(-1,0); break;
case VK_RIGHT: plane.accelerate(1,0); break;
```

The Window Procedure

In function WindowProc we need to clean up the sprite surfaces in response to the WM_DESTROY message at the end of the game. Notice once again how we enumerate the sprites using the ObjectType enumerated type.

```
for(int i=0; i<NUM_SPRITES; i++){ //for each sprite
  if(g_pSprite[i]) //if sprite exists
    g_pSprite[i]->Release(); //release sprite
  delete g_pSprite[i]; //delete sprite
}
```

The "if sprite exists" line is there to ensure that we only try to release sprites that actually exist. Naturally, this will only work if the sprite pointers have been initialized to NULL before we try to create the sprites. This is done in WinMain as an early part of the initialization before the game begins.

```
for(int i=0; i<NUM_SPRITES; i++) //null out sprites
  g_pSprite[i]=NULL;
```

Demo 4 Files

Code Files

The following files in Demo 4 are used without change from Demo 3:

- Bmp.h
- Bmp.cpp
- Bsprite.h
- Bsprite.cpp
- Defines.h
- Sbmp.h
- Sbmp.cpp
- Timer.h
- Timer.cpp

The following files in Demo 4 have been modified from Demo 3:

- Ddsetup.cpp
- Main.cpp
- Objects.h
- Objects.cpp

The following files are new in Demo 4:

- Csprite.h
- Csprite.cpp

Required Libraries

- Ddraw.lib
- Winmm.lib

Code Listings

Csprite.h

```
//csprite.h
//header file for clipped sprite class

//Copyright Ian Parberry, 1999
//Last updated September 29, 1999

#include "bsprite.h"

#ifndef __csprite_h__
#define __csprite_h__

class CClippedSprite: public CBaseSprite{
  private:
    RECT m_rectSource; //bounding rectangle
  public:
    CClippedSprite(int frames,int w,int h); //constructor
    virtual void draw(int frame,int x,int y,
      LPDIRECTDRAWSURFACE destination); //draw sprite
};

#endif
```

Csprite.cpp

```
//csprite.cpp: clipped sprite class functions

//Copyright Ian Parberry, 1999
//Last updated September 29, 1999

#include "csprite.h"

CClippedSprite::CClippedSprite(int frames,int w,int h):
CBaseSprite(frames,w,h){ //constructor
  //set bounding rectangle for use with Blt()
  m_rectSource.left=0; m_rectSource.right=w;
  m_rectSource.top=0; m_rectSource.bottom=h;
}

void CClippedSprite::draw(int frame,int x,int y,
                          LPDIRECTDRAWSURFACE dest){ //draw
  //compute destination rectangle
  RECT rectDest; //destination rectangle
  //horizontal extent
  rectDest.left=x-m_nWidth/2;
  rectDest.right=rectDest.left+m_nWidth;
  //vertical extent
```

```
    rectDest.top=y-m_nHeight+1;
    rectDest.bottom=y+1;
    //blit it
    dest->Blt(&rectDest,m_lpDDImage[frame],&m_rectSource,
      DDBLT_KEYSRC|DDBLT_WAIT,NULL);
}
```

Ddsetup.cpp

```
//ddsetup.cpp: directDraw setup and release
//Copyright Ian Parberry, 1999
//Last updated May 22, 2000

//system includes
#include <windows.h>
#include <windowsx.h>
#include <ddraw.h>

//custom includes
#include "defines.h"

//globals
extern LPDIRECTDRAW lpDirectDrawObject; //direct draw object
extern LPDIRECTDRAWSURFACE lpPrimary; //primary surface
extern LPDIRECTDRAWPALETTE lpPrimaryPalette; //its palette
extern LPDIRECTDRAWSURFACE lpSecondary; //back buffer
extern LPDIRECTDRAWPALETTE lpSecondaryPalette; //its palette
extern LPDIRECTDRAWSURFACE lpBackground; //background image

//helper functions

LPDIRECTDRAWPALETTE CreatePalette(LPDIRECTDRAWSURFACE surface){
//create surface palette
  PALETTEENTRY pe[COLORS]; //new palette
  LPDIRECTDRAWPALETTE lpDDPalette; //direct draw palette
  //construct pe[], set to black
  for(int i=0; i<COLORS; i++)
    pe[i].peRed=pe[i].peGreen=pe[i].peBlue=0;
  //create direct draw palette
  if(FAILED(lpDirectDrawObject->
  CreatePalette(DDPCAPS_8BIT,pe,&lpDDPalette,NULL)))
    return NULL;
  //load direct draw palette to surface
  surface->SetPalette(lpDDPalette);
  return lpDDPalette;
} //CreatePalette

BOOL InitDirectDraw(HWND hwnd){ //direct draw initialization
  //create and set up direct draw object
  if(FAILED(DirectDrawCreate(NULL,&lpDirectDrawObject,NULL)))
```

```
      return FALSE;
   //set cooperative level
   if(FAILED(lpDirectDrawObject->SetCooperativeLevel(hwnd,
   DDSCL_EXCLUSIVE|DDSCL_FULLSCREEN)))
      return FALSE;
   //change screen resolution
   if(FAILED(lpDirectDrawObject->
   SetDisplayMode(SCREEN_WIDTH,SCREEN_HEIGHT,COLOR_DEPTH)))
      return FALSE;
   //create the surfaces
   DDSURFACEDESC ddsd; //direct draw surface descriptor
   ddsd.dwSize=sizeof(ddsd);
   ddsd.dwFlags=DDSD_CAPS|DDSD_BACKBUFFERCOUNT;
   ddsd.ddsCaps.dwCaps=DDSCAPS_PRIMARYSURFACE|DDSCAPS_FLIP
      |DDSCAPS_COMPLEX;
   ddsd.dwBackBufferCount=1;
   if(FAILED(lpDirectDrawObject->
   CreateSurface(&ddsd,&lpPrimary,NULL)))
      return FALSE;
   //create its palette
   lpPrimaryPalette=CreatePalette(lpPrimary);
   //get pointer to the secondary surface
   DDSCAPS ddscaps;
   ddscaps.dwCaps=DDSCAPS_BACKBUFFER;
   if(FAILED(lpPrimary->
   GetAttachedSurface(&ddscaps,&lpSecondary)))
      return FALSE;
   //create its palette
   lpSecondaryPalette=CreatePalette(lpSecondary);
   //background surface
   ddsd.dwSize=sizeof(ddsd);
   ddsd.dwFlags=DDSD_CAPS|DDSD_HEIGHT|DDSD_WIDTH;
   ddsd.ddsCaps.dwCaps=DDSCAPS_OFFSCREENPLAIN;
   ddsd.dwHeight=SCREEN_HEIGHT; ddsd.dwWidth=SCREEN_WIDTH;
   if(FAILED(lpDirectDrawObject->
   CreateSurface(&ddsd,&lpBackground,NULL)))
      return FALSE;
   //create direct draw clipper
   LPDIRECTDRAWCLIPPER lpClipper; //pointer to the clipper
   if(FAILED(lpDirectDrawObject-> //create the clipper
   CreateClipper(NULL,&lpClipper,NULL)))
      return FALSE;
   //set to clip to window boundaries
   if(FAILED(lpClipper->SetHWnd(NULL,hwnd)))
      return FALSE;
   //attach clipper to secondary surface
   if(FAILED(lpSecondary->SetClipper(lpClipper)))
      return FALSE;
   return TRUE;
} //InitDirectDraw
```

```
long CALLBACK WindowProc(HWND hwnd,UINT message,
  WPARAM wParam,LPARAM lParam);

//windows system functions
HWND CreateDefaultWindow(char* name,HINSTANCE hInstance){
  WNDCLASS wc; //window registration info
  //register display window
  wc.style=CS_HREDRAW|CS_VREDRAW; //style
  wc.lpfnWndProc=WindowProc; //window message handler
  wc.cbClsExtra=wc.cbWndExtra=0;
  wc.hInstance=hInstance;
  wc.hIcon=LoadIcon(hInstance,IDI_APPLICATION);
  wc.hCursor=LoadCursor(NULL,IDC_ARROW);
  wc.hbrBackground=NULL;
  wc.lpszMenuName=NULL;
  wc.lpszClassName=name;
  RegisterClass(&wc);
  //create and set up fullscreen window
  return CreateWindowEx(WS_EX_TOPMOST,name,name,
    WS_POPUP,0,0,GetSystemMetrics(SM_CXSCREEN),
    GetSystemMetrics(SM_CYSCREEN),NULL,NULL,hInstance,NULL);
}
```

Main.cpp

```
//main.cpp

//Sprites are now clipped to the screen.
//Direct the plane with the left, right, up, and arrow keys
//to test clipping at all four edges of the screen.

//We now have two animated crows flying across the screen
//at different speeds.  Note that the fast crow also flaps
//its wings faster.  One crow is in front of plane, one
//is behind the plane.

//Copyright Ian Parberry, 1999
//Last updated May 22, 2000

//system includes
#include <windows.h>
#include <windowsx.h>
#include <ddraw.h>
#include <stdio.h>

//system defines
#define WIN32_LEAN_AND_MEAN

//custom includes
```

```
#include "defines.h" //global definitions
#include "bmp.h" //bmp file reader
#include "timer.h" //game timer
#include "csprite.h" //for clipped sprite class
#include "objects.h" //for object class

//globals

BOOL ActiveApp; //is this application active?

LPDIRECTDRAW lpDirectDrawObject=NULL; //direct draw object
LPDIRECTDRAWSURFACE lpPrimary=NULL; //primary surface
LPDIRECTDRAWPALETTE lpPrimaryPalette; //its palette
LPDIRECTDRAWSURFACE lpSecondary=NULL; //back buffer
LPDIRECTDRAWPALETTE lpSecondaryPalette; //its palette
LPDIRECTDRAWSURFACE lpBackground=NULL; //background image

CTimer Timer; //game timer

CBmpFileReader background; //background image
CBmpSpriteFileReader g_cSpriteImages; //sprite images

CObject plane; //plane object
CObject crow1,crow2; //crow objects
CClippedSprite *g_pSprite[NUM_SPRITES]; //sprites

//helper functions
LPDIRECTDRAWPALETTE CreatePalette(LPDIRECTDRAWSURFACE surface);
BOOL InitDirectDraw(HWND hwnd);
HWND CreateDefaultWindow(char* name,HINSTANCE hInstance);

BOOL LoadPlaneSprite(){ //load plane image
  return g_pSprite[PLANE_OBJECT]->load(&g_cSpriteImages,0,1,1);
} //LoadPlaneSprite

BOOL LoadCrowSprite(){
  BOOL result=TRUE;
  result=result&&g_pSprite[CROW_OBJECT]->
    load(&g_cSpriteImages,0,256,183); //frame 0
  result=result&&g_pSprite[CROW_OBJECT]->
    load(&g_cSpriteImages,1,320,183); //frame 1
  result=result&&g_pSprite[CROW_OBJECT]->
    load(&g_cSpriteImages,2,256,237); //frame 2
  result=result&&g_pSprite[CROW_OBJECT]->
    load(&g_cSpriteImages,3,323,237); //frame 3
  return result;
} //LoadCrowSprite

BOOL LoadImages(){ //load graphics from files to surfaces
  //get the background image
```

```
    if(!background.load("bckgnd.bmp"))return FALSE; //read file
    background.draw(lpBackground); //draw to background surface
    //set palettes in all surfaces
    if(!background.setpalette(lpPrimaryPalette))return FALSE;
    if(!background.setpalette(lpSecondaryPalette))return FALSE;
    //load the sprites...
    if(!g_cSpriteImages.load("sprites.bmp"))return FALSE;
    //...the plane
    g_pSprite[PLANE_OBJECT]=new CClippedSprite(1,121,72);
    if(!LoadPlaneSprite())return FALSE; //load plane images
    //...the crow
    g_pSprite[CROW_OBJECT]=new CClippedSprite(4,58,37);
    if(!LoadCrowSprite())return FALSE; //load crow images
    return TRUE;
} //LoadImages

void CreateObjects(){
    plane.create(PLANE_OBJECT,320,271,-1,0); //create plane
    crow1.create(CROW_OBJECT,400,100,-2,0); //create a crow
    crow2.create(CROW_OBJECT,300,100,-1,0); //another crow
} //CreateObjects

BOOL RestoreSurfaces(){ //restore all surfaces
    BOOL result=TRUE;
    if(SUCCEEDED(lpPrimary->Restore())) //if primary restored
      result=result&&background.draw(lpPrimary)&& //redraw image
        background.setpalette(lpPrimaryPalette); //set palette
    else return FALSE;
    if(SUCCEEDED(lpSecondary->Restore())) //if secondary restored
      result=result&&background.draw(lpSecondary)&& //redraw image
        background.setpalette(lpSecondaryPalette); //set palette
    else return FALSE;
    if(SUCCEEDED(lpBackground->Restore())) //if background restored
      result=result&&background.draw(lpBackground); //redraw image
    else return FALSE;
    if(g_pSprite[PLANE_OBJECT]->Restore()) //if plane restored
      result=result&&LoadPlaneSprite(); //redraw image
    else return FALSE;
    if(g_pSprite[CROW_OBJECT]->Restore()) //if crow restored
      result=result&&LoadCrowSprite(); //redraw image
    else return FALSE;
    return result;
} //RestoreSurfaces

BOOL PageFlip(){ //return TRUE if page flip succeeds
    if(lpPrimary->Flip(NULL,DDFLIP_WAIT)==DDERR_SURFACELOST)
      return RestoreSurfaces();
    return TRUE;
} //PageFlip
```

```
BOOL ComposeFrame(){ //compose a frame of animation
  //draw background
  RECT rect; //drawing rectangle
  rect.left=0; rect.right=SCREEN_WIDTH;
  rect.top=0; rect.bottom=SCREEN_HEIGHT;
  lpSecondary->Blt(&rect,lpBackground,&rect,DDBLT_WAIT,NULL);
  //move objects
  plane.move();
  crow1.move();
  crow2.move();
  //draw objects
  crow1.draw(lpSecondary);
  plane.draw(lpSecondary);
  crow2.draw(lpSecondary);
  return TRUE;
} //ComposeFrame

BOOL ProcessFrame(){ //process a frame of animation
  ComposeFrame(); //compose a frame in secondary surface
  return PageFlip(); //flip video memory surfaces
} //ProcessFrame

BOOL keyboard_handler(WPARAM keystroke){ //keyboard handler
  BOOL result=FALSE; //return TRUE if game is to end
  switch(keystroke){
    case VK_ESCAPE: result=TRUE; break; //exit game
    case VK_UP: plane.accelerate(0,-1); break;
    case VK_DOWN: plane.accelerate(0,1); break;
    case VK_LEFT: plane.accelerate(-1,0); break;
    case VK_RIGHT: plane.accelerate(1,0); break;
    default: break;
  }
  return result;
} //keyboard_handler

//message handler (window procedure)
long CALLBACK WindowProc(HWND hwnd,UINT message,
                         WPARAM wParam,LPARAM lParam){
  switch(message){
    case WM_ACTIVATEAPP: ActiveApp=wParam; break;
    case WM_CREATE: break;
    case WM_KEYDOWN: //keyboard hit
      if(keyboard_handler(wParam))DestroyWindow(hwnd);
      break;
    case WM_DESTROY: //end of game
      if(lpDirectDrawObject!=NULL){ //if DD object exists
        if(lpSecondary!=NULL) //if secondary surface exists
          lpSecondary->Release(); //release secondary surface
        if(lpPrimary!=NULL) //if primary surface exists
          lpPrimary->Release(); //release primary surface
```

```
            if(lpBackground!=NULL) //if background exists
              lpBackground->Release(); //release background
            for(int i=0; i<NUM_SPRITES; i++){ //for each sprite
              if(g_pSprite[i]) //if sprite exists
                g_pSprite[i]->Release(); //release sprite
              delete g_pSprite[i]; //delete sprite
            }
            lpDirectDrawObject->Release(); //release DD object
          }
          ShowCursor(TRUE); //show the mouse cursor
          PostQuitMessage(0); //and exit
          break;
        default: //default window procedure
          return DefWindowProc(hwnd,message,wParam,lParam);
    } //switch(message)
    return 0L;
} //WindowProc

int WINAPI WinMain(HINSTANCE hInstance,HINSTANCE hPrevInstance,
LPSTR lpCmdLine,int nCmdShow){
  MSG msg; //current message
  HWND hwnd; //handle to fullscreen window
  hwnd=CreateDefaultWindow("directX demo 4",hInstance);
  if(!hwnd)return FALSE;
  //set up window
  ShowWindow(hwnd,nCmdShow); UpdateWindow(hwnd);
  SetFocus(hwnd); //allow input from keyboard
  ShowCursor(FALSE); //hide the cursor
  //init graphics
  for(int i=0; i<NUM_SPRITES; i++) //null out sprites
    g_pSprite[i]=NULL;
  BOOL OK=InitDirectDraw(hwnd);//initialize DirectDraw
  if(OK)OK=LoadImages(); //load images from disk
  if(!OK){ //bail out if initialization failed
    DestroyWindow(hwnd); return FALSE;
  }
  //start game timer
  Timer.start();
  //create objects
  CreateObjects();
  //message loop
  while(TRUE)
    if(PeekMessage(&msg,NULL,0,0,PM_NOREMOVE)){
      if(!GetMessage(&msg,NULL,0,0))return msg.wParam;
      TranslateMessage(&msg); DispatchMessage(&msg);
    }
    else if(ActiveApp)ProcessFrame(); else WaitMessage();
} //WinMain
```

Objects.h

```
//objects.h: header file for CObject class

//Copyright Ian Parberry, 1999
//Last updated September 29, 1999

#ifndef __OBJECTS__
#define __OBJECTS__

#include "bsprite.h"

//object types
enum ObjectType{CROW_OBJECT=0,PLANE_OBJECT,NUM_SPRITES};
//note: NUM_SPRITES must be last

class CObject{ //class for a moving object
  private:
    int m_nX,m_nY; //current location
    int m_nXspeed,m_nYspeed; //current speed
    int m_nLastXMoveTime; //last time moved horizontally
    int m_nLastYMoveTime; //last time moved vertically
    CBaseSprite *m_pSprite; //pointer to sprite
    int m_nMinXSpeed,m_nMaxXSpeed; //min, max horizontal speeds
    int m_nMinYSpeed,m_nMaxYSpeed; //min,max vertical speeds
    int m_nCurrentFrame; //frame to be displayed
    int m_nFrameCount; //number of frames in animation
    int m_nLastFrameTime; //last time the frame was changed
    int m_nFrameInterval; //interval between frames
    BOOL m_bForwardAnimation; //is animation going forwards?
  public:
    CObject(); //constructor
    void draw(LPDIRECTDRAWSURFACE surface); //draw
    void create(ObjectType object,int x,int y,
      int xspeed,int yspeed); //create object
    void accelerate(int xdelta,int ydelta=0); //change speed
    void move(); //make a move depending on time and speed
};

#endif
```

Objects.cpp

```
//objects.cpp

//Copyright Ian Parberry, 1999
//Last updated October 5, 1999

#include "objects.h"
#include "timer.h" //game timer
```

```cpp
#include "csprite.h" //for clipped sprite class

extern CClippedSprite *g_pSprite[]; //sprites
extern CTimer Timer; //game timer

CObject::CObject(){ //constructor
  m_nX=m_nY=m_nXspeed=m_nYspeed=0;
  m_pSprite=NULL;
  m_nLastXMoveTime=m_nLastYMoveTime=0;
  m_nCurrentFrame=m_nFrameCount=m_nLastFrameTime=0;
  m_bForwardAnimation=TRUE;
  m_nFrameInterval=30;
}

void CObject::draw(LPDIRECTDRAWSURFACE surface){ //draw
  //draw the current frame
  m_pSprite->draw(m_nCurrentFrame,m_nX,m_nY,surface);
  //figure out which frame is next
  int t=m_nFrameInterval/(1+abs(m_nXspeed)); //frame interval
  if(m_nFrameCount>1&&Timer.elapsed(m_nLastFrameTime,t))
    if(m_bForwardAnimation){ //forward animation
      if(++m_nCurrentFrame>=m_nFrameCount){ //wrap
        m_nCurrentFrame=m_nFrameCount-2;
        m_bForwardAnimation=FALSE;
      }
    }
    else{ //backward animation
      if(--m_nCurrentFrame<0){ //wrap
        m_nCurrentFrame=1;
        m_bForwardAnimation=TRUE;
      }
    }
}

void CObject::create(ObjectType object,int x,int y,
                     int xspeed,int yspeed){
  m_nLastXMoveTime=m_nLastYMoveTime=Timer.time(); //time
  m_nX=x; m_nY=y; //location
  m_nXspeed=xspeed; m_nYspeed=yspeed; //speed
  m_pSprite=g_pSprite[object]; //sprite
  m_nFrameCount=m_pSprite->frame_count(); //frame count
  //customize properties of each object type
  switch(object){
    case PLANE_OBJECT:
      m_nMinXSpeed=-3; m_nMaxXSpeed=-1;
      m_nMinYSpeed=-4; m_nMaxYSpeed=4;
      break;
    case CROW_OBJECT:
      m_nMinXSpeed=-2; m_nMaxXSpeed=-1;
      m_nMinYSpeed=-1; m_nMaxYSpeed=1;
```

```
        m_nFrameInterval=250;
        break;
    }
}

void CObject::accelerate(int xdelta,int ydelta){
  //change speed
  //horizontal
  m_nXspeed+=xdelta;
  if(m_nXspeed<m_nMinXSpeed)m_nXspeed=m_nMinXSpeed;
  if(m_nXspeed>m_nMaxXSpeed)m_nXspeed=m_nMaxXSpeed;
  //vertical
  m_nYspeed+=ydelta;
  if(m_nYspeed<m_nMinYSpeed)m_nYspeed=m_nMinYSpeed;
  if(m_nYspeed>m_nMaxYSpeed)m_nYspeed=m_nMaxYSpeed;
}

void CObject::move(){ //move object
  const int XSCALE=16; //to scale back horizontal motion
  const int YSCALE=32; //to scale back vertical motion
  const int MARGIN=100; //margin on outside of page
  int xdelta,ydelta; //change in position
  int time=Timer.time(); //current time
  //horizontal motion
  int tfactor=time-m_nLastXMoveTime; //time since last move
  xdelta=(m_nXspeed*tfactor)/XSCALE; //x distance moved
  m_nX+=xdelta; //x motion
  if(m_nX<-MARGIN)m_nX=SCREEN_WIDTH+MARGIN; //wrap left
  if(m_nX>SCREEN_WIDTH+MARGIN)m_nX=-MARGIN; //wrap right
  if(xdelta||m_nXspeed==0) //record time of move
    m_nLastXMoveTime=time;
  //vertical motion
  tfactor=time-m_nLastYMoveTime; //time since last move
  ydelta=(m_nYspeed*tfactor)/YSCALE; //y distance moved
  m_nY+=ydelta; //y motion
  if(m_nY<-MARGIN)m_nY=-MARGIN; //wrap top
  if(m_nY>SCREEN_HEIGHT+MARGIN)
    m_nY=SCREEN_HEIGHT+MARGIN; //wrap bottom
  if(ydelta||m_nYspeed==0) //record time of move
    m_nLastYMoveTime=time;
}
```

Chapter 7

Here's what you'll learn:

- How to manage the player's viewpoint within the virtual universe with a viewpoint manager

- What parallax scrolling is and how to implement it

- How to get subpixel scrolling with integer arithmetic

- How to manage objects with an object manager

- What pseudorandom numbers are, why they are used, and how to generate them

Parallax Scrolling

In Demo 5, we learn how to do parallax scrolling. We manage the objects in a game using an object manager class. Our game now has six crows, and the viewpoint moves horizontally with the plane, displaying it in the middle of the screen at all times (see Figure 7.1). There is a farm drawn in the foreground. The background scrolls horizontally slower than the farm, giving an illusion of depth known as *parallax scrolling*. The plane sprite now has multiple frames of animation. The crow sprites have very few frames of animation—only four frames shown forward and backward for a total of six frames per wingbeat. This relatively low frame count means that the crows' wingbeats can easily become synchronized, which looks unnatural. To combat this problem, the crow sprite animations are desynchronized using a pseudorandom number generator.

Figure 7.1
Screen shot
of Demo 5

Experiment with Demo 5

Take a moment now to run Demo 5.

- You should see a plane and two groups of three crows flying from right to left across the background, one fast and one slow.

- Notice that the plane is at the center of the screen, no matter how you accelerate and decelerate it using the arrow keys.

- Notice that the background moves more slowly than the foreground.

- Notice that the wingbeats of the crows are never in synchrony for more than a few seconds even when the crows are flying at the same speed.

- Notice that as clouds scroll off the right of the screen, they appear immediately on the left of the screen. This is because the background image file Bckgnd.bmp was drawn by the artist so that the left side of the image wraps around to the right side seamlessly.

- Hit the Esc key to exit the program.

The Viewpoint Manager

Ned's Turkey Farm takes place in a two-dimensional virtual universe that is 1,280 pixels wide, twice as wide as the screen. Each object in the game is responsible for recording its position in the virtual universe in its CObject private member variables m_nX and m_nY. The player's viewpoint, to be displayed on the screen, is also free to move arbitrarily within the virtual universe, but we will tie it to the plane so that the plane stays in the center of the screen. The illusion of the plane moving to the left will be provided by having all of the stationary objects in the virtual universe move to the right.

Imagine yourself standing at the side window of a train as it moves, observing stationary objects. As you travel through the countryside, you will notice that things close to you appear to zip speedily across your field of vision, whereas things farther away move less quickly and things on the horizon seem to move hardly at all. This effect of having things cross your field of vision at a speed that is inversely proportional to their distance is called *parallax*. We will create the illusion of depth in our flat two-dimensional virtual universe by having the background scroll at a lower speed than objects in the foreground in a process known as *parallax scrolling*.

We will implement parallax scrolling using a single 640x480 background image. This implies that when part of the background image disappears off one edge of the screen, it must reappear on the other. For this to work properly, the artist must create the background image as if it were rolled into a cylinder, with the right edge of the image merging seamlessly with the left edge. This effect has been achieved in the file `Bckgnd.bmp`, which you may verify by examining Figure 7.2. At the top of that figure you can see three copies of `Bckgnd.bmp` that have been laid out side by side to make a long strip. Observe that no seam can be seen. A single copy of `Bckgnd.bmp` has been placed below the strip for comparison. In practice you should use a virtual universe that is wider than double the screen size, and a background image that is wider than the screen, but we have opted for the simplest example here as a teaching device.

Figure 7.2
Three copies of Bckgnd. bmp (top) pasted side by side to show continuity, with a single copy below

The viewpoint manager `CViewPoint` is charged with the task of maintaining and manipulating the player viewpoint. It must record and maintain the location of the viewpoint, provide information to objects about where they should be drawn on the screen (which depends on the relative location of the object and the viewpoint in the virtual universe), and implement parallax scrolling.

Viewpoint Manager Overview

The header file for `CViewPoint` is `View.h`, which begins with the declaration of the width of the virtual universe:

```
#define WORLD_WIDTH 1280 //width of the world
```

`CViewPoint` has three private member functions. The first is the x coordinate of the viewpoint in the virtual universe (which will be between 0 and `WORLD_WIDTH-1`, inclusive), the second is where the right side of the screen hits the background image, and the third is the last time the background was moved and redrawn (which helps the viewpoint manager to compute how far the background has moved since it was last moved).

```
int m_nX; //x coordinate of viewpoint
int m_nBgOffset; //offset of parallax scrolled background
int m_nLastTimeBgDrawn; //last time background was drawn
```

CViewPoint has five public member functions, the first of which is a constructor:

```
CViewPoint(); //constructor
```

The second CViewPoint public member function allows us to set the initial viewpoint to a specific x coordinate in the virtual universe:

```
void set_position(int x); //set current viewpoint
```

The third CViewPoint public member returns the screen-relative x coordinates of a given x coordinate in the virtual universe. This will be used by objects to determine where they should be drawn in the screen.

```
int screen(int x); //screen coords relative to viewpoint
```

The fourth CViewPoint public member function normalizes a given x coordinate in the virtual universe; that is, it rounds it off to a value that is no smaller than 0 and less than WORLD_WIDTH. Notice that the parameter x is a call-by-reference parameter, which means that changes to x in the body of function normalize will affect the calling parameter.

```
void normalize(int &x); //normalize location x
```

The fifth and final CViewPoint public member function draws the background surface pointed to by parameter lpSource to the surface pointed to by lpDestination using parallax scrolling with the background surface moving at the given speed:

```
void draw_background(LPDIRECTDRAWSURFACE lpSource,
    LPDIRECTDRAWSURFACE lpDestination,int speed);
```

Viewpoint Manager Code

The code file for CViewPoint is View.cpp. It begins with the CViewPoint constructor, which initializes the private member variables.

```
CViewPoint::CViewPoint(){ //constructor
  m_nX=0; m_nBgOffset=0; m_nLastTimeBgDrawn=0;
}
```

The CViewPoint set_position function sets the position of the background to a specified x coordinate x, after first calling the public member function normalize to ensure that x falls within the virtual universe:

```
void CViewPoint::set_position(int x){ //set current viewpoint
  normalize(x); m_nX=x;
}
```

The CViewPoint screen function returns the screen-relative value of an x coordinate x in the virtual universe. Basically, we want to find out how far x is from the player's viewpoint.

```
int CViewPoint::screen(int x){
```

At first glance, it may seem that all this function needs to do is to compute the difference between the parameter x and the x coordinate of the viewpoint, m_nX, a value that we will call delta. We begin by doing this.

```
int delta=x-m_nX;
```

However, in a circular world of width WORLD_WIDTH, no two things can be farther away from each other than WORLD_WIDTH/2. Think about it for a second—the Earth is about 25,000 miles around, which means that I can never be more than about 12,500 miles away from you as you read this book. Therefore, we need to normalize delta so that it is between -WORLD_WIDTH/2 and WORLD_WIDTH/2, inclusive.

```
if(delta>WORLD_WIDTH/2)delta-=WORLD_WIDTH;
if(delta<-WORLD_WIDTH/2)delta+=WORLD_WIDTH;
```

Finally, since m_nX is the x-coordinate of the left side of the screen, we will add SCREEN_WIDTH/2 to make distances relative to the center of the screen:

```
return SCREEN_WIDTH/2+delta;
}
```

The CViewPoint normalize function normalizes the call-by-reference parameter x to be within the virtual universe. Since under normal playing circumstances x will be only slightly outside the virtual universe if at all, we can use additions and subtractions instead of the slightly more costly remainder operator. This is a piece of essentially pointless optimization that dates from the days when multiplication and division hardware was hopelessly slow, but really doesn't make a difference in the performance of this game. Nonetheless, it costs us nothing.

```
void CViewPoint::normalize(int &x){ //nomrmalize to world
  while(x<0)x+=WORLD_WIDTH;
  while(x>=WORLD_WIDTH)x-=WORLD_WIDTH;
}
```

Drawing the Background

The most interesting function in this file is probably the CViewPoint
draw_background function, which has three parameters: a pointer lpSource
to a source surface containing the background image, a pointer lpDestination
to a destination surface to which it is to be drawn using parallax scrolling from the
player's viewpoint, and the speed that the background is to scroll:

```
void CViewPoint::draw_background(LPDIRECTDRAWSURFACE lpSource,
    LPDIRECTDRAWSURFACE lpDestination,int speed){
```

The private member function m_nBgOffset keeps track of where the right side
of the screen hits the source image. A strip of this width must be drawn from the
left side of the source to the right side of the destination, and the remainder of the
source must be drawn to the left side of the destination (see Figure 7.3). This will
be accomplished with two calls to the DirectDraw Blt function. We will start by
drawing the left side of the source to the right side of the destination. First, we
compute the destination rectangle.

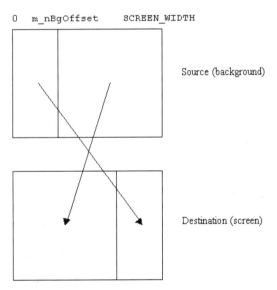

Figure 7.3
Drawing the
background

```
RECT rectDest; //destination rectangle
rectDest.left=SCREEN_WIDTH-m_nBgOffset;
rectDest.right=SCREEN_WIDTH;
rectDest.top=0;
rectDest.bottom=SCREEN_HEIGHT; //vertical extent
```

Then we compute the source rectangle:

```
RECT rectSource; //source rectangle
rectSource.left=0;
rectSource.right=m_nBgOffset;
rectSource.top=0;
rectSource.bottom=SCREEN_HEIGHT;
```

Then, we can do the first blit:

```
lpDestination->
  Blt(&rectDest,lpSource,&rectSource,DDBLT_WAIT,NULL);
```

Now we compute the destination rectangle for the second blit, which is the screen minus the rectangle drawn to by the first blit:

```
rectDest.left=0;
rectDest.right=SCREEN_WIDTH-m_nBgOffset;
rectDest.top=0;
rectDest.bottom=SCREEN_HEIGHT;
```

Then the source rectangle, which is the background image minus the rectangle taken in the first blit, is computed:

```
rectSource.left=m_nBgOffset;
rectSource.right=SCREEN_WIDTH;
rectSource.top=0;
rectSource.bottom=SCREEN_HEIGHT;
```

And we are ready for the second blit:

```
lpDestination->
  Blt(&rectDest,lpSource,&rectSource,DDBLT_WAIT,NULL);
```

Now that drawing has been completed, we are ready to scroll the background sideways to prepare for the next time it is drawn; that is, we need to update m_nBgOffset by the amount that the background is suppose to have moved. This change in m_nBgOffset depends on the parameter speed and the amount of time since the background was last drawn. We compute it in a local variable delta.

```
int delta=(speed*(Timer.time()-m_nLastTimeBgDrawn))/50;
```

If delta is zero, it means that the background is scrolling too slowly for it to have been moved in the current frame. If it has moved, we update m_nBgOffset, check that the new value is within range, and update the private member variable m_nLastTimeBgDrawn to record the last time the background was scrolled. Notice that we *don't* want to update m_nLastTimeBgDrawn when delta is zero. Updating m_nBgOffset when delta is zero would do no harm, but updating m_nLastTimeBgDrawn when delta is zero would make it impossible for us to perform *subpixel scrolling*, that is to scroll the background at a rate less than one pixel per frame. We can imagine a situation in which the frame rate is so high and the parameter speed is so low that the background scrolls only one pixel every second or third frame. For example, suppose that the game is running at 50 frames per second, that speed is 1, and that the background was scrolled in frame 0. In frame 1, 20 milliseconds later, delta is (1*20)/50, which gets rounded to zero. If m_nLastTimeBgDrawn is not changed, then 20 milliseconds later in frame 2, delta is (1*40)/50, which also gets rounded to zero. In frame 3, however, delta is (1*60)/50, which gets rounded to one, and the background moves by one pixel. If m_nLastTimeBgDrawn is changed when delta is zero, then delta *always* gets assigned (1*20)/50, which gets rounded to zero, and so the background *never* scrolls.

```
if(delta){ //if nonzero
  m_nBgOffset-=delta; //initial offset
  if(m_nBgOffset>SCREEN_WIDTH) //too positive
    m_nBgOffset=0;
  if(m_nBgOffset<0) //too negative
    m_nBgOffset=SCREEN_WIDTH-1;
  m_nLastTimeBgDrawn=Timer.time(); //record time of move
}
} //draw_background
```

The Object Manager

Managing objects is a significant component of any game. We will do this using an object manager class called CObjectManager whose task is to maintain and process a list of all game objects.

Object Manager Overview

The header file for CObjectManager is Objman.h. The object list will be implemented quite simply using a private array of pointers to CObject class instances. Initially we don't know how large that array has to be, so we will declare it as a pointer to a pointer to CObject, and will new enough space for the array later.

```
CObject **m_pObjectList; //list of objects in game
```

We will use the leading entries in the array to hold pointers to the objects in the list, and so we need a count of how many objects are in use:

```
int m_nCount; //how many objects in list
```

We also keep a record of how large the object array is, so that we can check for overflow:

```
int m_nMaxCount; //maximum number of objects
```

Finally, we will distinguish one object from all of the others and call it the *current object*. This object will represent the player.

```
int m_nCurrentObject; //index of the current object
```

All of the above variables are private member variables. The object manager has seven public member functions, including a constructor and a destructor. The constructor has a single parameter `max` that specifies the size of the object list. This gives us the ability (should we later choose to use it) to use a larger array for more advanced levels of the game that have more objects than earlier levels.

```
CObjectManager(int max); //constructor
~CObjectManager(); //destructor
```

The `CObjectManager` `create` function creates a new object, and has five parameters that specify the object type, its initial coordinates, and its initial horizontal and vertical speeds. It returns the index of the newly created object in the object list.

```
int create(ObjectType object,int x,int y,
   int xspeed,int yspeed); //create new object
```

The `CObjectManager` `animate` function will animate all of the objects in the object list to a DirectDraw surface (usually the secondary surface) given as the parameter `surface`:

```
void animate(LPDIRECTDRAWSURFACE surface);
```

The remaining three `CObjectManager` public member functions operate on the current object. Function `accelerate` changes the horizontal and vertical components of the current object's speed by specified amounts `xdelta` and `ydelta`, respectively, function `set_current` sets the current object to the object with a given `index` in the object list, and function `speed` returns the magnitude of the horizontal speed of the current object.

```
void accelerate(int xdelta,int ydelta=0); //change speed
void set_current(int index); //set current object
int speed(); //return magnitude of speed
```

The Constructor and Destructor

The code file for `CObjectManager` is `Objman.cpp`. The first declaration in `Objman.cpp` is an `extern` declaration for the viewpoint manager, which was described in the previous section.

```
extern CViewPoint Viewpoint; //player viewpoint
```

The `CObjectManager` constructor has a single parameter `max` that specifies the number of entries in the object list:

```
CObjectManager::CObjectManager(int max){ //constructor
```

We start out by recording this value in m_nMaxCount, setting m_nCount to 0 to indicate that the object list is empty, and setting m_nCurrentObject to 0 by default:

```
m_nMaxCount=max; m_nCount=0; m_nCurrentObject=0;
```

The array for the object list is created by allocating an array of max pointers to CObject. Once this has been done, we can address the object list as a normal array. For example, the first entry will be m_pObjectList[0].

```
m_pObjectList=new CObject*[max]; //object list
```

The last thing that the constructor does is to create empty objects for each slot in the object list. These will be initialized and used later.

```
for(int i=0; i<m_nMaxCount; i++) //create objects
  m_pObjectList[i]=new CObject;
}
```

The CObjectManager destructor deletes all of the memory allocated by the constructor. First, it deletes all of the CObject class instances pointed to by the object list.

```
for(int i=0; i<m_nMaxCount; i++) //for each object
  delete m_pObjectList[i]; //delete it
```

Then it deletes the array itself. Notice the use of delete[] to delete the whole array; using delete without the [] would just delete the first entry in the array instead of the whole array. Notice that we must delete the objects first, then the array, which is the reverse of the order in which they were created by the constructor.

```
delete[]m_pObjectList; //delete object list
```

The Create Function

The CObjectManager create function takes five parameters that specify the object's type, location, and speed:

```
int CObjectManager::create(ObjectType object,int x,int y,
                           int xspeed,int yspeed){
```

To avoid array overflow, it checks to see whether there is room in the object array for the new object:

```
if(m_nCount<m_nMaxCount){ //if room, create object
```

If there is room in the array, it uses the next unused object in the array (the one with index m_nCount) for the new object, which it initializes using the CObject create function:

```
m_pObjectList[m_nCount]->
  create(object,x,y,xspeed,yspeed);
```

It then returns the index of the new object, post-incrementing it to indicate that there is one more object in the array:

```
    return m_nCount++; //return index into object list
  }
```

Otherwise, there is no room in the object array for the new object, so it returns −1:

```
    else return -1; //no room
  }
```

The Animate Function

The `CObjectManager animate` function animates each of the objects in the object list to a specified surface. It encapsulates most of the work that was formerly done by the `ComposeFrame` function in `Main.cpp` of Demo 4.

```
void CObjectManager::animate(LPDIRECTDRAWSURFACE surface){
```

It first moves the objects:

```
    for(int i=0; i<m_nCount; i++)m_pObjectList[i]->move();
```

In Demo 5, we want the viewpoint to move with the plane so that the plane stays in the center of the screen. We do this by calling the viewpoint manager's `set_position` member function and giving it as a parameter the plane's horizontal location within the game world. Note that in order to give the object manager access to `CObject` private member variables such as `m_nX`, we have chosen to make `CObjectManager` a friend of class `CObject`. We will say more about this in a later section of this chapter in which we describe changes to the `CObject` class.

```
    Viewpoint.set_position(
      m_pObjectList[m_nCurrentObject]->m_nX);
```

Finally, it draws the objects in the object list. Note that the higher-indexed objects in the list are drawn over the lower-indexed objects.

```
    for(i=0; i<m_nCount; i++)m_pObjectList[i]->draw(surface);
  }
```

Other Member Functions

The `CObjectManager accelerate` function is simply a wrapper for the `CObject accelerate` function of the current object:

```
void CObjectManager::accelerate(int xdelta,int ydelta){
  //change speed of current object
```

```
m_pObjectList[m_nCurrentObject]->
   accelerate(xdelta,ydelta);
}
```

The `CObjectManager set_current` function sets `m_nCurrentObject` to the index provided as a parameter, provided the index is a valid one:

```
void CObjectManager::set_current(int index){
  //set current object
  if(index>=0&&index<m_nCount)m_nCurrentObject=index;
}
```

Finally, the `CObjectManager speed` function returns the absolute value of the horizontal component of the current object's speed. Once again, the fact that `CObjectManager` is a friend of `CObject` allows us to access the private member variable `m_nXspeed` of a `CObject` class instance.

```
int CObjectManager::speed(){
  //return magnitude of current object speed
  return abs(m_pObjectList[m_nCurrentObject]->m_nXspeed);
}
```

Generating Pseudorandom Numbers

A *pseudorandom number generator* is an algorithm for generating a sequence of numbers in which the next number in the sequence is difficult to predict from the previous ones. In a sense, those numbers "look random." They are not truly random—the generation of true random numbers requires specialized hardware not included with the typical PC—but they are good enough for many applications. The most popular pseudorandom number generator is called a *linear congruential random number generator.* If this generator is given an initial random number called a *seed*, it will generate a sequence of numbers that look progressively less random as time goes by. We will compensate for this drift away from randomness by reseeding the random number generator after a certain number of numbers have been generated—we will say that the generator has become *stale* when this happens.

But what will we use for a seed? In practice, a good thing to use is the current time as reported by the `timeGetTime` Windows API function. The linear congruential random number generator provided in the C standard library is encapsulated in the class `CRandom`. The `CRandom` header file is `Random.h`. The first declaration in `Random.h` is for the constant `STALE_RAND`, defined to be the number of expected calls to the linear congruential random number generator before it becomes stale. There is no mathematics for determining how to set this value, but 1,000 will do.

```
#define STALE_RAND 1000 //stale after this many calls
```

CRandom needs to keep track of how many pseudorandom numbers it has generated since it was last reseeded. It uses a private member variable called m_nCount for this purpose.

```
int m_nCount; //count of number of times used
```

Public member functions include a constructor, a function number(i,j) that returns a pseudorandom integer in the range i to j inclusive, and a function sowseed that reseeds the pseudorandom number generator using the current time:

```
CRandom(); //constructor
int number(int i,int j); //return random number in i..j
void sowseed(); //seed the random number generator
```

The code file for CRandom is Random.cpp. It begins with a constructor, which calls the public member function sowseed to seed the linear congruential random number generator.

```
CRandom::CRandom(){ //constructor
  sowseed(); //seed random number generator
}
```

Function sowseed seeds the linear congruential random number generator using the srand function provided in the C standard library. Function srand requires a random number to use as a seed; we will use the value returned by the Windows API function timeGetTime on the assumption that reseeding will take place at unpredictable times. Since the generator is no longer stale, it then resets m_nCount to zero.

```
void CRandom::sowseed(){ //seed random number generator
  srand(timeGetTime()); m_nCount=0;
}
```

Function number(i,j) returns a pseudorandom number in the range i to j inclusive, using the C standard library function rand. Unfortunately, rand is a legacy function that returns a positive signed short integer, which is only 15 bits long. This lets us generate pseudorandom numbers up to 32,767, which is a bit restrictive. We will write code to generate 30-bit random numbers by concatenating two consecutive 15-bit pseudorandom numbers generated by rand. In general, this is *not* a statistically good way to generate pseudorandom numbers, but it is good enough for many purposes. The first thing we do is to increment m_nCount and reseed if the generator is stale.

```
if(++m_nCount>STALE_RAND)sowseed(); //reseed if stale
```

If the random number requested is small, we use a single call to rand:

```
int sample; //random sample
//get a random sample
if(j<0x7FFF)sample=rand(); //15-bit
```

Otherwise we take the result from rand, left-shift it 15 bits, then OR a second result from rand into the lower-order 15 bits (which were left zero after the left-shift of the first sample):

```
else sample=((int)rand()<<15)|(int)rand(); //30-bit
```

Now we need to constrain the sample to be in the range i to j inclusive, that is, no smaller than i, and no larger than j. Taking the remainder modulo (j-i+1) makes it no smaller than 0 and no larger than j-i. Adding i to this makes it no smaller than i and no larger than j, as required.

```
return sample%(j-i+1)+i;
```

Changes to the Object Class

Changes to CObject in Demo 5 are fairly minimal. In Objects.h, the only changes are to insert two new entries, FARM_OBJECT and FIELD_OBJECT, in ObjectType for two new objects representing Ned's farm.

```
enum ObjectType{CROW_OBJECT=0,PLANE_OBJECT,FARM_OBJECT,
  FIELD_OBJECT,NUM_SPRITES};
```

As described earlier in this chapter, the following line of code is added to the declaration of CObject. This grants CObjectManager the right to access private and protected member variables of CObject. The friend class construct is a powerful one that can be abused through overuse, though it is legitimate to use it to give a manager class control over the objects that it is managing.

```
friend class CObjectManager;
```

In the CObject draw function in Objects.cpp, we change the first line of code so that it draws the object's sprite image m_pSprite to the correct location on the screen relative to the player's viewpoint instead of its absolute coordinates in the virtual universe, that is, to (Viewpoint.screen(m_nX),m_nY) instead of (m_nX,m_nY):

```
m_pSprite->draw(m_nCurrentFrame,Viewpoint.screen(m_nX),
  m_nY,surface);
```

In the CObject create function, we change the PLANE_OBJECT's frame interval to 250 milliseconds:

```
m_nFrameInterval=250;
```

The CROW_OBJECT wingbeat animations are desynchronized by starting each crow object at a random frame in its animation and setting its frame interval to a random number in the range 220 to 280 milliseconds. Since the random number generator may generate the same frame interval for different crows, some crows *may* remain synchronized. However, this is sufficiently unlikely. The probability of two crows getting the same frame interval is 1/61, which means that the probability of getting two synchronized crows is greater than 1/2 only when there are 30 crows or more, and in such a crowd of crows they are unlikely to be recognized unless the player is particularly looking for them. Crow wingbeats may also appear to be synchronized for short periods of time and then become asynchronous later due to the artificial quantization of time into discrete frames of varying lengths.

```
m_nCurrentFrame=Random.number(0,m_nFrameCount-1);
m_nFrameInterval=250+Random.number(-30,30);
```

We also introduce two new cases into the switch statement for the farm and field objects:

```
case FARM_OBJECT:
case FIELD_OBJECT:
m_nFrameCount=1;
break;
```

Finally, in the CObject move function, we change the definition of the constant YMARGIN:

```
const int YMARGIN=20; //vertical margin;
```

We add the following line of code to normalize the object's x-coordinate to within the virtual universe:

```
Viewpoint.normalize(m_nX); //normalize to world width
```

Finally, we constrain the object's vertical motion so that it remains below the top of the screen and above the bottom of the screen. Since the object's m_nY value is the y-coordinate of its bottom, we will make sure that m_nY is at least YMARGIN so that at least 20 pixels of the object will appear at the top of the screen (which will be large enough to show all of the small objects such as crows), and that m_nY is at most SCREEN_HEIGHT-1 so that it will stay above the bottom of the screen.

```
if(m_nY<YMARGIN)m_nY=YMARGIN;
if(m_nY>=SCREEN_HEIGHT)m_nY=SCREEN_HEIGHT-1;
```

Changes to Main.cpp

The changes to Main.cpp in Demo 5 begin with the declaration of a constant for the maximum number of objects allowed in the game:

```
#define MAX_OBJECTS 32 //max number of objects in game
```

We declare a new bmp sprite file reader to hold the foreground image depicting Ned's farm:

```
CBmpSpriteFileReader g_cFrgndImages; //foreground images
```

We declare an object manager of sufficient size to hold all of the objects:

```
CObjectManager ObjectManager(MAX_OBJECTS); //object manager
```

Then, we declare a viewpoint manager and a random number generator. In Demo 5, we will use the random number generator in the CObject class to desynchronize the crow wingbeats; we will find many other uses for it later.

```
CViewPoint Viewpoint; //player viewpoint
CRandom Random; //random number generator
```

Loading Sprites

The first code change is to the body of LoadPlaneSprite, which now loads six frames of plane animation from locations (1,1), (123,1), (245,1), (367,1), (489,1), and (17,74) of the image stored in the bmp sprite file reader g_cSpriteImages:

```
BOOL result=TRUE;
result=result&&g_pSprite[PLANE_OBJECT]->
  load(&g_cSpriteImages,0,1,1);
  result=result&&g_pSprite[PLANE_OBJECT]->
  load(&g_cSpriteImages,1,123,1);
  result=result&&g_pSprite[PLANE_OBJECT]->
  load(&g_cSpriteImages,2,245,1);
  result=result&&g_pSprite[PLANE_OBJECT]->
  load(&g_cSpriteImages,3,367,1);
  result=result&&g_pSprite[PLANE_OBJECT]->
  load(&g_cSpriteImages,4,489,1);
  result=result&&g_pSprite[PLANE_OBJECT]->
  load(&g_cSpriteImages,5,17,74);
  return result;
```

A new function, LoadFrgndSprites, loads the foreground images of the farm and the field into two sprites from the bmp sprite file reader g_cFrgndImages:

```
BOOL LoadFrgndSprites(){ //load foreground sprites
  BOOL result=TRUE;
  result=result&&g_pSprite[FARM_OBJECT]->
```

```
    load(&g_cFrgndImages,0,0,0); //load farm sprite
  result=result&&g_pSprite[FIELD_OBJECT]->
    load(&g_cFrgndImages,0,640,0); //load field sprite
  return result;
} //LoadFrgndSprites
```

We use this function to load the foreground sprites by adding four lines of code to the end of function `LoadImages`. We load the new bmp file `Farm.bmp` (see Figure 7.4) into the bmp sprite file reader `g_cFrgndImages`.

```
if(!g_cFrgndImages.load("farm.bmp"))return FALSE;
```

Figure 7.4 The foreground image Farm.bmp

We then create two clipped sprites for the farm and the field, and call function `LoadFrgndSprites` to load the images into the sprites from the bmp sprite file reader `g_cFrgndImages`:

```
g_pSprite[FARM_OBJECT]=new CClippedSprite(1,640,162);
g_pSprite[FIELD_OBJECT]=new CClippedSprite(1,640,162);
if(!LoadFrgndSprites())return FALSE; //load foreground
```

The CreateObjects Function

The body of function `CreateObjects` now requests the object manager to create the objects for us. First, the farm and field objects are placed side by side so as to fill up the virtual universe. The farm object is placed at (0,SCREEN_HEIGHT-1), and the field object is placed at (SCREEN_WIDTH,SCREEN_HEIGHT-1). The exact x-coordinates are not important provided one is SCREEN_WIDTH larger than the other is. The y-coordinates must be at the bottom of the screen. The farm and field objects have a horizontal and vertical velocity of zero.

```
ObjectManager.create(FARM_OBJECT,0,SCREEN_HEIGHT-1,0,0);
ObjectManager.create(FIELD_OBJECT,SCREEN_WIDTH,
  SCREEN_HEIGHT-1,0,0);
```

Three crow objects are placed, with horizontal speeds of -2 (recall that negative speeds are to the left):

```
ObjectManager.create(CROW_OBJECT,400,100,-2,0);
```

```
ObjectManager.create(CROW_OBJECT,420,80,-2,0);
ObjectManager.create(CROW_OBJECT,430,120,-2,0);
```

Then the plane object, which is made the current object using the `ObjectManager set_current` function, is created:

```
ObjectManager.set_current(
  ObjectManager.create(PLANE_OBJECT,320,271,-1,0));
```

Lastly, we create three slower crow objects in various places, with horizontal speeds of −1:

```
ObjectManager.create(CROW_OBJECT,320,100,-1,0);
ObjectManager.create(CROW_OBJECT,405,90,-1,0);
ObjectManager.create(CROW_OBJECT,255,125,-1,0);
```

Other Functions

The next function to be changed is `RestoreSurfaces`, in which we add code to restore the surfaces in the two new sprites:

```
if(g_pSprite[FARM_OBJECT]->Restore()&& //if farm and ...
  g_pSprite[FIELD_OBJECT]->Restore()) //... field restored
  result=result&&LoadFrgndSprites(); //redraw image
else return FALSE;
```

Function `ComposeFrame` is now a lot simpler than it was in Demo 4. The tasks of drawing the background and animating the objects have been given to the viewpoint manager and the object manager, respectively. `ComposeFrame` simply asks them to do their jobs, passing to the viewpoint manager the speed of the plane as reported by the object manager so that the background scrolls at a speed proportional to the plane's speed.

```
Viewpoint.draw_background(lpBackground,lpSecondary,
  ObjectManager.speed()); //draw scrolling background
ObjectManager.animate(lpSecondary); //draw objects
```

The last significant change to `Main.cpp` is that the `keyboard_handler` function must now request the object manager to accelerate the plane in response to the appropriate keystrokes from the player:

```
case VK_UP: ObjectManager.accelerate(0,-1); break;
case VK_DOWN: ObjectManager.accelerate(0,1); break;
case VK_LEFT: ObjectManager.accelerate(-1,0); break;
case VK_RIGHT: ObjectManager.accelerate(1,0); break;
```

Demo 5 Files

Code Files

The following files in Demo 5 are used without change from Demo 4:

- Bmp.h
- Bmp.cpp
- Bsprite.h
- Bsprite.cpp
- Csprite.h
- Csprite.cpp
- Defines.h
- Ddsetup.cpp
- Sbmp.h
- Sbmp.cpp
- Timer.h
- Timer.cpp

The following files in Demo 5 have been modified from Demo 4:

- Main.cpp
- Objects.h
- Objects.cpp

The following files are new in Demo 5:

- Objman.h
- Objman.cpp
- Random.h
- Random.cpp
- View.h
- View.cpp

Media Files

The following image files are new in Demo 5:

- Farm.bmp

Required Libraries

- Ddraw.lib
- Winmm.lib

Code Listings

Main.cpp

```
//main.cpp

//There is now an object manager to manage the objects.
//Note how much easier it is to add new objects to the
//game - we now have flocks of crows. A pseudorandom
//number generator is used to desynchronize crow wingbeats.
//Also animated plane, and parallax scrolling.

//Copyright Ian Parberry, 1999
//Last updated May 22, 2000

//system includes
#include <windows.h>
#include <windowsx.h>
#include <ddraw.h>
#include <stdio.h>

//system defines
#define WIN32_LEAN_AND_MEAN

//custom includes
#include "defines.h" //global definitions
#include "bmp.h" //bmp file reader
#include "timer.h" //game timer
#include "csprite.h" //for clipped sprite class
#include "objects.h" //for object class
#include "objman.h" //for object manager
#include "view.h" //for viewpoint class
#include "random.h" //for random number generator

//defines
#define MAX_OBJECTS 32 //max number of objects in game

//globals

BOOL ActiveApp; //is this application active?

LPDIRECTDRAW lpDirectDrawObject=NULL; //direct draw object
LPDIRECTDRAWSURFACE lpPrimary=NULL; //primary surface
LPDIRECTDRAWPALETTE lpPrimaryPalette; //its palette
```

```
LPDIRECTDRAWSURFACE lpSecondary=NULL; //back buffer
LPDIRECTDRAWPALETTE lpSecondaryPalette; //its palette
LPDIRECTDRAWSURFACE lpBackground=NULL; //background image

CTimer Timer; //game timer

CBmpFileReader background; //background image
CBmpSpriteFileReader g_cSpriteImages; //sprite images
CBmpSpriteFileReader g_cFrgndImages; //foreground images

CObjectManager ObjectManager(MAX_OBJECTS); //object manager

CClippedSprite *g_pSprite[NUM_SPRITES]; //sprites

CViewPoint Viewpoint; //player viewpoint
CRandom Random; //random number generator

//helper functions
LPDIRECTDRAWPALETTE CreatePalette(LPDIRECTDRAWSURFACE surface);
BOOL InitDirectDraw(HWND hwnd);
HWND CreateDefaultWindow(char* name,HINSTANCE hInstance);

BOOL LoadPlaneSprite(){
  BOOL result=TRUE;
  result=result&&g_pSprite[PLANE_OBJECT]->
    load(&g_cSpriteImages,0,1,1);
  result=result&&g_pSprite[PLANE_OBJECT]->
    load(&g_cSpriteImages,1,123,1);
  result=result&&g_pSprite[PLANE_OBJECT]->
    load(&g_cSpriteImages,2,245,1);
  result=result&&g_pSprite[PLANE_OBJECT]->
    load(&g_cSpriteImages,3,367,1);
  result=result&&g_pSprite[PLANE_OBJECT]->
    load(&g_cSpriteImages,4,489,1);
  result=result&&g_pSprite[PLANE_OBJECT]->
    load(&g_cSpriteImages,5,17,74);
  return result;
} //LoadPlaneSprite

BOOL LoadCrowSprite(){
  BOOL result=TRUE;
  result=result&&g_pSprite[CROW_OBJECT]->
    load(&g_cSpriteImages,0,256,183); //frame 0
  result=result&&g_pSprite[CROW_OBJECT]->
    load(&g_cSpriteImages,1,320,183); //frame 1
  result=result&&g_pSprite[CROW_OBJECT]->
    load(&g_cSpriteImages,2,256,237); //frame 2
  result=result&&g_pSprite[CROW_OBJECT]->
    load(&g_cSpriteImages,3,323,237); //frame 3
  return result;
```

```
} //LoadCrowSprite

BOOL LoadFrgndSprites(){ //load foreground sprites
  BOOL result=TRUE;
  result=result&&g_pSprite[FARM_OBJECT]->
    load(&g_cFrgndImages,0,0,0); //load farm sprite
  result=result&&g_pSprite[FIELD_OBJECT]->
    load(&g_cFrgndImages,0,640,0); //load field sprite
  return result;
} //LoadFrgndSprites

BOOL LoadImages(){ //load graphics from files to surfaces
  //get the background image
  if(!background.load("bckgnd.bmp"))return FALSE; //read file
  background.draw(lpBackground); //draw to background surface
  //set palettes in all surfaces
  if(!background.setpalette(lpPrimaryPalette))return FALSE;
  if(!background.setpalette(lpSecondaryPalette))return FALSE;
  //load the sprites...
  if(!g_cSpriteImages.load("sprites.bmp"))return FALSE;
  //...the plane
  g_pSprite[PLANE_OBJECT]=new CClippedSprite(6,121,72);
  if(!LoadPlaneSprite())return FALSE; //load plane images
  //...the crow
  g_pSprite[CROW_OBJECT]=new CClippedSprite(4,58,37);
  if(!LoadCrowSprite())return FALSE; //load crow images
  //...the foreground sprites
  if(!g_cFrgndImages.load("farm.bmp"))return FALSE;
  g_pSprite[FARM_OBJECT]=new CClippedSprite(1,640,162);
  g_pSprite[FIELD_OBJECT]=new CClippedSprite(1,640,162);
  if(!LoadFrgndSprites())return FALSE; //load foreground
  return TRUE;
} //LoadImages

void CreateObjects(){
  ObjectManager.create(FARM_OBJECT,0,SCREEN_HEIGHT-1,0,0);
  ObjectManager.create(FIELD_OBJECT,SCREEN_WIDTH,
    SCREEN_HEIGHT-1,0,0);
  ObjectManager.create(CROW_OBJECT,400,100,-2,0);
  ObjectManager.create(CROW_OBJECT,420,80,-2,0);
  ObjectManager.create(CROW_OBJECT,430,120,-2,0);
  ObjectManager.set_current(
    ObjectManager.create(PLANE_OBJECT,320,271,-1,0));
  ObjectManager.create(CROW_OBJECT,320,100,-1,0);
  ObjectManager.create(CROW_OBJECT,405,90,-1,0);
  ObjectManager.create(CROW_OBJECT,255,125,-1,0);
} //CreateObjects

BOOL RestoreSurfaces(){ //restore all surfaces
  BOOL result=TRUE;
```

```
    if(SUCCEEDED(lpPrimary->Restore())) //if primary restored
      result=result&&background.draw(lpPrimary)&& //redraw image
        background.setpalette(lpPrimaryPalette); //set palette
    else return FALSE;
    if(SUCCEEDED(lpSecondary->Restore())) //if secondary restored
      result=result&&background.draw(lpSecondary)&& //redraw image
        background.setpalette(lpSecondaryPalette); //set palette
    else return FALSE;
    if(SUCCEEDED(lpBackground->Restore())) //if background restored
      result=result&&background.draw(lpBackground); //redraw image
    else return FALSE;
    if(g_pSprite[PLANE_OBJECT]->Restore()) //if plane restored
      result=result&&LoadPlaneSprite(); //redraw image
    else return FALSE;
    if(g_pSprite[CROW_OBJECT]->Restore()) //if crow restored
      result=result&&LoadCrowSprite(); //redraw image
    else return FALSE;
    if(g_pSprite[FARM_OBJECT]->Restore()&& //if farm and ...
      g_pSprite[FIELD_OBJECT]->Restore()) //... field restored
      result=result&&LoadFrgndSprites(); //redraw image
    else return FALSE;
    return result;
} //RestoreSurfaces

BOOL PageFlip(){ //return TRUE if page flip succeeds
  if(lpPrimary->Flip(NULL,DDFLIP_WAIT)==DDERR_SURFACELOST)
    return RestoreSurfaces();
  return TRUE;
} //PageFlip

BOOL ComposeFrame(){ //compose a frame of animation
  Viewpoint.draw_background(lpBackground,lpSecondary,
    ObjectManager.speed()); //draw scrolling background
  ObjectManager.animate(lpSecondary); //draw objects
  return TRUE;
} //ComposeFrame

BOOL ProcessFrame(){ //process a frame of animation
  ComposeFrame(); //compose a frame in secondary surface
  return PageFlip(); //flip video memory surfaces
} //ProcessFrame

BOOL keyboard_handler(WPARAM keystroke){ //keyboard handler
  BOOL result=FALSE; //return TRUE if game is to end
  switch(keystroke){
    case VK_ESCAPE: result=TRUE; break; //exit game
    case VK_UP: ObjectManager.accelerate(0,-1); break;
    case VK_DOWN: ObjectManager.accelerate(0,1); break;
    case VK_LEFT: ObjectManager.accelerate(-1,0); break;
    case VK_RIGHT: ObjectManager.accelerate(1,0); break;
```

```
        default: break;
    }
    return result;
} //keyboard_handler

//message handler (window procedure)
long CALLBACK WindowProc(HWND hwnd,UINT message,
                         WPARAM wParam,LPARAM lParam){
    switch(message){
      case WM_ACTIVATEAPP: ActiveApp=wParam; break;
      case WM_CREATE: break;
      case WM_KEYDOWN: //keyboard hit
        if(keyboard_handler(wParam))DestroyWindow(hwnd);
        break;
      case WM_DESTROY: //end of game
        if(lpDirectDrawObject!=NULL){ //if DD object exists
          if(lpSecondary!=NULL) //if secondary surface exists
            lpSecondary->Release(); //release secondary surface
          if(lpPrimary!=NULL) //if primary surface exists
            lpPrimary->Release(); //release primary surface
          if(lpBackground!=NULL) //if background exists
            lpBackground->Release(); //release background
          for(int i=0; i<NUM_SPRITES; i++){ //for each sprite
            if(g_pSprite[i]) //if sprite exists
              g_pSprite[i]->Release(); //release sprite
            delete g_pSprite[i]; //delete sprite
          }
          lpDirectDrawObject->Release(); //release DD object
        }
        ShowCursor(TRUE); //show the mouse cursor
        PostQuitMessage(0); //and exit
        break;
      default: //default window procedure
        return DefWindowProc(hwnd,message,wParam,lParam);
    } //switch(message)
    return 0L;
} //WindowProc

int WINAPI WinMain(HINSTANCE hInstance,HINSTANCE hPrevInstance,
LPSTR lpCmdLine,int nCmdShow){
    MSG msg; //current message
    HWND hwnd; //handle to full-screen window
    hwnd=CreateDefaultWindow("directX demo 5",hInstance);
    if(!hwnd)return FALSE;
    //set up window
    ShowWindow(hwnd,nCmdShow); UpdateWindow(hwnd);
    SetFocus(hwnd); //allow input from keyboard
    ShowCursor(FALSE); //hide the cursor
    //init graphics
    for(int i=0; i<NUM_SPRITES; i++) //null out sprites
```

```
      g_pSprite[i]=NULL;
    BOOL OK=InitDirectDraw(hwnd);//initialize DirectDraw
    if(OK)OK=LoadImages(); //load images from disk
    if(!OK){ //bail out if initialization failed
      DestroyWindow(hwnd); return FALSE;
    }
    //start game timer
    Timer.start();
    //create objects
    CreateObjects();
    //message loop
    while(TRUE)
      if(PeekMessage(&msg,NULL,0,0,PM_NOREMOVE)){
        if(!GetMessage(&msg,NULL,0,0))return msg.wParam;
        TranslateMessage(&msg); DispatchMessage(&msg);
      }
      else if(ActiveApp)ProcessFrame(); else WaitMessage();
} //WinMain
```

Objects.h

```
//objects.h: header file for CObject class

//Copyright Ian Parberry, 1999
//Last updated October 5, 1999

#ifndef __OBJECTS__
#define __OBJECTS__

#include "bsprite.h"

//object types
enum ObjectType{CROW_OBJECT=0,PLANE_OBJECT,FARM_OBJECT,
  FIELD_OBJECT,NUM_SPRITES};
//note: NUM_SPRITES must be last

class CObject{ //class for a moving object
  friend class CObjectManager;
  private:
    int m_nX,m_nY; //current location
    int m_nXspeed,m_nYspeed; //current speed
    int m_nLastXMoveTime; //last time moved horizontally
    int m_nLastYMoveTime; //last time moved vertically
    CBaseSprite *m_pSprite; //pointer to sprite
    int m_nMinXSpeed,m_nMaxXSpeed; //min, max horizontal speeds
    int m_nMinYSpeed,m_nMaxYSpeed; //min, max vertical speeds
    int m_nCurrentFrame; //frame to be displayed
    int m_nFrameCount; //number of frames in animation
    int m_nLastFrameTime; //last time the frame was changed
    int m_nFrameInterval; //interval between frames
```

```
      BOOL m_bForwardAnimation; //is animation going forward?
    public:
      CObject(); //constructor
      void draw(LPDIRECTDRAWSURFACE surface); //draw
      void create(ObjectType object,int x,int y,
        int xspeed,int yspeed); //create object
      void accelerate(int xdelta,int ydelta=0); //change speed
      void move(); //move depending on time and speed
};

#endif
```

Objects.cpp

```
//objects.cpp

//Copyright Ian Parberry, 1999
//Last updated October 5, 1999

#include "objects.h"
#include "timer.h" //game timer
#include "csprite.h" //for clipped sprite class
#include "random.h" //for random number generator
#include "view.h" //for viewpoint class

extern CClippedSprite *g_pSprite[]; //sprites
extern CTimer Timer; //game timer
extern CRandom Random; //random number generator
extern CViewPoint Viewpoint; //player viewpoint

CObject::CObject(){ //constructor
  m_nX=m_nY=m_nXspeed=m_nYspeed=0;
  m_pSprite=NULL;
  m_nLastXMoveTime=m_nLastYMoveTime=0;
  m_nCurrentFrame=m_nFrameCount=m_nLastFrameTime=0;
  m_bForwardAnimation=TRUE;
  m_nFrameInterval=30;
}

void CObject::draw(LPDIRECTDRAWSURFACE surface){ //draw
  //draw the current frame
  m_pSprite->draw(m_nCurrentFrame,Viewpoint.screen(m_nX),
    m_nY,surface);
  //figure out which frame is next
  int t=m_nFrameInterval/(1+abs(m_nXspeed)); //frame interval
  if(m_nFrameCount>1&&Timer.elapsed(m_nLastFrameTime,t))
    if(m_bForwardAnimation){ //forward animation
      if(++m_nCurrentFrame>=m_nFrameCount){ //wrap
        m_nCurrentFrame=m_nFrameCount-2;
        m_bForwardAnimation=FALSE;
```

```
        }
      }
      else{ //backward animation
        if(--m_nCurrentFrame<0){ //wrap
          m_nCurrentFrame=1;
          m_bForwardAnimation=TRUE;
        }
      }
  }

  void CObject::create(ObjectType object,int x,int y,
                        int xspeed,int yspeed){
    m_nLastXMoveTime=m_nLastYMoveTime=Timer.time(); //time
    m_nX=x; m_nY=y; //location
    m_nXspeed=xspeed; m_nYspeed=yspeed; //speed
    m_pSprite=g_pSprite[object]; //sprite
    m_nFrameCount=m_pSprite->frame_count(); //frame count
    //customize properties of each object type
    switch(object){
      case PLANE_OBJECT:
        m_nMinXSpeed=-3; m_nMaxXSpeed=-1;
        m_nMinYSpeed=-4; m_nMaxYSpeed=4;
        m_nFrameInterval=250;
        break;
      case CROW_OBJECT:
        m_nMinXSpeed=-2; m_nMaxXSpeed=-1;
        m_nMinYSpeed=-1; m_nMaxYSpeed=1;
        m_nCurrentFrame=Random.number(0,m_nFrameCount-1);
        m_nFrameInterval=250+Random.number(-30,30);
        break;
      case FARM_OBJECT:
      case FIELD_OBJECT:
        m_nFrameCount=1;
        break;
    }
  }

  void CObject::accelerate(int xdelta,int ydelta){
  //change speed
    //horizontal
    m_nXspeed+=xdelta;
    if(m_nXspeed<m_nMinXSpeed)m_nXspeed=m_nMinXSpeed;
    if(m_nXspeed>m_nMaxXSpeed)m_nXspeed=m_nMaxXSpeed;
    //vertical
    m_nYspeed+=ydelta;
    if(m_nYspeed<m_nMinYSpeed)m_nYspeed=m_nMinYSpeed;
    if(m_nYspeed>m_nMaxYSpeed)m_nYspeed=m_nMaxYSpeed;
  }

  void CObject::move(){ //move object
```

```
const int XSCALE=16; //to scale back horizontal motion
const int YSCALE=32; //to scale back vertical motion
const int YMARGIN=20; //vertical margin;
int xdelta,ydelta; //change in position
int time=Timer.time(); //current time
//horizontal motion
int tfactor=time-m_nLastXMoveTime; //time since last move
xdelta=(m_nXspeed*tfactor)/XSCALE; //x distance moved
m_nX+=xdelta; //x motion
Viewpoint.normalize(m_nX); //normalize to world width
if(xdelta||m_nXspeed==0) //record time of move
  m_nLastXMoveTime=time;
//vertical motion
tfactor=time-m_nLastYMoveTime; //time since last move
ydelta=(m_nYspeed*tfactor)/YSCALE; //y distance moved
m_nY+=ydelta; //y motion
if(m_nY<YMARGIN)m_nY=YMARGIN;
if(m_nY>=SCREEN_HEIGHT)m_nY=SCREEN_HEIGHT-1;
if(ydelta||m_nYspeed==0) //record time of move
  m_nLastYMoveTime=time;
}
```

Objman.h

```
//objman.h: header file for the object manager
//Copyright Ian Parberry, 1999
//Last updated September 29, 1999

#ifndef __OBJMAN__
#define __OBJMAN__

#include <windows.h>
#include <windowsx.h>
#include <ddraw.h>

#include "objects.h"

class CObjectManager{
  private:
    CObject **m_pObjectList; //list of objects in game
    int m_nCount; //how many objects in list
    int m_nMaxCount; //maximum number of objects
    int m_nCurrentObject; //index of the current object
  public:
    CObjectManager(int max); //constructor
    ~CObjectManager(); //destructor
    int create(ObjectType object,int x,int y,
      int xspeed,int yspeed); //create new object
    //animate all objects
    void animate(LPDIRECTDRAWSURFACE surface);
```

```
                //the following functions operate on the current object
                void accelerate(int xdelta,int ydelta=0); //change speed
                void set_current(int index); //set current object
                int speed(); //return magnitude of speed
        };

        #endif
```

Objman.cpp

```
        //objman.cpp: object manager class
        //Copyright Ian Parberry, 1999
        //Last updated September 29, 1999

        #include "objman.h"
        #include "view.h" //for viewpoint class

        extern CViewPoint Viewpoint; //player viewpoint

        CObjectManager::CObjectManager(int max){ //constructor
          m_nMaxCount=max; m_nCount=0; m_nCurrentObject=0;
          m_pObjectList=new CObject*[max]; //object list
          for(int i=0; i<m_nMaxCount; i++) //create objects
            m_pObjectList[i]=new CObject;
        }

        CObjectManager::~CObjectManager(){ //destructor
          for(int i=0; i<m_nMaxCount; i++) //for each object
            delete m_pObjectList[i]; //delete it
          delete[]m_pObjectList; //delete object list
        }

        int CObjectManager::create(ObjectType object,int x,int y,
                                   int xspeed,int yspeed){
          if(m_nCount<m_nMaxCount){ //if room, create object
            m_pObjectList[m_nCount]->
              create(object,x,y,xspeed,yspeed);
            return m_nCount++; //return index into object list
          }
          else return -1; //no room
        }

        void CObjectManager::animate(LPDIRECTDRAWSURFACE surface){
          //move objects
          for(int i=0; i<m_nCount; i++)m_pObjectList[i]->move();
          //move viewpoint with plane
          Viewpoint.set_position(
            m_pObjectList[m_nCurrentObject]->m_nX);
          //draw objects
```

```
    for(i=0; i<m_nCount; i++)m_pObjectList[i]->draw(surface);
}

void CObjectManager::accelerate(int xdelta,int ydelta){
  //change speed of current object
  m_pObjectList[m_nCurrentObject]->
    accelerate(xdelta,ydelta);
}

void CObjectManager::set_current(int index){
  //set current object
  if(index>=0&&index<m_nCount)m_nCurrentObject=index;
}

int CObjectManager::speed(){
  //return magnitude of current object speed
  return abs(m_pObjectList[m_nCurrentObject]->m_nXspeed);
}
```

Random.h

```
// random.h
// header for random number generator

//Copyright Ian Parberry, 1999
//Last updated September 29, 1999


#ifndef __RANDOM__
#define __RANDOM__

#define STALE_RAND 1000 //stale after this many calls

class CRandom{
  private:
    int m_nCount; //count of number of times used
  public:
    CRandom(); //constructor
    int number(int i,int j); //return random number in i..j
    void sowseed(); //seed the random number generator
};

#endif
```

Random.cpp

```
// random.cpp
// random number generator

//Copyright Ian Parberry, 1998
//Last updated July 3, 1998
```

```
#include <windows.h>

#include "random.h"

CRandom::CRandom(){ //constructor
  sowseed(); //seed random number generator
}

void CRandom::sowseed(){ //seed random number generator
  srand(timeGetTime()); m_nCount=0;
}

int CRandom::number(int i,int j){
  //return random number in  i..j
  if(++m_nCount>STALE_RAND)sowseed(); //reseed if stale
  int sample; //random sample
  //get a random sample
  if(j<0x7FFF)sample=rand(); //15-bit
  else sample=((int)rand()<<15)|(int)rand(); //30-bit
  //compute result
  return sample%(j-i+1)+i;
}
```

View.h

```
//view.h: header file for viewpoint manager
//Copyright Ian Parberry, 1999
//Last updated October 5, 1999

#ifndef __VIEWPOINT__
#define __VIEWPOINT__

#include <windows.h>
#include <windowsx.h>
#include <ddraw.h>

#include "defines.h"

#define WORLD_WIDTH 1280 //width of the world

class CViewPoint{
  private:
    int m_nX; //x coordinate of viewpoint
    int m_nBgOffset; //offset of parallax scrolled background
    int m_nLastTimeBgDrawn; //last time background was drawn
  public:
    CViewPoint(); //constructor
    void set_position(int x); //set current viewpoint
    int screen(int x); //screen coords relative to viewpoint
```

```
        void normalize(int &x); //normalize location x
        void draw_background(LPDIRECTDRAWSURFACE lpSource,
          LPDIRECTDRAWSURFACE lpDestination,int speed);
};

#endif
```

View.cpp

```
//view.cpp: viewpoint manager
//Copyright Ian Parberry, 1999
//Last updated October 5, 1999

#include "view.h"
#include "timer.h" //game timer

extern CTimer Timer; //game timer

CViewPoint::CViewPoint(){ //constructor
  m_nX=0; m_nBgOffset=0; m_nLastTimeBgDrawn=0;
}

void CViewPoint::set_position(int x){ //set current viewpoint
  normalize(x); m_nX=x;
}

int CViewPoint::screen(int x){
  //screen coords relative to viewpoint
  int delta=x-m_nX;
  if(delta>WORLD_WIDTH/2)delta-=WORLD_WIDTH;
  if(delta<-WORLD_WIDTH/2)delta+=WORLD_WIDTH;
  return SCREEN_WIDTH/2+delta;
}

void CViewPoint::normalize(int &x){ //nomrmalize to world
  while(x<0)x+=WORLD_WIDTH;
  while(x>=WORLD_WIDTH)x-=WORLD_WIDTH;
}

void CViewPoint::draw_background(LPDIRECTDRAWSURFACE lpSource,
  LPDIRECTDRAWSURFACE lpDestination,int speed){
//draw scrolling background from surface lpSource to
//surface lpDestination
  //compute source rectangle
  RECT rectDest; //destination rectangle
  rectDest.left=SCREEN_WIDTH-m_nBgOffset;
  rectDest.right=SCREEN_WIDTH;
  rectDest.top=0;
  rectDest.bottom=SCREEN_HEIGHT; //vertical extent
  //compute source rectangle
```

```
RECT rectSource; //destination rectangle
rectSource.left=0;
rectSource.right=m_nBgOffset;
rectSource.top=0;
rectSource.bottom=SCREEN_HEIGHT;
//draw left half of screen
lpDestination->
  Blt(&rectDest,lpSource,&rectSource,DDBLT_WAIT,NULL);
//compute destination rectangle
rectDest.left=0;
rectDest.right=SCREEN_WIDTH-m_nBgOffset;
rectDest.top=0;
rectDest.bottom=SCREEN_HEIGHT;
//compute source rectangle
rectSource.left=m_nBgOffset;
rectSource.right=SCREEN_WIDTH;
rectSource.top=0;
rectSource.bottom=SCREEN_HEIGHT;
//draw right half of screen
lpDestination->
  Blt(&rectDest,lpSource,&rectSource,DDBLT_WAIT,NULL);
//compute new offset
int delta=(speed*(Timer.time()-m_nLastTimeBgDrawn))/50;
if(delta){ //if nonzero
  m_nBgOffset-=delta; //initial offset
  if(m_nBgOffset>SCREEN_WIDTH) //too positive
    m_nBgOffset=0;
  if(m_nBgOffset<0) //too negative
    m_nBgOffset=SCREEN_WIDTH-1;
  m_nLastTimeBgDrawn=Timer.time(); //record time of move
}
} //draw_background
```

Chapter 8

Here's what you'll learn:

- What a rule-based system is and how to implement it

- How to layer object intelligence on top of the code for dumb objects

- How to prevent intelligent objects from behaving identically using the timer and the pseudorandom number generator

- How to manage objects that are born and die during the course of the game

- How to implement a simple form of collision detection

Artificial Intelligence

In Demo 6, we learn how to create rudimentary artificial intelligence (AI for short) using a simple rule-based system augmented with randomness to make the behavior of the crows less predictable and more chaotic. Suddenly the game becomes more interesting. The crows react to the plane, changing speed and height to get away from it, and dropping behind the plane when the opportunity presents itself. The player can now fire bullets by pressing the Spacebar. When hit, the crows explode and turn into falling corpses (see Figure 8.1). This begins to complicate our object management. The exploding crow and the falling crow are treated as different objects from the flying crow. Whereas the crows and plane, as we have already seen, are animated by playing a single animation sequence forward and backward, the exploding crows have an animation that is played only once. The bullets and falling crows have a single frame of animation and a fixed lifetime.

Figure 8.1
Bullets and
an exploding
crow

Experiment with Demo 6

Take a moment now to run Demo 6.

- You should see a plane and a flock of crows in random places.
- Use the left and right arrow keys to make the plane accelerate and decelerate.
- Chase the crows that are ahead of you. Notice that they accelerate to get away from you, and change heights chaotically. If you chase one for long enough at maximum speed, it will eventually slow down as if it has become tired.
- Notice that the crows will gradually all fall behind you and drop to minimum speed so that you cannot chase them any more.
- Drop your speed to the minimum. Notice that the crows form two flocks, one ahead of you and one level with or behind you, and keep pace with the plane.
- Chase the flock ahead of you again, and see the crows scatter in alarm.
- Hit the Spacebar to fire a bullet. Hunt down a crow and shoot it. Watch it explode and change into a corpse that falls from the sky, accelerating due to gravity as it falls.
- Hit the Esc key to exit the program.

Intelligent Objects

Some of the objects in our game are intelligent, and some are not. Intelligence comes with a price—it costs in time to compute intelligent actions, and it costs in memory to store information from which to make intelligent choices. There are many different AI designs from which to choose. We will use one of the simplest, a *rule-based system*, which consists of a set of *states* that the intelligent object can be in, and a set of *rules* that determine which state it is in and what actions are to be taken while in those states. The good thing about a rule-based system is that it is easy to program and requires very little computing time to run. The bad thing about it is that it can lead to predictable, and even worse, identical behavior from the objects. This is bad enough when you meet the objects one at a time, but is worse when you have many of them on the screen at the same time. We want our crows to behave like real crows in that they should behave similarly but not identically. We will achieve this by using the pseudorandom number generator to modify their behavior.

Since not all of the objects in our game will be intelligent, we will derive an intelligent object class `CIntelligentObject` from our base object class `CObject`. Intelligent objects will have more private member variables than base objects, and therefore will use more memory. To save memory, we will use both

`CIntelligentObject` and `CObject` in our game, whichever is appropriate for each object.

Intelligent Object Overview

The header file for `CIntelligentObject` is `Ai.h`, which begins with the declaration of an enumerated type for the states that the intelligent objects can be in. `CRUISING_STATE` means that the object is simply cruising around, unaware of the plane. `AVOIDING_STATE` means that it is aware of the plane's nearby location and is trying to avoid it.

```
enum StateType{CRUISING_STATE,AVOIDING_STATE};
```

`CIntelligentObject` is derived from `Cobject`:

```
class CIntelligentObject: public CObject{
```

It has 11 private member variables. The first records the object's current state.

```
StateType m_eState; //state
```

The next three private member variables are associated with height changes. The first of these is the desired height that the object is currently at or moving toward. The second is the last time the object changed height. The third is the desired time between height changes.

```
int m_nDesiredHeight; //desired altitude
int m_nHeightTime; //time between height changes
int m_nHeightDelayTime; //time to next height change
```

The next two private member variables are associated with speed changes. The first of these is the last time the object changed speed. The second is the desired time between speed changes.

```
int m_nSpeedVariationTime; //last time speed varied
int m_nSpeedVariationDuration; //time to next speed variation
```

The next two private member variables are associated with the use of intelligence. Intelligent objects are not intelligent all of the time; they "zone out" for long periods, not paying much attention to what is going on about them. The first of these private member functions is the last time that the object paid attention, and the second is the amount of time that the object is allowed to "zone out."

```
int m_nLastAiTime; //last time AI was used
int m_nAiDelayTime; //time until AI next used
```

The next three private member variables are associated with the plane. The first is the distance to the plane, the second is the vertical distance, and the third is the horizontal distance. All distances are measured in pixels.

```
int m_nDistance; //distance to plane
int m_nVerticalDistance; //vertical distance from plane
int m_nHorizontalDistance; //horizontal distance from plane
```

`CIntelligentObject` has four private member functions. Function `ai` is the main artificial intelligence function. It consists of a `switch` statement based on the object's current state, which then determines which actions are appropriate.

```
void ai(); //artificial intelligence
```

The next two private member functions control the AI for the two possible states that the object can be in.

```
void cruising_ai(); //ai for cruising along
void avoiding_ai(); //ai for avoiding plane
```

The last private member function takes care of the housekeeping that must take place when an object changes state:

```
void set_state(StateType state); //change state
```

`CIntelligentObject` has three public member functions, starting with a constructor:

```
CIntelligentObject(ObjectType object,int x,int y,
    int xspeed,int yspeed); //constructor
```

The `move` function is declared `virtual void` because we are going to take advantage of the fact that, since `CIntelligentObject` is derived from `CObject`, a `CObject*` pointer p can also be used to point to a `CIntelligent-Object` at run time. The declaration of `move` as `virtual void` allows the compiler to tell at run time which `move` function to call in response to `p->move()`—the `CIntelligentObject` one if p is pointing to a `CIntelligentObject` or the `CObject` one if p is pointing to a `CObject`. Leaving out the `virtual void` would make the compiler call the `CObject` `move` function every time.

```
virtual void move(); //move depending on time and speed
```

The `plane` function is a writer function used to tell the object where the plane is and how far away it is:

```
void plane(int x,int y,int d); //relationship w/plane
};
```

Intelligent Object Code

The code file for `CIntelligentObject` is `Ai.cpp`, which begins with the declaration of some constants. The first two of these constants define when an object is to be considered "close to" and "far from" the plane. It is "close to" the plane when it is at most distance `CLOSE_DISTANCE` from the plane, and "far from" the plane when it is at least `FAR_DISTANCE` from the plane. These constants should be tuned during play testing.

```
const int CLOSE_DISTANCE=200; //close to plane
const int FAR_DISTANCE=300; //far from plane
```

If objects are in front of but much higher or much lower than the plane, they will reduce their speed with the intention of falling back behind the plane where it is safer. The *fallback distance* is the vertical separation that is considered high enough or low enough to attempt to fall back.

```
const int FALLBACK_DISTANCE=150;
```

Finally, when an object is behind the plane it is safe. When the center of the object is `BEHIND_DISTANCE` away from (in this case slightly in front of) the center of the plane, it considers itself to be behind the plane, and therefore safe from attack.

```
const int BEHIND_DISTANCE=-5;
```

The `CIntelligentObject` constructor passes its parameters on to the `CObject` constructor, then sets the `CIntelligentObject` private member variables to sensible initial values. The alert reader will notice the member variable `m_bIntelligent` that hasn't been discussed yet—it is a new member variable of `CObject` that we will talk about later.

```
CIntelligentObject::CIntelligentObject(ObjectType object,
  int x,int y,int xspeed,int yspeed):
CObject(object,x,y,xspeed,yspeed){ //constructor
  m_bIntelligent=TRUE;
  m_nDesiredHeight=240;
  m_nHeightTime=0;  m_nHeightDelayTime=0;
  m_nSpeedVariationTime=m_nSpeedVariationDuration=0;
  m_nDistance=m_nHorizontalDistance=m_nVerticalDistance=0;
  m_eState=CRUISING_STATE;
  m_nLastAiTime=0; m_nAiDelayTime=0;
}
```

Moving and Thinking

The `CIntelligentObject move` function calls the `CObject move` function to move like a dumb object, then calls the `CIntelligentObject ai` function to act intelligently. The idea is that the `ai` will simply change the private `CObject` member functions in an intelligent way, and leave the `CObject move` function to implement these changes. This division of labor makes sense; otherwise you might end up with both the `CObject` and the `CIntelligentObject` member functions trying to direct the object's actions, with potentially disastrous—or at least hilarious—results.

```
void CIntelligentObject::move(){ //move object
  CObject::move(); //move like a dumb object
  ai(); //act intelligently
}
```

Next, we see the `CIntelligentObject ai` function. If enough time has elapsed since the last time the object acted intelligently, then it calls the AI function corresponding to the object's current state. Notice that this modular design makes it easy to add more states to the state space, which we would definitely want to do if we were to introduce more object types into the game.

```
void CIntelligentObject::ai(){ //main AI function
  //do the following periodically
  if(Timer.elapsed(m_nLastAiTime,m_nAiDelayTime))
    switch(m_eState){ //behavior depends on state
      case CRUISING_STATE: cruising_ai(); break;
      case AVOIDING_STATE: avoiding_ai(); break;
      default: break;
    }
}
```

The Plane and Distance

The `CIntelligentObject plane` function is a method for introducing information about the plane. It has three parameters, the horizontal and vertical coordinates of the plane in the virtual universe, and the Euclidean distance from the plane to the object.

```
void CIntelligentObject::plane(int x, int y,int d){
```

It stores the Euclidean distance and the vertical distance in private member variables:

```
m_nDistance=d;
m_nVerticalDistance=abs(m_nY-y);
```

The horizontal distance requires a little more effort because, as explained in Chapter 7, no two things can be farther away from each other than WORLD_WIDTH/2:

```
m_nHorizontalDistance=m_nX-x;
if(m_nHorizontalDistance>WORLD_WIDTH/2)
  m_nHorizontalDistance-=WORLD_WIDTH;
if(m_nHorizontalDistance<-WORLD_WIDTH/2)
  m_nHorizontalDistance+=WORLD_WIDTH;
}
```

Changing State

The `CIntelligentObject set_state` function takes a single parameter containing the new state. It begins by changing the state member variable `m_eState` to the new state.

```
void CIntelligentObject::set_state(StateType state){
  m_eState=state; //change state
```

Most importantly, it takes care of the housekeeping associated with state changes using a `switch` statement:

```
switch(m_eState){ //change behavior settings
```

It begins with the cruising state:

```
case CRUISING_STATE:
```

In the cruising state, the object is lazy about acting intelligently, so `set_state` sets the delay time for intelligent acts to a random interval between 300 and 600 milliseconds:

```
m_nAiDelayTime=300+Random.number(0,300);
```

It's feeling pretty relaxed when it starts cruising, so drop the speed to the minimum:

```
m_nXspeed=-1;
```

Change height only every 8 to 13 seconds:

```
m_nHeightDelayTime=8000+Random.number(0,5000);
break;
```

In the avoiding state, things are faster. The AI delay time drops to 200 to 400 milliseconds.

```
case AVOIDING_STATE:
  m_nAiDelayTime=200+Random.number(0,200);
```

Speed increases to the maximum:

```
m_nXspeed=-3;
```

Choose a random height to move to, and change the height delay time to between 3 and 5 seconds:

```
m_nDesiredHeight=Random.number(100,400);
m_nHeightDelayTime=3000+Random.number(0,2000);
```

Change speed every 5 to 7 seconds to make things interesting. What it looks like in practice is that the objects get tired after flying at top speed for a while, then get a "second wind" later.

```
      m_nSpeedVariationDuration=5000+Random.number(0,2000);
      break;
   default: break;
   }
}
```

Cruising AI

The `CIntelligentObject cruising_ai` function takes care of AI when the object is cruising:

```
void CIntelligentObject::cruising_ai(){ //just cruising along
```

If the desired height is not too close to the current height, it sets the vertical speed in the correct direction:

```
if(m_nDesiredHeight<m_nY-20)m_nYspeed=-1;
else if(m_nDesiredHeight>m_nY+20)m_nYspeed=1;
else m_nYspeed=0;
```

If enough time has passed since the last height change, it initiates a new height change and sets the time until the next height change to a random number between 15 and 20 seconds:

```
if(Timer.elapsed(m_nHeightTime,m_nHeightDelayTime)){
  m_nDesiredHeight=Random.number(150,400);
  m_nHeightDelayTime=15000+Random.number(0,5000);
}
```

Finally, it looks for the plane. If the plane is close to but not in front of the object, it moves into the avoiding state.

```
if(m_nDistance<CLOSE_DISTANCE&&
m_nHorizontalDistance<BEHIND_DISTANCE)
  set_state(AVOIDING_STATE);
}
```

Avoidance AI

The `CIntelligentObject avoiding_ai` function takes care of AI when the object is avoiding the plane:

```
void CIntelligentObject::avoiding_ai(){ //avoiding plane
```

If enough time has passed since the last height change, it picks a new height, sets the vertical speed to the correct direction, which is a little faster than in the cruising state, then sets the height delay time to a random number between 3 and 5 seconds. Notice that the object will either overshoot the desired height or be reassigned a new height before it gets there, which will make it continually dither from one height to another.

```
if(Timer.elapsed(m_nHeightTime,m_nHeightDelayTime)){
  m_nDesiredHeight=Random.number(100,450);
  if(m_nDesiredHeight<m_nY)m_nYspeed=-2;
  if(m_nDesiredHeight>m_nY)m_nYspeed=2;
  m_nHeightDelayTime=3000+Random.number(0,2000);
}
```

Next, we have the code for the speed variation:

```
if(Timer.elapsed(m_nSpeedVariationTime,
m_nSpeedVariationDuration))
  if(m_nXspeed==-2){
    m_nXspeed=-3;
    m_nSpeedVariationDuration=10000+Random.number(0,3000);
  }
  else{
    m_nXspeed=-2;
    m_nSpeedVariationDuration=5000+Random.number(0,2000);
  }
```

If the object is behind the plane, it slows down:

```
if(m_nHorizontalDistance>BEHIND_DISTANCE) //if behind
  m_nXspeed=-1; //slow down
```

If the plane is far away from the object, or if the plane is close but at a sufficiently different height, then the object drops back to the cruising state. Notice that we will want FAR_DISTANCE to be sufficiently larger than CLOSE_DISTANCE to prevent the object from dithering between the two states (by which I mean swapping between the two states several times a second, resulting in jerky behavior).

```
if(m_nDistance>FAR_DISTANCE|| //if far away, or
(m_nDistance<CLOSE_DISTANCE&& //close and
m_nVerticalDistance>FALLBACK_DISTANCE)) //higher or lower
  set_state(CRUISING_STATE); //then back to cruising
}
```

Changes to the Object Class

Our object class needs substantial changes to handle the new kinds of object.

Declarations

In Objects.h, the ObjectType enumerated type is modified by adding the new object types for the bullet, the exploding crow, and the dead crow:

```
enum ObjectType{CROW_OBJECT=0,PLANE_OBJECT,FARM_OBJECT,
  FIELD_OBJECT,BULLET_OBJECT,EXPLODINGCROW_OBJECT,
  DEADCROW_OBJECT,NUM_SPRITES};
```

A new enumerated type `MortalityType` enumerates the different mortality choices for an object. `MORTAL` means having a fixed lifespan, `IMMORTAL` means having no fixed life expectancy (immortal objects can be killed, however; they just don't die of old age), and `ONESHOT_MORTAL` means that they live just long enough to play their animation sequence through once.

```
enum MortalityType{MORTAL,IMMORTAL,ONESHOT_MORTAL};
```

A new enumerated type `LocomotionType` enumerates the different locomotion choices for an object. `FLYING_MOTION` means that they fly, `FALLING_MOTION` means that they fall (accelerating due to gravity), and `NO_MOTION` means they don't move.

```
enum LocomotionType{FLYING_MOTION,FALLING_MOTION,NO_MOTION};
```

The `CObject` private member variables now become `protected` so that they can be inherited by `CIntelligentObject`. `CObject` gains some new protected member variables, starting with two that record the width and height of the sprite.

```
int m_nWidth,m_nHeight; //width and height of sprite
```

The next three protected member variables record the object's mode of locomotion, its object type, and its mortality type:

```
LocomotionType m_eLocomotion; //mode of travel
ObjectType m_eObject; //what kind of object is this?
MortalityType m_eMortality; //whether it dies or not
```

The next three protected member variables relate to the object's mortality: the time that it was born, its life expectancy, and whether it is vulnerable to bullets:

```
int m_nBirthTime; //time of creation
int m_nLifeTime; //time that object lives
BOOL m_bVulnerable; //vulnerable to bullets
```

The last new protected member variable was mentioned in the previous section: `m_bIntelligent` is set to `TRUE` if the object is intelligent, that is, if it is a `CIntelligentObject` class instance rather than a `CObject` class instance. This is because we will use a `CObject*` pointer to point to both `CObject` and `CIntelligentObject` class instances, but C++ provides no facility for telling which is which at run time. So, we will do it ourselves by setting `m_bIntelligent` to `FALSE` in the `CObject` constructor and resetting it to `TRUE` in the `CIntelligentObject` constructor.

```
BOOL m_bIntelligent; //TRUE if object is intelligent
```

Instead of having a constructor and a `create` function, `CObject` will now just have a constructor with the same parameters that function `create` had in Demo 5:

```
CObject(ObjectType object,int x,int y,
    int xspeed,int yspeed); //constructor
```

Finally, function move is made a virtual function, as was discussed in the previous section. As far as the compiler is concerned, once we have declared move to be a virtual function in CObject we don't need to list it as virtual again in CIntelligentObject, but it is a good idea to do so in both places as a reminder to the programmer.

```
virtual void move(); //move depending on time and speed
```

The Constructor

Changes to Objects.cpp begin with the new constructor, which now has the same parameters that function create had in Demo 5:

```
CObject::CObject(ObjectType object,int x,int y,
                 int xspeed,int yspeed){ //constructor
```

It begins by setting default values for some of the protected member variables including, as mentioned above, setting m_bIntelligent to FALSE:

```
m_nCurrentFrame=0; m_nLastFrameTime=Timer.time();
m_bForwardAnimation=TRUE; m_nFrameInterval=30;
m_eMortality=IMMORTAL; m_eLocomotion=NO_MOTION;
m_nLifeTime=1000; m_bVulnerable=FALSE;
m_bIntelligent=FALSE;
```

Next, we set the protected member variables that are common to all object types, starting with the object's type and motion characteristics:

```
m_eObject=object; //type of object
m_nLastXMoveTime=m_nLastYMoveTime=Timer.time(); //time
m_nX=x; m_nY=y; //location
m_nXspeed=xspeed; m_nYspeed=yspeed; //speed
```

Then, the object's image characteristics are set:

```
m_pSprite=g_pSprite[object];
m_nFrameCount=m_pSprite->frame_count();
m_nHeight=m_pSprite->height();
m_nWidth=m_pSprite->width();
```

The time that the object was created is recorded in a protected member variable so that we can cull the mortal objects that die of old age:

```
m_nBirthTime=Timer.time(); //time of creation
```

Next, we have the settings that depend on the object type, managed by a switch statement:

```
switch(object){
```

First, the plane object's speed limits and frame interval are set:

```
case PLANE_OBJECT:
  m_nMinXSpeed=-3; m_nMaxXSpeed=-1;
  m_nMinYSpeed=-4; m_nMaxYSpeed=4;
  m_nFrameInterval=250;
```

The plane is immortal, it flies, and it is not vulnerable to bullets:

```
m_eMortality=IMMORTAL;
m_eLocomotion=FLYING_MOTION;
m_bVulnerable=FALSE;
break;
```

Next, the crow object's speed limits, first frame, and frame interval are set:

```
case CROW_OBJECT:
  m_nMinXSpeed=-2; m_nMaxXSpeed=-1;
  m_nMinYSpeed=-1; m_nMaxYSpeed=1;
  m_nCurrentFrame=Random.number(0,m_nFrameCount-1);
  m_nFrameInterval=250+Random.number(-30,30);
```

The crow is immortal, it flies, and it is vulnerable to bullets:

```
m_eMortality=IMMORTAL;
m_eLocomotion=FLYING_MOTION;
m_bVulnerable=TRUE;
break;
```

The settings for the farm and field objects are self-explanatory:

```
case FARM_OBJECT:
case FIELD_OBJECT:
  m_nFrameCount=1;
  m_eMortality=IMMORTAL;
  m_eLocomotion=NO_MOTION;
  m_bVulnerable=FALSE;
  break;
```

The bullet object is mortal, it flies, it is not vulnerable, and its lifetime is a random number between 500 and 700 milliseconds. Making each bullet have a different lifetime makes things a little more interesting out at the extreme range of the plane's gun, so that some bullets travel farther than others.

```
case BULLET_OBJECT:
  m_nFrameCount=1;
  m_eMortality=MORTAL;
  m_eLocomotion=FLYING_MOTION;
  m_bVulnerable=FALSE;
  m_nLifeTime=500+Random.number(0,200);
  break;
```

The dead crow is mortal, it falls, it is not vulnerable (it's no use hitting it with bullets since it's already dead), and it has a lifetime of 1 second. It would be cleaner to have the dead crow culled when it hits ground level, and in fact, we will add code to implement this in the next chapter. The finite lifetime set here will act as a backup in case we mess up that code.

```
case DEADCROW_OBJECT:
  m_nCurrentFrame=0;
  m_eMortality=MORTAL;
  m_eLocomotion=FALLING_MOTION;
  m_bVulnerable=FALSE;
  m_nLifeTime=1000;
  break;
```

The exploding crow is mortal and lives for a single run through its animation sequence, it flies, and it is not vulnerable. This is the last `case` statement and ends the new `CObject` constructor.

```
case EXPLODINGCROW_OBJECT:
  m_nCurrentFrame=0;
  m_nFrameInterval=100;
  m_eMortality=ONESHOT_MORTAL;
  m_eLocomotion=FLYING_MOTION;
  m_bVulnerable=FALSE;
  break;
  }
}
```

Drawing and Moving

The `CObject draw` function changes slightly because the next frame of the new `ONESHOT_MORTAL` objects is computed differently from the others. Right after the call to the `m_pSprite->draw` function, we insert the following code. If the object is `ONESHOT_MORTAL`, then we increment the frame counter without wrapping it around the ends; this is so we can detect when the animation is over by checking whether `m_nCurrentFrame` is at least as large as `m_nFrameCount`.

```
if(m_eMortality==ONESHOT_MORTAL){ //animation plays once
  if(Timer.elapsed(m_nLastFrameTime,m_nFrameInterval))
    ++m_nCurrentFrame;
}
else{ //repeating animation
```

Otherwise, we perform the animation as in Demo 5.

The `CObject move` function is changed slightly because we now have different modes of locomotion. A switch statement is placed around the entire body of the function under the `case FLYING_MOTION`.

```
switch(m_eLocomotion){
  case FLYING_MOTION:
```

Then, a new case is created for falling objects:

```
    break;
  case FALLING_MOTION:
```

Horizontal speed is set to zero:

```
    m_nXspeed=0;
```

We compute the time since the object was born since the acceleration due to gravity means that vertical distance traveled is proportional to the amount of time that it has been falling:

```
    tfactor=time-m_nBirthTime;
```

The vertical distance traveled is scaled, recorded, and timed:

```
    ydelta=tfactor/YSCALE; m_nY+=ydelta;
    if(m_nY<YMARGIN)m_nY=YMARGIN;
    if(ydelta||m_nYspeed==0)  //record time of move
      m_nLastYMoveTime=time;
    break;
```

Objects with other modes of locomotion (such as NO_MOTION) don't move at all:

```
  default: break;
}
```

Changes to the Object Manager Class

Our object manager also needs substantial changes to handle the interactions between the new kinds of objects. The way we handle the object list will be substantially different. In Demo 5, we created a CObject class instance for every slot in the object list. Now, we will keep unused slots empty, new ourselves a CObject or CIntelligentObject class instance when an object is born, and delete it when it dies. Some purists will object to this reliance on the C++ operators new and delete, which can be slow. However, in defense of this approach, it should be observed that the birth and death of objects is a relatively infrequent occurrence, and therefore any attempt to optimize this code is probably a waste of time and effort.

Secondly, a reader who has taken a course on algorithm analysis may object to our naïve implementation of the object list as a simple array. While such an implementation is efficient for most of the operations used in our game, the insertion of a new object in the object list will in the worst case take time proportional to the number of objects already in the list. It is tempting to propose the use of more sophisticated data structures with a faster insertion time. For example, with a linked list, insertions could take place almost instantaneously. However, the extra overhead inherent in more sophisticated data structures will actually make them slower for the small number of objects that we have in our game. Remember, most data structures have the caveat that they are what is called *asymptotically faster*, that is, faster when the amount of data gets large. For small tasks, simpler is better. If your game has thousands of objects in it, however, you might want to review this decision.

Declarations

In `Objman.h`, the class `CObjectManager` gets a new private variable `m_nLastGunFireTime`, which records the last time that the gun fired. We will use this to make sure that the gun doesn't fire too often, to foil (for instance) a sophisticated user who increases the autorepeat rate to get a machine-gun effect by holding down the Spacebar.

```
int m_nLastGunFireTime; //time gun was last fired
```

`CObjectManager` has seven new private member functions, the first two of which compute distances in the virtual universe. One of these distance functions takes two sets of coordinates, `(x1,y1)` and `(x2,y2)`, and computes the Euclidean distance between them. The other function takes two indices, and returns the distance between the centers of the objects at those indices in the object list.

```
int distance(int x1,int y1,int x2,int y2); //in universe
int distance(int first,int second); //between objects
```

The next pair of functions handles collision detection. The first of these computes collisions between all objects, and the second computes collisions between a particular object at a given `index` in the object list with all other objects.

```
void collision_detection(); //all collisions
void collision_detection(int index); //with this object
```

The remaining three functions deal with dead objects. The `cull` function goes through the object list and removes those objects that have exceeded their allotted lifetimes (the Grim Reaper of the object list). The `kill` function takes an index as a parameter and removes the object at that index from the object list. The `replace` function takes an index as a parameter and replaces the object at that index with the next object in the sequence, if that object is part of a sequence (for example, crow, exploding crow, dead crow).

```
void cull(); //cull dead objects
void kill(int index); //remove object from list
void replace(int index); //replace by next in series
```

The Constructor

The changes to `Objman.cpp` begin with the `CObjectManager` constructor. The private member variable that records the last time the gun fired is set to zero, so that the gun is ready for immediate firing.

```
m_nLastGunFireTime=0;
```

Each pointer in the object list is set to `NULL` inside the `for` loop instead of being initialized with a `CObject` class instance the way it was in Demo 5. This is because some of them will be `CIntelligentObject` class instances instead. We'll create them later as needed.

```
m_pObjectList[i]=NULL;
```

In the `CObjectManager` `create` function, after testing to see if there is room for the new object, the following code is used. A local variable `i` is used to find the first unused slot in the object list, indicated by a `NULL` pointer.

```
int i=0; //index into object list
while(m_pObjectList[i]!=NULL)i++; //find first free slot
```

An intelligent object is created for a crow, and a base object is created for the other object types (such as the plane and the bullets):

```
if(object==CROW_OBJECT) //intelligent object
  m_pObjectList[i]=
    new CIntelligentObject(object,x,y,xspeed,yspeed);
else //dumb object
  m_pObjectList[i]=new CObject(object,x,y,xspeed,yspeed);
```

We then increment the object count and return the index of the new object:

```
m_nCount++;
return i;
```

The Animate Function

In the `CObjectManager` `animate` function, we begin by protecting the calls to `m_pObjectList[i]->move()` and `m_pObjectList[i]->draw(sur-face)` with an `if(m_pObjectList[i]!=NULL)` conditional. Failure to do this would obviously result in a nasty crash.

After the call to `m_pObjectList[i]->move()`, we insert the following code to notify intelligent objects about the plane's current position. Notice that we must cast the `CObject*` pointer `m_pObjectList[i]` to `CIntelligentObject*` before the compiler will let us call its `plane` member function. If `m_pObject-List[i]` points to `CObject` class instance, doing this will result in a crash, which is why we use the `CObject` private member variable `m_bIntelligent` to distinguish `CObject` class instances from `CIntelligentObject` class instances.

```
if(m_pObjectList[i]->m_bIntelligent) //if intelligent
    //tell object about plane current position
    ((CIntelligentObject*)m_pObjectList[i])->plane(
        m_pObjectList[m_nCurrentObject]->m_nX,
        m_pObjectList[m_nCurrentObject]->m_nY,
        distance(i,m_nCurrentObject));
```

Immediately before the objects are drawn, we do collision detection and cull the old objects (that is, remove the ones that have lived out their allotted lifespan):

```
collision_detection();
cull();
```

The Distance Functions

Now we have the new object manager functions. The first of the two `CObjectManager distance` functions takes two sets of coordinates, $(x1,y1)$ and $(x2,y2)$, and computes the Euclidean distance between them.

```
int CObjectManager::distance(int x1,int y1,int x2,int y2){
```

It begins by computing the x and y components of the distance:

```
int x=abs(x1-x2),y=abs(y1-y2);//x and y distance
```

Then it adjusts the horizontal component of the distance, remembering that in a circular world, no two objects can be farther apart than `WORLD_WIDTH/2`:

```
if(x>WORLD_WIDTH/2)x-=WORLD_WIDTH;
```

Finally, it returns the distance according to the well-known formula of Euclid:

```
return (int)sqrt((double)x*x+(double)y*y);
}
```

The second of the two `CObjectManager distance` functions takes two indices, `first` and `second`, and computes the distance between the objects at those indices in the object list:

```
int CObjectManager::distance(int first,int second){
```

First, it checks that the indices are within range. (Actually, in retrospect I should have checked that the object pointers at those indices are not `NULL` instead.)

```
if(first<0||first>=m_nMaxCount)return -1;
if(second<0||second>=m_nMaxCount)return -1;
```

Then it computes the coordinates of the centers of the objects in local variables `x1,y1` and `x2,y2`. Notice that we adjust the vertical coordinates by subtracting half of the height of the object so that the coordinates are those of the center of the object.

```
int x1,y1,x2,y2; //coordinates of objects
x1=m_pObjectList[first]->m_nX;
y1=m_pObjectList[first]->m_nY-
  m_pObjectList[first]->m_nHeight/2;
x2=m_pObjectList[second]->m_nX;
y2=m_pObjectList[second]->m_nY-
  m_pObjectList[second]->m_nHeight/2;
```

Finally, it calls the first distance function to do the hard work:

```
  return distance(x1,y1,x2,y2);
}
```

Killing and Firing the Gun

The CObjectManager kill function takes a single parameter index, and removes the object at that index in the object list by decrementing the counter, deleting the object, and setting its pointer to NULL:

```
void CObjectManager::kill(int index){ //remove object
  m_nCount--;
  delete m_pObjectList[index];
  m_pObjectList[index]=NULL;
}
```

The CObjectManager fire_gun function creates a bullet object 60 pixels to the left and 50 pixels above the bottom center of the plane, moving to the left at speed 5. This makes it appear to have been fired from the plane's gun. Note that if the artist decides to change the position of the gun, we would have to change this code. The timer's elapsed function is used to ensure that bullets can only be fired every 200 milliseconds.

```
void CObjectManager::fire_gun(){ //fire current object's gun
  CObject *plane= m_pObjectList[m_nCurrentObject];
  if(Timer.elapsed(m_nLastGunFireTime,200))
    create(BULLET_OBJECT,plane->m_nX-60,plane->m_nY-50,-5,0);
}
```

Culling Objects

The CObjectManager cull function kills all old objects. It declares a local variable object, which will be used to point to the current object.

```
void CObjectManager::cull(){ //cull old objects
  CObject *object;
```

Then, in a for loop that addresses each place in the object list, it sets object to point to the current object:

```
for(int i=0; i<m_nMaxCount; i++){ //for each object
    object=m_pObjectList[i]; //current object
```

It checks to see whether there is an object at that place in the object list. If not, it continues on to the next object in the list.

```
if(object!=NULL){
```

If there is an object there, it checks to see whether it should die of old age, that is, whether it is mortal and has lived long enough. By "lived long enough," we mean that the amount of time that it has been alive, which is the difference between the current time and its birth time `Timer.time()-object->m_nBirthTime`, is greater than its life expectancy, which is `object->m_nLifeTime`. If so, then it calls the `kill` member function to remove it from the object list.

```
if(object->m_eMortality==MORTAL&& //if mortal and ...
(Timer.time()-object->m_nBirthTime>object->m_nLifeTime))
    kill(i); //...then kill it
```

Otherwise, we check to see if it is a one-shot animation object that has been played through completely, that is, its current frame `object->m_nCurrent-Frame` is greater than or equal to its frame count `object->m_nFrameCount`. If so, then it calls the `replace` member function to replace the object with the next object in the appropriate sequence (which for now is limited to the sequence crow, exploding crow, dead crow), if there is one.

```
        else //one-shot animation
            if(object->m_eMortality==ONESHOT_MORTAL&&
            object->m_nCurrentFrame>=object->m_nFrameCount)
                replace(i); //...then replace the object
    }
  }
}
```

The Replace Function

The `CObjectManager` `replace` function takes an `index` as a parameter and replaces the object at that index in the object list with the next object in the sequence associated with that object type:

```
void CObjectManager::replace(int index){
```

It begins with three local variables, `object` to point to the current object as we scan the object list, `newtype` to record the type of the new object, and a Boolean `successor`, which is TRUE if the object has a successor in the object sequence (set TRUE initially until we learn otherwise):

```
CObject *object=m_pObjectList[index]; //current object
ObjectType newtype;
BOOL successor=TRUE; //assume it has a successor
```

A `switch` statement sets `newtype` to the next object type in the sequence, setting `successor` to `FALSE` if it doesn't have one. The only object sequence available in Demo 6 is `CROW_OBJECT`, `EXPLODINGCROW_OBJECT`, `DEADCROW_OBJECT`.

```
switch(object->m_eObject){
  case CROW_OBJECT: newtype=EXPLODINGCROW_OBJECT; break;
  case EXPLODINGCROW_OBJECT: newtype=DEADCROW_OBJECT; break;
  default: successor=FALSE; break; //has no successor
}
```

We then read the location and speed of the old object into local variables `x`, `y`, `xspeed`, and `yspeed`:

```
int x=object->m_nX,y=object->m_nY; //location
int xspeed=object->m_nXspeed;
int yspeed=object->m_nYspeed;
```

We then kill the old object, and if it has a successor, create a new one of type `newtype` with the same location and speed as the old object. Notice that the new object won't necessarily have the same index in the object list as the old object, but then that isn't a requirement.

```
kill(index); //kill old object
if(successor) //if it has a successor
  create(newtype,x,y,xspeed,yspeed); //create new one
}
```

Collision Detection

The last pair of functions in the object manager deals with collision detection, which at this stage simply means bullets colliding with crows. The first instance of this function has no parameters; it collides all objects with all other objects. It runs through the object list with a `for` loop. For each non-`NULL` entry, if the object there is a bullet, then it passes its index to the second `collision_detection` function which does the real work.

```
void CObjectManager::collision_detection(){
//check for all collisions
  for(int i=0; i<m_nMaxCount; i++) //for each object slot
    if(m_pObjectList[i]!=NULL) //if object exists
      if(m_pObjectList[i]->m_eObject==BULLET_OBJECT)
        collision_detection(i); //check for collisions
}
```

The second `CObjectManager` `collision_detection` function has a single parameter `index`, and takes care of collisions between the (bullet) object at that place in the object list with every other object in the list:

```
void CObjectManager::collision_detection(int index){
```

It has two local variables, an index i for the object that is checked for collision with object index and a Boolean variable finished that will be set to TRUE when a collision has been detected. We will design the code so that each object can collide with only one other object at a time, so when finished is TRUE we can exit the function.

```
int i=0; //index of object collided with
BOOL finished=FALSE; //finished when collision detected
```

We use a while loop to run i through the object list, allowing premature exit if finished ever becomes TRUE:

```
while(i<m_nMaxCount&&!finished){
```

We check to see that there is an object at index i of the object list, that this object is vulnerable, and that it is "close enough" to the object at index (where "close enough" was defined after some experimentation to be 15). This is very naïve collision detection that doesn't depend on the size of the object being hit. If you want to get more sophisticated, you can replace 15 by some function of the sprite size, thus creating an invisible bounding box or bounding circle around the vulnerable parts of the object.

```
if(m_pObjectList[i]!=NULL) //if i is a valid object index
  if(m_pObjectList[i]->m_bVulnerable&& //if vulnerable
    distance(index,i)<15){ //and close enough, then
```

If there is a collision, then we record a hit by setting finished to TRUE, calling member function replace to replace the object that was hit, and killing the object doing the hitting (in this case, a bullet). Notice that if we were to remove the statement kill(index), bullets could continue through the crows to potentially kill other crows. We have coded it in such a way that bullets remain lodged in crow corpses. This is a design decision that makes the game different, though not necessarily better.

```
      finished=TRUE; //hit found, so exit loop
      replace(i); //replace object that is hit
      kill(index); //kill object doing the hitting
    }
```

We then move on to the next object in the while loop, and exit the function after its termination:

```
    ++i; //next object
  }
}
```

Changes to Main.cpp

Changes to `Main.cpp` in Demo 6 mainly involve the processing of the new objects and their sprites.

Loading Sprites

Function `LoadDeadCrowSprite` loads the single frame of the dead crow sprite from location (453, 230) of the image in the bmp sprite file reader `g_cSpriteImages`:

```
BOOL LoadDeadCrowSprite(){ //load dead crow
  return g_pSprite[DEADCROW_OBJECT]->
    load(&g_cSpriteImages,0,453,230);
} //LoadDeadCrowSprite
```

Function `LoadExplodingCrowSprite` loads six frames of exploding crow animation from locations (257, 294), (321, 294), (386, 162), (453, 162), (386, 230), and (453, 230) of the image in the bmp sprite file reader `g_cSpriteImages`:

```
BOOL LoadExplodingCrowSprite(){ //load exploding crow
  BOOL result=TRUE;
  result=result&&g_pSprite[EXPLODINGCROW_OBJECT]->
    load(&g_cSpriteImages,0,257,294);
  result=result&&g_pSprite[EXPLODINGCROW_OBJECT]->
    load(&g_cSpriteImages,1,321,294);
  result=result&&g_pSprite[EXPLODINGCROW_OBJECT]->
    load(&g_cSpriteImages,2,386,162);
  result=result&&g_pSprite[EXPLODINGCROW_OBJECT]->
    load(&g_cSpriteImages,3,453,162);
  result=result&&g_pSprite[EXPLODINGCROW_OBJECT]->
    load(&g_cSpriteImages,4,386,230);
  result=result&&g_pSprite[EXPLODINGCROW_OBJECT]->
    load(&g_cSpriteImages,5,453,230);
  return result;
} //LoadExplodingCrowSprite
```

Function `LoadBulletSprite` loads the single frame of the bullet sprite from location (5, 123) of the image in the bmp sprite file reader `g_cSpriteImages`:

```
BOOL LoadBulletSprite(){ //load bullet
  return g_pSprite[BULLET_OBJECT]->
    load(&g_cSpriteImages,0,5,123);
} //LoadBulletSprite
```

Function `LoadImages` has the following new code to load the new sprite images. The dead crow sprite has a single frame of animation and is 62x53 pixels in size.

```
g_pSprite[DEADCROW_OBJECT]=new CClippedSprite(1,62,53);
LoadDeadCrowSprite(); //load dead crow images
```

The exploding crow sprite has six frames of animation and is also 62x53 pixels in size:

```
g_pSprite[EXPLODINGCROW_OBJECT]=new CClippedSprite(6,62,53);
LoadExplodingCrowSprite(); //load exploding crow images
```

The bullet sprite has a single frame of animation and is a tiny 5x3 pixels in size (which is why it is so hard to see in Sprites.bmp shown in Figure 5.2):

```
g_pSprite[BULLET_OBJECT]=new CClippedSprite(1,5,3);
LoadBulletSprite(); //load bullet images
```

The CreateObjects Function

Function CreateObjects gets its crow creation code replaced. The following code is used to create eight crows before the plane is created, so they are drawn behind the plane. The object manager is asked eight times to create a crow object at a random location, each crow initially moving slowly to the left.

```
for(i=0; i<8; i++)
  ObjectManager.create(CROW_OBJECT,
    Random.number(0,WORLD_WIDTH-1),
    Random.number(100,400),-1,0);
```

The same four lines of code is used again in function CreateObjects *after* the plane has been created, so that eight more crows are drawn in front of the plane.

Other Functions

Function RestoreSurfaces gets nine more lines of code to restore and reload the surfaces in the three new sprites. By now this type of code should be very familiar to you.

```
if(g_pSprite[DEADCROW_OBJECT]->Restore()) //if restored
  result=result&&LoadDeadCrowSprite(); //redraw image
else return FALSE;
if(g_pSprite[EXPLODINGCROW_OBJECT]->Restore()) //if restored
  result=result&&LoadExplodingCrowSprite(); //redraw image
else return FALSE;
if(g_pSprite[BULLET_OBJECT]->Restore()) //if restored
  result=result&&LoadBulletSprite(); //redraw image
else return FALSE;
```

The keyboard_handler function has a new case for the Spacebar added to its switch statement. In response to a space, the keyboard handler asks the object manager to fire the gun.

```
case VK_SPACE: ObjectManager.fire_gun(); break;
```

Demo 6 Files

Code Files

The following files in Demo 6 are used without change from Demo 5:

- Bmp.h
- Bmp.cpp
- Bsprite.h
- Bsprite.cpp
- Csprite.h
- Csprite.cpp
- Defines.h
- Ddsetup.cpp
- Random.h
- Random.cpp
- Sbmp.h
- Sbmp.cpp
- Timer.h
- Timer.cpp
- View.h
- View.cpp

The following files in Demo 6 have been modified from Demo 5:

- Main.cpp
- Objects.h
- Objects.cpp
- Objman.h
- Objman.cpp

The following files are new in Demo 6:

- Ai.h
- Ai.cpp

Required Libraries

- Ddraw.lib
- Winmm.lib

Code Listings

Ai.h

```cpp
//ai.h: header file for intelligent object class

//Copyright Ian Parberry, 1999
//Last updated October 25, 1999

#ifndef __AI__
#define __AI__

enum StateType{CRUISING_STATE,AVOIDING_STATE};

#include "objects.h"

class CIntelligentObject: public CObject{
  private:
    StateType m_eState; //state
    int m_nDesiredHeight; //desired altitude
    int m_nHeightTime; //time between height changes
    int m_nHeightDelayTime; //time to next height change
    int m_nSpeedVariationTime; //last time speed varied
    int m_nSpeedVariationDuration; //time to next speed vrn
    int m_nLastAiTime; //last time AI was used
    int m_nAiDelayTime; //time until AI next used
    int m_nDistance; //distance to plane
    int m_nVerticalDistance; //vertical distance from plane
    int m_nHorizontalDistance; //hor. distance from plane
    void ai(); //artificial intelligence
    void cruising_ai(); //ai for cruising along
    void avoiding_ai(); //ai for avoiding plane
    void set_state(StateType state); //change state
  public:
    CIntelligentObject(ObjectType object,int x,int y,
      int xspeed,int yspeed); //constructor
    virtual void move(); //move depending on time and speed
    void plane(int x,int y,int d); //relationship w/plane
};

#endif
```

Ai.cpp

```cpp
//ai.cpp: artificial intelligence

//Copyright Ian Parberry, 1999
//Last updated October 25, 1999
```

```
#include "ai.h"
#include "timer.h" //game timer
#include "random.h" //for random number generator
#include "view.h" //for viewpoint manager

extern CTimer Timer;  //game timer
extern CRandom Random; //random number generator

const int CLOSE_DISTANCE=200; //close to plane
const int FAR_DISTANCE=300; //far from plane

//fall back at this vertical distance from plane
const int FALLBACK_DISTANCE=150;

//horizontal distance considered to be behind plane
const int BEHIND_DISTANCE=-5;

CIntelligentObject::CIntelligentObject(ObjectType object,
  int x,int y,int xspeed,int yspeed):
CObject(object,x,y,xspeed,yspeed){ //constructor
  m_bIntelligent=TRUE;
  m_nDesiredHeight=240;
  m_nHeightTime=0;  m_nHeightDelayTime=0;
  m_nSpeedVariationTime=m_nSpeedVariationDuration=0;
  m_nDistance=m_nHorizontalDistance=m_nVerticalDistance=0;
  m_eState=CRUISING_STATE;
  m_nLastAiTime=0; m_nAiDelayTime=0;
}

void CIntelligentObject::move(){ //move object
  CObject::move(); //move like a dumb object
  ai(); //act intelligently
}
void CIntelligentObject::ai(){ //main AI function
  //do the following periodically
  if(Timer.elapsed(m_nLastAiTime,m_nAiDelayTime))
    switch(m_eState){ //behavior depends on state
      case CRUISING_STATE: cruising_ai(); break;
      case AVOIDING_STATE: avoiding_ai(); break;
      default: break;
    }
}

void CIntelligentObject::plane(int x, int y,int d){
//compute relationship with plane
  //distances from plane
  m_nDistance=d;
  m_nVerticalDistance=abs(m_nY-y);
  //horizontal distance
  m_nHorizontalDistance=m_nX-x;
```

```
    if(m_nHorizontalDistance>WORLD_WIDTH/2)
      m_nHorizontalDistance-=WORLD_WIDTH;
    if(m_nHorizontalDistance<-WORLD_WIDTH/2)
      m_nHorizontalDistance+=WORLD_WIDTH;
  }


void CIntelligentObject::set_state(StateType state){
  m_eState=state; //change state
  switch(m_eState){ //change behavior settings
    case CRUISING_STATE:
      m_nAiDelayTime=300+Random.number(0,300);
      m_nXspeed=-1;
      m_nHeightDelayTime=8000+Random.number(0,5000);
      break;
    case AVOIDING_STATE:
      m_nAiDelayTime=200+Random.number(0,200);
      m_nXspeed=-3;
      m_nDesiredHeight=Random.number(100,400);
      m_nHeightDelayTime=3000+Random.number(0,2000);
      m_nSpeedVariationDuration=5000+Random.number(0,2000);
      break;
    default: break;
  }
}


void CIntelligentObject::cruising_ai(){ //just cruising along
  //height variation
  if(m_nDesiredHeight<m_nY-20)m_nYspeed=-1;
  else if(m_nDesiredHeight>m_nY+20)m_nYspeed=1;
  else m_nYspeed=0;
  if(Timer.elapsed(m_nHeightTime,m_nHeightDelayTime)){
    m_nDesiredHeight=Random.number(150,400);
    m_nHeightDelayTime=15000+Random.number(0,5000);
  }
  //look for plane
  if(m_nDistance<CLOSE_DISTANCE&&
  m_nHorizontalDistance<BEHIND_DISTANCE)
    set_state(AVOIDING_STATE);
}

void CIntelligentObject::avoiding_ai(){ //avoiding plane
  //height variation
  if(Timer.elapsed(m_nHeightTime,m_nHeightDelayTime)){
    m_nDesiredHeight=Random.number(100,450);
    if(m_nDesiredHeight<m_nY)m_nYspeed=-2;
    if(m_nDesiredHeight>m_nY)m_nYspeed=2;
    m_nHeightDelayTime=3000+Random.number(0,2000);
  }
  //speed variation
  if(Timer.elapsed(m_nSpeedVariationTime,
```

```
      m_nSpeedVariationDuration))
        if(m_nXspeed==-2){
          m_nXspeed=-3;
          m_nSpeedVariationDuration=10000+Random.number(0,3000);
        }
        else{
          m_nXspeed=-2;
          m_nSpeedVariationDuration=5000+Random.number(0,2000);
        }
      if(m_nHorizontalDistance>BEHIND_DISTANCE) //if behind
        m_nXspeed=-1; //slow down
      //look for plane, maybe leave avoiding state
      if(m_nDistance>FAR_DISTANCE|| //if far away, or
       (m_nDistance<CLOSE_DISTANCE&& //close and
       m_nVerticalDistance>FALLBACK_DISTANCE)) //higher or lower
        set_state(CRUISING_STATE); //then back to cruising
    }
```

Main.cpp

```
//main.cpp


//Crows have AI.  They try to avoid the plane.
//Plane fires bullets, which have a fixed lifetime.
//When you hit the crows, they explode and turn into
//falling corpses.

//Copyright Ian Parberry, 1999
//Last updated May 22, 2000

//system includes
#include <windows.h>
#include <windowsx.h>
#include <ddraw.h>
#include <stdio.h>

//system defines
#define WIN32_LEAN_AND_MEAN

//custom includes
#include "defines.h" //global definitions
#include "bmp.h" //bmp file reader
#include "timer.h" //game timer
#include "csprite.h" //for clipped sprite class
#include "objects.h" //for object class
#include "objman.h" //for object manager
#include "view.h" //for viewpoint class
#include "random.h" //for random number generator

//defines
```

```
#define MAX_OBJECTS 32 //max number of objects in game

//globals

BOOL ActiveApp; //is this application active?

LPDIRECTDRAW lpDirectDrawObject=NULL; //direct draw object
LPDIRECTDRAWSURFACE lpPrimary=NULL; //primary surface
LPDIRECTDRAWPALETTE lpPrimaryPalette; //its palette
LPDIRECTDRAWSURFACE lpSecondary=NULL; //back buffer
LPDIRECTDRAWPALETTE lpSecondaryPalette; //its palette
LPDIRECTDRAWSURFACE lpBackground=NULL; //background image

CTimer Timer; //game timer

CBmpFileReader background; //background image
CBmpSpriteFileReader g_cSpriteImages; //sprite images
CBmpSpriteFileReader g_cFrgndImages; //foreground images

CObjectManager ObjectManager(MAX_OBJECTS); //object manager

CClippedSprite *g_pSprite[NUM_SPRITES]; //sprites

CViewPoint Viewpoint; //player viewpoint
CRandom Random; //random number generator

//helper functions
LPDIRECTDRAWPALETTE CreatePalette(LPDIRECTDRAWSURFACE surface);
BOOL InitDirectDraw(HWND hwnd);
HWND CreateDefaultWindow(char* name,HINSTANCE hInstance);

BOOL LoadPlaneSprite(){
  BOOL result=TRUE;
  result=result&&g_pSprite[PLANE_OBJECT]->
    load(&g_cSpriteImages,0,1,1);
  result=result&&g_pSprite[PLANE_OBJECT]->
    load(&g_cSpriteImages,1,123,1);
  result=result&&g_pSprite[PLANE_OBJECT]->
    load(&g_cSpriteImages,2,245,1);
  result=result&&g_pSprite[PLANE_OBJECT]->
    load(&g_cSpriteImages,3,367,1);
  result=result&&g_pSprite[PLANE_OBJECT]->
    load(&g_cSpriteImages,4,489,1);
  result=result&&g_pSprite[PLANE_OBJECT]->
    load(&g_cSpriteImages,5,17,74);
  return result;
} //LoadPlaneSprite

BOOL LoadCrowSprite(){
  BOOL result=TRUE;
```

```
  result=result&&g_pSprite[CROW_OBJECT]->
    load(&g_cSpriteImages,0,256,183); //frame 0
  result=result&&g_pSprite[CROW_OBJECT]->
    load(&g_cSpriteImages,1,320,183); //frame 1
  result=result&&g_pSprite[CROW_OBJECT]->
    load(&g_cSpriteImages,2,256,237); //frame 2
  result=result&&g_pSprite[CROW_OBJECT]->
    load(&g_cSpriteImages,3,323,237); //frame 3
  return result;
} //LoadCrowSprite

BOOL LoadFrgndSprites(){ //load foreground sprites
  BOOL result=TRUE;
  result=result&&g_pSprite[FARM_OBJECT]->
    load(&g_cFrgndImages,0,0,0); //load farm sprite
  result=result&&g_pSprite[FIELD_OBJECT]->
    load(&g_cFrgndImages,0,640,0); //load field sprite
  return result;
} //LoadFrgndSprites

BOOL LoadDeadCrowSprite(){ //load dead crow
  return g_pSprite[DEADCROW_OBJECT]->
    load(&g_cSpriteImages,0,453,230);
} //LoadDeadCrowSprite

BOOL LoadExplodingCrowSprite(){ //load exploding crow
  BOOL result=TRUE;
  result=result&&g_pSprite[EXPLODINGCROW_OBJECT]->
    load(&g_cSpriteImages,0,257,294);
  result=result&&g_pSprite[EXPLODINGCROW_OBJECT]->
    load(&g_cSpriteImages,1,321,294);
  result=result&&g_pSprite[EXPLODINGCROW_OBJECT]->
    load(&g_cSpriteImages,2,386,162);
  result=result&&g_pSprite[EXPLODINGCROW_OBJECT]->
    load(&g_cSpriteImages,3,453,162);
  result=result&&g_pSprite[EXPLODINGCROW_OBJECT]->
    load(&g_cSpriteImages,4,386,230);
  result=result&&g_pSprite[EXPLODINGCROW_OBJECT]->
    load(&g_cSpriteImages,5,453,230);
  return result;
} //LoadExplodingCrowSprite
BOOL LoadBulletSprite(){ //load bullet
  return g_pSprite[BULLET_OBJECT]->
    load(&g_cSpriteImages,0,5,123);
} //LoadBulletSprite

BOOL LoadImages(){ //load graphics from files to surfaces
  //get the background image
  if(!background.load("bckgnd.bmp"))return FALSE; //read file
  background.draw(lpBackground); //draw to background surface
```

```
        //set palettes in all surfaces
        if(!background.setpalette(lpPrimaryPalette))return FALSE;
        if(!background.setpalette(lpSecondaryPalette))return FALSE;
        //load the sprites...
        if(!g_cSpriteImages.load("sprites.bmp"))return FALSE;
        //...the plane
        g_pSprite[PLANE_OBJECT]=new CClippedSprite(6,121,72);
        if(!LoadPlaneSprite())return FALSE; //load plane images
        //...the crow
        g_pSprite[CROW_OBJECT]=new CClippedSprite(4,58,37);
        if(!LoadCrowSprite())return FALSE; //load crow images
        //..the dead crow
        g_pSprite[DEADCROW_OBJECT]=new CClippedSprite(1,62,53);
        LoadDeadCrowSprite(); //load dead crow images
        //...the exploding crow
        g_pSprite[EXPLODINGCROW_OBJECT]=new CClippedSprite(6,62,53);
        LoadExplodingCrowSprite(); //load exploding crow images
        //...the bullet
        g_pSprite[BULLET_OBJECT]=new CClippedSprite(1,5,3);
        LoadBulletSprite(); //load bullet images
        //...the foreground sprites
        if(!g_cFrgndImages.load("farm.bmp"))return FALSE;
        g_pSprite[FARM_OBJECT]=new CClippedSprite(1,640,162);
        g_pSprite[FIELD_OBJECT]=new CClippedSprite(1,640,162);
        if(!LoadFrgndSprites())return FALSE; //load foreground
        return TRUE;
} //LoadImages

void CreateObjects(){
    int i;
    ObjectManager.create(FARM_OBJECT,0,SCREEN_HEIGHT-1,0,0);
    ObjectManager.create(FIELD_OBJECT,SCREEN_WIDTH,
        SCREEN_HEIGHT-1,0,0);
    for(i=0; i<8; i++)
        ObjectManager.create(CROW_OBJECT,
            Random.number(0,WORLD_WIDTH-1),
            Random.number(100,400),-1,0);
    ObjectManager.set_current(
        ObjectManager.create(PLANE_OBJECT,320,271,-1,0));
    for(i=0; i<8; i++)
        ObjectManager.create(CROW_OBJECT,
            Random.number(0,WORLD_WIDTH-1),
            Random.number(100,400),-1,0);
} //CreateObjects

BOOL RestoreSurfaces(){ //restore all surfaces
    BOOL result=TRUE;
    if(SUCCEEDED(lpPrimary->Restore())) //if primary restored
        result=result&&background.draw(lpPrimary)&& //redraw image
            background.setpalette(lpPrimaryPalette); //set palette
```

```
      else return FALSE;
      if(SUCCEEDED(lpSecondary->Restore())) //if secondary restored
        result=result&&background.draw(lpSecondary)&& //redraw image
          background.setpalette(lpSecondaryPalette); //set palette
      else return FALSE;
      if(SUCCEEDED(lpBackground->Restore())) //if background restored
        result=result&&background.draw(lpBackground); //redraw image
      else return FALSE;
      if(g_pSprite[PLANE_OBJECT]->Restore()) //if plane restored
        result=result&&LoadPlaneSprite(); //redraw image
      else return FALSE;
      if(g_pSprite[CROW_OBJECT]->Restore()) //if crow restored
        result=result&&LoadCrowSprite(); //redraw image
      else return FALSE;
      if(g_pSprite[DEADCROW_OBJECT]->Restore()) //if restored
        result=result&&LoadDeadCrowSprite(); //redraw image
      else return FALSE;
      if(g_pSprite[EXPLODINGCROW_OBJECT]->Restore()) //if restored
        result=result&&LoadExplodingCrowSprite(); //redraw image
      else return FALSE;
      if(g_pSprite[BULLET_OBJECT]->Restore()) //if restored
        result=result&&LoadBulletSprite(); //redraw image
      else return FALSE;
      if(g_pSprite[FARM_OBJECT]->Restore()&& //if farm and ...
        g_pSprite[FIELD_OBJECT]->Restore()) //... field restored
        result=result&&LoadFrgndSprites(); //redraw image
      else return FALSE;
      return result;
    } //RestoreSurfaces

    BOOL PageFlip(){ //return TRUE if page flip succeeds
      if(lpPrimary->Flip(NULL,DDFLIP_WAIT)==DDERR_SURFACELOST)
        return RestoreSurfaces();
      return TRUE;
    } //PageFlip

    BOOL ComposeFrame(){ //compose a frame of animation
      Viewpoint.draw_background(lpBackground,lpSecondary,
        ObjectManager.speed()); //draw scrolling background
      ObjectManager.animate(lpSecondary); //draw objects
      return TRUE;
    } //ComposeFrame

    BOOL ProcessFrame(){ //process a frame of animation
      ComposeFrame(); //compose a frame in secondary surface
      return PageFlip(); //flip video memory surfaces
    } //ProcessFrame

    BOOL keyboard_handler(WPARAM keystroke){ //keyboard handler
      BOOL result=FALSE; //return TRUE if game is to end
```

```
      switch(keystroke){
        case VK_ESCAPE: result=TRUE; break; //exit game
        case VK_UP: ObjectManager.accelerate(0,-1); break;
        case VK_DOWN: ObjectManager.accelerate(0,1); break;
        case VK_LEFT: ObjectManager.accelerate(-1,0); break;
        case VK_RIGHT: ObjectManager.accelerate(1,0); break;
        case VK_SPACE: ObjectManager.fire_gun(); break;
        default: break;
      }
      return result;
    } //keyboard_handler

//message handler (window procedure)
long CALLBACK WindowProc(HWND hwnd,UINT message,
                         WPARAM wParam,LPARAM lParam){
    switch(message){
      case WM_ACTIVATEAPP: ActiveApp=wParam; break;
      case WM_CREATE: break;
      case WM_KEYDOWN: //keyboard hit
        if(keyboard_handler(wParam))DestroyWindow(hwnd);
        break;
      case WM_DESTROY: //end of game
        if(lpDirectDrawObject!=NULL){ //if DD object exists
          if(lpSecondary!=NULL) //if secondary surface exists
            lpSecondary->Release(); //release secondary surface
          if(lpPrimary!=NULL) //if primary surface exists
            lpPrimary->Release(); //release primary surface
          if(lpBackground!=NULL) //if background exists
            lpBackground->Release(); //release background
          for(int i=0; i<NUM_SPRITES; i++){ //for each sprite
            if(g_pSprite[i]) //if sprite exists
              g_pSprite[i]->Release(); //release sprite
            delete g_pSprite[i]; //delete sprite
          }
          lpDirectDrawObject->Release(); //release DD object
        }
        ShowCursor(TRUE); //show the mouse cursor
        PostQuitMessage(0); //and exit
        break;
      default: //default window procedure
        return DefWindowProc(hwnd,message,wParam,lParam);
    } //switch(message)
    return 0L;
} //WindowProc

int WINAPI WinMain(HINSTANCE hInstance,HINSTANCE hPrevInstance,
LPSTR lpCmdLine,int nCmdShow){
  MSG msg; //current message
  HWND hwnd; //handle to full-screen window
  hwnd=CreateDefaultWindow("directX demo 6",hInstance);
```

```
      if(!hwnd)return FALSE;
      //set up window
      ShowWindow(hwnd,nCmdShow); UpdateWindow(hwnd);
      SetFocus(hwnd); //allow input from keyboard
      ShowCursor(FALSE); //hide the cursor
      //init graphics
      for(int i=0; i<NUM_SPRITES; i++) //null out sprites
        g_pSprite[i]=NULL;
      BOOL OK=InitDirectDraw(hwnd);//initialize DirectDraw
      if(OK)OK=LoadImages(); //load images from disk
      if(!OK){ //bail out if initialization failed
        DestroyWindow(hwnd); return FALSE;
      }
      //start game timer
      Timer.start();
      //create objects
      CreateObjects();
      //message loop
      while(TRUE)
        if(PeekMessage(&msg,NULL,0,0,PM_NOREMOVE)){
          if(!GetMessage(&msg,NULL,0,0))return msg.wParam;
          TranslateMessage(&msg); DispatchMessage(&msg);
        }
        else if(ActiveApp)ProcessFrame(); else WaitMessage();
    } //WinMain
```

Objects.h

```
//objects.h: header file for CObject class


//Copyright Ian Parberry, 1999
//Last updated October 27, 1999

#ifndef __OBJECTS__
#define __OBJECTS__

#include "bsprite.h"
#include "bmp.h"

//object types
enum ObjectType{CROW_OBJECT=0,PLANE_OBJECT,FARM_OBJECT,
  FIELD_OBJECT,BULLET_OBJECT,EXPLODINGCROW_OBJECT,
  DEADCROW_OBJECT,NUM_SPRITES};
//note: NUM_SPRITES must be last

enum MortalityType{MORTAL,IMMORTAL,ONESHOT_MORTAL};
enum LocomotionType{FLYING_MOTION,FALLING_MOTION,NO_MOTION};

class CObject{ //class for a moving object
  friend class CObjectManager;
```

```
protected:
   int m_nX,m_nY; //current location
   int m_nXspeed,m_nYspeed; //current speed
   int m_nLastXMoveTime; //last time moved horizontally
   int m_nLastYMoveTime; //last time moved vertically
   CBaseSprite *m_pSprite; //pointer to sprite
   int m_nWidth,m_nHeight; //width and height of sprite
   int m_nMinXSpeed,m_nMaxXSpeed; //min, max horizontal speeds
   int m_nMinYSpeed,m_nMaxYSpeed; //min, max vertical speeds
   int m_nCurrentFrame; //frame to be displayed
   int m_nFrameCount; //number of frames in animation
   int m_nLastFrameTime; //last time the frame was changed
   int m_nFrameInterval; //interval between frames
   BOOL m_bForwardAnimation; //is animation going forward?
   LocomotionType m_eLocomotion; //mode of travel
   ObjectType m_eObject; //what kind of object is this?
   MortalityType m_eMortality; //whether it dies or not
   int m_nBirthTime; //time of creation
   int m_nLifeTime; //time that object lives
   BOOL m_bVulnerable; //vulnerable to bullets
   BOOL m_bIntelligent; //TRUE if object is intelligent
public:
   CObject(ObjectType object,int x,int y,
      int xspeed,int yspeed); //constructor
   void draw(LPDIRECTDRAWSURFACE surface); //draw
   void accelerate(int xdelta,int ydelta=0); //change speed
   virtual void move(); //move depending on time and speed
};

#endif
```

Objects.cpp

```
//objects.cpp


//Copyright Ian Parberry, 1999
//Last updated October 27, 1999

#include "objects.h"
#include "timer.h" //game timer
#include "csprite.h" //for clipped sprite class
#include "random.h" //for random number generator
#include "view.h" //for viewpoint class

extern CClippedSprite *g_pSprite[]; //sprites
extern CTimer Timer; //game timer
extern CRandom Random; //random number generator
extern CViewPoint Viewpoint; //player viewpoint

CObject::CObject(ObjectType object,int x,int y,
```

```
                   int xspeed,int yspeed){ //constructor
//defaults
m_nCurrentFrame=0; m_nLastFrameTime=Timer.time();
m_bForwardAnimation=TRUE; m_nFrameInterval=30;
m_eMortality=IMMORTAL; m_eLocomotion=NO_MOTION;
m_nLifeTime=1000; m_bVulnerable=FALSE;
m_bIntelligent=FALSE;
//common values
m_eObject=object; //type of object
m_nLastXMoveTime=m_nLastYMoveTime=Timer.time(); //time
m_nX=x; m_nY=y; //location
m_nXspeed=xspeed; m_nYspeed=yspeed; //speed
m_pSprite=g_pSprite[object];
m_nFrameCount=m_pSprite->frame_count();
m_nHeight=m_pSprite->height();
m_nWidth=m_pSprite->width();
m_nBirthTime=Timer.time(); //time of creation
//customized values
switch(object){
  case PLANE_OBJECT:
    m_nMinXSpeed=-3; m_nMaxXSpeed=-1;
    m_nMinYSpeed=-4; m_nMaxYSpeed=4;
    m_nFrameInterval=250;
    m_eMortality=IMMORTAL;
    m_eLocomotion=FLYING_MOTION;
    m_bVulnerable=FALSE;
    break;
  case CROW_OBJECT:
    m_nMinXSpeed=-2; m_nMaxXSpeed=-1;
    m_nMinYSpeed=-1; m_nMaxYSpeed=1;
    m_nCurrentFrame=Random.number(0,m_nFrameCount-1);
    m_nFrameInterval=250+Random.number(-30,30);
    m_eMortality=IMMORTAL;
    m_eLocomotion=FLYING_MOTION;
    m_bVulnerable=TRUE;
    break;
  case FARM_OBJECT:
  case FIELD_OBJECT:
    m_nFrameCount=1;
    m_eMortality=IMMORTAL;
    m_eLocomotion=NO_MOTION;
    m_bVulnerable=FALSE;
    break;
  case BULLET_OBJECT:
    m_nFrameCount=1;
    m_eMortality=MORTAL;
    m_eLocomotion=FLYING_MOTION;
    m_bVulnerable=FALSE;
    m_nLifeTime=500+Random.number(0,200);
    break;
```

```
      case DEADCROW_OBJECT:
        m_nCurrentFrame=0;
        m_eMortality=MORTAL;
        m_eLocomotion=FALLING_MOTION;
        m_bVulnerable=FALSE;
        m_nLifeTime=1000;
        break;
      case EXPLODINGCROW_OBJECT:
        m_nCurrentFrame=0;
        m_nFrameInterval=100;
        m_eMortality=ONESHOT_MORTAL;
        m_eLocomotion=FLYING_MOTION;
        m_bVulnerable=FALSE;
        break;
  }
}

void CObject::draw(LPDIRECTDRAWSURFACE surface){ //draw
  //draw the current frame
  m_pSprite->draw(m_nCurrentFrame,Viewpoint.screen(m_nX),
    m_nY,surface);
  //figure out which frame is next
  if(m_eMortality==ONESHOT_MORTAL){ //animation plays once
    if(Timer.elapsed(m_nLastFrameTime,m_nFrameInterval))
      ++m_nCurrentFrame;
  }
  else{ //repeating animation
    int t=m_nFrameInterval/(1+abs(m_nXspeed)); //frame interval
    if(m_nFrameCount>1&&Timer.elapsed(m_nLastFrameTime,t))
      if(m_bForwardAnimation){ //forward animation
        if(++m_nCurrentFrame>=m_nFrameCount){ //wrap
          m_nCurrentFrame=m_nFrameCount-2;
          m_bForwardAnimation=FALSE;
        }
      }
      else{ //backward animation
        if(--m_nCurrentFrame<0){ //wrap
          m_nCurrentFrame=1;
          m_bForwardAnimation=TRUE;
        }
      }
  }
}

void CObject::accelerate(int xdelta,int ydelta){
//change speed
  //horizontal
  m_nXspeed+=xdelta;
  if(m_nXspeed<m_nMinXSpeed)m_nXspeed=m_nMinXSpeed;
  if(m_nXspeed>m_nMaxXSpeed)m_nXspeed=m_nMaxXSpeed;
```

```
      //vertical
      m_nYspeed+=ydelta;
      if(m_nYspeed<m_nMinYSpeed)m_nYspeed=m_nMinYSpeed;
      if(m_nYspeed>m_nMaxYSpeed)m_nYspeed=m_nMaxYSpeed;
}

void CObject::move(){ //move object
   const int XSCALE=16; //to scale back horizontal motion
   const int YSCALE=32; //to scale back vertical motion
   const int YMARGIN=20; //vertical margin
   int xdelta,ydelta; //change in position
   int time=Timer.time(); //current time
   int tfactor; //time since last move
   switch(m_eLocomotion){
     case FLYING_MOTION:
       //horizontal motion
       tfactor=time-m_nLastXMoveTime; //time since last move
       xdelta=(m_nXspeed*tfactor)/XSCALE; //x distance moved
       m_nX+=xdelta; //x motion
       Viewpoint.normalize(m_nX); //normalize to world width
       if(xdelta||m_nXspeed==0) //record time of move
         m_nLastXMoveTime=time;
       //vertical motion
       tfactor=time-m_nLastYMoveTime; //time since last move
       ydelta=(m_nYspeed*tfactor)/YSCALE; //y distance moved
       m_nY+=ydelta; //y motion
       if(m_nY<YMARGIN)m_nY=YMARGIN;
       if(m_nY>=SCREEN_HEIGHT)m_nY=SCREEN_HEIGHT-1;
       if(ydelta||m_nYspeed==0) //record time of move
         m_nLastYMoveTime=time;
       break;
     case FALLING_MOTION:
       m_nXspeed=0;
       //time since born, for acceleration due to gravity
       tfactor=time-m_nBirthTime;
       //vertical motion
       ydelta=tfactor/YSCALE; m_nY+=ydelta;
       if(m_nY<YMARGIN)m_nY=YMARGIN;
       if(ydelta||m_nYspeed==0) //record time of move
         m_nLastYMoveTime=time;
       break;
     default: break;
   }
}
```

Objman.h

```
//objman.h: header file for the object manager

//Copyright Ian Parberry, 1999
```

```
//Last updated October 27, 1999

#ifndef __OBJMAN__
#define __OBJMAN__

#include <windows.h>
#include <windowsx.h>
#include <ddraw.h>

#include "objects.h"

class CObjectManager{
  private:
    CObject **m_pObjectList; //list of objects in game
    int m_nCount; //how many objects in list
    int m_nMaxCount; //maximum number of objects
    int m_nCurrentObject; //index of the current object
    int m_nLastGunFireTime; //time gun was last fired
    //distance functions
    int distance(int x1,int y1,int x2,int y2); //in universe
    int distance(int first,int second); //between objects
    //collision detection
    void collision_detection(); //all collisions
    void collision_detection(int index); //with this object
    //managing dead objects
    void cull(); //cull dead objects
    void kill(int index); //remove object from list
    void replace(int index); //replace by next in series
  public:
    CObjectManager(int max); //constructor
    ~CObjectManager(); //destructor
    int create(ObjectType object,int x,int y,
      int xspeed,int yspeed); //create new object
    //animate all objects
    void animate(LPDIRECTDRAWSURFACE surface);
    //the following functions operate on the current object
    void accelerate(int xdelta,int ydelta=0); //change speed
    void set_current(int index); //set current object
    int speed(); //return magnitude of speed
    void fire_gun(); //fire the gun
};

#endif
```

Objman.cpp

```
//objman.cpp: object manager class
//Copyright Ian Parberry, 1999
//Last updated October 28, 1999
```

```cpp
#include <math.h> //for sqrt

#include "objman.h"
#include "view.h" //for viewpoint class
#include "timer.h" //game timer
#include "ai.h" //for intelligent objects

extern CViewPoint Viewpoint; //player viewpoint
extern CTimer Timer; //game timer

CObjectManager::CObjectManager(int max){ //constructor
  m_nMaxCount=max; m_nCount=0; m_nCurrentObject=0;
  m_nLastGunFireTime=0;
  m_pObjectList=new CObject*[max]; //object list
  for(int i=0; i<m_nMaxCount; i++) //create objects
    m_pObjectList[i]=NULL;
}

CObjectManager::~CObjectManager(){ //destructor
  for(int i=0; i<m_nMaxCount; i++) //for each object
    delete m_pObjectList[i]; //delete it
  delete[]m_pObjectList; //delete object list
}

int CObjectManager::create(ObjectType object,int x,int y,
                           int xspeed,int yspeed){
  if(m_nCount<m_nMaxCount){ //if room, create object
    int i=0; //index into object list
    while(m_pObjectList[i]!=NULL)i++; //find first free slot
    if(object==CROW_OBJECT) //intelligent object
      m_pObjectList[i]=
        new CIntelligentObject(object,x,y,xspeed,yspeed);
    else //dumb object
      m_pObjectList[i]=new CObject(object,x,y,xspeed,yspeed);
    m_nCount++;
    return i;
  }
  else return -1;
}

void CObjectManager::animate(LPDIRECTDRAWSURFACE surface){
  //move objects
  for(int i=0; i<m_nMaxCount; i++) //for each object slot
    if(m_pObjectList[i]!=NULL){ //if there's an object there
      m_pObjectList[i]->move(); //move it
      if(m_pObjectList[i]->m_bIntelligent) //if intelligent
        //tell object about plane current position
        ((CIntelligentObject*)m_pObjectList[i])->plane(
          m_pObjectList[m_nCurrentObject]->m_nX,
          m_pObjectList[m_nCurrentObject]->m_nY,
```

```
            distance(i,m_nCurrentObject));
    }
  //move viewpoint with plane
  Viewpoint.set_position(
    m_pObjectList[m_nCurrentObject]->m_nX);
  //collision detection
  collision_detection();
  //cull old objects
  cull();
  //draw objects
  for(i=0; i<m_nMaxCount; i++) //for each object slot
    if(m_pObjectList[i]!=NULL) //if there's an object there
      m_pObjectList[i]->draw(surface); //draw it
}

void CObjectManager::accelerate(int xdelta,int ydelta){
  //change speed of current object
  m_pObjectList[m_nCurrentObject]->
    accelerate(xdelta,ydelta);
}

void CObjectManager::set_current(int index){
  //set current object
  if(index>=0&&index<m_nCount)m_nCurrentObject=index;
}

int CObjectManager::speed(){
  //return magnitude of current object speed
  return abs(m_pObjectList[m_nCurrentObject]->m_nXspeed);
}

int CObjectManager::distance(int x1,int y1,int x2,int y2){
//return distance in universe
  int x=abs(x1-x2),y=abs(y1-y2);//x and y distance
  //compensate for wrap-around world
  if(x>WORLD_WIDTH/2)x-=WORLD_WIDTH;
  //return result
  return (int)sqrt((double)x*x+(double)y*y);
}

int CObjectManager::distance(int first,int second){
//return distance between objects
  //bail if bad index
  if(first<0||first>=m_nMaxCount)return -1;
  if(second<0||second>=m_nMaxCount)return -1;
  //get coordinates of centers
  int x1,y1,x2,y2; //coordinates of objects
  x1=m_pObjectList[first]->m_nX;
  y1=m_pObjectList[first]->m_nY-
    m_pObjectList[first]->m_nHeight/2;
```

```
      x2=m_pObjectList[second]->m_nX;
      y2=m_pObjectList[second]->m_nY-
        m_pObjectList[second]->m_nHeight/2;
      //return distance between coordinates
      return distance(x1,y1,x2,y2);
    }

    void CObjectManager::kill(int index){ //remove object
      m_nCount--;
      delete m_pObjectList[index];
      m_pObjectList[index]=NULL;
    }

    void CObjectManager::fire_gun(){ //fire current object's gun
      CObject *plane= m_pObjectList[m_nCurrentObject];
      if(Timer.elapsed(m_nLastGunFireTime,200))
        create(BULLET_OBJECT,plane->m_nX-60,plane->m_nY-50,-5,0);
    }

    void CObjectManager::cull(){ //cull old objects
      CObject *object;
      for(int i=0; i<m_nMaxCount; i++){ //for each object
        object=m_pObjectList[i]; //current object
        if(object!=NULL){
          //died of old age
          if(object->m_eMortality==MORTAL&& //if mortal and ...
          //...lived long enough...
          (Timer.time()-object->m_nBirthTime>object->m_nLifeTime))
            kill(i); //...then kill it
          else //one-shot animation
            //if object played one time only...
            if(object->m_eMortality==ONESHOT_MORTAL&&
            //...and played once already...
            object->m_nCurrentFrame>=object->m_nFrameCount)
              replace(i); //...then replace the object
        }
      }
    }

    void CObjectManager::replace(int index){
    //replace object by next in series
      CObject *object=m_pObjectList[index]; //current object
      ObjectType newtype;
      BOOL successor=TRUE; //assume it has a successor
      //decide on new object type
      switch(object->m_eObject){
        case CROW_OBJECT: newtype=EXPLODINGCROW_OBJECT; break;
        case EXPLODINGCROW_OBJECT: newtype=DEADCROW_OBJECT; break;
        default: successor=FALSE; break; //has no successor
      }
```

```
      //replace old object with new one
      int x=object->m_nX,y=object->m_nY; //location
      int xspeed=object->m_nXspeed;
      int yspeed=object->m_nYspeed;
      kill(index); //kill old object
      if(successor) //if it has a successor
        create(newtype,x,y,xspeed,yspeed); //create new one
}

void CObjectManager::collision_detection(){
//check for all collisions
    for(int i=0; i<m_nMaxCount; i++) //for each object slot
      if(m_pObjectList[i]!=NULL) //if object exists
        if(m_pObjectList[i]->m_eObject==BULLET_OBJECT)
          collision_detection(i); //check for collisions
}

void CObjectManager::collision_detection(int index){
//check whether object with this index collides
    int i=0; //index of object collided with
    BOOL finished=FALSE; //finished when collision detected
    while(i<m_nMaxCount&&!finished){
      if(m_pObjectList[i]!=NULL) //if i is a valid object index
        if(m_pObjectList[i]->m_bVulnerable&& //if vulnerable
         distance(index,i)<15){ //and close enough, then
           finished=TRUE; //hit found, so exit loop
           replace(i); //replace object that is hit
           kill(index); //kill object doing the hitting
        }
      ++i; //next object
    }
}
```

Here's what you'll learn:

- What a game shell is, and how to wrap one around your game engine

- How to display a logo screen, title screen, and main menu

- How to make your game engine re-entrant

The Game Shell

In Demo 7, we learn how to wrap a game shell around our game. The game shell consists of a logo screen displaying the logo of the company that created the game (in this case, my lab at UNT), a title screen for the game, and a menu screen. The logo and title for *Ned's Turkey Farm* are simply bmp files that are displayed for a few seconds, whereas in a real game you should use fancy animations or a movie clip. However, it is a good idea to keep the title screen low-impact because is a good place to load up resources such as sound and images for use during the game and it gives the player something to look at while they are loading. In our game demo, however, the resource requirements are so low that this is not necessary. Since the player will eventually get tired of seeing the logo and title screens, no matter how entertaining they are, we allow the player to click out of them by hitting any key.

The part of the game that we started in Demos 0-6, where you actually play the game, is called the *game engine*. After the logo screen (Figure 9.1) and the title screen (Figure 9.2) are displayed, the player is dumped into the main menu screen (Figure 9.3). From there, the player has several options, only two of which actually work in Demo 7—entering the game engine for a new game by hitting the "N" key or quitting by using the "Q" key. Which key to hit is indicated by having the artist draw the appropriate letter of each menu item in a different color. Eventually, when we get mouse control, the player will be able to click on the buttons next to the menu items instead. The player can exit the game engine by hitting the Esc key or killing all of the crows, in which case he or she will land in the menu screen again.

Figure 9.1
The logo
screen,
Larc.bmp

Figure 9.2
The title
screen,
Title.bmp

Figure 9.3
The menu
screen,
Menu.bmp

Experiment with Demo 7

Take a moment now to run Demo 7.

- You should see the logo screen displayed for 7 seconds and the title screen displayed for 10 seconds. You will then see the menu screen.
- Hit the "N" key to play a game. Kill all of the crows. When the last corpse hits the ground, you will be sent back to the menu screen.
- Hit the "N" key to play a second game. You will see a new flock of crows to kill. This time quit the game by hitting the Esc key before killing all of the crows. You will end up back at the menu screen again.
- Hit the "Q" key or the Esc key to exit the program.
- Run Demo 7 again. Hit any key to exit the logo screen early. Do the same for the title screen. You may exit the program again by hitting the "Q" key or the Esc key at the menu screen.

Changes to the Object Manager

Changes to the object manager class in Demo 7 involve the insertion of two new public member functions. Since these changes are relatively minor, `Objman.cpp` and `Objman.h` are not listed at the end of this chapter with the other changed files.

The first new `CObjectManager` function is a `reset` function, which resets a (possibly used) object manager back to its initial conditions. We need this now because the player may conceivably re-enter the game from the menu screen; up until now the player could only play one game and then quit.

```
void CObjectManager::reset(){ //reset to original conditions
```

We begin by resetting to zero the number of objects, the current object, and the last time the gun fired:

```
m_nCount=0; m_nCurrentObject=0; m_nLastGunFireTime=0;
```

A `for` loop iterates through all of the objects in the object list, calls `delete` to destroy each one, then replaces the corresponding pointer in the object list with `NULL`. This code works even with empty slots in the object list because calling `delete` on a `NULL` pointer does nothing.

```
    for(int i=0; i<m_nMaxCount; i++){
      delete m_pObjectList[i];
      m_pObjectList[i]=NULL;
    }
  }
```

The second new `CObjectManager` function is `won`, which returns `TRUE` if the player has killed all of the enemies in the game. Because the object list may contain friends as well as enemies, we can't use the `m_nCount` member variable. Instead, we search the object list and count the number of crow-related objects. Including the exploding and dead crows in the count means that the game doesn't end until the last corpse has hit the ground.

```
BOOL CObjectManager::won(){ //TRUE if enemies all dead
    int count=0; //how many enemies left
    for(int i=0; i<m_nMaxCount; i++)
      if(m_pObjectList[i]!=NULL)
        switch(m_pObjectList[i]->m_eObject){
          case CROW_OBJECT:
          case EXPLODINGCROW_OBJECT:
          case DEADCROW_OBJECT:
            count++;
            break;
        }
    return count<=0;
  }
```

Phase Management

For want of a better term, we will refer to the various parts of the game—for example, the part where the logo screen is being displayed as opposed to the part where the title screen is being displayed—as *phases*. Defines.h contains a new enumerated type that names the four phases in Demo 7. We will add new phases in later chapters.

```
enum GamePhaseType{
  LOGO_PHASE,TITLE_PHASE,MENU_PHASE,PLAYING_PHASE
};
```

Main.cpp has three new global variables to help manage phase transitions. The first is the current phase GamePhase, and the second a Boolean variable endphase that will be set to TRUE when the current phase should end. We use endphase simply as a convenient way to ensure that phase changes actually take place at only one place in the code, whereas the necessity for a phase change might be discovered in a variety of places. The third new global variable is PhaseTime, which will help us measure the time spent in each phase.

```
GamePhaseType GamePhase; //current phase
BOOL endphase=FALSE; //should we abort current phase?
int PhaseTime=0; //time in phase
```

In function RestoreSurfaces, we need to change the way that the primary and secondary surfaces are restored. Up until now, we have assumed that they should be reloaded immediately after they have been restored. Now things are more complicated, however; the reloading process depends on what phase we are in. Rather than clutter up function RestoreSurfaces, we restore without reloading and deal with it later in the code.

```
if(FAILED(lpPrimary->Restore()))return FALSE;
if(FAILED(lpSecondary->Restore()))return FALSE;
```

The Display_screen Function

A new function display_screen displays an image from a bmp file. It has a single parameter filename that points to the name of the file from which the image should be read. We will use this function to display the logo and title screens.

```
void display_screen(char *filename){ //display bmp file
```

It has a local bmp file reader called image:

```
CBmpFileReader image; //file reader
```

We load the image into the file reader, and draw it to the secondary surface:

```
image.load(filename); //load from file
image.draw(lpSecondary); //draw to back buffer
```

The displayed image might have a different palette from the game engine—in fact, I encouraged the artist to do so in order to give him as much creative freedom as possible—so we should set the palette in the primary surface to be the same as the palette in the image:

```
image.setpalette(lpPrimaryPalette); //may have custom palette
```

Function `display_screen` ends by page flipping so that the image can be seen:

```
PageFlip(); //display it
} //display_screen
```

The Change_phase Function

There is always some housekeeping to be done when entering a new phase. We will create a function `change_phase` to put all of this code in a common place. Function `change_phase` has a single parameter `new_phase` that tells it which phase to change to.

```
void change_phase(GamePhaseType new_phase){ //start new phase
```

It begins by setting `GamePhase` to the new phase, setting `PhaseTime` to the current time, and setting `endphase` (which we assume triggered the call to `change_phase` by being TRUE) to FALSE:

```
GamePhase=new_phase; PhaseTime=Timer.time();
endphase=FALSE;
```

A `switch` statement on the current phase helps us write custom phase transition code for each phase. At the start of the logo, title, and menu phases, we need only display the appropriate image.

```
switch(GamePhase){
  case LOGO_PHASE:
    display_screen("larc.bmp");
    break;
  case TITLE_PHASE:
    display_screen("title.bmp");
    break;
  case MENU_PHASE:
    display_screen("menu.bmp");
    break;
```

At the start of the playing phase, we need to set up the game engine to begin play:

```
case PLAYING_PHASE: //prepare the game engine
```

Now that the player can re-enter the game engine from the menu phase, we must reset the object manager to remove any object left behind from any previous games (the player may have hit the Esc key, leaving any number of crows in the object list). Then we call `CreateObjects` to create the objects for a new game.

```
ObjectManager.reset(); //clear object manager
CreateObjects(); //create new objects
```

Before entering the game engine, we initialize the graphics by setting the palette for the primary surface to the background palette (recall that we are entering the game engine from the menu screen, which has a custom palette), then priming the frame pump by displaying a frame of animation. This ends the `switch` statement, and ends function `change_phase`.

```
background.setpalette(lpPrimaryPalette); //game palette
ComposeFrame(); PageFlip(); //prime animation pump
break;
    }
} //change_phase
```

The Redraw Function

Next, we have a function `Redraw`, which we will use to redraw the screen after surface loss. It consists of a `switch` statement with a `case` for each phase. For most of the phases, we simply need to draw the appropriate image to the screen. For the game engine we need do nothing; animation will resume soon enough from the message pump.

```
void Redraw(){ //redraw in response to surface loss
  switch(GamePhase){
    case LOGO_PHASE:
      display_screen("larc.bmp");
      break;
    case TITLE_PHASE:
      display_screen("title.bmp");
      break;
    case MENU_PHASE:
      display_screen("menu.bmp"); //display main menu
      break;
    case PLAYING_PHASE:
      //do nothing, next frame of animation will catch it
      break;
  }
}
```

The ProcessFrame Function

The body of function `ProcessFrame` has become more complicated. It begins with the declarations of two constants that define how long the logo screen and title screen should be displayed (7 seconds and 10 seconds, respectively).

```
const int LOGO_DISPLAY_TIME=7000; //duration of logo
const int TITLE_DISPLAY_TIME=10000; //duration of title
```

Instead of checking for surface loss as a result of a failed page flip, we will check explicitly at the next step in `ProcessFrame` using the primary surface's `IsLost` member function. If surface loss is detected, surfaces are restored and then redrawn using our new `Redraw` function.

```
if(lpPrimary->IsLost()){
  RestoreSurfaces(); Redraw();
}
```

Next, a switch statement is used to determine which phase we are in:

```
switch(GamePhase){ //what phase are we in?
```

In the logo phase, all we need to do is wait until the phase is over. Rather than wasting system resources by getting locked into a tight wait loop, we use the API function `Sleep`, which makes the game become inactive for a fixed period (100 milliseconds in this case), during which system resources are free for use by other processes running on the player's computer. Sleeping for a tenth of a second is a little drastic; a less drastic alternative would be to call `Sleep` with no parameter, which forces the scheduler to switch to the next active process without mandating a sleep period.

```
case LOGO_PHASE: //displaying logo screen
  Sleep(100); //surrender time to other processes
```

If `endphase` has been set to `TRUE` or enough time has elapsed, we change to the title phase. The use of `endphase` here is to give the player the option of clicking out of the logo screen. With this in place, the keyboard manager need only set `endphase` to `TRUE` in response to any keystroke during the logo phase.

```
if(endphase||Timer.elapsed(PhaseTime,LOGO_DISPLAY_TIME))
  change_phase(TITLE_PHASE); //go to title screen
break;
```

The title phase has the same code, but with a different display time and a different next phase (the menu phase this time):

```
case TITLE_PHASE: //displaying title screen
  Sleep(100); //surrender time to other processes
  if(endphase||Timer.elapsed(PhaseTime,TITLE_DISPLAY_TIME))
    change_phase(MENU_PHASE); //go to menu
break;
```

The menu phase is similar, but you can stay in it as long as you want. When the phase ends, we go into the playing phase. None of the other menu items work yet, except for quitting which we handle as a special case in the keyboard handler.

```
case MENU_PHASE: //main menu
  Sleep(100); //surrender time to other processes
  if(endphase)change_phase(PLAYING_PHASE); //play game
```

```
      break;
```

The code for the playing phase has the `ComposeFrame`/`PageFlip` pair of function calls from the old version of `ProcessFrame`, followed by a new pair of lines that change the phase back to the menu phase if `endphase` is `TRUE` (the player hit Esc or "Q"), or the object manager reports that the player has won (by killing all of the crows). This ends the body of `ProcessFrame`.

```
    case PLAYING_PHASE: //game engine
      ComposeFrame(); //compose a frame in back surface
      PageFlip(); //flip video memory surfaces
      if(endphase||ObjectManager.won()) //if end of phase
        change_phase(MENU_PHASE); //go to menu
      break;
  }
```

The Keyboard Handlers

The keyboard handler code must change, because any given key may have a different effect in different phases. The cleanest way to do this is to make a keyboard handler for different phases, with similar phases sharing a handler. The logo and title phases share a keyboard handler called the `intro_keyboard_handler`, which responds to any keystroke by ending the phase.

```
void intro_keyboard_handler(WPARAM keystroke){
  endphase=TRUE; //any key ends the phase
} //intro_keyboard_handler
```

The keyboard handler for the menu phase is called `menu_keyboard_handler`, which returns `TRUE` if the player wants to exit the game. It has a single parameter that contains the virtual keycode of the key that was pressed.

```
BOOL menu_keyboard_handler(WPARAM keystroke){
```

The function begins with the declaration of a local variable for the return value:

```
  BOOL result=FALSE;
```

Then, we have a `switch` statement on the `keystroke` parameter:

```
  switch(keystroke){
```

The game exits when the player hits either the Esc key or the "Q" key. When this happens, we want to return `TRUE`. Notice that the virtual keycode for letter keys is identical to the ASCII encoding of the uppercase version of the letter, which we get by using a character in single quotes.

```
    case VK_ESCAPE:
    case 'Q': //exit game
      result=TRUE;
      break;
```

To play a new game in response to the "N" key, we simply set endphase to TRUE, which works at the current point in development since the only place to go from the menu phase is the playing phase. In later chapters, we will need to add a facility that lets us go to different phases when the menu phase ends.

```
case 'N': //play new game
  endphase=TRUE;
  break;
default: break; //do nothing
}
```

Finally, we return the result and exit:

```
  return result;
} //menu_keyboard_handler
```

The game keyboard handler is identical to the keyboard handler from Demo 6:

```
void game_keyboard_handler(WPARAM keystroke){
  switch(keystroke){
    case VK_ESCAPE: endphase=TRUE; break;
    case VK_UP: ObjectManager.accelerate(0,-1); break;
    case VK_DOWN: ObjectManager.accelerate(0,1); break;
    case VK_LEFT: ObjectManager.accelerate(-1,0); break;
    case VK_RIGHT: ObjectManager.accelerate(1,0); break;
    case VK_SPACE: ObjectManager.fire_gun(); break;
    default: break;
  }
} //game_keyboard_handler
```

The body of the main keyboard handler is replaced by a switch statement that calls the appropriate phase keyboard handler to do the real work:

```
BOOL keyboard_handler(WPARAM keystroke){ //keyboard handler
  BOOL result=FALSE; //TRUE if we are to exit game
  switch(GamePhase){ //select handler for phase
    case LOGO_PHASE:
    case TITLE_PHASE:
      intro_keyboard_handler(keystroke);
      break;
    case MENU_PHASE:
      result=menu_keyboard_handler(keystroke);
      break;
    case PLAYING_PHASE:
      game_keyboard_handler(keystroke);
      break;
  }
  return result;
} //keyboard_handler
```

The last change to `Main.cpp` involves setting the initial phase immediately before entering the message loop. This is done with a single-line call to `change_phase`. The first phase is, of course, the logo phase, and the `change_phase` function takes care of the housekeeping that needs to be done on phase entry, such as showing the logo screen and starting to measure the time in phase.

```
change_phase(LOGO_PHASE);
```

Demo 7 Files

Code Files

The following files in Demo 7 are used without change from Demo 6:

- Ai.h
- Ai.cpp
- Bmp.h
- Bmp.cpp
- Bsprite.h
- Bsprite.cpp
- Csprite.h
- Csprite.cpp
- Ddsetup.cpp
- Objects.h
- Objects.cpp
- Random.h
- Random.cpp
- Sbmp.h
- Sbmp.cpp
- Timer.h
- Timer.cpp
- View.h
- View.cpp

The following files in Demo 7 have been modified from Demo 6:

- Defines.h
- Main.cpp

  ◎ Objman.h (changes minimal; not listed)

  ◎ Objman.cpp (changes minimal; not listed)

Media Files

The following image files are new in Demo 7:

  ◎ Larc.bmp

  ◎ Menu.bmp

  ◎ Title.bmp

Required Libraries

  ◎ Ddraw.lib

  ◎ Winmm.lib

Code Listings

Defines.h

```
//defines.h: essential defines
//Copyright Ian Parberry, 1999
//Last updated April 3, 2000

#ifndef __DEFINES_H__
#define __DEFINES_H__

#define SCREEN_WIDTH 640 //pixels wide
#define SCREEN_HEIGHT 480 //pixels high
#define COLORS 256 //number of colors
#define COLOR_DEPTH 8 //number of bits to store colors
#define TRANSPARENT_COLOR 255 //transparent palette position

enum GamePhaseType{
  LOGO_PHASE,TITLE_PHASE,MENU_PHASE,PLAYING_PHASE
};

#endif
```

Main.cpp

```
//main.cpp

//Now there is a game shell wrapped around the game engine.
//You see a logo screen, a title screen, and a menu screen.
//From the menu screen you can play a game (hit the N key)
//or exit (hit the Q key). After playing you return to the
//menu screen - if you hit ESC in the game engine,
```

```
//and after you kill the last crow.

//Copyright Ian Parberry, 1999
//Last updated May 22, 2000

//system includes
#include <windows.h>
#include <windowsx.h>
#include <ddraw.h>
#include <stdio.h>

//system defines
#define WIN32_LEAN_AND_MEAN

//custom includes
#include "defines.h" //global definitions
#include "bmp.h" //bmp file reader
#include "timer.h" //game timer
#include "csprite.h" //for clipped sprite class
#include "objects.h" //for object class
#include "objman.h" //for object manager
#include "view.h" //for viewpoint class
#include "random.h" //for random number generator

//defines
#define MAX_OBJECTS 32 //max number of objects in game

//globals

BOOL ActiveApp; //is this application active?

LPDIRECTDRAW lpDirectDrawObject=NULL; //direct draw object
LPDIRECTDRAWSURFACE lpPrimary=NULL; //primary surface
LPDIRECTDRAWPALETTE lpPrimaryPalette; //its palette
LPDIRECTDRAWSURFACE lpSecondary=NULL; //back buffer
LPDIRECTDRAWPALETTE lpSecondaryPalette; //its palette
LPDIRECTDRAWSURFACE lpBackground=NULL; //background image

CTimer Timer; //game timer

CBmpFileReader background; //background image
CBmpSpriteFileReader g_cSpriteImages; //sprite images
CBmpSpriteFileReader g_cFrgndImages; //foreground images

CObjectManager ObjectManager(MAX_OBJECTS); //object manager

CClippedSprite *g_pSprite[NUM_SPRITES]; //sprites

CViewPoint Viewpoint; //player viewpoint
CRandom Random; //random number generator
```

```
GamePhaseType GamePhase; //current phase
BOOL endphase=FALSE; //should we abort current phase?
int PhaseTime=0; //time in phase

//helper functions
LPDIRECTDRAWPALETTE CreatePalette(LPDIRECTDRAWSURFACE surface);
BOOL InitDirectDraw(HWND hwnd);
HWND CreateDefaultWindow(char* name,HINSTANCE hInstance);

BOOL LoadPlaneSprite(){
  BOOL result=TRUE;
  result=result&&g_pSprite[PLANE_OBJECT]->
    load(&g_cSpriteImages,0,1,1);
  result=result&&g_pSprite[PLANE_OBJECT]->
    load(&g_cSpriteImages,1,123,1);
  result=result&&g_pSprite[PLANE_OBJECT]->
    load(&g_cSpriteImages,2,245,1);
  result=result&&g_pSprite[PLANE_OBJECT]->
    load(&g_cSpriteImages,3,367,1);
  result=result&&g_pSprite[PLANE_OBJECT]->
    load(&g_cSpriteImages,4,489,1);
  result=result&&g_pSprite[PLANE_OBJECT]->
    load(&g_cSpriteImages,5,17,74);
  return result;
} //LoadPlaneSprite

BOOL LoadCrowSprite(){
  BOOL result=TRUE;
  result=result&&g_pSprite[CROW_OBJECT]->
    load(&g_cSpriteImages,0,256,183); //frame 0
  result=result&&g_pSprite[CROW_OBJECT]->
    load(&g_cSpriteImages,1,320,183); //frame 1
  result=result&&g_pSprite[CROW_OBJECT]->
    load(&g_cSpriteImages,2,256,237); //frame 2
  result=result&&g_pSprite[CROW_OBJECT]->
    load(&g_cSpriteImages,3,323,237); //frame 3
  return result;
} //LoadCrowSprite

BOOL LoadFrgndSprites(){ //load foreground sprites
  BOOL result=TRUE;
  result=result&&g_pSprite[FARM_OBJECT]->
    load(&g_cFrgndImages,0,0,0); //load farm sprite
  result=result&&g_pSprite[FIELD_OBJECT]->
    load(&g_cFrgndImages,0,640,0); //load field sprite
  return result;
} //LoadFrgndSprites

BOOL LoadDeadCrowSprite(){ //load dead crow
```

```
    return g_pSprite[DEADCROW_OBJECT]->
      load(&g_cSpriteImages,0,453,230);
} //LoadDeadCrowSprite

BOOL LoadExplodingCrowSprite(){ //load exploding crow
  BOOL result=TRUE;
  result=result&&g_pSprite[EXPLODINGCROW_OBJECT]->
    load(&g_cSpriteImages,0,257,294);
  result=result&&g_pSprite[EXPLODINGCROW_OBJECT]->
    load(&g_cSpriteImages,1,321,294);
  result=result&&g_pSprite[EXPLODINGCROW_OBJECT]->
    load(&g_cSpriteImages,2,386,162);
  result=result&&g_pSprite[EXPLODINGCROW_OBJECT]->
    load(&g_cSpriteImages,3,453,162);
  result=result&&g_pSprite[EXPLODINGCROW_OBJECT]->
    load(&g_cSpriteImages,4,386,230);
  result=result&&g_pSprite[EXPLODINGCROW_OBJECT]->
    load(&g_cSpriteImages,5,453,230);
  return result;
} //LoadExplodingCrowSprite

BOOL LoadBulletSprite(){ //load bullet
  return g_pSprite[BULLET_OBJECT]->
    load(&g_cSpriteImages,0,5,123);
} //LoadBulletSprite

BOOL LoadImages(){ //load graphics from files to surfaces
  //get the background image
  if(!background.load("bckgnd.bmp"))return FALSE; //read file
  background.draw(lpBackground); //draw to background surface
  //set palettes in all surfaces
  if(!background.setpalette(lpPrimaryPalette))return FALSE;
  if(!background.setpalette(lpSecondaryPalette))return FALSE;
  //load the sprites...
  if(!g_cSpriteImages.load("sprites.bmp"))return FALSE;
  //...the plane
  g_pSprite[PLANE_OBJECT]=new CClippedSprite(6,121,72);
  if(!LoadPlaneSprite())return FALSE; //load plane images
  //...the crow
  g_pSprite[CROW_OBJECT]=new CClippedSprite(4,58,37);
  if(!LoadCrowSprite())return FALSE; //load crow images
  //..the dead crow
  g_pSprite[DEADCROW_OBJECT]=new CClippedSprite(1,62,53);
  LoadDeadCrowSprite(); //load dead crow images
  //...the exploding crow
  g_pSprite[EXPLODINGCROW_OBJECT]=new CClippedSprite(6,62,53);
  LoadExplodingCrowSprite(); //load exploding crow images
  //...the bullet
  g_pSprite[BULLET_OBJECT]=new CClippedSprite(1,5,3);
  LoadBulletSprite(); //load bullet images
```

```
    //...the foreground sprites
    if(!g_cFrgndImages.load("farm.bmp"))return FALSE;
    g_pSprite[FARM_OBJECT]=new CClippedSprite(1,640,162);
    g_pSprite[FIELD_OBJECT]=new CClippedSprite(1,640,162);
    if(!LoadFrgndSprites())return FALSE; //load foreground
    return TRUE;
} //LoadImages

void CreateObjects(){
    int i;
    ObjectManager.create(FARM_OBJECT,0,SCREEN_HEIGHT-1,0,0);
    ObjectManager.create(FIELD_OBJECT,SCREEN_WIDTH,
        SCREEN_HEIGHT-1,0,0);
    for(i=0; i<8; i++)
        ObjectManager.create(CROW_OBJECT,
            Random.number(0,WORLD_WIDTH-1),
            Random.number(100,400),-1,0);
    ObjectManager.set_current(
        ObjectManager.create(PLANE_OBJECT,320,271,-1,0));
    for(i=0; i<8; i++)
        ObjectManager.create(CROW_OBJECT,
            Random.number(0,WORLD_WIDTH-1),
            Random.number(100,400),-1,0);
} //CreateObjects

BOOL RestoreSurfaces(){ //restore all surfaces
    BOOL result=TRUE;
    //primary and secondary surfaces
    if(FAILED(lpPrimary->Restore()))return FALSE;
    if(FAILED(lpSecondary->Restore()))return FALSE;
    //surfaces containing images
    if(SUCCEEDED(lpBackground->Restore())) //if background restored
        result=result&&background.draw(lpBackground); //redraw image
    else return FALSE;
    if(g_pSprite[PLANE_OBJECT]->Restore()) //if plane restored
        result=result&&LoadPlaneSprite(); //redraw image
    else return FALSE;
    if(g_pSprite[CROW_OBJECT]->Restore()) //if crow restored
        result=result&&LoadCrowSprite(); //redraw image
    else return FALSE;
    if(g_pSprite[DEADCROW_OBJECT]->Restore()) //if restored
        result=result&&LoadDeadCrowSprite(); //redraw image
    else return FALSE;
    if(g_pSprite[EXPLODINGCROW_OBJECT]->Restore()) //if restored
        result=result&&LoadExplodingCrowSprite(); //redraw image
    else return FALSE;
    if(g_pSprite[BULLET_OBJECT]->Restore()) //if restored
        result=result&&LoadBulletSprite(); //redraw image
    else return FALSE;
    if(g_pSprite[FARM_OBJECT]->Restore()&& //if farm and ...
```

```
      g_pSprite[FIELD_OBJECT]->Restore()) //... field restored
      result=result&&LoadFrgndSprites(); //redraw image
    else return FALSE;
    return result;
} //RestoreSurfaces

BOOL PageFlip(){ //return TRUE if page flip succeeds
  if(lpPrimary->Flip(NULL,DDFLIP_WAIT)==DDERR_SURFACELOST)
    return RestoreSurfaces();
  return TRUE;
} //PageFlip

BOOL ComposeFrame(){ //compose a frame of animation
  Viewpoint.draw_background(lpBackground,lpSecondary,
    ObjectManager.speed()); //draw scrolling background
  ObjectManager.animate(lpSecondary); //draw objects
  return TRUE;
} //ComposeFrame

void display_screen(char *filename){ //display bmp file
  CBmpFileReader image; //file reader
  image.load(filename); //load from file
  image.draw(lpSecondary); //draw to back buffer
  image.setpalette(lpPrimaryPalette); //may have custom palette
  PageFlip(); //display it
} //display_screen

void change_phase(GamePhaseType new_phase){ //start new phase
  //change to new phase
  GamePhase=new_phase; PhaseTime=Timer.time();
  endphase=FALSE;
  //start-of-phase housekeeping
  switch(GamePhase){
    case LOGO_PHASE:
      display_screen("larc.bmp");
      break;
    case TITLE_PHASE:
      display_screen("title.bmp");
      break;
    case MENU_PHASE:
      display_screen("menu.bmp");
      break;
    case PLAYING_PHASE: //prepare the game engine
      //create objects in game engine
      ObjectManager.reset(); //clear object manager
      CreateObjects(); //create new objects
      //initialize graphics
      background.setpalette(lpPrimaryPalette); //game palette
      ComposeFrame(); PageFlip(); //prime animation pump
      break;
```

```
  }
} //change_phase

void Redraw(){ //redraw in response to surface loss
  switch(GamePhase){
    case LOGO_PHASE:
      display_screen("larc.bmp");
      break;
    case TITLE_PHASE:
      display_screen("title.bmp");
      break;
    case MENU_PHASE:
      display_screen("menu.bmp"); //display main menu
      break;
    case PLAYING_PHASE:
      //do nothing, next frame of animation will catch it
      break;
  }
}

void ProcessFrame(){ //process a frame of animation
  const int LOGO_DISPLAY_TIME=7000; //duration of logo
  const int TITLE_DISPLAY_TIME=10000; //duration of title
  //check for lost surfaces, e.g., alt+tab
  if(lpPrimary->IsLost()){
    RestoreSurfaces(); Redraw();
  }
  switch(GamePhase){ //what phase are we in?
    case LOGO_PHASE: //displaying logo screen
      Sleep(100); //surrender time to other processes
      if(endphase||Timer.elapsed(PhaseTime,LOGO_DISPLAY_TIME))
        change_phase(TITLE_PHASE); //go to title screen
      break;
    case TITLE_PHASE: //displaying title screen
      Sleep(100); //surrender time to other processes
      if(endphase||Timer.elapsed(PhaseTime,TITLE_DISPLAY_TIME))
        change_phase(MENU_PHASE); //go to menu
      break;
    case MENU_PHASE: //main menu
      Sleep(100); //surrender time to other processes
      if(endphase)change_phase(PLAYING_PHASE); //play game
      break;
    case PLAYING_PHASE: //game engine
      ComposeFrame(); //compose a frame in back surface
      PageFlip(); //flip video memory surfaces
      if(endphase||ObjectManager.won()) //if end of phase
        change_phase(MENU_PHASE); //go to menu
      break;
  }
} //ProcessFrame
```

```
//keyboard handlers

void intro_keyboard_handler(WPARAM keystroke){
  endphase=TRUE; //any key ends the phase
} //intro_keyboard_handler

BOOL menu_keyboard_handler(WPARAM keystroke){
  BOOL result=FALSE;
  switch(keystroke){
    case VK_ESCAPE:
    case 'Q': //exit game
      result=TRUE;
      break;
    case 'N': //play new game
      endphase=TRUE;
      break;
    default: break; //do nothing
  }
  return result;
} //menu_keyboard_handler

void game_keyboard_handler(WPARAM keystroke){
  switch(keystroke){
    case VK_ESCAPE: endphase=TRUE; break;
    case VK_UP: ObjectManager.accelerate(0,-1); break;
    case VK_DOWN: ObjectManager.accelerate(0,1); break;
    case VK_LEFT: ObjectManager.accelerate(-1,0); break;
    case VK_RIGHT: ObjectManager.accelerate(1,0); break;
    case VK_SPACE: ObjectManager.fire_gun(); break;
    default: break;
  }
} //game_keyboard_handler

BOOL keyboard_handler(WPARAM keystroke){ //keyboard handler
  BOOL result=FALSE; //TRUE if we are to exit game
  switch(GamePhase){ //select handler for phase
    case LOGO_PHASE:
    case TITLE_PHASE:
      intro_keyboard_handler(keystroke);
      break;
    case MENU_PHASE:
      result=menu_keyboard_handler(keystroke);
      break;
    case PLAYING_PHASE:
      game_keyboard_handler(keystroke);
      break;
  }
  return result;
} //keyboard_handler
```

```
//message handler (window procedure)
long CALLBACK WindowProc(HWND hwnd,UINT message,
                         WPARAM wParam,LPARAM lParam){
  switch(message){
    case WM_ACTIVATEAPP: ActiveApp=wParam; break;
    case WM_CREATE: break;
    case WM_KEYDOWN: //keyboard hit
      if(keyboard_handler(wParam))DestroyWindow(hwnd);
      break;
    case WM_DESTROY: //end of game
      if(lpDirectDrawObject!=NULL){ //if DD object exists
        if(lpSecondary!=NULL) //if secondary surface exists
          lpSecondary->Release(); //release secondary surface
        if(lpPrimary!=NULL) //if primary surface exists
          lpPrimary->Release(); //release primary surface
        if(lpBackground!=NULL) //if background exists
          lpBackground->Release(); //release background
        for(int i=0; i<NUM_SPRITES; i++){ //for each sprite
          if(g_pSprite[i]) //if sprite exists
            g_pSprite[i]->Release(); //release sprite
          delete g_pSprite[i]; //delete sprite
        }
        lpDirectDrawObject->Release(); //release DD object
      }
      ShowCursor(TRUE); //show the mouse cursor
      PostQuitMessage(0); //and exit
      break;
    default: //default window procedure
      return DefWindowProc(hwnd,message,wParam,lParam);
  } //switch(message)
  return 0L;
} //WindowProc

int WINAPI WinMain(HINSTANCE hInstance,HINSTANCE hPrevInstance,
LPSTR lpCmdLine,int nCmdShow){
  MSG msg; //current message
  HWND hwnd; //handle to full-screen window
  hwnd=CreateDefaultWindow("directX demo 7",hInstance);
  if(!hwnd)return FALSE;
  //set up window
  ShowWindow(hwnd,nCmdShow); UpdateWindow(hwnd);
  SetFocus(hwnd); //allow input from keyboard
  ShowCursor(FALSE); //hide the cursor
  //init graphics
  for(int i=0; i<NUM_SPRITES; i++) //null out sprites
    g_pSprite[i]=NULL;
  BOOL OK=InitDirectDraw(hwnd);//initialize DirectDraw
  if(OK)OK=LoadImages(); //load images from disk
  if(!OK){ //bail out if initialization failed
```

```
      DestroyWindow(hwnd); return FALSE;
   }
   //start game timer
   Timer.start();
   //set initial phase
   change_phase(LOGO_PHASE);
   //message loop
   while(TRUE)
      if(PeekMessage(&msg,NULL,0,0,PM_NOREMOVE)){
         if(!GetMessage(&msg,NULL,0,0))return msg.wParam;
         TranslateMessage(&msg); DispatchMessage(&msg);
      }
      else if(ActiveApp)ProcessFrame(); else WaitMessage();
} //WinMain
```

Chapter 10

Here's what you'll learn:

- What the major issues are in deciding on sound quality
- What the Nyquist frequency is and how it affects the sample rate
- How to set up DirectSound
- What a DirectSound buffer is and how to load sounds into it from WAV files
- How to play and mix sounds with DirectSound
- How to play looping sounds with DirectSound
- How to stop playing sounds in DirectSound
- How to play multiple copies of a sound without duplicating sound data

Sound

In Demo 8, we learn how to play digitally sampled sounds from files in WAV format. DirectSound enables us to play multiple sounds at the same time by digitally mixing the sound for us. Sounds are played asynchronously, which means that gameplay continues while the sound is being played. Although DirectSound only allows us to play one copy of each sound at a time, it gives us the facility to make multiple copies of a sound that share data, thus saving memory. In this chapter, we develop a sound manager that takes care of managing all of these copies. If you ask it to play a sound, it tries to locate a copy of the sound that isn't currently being played, and if it finds one, it begins to play it.

Experiment with Demo 8

Take a moment now to run Demo 8.

- Listen to the sounds! (Assuming that you have a sound card and speakers.)
- The logo and title screens have long sound samples containing music and voice-overs. In the game engine, the crows caw, the exploding crows go "boom," the gun goes "bang," the crow corpses go "thunk" when they hit the ground, and the plane goes "putt-putt."
- Notice that the logo sound stops if you click out of the logo screen. Similarly for the title sound and the game engine sounds.
- Notice that the plane sound is a single short "putt" sample played repeatedly to give a "putt-putt-putt-putt..." effect. Change the plane speed and notice that the sound changes too.
- Chase the crows, and notice that they caw when they enter the avoiding state. Each crow sample contains multiple caws, which makes a pleasant mix of sounds when several crows go into the avoiding state at about the same time.
- Exit the game, then double-click on some of the sound files in the Demo 8 folder, particularly `Caw.wav` and `Putt0.wav`, to see what they sound like outside of *Ned's Turkey Farm*.

The Sound List

Sndlist.h contains a pair of enumerated types for sound lists used during the game. We will use one sound list for the introduction sequence (the logo and title screens) and one sound list for the game engine. Sndlist.h begins with an obscure #define; later we will see a DirectSound function in which a particular parameter must be set to TRUE to make a sound play repeatedly. Instead, we will set it to LOOP_SOUND to make it more readable.

```
#define LOOP_SOUND TRUE
```

The first sound list is GameSoundType, which enumerates the sounds used in the game engine. The sound files will later be read in this order.

```
enum GameSoundType{ //sounds used in game engine
   CAW_SOUND=0, //sound a crow makes
   GUN_SOUND, //sound of gun firing
   BOOM_SOUND, //sound of explosion
   THUMP_SOUND, //sound of object hitting the ground
   //next 3 sounds must be consecutive and in this order
   SLOWPUTT_SOUND, //sound of slow engine
   MEDIUMPUTT_SOUND, //sound of medium engine
   FASTPUTT_SOUND //sound of fast engine
};
```

The second sound list is IntroSoundType, which enumerates the sounds used in the introduction sequence:

```
enum IntroSoundType{ //sounds used during the intro
   TITLE_SOUND=0, //sound used during title screen
   LOGO_SOUND, //signature chord
};
```

Sound Quality

As part of the game design, you have three choices to make regarding the quality of the sound samples in your game. In each of them there is a tradeoff: higher quality of sound means more data, which means more memory devoted to sound samples when your game is playing, more space on your CD to deliver them to the user, more time needed to load your sounds when the game begins, and more of your CPU processing power and bus bandwidth needed to play them. (Forget what I said about processing power and bus bandwidth for that lucky fraction of your customers who have high-end sound cards; they will store the sounds in memory on the sound card and play them directly without much supervision from the CPU.)

The first choice is stereo versus mono sound. Stereo sound takes twice as much memory as mono sound, but of course sounds much better. If you want to use

DirectSound's 3D sound facilities (which are out of the scope of this book), you will need to use mono sound. Is stereo sound overkill for your game? Is halving the amount of space for the sounds more important than stereo sound? For *Ned's Turkey Farm,* we will choose compactness over coolness by opting for mono sound.

The second choice is the number of bits per sample, usually set at either 8 (for low-quality sound) or 16 (for high-quality sound). While 16-bit sound takes twice as much memory as 8-bit sound, it takes a good ear and an excellent sound system to tell the difference between the two. It is most important on parts of the sound sample that have very low volume. The most noticeable difference is usually a higher level of background hiss on the 8-bit sound samples.

The final choice is the sample rate, which is the rate at which the sound is digitally sampled. This is measured in Hertz (Hz for short), which means "samples per second." The most common sample rates in Hertz are 8000, 11025, 12000, 16000, 22050, 24000, 32000, 44100, and 48000 (usually referred to as 8, 11, 12, 16, 22, 24, 32, 44, and 48 kHz, although this is not strictly accurate). The higher the sample rate, the higher the quality of the sound reproduction. With a low sample rate, the high frequency sounds are missed completely. If you have a game in which all of the sounds are fairly low frequency (for example, with no female voices), then 11 kHz is enough. If you have a fairly normal mix of sound frequencies, then 22 kHz is enough. The frequency of sounds that can be reproduced at a given sample rate is called the *Nyquist frequency.* The Nyquist frequency is half the sample rate, so for example, 22 kHz sampling can reproduce sounds that have a frequency of up to 11 kHz. The amount of memory needed to store a sound increases with the sample rate—doubling the sample rate will double the memory requirements.

Take a moment now to compare the sound samples in the folder Sound Test. All of the folders referred to below (mono, bits, rate, and quality) are subfolders of Sound Test. Each folder contains two or more sound files. Double-clicking on each sound file will cause it to play using whatever default player is installed on your computer. The best way to listen for the differences in sound quality is to wear headphones while performing these tests.

- Start in folder Mono. First, play file Stereo.wav. An overblown panning effect has been used to make it sound truly *stereo.* Then, play Mono.wav. It sounds flat and uninteresting compared to the stereo version. Now look at the file sizes: 363 KB for the stereo version, 182 KB for the mono version.

- Go to folder Bits. First, play the 16-bit version 16bit.wav, then the 8-bit version 8bit.wav. Unless your ear is very good and your sound system is excellent, you may not be able to hear much difference between the files except for a higher level of hiss in 8bit.wav (you may need to crank the volume a little—but not too much—to hear it). Now look at the file sizes: 363 KB for the 16-bit version, 182 KB for the 8-bit version.

- Go to folder `Rate`. First, play `22KHz.wav`. Then, play `11KHz.wav`, which should sound a little muffled compared to `22KHz.wav`. Finally, play `8KHz.wav`, which should sound even more muffled. The muffled sound quality comes from the suppression of the high frequency part of Mikayla's voice due to the Nyquist frequency. Personally, I think that 22 kHz is acceptable; 11 kHz might be acceptable under certain circumstances but I would rather not use it; and 8 kHz is flat-out unacceptable. You might not agree with me. Now look at the file sizes: 363 KB for the 22 kHz version, 182 KB for the 11 kHz version, and 132 KB for the 8 kHz version.

- Go to folder `Quality`. Compare the sound of `High.wav` (16-bit stereo, 22 kHz) to that of `Low.wav` (8-bit mono, 11 kHz). Which sounds better? Now look at the file sizes: 363 KB for `High.wav`, and 46 KB for `Low.wav`. The low-quality sound sample is under 13% of the size of the high-quality one, smaller by a factor of more than nine.

Which is more important to the sales of your game—sound quality or size? It's up to you to decide. Changing your mind doesn't involve much programming. We will see in a moment that it just means changing a few constants and recompiling.

The Sound Manager

Sound Manager Overview

The header file for the sound manager class `CSoundManager` is `Sound.h`. It begins with a definition for the maximum number of different sound samples that the sound manager can store.

```
#define MAX_SOUNDS 64 //maximum number of different sounds
```

The next definition is the number of channels, which is related to the number of sounds that can be played simultaneously. Mono sound requires one channel per sound, and stereo requires two channels per sound.

```
#define DS_NUMCHANNELS 8 //number of channels
```

The next definition is the number of channels per sound, which is one for mono sound and two for stereo sound. With the settings you have seen so far, we will be able to play eight mono sounds simultaneously.

```
#define DS_CHANSPERSAMPLE 1 //mono sound
```

The next definition is the number of bits per sample, which we will set to 8 for low quality but compact sound:

```
#define DS_BITSPERSAMPLE 8 //8-bit sound
```

The final definition is the sample rate, which we will set to 22 kHz:

```
#define DS_SAMPLERATE 22050 //22KHz sampling
```

CSoundManager has five private member variables. We start with a counter for the number of distinct sounds loaded so far.

```
int m_nCount; //number of sounds loaded
```

The m_lpDirectSound member variable stores a pointer to the DirectSound object, which is the DirectX object that gives us direct access to the sound hardware on our computer:

```
LPDIRECTSOUND m_lpDirectSound; //DirectSound object
```

Just as the DirectDraw object stores images on surfaces, the DirectSound object stores sounds in *sound buffers*. The best way to think of a sound buffer is that it is like a cassette player. It contains a playback head that tells it where to start playing from, and it contains the media to play from—for a cassette player that's a cassette, and for the sound buffer it's a chunk of memory containing the digital sample. The CSoundManager member variable m_lpBuffer is an array of MAX_SOUNDS pointers, each of which will point to an array containing the appropriate number of pointers to the copies of a sound (see Figure 10.1).

```
LPLPDIRECTSOUNDBUFFER m_lpBuffer[MAX_SOUNDS]; //sound buffers
```

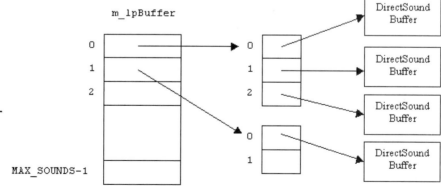

Figure 10.1
The CSound-Manager member variable m_lpBuffer in use

A parallel array m_nCopyCount (parallel to m_lpBuffer) will count the number of copies of each sound. By parallel array we mean that m_nCopyCount[i] will contain the number of copies of the sound number i, so that m_lpBuffer[i] points to an array of m_nCopyCount[i] pointers to sound buffers, each of which will contain a copy of the sound. For example, in Figure 10.1, m_nCopyCount[0] is 3, and m_nCopyCount[1] is 2.

```
int m_nCopyCount[MAX_SOUNDS]; //num copies of each sound
```

We keep a member variable m_bOperational, which will be set to TRUE if DirectSound was initialized correctly. We will use this to bail out of CSoundManager public member functions when DirectSound is not present (for example, if DirectX is not installed, or the computer has no sound card).

```
BOOL m_bOperational; //DirectSound initialized correctly
```

CSoundManager has four private member functions for managing sound buffers. Function CreateBuffer has three integer parameters, index, length, and copies. It creates an array of copies pointers to DirectSound sound buffers, one for each copy of sound number index, and makes m_lpBuffer[index] point to this array. It then creates a DirectSound sound buffer to store a sample of the given length, and sets m_lpBuffer[index][0] to point to the new buffer. The sound buffers for the other copies will be created later by CSoundManager function CopyBuffer (see Figure 10.1).

```
BOOL CreateBuffer(int index,int length,int copies);
```

The next three private member functions LoadBuffer, LoadSound, and CopyBuffer take care of loading sounds into the DirectSound sound buffers. The three-step process is illustrated in Figure 10.2.

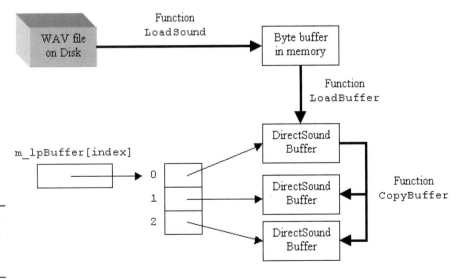

Figure 10.2
The process of loading a sound

Function `LoadBuffer` has three parameters, the integer `index` of a sound, a byte `buffer` containing sound data, and the integer `length` of the byte buffer. It copies the sound data from the `buffer` into the data area of the first copy of the sound in `m_lpBuffer[index]` (that is, to the DirectSound sound buffer pointed to by `*m_lpBuffer[index]`, equivalently, `m_lpBuffer[index][0]`).

```
BOOL LoadBuffer(int index,BYTE *buffer,int length);
```

Function `LoadSound` has two parameters, the name of a file in WAV format as a character string `filename` and the address of a pointer to a byte buffer to receive the sound data, called `sound`. This function queries the file to find the size of the sound data, allocates a large enough buffer to hold it, and loads the sound data from the file into the buffer. It also returns a pointer to the start of the buffer through the parameter `sound` (which is declared as a pointer to a pointer to a byte buffer to facilitate this return) and returns the length of the buffer in the conventional way.

```
int LoadSound(char *filename,BYTE **sound); //load from file
```

Function `CopyBuffer` uses the DirectSound function `DuplicateSound-Buffer` to copy the sound from the DirectSound buffer pointed to by `m_lpBuffer[index][0]` to the DirectSound buffers pointed to by `m_lpBuffer[index][i]` for i ranging from 1 to `copies-1`, inclusive. It does so without duplicating the sound data, which will be shared from the first copy to the other copies. Each copy can independently play from arbitrary points in the same sound data (see Figure 10.3).

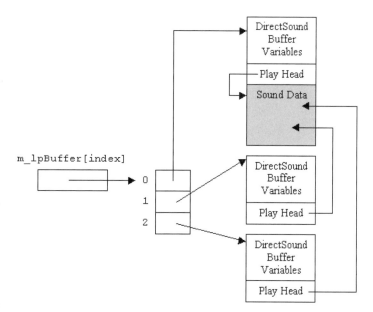

Figure 10.3
CopyBuffer creates copies that share sound data

```
BOOL CopyBuffer(int index,int copies); //copy sound
```

CSoundManager has seven public member functions, including a constructor and a destructor:

```
CSoundManager(HWND hwnd); //constructor
~CSoundManager(); //destructor
```

Function clear clears all sounds, reclaiming all of the memory used to store the sound data:

```
void clear(); //clear all sounds
```

Function load has two parameters, the name of a file in WAV format as a character string filename and an integer number of copies of that sound needed (which defaults to 1 if it is not provided). It uses the private member functions to load that many copies of the sound in the file to the next available slot in the sound list m_lpBuffer. Slots in the sound list will be filled in numerical order from slot 0 to slot MAX_SOUNDS-1.

```
void load(char *filename,int copies=1); //load from file
```

Function play has two parameters, the first of which is an integer index. It plays the next unused copy of the sound from the copies in the array pointed to by m_lpBuffer[index]. If the second parameter (which defaults to FALSE if it is not provided) is TRUE, the sound is played looping.

```
void play(int index,BOOL looping=FALSE); //play sound
```

There are two versions of the stop function. The first has a single parameter, an integer index. It stops all copies of the sound m_lpBuffer[index] that are currently playing and resets their play heads back to the start of the sample. The second version of the stop function has no parameters. It does the same thing to all sounds, that is, to all copies of all currently playing sounds.

```
void stop(int index); //stop playing sound
void stop(void); //stop playing all sounds
```

The Constructor and Destructor

The code file for the sound manager class CSoundManager is Sound.cpp. It begins with the CSoundManager constructor, which has a window handle as a single parameter. It begins by setting the number of loaded sounds to zero.

```
CSoundManager::CSoundManager(HWND hwnd){ //constructor
  m_nCount=0; //no sounds yet
```

Next, it NULLs out the sound buffer copy pointers and zeros the copy counts:

```
//null out sound buffers and flags
for(int i=0; i<MAX_SOUNDS; i++){
```

```
    m_lpBuffer[i]=NULL; m_nCopyCount[i]=0;
  }
```

Starting DirectSound looks quite a bit like starting DirectDraw. First, we call the DirectSound `DirectSoundCreate` function, which has three parameters. The first parameter is the GUID of a sound device, which can be set to `NULL` for the default device. The second parameter is the address of a place to put a pointer to the DirectSound object; we ask `DirectSoundCreate` to put this pointer into the private member variable `m_lpDirectSound`. The third parameter must be set to `NULL`. `DirectSoundCreate` will return the DirectX defined constant `DS_OK` if it succeeds. We bail out if it fails.

```
    m_bOperational=SUCCEEDED(
      DirectSoundCreate(NULL,&m_lpDirectSound,NULL));
    if(!m_bOperational)return;
```

The next thing that must be done is to set the cooperative level by calling the DirectSound object's `SetCooperativeLevel` member function. The first parameter of this function is the window handle of our application (which is why we specify it as a parameter to the constructor). The second parameter is a cooperative level, which we set to allow the maximum amount of sharing of the sound hardware with other applications.

```
    m_bOperational=SUCCEEDED(m_lpDirectSound->
      SetCooperativeLevel(hwnd,DSSCL_NORMAL));
  }
```

Next, we have the `CSoundManager` destructor, which (provided the DirectSound object exists) calls the `CSoundManager` `clear` member function to dispose of all of the sound buffers, and then calls the DirectSound object's `Release` member function to release the DirectSound object:

```
CSoundManager::~CSoundManager(){ //destructor
  if(!m_bOperational)return;
  clear(); //clear all buffers
  (void)m_lpDirectSound->Release(); //release DirectSound
}
```

The Clear Function

The `CSoundManager` `clear` function resets the sound manager so that it is ready to load new sounds. It bails out if the sound manager is not operational.

```
void CSoundManager::clear(){ //clear all sounds
  if(!m_bOperational)return;
```

We call the `CSoundManager` `stop` function without any parameters to stop all sounds:

```
  stop(); //stop all sounds (paranoia)
```

For each sound, we do the following:

```
for(int i=0; i<m_nCount; i++){ //for each sound
```

For each copy of each sound, we call the DirectSound sound buffer's `Release` function to release the buffer:

```
for(int j=0; j<m_nCopyCount[i]; j++){ //for each copy
  m_lpBuffer[i][j]->Release(); //release the sound
  m_lpBuffer[i][j]=NULL; //probably not needed
}
```

We then delete the array created in the constructor for the pointers to the copies of the current sound:

```
delete[]m_lpBuffer[i];
}
```

We set the count member variable to zero to indicate that there are no sounds currently loaded, and exit:

```
m_nCount=0; //no sounds left (hopefully)
}
```

The Load Function

The `CSoundManager` load function has two parameters, the `filename` of a file to load and the number of `copies` of that sound that we want to be able to play simultaneously:

```
void CSoundManager::load(char *filename,int copies){
```

It has two local variables, one for the length of the sound data (which we will get from the file), and a byte pointer that we will use to allocate a byte buffer of that length:

```
int length; //length of sound
BYTE *sound=NULL; //temporary buffer to hold sound data
```

We bail out if there is no DirectSound object, or if there is no space left in the sound list:

```
if(!m_bOperational)return; //bail if not initialized
if(m_nCount>=MAX_SOUNDS)return; //bail if no space left
```

We call the `CSoundManager` private member function `LoadSound` to load the sound from the file named `filename` into a byte buffer of the appropriate size, putting a pointer to the buffer in the local variable `sound` and the length of the buffer in the local variable `length`:

```
length=LoadSound(filename,&sound); //load sound from file
```

Next, we call the `CSoundManager` private member function `CreateBuffer` to create `copies` DirectSound sound buffers of length `length`, pointed to by `m_lpBuffer[m_nCount]`, the next empty slot in the sound list (see Figure 10.1):

```
CreateBuffer(m_nCount,length,copies); //create buffers
```

A call to the `CSoundManager` private member function `LoadBuffer` loads the sound from the byte buffer `sound` of length `length` into the first of the copy buffers pointed to by `m_lpBuffer[m_nCount]`.

```
LoadBuffer(m_nCount,sound,length); //load into buffer
```

Finally, a call to the `CSoundManager` private member function `CopyBuffer` creates duplicates of the sound buffer pointed to by `*m_lpBuffer[m_nCount][0]` for the remaining `copies-1` copies of that sound. (For an overview of the `LoadSound`—`LoadBuffer`—`CopyBuffer` process, refer back to Figure 10.2.)

```
CopyBuffer(m_nCount,copies); //make copies of contents
```

Cleanup consists of deleting the byte buffer created by the call to `LoadSound` and incrementing the counter so that the next call to the `CSoundManager` load function will load into the next slot in the sound list. This ends the `CSoundManager` load function.

```
//clean up and exit
delete[]sound; //delete temporary sound buffer
m_nCount++; //increment counter
}
```

The Play Function

The `CSoundManager` play function plays the next unused copy of the sound from the copies in the array pointed to by `m_lpBuffer[index]`, looping if `looping` is `TRUE`. It bails out if there is no DirectSound object or if the `index` is out of range.

```
void CSoundManager::play(int index,BOOL looping){ //play sound
  if(!m_bOperational)return; //bail if not initialized
  if(index<0||index>=m_nCount)return; //bail if bad index
```

It has two local variables, an index variable called `copy` in which we will store the index of the current copy and a `status` word that we will use to store the playing status of the current copy:

```
int copy=0; //current copy
DWORD status; //status of that copy
```

We begin by getting the status of the first copy of the sound (copy 0). This is done by calling the GetStatus member function of the DirectSound buffer holding the copy. This function takes as a parameter the address of a DWORD variable in which to place a status word and returns DS_OK if it succeeds in getting the status. If it fails, we will assume that the copy is currently playing, so that it is skipped over in the search for a copy to play.

```
if(FAILED(m_lpBuffer[index][copy]->GetStatus(&status)))
  status=DSBSTATUS_PLAYING; //assume playing if failed
```

If the copy is playing, the DSBSTATUS_PLAYING bit of status will be set. As is normal in windows flags, each bit of status corresponds to some property that is either on (if the bit is set) or off (if the bit is unset). The DirectSound constant DSBSTATUS_PLAYING is a power of two (it doesn't matter which one), which means that its binary representation has exactly one bit set, and so the way to check whether that particular bit is set in status is to use the bitwise logical AND operator "&", and check for a nonzero result. So, we use a while loop to march copy from 1 (we did 0 already) to the number of remaining copies m_nCopyCount[index]-1, exiting the loop when either copy goes out of range or we find a copy that is not being currently played.

```
while(copy<m_nCopyCount[index]&&
(status&DSBSTATUS_PLAYING)){ //while current copy in use
```

We increment copy, and check to see that it is still in range (note the pre-increment):

```
if(++copy<m_nCopyCount[index]) //go to next copy
```

We get the status of this new copy and loop back to test the status again:

```
    if(FAILED(m_lpBuffer[index][copy]->GetStatus(&status)))
      status=DSBSTATUS_PLAYING; //assume playing if failed
}
```

Having exited the while loop, we check to see whether copy is in range:

```
if(copy<m_nCopyCount[index]) //if unused copy found
```

If it is, then this copy must not be playing. We play it using the DirectSound buffer's Play member function, which has three parameters. The first parameter must be zero. The second parameter is a priority for the sound, which must be set to zero because we are not using prioritized sound in *Ned's Turkey Farm*. The third parameter is a flags word, in which we set the DSBPLAY_LOOPING bit if the parameter looping is TRUE. This ends the CSoundManager play function.

```
m_lpBuffer[index][copy]->
  Play(0,0,looping?DSBPLAY_LOOPING:0); //play it
}
```

The Stop Functions

The first of two CSoundManager stop functions has as a parameter the index of the sound that we wish to stop playing. As always, it bails out if necessary.

```
void CSoundManager::stop(int index){ //stop playing sound
  if(!m_bOperational)return; //bail if not initialized
  if(index<0||index>=m_nCount)return; //bail if bad index
```

For each copy of the sound, we stop it by calling the DirectSound buffer's Stop member function. Calling Stop on a nonplaying sound has no effect, so we can go ahead and call it for all copies. Just like a cassette player, the DirectSound Stop function stops the tape and leaves the play head somewhere in the middle of the sound. If we were to play this copy again, it would start playing from where it left off. We will use this facility in Chapter 15 to pause the sounds, but here we will rewind the sound back to the beginning by calling the DirectSound buffer's SetCurrentPosition function to rewind back to zero.

```
for(int i=0; i<m_nCopyCount[index]; i++){ //for each copy
  m_lpBuffer[index][i]->Stop(); //stop playing
  m_lpBuffer[index][i]->SetCurrentPosition(0); //rewind
  }
}
```

The second CSoundManager stop function stops all sounds by calling the first stop function once for each sound:

```
void CSoundManager::stop(void){ //stop playing sound
  if(!m_bOperational)return; //bail if not initialized
  for(int index=0; index<m_nCount; index++) //for each sound
    stop(index); //stop that sound
}
```

The CopyBuffer Function

The CSoundManager CopyBuffer function makes duplicates of the sound from the first sound buffer for the other copies. It does so without duplicating the sound data (see Figure 10.3). CopyBuffer has two parameters containing the index of the sound and the number of copies, respectively. It returns TRUE if it succeeds.

```
BOOL CSoundManager::CopyBuffer(int index,int copies){
```

It bails out if DirectSound is not operational:

```
if(!m_bOperational)return FALSE; //bail if not initialized
```

A local variable result holds the return result:

```
BOOL result=TRUE; //TRUE if everything went OK
```

The number of copies is recorded in the appropriate place:

```
m_nCopyCount[index]=copies; //record number of copies
```

The copies are made using the DirectSound object's `DuplicateSoundBuffer` function to duplicate the sound buffer from the first copy of the sound to all of the others. The same buffer memory is used for all of the copies; think of them as a collection of cassette players that share a single tape. Each one can be played, stopped, and rewound independently; they just share the same media.

```
for(int i=1; i<copies; i++) //for each copy
   result=result&& //copy the sound
      SUCCEEDED(m_lpDirectSound->
         DuplicateSoundBuffer(*m_lpBuffer[index],
         &(m_lpBuffer[index][i])));
```

If any one or more of the calls to `DuplicateSoundBuffer` returned a value other than `DS_OK`, then `result` was set to `FALSE`. When the copies have been made, the `CSoundManager CopyBuffer` function returns `result` and exits.

```
   return result;
}
```

The CreateBuffer Function

Function `CreateBuffer` creates the sound buffers for sound number `index`, of length `length`, with `copies` copies:

```
BOOL CSoundManager::CreateBuffer(int index,int length,
                                 int copies){
   if(!m_bOperational)return FALSE; //bail if not initialized
```

Local variables include a DirectSound buffer descriptor and a PCM wave format structure from the Windows API:

```
DSBUFFERDESC dsbdesc;
PCMWAVEFORMAT pcmwf;
```

This next line of code should probably be moved to the front of the function:

```
if(length<=0)return FALSE; //bail if length info wrong
```

First, we zero out the wave format structure:

```
memset(&pcmwf,0,sizeof(PCMWAVEFORMAT));
```

Then, we start filling out the fields. The `wf` field is a `WAVEFORMAT` structure. The first field in this substructure is `wFormatTag`, the format tag, which must be set to `WAVE_FORMAT_PCM`—there is no other choice.

```
pcmwf.wf.wFormatTag=WAVE_FORMAT_PCM;
```

The nChannels field is set to the number of channels, indicating mono or stereo:

```
pcmwf.wf.nChannels=DS_CHANSPERSAMPLE;
```

The nSamplesPerSec field is set to the sample rate:

```
pcmwf.wf.nSamplesPerSec=DS_SAMPLERATE;
```

The nBlockAlign field is set to the number of bytes per sample:

```
pcmwf.wf.nBlockAlign=
    DS_CHANSPERSAMPLE*DS_BITSPERSAMPLE/8;
```

The nAvgBytesPerSec field is set to the sample rate multiplied by bytes per sample:

```
pcmwf.wf.nAvgBytesPerSec=
    pcmwf.wf.nSamplesPerSec*pcmwf.wf.nBlockAlign;
```

This completes the wf field of pcmwf. The wBitsPerSample field of pcmwf is set to the number of bits per sample.

```
pcmwf.wBitsPerSample=DS_BITSPERSAMPLE;
```

Next, we fill in the DirectSound buffer descriptor dsbdesc, starting by zeroing it out and setting its size field:

```
memset(&dsbdesc,0,sizeof(DSBUFFERDESC));
dsbdesc.dwSize=sizeof(DSBUFFERDESC);
```

The dwFlags field must be set to request the capabilities of the requested buffers. We set it to DSBCAPS_STATIC, which means that the sound in these buffers will not be edited, and thus that it is a candidate to be loaded to the sound card's memory, if such a thing exists.

```
dsbdesc.dwFlags=DSBCAPS_STATIC;
```

The dwBufferBytes field is set to the length of the buffer, which is provided by the parameter length:

```
dsbdesc.dwBufferBytes=length;
```

The lpwfxFormat is set to the address of the WAVEFORMAT structure that we filled in above. This tells it important things like the playback sample rate.

```
dsbdesc.lpwfxFormat=(LPWAVEFORMATEX)&pcmwf;
```

Before actually creating the buffers to these specifications, we create space for the pointers to the buffers for the copies of the current sound (the blocks at the center of Figure 10.1):

```
m_lpBuffer[index]=new LPDIRECTSOUNDBUFFER[copies];
```

We NULL out the pointers to indicate that there are no buffers yet:

```
for(int i=0; i<copies; i++)m_lpBuffer[index][i]=NULL;
```

Finally, we ask the DirectSound object to create a sound buffer for the first copy of the sound according to the specifications set in dsbdesc. Don't be confused by the second parameter; it is asking that a pointer to the sound buffer be placed in *m_lpBuffer[index], not m_lpBuffer[index] itself. The last parameter of CreateSoundBuffer is yet another "this must be NULL" parameter. Function CreateBuffer then returns TRUE if this call to CreateSoundBuffer is DS_OK.

```
  return SUCCEEDED(m_lpDirectSound->
    CreateSoundBuffer(&dsbdesc,m_lpBuffer[index],NULL));
}
```

The LoadBuffer Function

Function LoadBuffer loads sound data from a byte buffer sound of length length into the DirectSound buffer pointed to by *m_lpBuffer[index].

```
BOOL CSoundManager::LoadBuffer(int index,BYTE *sound,int length){
  if(!m_bOperational)return FALSE; //bail if not initialized
```

Up until now you may have assumed that loading a DirectSound buffer simply involves copying the sound data from the byte buffer to the data field of the DirectSound buffer using either the C standard library function memcpy or the Windows API function CopyMemory. Unfortunately, it is not quite this easy. The sound data inside the DirectSound buffer may be circularly shifted within the buffer by an arbitrary amount, so we will need to use two calls to the CopyMemory function to load the sound data. Before we can load the data, we will need to lock down the DirectSound buffer using its Lock function (which is analogous to locking down a DirectDraw surface). This function will return two pointers w1,w2 and two lengths 11,12 (Note: This is *ell-one* and *ell-two*, *not* eleven and twelve), one for each block of data in the DirectSound buffer (see Figure 10.4). We begin by declaring local variables to hold these values.

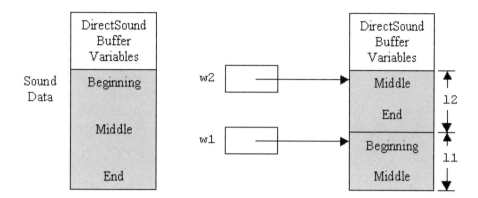

Figure 10.4
How we would like DirectSound buffers to be (left), and how they actually are (right), showing how the DirectSound buffer Lock function sets the local variables w1, w2, l1, and l2 in the CSoundManager LoadBuffer function.

```
LPVOID w1,w2; //write pointer (use 2 for buffer wraparound)
DWORD l1,l2; //length of sound to be written to write pointers
```

We get a pointer directly to the DirectSound buffer into which we're going to be loading data:

```
LPDIRECTSOUNDBUFFER buffer=*m_lpBuffer[index];
```

Just to be paranoid, we make sure that the length information is sensible:

```
if(length<=0)return FALSE; //bail if length info wrong
```

Now, we use the DirectSound buffer's Lock function to lock down the buffer so that we can write to it. The first two parameters of this function are the index of the first byte and the length of the area to be locked. We can use this to lock down only a portion of the sound buffer, but here we are locking down the whole thing. The next four parameters are the addresses of two pointers and two lengths as depicted in Figure 10.4. The last parameter is a flags word, which we are ignoring. If the lock fails due to a lost buffer (similar to losing a DirectDraw surface), we try restoring the buffer once and try the lock again. If that fails, then we bail out of the CSoundManager LoadBuffer function.

```
if(buffer->Lock(0,length,&w1,&l1,&w2,&l2,0)//lock down buffer
==DSERR_BUFFERLOST){ //if buffer lost
```

```
    buffer->Restore(); //restore, then try again
    if(FAILED(buffer->Lock(0,length,&w1,&l1,&w2,&l2,0)))
      return FALSE; //abort if failed the second time
  }
```

Now that we have the buffer locked down, we can load the first 11 bytes of sound to w1:

```
    CopyMemory(w1,sound,l1); //load first half
```

Now, things just might look like the left side of Figure 10.4 if we're lucky, in which case w2 will be NULL. If it is, we are finished already. Otherwise, we need to copy the last 12 bytes of sound to w2.

```
    if(w2!=NULL)CopyMemory(w2,sound+l1,l2); //load second half
```

Finally, we unlock the buffer and return:

```
    if(FAILED(buffer->Unlock(w1,l1,w2,l2)))return FALSE;
    return TRUE;
  }
```

The LoadSound Function

The last CSoundManager function in Sound.cpp is LoadSound, which loads a sound from a WAV file into a byte buffer. This function uses Windows MMIO functions, which are outside the scope of this book. If you *really* want to know what is going on inside that function, the code is listed at the end of this chapter.

Changes to the Object Classes

Now that we have a sound manager, we can use it to play sounds. It can be very tempting to splatter "play sound" code all through your game, which can make it difficult to maintain. To reduce the amount of code clutter, I have adopted the following simple policy: every object in the game is responsible for playing its own sounds. I could have chosen to have the object manager play the sounds, or have them played in Main.cpp, but it is easier (and intellectually satisfying) to have the low-level CObject and CIntelligentObject classes responsible for their own noises.

Changes to the Base Object

Some objects make a sound when they are created. This sound code goes into the CObject constructor. In the switch statement that separates the code by object type, we add the following to the appropriate cases. For the plane, since it starts out moving slowly, we play the slow engine noise sound. Recall that LOOP_SOUND was aliased to TRUE in Sound.h, so that the sound is played looped.

```
SoundManager->play(SLOWPUTT_SOUND,LOOP_SOUND);
```

The creation of a bullet is accompanied by the sound of gunfire:

```
SoundManager->play(GUN_SOUND); //sound of gun firing
```

The creation of an exploding crow is accompanied by the sound of an explosion:

```
SoundManager->play(BOOM_SOUND); //sound of explosion
```

The CObject accelerate function must take care of changing the engine sound when the plane changes speed. First, it saves the old horizontal speed in a local variable old_xspeed.

```
int old_xspeed=m_nXspeed; //old speed
```

We check that the object is indeed the plane and it has actually changed speed. Why do we check that the speed has actually changed? Because the player may hit the accelerate key when the plane is already at maximum speed, and if we are not careful, our code may restart the engine sound anyway, making the engine seem to stutter. The old_xspeed!=m_nXspeed check prevents this from happening.

```
if(m_eObject==PLANE_OBJECT&&old_xspeed!=m_nXspeed){
```

We stop all of the engine sounds (it is faster to stop them all than it is to find out which one is actually playing, and then stop just that one):

```
SoundManager->stop(SLOWPUTT_SOUND);
SoundManager->stop(MEDIUMPUTT_SOUND);
SoundManager->stop(FASTPUTT_SOUND);
```

Now we restart the engine sound. Which one? Well, the comments in Sndlist.h indicate that the three engine sound definitions should be consecutive, so that SLOWPUTT_SOUND+1 is MEDIUMPUTT_SOUND, and MEDIUMPUTT_SOUND+1 is FASTPUTT_SOUND. If m_nXspeed is -1, we want to play SLOWPUTT_SOUND. If m_nXspeed is -2, we want to play MEDIUMPUTT_SOUND, which is SLOWPUTT_SOUND+1. If m_nXspeed is -3, we want to play FASTPUTT_SOUND, which is SLOWPUTT_SOUND+2. Therefore, we play sound SLOWPUTT_SOUND-1 +abs(m_nXspeed). This completes the changes to the CObject accelerate function.

```
SoundManager->
    play(SLOWPUTT_SOUND-1+abs(m_nXspeed),LOOP_SOUND);
}
```

The last sound change to the object class involves the CObject move function. In FALLING_MOTION case, we want things that fall to go "thunk" when they hit the bottom of the screen. This is a good time to force falling objects to be culled then too. If the object's m_nY coordinate is greater than SCREEN_HEIGHT, we play the sound and force a cull by making the object mortal with a lifespan of zero.

This ensures that it will be culled the next time that the object manager's `cull` function is called (see Chapter 8).

```
if(m_nY>SCREEN_HEIGHT){
  SoundManager->play(THUMP_SOUND); //object hitting ground
  m_nLifeTime=0; m_eMortality=MORTAL; //force cull
}
```

Changes to the Intelligent Object

Since the changes to `CIntelligentObject` in Demo 8 are extremely minor—the addition of a single line of code—`Ai.cpp` is not listed at the end of this chapter with the other changed files. The change makes the crows caw when they enter the avoiding state. In the `CIntelligentObject set_state` function, under the `AVOIDING_STATE` case, we add a call to `SoundManager-> play(CAW_SOUND)`. The entire function is listed below so you can see this line of code in the correct context.

```
void CIntelligentObject::set_state(StateType state){
  m_eState=state; //change state
  switch(m_eState){ //change behavior settings
    case CRUISING_STATE:
      m_nAiDelayTime=300+Random.number(0,300);
      m_nXspeed=-1;
      m_nHeightDelayTime=8000+Random.number(0,5000);
      break;
    case AVOIDING_STATE:
      SoundManager->play(CAW_SOUND); //sound of crow cawing
      m_nAiDelayTime=200+Random.number(0,200);
      m_nXspeed=-3;
      m_nDesiredHeight=Random.number(100,400);
      m_nHeightDelayTime=3000+Random.number(0,2000);
      m_nSpeedVariationDuration=5000+Random.number(0,2000);
      break;
    default: break;
  }
}
```

Changes to Main.cpp

Changes to `Main.cpp` involve creating and setting up the sound manager. Near the top of `Main.cpp`, we add the declaration of a pointer to a sound manager. Why have we declared a pointer to a sound manager instead of declaring a sound manager? Because if we did the latter, the `CSoundManager` constructor would run before `WinMain`. However, the constructor needs a window handle to pass along to DirectSound, and we won't have a window handle until the window is created in

`WinMain`. Therefore, we'll actually create the sound manager later, when a window handle is available.

```
CSoundManager* SoundManager; //sound manager
```

Function `LoadSounds` loads the sounds for a particular level. We are not going to use its functionality to have different sounds for different levels, but we will use level 0 for intro sounds and level 1 for all of the other sounds.

```
void LoadSounds(int level=0){ //load sounds for level
```

We'll arbitrarily say that if we keep multiple copies of a sound, we will keep four copies of it. This number was chosen because it just sounded right during play testing. You may want to set this as high as eight.

```
const int copies=4; //copies of repeatable sounds
```

We have the ability to load a different set of sounds for different levels using a `switch` statement on the parameter `level`:

```
switch(level){
```

The intro sounds must be loaded in the same order as the constants in the enumerated type `IntroSoundType` in `Sndlist.h`. This sounds a little clumsy and difficult to maintain, but usually the only changes that are made to the load sequence is to add new sounds to the end of the list. Very rarely is it necessary to reorder the loading order, so why make the code more complicated than necessary?

```
case 0: //intro sounds
  SoundManager->load("intro.wav");
  SoundManager->load("larc.wav");
  break;
```

The game sounds must be loaded in the same order as the constants in the enumerated type `GameSoundType` in `Sndlist.h`. We create multiple copies of the sounds made by the crows, the gun, the exploding crows, and the dead crows.

```
case 1: //game engine sounds
  SoundManager->load("caw.wav",copies);
  SoundManager->load("gun.wav",copies);
  SoundManager->load("boom.wav",copies);
  SoundManager->load("thump.wav",copies);
  SoundManager->load("putt0.wav");
  SoundManager->load("putt1.wav");
  SoundManager->load("putt2.wav");
  break;
  }
}
```

Function `change_phase` must be modified to load the sounds for each phase. To the `LOGO_PHASE` case of the switch statement, we add code to load the intro sounds and begin playing the logo sound.

```
LoadSounds(); //load sounds for intro sequence
SoundManager->play(LOGO_SOUND); //signature chord
```

To the `TITLE_PHASE` case we add code to stop playing all sounds (in case the player clicked out of the logo phase) and begin playing the title sound:

```
SoundManager->stop(); //silence previous phase
SoundManager->play(TITLE_SOUND); //title sound
```

To the `MENU_PHASE` case, we add code to stop playing all sounds (in case the player clicked out of the title phase):

```
SoundManager->stop(); //silence previous phase
```

To the `PLAYING_PHASE` case we add code to stop playing all sounds (out of pure paranoia, since no sounds will be playing), clear the sound manager, and load the game sounds. This ends the changes to function `change_phase`.

```
SoundManager->stop(); //silence previous phase
SoundManager->clear(); //clear out old sounds
LoadSounds(1); //load game sounds
```

In `WindowProc`, we add code to shut down the sound manager in response to the `WM_DESTROY` message:

```
delete SoundManager; //reclaim sound manager memory
```

In `WinMain`, we can create a sound manager at any time after we have a handle to the application window and before the message loop:

```
SoundManager=new CSoundManager(hwnd);
```

Demo 8 Files

Code Files

The following files in Demo 8 are used without change from Demo 7:

- Ai.h
- Bmp.h
- Bmp.cpp
- Bsprite.h
- Bsprite.cpp
- Csprite.h
- Csprite.cpp

- Defines.h
- Ddsetup.cpp
- Objects.h
- Objman.h
- Objman.cpp
- Random.h
- Random.cpp
- Sbmp.h
- Sbmp.cpp
- Timer.h
- Timer.cpp
- View.h
- View.cpp

The following files in Demo 8 have been modified from Demo 7:

- Ai.cpp (changes minimal; not listed)
- Main.cpp
- Objects.cpp

The following files are new in Demo 8:

- Sndlist.h
- Sound.h
- Sound.cpp

Media Files

The following sound files are new in Demo 8:

- Boom.wav
- Caw.wav
- Gun.wav
- Intro.wav
- Larc.wav
- Putt0.wav
- Putt1.wav
- Putt2.wav
- Thump.wav

Required Libraries

- Ddraw.lib
- Dsound.lib
- Winmm.lib

Code Listings

Main.cpp

```cpp
//main.cpp

//Copyright Ian Parberry, 1999
//Last updated May 22, 2000

//Now we have sound, managed by CSoundManager. The plane
//engine sound loops, other sounds are mixed multiple times
//onto the sound track. Each object in the game is
//responsible for playing its own sounds.

//Don't forget to add dsound.lib to your linker settings!

//system includes
#include <windows.h>
#include <windowsx.h>
#include <ddraw.h>
#include <stdio.h>

//system defines
#define WIN32_LEAN_AND_MEAN

//custom includes
#include "defines.h" //global definitions
#include "bmp.h" //bmp file reader
#include "timer.h" //game timer
#include "csprite.h" //for clipped sprite class
#include "objects.h" //for object class
#include "objman.h" //for object manager
#include "view.h" //for viewpoint class
#include "random.h" //for random number generator
#include "sound.h" //for sound manager

//defines
#define MAX_OBJECTS 32 //max number of objects in game

enum GamePhaseType{
  LOGO_PHASE,TITLE_PHASE,MENU_PHASE,PLAYING_PHASE
};
```

```
//globals

BOOL ActiveApp; //is this application active?

LPDIRECTDRAW lpDirectDrawObject=NULL; //direct draw object
LPDIRECTDRAWSURFACE lpPrimary=NULL; //primary surface
LPDIRECTDRAWPALETTE lpPrimaryPalette; //its palette
LPDIRECTDRAWSURFACE lpSecondary=NULL; //back buffer
LPDIRECTDRAWPALETTE lpSecondaryPalette; //its palette
LPDIRECTDRAWSURFACE lpBackground=NULL; //background image

CTimer Timer; //game timer

CBmpFileReader background; //background image
CBmpSpriteFileReader g_cSpriteImages; //sprite images
CBmpSpriteFileReader g_cFrgndImages; //foreground images

CObjectManager ObjectManager(MAX_OBJECTS); //object manager

CClippedSprite *g_pSprite[NUM_SPRITES]; //sprites

CViewPoint Viewpoint; //player viewpoint
CRandom Random; //random number generator

GamePhaseType GamePhase; //current phase
BOOL endphase=FALSE; //should we abort current phase?
int PhaseTime=0; //time in phase

CSoundManager* SoundManager; //sound manager

//helper functions
LPDIRECTDRAWPALETTE CreatePalette(LPDIRECTDRAWSURFACE surface);
BOOL InitDirectDraw(HWND hwnd);
HWND CreateDefaultWindow(char* name,HINSTANCE hInstance);

BOOL LoadPlaneSprite(){
  BOOL result=TRUE;
  result=result&&g_pSprite[PLANE_OBJECT]->
    load(&g_cSpriteImages,0,1,1);
  result=result&&g_pSprite[PLANE_OBJECT]->
    load(&g_cSpriteImages,1,123,1);
  result=result&&g_pSprite[PLANE_OBJECT]->
    load(&g_cSpriteImages,2,245,1);
  result=result&&g_pSprite[PLANE_OBJECT]->
    load(&g_cSpriteImages,3,367,1);
  result=result&&g_pSprite[PLANE_OBJECT]->
    load(&g_cSpriteImages,4,489,1);
  result=result&&g_pSprite[PLANE_OBJECT]->
    load(&g_cSpriteImages,5,17,74);
```

```
    return result;
} //LoadPlaneSprite

BOOL LoadCrowSprite(){
  BOOL result=TRUE;
  result=result&&g_pSprite[CROW_OBJECT]->
    load(&g_cSpriteImages,0,256,183); //frame 0
  result=result&&g_pSprite[CROW_OBJECT]->
    load(&g_cSpriteImages,1,320,183); //frame 1
  result=result&&g_pSprite[CROW_OBJECT]->
    load(&g_cSpriteImages,2,256,237); //frame 2
  result=result&&g_pSprite[CROW_OBJECT]->
    load(&g_cSpriteImages,3,323,237); //frame 3
  return result;
} //LoadCrowSprite

BOOL LoadFrgndSprites(){ //load foreground sprites
  BOOL result=TRUE;
  result=result&&g_pSprite[FARM_OBJECT]->
    load(&g_cFrgndImages,0,0,0); //load farm sprite
  result=result&&g_pSprite[FIELD_OBJECT]->
    load(&g_cFrgndImages,0,640,0); //load field sprite
  return result;
} //LoadFrgndSprites

BOOL LoadDeadCrowSprite(){ //load dead crow
  return g_pSprite[DEADCROW_OBJECT]->
    load(&g_cSpriteImages,0,453,230);
} //LoadDeadCrowSprite

BOOL LoadExplodingCrowSprite(){ //load exploding crow
  BOOL result=TRUE;
  result=result&&g_pSprite[EXPLODINGCROW_OBJECT]->
    load(&g_cSpriteImages,0,257,294);
  result=result&&g_pSprite[EXPLODINGCROW_OBJECT]->
    load(&g_cSpriteImages,1,321,294);
  result=result&&g_pSprite[EXPLODINGCROW_OBJECT]->
    load(&g_cSpriteImages,2,386,162);
  result=result&&g_pSprite[EXPLODINGCROW_OBJECT]->
    load(&g_cSpriteImages,3,453,162);
  result=result&&g_pSprite[EXPLODINGCROW_OBJECT]->
    load(&g_cSpriteImages,4,386,230);
  result=result&&g_pSprite[EXPLODINGCROW_OBJECT]->
    load(&g_cSpriteImages,5,453,230);
  return result;
} //LoadExplodingCrowSprite

BOOL LoadBulletSprite(){ //load bullet
  return g_pSprite[BULLET_OBJECT]->
    load(&g_cSpriteImages,0,5,123);
```

```
    } //LoadBulletSprite

BOOL LoadImages(){ //load graphics from files to surfaces
    //get the background image
    if(!background.load("bckgnd.bmp"))return FALSE; //read file
    background.draw(lpBackground); //draw to background surface
    //set palettes in all surfaces
    if(!background.setpalette(lpPrimaryPalette))return FALSE;
    if(!background.setpalette(lpSecondaryPalette))return FALSE;
    //load the sprites...
    if(!g_cSpriteImages.load("sprites.bmp"))return FALSE;
    //...the plane
    g_pSprite[PLANE_OBJECT]=new CClippedSprite(6,121,72);
    if(!LoadPlaneSprite())return FALSE; //load plane images
    //...the crow
    g_pSprite[CROW_OBJECT]=new CClippedSprite(4,58,37);
    if(!LoadCrowSprite())return FALSE; //load crow images
    //..the dead crow
    g_pSprite[DEADCROW_OBJECT]=new CClippedSprite(1,62,53);
    LoadDeadCrowSprite(); //load dead crow images
    //...the exploding crow
    g_pSprite[EXPLODINGCROW_OBJECT]=new CClippedSprite(6,62,53);
    LoadExplodingCrowSprite(); //load exploding crow images
    //...the bullet
    g_pSprite[BULLET_OBJECT]=new CClippedSprite(1,5,3);
    LoadBulletSprite(); //load bullet images
    //...the foreground sprites
    if(!g_cFrgndImages.load("farm.bmp"))return FALSE;
    g_pSprite[FARM_OBJECT]=new CClippedSprite(1,640,162);
    g_pSprite[FIELD_OBJECT]=new CClippedSprite(1,640,162);
    if(!LoadFrgndSprites())return FALSE; //load foreground
    return TRUE;
} //LoadImages

void CreateObjects(){
    int i;
    ObjectManager.create(FARM_OBJECT,0,SCREEN_HEIGHT-1,0,0);
    ObjectManager.create(FIELD_OBJECT,SCREEN_WIDTH,
      SCREEN_HEIGHT-1,0,0);
    for(i=0; i<8; i++)
      ObjectManager.create(CROW_OBJECT,
        Random.number(0,WORLD_WIDTH-1),
        Random.number(100,400),-1,0);
    ObjectManager.set_current(
      ObjectManager.create(PLANE_OBJECT,320,271,-1,0));
    for(i=0; i<8; i++)
      ObjectManager.create(CROW_OBJECT,
        Random.number(0,WORLD_WIDTH-1),
        Random.number(100,400),-1,0);
} //CreateObjects
```

```
BOOL RestoreSurfaces(){ //restore all surfaces
  BOOL result=TRUE;
  //primary and secondary surfaces
  if(FAILED(lpPrimary->Restore()))return FALSE;
  if(FAILED(lpSecondary->Restore()))return FALSE;
  //surfaces containing images
  if(SUCCEEDED(lpBackground->Restore())) //if background restored
    result=result&&background.draw(lpBackground); //redraw image
  else return FALSE;
  if(g_pSprite[PLANE_OBJECT]->Restore()) //if plane restored
    result=result&&LoadPlaneSprite(); //redraw image
  else return FALSE;
  if(g_pSprite[CROW_OBJECT]->Restore()) //if crow restored
    result=result&&LoadCrowSprite(); //redraw image
  else return FALSE;
  if(g_pSprite[DEADCROW_OBJECT]->Restore()) //if restored
    result=result&&LoadDeadCrowSprite(); //redraw image
  else return FALSE;
  if(g_pSprite[EXPLODINGCROW_OBJECT]->Restore()) //if restored
    result=result&&LoadExplodingCrowSprite(); //redraw image
  else return FALSE;
  if(g_pSprite[BULLET_OBJECT]->Restore()) //if restored
    result=result&&LoadBulletSprite(); //redraw image
  else return FALSE;
  if(g_pSprite[FARM_OBJECT]->Restore()&& //if farm and ...
    g_pSprite[FIELD_OBJECT]->Restore()) //... field restored
    result=result&&LoadFrgndSprites(); //redraw image
  else return FALSE;
  return result;
} //RestoreSurfaces

void LoadSounds(int level=0){ //load sounds for level
  const int copies=4; //copies of repeatable sounds
  switch(level){
    case 0: //intro sounds
      SoundManager->load("intro.wav");
      SoundManager->load("larc.wav");
      break;
    case 1: //game engine sounds
      SoundManager->load("caw.wav",copies);
      SoundManager->load("gun.wav",copies);
      SoundManager->load("boom.wav",copies);
      SoundManager->load("thump.wav",copies);
      SoundManager->load("putt0.wav");
      SoundManager->load("putt1.wav");
      SoundManager->load("putt2.wav");
      break;
  }
}
```

```
BOOL PageFlip(){ //return TRUE if page flip succeeds
  if(lpPrimary->Flip(NULL,DDFLIP_WAIT)==DDERR_SURFACELOST)
    return RestoreSurfaces();
  return TRUE;
} //PageFlip

BOOL ComposeFrame(){ //compose a frame of animation
  Viewpoint.draw_background(lpBackground,lpSecondary,
    ObjectManager.speed()); //draw scrolling background
  ObjectManager.animate(lpSecondary); //draw objects
  return TRUE;
} //ComposeFrame

void display_screen(char *filename){ //display bmp file
  CBmpFileReader image; //file reader
  image.load(filename); //load from file
  image.draw(lpSecondary); //draw to back buffer
  image.setpalette(lpPrimaryPalette); //may have custom palette
  PageFlip(); //display it
} //display_screen

void change_phase(GamePhaseType new_phase){ //start new phase
  //change to new phase
  GamePhase=new_phase; PhaseTime=Timer.time();
  endphase=FALSE;
  //start-of-phase housekeeping
  switch(GamePhase){
    case LOGO_PHASE:
      display_screen("larc.bmp");
      LoadSounds(); //load sounds for intro sequence
      SoundManager->play(LOGO_SOUND); //signature chord
      break;
    case TITLE_PHASE:
      display_screen("title.bmp");
      SoundManager->stop(); //silence previous phase
      SoundManager->play(TITLE_SOUND); //title sound
      break;
    case MENU_PHASE:
      SoundManager->stop(); //silence previous phase
      display_screen("menu.bmp");
      break;
    case PLAYING_PHASE: //prepare the game engine
      //start sounds
      SoundManager->stop(); //silence previous phase
      SoundManager->clear(); //clear out old sounds
      LoadSounds(1); //load game sounds
      //create objects in game engine
      ObjectManager.reset(); //clear object manager
      CreateObjects(); //create new objects
```

```
      //initialize graphics
      background.setpalette(lpPrimaryPalette); //game palette
      ComposeFrame(); PageFlip(); //prime animation pump
      break;
  }
} //change_phase

void Redraw(){ //redraw in response to surface loss
  switch(GamePhase){
    case LOGO_PHASE:
      display_screen("larc.bmp");
      break;
    case TITLE_PHASE:
      display_screen("title.bmp");
      break;
    case MENU_PHASE:
      display_screen("menu.bmp"); //display main menu
      break;
    case PLAYING_PHASE:
      //do nothing, next frame of animation will catch it
      break;
  }
}

void ProcessFrame(){ //process a frame of animation
  const int LOGO_DISPLAY_TIME=8500; //duration of logo
  const int TITLE_DISPLAY_TIME=10000; //duration of title
  //check for lost surfaces, eg alt+tab
  if(lpPrimary->IsLost()){
    RestoreSurfaces(); Redraw();
  }
  //phase-related processing
  switch(GamePhase){ //what phase are we in?
    case LOGO_PHASE: //displaying logo screen
      Sleep(100); //surrender time to other processes
      if(endphase||Timer.elapsed(PhaseTime,LOGO_DISPLAY_TIME))
        change_phase(TITLE_PHASE); //go to title screen
      break;
    case TITLE_PHASE: //displaying title screen
      Sleep(100); //surrender time to other processes
      if(endphase||Timer.elapsed(PhaseTime,TITLE_DISPLAY_TIME))
        change_phase(MENU_PHASE); //go to menu
      break;
    case MENU_PHASE: //main menu
      Sleep(100); //surrender time to other processes
      if(endphase)change_phase(PLAYING_PHASE); //play game
      break;
    case PLAYING_PHASE: //game engine
      ComposeFrame(); //compose a frame in back surface
      PageFlip(); //flip video memory surfaces
```

```
        if(endphase||ObjectManager.won()) //if end of phase
          change_phase(MENU_PHASE); //go to menu
        break;
    }
} //ProcessFrame

//keyboard handlers

void intro_keyboard_handler(WPARAM keystroke){
  endphase=TRUE; //any key ends the phase
} //intro_keyboard_handler

BOOL menu_keyboard_handler(WPARAM keystroke){
  BOOL result=FALSE;
  switch(keystroke){
    case VK_ESCAPE:
    case 'Q': //exit game
      result=TRUE;
      break;
    case 'N': //play new game
      endphase=TRUE;
      break;
    default: break; //do nothing
  }
  return result;
} //menu_keyboard_handler

void game_keyboard_handler(WPARAM keystroke){
  switch(keystroke){
    case VK_ESCAPE: endphase=TRUE; break;
    case VK_UP: ObjectManager.accelerate(0,-1); break;
    case VK_DOWN: ObjectManager.accelerate(0,1); break;
    case VK_LEFT: ObjectManager.accelerate(-1,0); break;
    case VK_RIGHT: ObjectManager.accelerate(1,0); break;
    case VK_SPACE: ObjectManager.fire_gun(); break;
    default: break;
  }
} //game_keyboard_handler

BOOL keyboard_handler(WPARAM keystroke){ //keyboard handler
  BOOL result=FALSE; //TRUE if we are to exit game
  switch(GamePhase){ //select handler for phase
    case LOGO_PHASE:
    case TITLE_PHASE:
      intro_keyboard_handler(keystroke);
      break;
    case MENU_PHASE:
      result=menu_keyboard_handler(keystroke);
      break;
    case PLAYING_PHASE:
```

```
        game_keyboard_handler(keystroke);
        break;
  }
  return result;
} //keyboard_handler

//message handler (window procedure)
long CALLBACK WindowProc(HWND hwnd,UINT message,
                         WPARAM wParam,LPARAM lParam){
  switch(message){
    case WM_ACTIVATEAPP: ActiveApp=wParam; break;
    case WM_CREATE: break;
    case WM_KEYDOWN: //keyboard hit
      if(keyboard_handler(wParam))DestroyWindow(hwnd);
      break;
    case WM_DESTROY: //end of game
      if(lpDirectDrawObject!=NULL){ //if DD object exists
        if(lpSecondary!=NULL) //if secondary surface exists
          lpSecondary->Release(); //release secondary surface
        if(lpPrimary!=NULL) //if primary surface exists
          lpPrimary->Release(); //release primary surface
        if(lpBackground!=NULL) //if background exists
          lpBackground->Release(); //release background
        for(int i=0; i<NUM_SPRITES; i++){ //for each sprite
          if(g_pSprite[i]) //if sprite exists
            g_pSprite[i]->Release(); //release sprite
          delete g_pSprite[i]; //delete sprite
        }
        lpDirectDrawObject->Release(); //release DD object
      }
      delete SoundManager; //reclaim sound manager memory
      ShowCursor(TRUE); //show the mouse cursor
      PostQuitMessage(0); //and exit
      break;
    default: //default window procedure
      return DefWindowProc(hwnd,message,wParam,lParam);
  } //switch(message)
  return 0L;
} //WindowProc

int WINAPI WinMain(HINSTANCE hInstance,HINSTANCE hPrevInstance,
LPSTR lpCmdLine,int nCmdShow){
  MSG msg; //current message
  HWND hwnd; //handle to fullscreen window
  hwnd=CreateDefaultWindow("directX demo 8",hInstance);
  if(!hwnd)return FALSE;
  //set up window
  ShowWindow(hwnd,nCmdShow); UpdateWindow(hwnd);
  SetFocus(hwnd); //allow input from keyboard
  ShowCursor(FALSE); //hide the cursor
```

```
      //init graphics
      for(int i=0; i<NUM_SPRITES; i++) //null out sprites
        g_pSprite[i]=NULL;
      BOOL OK=InitDirectDraw(hwnd);//initialize DirectDraw
      if(OK)OK=LoadImages(); //load images from disk
      if(!OK){ //bail out if initialization failed
        DestroyWindow(hwnd); return FALSE;
      }
      //start game timer
      Timer.start();
      //init sound
      SoundManager=new CSoundManager(hwnd);
      //set initial phase
      change_phase(LOGO_PHASE);
      //message loop
      while(TRUE)
        if(PeekMessage(&msg,NULL,0,0,PM_NOREMOVE)){
          if(!GetMessage(&msg,NULL,0,0))return msg.wParam;
          TranslateMessage(&msg); DispatchMessage(&msg);
        }
        else if(ActiveApp)ProcessFrame(); else WaitMessage();
    } //WinMain
```

Objects.cpp

```
    //objects.cpp

//Copyright Ian Parberry, 1999
//Last updated November 2, 1999

#include "objects.h"
#include "timer.h" //game timer
#include "csprite.h" //for clipped sprite class
#include "random.h" //for random number generator
#include "view.h" //for viewpoint class
#include "sound.h" //for sound manager

extern CClippedSprite *g_pSprite[]; //sprites
extern CTimer Timer; //game timer
extern CRandom Random; //random number generator
extern CViewPoint Viewpoint; //player viewpoint
extern CSoundManager* SoundManager; //sound manager

CObject::CObject(ObjectType object,int x,int y,
                 int xspeed,int yspeed){ //constructor
  //defaults
  m_nCurrentFrame=0; m_nLastFrameTime=Timer.time();
  m_bForwardAnimation=TRUE; m_nFrameInterval=30;
  m_eMortality=IMMORTAL; m_eLocomotion=NO_MOTION;
  m_nLifeTime=1000; m_bVulnerable=FALSE;
```

```
m_bIntelligent=FALSE;
//common values
m_eObject=object; //type of object
m_nLastXMoveTime=m_nLastYMoveTime=Timer.time(); //time
m_nX=x; m_nY=y; //location
m_nXspeed=xspeed; m_nYspeed=yspeed; //speed
m_pSprite=g_pSprite[object];
m_nFrameCount=m_pSprite->frame_count();
m_nHeight=m_pSprite->height();
m_nWidth=m_pSprite->width();
m_nBirthTime=Timer.time(); //time of creation
//customized values
switch(object){
  case PLANE_OBJECT:
    SoundManager->play(SLOWPUTT_SOUND,LOOP_SOUND);
    m_nMinXSpeed=-3; m_nMaxXSpeed=-1;
    m_nMinYSpeed=-4; m_nMaxYSpeed=4;
    m_nFrameInterval=250;
    m_eMortality=IMMORTAL;
    m_eLocomotion=FLYING_MOTION;
    m_bVulnerable=FALSE;
    break;
  case CROW_OBJECT:
    m_nMinXSpeed=-2; m_nMaxXSpeed=-1;
    m_nMinYSpeed=-1; m_nMaxYSpeed=1;
    m_nCurrentFrame=Random.number(0,m_nFrameCount-1);
    m_nFrameInterval=250+Random.number(-30,30);
    m_eMortality=IMMORTAL;
    m_eLocomotion=FLYING_MOTION;
    m_bVulnerable=TRUE;
    break;
  case FARM_OBJECT:
  case FIELD_OBJECT:
    m_nFrameCount=1;
    m_eMortality=IMMORTAL;
    m_eLocomotion=NO_MOTION;
    m_bVulnerable=FALSE;
    break;
  case BULLET_OBJECT:
    SoundManager->play(GUN_SOUND); //sound of gun firing
    m_nFrameCount=1;
    m_eMortality=MORTAL;
    m_eLocomotion=FLYING_MOTION;
    m_bVulnerable=FALSE;
    m_nLifeTime=500+Random.number(0,200);
    break;
  case DEADCROW_OBJECT:
    m_nCurrentFrame=0;
    m_eMortality=MORTAL;
    m_eLocomotion=FALLING_MOTION;
```

```
            m_bVulnerable=FALSE;
            m_nLifeTime=1000;
            break;
        case EXPLODINGCROW_OBJECT:
            SoundManager->play(BOOM_SOUND); //sound of explosion
            m_nCurrentFrame=0;
            m_nFrameInterval=100;
            m_eMortality=ONESHOT_MORTAL;
            m_eLocomotion=FLYING_MOTION;
            m_bVulnerable=FALSE;
            break;
    }
}

void CObject::draw(LPDIRECTDRAWSURFACE surface){ //draw
    //draw the current frame
    m_pSprite->draw(m_nCurrentFrame,Viewpoint.screen(m_nX),
        m_nY,surface);
    //figure out which frame is next
    if(m_eMortality==ONESHOT_MORTAL){ //animation plays once
        if(Timer.elapsed(m_nLastFrameTime,m_nFrameInterval))
            ++m_nCurrentFrame;
    }
    else{ //repeating animation
        int t=m_nFrameInterval/(1+abs(m_nXspeed)); //frame interval
        if(m_nFrameCount>1&&Timer.elapsed(m_nLastFrameTime,t))
            if(m_bForwardAnimation){ //forward animation
                if(++m_nCurrentFrame>=m_nFrameCount){ //wrap
                    m_nCurrentFrame=m_nFrameCount-2;
                    m_bForwardAnimation=FALSE;
                }
            }
            else{ //backward animation
                if(--m_nCurrentFrame<0){ //wrap
                    m_nCurrentFrame=1;
                    m_bForwardAnimation=TRUE;
                }
            }
    }
}

void CObject::accelerate(int xdelta,int ydelta){
//change speed
    int old_xspeed=m_nXspeed; //old speed
    //horizontal
    m_nXspeed+=xdelta;
    if(m_nXspeed<m_nMinXSpeed)m_nXspeed=m_nMinXSpeed;
    if(m_nXspeed>m_nMaxXSpeed)m_nXspeed=m_nMaxXSpeed;
    //vertical
    m_nYspeed+=ydelta;
```

```
        if(m_nYspeed<m_nMinYSpeed)m_nYspeed=m_nMinYSpeed;
        if(m_nYspeed>m_nMaxYSpeed)m_nYspeed=m_nMaxYSpeed;
        //change plane sound
        if(m_eObject==PLANE_OBJECT&&old_xspeed!=m_nXspeed){
          //stop old sound (one of these will work)
          SoundManager->stop(SLOWPUTT_SOUND);
          SoundManager->stop(MEDIUMPUTT_SOUND);
          SoundManager->stop(FASTPUTT_SOUND);
          //start new sound
          SoundManager->
            play(SLOWPUTT_SOUND-1+abs(m_nXspeed),LOOP_SOUND);
        }
      }

  void CObject::move(){ //move object
    const int XSCALE=16; //to scale back horizontal motion
    const int YSCALE=32; //to scale back vertical motion
    const int YMARGIN=20; //vertical margin;
    int xdelta,ydelta; //change in position
    int time=Timer.time(); //current time
    int tfactor; //time since last move
    switch(m_eLocomotion){
      case FLYING_MOTION:
        //horizontal motion
        tfactor=time-m_nLastXMoveTime; //time since last move
        xdelta=(m_nXspeed*tfactor)/XSCALE; //x distance moved
        m_nX+=xdelta; //x motion
        Viewpoint.normalize(m_nX); //normalize to world width
        if(xdelta||m_nXspeed==0) //record time of move
          m_nLastXMoveTime=time;
        //vertical motion
        tfactor=time-m_nLastYMoveTime; //time since last move
        ydelta=(m_nYspeed*tfactor)/YSCALE; //y distance moved
        m_nY+=ydelta; //y motion
        if(m_nY<YMARGIN)m_nY=YMARGIN;
        if(m_nY>=SCREEN_HEIGHT)m_nY=SCREEN_HEIGHT-1;
        if(ydelta||m_nYspeed==0) //record time of move
          m_nLastYMoveTime=time;
        break;
      case FALLING_MOTION:
        m_nXspeed=0;
        //time since born, for acceleration due to gravity
        tfactor=time-m_nBirthTime;
        //vertical motion
        ydelta=tfactor/YSCALE; m_nY+=ydelta;
        if(m_nY<YMARGIN)m_nY=YMARGIN;
        if(ydelta||m_nYspeed==0) //record time of move
          m_nLastYMoveTime=time;
        //kill objects that have fallen below the screen
        if(m_nY>SCREEN_HEIGHT){
```

```
        SoundManager->play(THUMP_SOUND); //object hitting ground
        m_nLifeTime=0; m_eMortality=MORTAL; //force cull
      }
    break;
  default: break;
  }
}
```

Sndlist.h

```
//sndlist.h: list of sound definitions

//Copyright Ian Parberry, 1999
//Last updated November 2, 1999

#ifndef __SNDLIST__
#define __SNDLIST__

#define LOOP_SOUND TRUE

enum GameSoundType{ //sounds used in game engine
  CAW_SOUND=0, //sound a crow makes
  GUN_SOUND, //sound of gun firing
  BOOM_SOUND, //sound of explosion
  THUMP_SOUND, //sound of object hitting the ground
  //next 3 sounds must be consecutive and in this order
  SLOWPUTT_SOUND, //sound of slow engine
  MEDIUMPUTT_SOUND, //sound of medium engine
  FASTPUTT_SOUND //sound of fast engine
};

enum IntroSoundType{ //sounds used during the intro
  TITLE_SOUND=0, //sound used during title screen
  LOGO_SOUND, //signature chord
};

#endif
```

Sound.h

```
//sound.h: header class for sound.cpp
//CSoundManager allows you to play multiple copies of each
//sound simultaneously

//Copyright Ian Parberry, 1999
//Last updated November 2, 1999

#ifndef __SOUND__
#define __SOUND__
```

```
#ifndef WIN32
  //this seems to be necessary for correct compile,
  //but generates warnings
  #define WIN32
#endif

#include <dsound.h> //direct sound
#include "sndlist.h" //list of sound names

#define MAX_SOUNDS 64 //maximum number of different sounds

#define DS_NUMCHANNELS 8 //number of channels
#define DS_CHANSPERSAMPLE 1 //mono sound
#define DS_BITSPERSAMPLE 8 //8 bit sound
#define DS_SAMPLERATE 22050 //22KHz sampling

class CSoundManager{ //sound manager
  private:
    int m_nCount; //number of sounds loaded
    LPDIRECTSOUND m_lpDirectSound; //directSound object
    LPLPDIRECTSOUNDBUFFER m_lpBuffer[MAX_SOUNDS]; //sound buffers
    int m_nCopyCount[MAX_SOUNDS]; //num copies of each sound
    BOOL m_bOperational; //directSound initialized correctly
    BOOL CreateBuffer(int index,int length,int copies);
    BOOL LoadBuffer(int index,BYTE *buffer,int length);
    int LoadSound(char *filename,BYTE **sound); //load from file
    BOOL CopyBuffer(int index,int copies); //copy sound
  public:
    CSoundManager(HWND hwnd); //constructor
    ~CSoundManager(); //destructor
    void clear(); //clear all sounds
    void load(char *filename,int copies=1); //load from file
    void play(int index,BOOL looping=FALSE); //play sound
    void stop(int index); //stop playing sound
    void stop(void); //stop playing all sounds
};

#endif
```

Sound.cpp

```
//sound.cpp: sound manager

//Copyright Ian Parberry, 2000
//Last updated May 22, 2000

#include <stdio.h>
#include "sound.h"

CSoundManager::CSoundManager(HWND hwnd){ //constructor
```

```
      m_nCount=0; //no sounds yet
      //null out sound buffers and flags
      for(int i=0; i<MAX_SOUNDS; i++){
        m_lpBuffer[i]=NULL; m_nCopyCount[i]=0;
      }
      //start direct sound
      m_bOperational=SUCCEEDED(
        DirectSoundCreate(NULL,&m_lpDirectSound,NULL));
      if(!m_bOperational)return;
      m_bOperational=SUCCEEDED(m_lpDirectSound->
        SetCooperativeLevel(hwnd,DSSCL_NORMAL));
    }

CSoundManager::~CSoundManager(){ //destructor
      if(!m_bOperational)return;
      clear(); //clear all buffers
      (void)m_lpDirectSound->Release(); //release direct sound
    }

void CSoundManager::clear(){ //clear all sounds
      if(!m_bOperational)return;
      stop(); //stop all sounds (paranoia)
      for(int i=0; i<m_nCount; i++){ //for each sound
        for(int j=0; j<m_nCopyCount[i]; j++){ //for each copy
          m_lpBuffer[i][j]->Release(); //release the sound
          m_lpBuffer[i][j]=NULL; //probably not needed
        }
        //reclaim memory
        delete[]m_lpBuffer[i];
      }
      m_nCount=0; //no sounds left (hopefully)
    }

void CSoundManager::load(char *filename,int copies){
    //load sound from file
    //copies is how many copies of sound are to play simultaneously
      int length; //length of sound
      BYTE *sound=NULL; //temporary buffer to hold sound data
      //bail out if necessary
      if(!m_bOperational)return; //bail if not initialized
      if(m_nCount>=MAX_SOUNDS)return; //bail if no space left
      //load sound data from file
      length=LoadSound(filename,&sound); //load sound from file
      CreateBuffer(m_nCount,length,copies); //create buffers
      LoadBuffer(m_nCount,sound,length); //load into buffer
      CopyBuffer(m_nCount,copies); //make copies of contents
      //clean up and exit
      delete[]sound; //delete temporary sound buffer
      m_nCount++; //increment counter
    }
```

```
void CSoundManager::play(int index,BOOL looping){ //play sound
  if(!m_bOperational)return; //bail if not initialized
  if(index<0||index>=m_nCount)return; //bail if bad index
  int copy=0; //current copy
  DWORD status; //status of that copy
  //get status of first copy
  if(FAILED(m_lpBuffer[index][copy]->GetStatus(&status)))
    status=DSBSTATUS_PLAYING; //assume playing if failed
  //find next unplayed copy, if any
  while(copy<m_nCopyCount[index] &&
  (status&DSBSTATUS_PLAYING)){ //while current copy in use
    if(++copy<m_nCopyCount[index]) //go to next copy
      if(FAILED(m_lpBuffer[index][copy]->GetStatus(&status)))
        status=DSBSTATUS_PLAYING; //assume playing if failed
  }
  //play copy
  if(copy<m_nCopyCount[index]) //if unused copy found
    m_lpBuffer[index][copy]->
      Play(0,0,looping?DSBPLAY_LOOPING:0); //play it
}

void CSoundManager::stop(int index){ //stop playing sound
  if(!m_bOperational)return; //bail if not initialized
  if(index<0||index>=m_nCount)return; //bail if bad index
  for(int i=0; i<m_nCopyCount[index]; i++){ //for each copy
    m_lpBuffer[index][i]->Stop(); //stop playing
    m_lpBuffer[index][i]->SetCurrentPosition(0); //rewind
  }
}

void CSoundManager::stop(void){ //stop playing sound
  if(!m_bOperational)return; //bail if not initialized
  for(int index=0; index<m_nCount; index++) //for each sound
    stop(index); //stop that sound
}

BOOL CSoundManager::CopyBuffer(int index,int copies){
//make copies of buffer
  if(!m_bOperational)return FALSE; //bail if not initialized
  BOOL result=TRUE; //TRUE if everything went OK
  m_nCopyCount[index]=copies; //record number of copies
  for(int i=1; i<copies; i++) //for each copy
    result=result&& //copy the sound
      SUCCEEDED(m_lpDirectSound->
        DuplicateSoundBuffer(*m_lpBuffer[index],
        &(m_lpBuffer[index][i])));
  return result;
}
```

```
BOOL CSoundManager::CreateBuffer(int index,int length,
                                 int copies){
  if(!m_bOperational)return FALSE; //bail if not initialized
  DSBUFFERDESC dsbdesc;
  PCMWAVEFORMAT pcmwf;
  if(length<=0)return FALSE; //bail if length info wrong
  //init pcmwf, wave format descriptor
  memset(&pcmwf,0,sizeof(PCMWAVEFORMAT));
  pcmwf.wf.wFormatTag=WAVE_FORMAT_PCM;
  pcmwf.wf.nChannels=DS_CHANSPERSAMPLE;
  pcmwf.wf.nSamplesPerSec=DS_SAMPLERATE;
  pcmwf.wf.nBlockAlign=
    DS_CHANSPERSAMPLE*DS_BITSPERSAMPLE/8;
  pcmwf.wf.nAvgBytesPerSec=
    pcmwf.wf.nSamplesPerSec*pcmwf.wf.nBlockAlign;
  pcmwf.wBitsPerSample=DS_BITSPERSAMPLE;
  //init dsbdesc, direct sound buffer descriptor
  memset(&dsbdesc,0,sizeof(DSBUFFERDESC));
  dsbdesc.dwSize=sizeof(DSBUFFERDESC);
  dsbdesc.dwFlags=DSBCAPS_STATIC;
  dsbdesc.dwBufferBytes=length;
  dsbdesc.lpwfxFormat=(LPWAVEFORMATEX)&pcmwf;
  //create sound buffers and return success code
  m_lpBuffer[index]=new LPDIRECTSOUNDBUFFER[copies];
  for(int i=0; i<copies; i++)m_lpBuffer[index][i]=NULL;
  return SUCCEEDED(m_lpDirectSound->
    CreateSoundBuffer(&dsbdesc,m_lpBuffer[index],NULL));
}

BOOL CSoundManager::LoadBuffer(int index,BYTE *sound,int length){
  if(!m_bOperational)return FALSE; //bail if not initialized
  LPVOID w1,w2; //write pointer (use 2 for buffer wraparound)
  DWORD l1,l2; //length of sound to be written to write pointers
  LPDIRECTSOUNDBUFFER buffer=*m_lpBuffer[index];
  if(length<=0)return FALSE; //bail if length info wrong
  if(buffer->Lock(0,length,&w1,&l1,&w2,&l2,0) //lock down buffer
  ==DSERR_BUFFERLOST){ //if buffer lost
    buffer->Restore(); //restore, then try again
    if(FAILED(buffer->Lock(0,length,&w1,&l1,&w2,&l2,0)))
      return FALSE; //abort if failed the second time
  }
  CopyMemory(w1,sound,l1); //load first half
  if(w2!=NULL)CopyMemory(w2,sound+l1,l2); //load  second half
  //unlock the buffer and return
  if(FAILED(buffer->Unlock(w1,l1,w2,l2)))return FALSE;
  return TRUE;
}

int CSoundManager::LoadSound(char *filename,BYTE **buffer){
  if(!m_bOperational)return 0; //bail if not initialized
```

```
HMMIO hmfr;
MMCKINFO parent,child;
WAVEFORMATEX wfmtx;
int size=0;
//reclaim memory from buffer, if already used
delete[]*buffer;
//init parent and child MMCKINFOs
parent.ckid=(FOURCC)0;
parent.cksize=0;
parent.fccType=(FOURCC)0;
parent.dwDataOffset=0;
parent.dwFlags=0;
child=parent;
//open sound file
hmfr=mmioOpen(filename,NULL,MMIO_READ|MMIO_ALLOCBUF);
if(hmfr==NULL)return NULL;
//descend into the RIFF
parent.fccType=mmioFOURCC('W','A','V','E');
if(mmioDescend(hmfr,&parent,NULL,MMIO_FINDRIFF)){
  mmioClose(hmfr,0); return NULL; //not a wave file
}
//descend to the WAVEfmt
child.ckid=mmioFOURCC('f','m','t',' ');
if(mmioDescend(hmfr,&child,&parent,0)){
  mmioClose(hmfr,0); return NULL; //file has no fmt chunk
}
//read the WAVEFMT from the wave file
if(mmioRead(hmfr,(char*)&wfmtx,sizeof(wfmtx))!=sizeof(wfmtx)){
  mmioClose(hmfr,0); return NULL; //unable to read fmt chunk
}
//check wave format
if(wfmtx.wFormatTag!=WAVE_FORMAT_PCM){
  mmioClose(hmfr,0); return NULL; //WAVE file is not PCM format
}
//ascend back to RIFF level
if(mmioAscend(hmfr,&child,0)){
  mmioClose(hmfr,0); return NULL; //unable to ascend
}
//descend to the data chunk
child.ckid=mmioFOURCC('d','a','t','a');
if(mmioDescend(hmfr,&child,&parent,MMIO_FINDCHUNK)){
  mmioClose(hmfr,0); return NULL; //WAVE file has no data chunk
}
//grab memory to store sound
size=child.cksize;
*buffer=new BYTE[size];
if(*buffer==NULL){
  mmioClose(hmfr,0); return NULL; //out of memory
}
//read the wave data
```

```
if((int)mmioRead(hmfr,(char *)*buffer,size)!=size){
  //data read failed
  mmioClose(hmfr,0); delete[]*buffer; return NULL;
}
//close file and return
mmioClose(hmfr,0);
return size;
```

Chapter 11

Here's what you'll learn:

- Why you may not see a mouse cursor in DirectDraw and what to do about it

- How to add mouse control to your game using Windows API mouse messages

- How to use the mouse to click on buttons

- How to manage and animate buttons

- How to handle radio buttons

- How to use the mouse as a joystick

- How to manage input with an input manager

- How to implement a device menu

The Mouse

In Demo 9, we learn how to process input from the mouse by responding to Windows API mouse messages. The mouse can be used to navigate the main menu by clicking on the menu buttons for action. You can also play the game using the mouse as a joystick with the invisible cursor position controlling the plane's speed and height and the left mouse button firing the gun. There is now a device menu that lets you choose whether to play using the keyboard, the mouse, or (in the next chapter) the joystick (see Figure 11.1). The buttons on the main menu page are normal buttons, while the top three buttons on the device menu page are radio buttons, meaning that one of the buttons is down while the others are up (in Figure 11.1, however, they are all drawn in the up position). Response to the mouse using mouse messages is fast enough for a game of this type. However, if you need faster response time, you must use DirectInput, which is out of the scope of this book.

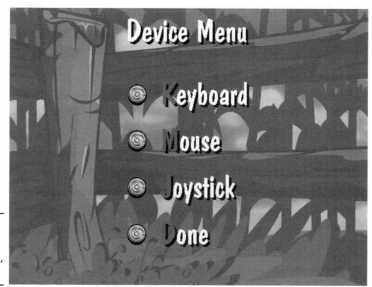

Figure 11.1
The device
menu screen,
Dmenu.bmp

Experiment with Demo 9

Take a moment now to run Demo 9.

- Click out of the intro screens using the left mouse button. You should now see the main menu. Notice that the mouse cursor is visible now.

- Click on the "Saved Game" button a few times; the button seems to get pressed into the screen. Notice the click sound when you press it down and a different click when you release it.

- Click down on the "Devices" button with the left mouse button, then move the mouse cursor off the button without releasing it. The button stays down.

- Now release it. It pops up, but no action is taken. Try releasing it on the menu screen, and within a different button.

- Now, click down on the "Devices" button and release it. You should now see the device menu, which should look like Figure 11.1 except that the first button is down. Notice that when you click on the "Mouse" button, the "Keyboard" button pops up, and vice versa. Push the "Mouse" button down and then click on the "Done" button. You should now be back at the main menu.

- Start a new game by clicking on the "New Game" button. You will now be able to play using the mouse (provided you followed the previous step of the instructions and selected "Mouse" from the device menu; if not, exit back to the main menu and try again from the previous step). Moving the mouse up moves the plane up, and moving it down moves the plane down. Moving the mouse left accelerates the plane, moving it right decelerates it. Clicking the left mouse button fires the gun. Notice that the keyboard controls for the plane are disabled while playing with the mouse.

- Exit back to the main menu by either hitting the Esc key or killing all of the crows. Notice that the mouse cursor disappeared while you were playing the game and reappears again on the main menu screen.

- Now, click on the "Quit" button to exit the program.

The Elusive DirectDraw Mouse Cursor

DirectDraw does not cooperate with software mouse cursors. This is in part because the API draws the software mouse cursor to what it thinks of as the primary surface and is blithely unaware of page flipping. This means that some of the time it is drawing it to the primary surface and sometimes to the secondary surface, resulting in an essentially useless mouse cursor that pulses dozens of times a second.

Most video cards have a hardware mouse cursor. The Windows Standard mouse cursor is implemented in hardware on most video cards, as is Animated Hourglasses, but not 3D Pointers. If you have trouble with the mouse cursor in Demo 9, go to the Mouse Properties box in the Control Panel and select the Windows Standard mouse cursor on the Pointers tab (see Figure 11.2).

What should you do about this in your game? You really only have three options.

The first option, which is easiest on you but hardest on your customers, is to ignore the problem in your program and add a note in your Help files saying that the player had better not use a software mouse pointer while playing your game. This is essentially what I am doing here.

The second option is to force the mouse cursor to be the Windows Standard cursor while your game is playing. This cursor has the best chance of actually being implemented in hardware. You can do this with the following obscure API function call.

```
SetSystemCursor(LoadCursor(NULL,IDC_ARROW),32512);
```

However, having done that you really should reset the cursor back to its old style when you exit your game. You can find out what the old style was by consulting the `Arrow` value in the `Control Panel\Cursors` subkey of `HKEY_CURRENT_USER` in the Windows registry. However, we are getting a little ahead of ourselves here; we won't be meeting the registry until Chapter 14.

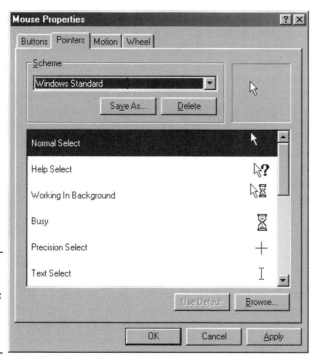

Figure 11.2
Selecting the Windows Standard mouse cursor

The third option is to turn the mouse cursor off and draw it yourself. All you need is a clipped sprite that is drawn last. You must store the mouse position in a global variable, updating it in response to WM_MOUSEMOVE messages. Of course, that means you'll have to animate screens that are currently not animated.

The Button Manager

The button manager maintains a list of buttons on a menu page and takes care of detecting clicks on them, animating them, and making the appropriate sounds. In *Ned's Turkey Farm*, each button is surrounded by a rectangle called a *hotspot*. The player clicks on a button by placing the mouse cursor inside the hotspot and clicking the left mouse button. If we were more sophisticated, we could code an arbitrarily shaped hotspot for each button—in our case, a round hotspot—instead of a bounding rectangle, but rectangles are quicker and easier to code. We will use a different instance of the button manager for each menu page, for instance, one button manager for the main menu and another for the device menu.

Button Manager Overview

The header file for the button manager class CButtonManager is Buttons.h. CButtonManager has ten private member variables. The first of these is an array of Windows API RECT structures that define the rectangular hotspots for each button on the screen. We don't know how many buttons there will be for any particular instance of the button manager, so we declare the array as a pointer for now, and we'll allocate memory for the array in the CButtonManager constructor.

```
RECT *m_rectHotspot; //hotspot locations
```

A parallel array of Boolean variables records whether each button is currently down. For example, button i will have hotspot m_rectHotspot[i], and m_bDown[i] will be TRUE if it is down.

```
BOOL *m_bDown; //is button held down?
```

The variable m_nMaxCount records the maximum number of hotspots allowed in the button manager:

```
int m_nMaxCount; //number of hotspots allowed
```

The variable m_nCount records how many hotspots have been allocated so far:

```
int m_nCount; //number of current hotspots
```

We assume that all of the buttons will have the same size, and allocate a Windows API SIZE structure to hold it. SIZE has two fields, cx and cy, which record the width and height of a rectangle:

```
SIZE m_sizeButton; //size of buttons, if all the same size
```

Next, we have a pointer to the button sprite for the buttons. The button manager will use the same sprite for each button. We use a base sprite object as opposed to a clipped sprite object because our buttons will always be completely on the screen, and so never need to be clipped. The actual sprite will be created by the constructor.

```
CBaseSprite* m_spriteDefault; //default button sprite
```

We will store the image of the buttons in a bmp sprite file reader in case the button sprite surfaces ever need to be restored and reloaded:

```
CBmpSpriteFileReader m_cImage; //button images
```

The next two private member variables record the indices of the sounds used when the button is pushed down and when it pops up:

```
int m_nButtonDownSound; //sound index for button down
int m_nButtonUpSound; //sound index for button up
```

The last private member variable records whether the buttons are radio buttons (except the last button on the screen, which is assumed to be "Quit" or "Done") or normal buttons:

```
BOOL m_bRadio; //TRUE for radio buttons
```

CButtonManager has five private member functions. The first of these, PointInRect, has two parameters, the first of which is a Windows API RECT structure rect, and the second of which is a Windows API POINT structure point. The POINT structure has two fields x and y which represent the coordinates of a two-dimensional point. PointInRect returns TRUE if point is inside rect.

```
BOOL PointInRect(RECT rect,POINT point); //is point in rect?
```

The CButtonManager addbutton function has a single parameter rect. It adds a new button with hotspot rect to the end of the button list, returning TRUE if it succeeds.

```
BOOL addbutton(RECT rect); //add button to list
```

Function loadsprite loads the button sprite from a file whose name is given as the parameter filename. It creates the CBaseSprite class to hold the sprite, loads the file into the private member variable m_cImage, and calls private member function loadimages to load the images from the bmp sprite file read to the sprite. Function loadimages assumes that the button sprite file image is m_sizeButton.cx pixels wide and 2*m_sizeButton.cy high, large enough to hold two copies of the button image, one above the other. The upper image will be loaded to frame 0 of the button sprite and will be displayed when the button is up. The lower image will be loaded to frame 1 of the button sprite and will be displayed when the button is down. See Figure 11.3 for an example.

```
BOOL loadsprite(char *filename); //load button sprite
void loadimages(); //load button images
```

Figure 11.3
The button file Buttons.bmp

Function `display_menu` draws all of the buttons in their current states (up or down) to the secondary surface and flips it to the primary surface, the assumption being that the menu screen will only be redrawn when a button state changes. It assumes that the menu background has already been drawn to both the primary and secondary surfaces.

```
void display_menu(); //display menu page
```

`CButtonManager` has 15 public member functions, including two constructors and a destructor. The first constructor has three parameters, and creates `count` buttons of size `size` with sprite image from a file named `filename`. The position of these buttons will be specified later. The second constructor has five parameters, including the three already named. The two extra parameters are a point `first` and a distance `ydelta`. These specify that the first button will be placed at point `first` on the screen, and the other buttons (`count` in all) will be placed below it, each at distance `ydelta` below the previous one. Ideally, it would be nice to only use the second version of the constructor. However, since artists (particularly those who, like you, are just learning their trade) are occasionally off by one or two pixels in the positioning of their buttons, the first constructor allows us to place the buttons arbitrarily on the screen. The alternative is going to the trouble and expense of having the artwork redrawn so that the buttons are exactly evenly spaced out, which is a moot point because usually nobody will notice if a button is one or two pixels away from where it should be. If you are lucky enough to have an artist to help you create your first game demo, it might be a good idea not to stress him or her out over a few pixels when it doesn't really make much difference to the game, and you can adapt to it with just a few extra lines of code.

```
CButtonManager(int count,SIZE size,char *filename);
CButtonManager(int count,SIZE size,POINT first,
  int ydelta,char *filename); //constructor
~CButtonManager(); //destructor
```

Function `addbutton` lets you add a button at an arbitrary `point` on the screen. It is designed to be used with the first `CButtonManager` constructor. It returns `TRUE` if it succeeds (it fails if there is not enough room in the button list for a new button). Notice that it is different from the private member function with the same name; the private version of the function takes a `RECT` variable as a parameter.

```
BOOL addbutton(POINT point); //add button of default size
```

If `point` is inside the hotspot of a button, function `hit` returns the index of that button; otherwise it returns -1. We will use this to detect when the left mouse button is pressed down with the mouse cursor inside a button.

```
int hit(POINT point); //return hit, if any
```

If `point` is inside the hotspot of a button that is currently down, function `release` returns the index of that button; otherwise it returns -1. We will use this to detect when the left mouse button is released with the mouse cursor inside the same button that it clicked down on.

```
int release(POINT point); //return hit on down button
```

If `point` is inside the hotspot of a button, the first version of function `buttondown` animates the button going down and returns TRUE; otherwise it returns FALSE:

```
BOOL buttondown(POINT point); //animate button down
```

The second version of function `buttondown` animates a particular button going down, the one with a given `index` in the button list. The second parameter specifies whether a sound is to be played; it defaults to TRUE if it is not provided.

```
BOOL buttondown(int index,BOOL sound=TRUE); //animate
```

The two versions of `buttonup` do the same things for a button going up:

```
BOOL buttonup(POINT point); //animate button up
BOOL buttonup(int index); //animate button up
```

Function `allbuttonsup` animates all of the buttons going up:

```
void allbuttonsup(); //animate all buttons up
```

Function `setsounds` provides the indices (in the sound manager's sound list) of the sounds to be played when a button is pressed down and when it pops up:

```
void setsounds(int down,int up); //set sounds
```

Function `set_radio` can be used to specify radio buttons or normal buttons:

```
void set_radio(BOOL on=TRUE); //set to radio buttons
```

Finally, `CButtonManager` has two public member functions that are required by every class that has private surfaces, a `Restore` and a `Release` function that respectively restore and release those surfaces. (`CButtonManager` has its surfaces contained in the button sprite class.)

```
BOOL Restore(); //restore surfaces
void Release(); //release surfaces
```

The Constructors and the Destructor

The code file for CButtonManager is Buttons.cpp. It begins with the code for the first of two constructors.

```
CButtonManager::CButtonManager(int count,SIZE size,
                              char *filename){
```

The constructor reserves space for the hotspot list and the button state list and sets all buttons in the down position:

```
m_rectHotspot=new RECT[m_nMaxCount=count]; //hotspot space
m_bDown=new BOOL[m_nMaxCount]; //whether button is down
for(int i=0; i<m_nMaxCount; i++)
  m_bDown[i]=FALSE; //all buttons up
```

It then sets some private member variables and loads the button sprite:

```
m_sizeButton=size; //size of buttons loaded
m_nCount=0; //number of buttons loaded
loadsprite(filename); //load the sprite
m_nButtonDownSound=m_nButtonUpSound=-1; //no sounds yet
m_bRadio=FALSE; //not radio buttons
}
```

The second CButtonManager constructor has an additional two parameters that specify the point at which the first button is to be drawn and the vertical separation ydelta between the buttons:

```
CButtonManager::CButtonManager(int count,SIZE size,
                POINT point,int ydelta,char *filename){
```

It has the same initial code as the first constructor, plus the addition of the following four lines of code that call the public member function addbutton to add the remaining buttons:

```
m_nCount=0; addbutton(point);
for(i=0; i<count-1; i++){
  point.y+=ydelta; addbutton(point);
}
```

The CButtonManager destructor deletes the things that were newed in the constructors:

```
CButtonManager::~CButtonManager(){ //destructor
  delete[]m_rectHotspot;
  delete m_spriteDefault;
  delete[]m_bDown;
}
```

The Set_radio and Addbutton Functions

The CButtonManager set_radio function is a simple writer function; it writes its parameter to the private member variable m_bRadio:

```
void CButtonManager::set_radio(BOOL on){ //set to radio buttons
  m_bRadio=on;
}
```

The CButtonManager private addbutton function adds a new button to the end of the button list and sets its hotspot to the rectangle rect:

```
BOOL CButtonManager::addbutton(RECT rect){
//add a hotspot in this rectangle
  if(m_nCount>=m_nMaxCount)return FALSE; //bail if no space
  m_rectHotspot[m_nCount++]=rect; //insert hotspot
  return TRUE;
}
```

The CButtonManager public addbutton function adds a new button to the end of the button list and creates a rectangular hotspot for it with the top left corner of the hotspot at point:

```
BOOL CButtonManager::addbutton(POINT point){
```

It first creates the bounding rectangle in a local variable rect:

```
RECT rect; //bounding rectangle
rect.left=point.x; rect.right=point.x+m_sizeButton.cx;
rect.top=point.y; rect.bottom=point.y+m_sizeButton.cy;
```

Then it calls the private addbutton function to do the real work:

```
  return addbutton(rect); //add hotspot in this rectangle
}
```

The Hit Function

The CButtonManager hit function has a single parameter point. If point is inside a hotspot, then it returns the index of that hotspot. Otherwise, it returns −1.

```
int CButtonManager::hit(POINT point){
```

It has two local variables, the return result (initially set to −1 indicating "no hit") and an index variable i:

```
int result=-1; //start by assuming no hit
int i=0; //index
```

A `while` loop exits either when we run out of buttons to check or when we detect a hit:

```
while(i<m_nCount&&result<0) //for each button
```

It uses the local member function `PointInRect` to check whether `point` is inside the ith hotspot `m_rectHotspot[i]`.

```
if(PointInRect(m_rectHotspot[i],point)) //check for hit
```

If so, it stores the index of the hit in local variable `result`.

```
result=i; //record hit
```

Otherwise, it moves on to the next button:

```
else i++; //next button
```

When the `while` loop terminates, we return the result:

```
return result;
}
```

The Release and PointInRect Functions

The `CButtonManager` `release` function is almost exactly the same as the `CButtonManager` `hit` function, except it looks for hits inside buttons that are currently down. The `if` statement in `hit` is replaced by the following.

```
if(m_bDown[i]&&PointInRect(m_rectHotspot[i],point))
```

The `CButtonManager` `PointInRect` function returns `TRUE` if `point` is inside `rect`. It simply checks the coordinates of `point` against the boundaries of `rect`.

```
BOOL CButtonManager::PointInRect(RECT rect,POINT point){
//is point in rectangle?
  return point.x>=rect.left&&point.x<=rect.right&&
    point.y>=rect.top&&point.y<=rect.bottom;
}
```

The LoadImages and Loadsprite Functions

The `CButtonManager` `loadimages` function loads the button sprite images from the private bmp sprite file reader `m_cImage`. The first frame shows the button in the up position, which is located at the top of the image with top left pixel at `(0,0)`. The second frame shows the button in the down position, which is located below the first frame, with the top left pixel at `(0,m_sizeButton.cy)` (see Figure 11.3).

```
void CButtonManager::loadimages(){ //load button images
  m_spriteDefault->load(&m_cImage,0,0,0); //up
```

```
   m_spriteDefault->load(&m_cImage,1,0,m_sizeButton.cy); //down
}
```

The CButtonManager loadsprite function is given the filename of a file containing the sprite images:

```
BOOL CButtonManager::loadsprite(char *filename){
```

It bails out if the button size member variable hasn't been reset since the constructor ran:

```
if(m_sizeButton.cx==0&&m_sizeButton.cy==0)return FALSE;
```

It asks bmp sprite file reader member variable m_cImage to load the button sprite file, and if it fails, loadimages bails out:

```
if(!m_cImage.load(filename))return FALSE;
```

If the file loaded correctly, it goes ahead and creates a two-frame button sprite of size m_sizeButton in private member variable m_spriteDefault.

```
m_spriteDefault=
  new CClippedSprite(2,m_sizeButton.cx,m_sizeButton.cy);
```

Finally, it calls private member function loadimages to load the sprite images from the bmp file reader to the button sprite, then reports success:

```
loadimages();
return TRUE;
}
```

The Restore and Release Functions

The CButtonManager Restore function restores the sprite surfaces by calling the CBaseSprite Restore function, then reloads the images by calling the CButtonManager private member function loadimages. It returns TRUE if it succeeds.

```
BOOL CButtonManager::Restore(){ //restore surfaces
  if(m_spriteDefault->Restore()){
    loadimages();
    return TRUE;
  }
  else return FALSE;
}
```

The CButtonManager Release function releases the sprite surfaces by calling the CBaseSprite Release function:

```
void CButtonManager::Release(){ //release surfaces
  m_spriteDefault->Release();
}
```

The Buttondown Functions

The `CButtonManager` public `buttondown` function returns `TRUE` if `point` is within a button hotspot, and if so, takes care of animating the button going down. It calls the `CButtonManager` member function `hit` to return the index of the hit hotspot, if there is one, and passes this index to the `CButtonManager` private `buttondown` function, which does the real work.

```
BOOL CButtonManager::buttondown(POINT point){
  return buttondown(hit(point));
}
```

The `CButtonManager` private `buttondown` function returns `TRUE` if button `index` is a valid button index, and if so, that button is not down. The second parameter `sound`, which defaults to `TRUE` if it is missing, tells it whether to play a sound. Notice that in the `CButtonManager` public `buttondown` function, this function is passed the index returned by the `CButtonManager` `hit` function, and so it should expect to occasionally receive an index of -1 indicating a mouse click outside of a button (in which case it should do nothing but return `FALSE`).

```
BOOL CButtonManager::buttondown(int index,BOOL sound){
```

It first checks that the `index` is within range, and if so, that the button is up. If either of these fails, it will do nothing.

```
if(index>=0&&index<m_nCount&&!m_bDown[index]){
```

If everything looks kosher, it plays the button down sound if required to do so by parameter `sound`:

```
if(sound)SoundManager->play(m_nButtonDownSound);
```

If the buttons are radio buttons and the one pressed down is not the last one (which is assumed to be "Done" or "Quit" and hence not strictly part of the radio button set), then it pops up all of the radio buttons and puts down the one that was just clicked on:

```
if(m_bRadio&&index<m_nCount-1) //if radio button (not last)
  for(int i=0; i<m_nCount-1; i++)
    m_bDown[i]=FALSE; //pop up other radio buttons
m_bDown[index]=TRUE; //button is now down
```

It then calls the `CButtonManager` private `display_menu` function to draw the buttons in their new positions and returns `TRUE`. The purist might argue that, since `display_menu` draws all of the buttons, we are wasting time drawing buttons whose state doesn't change. However, it really isn't worth the effort to recode `display_menu` to draw only the buttons whose state has changed, since we only call it once every few seconds (whenever the user clicks), and it has very little work to do as it is.

```
    display_menu(); //display menu page
    return TRUE;
  }
```

Otherwise, if there's no action, it returns FALSE:

```
    else return FALSE;
  }
```

The Buttonup and Allbuttonsup Functions

The two CButtonManager buttonup functions do the same thing for up buttons:

```
BOOL CButtonManager::buttonup(POINT point){
  return buttonup(hit(point));
}
```

Aside from the obvious changes involved in changing "down" to "up," we also want to disable radio buttons from popping up when the mouse button is released. That is, they are allowed to pop up only if they are not radio buttons or they are the last button on a radio button page. This is enforced by adding the condition (!m_bRadio||index==m_nCount-1) to the if statement in the private CButtonManager buttonup function.

```
BOOL CButtonManager::buttonup(int index){
  if((!m_bRadio||index==m_nCount-1)&&
  index>=0&&index<m_nCount&&m_bDown[index]){ //if valid
    SoundManager->play(m_nButtonUpSound);
    m_bDown[index]=FALSE; //button is up
    display_menu(); //display menu page
    return TRUE;
  }
  else return FALSE;
}
```

The CButtonManager allbuttonsup function pops up all buttons and plays the button up sound if anything actually popped up:

```
void CButtonManager::allbuttonsup(){
```

It has a local index variable i:

```
  int i; //index
```

If the screen contains radio buttons, it pops up only the last ("Exit" or "Done") button:

```
  if(m_bRadio){ //don't pop up radio buttons
    if(m_bDown[m_nCount-1]){ //pop up quit button if down
      m_bDown[m_nCount-1]=FALSE;
```

```
        SoundManager->play(m_nButtonUpSound);
      }
    }
```

Otherwise, it attempts to pop up all of the buttons, playing a sound only if one of them was down:

```
else{ //not radio buttons, so pop up all of them
```

A local variable found (initially FALSE) is set to TRUE if it finds that one of the buttons was down:

```
BOOL found=FALSE; //to make sure sound played only once
```

It loops through each of the button indices i with a for loop:

```
for(i=0; i<m_nCount; i++) //for each button
```

If button i is down, it pops it up and records that it found a down button:

```
if(m_bDown[i]){ //if valid down button
  found=TRUE; //will play sound later
  m_bDown[i]=FALSE; //button is up
}
```

On exit from the for loop, it plays the button up sound, provided a button actually popped up:

```
if(found)SoundManager->play(m_nButtonUpSound);
}
```

Finally, it redraws all of the buttons (whether it needs to or not) by calling the CButtonManager display_menu function:

```
display_menu(); //display menu page
}
```

The Display_menu Function

The CButtonManager display_menu function draws the buttons to the secondary surface, assuming that the background is already drawn there, and flips it to the primary surface:

```
void CButtonManager::display_menu(){ //display menu page
```

It loops through all of the buttons with a for loop:

```
for(int i=0; i<m_nCount; i++) //for each button
```

It checks whether the i th button is down:

```
if(m_bDown[i]) //draw button down
```

If so, it draws frame 1 to the secondary surface, being careful to map from the top left corner of the bounding rectangle to the bottom center pixel of the sprite:

```
m_spriteDefault->
    draw(1,m_rectHotspot[i].left+m_sizeButton.cx/2,
        m_rectHotspot[i].top+m_sizeButton.cy,lpSecondary);
```

If it's down, it draws frame 0 to the secondary surface instead:

```
else //draw button up
    m_spriteDefault->
        draw(0,m_rectHotspot[i].left+m_sizeButton.cx/2,
            m_rectHotspot[i].top+m_sizeButton.cy,lpSecondary);
```

When all the buttons have been drawn, it flips the secondary surface to the primary surface using the PageFlip function from Main.cpp:

```
PageFlip(); //flip back buffer to front
}
```

The Setsounds Function

The last CButtonManager function is setsounds, which writes the indices of the button sounds to the appropriate private member variables:

```
void CButtonManager::setsounds(int down,int up){ //set sounds
    m_nButtonDownSound=down; m_nButtonUpSound=up;
}
```

The Input Manager

Processing the input to our game is starting to get a little complicated, so we'll create an input manager CInputManager to handle it, and move the input handling functions out of Main.cpp. Now that we've got more than one input device, we add a new enumerated type to Defines.h.

```
enum InputDeviceType{KEYBOARD_INPUT=0,MOUSE_INPUT=1};
```

Input Manager Overview

The header file for CInputManager is Input.h. CInputManager has two private member functions. The first of these is InputDevice, which records the input device that the player currently wishes to use in the game engine. The second is a pointer to a button manager, which will be created and customized when a menu screen is being displayed, and will be disposed of afterward.

```
InputDeviceType InputDevice; //current input device
CButtonManager *ButtonManager; //for managing menu buttons
```

CInputManager has 15 private member functions. The first three of these are helper functions. The is_function_key function takes a keystroke as a parameter and returns TRUE if the keystroke is a function key (either Esc, or F1, F2, etc., at the top of the standard keyboard). The decode function takes an `lparam` sent by the operating system in response to a mouse event, and decodes from it the coordinates of the mouse pointer into a parameter `point`. The `set_plane_speed` function takes a mouse cursor location `point` within the screen `extent`, and uses it like a digital joystick to set the plane's horizontal speed and vertical speed.

```
BOOL is_function_key(WPARAM keystroke); //TRUE if functn key
void decode(LPARAM lparam,POINT &point); //decode mouse click
void set_plane_speed(POINT point,SIZE extent);
```

Each menu screen has its own private member function to set up the button manager pointed to by the private member variable `ButtonManager`. Since we have two menu screens, we have two of these functions, `SetupMainMenuButtons` and `SetupDeviceMenuButtons`.

```
void SetupMainMenuButtons(); //main menu button manager
void SetupDeviceMenuButtons(); //device menu button manager
```

The rest of the `CInputManager` private member functions are handlers for a particular device event in a particular phase. Devoting one function for each device in each phase makes the code easier to read and maintain. The next four private member functions are keyboard handlers, one for each phase. These are mostly lifted from `Main.cpp` in Demo 8.

```
void IntroKeyboard(WPARAM keystroke); //keyboard handler
BOOL MainMenuKeyboard(WPARAM keystroke); //keyboard handler
void DeviceMenuKeyboard(WPARAM keystroke); //keyboard handler
void GameKeyboard(WPARAM keystroke); //keyboard handler
```

Analogously, we have handlers for when the left mouse button goes down in the main menu, the device menu, and the game engine. Each of these functions has the mouse cursor location as a parameter.

```
void MainMenuLMouseDown(POINT point); //mouse down handler
void DeviceMenuLMouseDown(POINT point); //mouse down handler
void GameLMouseDown(POINT point); //mouse down handler
```

Then, we have handlers for the left mouse button going up during the intro phases, the main menu phase, and the device menu phase:

```
void IntroLMouseUp(POINT point); //mouse up handler
BOOL MainMenuLMouseUp(POINT point); //mouse up handler
void DeviceMenuLMouseUp(POINT point); //mouse up handler
```

The input manager has nine public member functions, including a constructor and a destructor:

```
CInputManager(); //constructor
~CInputManager(); //destructor
```

Next, we see the mandatory `Restore` and `Release` functions for the surfaces in the input manager. But where *are* the input manager surfaces? In the button manager.

```
BOOL Restore(); //restore surfaces
void Release(); //release surfaces
```

Function `SetupButtons` sets up the button manager for a given `phase`. It will call the appropriate private member function to do the real work.

```
void SetupButtons(GamePhaseType phase); //set up menu buttons
```

The main keyboard handler `Keyboard` parcels out the work to the keyboard manager private member function for the current phase. The keyboard handler will be disabled when the player is playing using the mouse; otherwise, he or she might try to confuse things by pressing the left and right arrow keys while simultaneously using the mouse to control speed. Rather than write code to handle this case, which the user really has no legitimate reason to try (other than jerking your chain, and believe me, some of them will take pleasure in doing exactly that), it is easier just to deactivate the keyboard handler. However, although the *player* has no business using the keyboard handler when playing with the mouse, *you* as programmer may find it convenient to issue fake keystrokes called *virtual keystrokes* (not to be confused with the Windows API virtual key*codes*). These special keystrokes should *not* be disabled. We handle this by giving function `Keyboard` an extra Boolean parameter `virtual_keystroke` that we will set to `TRUE` for virtual keystrokes and default to `FALSE` when it is missing.

```
BOOL Keyboard(WPARAM keystroke,
  BOOL virtual_keystroke=FALSE); //keyboard handler
```

Finally, we have main handlers for the mouse events, including left button down, left button up, and mouse motion:

```
void LMouseDown(LPARAM lparam); //main mouse down handler
BOOL LMouseUp(LPARAM lparam); //main mouse up handler
void MouseMove(LPARAM lparam); //handle mouse motion
```

The Constructor and Destructor

The code file for `CInputManager` is `Input.cpp`. It begins with the constructor, which sets the input device to the keyboard, and sets the button manager pointer to `NULL` so that if the destructor runs before a button manager has been created, the `delete` does not fail. The destructor's only job is to `delete` the button manager.

```
CInputManager::CInputManager(){ //constructor
  InputDevice=KEYBOARD_INPUT; //current input device
  ButtonManager=NULL; //for managing menu buttons
```

```
  }

  CInputManager::~CInputManager(){ //destructor
    delete ButtonManager;
  }
```

The Restore and Release Functions

The `CInputManager` `Restore` and `Release` functions respectively call the button manager's `Restore` and `Release` member functions:

```
BOOL CInputManager::Restore(){ //restore surfaces
  return ButtonManager->Restore();
}

void CInputManager::Release(){ //release surfaces
  ButtonManager->Release();
}
```

Setting Up Buttons

The `CInputManager` `SetupMainMenuButtons` function sets up a button manager for the main menu screen:

```
void CInputManager::SetupMainMenuButtons(){
```

It begins with two constants, the vertical separation between the buttons and the number of buttons that appear on the main menu:

```
const int YDELTA=70; //y separation between buttons
const int BUTTONCOUNT=6; //number of buttons
```

Next, we declare and initialize a `SIZE` structure for the size of the buttons, which are 40 pixels wide and 40 pixels high:

```
SIZE size; //size of buttons
size.cx=40; size.cy=40; //size of buttons
```

Similarly, a `POINT` structure holds the location of the top left corner of the first button:

```
POINT point; //top left corner of first button
point.x=111; point.y=46; //first button location
```

We delete the old button manager if there is one (as I've mentioned already, calling `delete` on a `NULL` pointer is harmless), and create a new one using the second `CButtonManager` constructor:

```
delete ButtonManager; //delete any old one
ButtonManager=new //create new button manager
  CButtonManager(BUTTONCOUNT,size,point,YDELTA,
    "buttons.bmp");
```

Finally, we set the button sounds, which are added to the end of the list of game sounds in `Sndlist.h`.

```
//set button sounds
 ButtonManager->
   setsounds(BIGCLICK_SOUND,SMALLCLICK_SOUND);
}
```

The `CInputManager SetupDeviceMenuButtons` function sets up a button manager for the device menu screen:

```
void CInputManager::SetupDeviceMenuButtons(){
```

It begins with a constant declaring the number of buttons that appear on the device menu:

```
const int BUTTONCOUNT=4;
```

It deletes the old button manager and sets up a `SIZE` structure for the buttons:

```
delete ButtonManager; //if there is one already, delete it
SIZE size; //size of buttons
size.cx=40; size.cy=40; //size of buttons
```

Since the locations of the buttons on the device menu are not quite perfect, we use the first `ButtonManager` constructor, the one that does not set up the initial button positions:

```
ButtonManager=new
   CButtonManager(BUTTONCOUNT,size,"buttons.bmp");
```

We set the sounds and make the buttons into radio buttons:

```
ButtonManager->setsounds(BIGCLICK_SOUND,SMALLCLICK_SOUND);
ButtonManager->set_radio(); //radio buttons
```

Then, we add the buttons into the button manager by hand, with their top left pixels at positions (209,130), (209,210), (209,291), and (209,372). (The first two buttons are separated by 80 pixels, but the rest are separated by 82 pixels. Did you notice that the first time you saw Figure 11.1?)

```
POINT point;
point.x=209; point.y=130;
ButtonManager->addbutton(point);
point.x=209; point.y=210;
ButtonManager->addbutton(point);
point.x=209; point.y=291;
ButtonManager->addbutton(point);
point.x=209; point.y=372;
ButtonManager->addbutton(point);
```

Finally, we push down the radio button corresponding to the current input device using the button manager's `buttondown` function. Naturally, we don't want any sound to be played; that's why we wrote the `buttondown` to play sounds optionally. We want a sound to be played when the player presses down a button, but not when the computer presses it down during initialization.

```
    ButtonManager->buttondown(InputDevice,FALSE); //no sound
  }
```

The `CInputManager SetupButtons` public member function consists of a `switch` statement that calls the appropriate `CInputManager` private member function to do the real work:

```
void CInputManager::SetupButtons(GamePhaseType phase){
//set up menu buttons
  switch(phase){
    case MENU_PHASE: SetupMainMenuButtons(); break;
    case DEVICEMENU_PHASE: SetupDeviceMenuButtons(); break;
  }
}
```

Keyboard Handlers

The `CInputManager IntroKeyboard` function is lifted from `Main.cpp` in Demo 8.

```
void CInputManager::IntroKeyboard(WPARAM keystroke){
//keyboard handler for intro
  endphase=TRUE; //any key ends the phase
}
```

There are some changes to the `CInputManager MainMenuKeyboard` from its counterpart in Demo 8's `Main.cpp`. Now that there is more than one phase that we can go to at the end of the main menu phase (either the new device menu phase or the playing phase), we need some method for indicating which phase is next. We do this with a global variable `NextPhase` that, when `endphase` is `TRUE`, indicates the next phase. Purists may object to this use of global variables. I like to use them to avoid getting tangled in a Byzantine return structure. I find that in practice, global variables are fine for unique things (meaning that there can be only one in a program), when they simplify programming, and provided they are not overused. Function `MainMenuKeyboard` also has a new case for the "D" key, which sends the player from the main menu to the device menu.

```
BOOL CInputManager::MainMenuKeyboard(WPARAM keystroke){
//keyboard handler for menu
  BOOL result=FALSE;
  switch(keystroke){
    case VK_ESCAPE:
    case 'Q': //exit the game
```

```
      result=TRUE;
      break;
    case 'N': //play new game
      NextPhase=PLAYING_PHASE; endphase=TRUE;
      break;
    case 'D':
      NextPhase=DEVICEMENU_PHASE; endphase=TRUE;
    default: break; //do nothing
  }
  return result;
}
```

The `CInputManager DeviceMenuKeyboard` function is the keyboard handler for the device menu:

```
void CInputManager::DeviceMenuKeyboard(WPARAM keystroke){
```

It consists of a `switch` statement with a `case` for each legal `keystroke`.

```
switch(keystroke){
```

The Esc key and the "D" key exit the device menu by setting `endphase` to `TRUE`.

```
case VK_ESCAPE:
case 'D': //exit menu
  endphase=TRUE;
  break;
```

The second `case` sets the private member variable `InputDevice` to indicate keyboard input, then puts the appropriate button down using the private button manager. Since the button manager's `m_bRadio` private member variable is set, it automatically pops up whichever button was previously down.

```
case 'K': //play using keyboard
  InputDevice=KEYBOARD_INPUT; //set device
  ButtonManager->buttondown(KEYBOARD_INPUT);
  break;
```

The third `case` does the same when the player chooses mouse input:

```
case 'M': //play using mouse
  InputDevice=MOUSE_INPUT; //set device
  ButtonManager->buttondown(MOUSE_INPUT);
  break;
default: break;
  }
}
```

The `CInputManager GameKeyboard` function is lifted from `Main.cpp` in Demo 8:

```
void CInputManager::GameKeyboard(WPARAM keystroke){
//keyboard handler for game play
```

```
switch(keystroke){
  case VK_ESCAPE: endphase=TRUE; break;
  case VK_UP: ObjectManager.accelerate(0,-1); break;
  case VK_DOWN: ObjectManager.accelerate(0,1); break;
  case VK_LEFT: ObjectManager.accelerate(-1,0); break;
  case VK_RIGHT: ObjectManager.accelerate(1,0); break;
  case VK_SPACE: ObjectManager.fire_gun(); break;
  default: break;
  }
}
```

The `CInputManager is_function_key` function returns TRUE when keystroke is a function key. It uses the handy Windows API constants for the function keys, which are fortunately contiguous in the ASCII table. This means that it only has to return TRUE when keystroke is equal to VK_ESCAPE, or keystroke is between VK_F1 and VK_F12, inclusive.

```
BOOL CInputManager::is_function_key(WPARAM keystroke){
  return keystroke==VK_ESCAPE||
    (keystroke>=VK_F1&&keystroke<=VK_F12);
}
```

The `CInputManager Keyboard` function is the main keyboard handler. It consists of a switch statement that selects the keyboard handler for the current phase using the global variable GamePhase. Most cases just pass the keystroke to the appropriate private member function without further work.

```
BOOL CInputManager::Keyboard(WPARAM keystroke,
  BOOL virtual_keystroke){ //keyboard handler
  BOOL result=FALSE;
  switch(GamePhase){
    case LOGO_PHASE:
    case TITLE_PHASE:
      IntroKeyboard(keystroke);
      break;
    case MENU_PHASE:
      result=MainMenuKeyboard(keystroke);
      break;
    case DEVICEMENU_PHASE:
      DeviceMenuKeyboard(keystroke);
      break;
```

However, the playing phase is different. We only pass on keystrokes to the private member function GameKeyboard if the input device is the keyboard, the key is a function key (for example, we still want the Esc key to work when the player is using the mouse), or the keystroke is a virtual keystroke.

```
    case PLAYING_PHASE:
      if(InputDevice==KEYBOARD_INPUT||
      is_function_key(keystroke)||virtual_keystroke)
```

```
        GameKeyboard(keystroke);
      break;
  }
  return result;
}
```

Mouse Handlers

Next, we have the `CInputManager` mouse left button down handlers. The main menu left button down handler `MainMenuLMouseDown` is relatively simple; if `point` is within a button's hotspot, then that button goes down. No real action is taken; for regular buttons, the action happens when the mouse button is released.

```
void CInputManager::MainMenuLMouseDown(POINT point){
//mouse down handler for menu
  if(ButtonManager->hit(point)>=0) //if a valid hit
    ButtonManager->buttondown(point); //animate a button down
}
```

The `CInputManager` `DeviceMenuLMouseDown` function is different because with radio buttons the action happens when the button goes down:

```
void CInputManager::DeviceMenuLMouseDown(POINT point){
```

It begins by checking whether `point` is inside a hotspot:

```
int hit=ButtonManager->hit(point);
```

Then, a switch statement takes different action for each hotspot:

```
switch(hit){
```

Here we come face to face with a design decision. If `hit` is 0, it means that the player clicked in the topmost button on the screen. This means that they want to play using the keyboard instead of the mouse or the joystick. We could insert code here to set `InputDevice` to `KEYBOARD_INPUT`, and animate the button going down, just like in the "K" `case` of the `switch` statement in the device menu keyboard handler. Instead, we are going to pretend that the player hit the "K" key by calling the keyboard manager with parameter 'K'. Our design philosophy will be that the keyboard handler is in charge of mapping player choices to game actions. Other device handlers will ask the keyboard to take the appropriate action. Why? It means we don't duplicate the code in two places, which would make maintenance a pain; every time we needed to make a change to the code, we'd have to remember to make the changes in two or more places. The obvious alternative would be to create lots of little functions instead, one for each action, but that in itself would make maintenance a bother. This solution is much easier, although it does make the assumption that for every mouse action in the menus, there is a corresponding keyboard command. This, however, is not a bad thing. Although these days everybody has a mouse, not everybody likes to use it all the time.

```
case 0: Keyboard('K'); break; //keyboard
```

Similarly for button 1, which calls for mouse play:

```
case 1: Keyboard('M'); break; //mouse
```

There is no `case` 2 because that button (joystick play) doesn't work yet. Case 3 is the "Done" button, which exits the menu.

```
case 3:
  ButtonManager->buttondown(hit); //quit button down
  break;
```

The `default` case is when the player clicked outside an active button, in which case `hit` is -1. We do nothing.

```
    default: break;
  }
}
```

The `CInputManager` game left mouse button handler `GameLMouseDown` sends a Spacebar virtual keystroke to the keyboard handler. Why a virtual keystroke? Because our keyboard handler is disabled during mouse play.

```
void CInputManager::GameLMouseDown(POINT point){
//mouse down handler for game
  Keyboard(VK_SPACE,TRUE);
}
```

The Windows API `WM_LBUTTONDOWN` message that is delivered to your message handler in `Main.cpp` when the left mouse button goes down comes with an `LPARAM` parameter that contains the mouse coordinates encoded as a 32-bit integer. The high 16 bits of this word contain the y coordinate, and the low 16 bits contain the x coordinate. We could shift and mask this integer to extract the fields we want, but the Windows API fortunately contains two macros, `LOWORD` and `HIWORD`, that do the job for us. The `CInputManager` decode helper function decodes `lparam` into `point` (note that `point` is a call-by-reference parameter).

```
void CInputManager::decode(LPARAM lparam,POINT &point){
//decode mouse click lparam to point
  point.x=LOWORD(lparam); point.y=HIWORD(lparam);
}
```

The `CInputManager` left mouse button down handler `LMouseDown` takes as a parameter the `LPARAM` parameter that accompanies the `WM_LBUTTONDOWN` message:

```
void CInputManager::LMouseDown(LPARAM lparam){
```

It decodes `lparam` into a local variable `point`:

```
POINT point; //mouse location on screen
decode(lparam,point); //decode mouse point
```

The main body of `LMouseDown` is a `switch` statement that passes `point` to the left mouse button down handler for the current phase, which is stored in the global variable `GamePhase`:

```
switch(GamePhase){
  case MENU_PHASE:
    MainMenuLMouseDown(point);
    break;
  case DEVICEMENU_PHASE:
    DeviceMenuLMouseDown(point);
    break;
  case PLAYING_PHASE:
    if(InputDevice==MOUSE_INPUT)
      GameLMouseDown(point);
    break;
  }
}
```

Next, we have the `CInputManager` left mouse button up handlers. There is a left button *up* handler for the intro sequence, but not a left button *down* handler because the action will take place when the left mouse button is released, not when it is pressed down. The `CInputManager IntroLMouseUp` function simply ends the current phase by setting the global `endphase` variable to `TRUE`.

```
void CInputManager::IntroLMouseUp(POINT point){
//mouse left button up handler for intro
  endphase=TRUE;
}
```

The action for the main menu takes place when a button is released. Why not when a button is pressed down? Because the player may mash down on a button and then change his or her mind; they can back out of it by moving the mouse cursor off the button and releasing it elsewhere on the screen. Our code requires that the player mash down on a button *and* release the left mouse button with the cursor on the same screen button to get an action. The `CInputManager MainMenuLMouseUp` function is the left mouse button up handler for the main menu. It returns `TRUE` if the main menu phase is to end because the player clicked on the last button on the screen.

```
BOOL CInputManager::MainMenuLMouseUp(POINT point){
```

It sets local variable `hit` to the index of the button that the cursor was in when the left mouse button was released, provided that button was down:

```
int hit=ButtonManager->release(point); //get button hit
```

It has a local variable `result` for the return result.

```
BOOL result=FALSE;
```

A `switch` statement maps the buttons to keyboard events. The last button is treated differently because it is the "Quit" button.

```
switch(hit){ //depending on which button was hit
  case 0: Keyboard('N'); break; //new game
  case 1: Keyboard('S'); break; //saved game
  case 2: Keyboard('D'); break; //devices
  case 3: Keyboard('L'); break; //high score list
  case 4: Keyboard('H'); break; //help
  case 5: result=Keyboard(VK_ESCAPE); break; //quit
  default: break;
}
```

If there was a legitimate hit, we animate the hit button going up. Otherwise, we animate all the buttons going up, because there may be a down button that the player moved the mouse cursor off prior to releasing the left mouse button. Then, we return the result and exit.

```
  //animate button images
  if(hit>=0)ButtonManager->buttonup(hit); //hit
  else ButtonManager->allbuttonsup(); //nonhit
  return result;
}
```

The `CInputManager` device menu left mouse button up function `DeviceMenuLMouseUp` is similar, but it only has to take action for the "Done" button because all of the other buttons on the screen are radio buttons, which means that their actions are handled by the `CInputManager` device menu left mouse button down function `DeviceMenuLMouseDown`:

```
void CInputManager::DeviceMenuLMouseUp(POINT point){
//mouse left button up handler for device menu
  int hit=ButtonManager->release(point);
  switch(hit){
    case 3: //quit button up
      ButtonManager->buttonup(hit); //show quit button up
      Keyboard(VK_ESCAPE);
      break;
  }
  if(hit<0)ButtonManager->allbuttonsup(); //no hit
}
```

The CInputManager main left mouse button up function LMouseUp is similar to the CInputManager main left mouse button down function LMouseDown. It decodes lparam into a point, then uses a switch statement to send it to the left mouse button down handler for the current phase.

```
BOOL CInputManager::LMouseUp(LPARAM lparam){
//main mouse left button up handler
  BOOL result=FALSE;
  POINT point; //mouse location on screen
  decode(lparam,point); //decode mouse point
  switch(GamePhase){
    case LOGO_PHASE:
    case TITLE_PHASE:
      IntroLMouseUp(point);
      break;
    case MENU_PHASE:
      result=MainMenuLMouseUp(point);
      break;
    case DEVICEMENU_PHASE:
      DeviceMenuLMouseUp(point);
      break;
  }
  return result;
}
```

The Mouse as Digital Joystick

The last two CInputManager functions deal with the use of the mouse as a digital joystick to control the plane's vertical and horizontal speed. We will divide the screen into rectilinear bands, and set the plane's speed according to which band the invisible mouse cursor is in currently. The CInputManager set_plane_speed function sets the plane's speed using the position of point within the screen extent.

```
void CInputManager::set_plane_speed(POINT point,SIZE extent){
```

It has four local variables that it sets to the plane's minimum and maximum horizontal and vertical speeds by calling a new CObjectManager speed_limits function (all four parameters of this function are call-by-reference):

```
int xmin,xmax,ymin,ymax; //plane speed limits
ObjectManager.speed_limits(xmin,xmax,ymin,ymax); //get them
```

The plane has xmax-xmin+1 different horizontal speeds, and so the screen should be divided into xmax-xmin+1 different bands, each of width XBANDWIDTH, where the constant XBANDWIDTH is defined as follows:

```
const int XBANDWIDTH=extent.cx/(xmax-xmin+1);
```

Similarly for the vertical bands:

```
const int YBANDWIDTH=extent.cy/(ymax-ymin+1);
```

Next, we have two local variables for the desired speed of the plane:

```
int xspeed,yspeed; //speed of plane
```

We start by dividing the x coordinate of the point by XBANDWIDTH to get the index of the vertical band containing the mouse pointer, which will be in the range 0 through xmax-xmin, inclusive (see Figure 11.4, in which the band index is listed at the top of each band). The leftmost band, with index 0, corresponds to a speed of xmin (since speeds to the left are negative, xmin is the largest negative speed, corresponding to moving leftward fastest). The rightmost band, with index xmax-xmin, corresponds to a speed of xmax (see Figure 11.4, in which the corresponding speed is listed toward the middle of each band). Therefore, we need to add xmin to the band index point.x/XBANDWIDTH to get the corresponding horizontal speed.

```
xspeed=point.x/XBANDWIDTH+xmin; //horizontal speed
```

Exactly the same argument holds for the vertical speed:

```
yspeed=point.y/YBANDWIDTH+ymin; //vertical speed
```

Finally, having computed the plane's speed, we set it using the new CObjectManager set_speed function:

```
ObjectManager.set_speed(xspeed,yspeed); //pass to plane
}
```

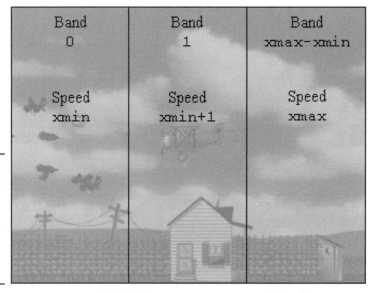

Figure 11.4
Dividing the screen into bands corresponding to horizontal speed

The `CInputManager MouseMove` function is the handler for mouse motion. Its `lparam` parameter carries the mouse cursor's new position on the screen encoded in the same way as for the mouse button handler functions.

```
void CInputManager::MouseMove(LPARAM lparam){
```

If the player isn't using the mouse to play the game, then we bail out; the mouse joystick is not needed:

```
if(InputDevice!=MOUSE_INPUT)return; //bail if not needed
if(GamePhase!=PLAYING_PHASE)return; //bail if not playing
```

We decode the parameter `lparam` into a local variable `point`:

```
POINT point; //mouse location on screen
decode(lparam,point); //decode mouse point
```

We create a local variable to hold the screen extent:

```
SIZE extent; //extent that mouse moves in
extent.cx=SCREEN_WIDTH;
extent.cy=SCREEN_HEIGHT;
```

Then we call the `CInputManager set_plane_speed` function to set the plane's speed using the position of `point` within the screen `extent`:

```
set_plane_speed(point,extent);
}
```

Changes to the Object and Object Manager Classes

There are some small changes to the `CObject` and `CObjectManager` classes—the addition of three new functions (in total) to facilitate the use of the mouse as a digital joystick. Since these changes are so small, we won't list the requisite files—`Objects.h`, `Objects.cpp`, `Objman.h`, and `Objman.cpp`—with the other new and changed files at the end of this chapter.

`CObject` has a new public member function `set_speed` to be used by the mouse move handler to transfer the plane's speed from the mouse to the plane. It calls the `CObject accelerate` member function to add `xspeed-m_nXspeed` to `m_nXspeed`, thereby changing it to `xspeed` (similarly for `yspeed` and `m_nYspeed`).

```
void CObject::set_speed(int xspeed,int yspeed){ //set speed
  accelerate(xspeed-m_nXspeed,yspeed-m_nYspeed);
}
```

`CObjectManager` has two new public member functions also for use by the mouse move handler. Function `set_speed` sets the plane's speed by calling the plane object's `set_speed` member function, which was described in the previous paragraph.

```
void CObjectManager::set_speed(int xdelta,int ydelta){
  m_pObjectList[m_nCurrentObject]->set_speed(xdelta,ydelta);
}
```

The `CObjectManager speed_limits` function is a reader function that sets its four call-by-reference parameters to the current object's minimum and maximum horizontal and vertical speeds:

```
void CObjectManager::speed_limits(int &xmin,int &xmax,
                                  int &ymin,int &ymax){
//return speed limits on current object
  CObject *plane=m_pObjectList[m_nCurrentObject];
  xmin=plane->m_nMinXSpeed; xmax=plane->m_nMaxXSpeed;
  ymin=plane->m_nMinYSpeed; ymax=plane->m_nMaxYSpeed;
}
```

Changes to Main.cpp

As we have mentioned already, `Main.cpp` now has a new global variable `NextPhase` that will be used to store the required next phase when the end of the current phase is signaled by setting `endphase` to `TRUE`:

```
GamePhaseType NextPhase; //next phase of game
```

We also need a global input manager:

```
CInputManager InputManager; //device input manager
```

Function `RestoreSurfaces` has the following line of code added to the end to restore the surfaces in the button sprite in the input manager's button manager:

```
if(!InputManager.Restore())return FALSE;
```

Function `LoadSounds` has the following two lines of code added to `case 1` of the `switch` statement. These load the sounds for the buttons going down (a big click) and up (a small click).

```
        SoundManager->load("bgclk.wav",2);
        SoundManager->load("smclk.wav",2);
```

Function `display_screen`, which is used to display the intro screens and the background for the menu screens, also needs a small modification. The code for animating the buttons going up and down assumes that the background screen has been drawn to both the primary and secondary surfaces. In Demo 8, function `display_screen` draws it to the secondary surface, then flips it up to the primary surface, leaving the secondary surface with whatever was in the primary surface before. We add the following extra line of code to the end of `display_screen` to bring it up to spec.

```
image.draw(lpSecondary);
```

The Change_phase Function

Function `change_phase` has been made more complicated by the fact that you can enter more than one phase from the main menu, and of course by the addition of a new phase for the device menu. In Demo 8, it started with the following two lines of code to change the phase. These are now moved to the end of the function because the `switch` statement now needs access to the current phase information to determine what to do.

```
GamePhase=new_phase; PhaseTime=Timer.time();
endphase=FALSE;
```

Because the current phase has not yet been changed to the new phase, the switch statement itself must now look at the new phase, not the current one:

```
switch(new_phase){
```

The case for the `MENU_PHASE` had become much more elaborate:

```
case MENU_PHASE:
```

We begin by setting up the buttons for the main menu phase:

```
InputManager.SetupButtons(MENU_PHASE);
```

What is done to the sound depends on the current phase. If we are leaving the title phase to enter the main menu phase, the title sound needs to be stopped in case the player clicked out of the title screen, and we will load the sounds for level 1 now instead of later because these sounds now include the mouse clicks for the menu pages. If we are leaving the playing phase for the main menu, we need only stop the sounds.

```
switch(GamePhase){ //depending on previous phase
  case TITLE_PHASE: //from intro phase
    SoundManager->stop(); //silence previous phase
    SoundManager->clear(); //clear out old sounds
    LoadSounds(1); //set up game sounds
    break;
  case PLAYING_PHASE: //from game engine
    SoundManager->stop(); //silence game engine
    break;
   case DEVICEMENU_PHASE: //device menu, do nothing
    break;
}
```

We then display the main menu screen from file `Menu.bmp`.

```
display_screen("menu.bmp"); //display main menu
```

The mouse cursor needs to be shown if we are entering the main menu phase (which needs the mouse cursor on) from the playing or title phases (which have the mouse cursor off), but not from the device menu page (which has the mouse cursor on). Some care must be taken with the use of the Windows API function calls `ShowCursor(TRUE)` and `ShowCursor(FALSE)`. Recall from Chapter 2 that instead of setting and unsetting a Boolean value, `ShowCursor(TRUE)` increments a counter and `ShowCursor(FALSE)` decrements it. The counter must be positive for the mouse cursor to be shown. Therefore, if you call `ShowCursor(FALSE)` twice in succession, you must call `ShowCursor(TRUE)` twice before the mouse cursor will reappear (remember these words when your mouse cursor fails to appear when you expect it to). This ends the `case MENU_PHASE` in the main switch statement.

```
switch(GamePhase){ //what phase did we come in from?
  case PLAYING_PHASE:
  case TITLE_PHASE:
    ShowCursor(TRUE); //activate the mouse cursor
    break;
}
break;
```

There is a new `case` for the `DEVICEMENU_PHASE`, which displays the device menu screen and sets up the buttons for the device menu:

```
case DEVICEMENU_PHASE:
  //display button background
  display_screen("dmenu.bmp");
  //set up the button manager
  InputManager.SetupButtons(DEVICEMENU_PHASE);
  break;
```

The `case PLAYING_PHASE` has two new lines of code to set up the cursor position and turn off the mouse cursor (which in Demo 8 was turned off at the start of the game and left off; now it will be turned on in the main menu and must be turned off when entering the game engine). The cursor position is set using the Windows API function `SetCursorPos`.

```
SetCursorPos(SCREEN_WIDTH-1,SCREEN_HEIGHT/2); //throttle
ShowCursor(FALSE); //hide the mouse cursor
```

Other Functions

Function `Redraw` has the following case added to its `switch` statement to redraw the device menu screen:

```
case DEVICEMENU_PHASE:
  display_screen("dmenu.bmp");
  InputManager.SetupButtons(DEVICEMENU_PHASE);
  break;
```

The new global variable `NextPhase` gets used in function `ProcessFrame` to set the next phase when exiting the main menu screen. In the `case MENU_PHASE` in its `switch` statement, the call to `change_phase` is changed from `change_phase(PLAYING_PHASE)` in Demo 8 to `change_phase(NextPhase)`. We also add a new `case` for the device menu; when the device menu phase ends, we go to the main menu.

```
case DEVICEMENU_PHASE:
  if(endphase) change_phase(MENU_PHASE); //go to menu phase
  break;
```

There are several changes to the window procedure `WindowProc`. The first is minor; in response to the `WM_KEYDOWN` message, it now uses the input manager's keyboard handler instead of having the keyboard handler functions in `Main.cpp`.

```
case WM_KEYDOWN: //keyboard hit
  if(InputManager.Keyboard(wParam))
    DestroyWindow(hwnd);
  break;
```

There are three new cases for mouse messages, beginning with the left mouse button down message `WM_LBUTTONDOWN`. The `lParam` parameter containing the mouse cursor coordinates is passed on to the input manager's `LMouseDown` function.

```
case WM_LBUTTONDOWN: //left mouse button down
  InputManager.LMouseDown(lParam); //handle it
  break;
```

The response to the left mouse button up handler is similar, with the addition that the input manager's `LMouseUp` function will return `TRUE` if the player wants to exit the program, which, as always, we do with a call to the Windows API function `DestroyWindow`:

```
case WM_LBUTTONUP: //left mouse button up
  if(InputManager.LMouseUp(lParam))
    DestroyWindow(hwnd);
  break;
```

The mouse move message `WM_MOUSEMOVE` is handled similarly:

```
case WM_MOUSEMOVE: //mouse move
  InputManager.MouseMove(lParam);
  break;
```

One line of code is added to the `case WM_DESTROY` to release the input manager's surfaces:

```
InputManager.Release(); //button surfaces
```

Demo 9 Files

Code Files

The following files in Demo 9 are used without change from Demo 8:

- Ai.h
- Ai.cpp
- Bmp.h
- Bmp.cpp
- Bsprite.h
- Bsprite.cpp
- Csprite.h
- Csprite.cpp
- Ddsetup.cpp
- Random.h
- Random.cpp
- Sbmp.h
- Sbmp.cpp
- Sound.h
- Sound.cpp
- Timer.h
- Timer.cpp
- View.h
- View.cpp

The following files in Demo 9 have been modified from Demo 8:

- Defines.h
- Main.cpp
- Objects.h (changes minimal; not listed)

- Objects.cpp (changes minimal; not listed)
- Objman.h (changes minimal; not listed)
- Objman.cpp (changes minimal; not listed)
- Sndlist.h

The following files are new in Demo 9:

- Buttons.h
- Buttons.cpp
- Input.h
- Input.cpp

Media Files

The following image files are new in Demo 9:

- Buttons.bmp
- Dmenu.bmp

The following sound files are new in Demo 9:

- Bgclk.wav
- Smclk.wav

Required Libraries

- Ddraw.lib
- Dsound.lib
- Winmm.lib

Code Listings

Buttons.h

```
//buttons.h: header file for button class

//Copyright Ian Parberry, 1999
//Last updated March 15, 2000

#ifndef __BUTTONS__
#define __BUTTONS__

#include <windows.h>
#include <ddraw.h>
#include "csprite.h"
```

```
class CButtonManager{ //button manager class
  private:
    RECT *m_rectHotspot; //hotspot locations
    BOOL *m_bDown; //is button held down?
    int m_nMaxCount; //number of hotspots allowed
    int m_nCount; //number of current hotspots
    SIZE m_sizeButton; //size of buttons, if all the same size
    CBaseSprite* m_spriteDefault; //default button sprite
    CBmpSpriteFileReader m_cImage; //button images
    int m_nButtonDownSound; //sound index for button down
    int m_nButtonUpSound; //sound index for button up
    BOOL m_bRadio; //TRUE for radio buttons
    BOOL PointInRect(RECT rect,POINT point); //is point in rect?
    BOOL addbutton(RECT rect); //add button to list
    BOOL loadsprite(char *filename); //load button sprite
    void loadimages(); //load button images
    void display_menu(); //display menu page
  public:
    CButtonManager(int count,SIZE size,char *filename);
    CButtonManager(int count,SIZE size,POINT first,
      int ydelta,char *filename); //constructor
    ~CButtonManager(); //destructor
    BOOL addbutton(POINT point); //add button of default size
    int hit(POINT point); //return hit, if any
    int release(POINT point); //return hit on down button
    BOOL buttondown(POINT point); //animate button down
    BOOL buttondown(int index,BOOL sound=TRUE); //animate
    BOOL buttonup(POINT point); //animate button up
    BOOL buttonup(int index); //animate button up
    void allbuttonsup(); //animate all buttons up
    void setsounds(int down,int up); //set sounds
    void set_radio(BOOL on=TRUE); //set to radio buttons
    BOOL Restore(); //restore surfaces
    void Release(); //release surfaces
};
#endif
```

Buttons.cpp

```
//buttons.cpp: button class
//assumes that the menu background has been drawn to
//both primary and secondary surfaces

//Copyright Ian Parberry, 1999
//Last updated March 15, 2000

#include "buttons.h"
#include "sound.h" //for sound manager

extern LPDIRECTDRAWSURFACE lpPrimary; //primary surface
```

```
extern LPDIRECTDRAWSURFACE lpSecondary; //back buffer
extern CSoundManager* SoundManager; //sound manager

BOOL PageFlip(); //from demo??.cpp
CButtonManager::CButtonManager(int count,SIZE size,
                               char *filename){
  m_rectHotspot=new RECT[m_nMaxCount=count]; //hotspot space
  m_bDown=new BOOL[m_nMaxCount]; //whether button is down
  for(int i=0; i<m_nMaxCount; i++)
    m_bDown[i]=FALSE; //all buttons up
  m_sizeButton=size; //size of buttons loaded
  m_nCount=0; //number of buttons loaded
  loadsprite(filename); //load the sprite
  m_nButtonDownSound=m_nButtonUpSound=-1; //no sounds yet
  m_bRadio=FALSE; //not radio buttons
}

CButtonManager::CButtonManager(int count,SIZE size,
               POINT point,int ydelta,char *filename){
  m_rectHotspot=new RECT[m_nMaxCount=count]; //hotspot space
  m_bDown=new BOOL[m_nMaxCount]; //whether button is down
  for(int i=0; i<m_nMaxCount; i++)
    m_bDown[i]=FALSE; //all buttons up
  m_sizeButton=size; //size of buttons
  loadsprite(filename); //load the sprite
  m_nButtonDownSound=m_nButtonUpSound=-1; //no sounds yet
  m_bRadio=FALSE; //not radio buttons
  //add the buttons
  m_nCount=0; addbutton(point);
  for(i=0; i<count-1; i++){
    point.y+=ydelta; addbutton(point);
  }
}

CButtonManager::~CButtonManager(){ //destructor
  delete[]m_rectHotspot;
  delete m_spriteDefault;
  delete[]m_bDown;
}

void CButtonManager::set_radio(BOOL on){ //set to radio buttons
  m_bRadio=on;
}

BOOL CButtonManager::addbutton(RECT rect){
//add a hotspot in this rectangle
  if(m_nCount>=m_nMaxCount)return FALSE; //bail if no space
  m_rectHotspot[m_nCount++]=rect; //insert hotspot
  return TRUE;
}
```

```
BOOL CButtonManager::addbutton(POINT point){
//add a hotspot with top left at point
  RECT rect; //bounding rectangle
  rect.left=point.x; rect.right=point.x+m_sizeButton.cx;
  rect.top=point.y; rect.bottom=point.y+m_sizeButton.cy;
  return addbutton(rect); //add hotspot in this rectangle
}

int CButtonManager::hit(POINT point){
//return index of button hit (-1 if no hit)
  int result=-1; //start by assuming no hit
  int i=0; //index
  while(i<m_nCount&&result<0) //for each button
    if(PointInRect(m_rectHotspot[i],point)) //check for hit
      result=i; //record hit
    else i++; //next button
  return result;
}

int CButtonManager::release(POINT point){
//return index of button for mouse release
  int result=-1; //start by assuming no hit
  int i=0; //index
  while(i<m_nCount&&result<0) //for each button
    if(m_bDown[i]&&PointInRect(m_rectHotspot[i],point))
      result=i; //a hit
    else i++; //next button
  return result;
}

BOOL CButtonManager::PointInRect(RECT rect,POINT point){
//is point in rectangle?
  return point.x>=rect.left&&point.x<=rect.right&&
    point.y>=rect.top&&point.y<=rect.bottom;
}

void CButtonManager::loadimages(){ //load button images
  m_spriteDefault->load(&m_cImage,0,0,0); //up
  m_spriteDefault->load(&m_cImage,1,0,m_sizeButton.cy); //down
}

BOOL CButtonManager::loadsprite(char *filename){
  //bail if size not set
  if(m_sizeButton.cx==0&&m_sizeButton.cy==0)return FALSE;
  //bail if can't load file
  if(!m_cImage.load(filename))return FALSE;
  //make sprite
  m_spriteDefault=
```

```
    new CClippedSprite(2,m_sizeButton.cx,m_sizeButton.cy);
  //load button images
  loadimages();
  return TRUE;
}

BOOL CButtonManager::Restore(){ //restore surfaces
  if(m_spriteDefault->Restore()){
    loadimages();
    return TRUE;
  }
  else return FALSE;
}

void CButtonManager::Release(){ //release surfaces
  m_spriteDefault->Release();
}

BOOL CButtonManager::buttondown(POINT point){
  return buttondown(hit(point));
}

BOOL CButtonManager::buttondown(int index,BOOL sound){
  if(index>=0&&index<m_nCount&&!m_bDown[index]){
    if(sound)SoundManager->play(m_nButtonDownSound);
    if(m_bRadio&&index<m_nCount-1) //if radio button (not last)
      for(int i=0; i<m_nCount-1; i++)
        m_bDown[i]=FALSE; //pop up other radio buttons
    m_bDown[index]=TRUE; //button is now down
    display_menu(); //display menu page
    return TRUE;
  }
  else return FALSE;
}

BOOL CButtonManager::buttonup(POINT point){
  return buttonup(hit(point));
}

BOOL CButtonManager::buttonup(int index){
  if((!m_bRadio||index==m_nCount-1) &&
  index>=0&&index<m_nCount&&m_bDown[index]){ //if valid
    SoundManager->play(m_nButtonUpSound);
    m_bDown[index]=FALSE; //button is up
    display_menu(); //display menu page
    return TRUE;
```

```
    }
    else return FALSE;
}

void CButtonManager::allbuttonsup(){
  int i; //index
  if(m_bRadio){ //don't pop up radio buttons
    if(m_bDown[m_nCount-1]){ //pop up quit button if down
      m_bDown[m_nCount-1]=FALSE;
      SoundManager->play(m_nButtonUpSound);
    }
  }
  else{ //not radio buttons, so pop up all of them
    BOOL found=FALSE; //to make sure sound played only once
    for(i=0; i<m_nCount; i++) //for each button
      if(m_bDown[i]){ //if valid down button
        found=TRUE; //will play sound later
        m_bDown[i]=FALSE; //button is up
      }
    if(found)SoundManager->play(m_nButtonUpSound);
  }
  display_menu(); //display menu page
}

void CButtonManager::display_menu(){ //display menu page
  for(int i=0; i<m_nCount; i++) //for each button
    if(m_bDown[i]) //draw button down
      m_spriteDefault->
        draw(1,m_rectHotspot[i].left+m_sizeButton.cx/2,
          m_rectHotspot[i].top+m_sizeButton.cy,lpSecondary);
    else //draw button up
      m_spriteDefault->
        draw(0,m_rectHotspot[i].left+m_sizeButton.cx/2,
          m_rectHotspot[i].top+m_sizeButton.cy,lpSecondary);
  PageFlip(); //flip back buffer to front
}

void CButtonManager::setsounds(int down,int up){ //set sounds
  m_nButtonDownSound=down; m_nButtonUpSound=up;
}
```

Defines.h

```
//defines.h: essential defines
//Copyright Ian Parberry, 1999
//Last updated November 9, 1999

#ifndef __DEFINES_H__
#define __DEFINES_H__

#define SCREEN_WIDTH 640 //pixels wide
#define SCREEN_HEIGHT 480 //pixels high
#define COLORS 256 //number of colors
#define COLOR_DEPTH 8 //number of bits to store colors
#define TRANSPARENT_COLOR 255 //transparent palette position

enum GamePhaseType{
  LOGO_PHASE,TITLE_PHASE,MENU_PHASE,PLAYING_PHASE,
  DEVICEMENU_PHASE
};

enum InputDeviceType{KEYBOARD_INPUT=0,MOUSE_INPUT=1};

#endif
```

Input.h

```
//input.h: header file for input class

//Copyright Ian Parberry, 1999
//Last updated March 17, 2000

#include <windows.h>
#include <windowsx.h>

#include "defines.h"
#include "buttons.h" //for button manager

#ifndef __INPUT_H__
#define __INPUT_H__
```

```
class CInputManager{
  private:
    InputDeviceType InputDevice; //current input device
    CButtonManager *ButtonManager; //for managing menu buttons
    //helper functions
    BOOL is_function_key(WPARAM keystroke); //TRUE if function
key
    void decode(LPARAM lparam,POINT &point); //decode mouse click
    void set_plane_speed(POINT point,SIZE extent);
    //set up buttons for menus
    void SetupMainMenuButtons(); //main menu button manager
    void SetupDeviceMenuButtons(); //device menu button manager
    //keyboard handlers
    void IntroKeyboard(WPARAM keystroke); //keyboard handler
    BOOL MainMenuKeyboard(WPARAM keystroke); //keyboard handler
    void DeviceMenuKeyboard(WPARAM keystroke); //keyboard handler
    void GameKeyboard(WPARAM keystroke); //keyboard handler
    //left mouse button down handlers
    void MainMenuLMouseDown(POINT point); //mouse down handler
    void DeviceMenuLMouseDown(POINT point); //mouse down handler
    void GameLMouseDown(POINT point); //mouse down handler
    //left mouse button up handlers
    void IntroLMouseUp(POINT point); //mouse up handler
    BOOL MainMenuLMouseUp(POINT point); //mouse up handler
    void DeviceMenuLMouseUp(POINT point); //mouse up handler
  public:
    CInputManager(); //constructor
    ~CInputManager(); //destructor
    BOOL Restore(); //restore surfaces
    void Release(); //release surfaces
    void SetupButtons(GamePhaseType phase); //set up menu buttons
    BOOL Keyboard(WPARAM keystroke,
      BOOL virtual_keystroke=FALSE); //keyboard handler
    void LMouseDown(LPARAM lparam); //main mouse down handler
    BOOL LMouseUp(LPARAM lparam); //main mouse up handler
    void MouseMove(LPARAM lparam); //handle mouse motion
};

#endif
```

Input.cpp

```
//input.cpp: program file for input class

//Copyright Ian Parberry, 1999
//Last updated March 17, 2000

#include "input.h"
#include "objman.h" //for object manager
#include "sndlist.h" //for list of sounds

extern GamePhaseType GamePhase; //current phase
extern GamePhaseType NextPhase; //next phase of game
extern BOOL endphase; //should we abort current phase?
extern CObjectManager ObjectManager; //object manager

CInputManager::CInputManager(){ //constructor
  InputDevice=KEYBOARD_INPUT; //current input device
  ButtonManager=NULL; //for managing menu buttons
}

CInputManager::~CInputManager(){ //destructor
  delete ButtonManager;
}
BOOL CInputManager::Restore(){ //restore surfaces
  return ButtonManager->Restore();
}

void CInputManager::Release(){ //release surfaces
    ButtonManager->Release();
}

void CInputManager::SetupMainMenuButtons(){
//set up main menu button manager
  const int YDELTA=70; //y separation between buttons
  const int BUTTONCOUNT=6; //number of buttons
  SIZE size; //size of buttons
  size.cx=40; size.cy=40; //size of buttons
  POINT point; //top left corner of first button
  point.x=111; point.y=46; //first button location
  delete ButtonManager; //delete any old one
  ButtonManager=new //create new button manager
    CButtonManager(BUTTONCOUNT,size,point,YDELTA,
      "buttons.bmp");
 //set button sounds
  ButtonManager->
    setsounds(BIGCLICK_SOUND,SMALLCLICK_SOUND);
}
```

```
void CInputManager::SetupDeviceMenuButtons(){
//set up device menu button manager
  const int BUTTONCOUNT=4;
  delete ButtonManager; //if there is one already, delete it
  SIZE size; //size of buttons
  size.cx=40; size.cy=40; //size of buttons
  ButtonManager=new
    CButtonManager(BUTTONCOUNT,size,"buttons.bmp");
  ButtonManager->setsounds(BIGCLICK_SOUND,SMALLCLICK_SOUND);
  ButtonManager->set_radio(); //radio buttons
  //add buttons
  POINT point;
  point.x=209; point.y=130;
  ButtonManager->addbutton(point);
  point.x=209; point.y=210;
  ButtonManager->addbutton(point);
  point.x=209; point.y=291;
  ButtonManager->addbutton(point);
  point.x=209; point.y=372;
  ButtonManager->addbutton(point);
  //initialize image of radio button
  ButtonManager->buttondown(InputDevice,FALSE); //no sound
}
void CInputManager::SetupButtons(GamePhaseType phase){
//set up menu buttons
  switch(phase){
    case MENU_PHASE: SetupMainMenuButtons(); break;
    case DEVICEMENU_PHASE: SetupDeviceMenuButtons(); break;
  }
}

//keyboard handlers

void CInputManager::IntroKeyboard(WPARAM keystroke){
//keyboard handler for intro
  endphase=TRUE; //any key ends the phase
}
BOOL CInputManager::MainMenuKeyboard(WPARAM keystroke){
//keyboard handler for menu
  BOOL result=FALSE;
  switch(keystroke){
    case VK_ESCAPE:
    case 'Q': //exit the game
      result=TRUE;
      break;
    case 'N': //play new game
      NextPhase=PLAYING_PHASE; endphase=TRUE;
      break;
    case 'D':
      NextPhase=DEVICEMENU_PHASE; endphase=TRUE;
```

```
        default: break; //do nothing
      }
    return result;
  }

void CInputManager::DeviceMenuKeyboard(WPARAM keystroke){
//keyboard handler //for device menu
  switch(keystroke){
    case VK_ESCAPE:
    case 'D': //exit menu
      endphase=TRUE;
      break;
    case 'K': //play using keyboard
      InputDevice=KEYBOARD_INPUT; //set device
      ButtonManager->buttondown(KEYBOARD_INPUT);
      break;
    case 'M': //play using mouse
      InputDevice=MOUSE_INPUT; //set device
      ButtonManager->buttondown(MOUSE_INPUT);
      break;
    default: break;
  }
}
void CInputManager::GameKeyboard(WPARAM keystroke){
//keyboard handler for game play
  switch(keystroke){
    case VK_ESCAPE: endphase=TRUE; break;
    case VK_UP: ObjectManager.accelerate(0,-1); break;
    case VK_DOWN: ObjectManager.accelerate(0,1); break;
    case VK_LEFT: ObjectManager.accelerate(-1,0); break;
    case VK_RIGHT: ObjectManager.accelerate(1,0); break;
    case VK_SPACE: ObjectManager.fire_gun(); break;
    default: break;
  }
}

BOOL CInputManager::is_function_key(WPARAM keystroke){
  return keystroke==VK_ESCAPE||
    (keystroke>=VK_F1&&keystroke<=VK_F12);
}

BOOL CInputManager::Keyboard(WPARAM keystroke,
  BOOL virtual_keystroke){ //keyboard handler
  BOOL result=FALSE;
  switch(GamePhase){
    case LOGO_PHASE:
    case TITLE_PHASE:
      IntroKeyboard(keystroke);
      break;
    case MENU_PHASE:
```

```
        result=MainMenuKeyboard(keystroke);
        break;
    case DEVICEMENU_PHASE:
      DeviceMenuKeyboard(keystroke);
      break;
    case PLAYING_PHASE:
      if(InputDevice==KEYBOARD_INPUT||
      is_function_key(keystroke)||virtual_keystroke)
        GameKeyboard(keystroke);
      break;
  }
  return result;
}

//mouse left button down handlers

void CInputManager::MainMenuLMouseDown(POINT point){
//mouse down handler for menu
  if(ButtonManager->hit(point)>=0) //if a valid hit
    ButtonManager->buttondown(point); //animate a button down
}
void CInputManager::DeviceMenuLMouseDown(POINT point){
//mouse down handler for device menu
  int hit=ButtonManager->hit(point);
  switch(hit){
    case 0: Keyboard('K'); break; //keyboard
    case 1: Keyboard('M'); break; //mouse
    case 3:
      ButtonManager->buttondown(hit); //quit button down
      break;
    default: break;
  }
}

void CInputManager::GameLMouseDown(POINT point){
//mouse down handler for game
  Keyboard(VK_SPACE,TRUE);
}

void CInputManager::decode(LPARAM lparam,POINT &point){
//decode mouse click lparam to point
  point.x=LOWORD(lparam); point.y=HIWORD(lparam);
}

void CInputManager::LMouseDown(LPARAM lparam){
//main mouse left button down handler
  POINT point; //mouse location on screen
  decode(lparam,point); //decode mouse point
  switch(GamePhase){
    case MENU_PHASE:
```

```
      MainMenuLMouseDown(point);
      break;
    case DEVICEMENU_PHASE:
      DeviceMenuLMouseDown(point);
      break;
    case PLAYING_PHASE:
      if(InputDevice==MOUSE_INPUT)
        GameLMouseDown(point);
      break;
  }
}


//mouse left button up handlers

void CInputManager::IntroLMouseUp(POINT point){
//mouse left button up handler for intro
  endphase=TRUE;
}
BOOL CInputManager::MainMenuLMouseUp(POINT point){
//mouse left button up handler for menu
  int hit=ButtonManager->release(point); //get button hit
  BOOL result=FALSE;
  //take action depending on which button was hit
  switch(hit){ //depending on which button was hit
    case 0: Keyboard('N'); break; //new game
    case 1: Keyboard('S'); break; //saved game
    case 2: Keyboard('D'); break; //devices
    case 3: Keyboard('L'); break; //high score list
    case 4: Keyboard('H'); break; //help
    case 5: result=Keyboard(VK_ESCAPE); break; //quit
    default: break;
  }
  //animate button images
  if(hit>=0)ButtonManager->buttonup(hit); //hit
  else ButtonManager->allbuttonsup(); //nonhit
  return result;
}

void CInputManager::DeviceMenuLMouseUp(POINT point){
//mouse left button up handler for device menu
  int hit=ButtonManager->release(point);
  switch(hit){
    case 3: //quit button up
      ButtonManager->buttonup(hit); //show quit button up
      Keyboard(VK_ESCAPE);
      break;
  }
  if(hit<0)ButtonManager->allbuttonsup(); //no hit
}
```

```
BOOL CInputManager::LMouseUp(LPARAM lparam){
//main mouse left button up handler
  BOOL result=FALSE;
  POINT point; //mouse location on screen
  decode(lparam,point); //decode mouse point
  switch(GamePhase){
    case LOGO_PHASE:
    case TITLE_PHASE:
      IntroLMouseUp(point);
      break;
    case MENU_PHASE:
      result=MainMenuLMouseUp(point);
      break;
    case DEVICEMENU_PHASE:
      DeviceMenuLMouseUp(point);
      break;
  }
  return result;
}

//mouse motion handler

void CInputManager::set_plane_speed(POINT point,SIZE extent){
//set plane speed based on point's position in extent
  int xmin,xmax,ymin,ymax; //plane speed limits
  ObjectManager.speed_limits(xmin,xmax,ymin,ymax); //get them
  //bands for speed assignment
  const int XBANDWIDTH=extent.cx/(xmax-xmin+1);
  const int YBANDWIDTH=extent.cy/(ymax-ymin+1);
  int xspeed,yspeed; //speed of plane
  xspeed=point.x/XBANDWIDTH+xmin; //horizontal speed
  yspeed=point.y/YBANDWIDTH+ymin; //vertical speed
  ObjectManager.set_speed(xspeed,yspeed); //pass to plane
}

void CInputManager::MouseMove(LPARAM lparam){
  if(InputDevice!=MOUSE_INPUT)return; //bail if not needed
  if(GamePhase!=PLAYING_PHASE)return; //bail if not playing
  POINT point; //mouse location on screen
  decode(lparam,point); //decode mouse point
  //set extent
  SIZE extent; //extent that mouse moves in
  extent.cx=SCREEN_WIDTH;
  extent.cy=SCREEN_HEIGHT;
  //set plane speed based on point and extent
  set_plane_speed(point,extent);
}
```

Main.cpp

```
//main.cpp

//Copyright Ian Parberry, 1999
//Last updated May 22, 2000

//Now the input can come from the mouse. Navigate the
//menu with the mouse, clicking on the buttons. Note that
//animation occurs on button down, action on button up.
//Watch what happens when you move the mouse pointer onto
//or off of a button between pressing and releasing the
//left mouse button.

//You can also play the game using the mouse, with the
//invisible cursor position controlling speed and height,
//and the left mouse button firing the gun.

//system includes
#include <windows.h>
#include <windowsx.h>
#include <ddraw.h>
#include <stdio.h>

//system defines
#define WIN32_LEAN_AND_MEAN

//custom includes
#include "defines.h" //global definitions
#include "bmp.h" //bmp file reader
#include "timer.h" //game timer
#include "csprite.h" //for clipped sprite class
#include "objects.h" //for object class
#include "objman.h" //for object manager
#include "view.h" //for viewpoint class
#include "random.h" //for random number generator
#include "sound.h" //for sound manager
#include "input.h" //for input manager

//defines
#define MAX_OBJECTS 32 //max number of objects in game

//globals

BOOL ActiveApp; //is this application active?

LPDIRECTDRAW lpDirectDrawObject=NULL; //DirectDraw object
LPDIRECTDRAWSURFACE lpPrimary=NULL; //primary surface
```

```
LPDIRECTDRAWPALETTE lpPrimaryPalette; //its palette
LPDIRECTDRAWSURFACE lpSecondary=NULL; //back buffer
LPDIRECTDRAWPALETTE lpSecondaryPalette; //its palette
LPDIRECTDRAWSURFACE lpBackground=NULL; //background image

CTimer Timer; //game timer

CBmpFileReader background; //background image
CBmpSpriteFileReader g_cSpriteImages; //sprite images
CBmpSpriteFileReader g_cFrgndImages; //foreground images

CObjectManager ObjectManager(MAX_OBJECTS); //object manager

CClippedSprite *g_pSprite[NUM_SPRITES]; //sprites

CViewPoint Viewpoint; //player viewpoint
CRandom Random; //random number generator

GamePhaseType GamePhase; //current phase
GamePhaseType NextPhase; //next phase of game
BOOL endphase=FALSE; //should we abort current phase?
int PhaseTime=0; //time in phase

CSoundManager* SoundManager; //sound manager
CInputManager InputManager; //device input manager

//helper functions
LPDIRECTDRAWPALETTE CreatePalette(LPDIRECTDRAWSURFACE surface);
BOOL InitDirectDraw(HWND hwnd);
HWND CreateDefaultWindow(char* name,HINSTANCE hInstance);

BOOL LoadPlaneSprite(){
  BOOL result=TRUE;
  result=result&&g_pSprite[PLANE_OBJECT]->
    load(&g_cSpriteImages,0,1,1);
  result=result&&g_pSprite[PLANE_OBJECT]->
    load(&g_cSpriteImages,1,123,1);
  result=result&&g_pSprite[PLANE_OBJECT]->
    load(&g_cSpriteImages,2,245,1);
  result=result&&g_pSprite[PLANE_OBJECT]->
    load(&g_cSpriteImages,3,367,1);
  result=result&&g_pSprite[PLANE_OBJECT]->
    load(&g_cSpriteImages,4,489,1);
  result=result&&g_pSprite[PLANE_OBJECT]->
    load(&g_cSpriteImages,5,17,74);
  return result;
} //LoadPlaneSprite
```

```
BOOL LoadCrowSprite(){
  BOOL result=TRUE;
  result=result&&g_pSprite[CROW_OBJECT]->
    load(&g_cSpriteImages,0,256,183); //frame 0
  result=result&&g_pSprite[CROW_OBJECT]->
    load(&g_cSpriteImages,1,320,183); //frame 1
  result=result&&g_pSprite[CROW_OBJECT]->
    load(&g_cSpriteImages,2,256,237); //frame 2
  result=result&&g_pSprite[CROW_OBJECT]->
    load(&g_cSpriteImages,3,323,237); //frame 3
  return result;
} //LoadCrowSprite

BOOL LoadFrgndSprites(){ //load foreground sprites
  BOOL result=TRUE;
  result=result&&g_pSprite[FARM_OBJECT]->
    load(&g_cFrgndImages,0,0,0); //load farm sprite
  result=result&&g_pSprite[FIELD_OBJECT]->
    load(&g_cFrgndImages,0,640,0); //load field sprite
  return result;
} //LoadFrgndSprites

BOOL LoadDeadCrowSprite(){ //load dead crow
  return g_pSprite[DEADCROW_OBJECT]->
    load(&g_cSpriteImages,0,453,230);
} //LoadDeadCrowSprite

BOOL LoadExplodingCrowSprite(){ //load exploding crow
  BOOL result=TRUE;
  result=result&&g_pSprite[EXPLODINGCROW_OBJECT]->
    load(&g_cSpriteImages,0,257,294);
  result=result&&g_pSprite[EXPLODINGCROW_OBJECT]->
    load(&g_cSpriteImages,1,321,294);
  result=result&&g_pSprite[EXPLODINGCROW_OBJECT]->
    load(&g_cSpriteImages,2,386,162);
  result=result&&g_pSprite[EXPLODINGCROW_OBJECT]->
    load(&g_cSpriteImages,3,453,162);
  result=result&&g_pSprite[EXPLODINGCROW_OBJECT]->
    load(&g_cSpriteImages,4,386,230);
  result=result&&g_pSprite[EXPLODINGCROW_OBJECT]->
    load(&g_cSpriteImages,5,453,230);
  return result;
} //LoadExplodingCrowSprite

BOOL LoadBulletSprite(){ //load bullet
  return g_pSprite[BULLET_OBJECT]->
    load(&g_cSpriteImages,0,5,123);
} //LoadBulletSprite
```

```
BOOL LoadImages(){ //load graphics from files to surfaces
  //get the background image
  if(!background.load("bckgnd.bmp"))return FALSE; //read file
  background.draw(lpBackground); //draw to background surface
  //set palettes in all surfaces
  if(!background.setpalette(lpPrimaryPalette))return FALSE;
  if(!background.setpalette(lpSecondaryPalette))return FALSE;
  //load the sprites...
  if(!g_cSpriteImages.load("sprites.bmp"))return FALSE;
  //...the plane
  g_pSprite[PLANE_OBJECT]=new CClippedSprite(6,121,72);
  if(!LoadPlaneSprite())return FALSE; //load plane images
  //...the crow
  g_pSprite[CROW_OBJECT]=new CClippedSprite(4,58,37);
  if(!LoadCrowSprite())return FALSE; //load crow images
  //..the dead crow
  g_pSprite[DEADCROW_OBJECT]=new CClippedSprite(1,62,53);
  LoadDeadCrowSprite(); //load dead crow images
  //...the exploding crow
  g_pSprite[EXPLODINGCROW_OBJECT]=new CClippedSprite(6,62,53);
  LoadExplodingCrowSprite(); //load exploding crow images
  //...the bullet
  g_pSprite[BULLET_OBJECT]=new CClippedSprite(1,5,3);
  LoadBulletSprite(); //load bullet images
  //...the foreground sprites
  if(!g_cFrgndImages.load("farm.bmp"))return FALSE;
  g_pSprite[FARM_OBJECT]=new CClippedSprite(1,640,162);
  g_pSprite[FIELD_OBJECT]=new CClippedSprite(1,640,162);
  if(!LoadFrgndSprites())return FALSE; //load foreground
  return TRUE;
} //LoadImages

void CreateObjects(){
  int i;
  ObjectManager.create(FARM_OBJECT,0,SCREEN_HEIGHT-1,0,0);
  ObjectManager.create(FIELD_OBJECT,SCREEN_WIDTH,
    SCREEN_HEIGHT-1,0,0);
  for(i=0; i<8; i++)
    ObjectManager.create(CROW_OBJECT,
      Random.number(0,WORLD_WIDTH-1),
      Random.number(100,400),-1,0);
  ObjectManager.set_current(
    ObjectManager.create(PLANE_OBJECT,320,271,-1,0));
  for(i=0; i<8; i++)
    ObjectManager.create(CROW_OBJECT,
      Random.number(0,WORLD_WIDTH-1),
      Random.number(100,400),-1,0);
} //CreateObjects
```

```
BOOL RestoreSurfaces(){ //restore all surfaces
  BOOL result=TRUE;
  //primary and secondary surfaces
  if(FAILED(lpPrimary->Restore()))return FALSE;
  if(FAILED(lpSecondary->Restore()))return FALSE;
  //surfaces containing images
  if(SUCCEEDED(lpBackground->Restore())) //if background restored
    result=result&&background.draw(lpBackground); //redraw image
  else return FALSE;
  if(g_pSprite[PLANE_OBJECT]->Restore()) //if plane restored
    result=result&&LoadPlaneSprite(); //redraw image
  else return FALSE;
  if(g_pSprite[CROW_OBJECT]->Restore()) //if crow restored
    result=result&&LoadCrowSprite(); //redraw image
  else return FALSE;
  if(g_pSprite[DEADCROW_OBJECT]->Restore()) //if restored
    result=result&&LoadDeadCrowSprite(); //redraw image
  else return FALSE;
  if(g_pSprite[EXPLODINGCROW_OBJECT]->Restore()) //if restored
    result=result&&LoadExplodingCrowSprite(); //redraw image
  else return FALSE;
  if(g_pSprite[BULLET_OBJECT]->Restore()) //if restored
    result=result&&LoadBulletSprite(); //redraw image
  else return FALSE;
  if(g_pSprite[FARM_OBJECT]->Restore()&& //if farm and ...
    g_pSprite[FIELD_OBJECT]->Restore()) //... field restored
    result=result&&LoadFrgndSprites(); //redraw image
  else return FALSE;
  //input manager has button sprites
  if(!InputManager.Restore())return FALSE;
  return result;
} //RestoreSurfaces

void LoadSounds(int level=0){ //load sounds for level
  const int copies=4; //copies of repeatable sounds
  switch(level){
    case 0: //intro sounds
      SoundManager->load("intro.wav");
      SoundManager->load("larc.wav");
      break;
    case 1: //game engine sounds
      SoundManager->load("caw.wav",copies);
      SoundManager->load("gun.wav",copies);
      SoundManager->load("boom.wav",copies);
      SoundManager->load("thump.wav",copies);
      SoundManager->load("putt0.wav");
      SoundManager->load("putt1.wav");
      SoundManager->load("putt2.wav");
      SoundManager->load("bgclk.wav",2);
```

```
      SoundManager->load("smclk.wav",2);
      break;
  }
}

BOOL PageFlip(){ //return TRUE if page flip succeeds
  if(lpPrimary->Flip(NULL,DDFLIP_WAIT)==DDERR_SURFACELOST)
    return RestoreSurfaces();
  return TRUE;
} //PageFlip

BOOL ComposeFrame(){ //compose a frame of animation
  Viewpoint.draw_background(lpBackground,lpSecondary,
    ObjectManager.speed()); //draw scrolling background
  ObjectManager.animate(lpSecondary); //draw objects
  return TRUE;
} //ComposeFrame

void display_screen(char *filename){ //display bmp file
  CBmpFileReader image; //filc reader
  image.load(filename); //load from file
  image.draw(lpSecondary); //draw to back buffer
  image.setpalette(lpPrimaryPalette); //may have custom palette
  PageFlip(); //display it
  //draw to back buffer again for button animation
  image.draw(lpSecondary);
} //display_screen

void change_phase(GamePhaseType new_phase){ //go to new phase
  switch(new_phase){
    case LOGO_PHASE:
      display_screen("larc.bmp");
      LoadSounds(); //load sounds for intro sequence
      SoundManager->play(LOGO_SOUND); //signature chord
      break;
    case TITLE_PHASE:
      display_screen("title.bmp");
      SoundManager->stop(); //silence previous phase
      SoundManager->play(TITLE_SOUND); //title sound
      break;
    case MENU_PHASE:
      //set up buttons for menu
      InputManager.SetupButtons(MENU_PHASE);
      //sound
      switch(GamePhase){ //depending on previous phase
        case TITLE_PHASE: //from intro phase
          SoundManager->stop(); //silence previous phase
          SoundManager->clear(); //clear out old sounds
          LoadSounds(1); //set up game sounds
```

```
            break;
          case PLAYING_PHASE: //from game engine
            SoundManager->stop(); //silence game engine
            break;
          case DEVICEMENU_PHASE: //device menu, do nothing
            break;
        }
        //display background
        display_screen("menu.bmp"); //display main menu
        //mouse cursor
        switch(GamePhase){ //what phase did we come in from?
          case PLAYING_PHASE:
          case TITLE_PHASE:
            ShowCursor(TRUE); //activate the mouse cursor
            break;
        }
        break;
      case DEVICEMENU_PHASE:
        //display button background
        display_screen("dmenu.bmp");
        //set up the button manager
        InputManager.SetupButtons(DEVICEMENU_PHASE);
        break;
      case PLAYING_PHASE: //prepare the game engine
        //mouse cursor
        SetCursorPos(SCREEN_WIDTH-1,SCREEN_HEIGHT/2); //throttle
        ShowCursor(FALSE); //hide the mouse cursor
        //start sounds
        SoundManager->stop(); //silence previous phase
        //create objects in game engine
        ObjectManager.reset(); //clear object manager
        CreateObjects(); //create new objects
        //initialize graphics
        background.setpalette(lpPrimaryPalette); //game palette
        ComposeFrame(); PageFlip(); //prime animation pump
        break;
    }
    //change to new phase
    GamePhase=new_phase; PhaseTime=Timer.time();
    endphase=FALSE;
} //change_phase

void Redraw(){ //redraw in response to surface loss
  switch(GamePhase){
    case LOGO_PHASE:
      display_screen("larc.bmp");
      break;
    case TITLE_PHASE:
```

```
          display_screen("title.bmp");
          break;
        case MENU_PHASE:
          display_screen("menu.bmp"); //display main menu
          break;
        case PLAYING_PHASE:
          //do nothing, next frame of animation will catch it
          break;
        case DEVICEMENU_PHASE:
          display_screen("dmenu.bmp");
          InputManager.SetupButtons(DEVICEMENU_PHASE);
          break;
    }
}

void ProcessFrame(){ //process a frame of animation
  const int LOGO_DISPLAY_TIME=8500; //duration of logo
  const int TITLE_DISPLAY_TIME=10000; //duration of title
  //check for lost surfaces, e.g., alt+tab
  if(lpPrimary->IsLost()){
    RestoreSurfaces(); Redraw();
  }
  //phase-related processing
  switch(GamePhase){ //what phase are we in?
    case LOGO_PHASE: //displaying logo screen
      Sleep(100); //surrender time to other processes
      if(endphase||Timer.elapsed(PhaseTime,LOGO_DISPLAY_TIME))
        change_phase(TITLE_PHASE); //go to title screen
      break;
    case TITLE_PHASE: //displaying title screen
      Sleep(100); //surrender time to other processes
      if(endphase||Timer.elapsed(PhaseTime,TITLE_DISPLAY_TIME))
        change_phase(MENU_PHASE); //go to menu
      break;
    case MENU_PHASE: //main menu
      Sleep(100); //surrender time to other processes
      if(endphase)change_phase(NextPhase); //change phase
      break;
    case DEVICEMENU_PHASE:
      if(endphase)change_phase(MENU_PHASE); //go to menu phase
      break;
    case PLAYING_PHASE: //game engine
      ComposeFrame(); //compose a frame in back surface
      PageFlip(); //flip video memory surfaces
      if(endphase||ObjectManager.won()) //if end of phase
        change_phase(MENU_PHASE); //go to menu
      break;
  }
} //ProcessFrame
```

```
//message handler (window procedure)
long CALLBACK WindowProc(HWND hwnd,UINT message,
                         WPARAM wParam,LPARAM lParam){
  switch(message){
    case WM_ACTIVATEAPP: ActiveApp=wParam; break;
    case WM_CREATE: break;
    case WM_KEYDOWN: //keyboard hit
      if(InputManager.Keyboard(wParam))
        DestroyWindow(hwnd);
      break;
    case WM_LBUTTONDOWN: //left mouse button down
      InputManager.LMouseDown(lParam); //handle it
      break;
    case WM_LBUTTONUP: //left mouse button up
      if(InputManager.LMouseUp(lParam))
        DestroyWindow(hwnd);
      break;
    case WM_MOUSEMOVE: //mouse move
      InputManager.MouseMove(lParam);
      break;
    case WM_DESTROY: //end of game
      if(lpDirectDrawObject!=NULL){ //if DD object exists
        if(lpSecondary!=NULL) //if secondary surface exists
          lpSecondary->Release(); //release secondary surface
        if(lpPrimary!=NULL) //if primary surface exists
          lpPrimary->Release(); //release primary surface
        if(lpBackground!=NULL) //if background exists
          lpBackground->Release(); //release background
        for(int i=0; i<NUM_SPRITES; i++){ //for each sprite
          if(g_pSprite[i]) //if sprite exists
            g_pSprite[i]->Release(); //release sprite
          delete g_pSprite[i]; //delete sprite
        }
        InputManager.Release(); //button surfaces
        lpDirectDrawObject->Release(); //release DD object
      }
      delete SoundManager; //reclaim sound manager memory
      ShowCursor(TRUE); //show the mouse cursor
      PostQuitMessage(0); //and exit
      break;
    default: //default window procedure
      return DefWindowProc(hwnd,message,wParam,lParam);
  } //switch(message)
  return 0L;
} //WindowProc
```

```cpp
int WINAPI WinMain(HINSTANCE hInstance,HINSTANCE hPrevInstance,
LPSTR lpCmdLine,int nCmdShow){
  MSG msg; //current message
  HWND hwnd; //handle to full-screen window
  hwnd=CreateDefaultWindow("directX demo 9",hInstance);
  if(!hwnd)return FALSE;
  //set up window
  ShowWindow(hwnd,nCmdShow); UpdateWindow(hwnd);
  SetFocus(hwnd); //allow input from keyboard
  ShowCursor(FALSE); //hide the cursor
  //init graphics
  for(int i=0; i<NUM_SPRITES; i++) //null out sprites
    g_pSprite[i]=NULL;
  BOOL OK=InitDirectDraw(hwnd);//initialize DirectDraw
  if(OK)OK=LoadImages(); //load images from disk
  if(!OK){ //bail out if initialization failed
    DestroyWindow(hwnd); return FALSE;
  }
  //start game timer
  Timer.start();
  //init sound
  SoundManager=new CSoundManager(hwnd);
  //set initial phase
  change_phase(LOGO_PHASE);
  //message loop
  while(TRUE)
    if(PeekMessage(&msg,NULL,0,0,PM_NOREMOVE)){
      if(!GetMessage(&msg,NULL,0,0))return msg.wParam;
      TranslateMessage(&msg); DispatchMessage(&msg);
    }
    else if(ActiveApp)ProcessFrame(); else WaitMessage();
} //WinMain
```

Sndlist.h

```
//sndlist.h: list of sound definitions

//Copyright Ian Parberry, 1999
//Last updated November 9, 1999

#ifndef __SNDLIST__
#define __SNDLIST__

#define LOOP_SOUND TRUE

enum GameSoundType{ //sounds used in game engine
  CAW_SOUND=0, //sound a crow makes
  GUN_SOUND, //sound of gun firing
  BOOM_SOUND, //sound of explosion
  THUMP_SOUND, //sound of object hitting the ground
  //next 3 sounds must be consecutive and in this order
  SLOWPUTT_SOUND, //sound of slow engine
  MEDIUMPUTT_SOUND, //sound of medium engine
  FASTPUTT_SOUND, //sound of fast engine
  //mouse clicks
  BIGCLICK_SOUND, //loud click
  SMALLCLICK_SOUND, //soft click
};

enum IntroSoundType{ //sounds used during the intro
  TITLE_SOUND=0, //sound used during title screen
  LOGO_SOUND, //signature chord
};

#endif
```

Chapter 12

Here's what you'll learn:

- How the joystick hardware works

- What can go wrong with your joystick handler

- How to access the joystick using the Windows API

- How to get configuration information from the joystick

- How to poll the joystick position

- How to poll the joystick buttons

The Joystick

In Demo 10, we learn how to process input from the joystick. I assume that you do have a joystick attached to your computer. If not, then this chapter is going to be a little boring for you. We will use the joystick position to control the plane's speed, and we will use button 1 on the joystick to fire the gun. The joystick is radically different from any other device attached to your computer—it is analog instead of digital. This introduces some unique programming challenges. Rather than use the Windows API message-passing system, we will poll the joystick hardware directly.

Experiment with Demo 10

Take a moment now to run Demo 10.

- If you haven't done so recently, calibrate your joystick. Start by double-clicking on the Game Controllers icon in the Control Panel of your computer. Select a joystick from the list displayed there, and click on the Properties button. You will then see the Game Controller Properties dialog box, which will look similar to Figure 12.1. On the Settings tab, click on the Calibrate button. You will then see the Controller Calibration dialog box, which will look similar to Figure 12.2. Follow the instructions there.

- Run Demo 10. Notice that you can click out of the logo and title screens by clicking on button 1 on the joystick.

- Go to the device menu and click on the Joystick button. If that button does not depress, it means that something is wrong with your joystick; it is either broken, unplugged, or misconfigured. You should exit Demo 10 before you attempt to rectify this problem.

- Now, play a game. Notice that the joystick position controls the plane's speed, and button 1 fires the gun. Notice that the mouse and keyboard controls for the plane are disabled.

- Hold the joystick button down for several seconds. Notice that the gun is fired only once. To fire it again, you must first release the button.

- Exit from Demo 10, unplug your joystick, and try again. The Joystick button on the device menu should now be inactive.

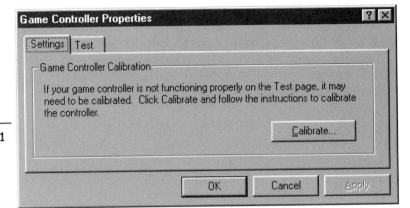

Figure 12.1
The Game
Controller
Properties
dialog box

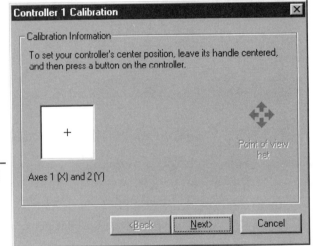

Figure 12.2
The
Controller
Calibration
dialog box

How the Joystick Works

Imagine a manager working on a noisy factory floor. He has a bunch of paperwork to do, and he has to oversee his employees at the same time. He's the CPU. He has a bunch of flunkies who constantly tap him on the shoulder and pass him pieces of information. They get his attention for a few seconds, during which time he records their information, then gets back to his paperwork. They are the digital devices on your computer, such as the mouse and the keyboard. The mouse and the keyboard behave exactly in this manner, constantly interrupting the CPU, which must break off from its regular work to service their interrupts.

The joystick is like a roving employee out on the factory floor who needs to report a number to the manager periodically. However, the employee is too far away to be able to send interrupts to the manager. Every so often, the manager calls out to him, and he responds by shouting back his number. However, it's noisy out there on the factory floor, so although the manager can hear when the employee shouts, he can't tell exactly what he's saying. Therefore, they've evolved a system. If the employee wants to communicate the number "5," he waits for 5 seconds after he hears the manager's query, and then answers. If he wants to communicate "10," he waits 10 seconds before responding. The manager notes the time when he sends his request and counts the number of seconds until the employee responds. This gives him the number that the employee wants to shout to him.

The manager has to actively listen for the employee to be able to distinguish his voice over the noise, so, in addition to being taken away from his paperwork, he has to disable all interrupts while he's listening. Otherwise he might miss a response that comes in while he is working or servicing an interrupt. Disabling interrupts is not in general a good idea because it potentially shuts out all sorts of time-sensitive information, but it is acceptable if it is not done too often, or for too long. This means that if for some reason the roving employee doesn't respond at all, the manager needs to time-out after waiting for a period of time that is long enough for any reasonable response, but not long enough to interfere with normal work or important interrupts.

This is how the joystick communicates with the CPU. It doesn't do so because of noise, of course, but because that's the way the analog hardware works. Periodically the CPU must turn off interrupts, send a signal to the joystick, and then wait a reasonable amount of time (measured in milliseconds this time, not seconds) for the joystick to respond. It then decodes the information sent (such as the joystick coordinates) from the amount of time that elapses before a signal returns. This process is called *polling* the joystick.

Turning off interrupts can be *very* dangerous. For example, consider the *RAM refresh interrupt*. The RAM on your computer is volatile and needs to be refreshed periodically by the CPU. A failure to respond to this interrupt in a timely fashion will result in the contents of your computer's memory being sent to the Great Bit-bucket in the Sky. Therefore, you really don't want to poll the joystick too frequently or set the time-out value too high.

Here's an example of the kind of weird thing that can happen when you code for the joystick. The first joystick code that I wrote was under DOS on an old 66MHZ 486. Initially, I had the polling interval and the time-out value a little too high. As a result, the processor spent far too much of its time waiting for the joystick to respond. It also had a cool side effect. The game was playing MIDI music at the time, which involves having the CPU send a signal to the sound card at the beginning and end of every note. The joystick code interfered with the timing of this process by making the CPU too busy to send the MIDI signals on time, and since the amount of time that the CPU must wait for the joystick is longer when the joystick is sending a larger number (for example, more when the joystick is in the back-right corner than the forward-left corner), the degree of interference was dependent on the joystick's position. The result was that the joystick unintentionally acted as a tempo controller—waggling the joystick made the tempo of the music go up and down in response!

Coding for the joystick in Windows is a lot easier than it was back in the old DOS days. The API provides you with a lot of support. We will use the Windows API to poll the joystick hardware directly. Alternatively, you can (by calling the Windows API `JoySetCapture` function) get Windows to make the joystick appear to send messages. The messages you receive from the joystick have a prefix of "`MM_`", for example, `MM_JOY1MOVE` for joystick motion. The mouse messages that we saw in Chapter 11 are generated by interrupts from the mouse, whereas with the joystick, the Windows API is taking care of polling the joystick behind the scenes and faking the joystick messages for you, just as if the joystick were interrupt driven.

There's one more thing about joysticks that the programmer should know. They contain two variable resistors, one measuring side-to-side motion, and the other measuring front-to-back motion. These variable resistors have different physical properties from one joystick to another, even when they are made by the same manufacturer. Even worse, they will behave differently from one day to the next, depending on the ambient temperature and humidity. If you think *that's* bad, listen to this: Electrical resistance is inversely proportional to temperature. Moving the joystick creates friction, which raises the temperature of its components, so it can behave differently during a *single play session* depending on how heavily it is used. The numbers returned by the joystick at the forward-left position will almost never be exactly the same each time you poll it. The same for back-right, or even the at-rest position in the middle.

The Joystick Manager

The joystick manager class `CJoystickManager` handles the joystick polling functions for *Ned's Turkey Farm*.

Joystick Manager Overview

The header file for the joystick manager is `Joystick.h`. It begins with an unusual `include` that we haven't seen before—the header `Mmsystem.h`, which we need to access joystick support in the Windows API.

```
#include <mmsystem.h>
```

Then we define the joystick poll interval constant `JOYSTICKPOLLINTERVAL`, which is the number of milliseconds between polls of the joystick. Setting this to 100 milliseconds means that we poll ten times per second, which is adequate for a game of this kind.

```
#define JOYSTICKPOLLINTERVAL 100 //time between polls
```

`CJoystickManager` has 12 private member variables. The first is a Windows API `JOYINFOEX` structure `m_joyInfo`. This is the structure that the joystick polling function will use to pass information back to our program.

```
JOYINFOEX m_joyInfo; //current joystick state
```

The next eight private member variables are places into which we will parse the `JOYINFOEX` information to make it more accessible. The first of these is the joystick identifier; the API allows us to use multiple joysticks if we wish.

```
UINT m_uJoystickid; //joystick id
```

Next, are the joystick coordinates stored as percentages, from zero to one hundred percent, inclusive. The joystick manager uses percentages so that the joystick coordinates it delivers to your program are always within the same extent, even though (as we noted already) this cannot be said of the hardware.

```
int m_nX, m_nY; //x and y coordinates as percentages
```

Next, the joystick extents, as reported by the hardware:

```
int m_nXmax, m_nYmax; //maximum x and y from h/w
int m_nXmin, m_nYmin; //minimum x and y from h/w
```

Finally, the positions of up to four joystick buttons are stored in a Boolean array. Note that while we will be indexing these buttons 0 through 3, the joystick indexes them 1 through 4 (joysticks have obviously never heard of C).

```
BOOL m_bButton[4]; //buttons down?
```

A parallel array stores Boolean values that indicate whether a down button has been serviced. We only want to fire a bullet when the button is polled *going down*, that is, it is up on one poll and down on the next. Once it has been serviced, no more bullets will be fired if it remains down on subsequent polls. That is, unless we allow the joystick buttons to *autorepeat*.

```
BOOL m_bServiced[4]; //whether down button was serviced
```

The Boolean variable m_bOperational will be set to TRUE if the joystick was successfully initialized:

```
BOOL m_bOperational; //was init successful?
```

Next, m_nLastPollTime records the last time that the joystick was polled:

```
int m_nLastPollTime; //last time joystick was polled
```

The last private member variable is set to TRUE if we want the joystick buttons to autorepeat when they are held down:

```
BOOL m_bAutoRepeat; //allow autorepeat
```

CJoystickManager has one private member function load_data, which parses information from the JOYINFOEX structure into the private member variables:

```
void load_data(); //process data from m_joyInfo
```

The joystick manager has seven public member functions, including a constructor:

```
CJoystickManager(); //constructor
```

The initialize function initializes the joystick manager by checking whether there is a joystick available, and if so, it gets information about the joystick:

```
BOOL initialize(); //initialize settings
```

The poll function polls the joystick state, returning TRUE if new information was successfully received from the joystick:

```
BOOL poll(); //poll joystick state
```

The button_down function has an integer parameter button in the range 1 through 4, and returns TRUE if that button was down the last time the joystick was polled and has not yet been serviced:

```
BOOL button_down(int button); //is button down?
```

The position function delivers the position of the joystick as a POINT structure provided as a call-by-reference parameter, with the coordinates of that structure expressed as percentages. It returns FALSE if the joystick is not operational.

```
BOOL position(POINT &point); //position as percentage
```

The `autorepeat` function sets and unsets autorepeat on the joystick buttons:

```
void autorepeat(BOOL setting=TRUE); //un/set autorepeat
```

Finally, the `exists` function returns `TRUE` if the joystick is operational:

```
BOOL exists(); //TRUE if joystick exists
```

Initializing the Joystick Manager

The code file for the joystick manager is `Joystick.cpp`. It begins with the constructor, which simply sets the private member variables to sensible initial values.

```
CJoystickManager::CJoystickManager(){ //constructor
  m_nLastPollTime=0; //not polled yet
  m_bOperational=FALSE; //not initialized yet
  m_uJoystickid=0; m_bAutoRepeat=TRUE;
  m_nX=m_nY=0; m_nXmax=m_nYmax=m_nXmin=m_nYmin=0;
  for(int i=0; i<4; i++) //init button positions
    m_bServiced[i]=m_bButton[i]=FALSE;
}
```

The `CJoystickManager initialize` function gets information about the joystick, setting the private member variable `m_bOperational` to `TRUE` and returning `TRUE` if it finds an operational joystick:

```
BOOL CJoystickManager::initialize(){ //init joystick
  m_bOperational=FALSE; //assume failure
```

A call to the Windows API function `joyGetNumDevs` returns the number of joysticks. If this is zero, we bail out.

```
if(!joyGetNumDevs())return FALSE; //bail if no joysticks
```

Next, we set up the `JOYINFOEX` private member variable `m_joyInfo` by setting all fields to zero, then setting its size field:

```
memset(&m_joyInfo,0,sizeof(JOYINFOEX));
m_joyInfo.dwSize=sizeof(JOYINFOEX);
```

The flags field in `m_joyInfo` is set to indicate that we will be querying the joystick buttons and coordinates:

```
m_joyInfo.dwFlags=JOY_RETURNBUTTONS|JOY_RETURNX|JOY_RETURNY;
```

The API allows us to access at most two joysticks. We next see which, if any, of the two possible joysticks is available. We do this by calling the API function `joyGetPosEx`, which will attempt to get us the joystick position and button states, failing if the joystick is not available. The first parameter of `joyGetPosEx` is the joystick identifier, for which the API kindly provides us two constants, `JOYSTICKID1` and `JOYSTICKID2`. The second parameter is a pointer to a `JOYINFOEX` structure that receives the joystick information. We try joystick 1 first, and if we get a return of JOYERR_NOERROR, indicating the joystick exists and is operational, we set the private member variable m_uJoystickid to JOYSTICKID1.

```
if(joyGetPosEx(JOYSTICKID1,&m_joyInfo)==JOYERR_NOERROR)
  m_uJoystickid=JOYSTICKID1;
```

Otherwise, we try the same thing with joystick 2:

```
else if(joyGetPosEx(JOYSTICKID2,&m_joyInfo)==JOYERR_NOERROR)
  m_uJoystickid=JOYSTICKID2;
```

If both attempts fail, we bail. Strictly speaking, if we identify two working joysticks, we should ask the player which one they would like to use, but for a simple demo like this, it is good enough to be lazy and just use the first one that works.

```
else return FALSE;
```

Now that we've identified a working joystick, we need to get its minimum and maximum extents. We declare a local structure of type JOYCAPS for the joystick's capabilities.

```
JOYCAPS joycaps;
```

We call the API function joyGetDevCaps to put the joystick capabilities into joycaps, and bail out if it fails to do so:

```
if(joyGetDevCaps(m_uJoystickid,&joycaps,
sizeof(joycaps))!=JOYERR_NOERROR)
  return FALSE; //bail if can't get caps info
```

From joycaps we extract the joystick extents and store them in the appropriate private member variables:

```
m_nXmax=joycaps.wXmax; m_nYmax=joycaps.wYmax; //max extent
m_nXmin=joycaps.wXmin; m_nYmin=joycaps.wYmin; //min extent
```

Now we call the CJoystickManager member function load_data to extract joystick position and button data from the m_joyInfo member variable. This information was placed there by the earlier call to joyGetPosEx, but we couldn't process it until we obtained the joystick extents from which we can compute the joystick coordinates as percentages.

```
load_data();
```

Finally, we record that the joystick is ready for use:

```
return m_bOperational=TRUE;
}
```

Getting Data From the Joystick

The CJoystickManager load_data function takes care of processing information from the JOYINFOEX information private member variable m_joyInfo into the other private member variables:

```
void CJoystickManager::load_data(){ //process joystick data
```

Each button state is recorded in a single bit of the dwButtons field of m_joyInfo, so we extract each one by performing a bitwise AND of m_joyInfo.dwButtons with the appropriate power of two:

```
m_bButton[0]=m_joyInfo.dwButtons&1;
m_bButton[1]=m_joyInfo.dwButtons&2;
m_bButton[2]=m_joyInfo.dwButtons&4;
m_bButton[3]=m_joyInfo.dwButtons&8;
```

After a test to eliminate the possibility of a divide-by-zero error, we normalize the x coordinate of the joystick to between 0 and 100. Notice that if the joystick's x coordinate m_joyInfo.dwXpos is at the far left extent, stored in m_nXmin, then m_nX is set to zero. Similarly, if m_joyInfo.dwXpos is at the far right extent, stored in m_nXmax, then m_nX is set to 100.

```
if(m_nXmax!=m_nXmin)
  m_nX=(100*(m_joyInfo.dwXpos-m_nXmin))/(m_nXmax-m_nXmin);
```

However, the joystick extents were stored in the private member variables m_nXmax and m_nXmin back when the CJoystickManager initialize function was called, which may have been a long time ago. The joystick's temperature may have changed since then, which means that the joystick may report an x coordinate that is larger than m_nXmax or smaller than m_nXmin. However, it won't be off by much, so we will simply truncate the percentages at 0 and 100.

```
if(m_nX<0)m_nX=0;  if(m_nX>100)m_nX=100;
```

The joystick's Y coordinate is handled similarly.

```
if(m_nYmax!=m_nYmin)
  m_nY=(100*(m_joyInfo.dwYpos-m_nYmin))/(m_nYmax-m_nYmin);
if(m_nY<0)m_nY=0;  if(m_nY>100)m_nY=100;
}
```

The CJoystickManager poll function polls the joystick state using the API function joyGetPosEx. It returns TRUE if new data was received from the joystick.

```
BOOL CJoystickManager::poll(){ //poll joystick state
```

It bails out if the joystick is not operational:

```
if(!m_bOperational)return FALSE; //bail if not initialized
```

It uses the timer to ensure that the joystick is not polled too often:

```
if(!Timer.elapsed(m_nLastPollTime,JOYSTICKPOLLINTERVAL))
    return FALSE;
```

If everything is OK, it calls `joyGetPosEx` to put joystick information in `m_joyInfo`, and bails out if the joystick was unplugged by the player:

```
if(joyGetPosEx(m_uJoystickid,&m_joyInfo)==JOYERR_UNPLUGGED)
    return FALSE; //bail if cannot get data from joystick
```

It parses the `m_joyInfo` information into the other private member variables:

```
load_data();
```

Then it marks all of the up buttons as unserviced, so that they get serviced the next time they are down:

```
for(int i=0; i<4; i++)
    if(!m_bButton[i])m_bServiced[i]=FALSE;
```

Having succeeded, it returns TRUE:

```
    return TRUE;
}
```

Other Member Functions

The next two `CJoystickManager` member functions `button_down` and `position` report on the joystick state from the information parsed out of the `JOYINFOEX` structure. The `CJoystickManager` `button_down` function reports the state of a joystick button. The parameter `button` uses the joystick standard, not the C standard, in that it starts at 1 instead of 0.

```
BOOL CJoystickManager::button_down(int button){
```

We declare a local variable for the returned `result`, decrement `button` so that it can be used as an array index, and then bail out if the joystick is not operational or `button` is out of range:

```
BOOL result;
button--; //adjust for 0-based array
if(!m_bOperational)return FALSE; //bail if not initialized
if(button<0||button>=4)return FALSE; //bail if wrong number
```

We set `result` to TRUE if `button` is down:

```
result=m_bButton[button]; //is button down?
```

We pop it up, so that it is not recorded as being down the next time the button is queried even though the joystick may not have been polled in the meantime:

```
m_bButton[button]=FALSE; //pop it up
```

If autorepeat is disabled, and the button was down and has been serviced, then we return FALSE (reporting that the button is up):

```
if(!m_bAutoRepeat&&result&&m_bServiced[button])
  return FALSE; //prevent button bounce
```

Otherwise, if the button is down, then we mark it as serviced. This prevents it from being serviced again until the poll function sees that it has been released and sets m_bServiced[button] to FALSE.

```
if(result) //if button is down
  m_bServiced[button]=TRUE; //mark as serviced
```

Finally, we return the result:

```
  return result;
}
```

The CJoystickManager position function is a simple reader function that reports the joystick coordinates from the private member variables m_nX and m_nY:

```
BOOL CJoystickManager::position(POINT &point){
  if(!m_bOperational)return FALSE; //bail if not initialized
  point.x=m_nX; point.y=m_nY;
  return TRUE;
}
```

The function CJoystickManager autorepeat function changes the autorepeat settings and resets the service flags:

```
void CJoystickManager::autorepeat(BOOL setting){
  m_bAutoRepeat=setting; //allow autorepeat
  for(int i=0; i<4; i++) //reset buttons
    m_bServiced[i]=m_bButton[i]=FALSE;
}
```

The CJoystickManager exists function returns TRUE if an operational joystick exists:

```
BOOL CJoystickManager::exists(){
  //TRUE if joystick apparently exists
  return m_bOperational;
}
```

Changes to the Input Manager

Some changes to the input manager class `CInputManager` are needed to incorporate the joystick code.

Declarations

In `Defines.h`, we add a new entry `JOYSTICK_INPUT` to the enumerated type `InputDeviceType`:

```
enum InputDeviceType{KEYBOARD_INPUT=0,MOUSE_INPUT,
  JOYSTICK_INPUT};
```

The changes to `Input.h` begin with the declaration of a joystick manager as a private member variable:

```
CJoystickManager JoystickManager; //joystick manager
```

Two new private member functions `IntroJoystick` and `GameJoystick` act as joystick handlers during the intro and during gameplay, respectively:

```
void IntroJoystick(); //joystick handler
void GameJoystick(); //joystick handler
```

The main joystick handler is a `CInputManager` public member function `Joystick`:

```
void Joystick(); //main joystick handler
```

Changes to the Code

Changes to the `CInputManager` code in `Input.cpp` begin with the constructor, which has two additional lines of code to initialize the joystick manager member variable and set autorepeat on the joystick buttons to `FALSE`:

```
JoystickManager.initialize(); //set up joystick
JoystickManager.autorepeat(FALSE); //disable autorepeat
```

In the `CInputManager DeviceMenuKeyboard` function, we add a new `case` to the `switch` statement so that the joystick option is selected when the player hits the "J" key. It checks that the joystick exists by calling the joystick manager's `exists` member function, then sets the input device to `JOYSTICK_INPUT` before drawing the joystick radio button on the screen in the down position.

```
case 'J': //play using joystick
  if(JoystickManager.exists()){ //if joystick exists
    InputDevice=JOYSTICK_INPUT;
    ButtonManager->buttondown(JOYSTICK_INPUT);
  }
  break;
```

Similarly, we add a new `case` to the `switch` statement in the `CInputManager DeviceMenuLMouseDown` function so that the player can click on the "Joystick" button with the mouse. As with the other cases, it relies on the keyboard manager to effect the change by sending it a "J" character.

```
case 2: Keyboard('J'); break; //joystick
```

The remaining three new member functions are the joystick handlers. The `CInputManager GameJoystick` function handles the joystick during gameplay.

```
void CInputManager::GameJoystick(){
```

It bails out if the joystick is not being used:

```
if(InputDevice!=JOYSTICK_INPUT)return; //bail if unneeded
```

If button 1 is down, it fires the gun. Notice that the joystick manager takes care of making sure that the gun is fired once per click.

```
if(JoystickManager.button_down(1)) //button 1...
  Keyboard(VK_SPACE,TRUE); //...fires bullets
```

The next line of code never actually gets used, but it's in there just to provide safety during debugging:

```
if(GamePhase!=PLAYING_PHASE)return; //bail if not playing
```

We declare a local variable `point` to hold the joystick's current coordinates from the joystick manager:

```
POINT point; //coordinates of joystick
JoystickManager.position(point); //get coordinates
```

We set a local variable `extent` for the joystick extent, and pass both `point` and `extent` to the input manager's `set_plane_speed` function to set the plane's speed:

```
SIZE extent; //extent that joystick indicator moves in
extent.cx=100; extent.cy=100; //set extent
set_plane_speed(point,extent); //set plane speed
}
```

The `CInputManager IntroJoystick` function allows the player to click out of the intro screens using the joystick button:

```
void CInputManager::IntroJoystick(){
//joystick handler for intro
  if(JoystickManager.button_down(1)) //click out
    Keyboard(VK_ESCAPE);
}
```

The `CInputManager Joystick` function is the main joystick handler. As with the other `CInputManager` device handlers, it consists of a `switch` statement that selects the private member function for the current phase. First, however, it attempts to poll the joystick by calling the joystick manager's `poll` function.

Recall that the timer is used in the `CJoystickManager poll` function to make sure that the joystick is not polled too often.

```
void CInputManager::Joystick(){ //main joystick handler
  JoystickManager.poll(); //poll joystick
  switch(GamePhase){ //call joystick handler for phase
    case PLAYING_PHASE: GameJoystick(); break;
    case LOGO_PHASE:
    case TITLE_PHASE: IntroJoystick(); break;
    case DEVICEMENU_PHASE:
    case MENU_PHASE:
      break; //do nothing
  }
}
```

To ensure that the joystick gets polled regularly, we add a line of code to function `ProcessFrame` in `Main.cpp` to process the joystick input:

```
InputManager.Joystick(); //process joystick input
```

Demo 10 Files

Code Files

The following files in Demo 10 are used without change from Demo 9:

- `Ai.h`
- `Ai.cpp`
- `Bmp.h`
- `Bmp.cpp`
- `Bsprite.h`
- `Bsprite.cpp`
- `Buttons.h`
- `Buttons.cpp`
- `Csprite.h`
- `Csprite.cpp`
- `Ddsetup.cpp`
- `Objects.h`
- `Objects.cpp`

- Objman.h
- Objman.cpp
- Random.h
- Random.cpp
- Sbmp.h
- Sbmp.cpp
- Sndlist.h
- Sound.h
- Sound.cpp
- Timer.h
- Timer.cpp
- View.h
- View.cpp

The following files in Demo 10 have been modified from Demo 9:

- Defines.h
- Input.h
- Input.cpp
- Main.cpp (changes minimal; not listed)

The following files are new in Demo 10:

- Joystick.h
- Joystick.cpp

Required Libraries

- Ddraw.lib
- Dsound.lib
- Winmm.lib

Code Listings

Defines.h

```
//defines.h: essential defines
//Copyright Ian Parberry, 1999
//Last updated November 9, 1999

#ifndef __DEFINES_H__
#define __DEFINES_H__
```

```
#define SCREEN_WIDTH 640 //pixels wide
#define SCREEN_HEIGHT 480 //pixels high
#define COLORS 256 //number of colors
#define COLOR_DEPTH 8 //number of bits to store colors
#define TRANSPARENT_COLOR 255 //transparent palette position

enum GamePhaseType{
  LOGO_PHASE,TITLE_PHASE,MENU_PHASE,PLAYING_PHASE,
  DEVICEMENU_PHASE
};

enum InputDeviceType{KEYBOARD_INPUT=0,MOUSE_INPUT,
  JOYSTICK_INPUT};

#endif
```

Input.h

```
//input.h: header file for input class

//Copyright Ian Parberry, 1999
//Last updated March 17, 2000

#include <windows.h>
#include <windowsx.h>

#include "defines.h"
#include "buttons.h" //for button manager
#include "joystick.h" //for joystick manager


#ifndef __INPUT_H__
#define __INPUT_H__

class CInputManager{
  private:
    InputDeviceType InputDevice; //current input device
    CButtonManager *ButtonManager; //for managing menu buttons
    CJoystickManager JoystickManager; //joystick manager
    //helper functions
    BOOL is_function_key(WPARAM keystroke); //TRUE if function
key
    void decode(LPARAM lparam,POINT &point); //decode mouse click
    void set_plane_speed(POINT point,SIZE extent);
    //set up buttons for menus
    void SetupMainMenuButtons(); //main menu button manager
    void SetupDeviceMenuButtons(); //device menu button manager
    //keyboard handlers
    void IntroKeyboard(WPARAM keystroke); //keyboard handler
```

```
      BOOL MainMenuKeyboard(WPARAM keystroke); //keyboard handler
      void DeviceMenuKeyboard(WPARAM keystroke); //keyboard handler
      void GameKeyboard(WPARAM keystroke); //keyboard handler
      //left mouse button down handlers
      void MainMenuLMouseDown(POINT point); //mouse down handler
      void DeviceMenuLMouseDown(POINT point); //mouse down handler
      void GameLMouseDown(POINT point); //mouse down handler
      //left mouse button up handlers
      void IntroLMouseUp(POINT point); //mouse up handler
      BOOL MainMenuLMouseUp(POINT point); //mouse up handler
      void DeviceMenuLMouseUp(POINT point); //mouse up handler
      //joystick handlers
      void IntroJoystick(); //joystick handler
      void GameJoystick(); //joystick handler
    public:
      CInputManager(); //constructor
      ~CInputManager(); //destructor
      BOOL Restore(); //restore surfaces
      void Release(); //release surfaces
      void SetupButtons(GamePhaseType phase); //set up menu buttons
      BOOL Keyboard(WPARAM keystroke,
        BOOL virtual_keystroke=FALSE); //keyboard handler
      void LMouseDown(LPARAM lparam); //main mouse down handler
      BOOL LMouseUp(LPARAM lparam); //main mouse up handler
      void MouseMove(LPARAM lparam); //handle mouse motion
      void Joystick(); //main joystick handler
};

#endif
```

Input.cpp

```
//input.cpp: program file for input class

//Copyright Ian Parberry, 1999
//Last updated March 17, 2000

#include "input.h"
#include "objman.h" //for object manager
#include "sndlist.h" //for list of sounds

extern GamePhaseType GamePhase; //current phase
extern GamePhaseType NextPhase; //next phase of game
extern BOOL endphase; //should we abort current phase?
extern CObjectManager ObjectManager; //object manager

CInputManager::CInputManager(){ //constructor
  InputDevice=KEYBOARD_INPUT; //current input device
  ButtonManager=NULL; //for managing menu buttons
  JoystickManager.initialize(); //set up joystick
```

```
    JoystickManager.autorepeat(FALSE); //disable autorepeat
}

CInputManager::~CInputManager(){ //destructor
  delete ButtonManager;
}

BOOL CInputManager::Restore(){ //restore surfaces
  return ButtonManager->Restore();
}

void CInputManager::Release(){ //release surfaces
    ButtonManager->Release();
}

void CInputManager::SetupMainMenuButtons(){
//set up main menu button manager
  const int YDELTA=70; //y separation between buttons
  const int BUTTONCOUNT=6; //number of buttons
  SIZE size; //size of buttons
  size.cx=40; size.cy=40; //size of buttons
  POINT point; //top left corner of first button
  point.x=111; point.y=46; //first button location
  delete ButtonManager; //delete any old one
  ButtonManager=new //create new button manager
    CButtonManager(BUTTONCOUNT,size,point,YDELTA,
      "buttons.bmp");
 //set button sounds
  ButtonManager->
    setsounds(BIGCLICK_SOUND,SMALLCLICK_SOUND);
}

void CInputManager::SetupDeviceMenuButtons(){
//set up device menu button manager
  const int BUTTONCOUNT=4;
  delete ButtonManager; //if there is one already, delete it
  SIZE size; //size of buttons
  size.cx=40; size.cy=40; //size of buttons
  ButtonManager=new
    CButtonManager(BUTTONCOUNT,size,"buttons.bmp");
  ButtonManager->setsounds(BIGCLICK_SOUND,SMALLCLICK_SOUND);
  ButtonManager->set_radio(); //radio buttons
  //add buttons
  POINT point;
  point.x=209; point.y=130;
  ButtonManager->addbutton(point);
  point.x=209; point.y=210;
  ButtonManager->addbutton(point);
  point.x=209; point.y=291;
  ButtonManager->addbutton(point);
```

```
    point.x=209; point.y=372;
    ButtonManager->addbutton(point);
    //initialize image of radio button
    ButtonManager->buttondown(InputDevice,FALSE); //no sound
}

void CInputManager::SetupButtons(GamePhaseType phase){
//set up menu buttons
    switch(phase){
        case MENU_PHASE: SetupMainMenuButtons(); break;
        case DEVICEMENU_PHASE: SetupDeviceMenuButtons(); break;
    }
}


//keyboard handlers

void CInputManager::IntroKeyboard(WPARAM keystroke){
//keyboard handler for intro
    endphase=TRUE; //any key ends the phase
}

BOOL CInputManager::MainMenuKeyboard(WPARAM keystroke){
//keyboard handler for menu
    BOOL result=FALSE;
    switch(keystroke){
        case VK_ESCAPE:
        case 'Q': //exit the game
            result=TRUE;
            break;
        case 'N': //play new game
            NextPhase=PLAYING_PHASE; endphase=TRUE;
            break;
        case 'D':
            NextPhase=DEVICEMENU_PHASE; endphase=TRUE;
        default: break; //do nothing
    }
    return result;
}

void CInputManager::DeviceMenuKeyboard(WPARAM keystroke){
//keyboard handler //for device menu
    switch(keystroke){
        case VK_ESCAPE:
        case 'D': //exit menu
            endphase=TRUE;
            break;
        case 'K': //play using keyboard
            InputDevice=KEYBOARD_INPUT; //set device
            ButtonManager->buttondown(KEYBOARD_INPUT);
            break;
```

```
          case 'M': //play using mouse
            InputDevice=MOUSE_INPUT; //set device
            ButtonManager->buttondown(MOUSE_INPUT);
            break;
          case 'J': //play using joystick
            if(JoystickManager.exists()){ //if joystick exists
              InputDevice=JOYSTICK_INPUT;
              ButtonManager->buttondown(JOYSTICK_INPUT);
            }
            break;
          default: break;
      }
}
void CInputManager::GameKeyboard(WPARAM keystroke){
//keyboard handler for game play
  switch(keystroke){
    case VK_ESCAPE: endphase=TRUE; break;
    case VK_UP: ObjectManager.accelerate(0,-1); break;
    case VK_DOWN: ObjectManager.accelerate(0,1); break;
    case VK_LEFT: ObjectManager.accelerate(-1,0); break;
    case VK_RIGHT: ObjectManager.accelerate(1,0); break;
    case VK_SPACE: ObjectManager.fire_gun(); break;
    default: break;
  }
}

BOOL CInputManager::is_function_key(WPARAM keystroke){
  return keystroke==VK_ESCAPE||
    (keystroke>=VK_F1&&keystroke<=VK_F12);
}

BOOL CInputManager::Keyboard(WPARAM keystroke,
  BOOL virtual_keystroke){ //keyboard handler
  BOOL result=FALSE;
  switch(GamePhase){
    case LOGO_PHASE:
    case TITLE_PHASE:
      IntroKeyboard(keystroke);
      break;
    case MENU_PHASE:
      result=MainMenuKeyboard(keystroke);
      break;
    case DEVICEMENU_PHASE:
      DeviceMenuKeyboard(keystroke);
      break;
    case PLAYING_PHASE:
      if(InputDevice==KEYBOARD_INPUT||
      is_function_key(keystroke)||virtual_keystroke)
        GameKeyboard(keystroke);
      break;
```

```cpp
  }
  return result;
}


//mouse left button down handlers

void CInputManager::MainMenuLMouseDown(POINT point){
//mouse down handler for menu
  if(ButtonManager->hit(point)>=0) //if a valid hit
    ButtonManager->buttondown(point); //animate a button down
}

void CInputManager::DeviceMenuLMouseDown(POINT point){
//mouse down handler for device menu
  int hit=ButtonManager->hit(point);
  switch(hit){
    case 0: Keyboard('K'); break; //keyboard
    case 1: Keyboard('M'); break; //mouse
    case 2: Keyboard('J'); break; //joystick
    case 3:
      ButtonManager->buttondown(hit); //quit button down
      break;
    default: break;
  }
}

void CInputManager::GameLMouseDown(POINT point){
//mouse down handler for game
  Keyboard(VK_SPACE,TRUE);
}

void CInputManager::decode(LPARAM lparam,POINT &point){
//decode mouse click lparam to point
  point.x=LOWORD(lparam); point.y=HIWORD(lparam);
}

void CInputManager::LMouseDown(LPARAM lparam){
//main mouse left button down handler
  POINT point; //mouse location on screen
  decode(lparam,point); //decode mouse point
  switch(GamePhase){
    case MENU_PHASE:
      MainMenuLMouseDown(point);
      break;
    case DEVICEMENU_PHASE:
      DeviceMenuLMouseDown(point);
      break;
    case PLAYING_PHASE:
      if(InputDevice==MOUSE_INPUT)
        GameLMouseDown(point);
```

```
      break;
    }
  }

//mouse left button up handlers

void CInputManager::IntroLMouseUp(POINT point){
//mouse left button up handler for intro
  endphase=TRUE;
}

BOOL CInputManager::MainMenuLMouseUp(POINT point){
//mouse left button up handler for menu
  int hit=ButtonManager->release(point); //get button hit
  BOOL result=FALSE;
  //take action depending on which button was hit
  switch(hit){ //depending on which button was hit
    case 0: Keyboard('N'); break; //new game
    case 1: Keyboard('S'); break; //saved game
    case 2: Keyboard('D'); break; //devices
    case 3: Keyboard('L'); break; //high score list
    case 4: Keyboard('H'); break; //help
    case 5: result=Keyboard(VK_ESCAPE); break; //quit
    default: break;
  }
  //animate button images
  if(hit>=0)ButtonManager->buttonup(hit); //hit
  else ButtonManager->allbuttonsup(); //nonhit
  return result;
}

void CInputManager::DeviceMenuLMouseUp(POINT point){
//mouse left button up handler for device menu
  int hit=ButtonManager->release(point);
  switch(hit){
    case 3: //quit button up
      ButtonManager->buttonup(hit); //show quit button up
      Keyboard(VK_ESCAPE);
      break;
  }
  if(hit<0)ButtonManager->allbuttonsup(); //no hit
}

BOOL CInputManager::LMouseUp(LPARAM lparam){
//main mouse left button up handler
  BOOL result=FALSE;
  POINT point; //mouse location on screen
  decode(lparam,point); //decode mouse point
  switch(GamePhase){
    case LOGO_PHASE:
```

```
      case TITLE_PHASE:
        IntroLMouseUp(point);
        break;
      case MENU_PHASE:
        result=MainMenuLMouseUp(point);
        break;
      case DEVICEMENU_PHASE:
        DeviceMenuLMouseUp(point);
        break;
    }
    return result;
}


//mouse motion handler

void CInputManager::set_plane_speed(POINT point,SIZE extent){
//set plane speed based on point's position in extent
  int xmin,xmax,ymin,ymax; //plane speed limits
  ObjectManager.speed_limits(xmin,xmax,ymin,ymax); //get them
  //bands for speed assignment
  const int XBANDWIDTH=extent.cx/(xmax-xmin+1);
  const int YBANDWIDTH=extent.cy/(ymax-ymin+1);
  int xspeed,yspeed; //speed of plane
  xspeed=point.x/XBANDWIDTH+xmin; //horizontal speed
  yspeed=point.y/YBANDWIDTH+ymin; //vertical speed
  ObjectManager.set_speed(xspeed,yspeed); //pass to plane
}

void CInputManager::MouseMove(LPARAM lparam){
  if(InputDevice!=MOUSE_INPUT)return; //bail if not needed
  if(GamePhase!=PLAYING_PHASE)return; //bail if not playing
  POINT point; //mouse location on screen
  decode(lparam,point); //decode mouse point
  //set extent
  SIZE extent; //extent that mouse moves in
  extent.cx=SCREEN_WIDTH;
  extent.cy=SCREEN_HEIGHT;
  //set plane speed based on point and extent
  set_plane_speed(point,extent);
}


//joystick handlers

void CInputManager::GameJoystick(){
//joystick handler for game play
  if(InputDevice!=JOYSTICK_INPUT)return; //bail if unneeded
  //buttons
  if(JoystickManager.button_down(1)) //button 1...
    Keyboard(VK_SPACE,TRUE); //...fires bullets
  //stick
```

```
    if(GamePhase!=PLAYING_PHASE)return; //bail if not playing
    POINT point; //coordinates of joystick
    JoystickManager.position(point); //get coordinates
    SIZE extent; //extent that joystick indicator moves in
    extent.cx=100; extent.cy=100; //set extent
    set_plane_speed(point,extent); //set plane speed
}

void CInputManager::IntroJoystick(){
//joystick handler for intro
    if(JoystickManager.button_down(1)) //click out
        Keyboard(VK_ESCAPE);
}

void CInputManager::Joystick(){ //main joystick handler
    JoystickManager.poll(); //poll joystick
    switch(GamePhase){ //call joystick handler for phase
        case PLAYING_PHASE: GameJoystick(); break;
        case LOGO_PHASE:
        case TITLE_PHASE: IntroJoystick(); break;
        case DEVICEMENU_PHASE:
        case MENU_PHASE:
            break; //do nothing
    }
}
```

Joystick.h

```
//joystick.h: header file for joystick.cpp
//joystick manager class

//Copyright Ian Parberry, 1999
//Last updated February 14, 2000

#ifndef __JOYSTICK__
#define __JOYSTICK__

#include <windows.h>
#include <mmsystem.h>

#define JOYSTICKPOLLINTERVAL 100 //time between polls

class CJoystickManager{
  private:
    JOYINFOEX m_joyInfo; //current joystick state
    UINT m_uJoystickid; //joystick id
    int m_nX, m_nY; //x and y coordinates as percentages
    int m_nXmax, m_nYmax; //maximum x and y from h/w
    int m_nXmin, m_nYmin; //minimum x and y from h/w
    BOOL m_bButton[4]; //buttons down?
```

```
      BOOL m_bServiced[4]; //whether down button was serviced
      BOOL m_bOperational; //was init successful?
      int m_nLastPollTime; //last time joystick was polled
      BOOL m_bAutoRepeat; //allow autorepeat
      void load_data(); //process data from m_joyInfo
   public:
      CJoystickManager(); //constructor
      BOOL initialize(); //initialize settings
      BOOL poll(); //poll joystick state
      BOOL button_down(int button); //is button down?
      BOOL position(POINT &point); //position as percentage
      void autorepeat(BOOL setting=TRUE); //un/set autorepeat
      BOOL exists(); //TRUE if joystick exists
};

#endif
```

Joystick.cpp

```
//joystick.cpp: simple joystick handler

//Copyright Ian Parberry, 1999
//Last updated November 16, 1999

#include "joystick.h"
#include "timer.h" //game timer

extern CTimer Timer; //game timer

CJoystickManager::CJoystickManager(){ //constructor
  m_nLastPollTime=0; //not polled yet
  m_bOperational=FALSE; //not initialized yet
  m_uJoystickid=0; m_bAutoRepeat=TRUE;
  m_nX=m_nY=0; m_nXmax=m_nYmax=m_nXmin=m_nYmin=0;
  for(int i=0; i<4; i++) //init button positions
    m_bServiced[i]=m_bButton[i]=FALSE;
}

BOOL CJoystickManager::initialize(){ //init joystick
  m_bOperational=FALSE; //assume failure
  //attempt to init joystick
  if(!joyGetNumDevs())return FALSE; //bail if no joysticks
  //init JOYINFOEX
  memset(&m_joyInfo,0,sizeof(JOYINFOEX));
  m_joyInfo.dwSize=sizeof(JOYINFOEX);
  m_joyInfo.dwFlags=JOY_RETURNBUTTONS|JOY_RETURNX|JOY_RETURNY;
  //get id of first of 2 possible joysticks
  if(joyGetPosEx(JOYSTICKID1,&m_joyInfo)==JOYERR_NOERROR)
    m_uJoystickid=JOYSTICKID1;
  else if(joyGetPosEx(JOYSTICKID2,&m_joyInfo)==JOYERR_NOERROR)
```

```
      m_uJoystickid=JOYSTICKID2;
    else return FALSE;
    //get min and max extents of joystick
    JOYCAPS joycaps;
    if(joyGetDevCaps(m_uJoystickid,&joycaps,
    sizeof(joycaps))!=JOYERR_NOERROR)
      return FALSE; //bail if can't get caps info
    m_nXmax=joycaps.wXmax; m_nYmax=joycaps.wYmax; //max extent
    m_nXmin=joycaps.wXmin; m_nYmin=joycaps.wYmin; //min extent
    //init data fields with fresh info
    load_data();
    //record success
    return m_bOperational=TRUE;
}

void CJoystickManager::load_data(){ //process joystick data
    //buttons
    m_bButton[0]=m_joyInfo.dwButtons&1;
    m_bButton[1]=m_joyInfo.dwButtons&2;
    m_bButton[2]=m_joyInfo.dwButtons&4;
    m_bButton[3]=m_joyInfo.dwButtons&8;
    //X position: normalize to range 0..100
    if(m_nXmax!=m_nXmin)
      m_nX=(100*(m_joyInfo.dwXpos-m_nXmin))/(m_nXmax-m_nXmin);
    if(m_nX<0)m_nX=0; if(m_nX>100)m_nX=100;
    //Y position: normalize to range 0..100
    if(m_nYmax!=m_nYmin)
      m_nY=(100*(m_joyInfo.dwYpos-m_nYmin))/(m_nYmax-m_nYmin);
    if(m_nY<0)m_nY=0; if(m_nY>100)m_nY=100;
}

BOOL CJoystickManager::poll(){ //poll joystick state
    if(!m_bOperational)return FALSE; //bail if not initialized
    //allow only infrequent polls
    if(!Timer.elapsed(m_nLastPollTime,JOYSTICKPOLLINTERVAL))
      return FALSE;
    //get new data into JOYINFOEX member
    if(joyGetPosEx(m_uJoystickid,&m_joyInfo)==JOYERR_UNPLUGGED)
      return FALSE; //bail if cannot get data from joystick
    //decode data into member variables
    load_data();
    //init serviced flags for noautorepeat
    for(int i=0; i<4; i++)
      if(!m_bButton[i])m_bServiced[i]=FALSE;
    //done
    return TRUE;
}

BOOL CJoystickManager::button_down(int button){
//is button down?
```

```
  BOOL result;
  button--; //adjust for 0-based array
  if(!m_bOperational)return FALSE; //bail if not initialized
  if(button<0||button>=4)return FALSE; //bail if wrong number
  result=m_bButton[button]; //is button down?
  m_bButton[button]=FALSE; //pop it up
  if(!m_bAutoRepeat&&result&&m_bServiced[button])
    return FALSE; //prevent button bounce
  if(result) //if button is down
    m_bServiced[button]=TRUE; //mark as serviced
  return result;
}

BOOL CJoystickManager::position(POINT &point){
  if(!m_bOperational)return FALSE; //bail if not initialized
  point.x=m_nX; point.y=m_nY;
  return TRUE;
}

void CJoystickManager::autorepeat(BOOL setting){
  m_bAutoRepeat=setting; //allow autorepeat
  for(int i=0; i<4; i++) //reset buttons
    m_bServiced[i]=m_bButton[i]=FALSE;
}

BOOL CJoystickManager::exists(){
  //TRUE if joystick apparently exists
  return m_bOperational;
}
```

Here's what you'll learn:

- How to add levels to your game

- How to make the player win or lose

- How to deal with the increasing complexity of your game

- How to manage the player's score, health, and lives

- How to display text on the screen using sprites

- How to keep track of the frame rate

Winning and Losing

A game is not truly a game unless there are rewards for success, with subgoals that can be met along the way to give the player a sense of making progress. In Demo 11, we learn how to add levels to the game, with more adversaries to destroy as the player advances in level. When a player completes a level successfully by killing all of the crows, a success screen is displayed and a success sound is played before the player is allowed to progress to the next level.

A game is also not truly a game unless you can die. In Demo 11, the player has health and lives, which are managed by a score manager. The player can be hit by crows, losing a health point each time. After three health points are lost, the player loses a life. Lose enough lives and he or she is out of the game. Lives can be gained when enough points are scored—points are scored for each crow killed and for completing each level. Naturally, the player wants to keep track of his or her statistics, so a text bar at the top of the screen shows the current level number, the number of adversaries left to kill, and the player's score, health, and lives (see Figure 13.1). The F1 key toggles a frame rate display in the lower right-hand corner of the screen, in frames per second. The screen text is handled by a text manager.

Figure 13.1
Screen shot
of Demo 11

Experiment with Demo 11

Take a moment now to run Demo 11.

- Play a game. Notice the text at the top of the screen.
- Kill some crows and notice that your score increases each time a crow corpse hits the ground.
- Kill all of the crows to progress to the next level. Notice that you get ten extra points for completing a level. Notice that there are more crows each time, until you eventually reach a maximum.
- Run into a crow to see what happens. Do it three times and you die. Notice that each time you get a new incarnation, you get a small grace period of a few seconds in which it is impossible to run into crows. Why? Because the plane is out of control when it explodes and dies, which means that we need to give the player a few seconds to dodge crows when control returns.
- Keep playing. Notice that you get a new life with each 100 points scored.
- Use the F1 key to toggle the frame rate indicator at the lower right corner of the screen. Notice that it is updated once a second.
- Exit back to the main menu. Start a new game, but do not fire the gun. Instead, kill all of the crows by running into them. Progress to level two and keep killing them until you run out of lives and health. What happens then?

The Score Manager

The score manager's job is to take care of the player's score and health. We create a class called CScoreManager for the score manager.

Score Manager Overview

The header file for the score manager is Score.h. It begins with the declaration of a constant LEVEL_BONUS_SCORE for the number of extra points earned by completing a level.

```
const int LEVEL_BONUS_SCORE=10; //pts for level completion
```

The score manager class CScoreManager has three private member variables to hold the player's statistics: m_nScore, the number of points scored; m_nHealth, the amount of health that the player has; and m_nLives, the number of lives that the player has left after the current one:

```
int m_nScore; //points scored
int m_nHealth; //how many times plane has been hit
int m_nLives; //how many lives the player has
```

`CScoreManager` has nine public member functions, beginning with a constructor:

```
CScoreManager(); //constructor
```

The `reset` function resets the score manager for the start of a game:

```
void reset(); //reset to start conditions
```

The `score`, `health`, and `lives` functions are reader functions that return the player's current score, health, and number of lives, respectively:

```
int score(); //return current points score
int health(); //return plane health
int lives(); //return number of lives
```

There are two `add_to_score` functions, the first of which adds a specific number of points `delta` to the player's score. This will be used to add in the level-end bonus, for example. The second version takes an object type `object` as a parameter, and adds to the player's score an appropriate bounty for killing that type of object.

```
void add_to_score(int delta); //add delta to score
void add_to_score(ObjectType object); //for killing object
```

The `collision` function deducts from the player's health due to a collision:

```
void collision(); //collision, bad for health
```

The `deduct_life` function deducts a life from a player whose health is bad.

```
void deduct_life(); //lose a life if health bad
```

Score Manager Code

The code file for the score manager is `Score.cpp`. It begins with the declaration of three constants: `START_LIVES`, the number of lives that the player starts with; `MAX_HEALTH`, the maximum health that the player can have (the minimum is zero); and `SCORE_PER_LIFE`, the number of points that it takes to earn an extra life.

```
const int START_LIVES=3; //initial number of lives
const int MAX_HEALTH=3; //maximum plane health
const int SCORE_PER_LIFE=100; //pts to earn another life
```

The `CScoreManager` constructor calls the `reset` member function:

```
CScoreManager::CScoreManager(){ //constructor
  reset();
}
```

The CScoreManager reset function sets the player's statistics stored in the three private member variables back to their initial conditions:

```
void CScoreManager::reset(){ //reset to start conditions
  m_nScore=0; m_nHealth=MAX_HEALTH; m_nLives=START_LIVES;
}
```

The first of two CScoreManager add_to_score functions adds a point count delta to the player's score, and awards a new life if one has been earned:

```
void CScoreManager::add_to_score(int delta){
```

It takes a snapshot of the current score in a local variable oldscore, then adds delta to m_nScore:

```
int oldscore=m_nScore; //old score
m_nScore+=delta; //add to score
```

It computes the number of new lives earned, and stores the result in a local variable newlives. The number of new lives earned is the number of lives divided by the new score (m_nScore/SCORE_PER_LIFE) minus the number of lives divided by the old score (oldscore/SCORE_PER_LIFE).

```
int newlives= //new lives earned
  m_nScore/SCORE_PER_LIFE-oldscore/SCORE_PER_LIFE;
```

If the number of new lives is nonzero, a special sound is played:

```
if(newlives) //play sound if nonzero
  SoundManager->play(NEWLIFE_SOUND);
```

The number of new lives (usually zero) is added to the player's life counter, and then the function returns:

```
m_nLives+=newlives; //add new lives to counter
}
```

The second of two CScoreManager add_to_score functions has an ObjectType parameter object. It adds to the player's score the number of points earned by killing an object of that type.

```
void CScoreManager::add_to_score(ObjectType object){
```

It begins with the declaration of a constant that defines the bounty for killing a crow:

```
const int CROW_SCORE=3; //score for killing crow
```

A switch statement breaks up the code by object type. This is pretty boring with only one object type, but it is all set up for the addition of more object types later.

```
switch(object){ //score depends on object
  case DEADCROW_OBJECT: add_to_score(CROW_SCORE); break;
  default: break; //default is nothing
```

```
      }
   }
```

The CScoreManager collision function deducts a point from the player's health, and if the health is nonzero, it plays an appropriate sound:

```
void CScoreManager::collision(){ //collision, bad for health
  if(--m_nHealth>0) //deduct from health
    SoundManager->play(STINGS_SOUND); //play sound
}
```

The CScoreManager deduct_life function deducts a life if the player's health is bad enough:

```
void CScoreManager::deduct_life(){ //lose a life
```

It checks whether the player's health is low:

```
    if(m_nHealth<=0){ //if health bad
```

If it is low, it resets the player's health to the maximum for the start of a new incarnation:

```
      m_nHealth=MAX_HEALTH; //make healthy
```

It deducts a life, and if there are no more lives left, it ends the playing phase:

```
      if(--m_nLives<0) //deduct a life, if last
        endphase=TRUE; //end of game
    }
}
```

The last three CScoreManager functions are reader functions that return the player's current lives, score, and health, respectively:

```
int CScoreManager::lives(){ //return number of lives
  return m_nLives;
}
int CScoreManager::score(){ //return score
  return m_nScore;
}

int CScoreManager::health(){ //return score
  return m_nHealth;
}
```

The Text Manager

The text manager's job is to take care of drawing text on the screen. Rather than using slow Windows API functions such as `DrawText` to draw text on the screen, we will use text sprites. This has the added advantage of allowing your artist to create more colorful and dramatic text than can be managed with a Windows screen font. We create a class called `CTextManager` for the text manager.

Text Manager Overview

The header file for the text manager is `Text.h`. It begins with the declaration of an enumerated type for the printable characters—the alphabetic and numeric characters only.

```
enum chartype{CHAR_A=0,CHAR_B,CHAR_C,CHAR_D,CHAR_E,CHAR_F,
    CHAR_G,CHAR_H,CHAR_I,CHAR_J,CHAR_K,CHAR_L,CHAR_M,CHAR_N,
    CHAR_O,CHAR_P,CHAR_Q,CHAR_R,CHAR_S,CHAR_T,CHAR_U,CHAR_V,
    CHAR_W,CHAR_X,CHAR_Y,CHAR_Z,CHAR_0,CHAR_1,CHAR_2,CHAR_3,
    CHAR_4,CHAR_5,CHAR_6,CHAR_7,CHAR_8,CHAR_9,NUM_CHARS};
```

`CTextManager` has five private member variables. The first is an array of pointers to clipped sprites with an entry for each character. Note the use of `NUM_CHARS` from our enumerated type `chartype`.

```
CClippedSprite *character[NUM_CHARS]; //char sprites
```

The next two private member variables are the width and height of the character sprites. Notice that we are using *fixed width* characters, which means that every character has the same width. Fixed width characters can look very ugly, since a narrow character such as "I" must have a lot of empty space to make it as wide as a character like "W." This problem can be alleviated by having your artist put a drop-shadow on each character, which makes it look like the character has been raised off the page so that it casts a shadow (see Figure 13.2).

```
int width,height; //width and height of chars
```

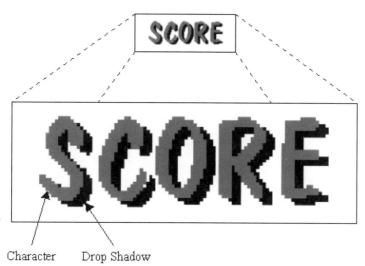

Figure 13.2
Text with a
drop shadow

Character   Drop Shadow

The text manager acts like a typewriter. It has a print head, referred to as the text *cursor*, that invisibly marks the place where the text manager will put text next. The private member variables x and y store the screen coordinates of the text cursor.

```
int x,y; //current cursor location
```

CTextManager has a private member function draw with two parameters, a character c and a pointer to a DirectDraw surface surface. It draws the character on the surface at the location specified by the text cursor. To be precise, the text cursor indicates the lower left pixel of the next character.

```
void draw(chartype c,LPDIRECTDRAWSURFACE surface);
```

CTextManager has seven public member functions, starting with a constructor and a destructor. The constructor has parameters wdth and ht, specifying respectively the width and height of the character sprites.

```
CTextManager(int wdth,int ht); //constructor
~CTextManager(); //destructor
```

The load function takes three parameters, a pointer to a bmp sprite file reader file, and the x and y coordinates of the first character image in that file. It returns TRUE if the load succeeds.

```
BOOL load(CBmpSpriteFileReader *file,
  int x,int y); //load sprites from file at (x,y)
```

The `jump` function moves the text cursor to position (`xloc`, `yloc`):

```
void jump(int xloc,int yloc); //move cursor to here
```

The public `draw` function draws a text `string` to a specified `surface`:

```
void draw(char* string,
    LPDIRECTDRAWSURFACE surface); //draw string
```

The last two public member functions are the mandatory `Restore` and `Release` functions, which respectively restore and release the text sprite surfaces:

```
BOOL Restore(); //restore sprite surfaces
void Release(); //release sprite surfaces
```

Text Manager Code

The code file for the text manager is `Text.cpp`. It begins with the `CTextManager` constructor.

```
CTextManager::CTextManager(int wdth,int ht){ //constructor
```

We store the text width and height into private member variables `width` and `height`:

```
width=wdth; height=ht; x=y=0;
```

Then, we create a single-frame clipped sprite object for each text character, and store a pointer to it in the private array `character`:

```
for(int i=0; i<NUM_CHARS; i++)
    character[i]=new CClippedSprite(1,width,height);
}
```

The `CTextManager` destructor `deletes` the sprites created by the constructor. Here's a test to see whether you have been paying attention. Why don't we release the sprite surfaces in the destructor too? After all, they must be released before we delete the sprites, so here would be a good place to do it. The way I've coded it, we have an explicit series of `Release` calls in `WindowProc` in response to the `WM_DESTROY` message, and we'll have to remember to go there later and add a call to the `CTextManager Release` function. Think about it before reading the answer in the next paragraph.

```
CTextManager::~CTextManager(){ //destructor
    for(int i=0; i<NUM_CHARS; i++)delete character[i];
}
```

The answer is, of course, that we need the DirectDraw object to still exist (that is, not to have been released itself) when surfaces are released. Destructors are the last things executed in this program, and so by the time the `CTextManager` destructor runs, the DirectDraw object will be long gone. We could, as some programmers do, encapsulate the DirectDraw management into a C++ class and release the DirectDraw object in its destructor; then we must make sure that it is declared first so that the destructor runs last.

The `CTextManager load` function loads the text images from a bmp sprite file reader pointed to by `bmp`, with the image of the first character starting at (`x, y`) in the image. It returns `TRUE` if it succeeds. This function assumes that the numeric characters are arranged in order in a single row, separated by a single pixel for the bounding box, and that the alphabetic characters are similarly arranged beneath them (see Figure 13.3).

Figure 13.3
The text sprite layout

```
BOOL CTextManager::load(CBmpSpriteFileReader *bmp,
                        int x,int y){ //load sprites
```

We declare a local variable to hold the return `result`, and two indices `cx, cy` into the sprite file.

```
BOOL result=TRUE;
int cx=x,cy=y; //location to read from
```

We run through the digit characters with a `for` loop:

```
for(int c=CHAR_0; c<=CHAR_9; c++){
```

We load character `c` from position (`cx, cy`) in the sprite file using the `CBmpSpriteFileReader load` function:

```
result=result&&character[c]->load(bmp,0,cx,cy);
```

We then move horizontally to the next character image in the file by adding the sprite `width` to `cx`, plus 1 for the bounding box:

```
cx+=width+1;
}
```

Having loaded the digits, we move to the letters on the next row (as depicted in Figure 13.3) by setting `cy` to `y` (the original origin) plus `height` (the height of the digits) plus 1 (for the bounding box):

```
cx=x; cy=y+height+1; //assume letters below numbers
```

The letters are loaded with a `for` loop, similarly to the way we loaded the digits:

```
for(c=CHAR_A; c<=CHAR_Z; c++){
  result=result&&character[c]->load(bmp,0,cx,cy);
  cx+=width+1;
}
```

Having attempted to load all of the digits and letters, we return the `result`:

```
  return result;
}
```

The `CTextManager` `jump` function moves the invisible text cursor to `(xloc,yloc)`:

```
void CTextManager::jump(int xloc,int yloc){ //jump to here
  x=xloc; y=yloc;
}
```

The `CTextManager` private `draw` function draws a character `c` with its lower left pixel at the location of the text cursor on `surface`:

```
void CTextManager::draw(chartype c,
    LPDIRECTDRAWSURFACE surface){ //draw char to surface
```

Since the location of sprites is actually the location of their lower middle pixel whereas the text cursor indicates the position of the lower left pixel, we shift the sprite location to the right by half of its width:

```
  int cx=x+width/2,cy=y; //compute location
```

We check that `c` is a valid character index before drawing it using the `CClippedSprite` `draw` function:

```
  if(c>=0&&c<NUM_CHARS)
    character[c]->draw(0,cx,cy,surface); //draw
```

Having drawn it, we move the cursor to the right by the width of one character:

```
  x+=width; //advance to next char
}
```

The `CTextManager` public `draw` function draws a `string` with its lower left pixel at the location of the text cursor on `surface`:

```
void CTextManager::draw(char* string,
    LPDIRECTDRAWSURFACE surface){ //draw string to surface
```

We loop through each character in the string with a `for` loop on `i`:

```
  for(int i=0; i<(int)strlen(string); i++){ //for each char
```

A local character variable `c` stores the current character from `string`:

```
    char c=string[i]; //grab character
```

If it is a digit, we use the `CTextManager` private `draw` function to draw it:

```
if(c>='0'&&c<='9') //number
  draw((chartype)(CHAR_0+c-'0'),surface);
```

Similarly for uppercase letters:

```
else if(c>='A'&&c<='Z') //uppercase
  draw((chartype)(CHAR_A+c-'A'),surface);
```

Similarly for lowercase letters, noting that since we don't have lowercase characters in our sprite font, we will draw them in uppercase:

```
else if(c>='a'&&c<='z') //lowercase
  draw((chartype)(CHAR_A+c-'a'),surface);
```

The only punctuation character allowed is a space, which is easily drawn by advancing the text cursor to the right:

```
    else if(c==' ')x+=width; //space
  }
}
```

Finally, we have the obligatory `Restore` and `Release` member functions:

```
BOOL CTextManager::Restore(){ //restore sprite surfaces
  BOOL result=TRUE;
  for(int c=0; c<NUM_CHARS; c++) //for each char sprite
    result=result&&character[c]->Restore(); //restore it
  return result;
}

void CTextManager::Release(){ //release sprite surfaces
  for(int c=0; c<NUM_CHARS; c++) //for each char sprite
    character[c]->Release(); //release it
}
```

Changes to Defines.h and Sndlist.h

When the player completes a level we will briefly display a success screen (see Figure 13.4). This entails a new phase called the *success phase*, for which we add the declaration of SUCCESS_PHASE to the end of the enumerated type GamePhaseType in Defines.h.

```
enum GamePhaseType{
  LOGO_PHASE,TITLE_PHASE,MENU_PHASE,PLAYING_PHASE,
  DEVICEMENU_PHASE,SUCCESS_PHASE
};
```

Figure 13.4
The success
screen

In `Sndlist.h`, we add the following new sounds to the enumerated type `GameSoundType`. On the completion of a level, we play `SUCCESS_SOUND` if the player succeeded in killing all of the varmints, and `FAILED_SOUND` if he or she got killed for the last time.

```
SUCCESS_SOUND, //completion of level
FAILED_SOUND, //sound of failing
```

We play `NEWLIFE_SOUND` when the player earns a new life:

```
NEWLIFE_SOUND, //sound of getting a new life
```

The first two times that the plane takes damage, we play a voice-over that says "That stings." The third time, it says "That smarts."

```
STINGS_SOUND, //that stings (damage)
SMARTS_SOUND, //that smarts (damage)
```

Changes to the Input Manager

A few minor changes to the input manager are necessary to handle the "show frame rate" key F1 and the new success phase. `Input.cpp` now must include an `extern` declaration for a global Boolean variable `show_framerate`.

```
extern BOOL show_framerate;
```

The CInputManager GameKeyboard function has an extra case added to its switch statement for the F1 key, whose virtual keycode is VK_F1. It toggles the show_framerate flag.

```
case VK_F1: show_framerate=!show_framerate; break;
```

The success phase is treated exactly like the intro phases by the input manager. The player is allowed to click out of the success screen by hitting any key, clicking the left mouse button, or clicking joystick button 1. Therefore, we simply need to add a new case label for SUCCESS_PHASE immediately after the case label for TITLE_PHASE in the CInputManager functions Keyboard, LMouseUp, and Joystick.

Changes to the Object Class

Our object class CObject needs some modifications to handle the new objects—the damaged plane, exploding plane, and dead plane objects.

Declarations

In Objects.h, we add constants for the damaged plane (DAMAGED-PLANE_OBJECT), the exploding plane (EXPLODINGPLANE_OBJECT), and the dead plane (DEADPLANE_OBJECT) to the ObjectType enumerated type:

```
enum ObjectType{CROW_OBJECT=0,PLANE_OBJECT,
   DAMAGEDPLANE_OBJECT,EXPLODINGPLANE_OBJECT,
   DEADPLANE_OBJECT,FARM_OBJECT,FIELD_OBJECT,BULLET_OBJECT,
   EXPLODINGCROW_OBJECT,DEADCROW_OBJECT,NUM_SPRITES};
```

In the declaration of CObject, the object class gets a destructor. We'll see why later.

```
~CObject(); //destructor
```

The Constructor and Destructor

In Objects.cpp, the CObject constructor needs some changes. In the switch statement that deals with customized values, the plane engine sound now needs to be set according to the plane's speed. Why do we need this in Demo 11, when we didn't need it in Demo 10? Well, in Demo 10, the plane was created at the start of a level, and it didn't die. It always started out moving at the slowest speed. In Demo 11, the plane object can die, and be replaced in succession by the damaged, exploding, and dead plane objects, after which a new plane object is created. The new plane object will move at the same speed as the old one, which may no longer necessarily be the slowest speed. Therefore, we add the following code to the PLANE_OBJECT case in the switch statement for the customized values in the CObject constructor.

```
switch(abs(m_nXspeed)){ //depending on horizontal speed
  case 1:
    SoundManager->play(SLOWPUTT_SOUND,LOOP_SOUND);
    break;
  case 2:
    SoundManager->play(MEDIUMPUTT_SOUND,LOOP_SOUND);
    break;
  case 3:
    SoundManager->play(FASTPUTT_SOUND,LOOP_SOUND);
    break;
}
```

We also need to add new cases for the exploding plane object:

```
case EXPLODINGPLANE_OBJECT:
```

We kill its vertical speed:

```
m_nYspeed=0;
```

The speed limits are not absolutely necessary since we won't be changing its speed, but here they are anyway:

```
m_nMinXSpeed=-3; m_nMaxXSpeed=-1;
m_nMinYSpeed=-4; m_nMaxYSpeed=4;
```

The frame interval is one-fifth of a second:

```
m_nFrameInterval=200;
```

Its mortality is one-shot mortal (the animation is played once, then it dies), it is not vulnerable to bullets, and it flies:

```
m_eMortality=ONESHOT_MORTAL; m_bVulnerable=FALSE;
m_eLocomotion=FLYING_MOTION;
break;
```

The dead plane object is similar, except that its single frame is displayed for 3 seconds, and it plays a special sound ("that smarts"):

```
case DEADPLANE_OBJECT:
  SoundManager->play(SMARTS_SOUND);
  m_nYspeed=0;
  m_nMinXSpeed=-3; m_nMaxXSpeed=-1;
  m_nMinYSpeed=-4; m_nMaxYSpeed=4;
  m_nFrameInterval=3000;
  m_eMortality=ONESHOT_MORTAL; m_bVulnerable=FALSE;
  m_eLocomotion=FLYING_MOTION;
  break;
```

You may have noticed that there are two things that you expected to see but didn't. The first is, why doesn't the exploding plane play a sound? The answer is that the plane explodes after colliding with a crow, and the crow already makes an explosion sound. Another explosion sound would be redundant. The second is that there is no case for the damaged plane object. Why? Well, we'll treat the damaged plane differently from other objects. To save memory, the damaged plane will be the same as the old plane, but overlaid with an image (stored in the damaged plane sprite) showing damage. This saves having to provide six frames of animation for each of the two versions of the damaged plane. Instead, the overlays will draw over the non-moving parts of the plane (specifically, everything except the propeller, the big wheel, and Ned's scarf). The two damaged overlays and the various versions of the plane are shown in Figure 13.5.

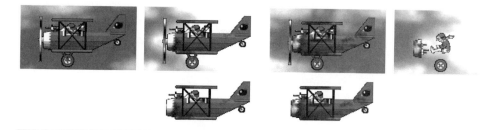

Figure 13.5
From left to right at top: undamaged plane, slightly damaged plane, more damaged plane, and dead plane. At bottom: overlays for the two versions of the damaged plane.

CObject now has a destructor. The only object that really needs a destructor is the plane object—we want to turn off the engine sound when the plane explodes. We'll keep the plane object around when it is damaged, and replace it with the exploding plane when the time comes, so the appropriate time to turn off the plane engine sound is when the plane's destructor runs. Again, we stop all three sounds, even though only one of them will be playing.

```
CObject::~CObject(){ //destructor
  if(m_eObject==PLANE_OBJECT){ //kill plane engine sounds
    SoundManager->stop(SLOWPUTT_SOUND);
    SoundManager->stop(MEDIUMPUTT_SOUND);
    SoundManager->stop(FASTPUTT_SOUND);
  }
}
```

The Draw Function

The CObject draw function needs code appended to the end for the abovementioned plane damage overlay. It first checks that we are drawing the plane.

```
if(m_eObject==PLANE_OBJECT){
```

If so, there's a switch statement on the player's health, as reported by the CScoreManager health function:

```
switch(ScoreManager.health()){ //depending on health
```

A health level of 1 means heavy damage. We draw damaged plane sprite frame 1 to the plane's location where it partially overwrites the plane sprite that has already been drawn there.

```
case 1: //heavy damage
  g_pSprite[DAMAGEDPLANE_OBJECT]->
    draw(1,Viewpoint.screen(m_nX),m_nY,surface);
  break;
```

A health level of 2 means mild damage. We draw damaged plane sprite frame 0 to the plane's location, where it partially overwrites the plane sprite that has already been drawn there.

```
case 2: //mild damage
  g_pSprite[DAMAGEDPLANE_OBJECT]->
    draw(0,Viewpoint.screen(m_nX),m_nY,surface);
  break;
```

The default is to do nothing:

```
    default: break;
  }
}
```

Changes to the Object Manager Class

Declarations

There are four changes to the object manager declarations in Objman.h. CObjectManager has a new private member variable that records the starting time of the player's invulnerable period. Recall that the player is invulnerable to collisions with crows for a few seconds after he or she dies and gets a new incarnation.

```
int m_nStartInvulnerableTime; //time level started
```

We change the second `collision_detection` function to return TRUE when there has been a collision:

```
BOOL collision_detection(int index); //with this object
```

We add a new version of the `create` function with the same parameters as the old one, plus an additional parameter `index` that specifies which index to use in the object list for the newly created object:

```
int create(int index,ObjectType object,
    int x,int y,int xspeed,int yspeed); //create at index
```

A new public member function `enemies` returns the number of varmints left to be killed:

```
int enemies(); //number of enemies left
```

The Constructor and the Create Functions

Changes to the `CObjectManager` code file `Objman.cpp` begin with the declaration of a constant for the amount of time that the player is invulnerable after a new plane has been created, currently set to 3 seconds:

```
const int INITIAL_INVULNERABLE_TIME=3000;
```

In the `CObjectManager` constructor, we need to add a line of code to record when the plane first became invulnerable:

```
m_nStartInvulnerableTime=Timer.time(); //start invulnerable
```

As mentioned already, `CObjectManager` now has a new `create` function that specifies the index to use in the object array. With the addition of that function, we can rewrite the old version of `create` to use the new version to do the actual work. It begins as before.

```
int CObjectManager::create(ObjectType object,int x,int y,
                            int xspeed,int yspeed){
//create object at first available index
  if(m_nCount<m_nMaxCount){ //if room, create object
    int i=0;//index into object list
    while(m_pObjectList[i]!=NULL)i++; //find first free slot
```

Once the index of an empty slot has been identified, the next line of code passes it on to the new `CObjectManager` `create` function:

```
return create(i,object,x,y,xspeed,yspeed); //create it there
```

The rest of the function is as before:

```
  }
  else return -1;
}
```

The new `CObjectManager` `create` function has the additional parameter
`index`:

```
int CObjectManager::create(int index,ObjectType object,
                        int x,int y,int xspeed,int yspeed){
```

First, we check that the index is valid. This check is not strictly necessary, but it's
a good coding practice.

```
if(m_nCount<m_nMaxCount&&m_pObjectList[index]==NULL){
```

If the index is valid, we create either an intelligent or a regular object, increment
the counter, and return the index of the new object:

```
if(object==CROW_OBJECT)
  m_pObjectList[index]=
    new CIntelligentObject(object,x,y,xspeed,yspeed);
else
  m_pObjectList[index]=new CObject(object,x,y,xspeed,yspeed);
m_nCount++;
return index;
}
else return -1;
}
```

The Accelerate, Kill, and Fire_gun Functions

The `CObjectManager` `accelerate` function now checks that the current
object is a plane object (as opposed to an exploding plane or a dead plane) before
allowing the acceleration to take place. This is so that the plane ignores all player
input and continues at constant horizontal speed as it explodes and dies.

```
void CObjectManager::accelerate(int xdelta,int ydelta){
  //change speed of current object
  CObject *plane= m_pObjectList[m_nCurrentObject];
  if(plane->m_eObject==PLANE_OBJECT) //if not dead or exploding
    plane->accelerate(xdelta,ydelta);
}
```

The `CObjectManager` `kill` function has a new line of code that adds to the
player's score the appropriate number of points for the type of the object that was
killed. Obviously, this must be done before the object is removed from the object
list so that we can query its type.

```
ScoreManager.add_to_score(m_pObjectList[index]->m_eObject);
```

The `CObjectManager` `fire_gun` function has an extra line of code that fires
the gun only if the current object is a plane object—exploding and dead planes
don't fire guns:

```
if(plane->m_eObject==PLANE_OBJECT) //if not dead or exploding
```

The Replace Function

The `CObjectManager replace` function needs code for the new plane object series: plane, to exploding plane, to dead plane. The `switch` statement gets a new `case` for the plane object, stating that the next object type in the series, `newtype`, is the exploding plane object.

```
case PLANE_OBJECT: newtype=EXPLODINGPLANE_OBJECT; break;
```

The exploding plane is replaced by the dead plane and we deduct a life from the score manager:

```
case EXPLODINGPLANE_OBJECT:
  newtype=DEADPLANE_OBJECT; //you're dead
  ScoreManager.deduct_life(); //deduct a life from score
  break;
```

The dead plane reincarnates as an ordinary plane and starts out invulnerable:

```
case DEADPLANE_OBJECT: //you're done being dead
  newtype=PLANE_OBJECT; //reincarnate as a regular plane
  m_nStartInvulnerableTime=Timer.time(); //start invulnerable
  break;
```

We modify the code that creates the new object so that it reuses the slot in the object list that was vacated by the old object. In Demo 10 it didn't matter where the new object was created, but now that the plane can die, it is convenient to have the new plane created in the same slot so that we don't have to change the current object index. This is why we made the new version of the `create` function.

```
if(successor) //if it has a successor
  create(index,newtype,x,y,xspeed,yspeed); //create new one
```

Collision Detection

The core of the first `CObjectManager collision_detection` function has been rewritten so that collisions now include objects colliding with the plane, in addition to the collisions with bullets that we inherited from Demo 10. After checking that the object exists, we have a new `switch` statement on the object type.

```
switch(m_pObjectList[i]->m_eObject){ //depending on type
```

If object `i` is a bullet, we call the second `collision_detection` function to see whether anything has collided with object `i`. If so, we kill the bullet.

```
case BULLET_OBJECT: //if it is a bullet
  if(collision_detection(i)) //if object hit something
    kill(i); //kill object doing the hitting
  break;
```

If object i is the plane, we first check that the plane is not in its invulnerable period:

```
case PLANE_OBJECT: //if it was the plane
    if(Timer.time()>=m_nStartInvulnerableTime+
    INITIAL_INVULNERABLE_TIME) //if plane is vulnerable
```

If the plane is vulnerable, we check whether the plane hit something:

```
if(collision_detection(i)){ //if plane hit something
```

If the plane did hit something, we check the player's health. If it is low, the plane explodes.

```
if(ScoreManager.health()<=1) //if health low
    replace(m_nCurrentObject); //explosion
```

Then, we tell the score manager that the player has been involved in a collision, so that it can deduct from the player's health:

```
        ScoreManager.collision(); //register collision
    }
    break;
}
```

The second CObjectManager collision_detection function, the one that has a parameter index, and checks for collisions between that object and all of the other objects in the object list, gets two modifications. First, we update the distance check, which in Demo 10 merely check that the objects were at most 15 pixels apart. Instead of using an arbitrary threshold of 15 pixels, we use half the sum of the objects' heights.

```
if(m_pObjectList[i]->m_bVulnerable&& //if vulnerable
    distance(index,i)<m_pObjectList[i]->m_nHeight/2+
    m_pObjectList[index]->m_nHeight/2){ //and close enough
```

It also returns the value from the local variable finished when it is done:

```
return finished;
```

Other Member Functions

The CObjectManager reset function now restarts the plane's invulnerable time:

```
m_nStartInvulnerableTime=Timer.time(); //start invulnerable
```

The CObjectManager set_speed function, which is used by the mouse and joystick to change the plane's speed, is now allowed to do so only for the plane object. (Recall that we already did this for the CObjectManager accelerate function, which is used by the keyboard for the same purpose.)

```
void CObjectManager::set_speed(int xdelta,int ydelta){
  CObject *plane=m_pObjectList[m_nCurrentObject];
  if(plane->m_eObject==PLANE_OBJECT)
    plane->set_speed(xdelta,ydelta);
}
```

Finally, CObjectManager has a new public member function enemies that returns the number of varmints remaining. It runs through the object list, counting the number of crows, dead crows, and exploding crows that remain.

```
int CObjectManager::enemies(){ //return number of enemies
  int count=0; //how many enemies left
  for(int i=0;  i<m_nMaxCount; i++)
    if(m_pObjectList[i]!=NULL)
      switch(m_pObjectList[i]->m_eObject){
        case CROW_OBJECT:
        case EXPLODINGCROW_OBJECT:
        case DEADCROW_OBJECT:
          count++;
          break;
      }
  return count;
}
```

Changes to Main.cpp

Changes to Main.cpp begin with the declaration of some new global variables.

Declarations

First, we have the declaration of a new bmp sprite file reader g_cTextImages for the text images:

```
CBmpSpriteFileReader g_cTextImages; //text images
```

Next, a global variable level records the current level of play:

```
int level=1; //current level
```

The next four global variables are associated with the frame timer, which is designed to display the number of frames of animation displayed in the previous second while counting up the number of frames displayed so far in the current second. The Boolean variable show_framerate is toggled to TRUE if the frame rate is to be displayed.

```
BOOL show_framerate=FALSE; //TRUE to show the frame rate
```

The `framerate_timer` is used to record when the previous second ended and the current second began:

```
int framerate_timer=0; //timer for updating frame rate display
```

The `framecount` variable is used to record the number of frames displayed so far in the current second:

```
int framecount=0; //number of frames in this interval (so far)
```

The `last_framecount` variable is used to record the number of frames displayed in the previous second. This is the frame count that will be displayed on the screen.

```
int last_framecount=0; //number of frames in last full interval
```

We also need a new text manager and a new score manager. The score manager can be created immediately, but the text manager (since it contains surfaces) can only be created after the DirectDraw object has been created, so we must content ourselves with a pointer to a text manager for now.

```
CTextManager *Text; //text manager
CScoreManager ScoreManager; //score manager
```

Loading Sprites

`Main.cpp` has a new `LoadDamagedPlaneSprite` function to load the two frames of the damaged plane sprite. These are overlays to the main plane sprite, showing damage to the plane. (See Figure 13.5.)

```
BOOL LoadDamagedPlaneSprite(){
  BOOL result=TRUE;
```

It loads frame 0 from location (387, 288) of the image stored in the global bmp sprite file reader `g_pSprite`:

```
result=result&&g_pSprite[DAMAGEDPLANE_OBJECT]->
  load(&g_cSpriteImages,0,387,288);
```

Then, it loads frame 1 from location (509, 288):

```
result=result&&g_pSprite[DAMAGEDPLANE_OBJECT]->
  load(&g_cSpriteImages,1,509,288);
  return result;
} //LoadDamagedPlaneSprite
```

The `LoadExplodingPlaneSprite` function loads the four frames of the exploding plane from positions (139, 74), (261, 74), (383, 74), and (505, 74) of the image stored in the global bmp sprite file reader `g_pSprite`:

```
BOOL LoadExplodingPlaneSprite(){
  BOOL result=TRUE;
  result=result&&g_pSprite[EXPLODINGPLANE_OBJECT]->
```

```
        load(&g_cSpriteImages,0,139,74);
    result=result&&g_pSprite[EXPLODINGPLANE_OBJECT]->
        load(&g_cSpriteImages,1,261,74);
    result=result&&g_pSprite[EXPLODINGPLANE_OBJECT]->
        load(&g_cSpriteImages,2,383,74);
    result=result&&g_pSprite[EXPLODINGPLANE_OBJECT]->
        load(&g_cSpriteImages,3,505,74);
    return result;
} //LoadExplodingPlaneSprite
```

The `LoadDeadPlaneSprite` function loads the single frame of the dead plane from position (120, 237) of the image stored in the global bmp sprite file reader g_pSprite. (See Figure 13.5.)

```
BOOL LoadDeadPlaneSprite(){
    return g_pSprite[DEADPLANE_OBJECT]->
        load(&g_cSpriteImages,0,120,237);
} //LoadDeadPlaneSprite
```

The `LoadImages` function gets additional code to load the new sprites. We begin with the text sprites. We first load them from the file Text.bmp into the new bmp sprite file reader g_cTextImages.

```
if(!g_cTextImages.load("text.bmp"))return FALSE;//read file
```

Then we create the text manager, specifying that the text sprites will be 19 pixels wide and 30 pixels high:

```
Text=new CTextManager(19,30); //text manager
```

Next we call the function to load the text sprites from g_cTextImages into the text manager *Text:

```
LoadTextSprites();
```

After the code that loads the plane sprite, we add code to create and load the damaged plane sprite, which has 2 frames and is 121 pixels wide, 72 pixels high:

```
g_pSprite[DAMAGEDPLANE_OBJECT]=new CClippedSprite(2,121,72);
LoadDamagedPlaneSprite();
```

Then, we do the same for the exploding plane sprite, which has 4 frames and is 121 pixels wide, 72 pixels high:

```
g_pSprite[EXPLODINGPLANE_OBJECT]=new CClippedSprite(4,121,72);
LoadExplodingPlaneSprite();
```

Finally, we do the same for the dead plane sprite, which has 1 frame and is 119 pixels wide, 54 pixels high:

```
g_pSprite[DEADPLANE_OBJECT]=new CClippedSprite(1,119,54);
LoadDeadPlaneSprite();
```

The CreateObjects Function

The `CreateObjects` function is now more sophisticated; it creates more crows as the player progresses through the levels of the game. Two new constants define the number of reserved slots in the object manager for nonvermin—including bullets—and the number of crows as a function of the global `level` number.

```
const int reserved=6; //reserved positions for nonvermin
int crowcount=5+level*3; //number of crows per level
```

A few lines of code ensure that `crowcount` is within reasonable bounds.

```
if(crowcount>MAX_OBJECTS-reserved)
  crowcount=MAX_OBJECTS-reserved;
if(crowcount<0)crowcount=0;
```

Finally, the bounds on the two `for` loops that create crows are changed from 8 in Demo 10 to `crowcount/2` and `crowcount-crowcount/2`, respectively, in Demo 11. It may be tempting to set both to `crowcount/2`, but that would leave us with one fewer crow when `crowcount` is odd.

The RestoreSurfaces Function

Function `RestoreSurfaces` now has more surfaces to restore and reload. First, the new plane sprites.

```
if(g_pSprite[DAMAGEDPLANE_OBJECT]->Restore()) //if restored
  result=result&&LoadDamagedPlaneSprite(); //redraw image
else return FALSE;
if(g_pSprite[EXPLODINGPLANE_OBJECT]->Restore()) //if restored
  result=result&&LoadExplodingPlaneSprite(); //redraw image
else return FALSE;
if(g_pSprite[DEADPLANE_OBJECT]->Restore()) //if restored
  result=result&&LoadDeadPlaneSprite(); //redraw image
else return FALSE;
```

The text manager also has surfaces that need to be restored and reloaded:

```
if(Text->Restore())
  result=result&&LoadTextSprites();
else return FALSE;
```

The LoadSounds Function

Function `LoadSounds` has five new lines of code added to `case 1` of the `switch` statement to load the new sounds:

```
SoundManager->load("success.wav");
SoundManager->load("failed.wav");
SoundManager->load("life.wav");
SoundManager->load("stings.wav");
```

```
SoundManager->load("smarts.wav");
```

Drawing Numbers

Main.cpp has three new functions associated with drawing text on the screen. Function chars_in_number has a single parameter n, and returns the number of characters needed to print n.

```
int chars_in_number(int n){ //return number of chars
```

Zero is a special case:

```
if(n==0)return 1; //0 has one character
```

A local variable count is used to count digits:

```
int count=0; //count of number of characters
```

Although I plan to use this only for positive numbers, I'd better be careful:

```
n=abs(n); //positive numbers only
```

We tally the number of decimal digits in n by repeatedly dividing by 10 in integer arithmetic, which rounds down:

```
while(n>0){n/=10; count++;} //tally number of chars
```

When we're done, we return count:

```
    return count;
} //chars_in_number
```

Function draw_number is used to draw a number near the top of the screen. It has four parameters. The first parameter is n, the number to be drawn. The second parameter is center; the center of the number is to be that many characters from the left of the screen. The third parameter is surface, a pointer to the surface on which the number is to be drawn. The fourth and last parameter is a Boolean value middle. If middle is TRUE, then the number will be shifted left by half a character width, which is useful for aligning numbers beneath the center of a word with an even number of letters (such as "Varmints" and "Health" in Figure 13.1).

```
void draw_number(int n,int center,
    LPDIRECTDRAWSURFACE surface,BOOL middle=FALSE){
```

Half a character width is defined to be 10 pixels:

```
const int HALF_CHAR_WIDTH=10;
```

We declare two buffers, one for display on the screen and the other a temporary buffer:

```
char buffer[64]; //for display on screen
char buffer2[16]; //temp buffer
```

The left margin is defined to be 7 pixels in. It is declared as int—not const int—because we may modify it in the body of the function.

```
int margin=7;
```

A local variable width holds the width of the number in characters, computed by calling the chars_in_number function:

```
int width=chars_in_number(n); //width of number in chars
```

We fill buffer with enough leading spaces to center the number and terminate the string:

```
for(int i=0; i<center-width/2-1; i++)
  buffer[i]=' '; //shift right
buffer[i]=0; //end of string
```

We use the C standard library function sprintf to convert n into a string in buffer2, then concatenate buffer2 to the end of buffer using the C standard library function strcat:

```
sprintf(buffer2,"%d",n);
strcat(buffer,buffer2); //n to buffer
```

We adjust the margin right by half a character width if width is even, meaning the number has an even number of characters and hence cannot be centered exactly by using leading spaces:

```
if(!(width&1))margin+=HALF_CHAR_WIDTH;
```

As described above, the margin is moved left by half a character width if the parameter middle is TRUE:

```
if(middle)margin-=HALF_CHAR_WIDTH;
```

We move the text cursor to the second row of text (which is 75 pixels down), margin pixels from the left, and draw the numeric string (with leading spaces to center it as required) from buffer to the surface using the text manager:

```
Text->jump(margin,75); //start of line
Text->draw(buffer,surface); //print number
}
```

Drawing the Text Header and Player Statistics

The draw_text_header function draws the two lines of the text header and player statistics (see Figure 13.1) to surface:

```
void draw_text_header(LPDIRECTDRAWSURFACE surface){
```

Again, the left margin is set to 7 pixels in from the left of the screen:

```
const int margin=7;
```

We move the text cursor to the top row of text (which is 40 pixels down), and draw the headings using the text manager:

```
Text->jump(margin,40);
Text->draw("level varmints score health lives",surface);
```

We use the `draw_number` function to draw the numbers under the headings, and return:

```
draw_number(level,3,surface);
draw_number(ObjectManager.enemies(),11,surface,TRUE);
draw_number(ScoreManager.score(),18,surface);
draw_number(ScoreManager.health(),25,surface,TRUE);
draw_number(ScoreManager.lives(),31,surface);
}
```

The text header is actually drawn in function `ComposeFrame`. After the background and game objects have been drawn, we insert code for the text header using the `draw_text_header` function.

```
draw_text_header(lpSecondary); //draw text header
```

Next, we add code to draw the frame rate. First, we check whether we should draw it by examining the global variable `show_framerate`.

```
if(show_framerate){ //if we need to show the frame count
```

A local variable `buffer` holds the string representing the frame rate:

```
char buffer[4];
```

We hit `ComposeFrame` once per frame, so we can increment the frame counter:

```
framecount++; //count frame
```

If a second has elapsed since the last time we did this, we take a snapshot of `framecount` in `last_framecount`, then reset `framecount` to zero:

```
if(Timer.elapsed(framerate_timer,1000)){
  last_framecount=framecount; framecount=0;
}
```

We move the text cursor down near the bottom right corner of the screen, use `sprintf` to convert `last_framecount` to a string in `buffer`, then draw `buffer` to the screen using the text manager:

```
Text->jump(580,470);
sprintf(buffer,"%d",last_framecount);
Text->draw(buffer,lpSecondary);
}
```

The Change_phase Function

The majority of the remaining changes to Main.cpp concern what happens when you succeed (the success phase) and when you don't. The first of these involves the change_phase function. When entering the menu phase from the playing phase, we check to see whether the user was forcibly ejected from the game because they used up their last life, and if so, play the failure sound.

```
if(ScoreManager.lives()<0)
    SoundManager->play(FAILED_SOUND);
```

Now we add a second-level switch statement to the PLAYING_PHASE case because there are now two ways to enter the playing phase—the old way from the main menu and the new way from the success phase:

```
switch(GamePhase){//depending on previous phase
```

When entering the game phase from the menu phase, we hide the mouse cursor and set things up for a new game: set the level counter to 1, and reset the score manager:

```
case MENU_PHASE:
    ShowCursor(FALSE); //deactivate the mouse cursor
    level=1; ScoreManager.reset(); //reset score
    break;
```

When entering the game phase from the success phase, we increment the level counter and ask the score manager to add a bonus score for completing the previous level:

```
case SUCCESS_PHASE:
    level++; //go to next level
    //add score for level completion
    ScoreManager.add_to_score(LEVEL_BONUS_SCORE);
    break;
}
```

We also need to add a new case to the switch statement for the new success phase. It stops the game sounds, starts playing a success sound, and displays the success screen (shown in Figure 13.4).

```
case SUCCESS_PHASE: //successful completion of level
    SoundManager->stop(); //stop sounds from previous phase
    SoundManager->play(SUCCESS_SOUND); //jubilation
    display_screen("success.bmp"); //display success screen
    break;
```

The Redraw and ProcessFrame Functions

The Redraw function also needs a new case for the success phase, in which it redraws the success screen from Success.bmp:

```
case SUCCESS_PHASE:
  display_screen("success.bmp"); //display success screen
  break;
```

Changes to function ProcessFrame for the success phase begin with the declaration of a new constant SUCCESS_DISPLAY_TIME that defines the amount of time that the success screen is displayed:

```
const int SUCCESS_DISPLAY_TIME=4500; //duration of success
```

At the end of the PLAYING_PHASE case of the switch statement, we add code to determine what is to happen at the end of the playing phase. We start by asking the object manager whether the player has won, and if so, enter the success phase.

```
if(ObjectManager.won()) //completed level
  change_phase(SUCCESS_PHASE);
```

Otherwise, if the phase has ended, we return the player to the main menu:

```
else if(endphase) //quit, go to menu
  change_phase(MENU_PHASE);
```

A new case for the success phase has code that is similar to the logo and title screens. At the end of the success phase, the player returns to the playing phase to play the next level.

```
case SUCCESS_PHASE: //displaying title screen
  Sleep(100); //surrender time to other processes
  if(endphase|| //if end of phase
  Timer.elapsed(PhaseTime,SUCCESS_DISPLAY_TIME))
    change_phase(PLAYING_PHASE); //start playing
  break;
```

The Window Procedure

There's a little more for us to do in the window procedure WindowProc in response to the WM_DESTROY message. First, we must call the object manager's reset function to reclaim the objects in it.

```
ObjectManager.reset(); //clear objects
```

Before releasing the DirectDraw object, we release the text manager:

```
Text->Release(); //release text manager sprites
```

Later, we delete the text manager itself:

```
delete Text; //reclaim text manager memory
```

Demo 11 Files

Code Files

The following files in Demo 11 are used without change from Demo 10:

- Ai.h
- Ai.cpp
- Bmp.h
- Bmp.cpp
- Bsprite.h
- Bsprite.cpp
- Buttons.cpp
- Buttons.h
- Csprite.h
- Csprite.cpp
- Ddsetup.cpp
- Input.h
- Joystick.h
- Joystick.cpp
- Random.h
- Random.cpp
- Sbmp.h
- Sbmp.cpp
- Sound.h
- Sound.cpp
- Timer.h
- Timer.cpp
- View.h
- View.cpp

The following files in Demo 11 have been modified from Demo 10:

- Defines.h
- Input.cpp
- Main.cpp
- Objects.h

- ◎ `Objects.cpp`
- ◎ `Objman.h`
- ◎ `Objman.cpp`
- ◎ `Sndlist.h`

The following files are new in Demo 11:

- ◎ `Score.h`
- ◎ `Score.cpp`
- ◎ `Text.h`
- ◎ `Text.cpp`

Media Files

The following image files are new in Demo 11:

- ◎ `Success.bmp`
- ◎ `Text.bmp`

The following sound files are new in Demo 11:

- ◎ `Failed.wav`
- ◎ `Life.wav`
- ◎ `Smarts.wav`
- ◎ `Stings.wav`
- ◎ `Success.wav`

Required Libraries

- ◎ `Ddraw.lib`
- ◎ `Dsound.lib`
- ◎ `Winmm.lib`

Code Listings

Defines.h

```
//defines.h: essential defines
//Copyright Ian Parberry, 1999
//Last updated December 7, 1999

#ifndef __DEFINES_H__
#define __DEFINES_H__

#define SCREEN_WIDTH 640 //pixels wide
```

```
#define SCREEN_HEIGHT 480 //pixels high
#define COLORS 256 //number of colors
#define COLOR_DEPTH 8 //number of bits to store colors
#define TRANSPARENT_COLOR 255 //transparent palette position

enum GamePhaseType{
  LOGO_PHASE,TITLE_PHASE,MENU_PHASE,PLAYING_PHASE,
  DEVICEMENU_PHASE,SUCCESS_PHASE
};

enum
InputDeviceType{KEYBOARD_INPUT=0,MOUSE_INPUT,JOYSTICK_INPUT};

#endif
```

Input.cpp

```
//input.cpp: program file for input class

//Copyright Ian Parberry, 1999
//Last updated March 17, 2000

#include "input.h"
#include "objman.h" //for object manager
#include "sndlist.h" //for list of sounds

extern GamePhaseType GamePhase; //current phase
extern GamePhaseType NextPhase; //next phase of game
extern BOOL endphase; //should we abort current phase?
extern CObjectManager ObjectManager; //object manager

extern BOOL show_framerate;

CInputManager::CInputManager(){ //constructor
  InputDevice=KEYBOARD_INPUT; //current input device
  ButtonManager=NULL; //for managing menu buttons
  JoystickManager.initialize(); //set up joystick
  JoystickManager.autorepeat(FALSE); //disable autorepeat
}

CInputManager::~CInputManager(){ //destructor
  delete ButtonManager;
}

BOOL CInputManager::Restore(){ //restore surfaces
  return ButtonManager->Restore();
}
void CInputManager::Release(){ //release surfaces
  ButtonManager->Release();
}
```

```
void CInputManager::SetupMainMenuButtons(){
//set up main menu button manager
  const int YDELTA=70; //y separation between buttons
  const int BUTTONCOUNT=6; //number of buttons
  SIZE size; //size of buttons
  size.cx=40; size.cy=40; //size of buttons
  POINT point; //top left corner of first button
  point.x=111; point.y=46; //first button location
  delete ButtonManager; //delete any old one
  ButtonManager=new //create new button manager
    CButtonManager(BUTTONCOUNT,size,point,YDELTA,
      "buttons.bmp");
 //set button sounds
  ButtonManager->
    setsounds(BIGCLICK_SOUND,SMALLCLICK_SOUND);
}


void CInputManager::SetupDeviceMenuButtons(){
//set up device menu button manager
  const int BUTTONCOUNT=4;
  delete ButtonManager; //if there is one already, delete it
  SIZE size; //size of buttons
  size.cx=40; size.cy=40; //size of buttons
  ButtonManager=new
    CButtonManager(BUTTONCOUNT,size,"buttons.bmp");
  ButtonManager->setsounds(BIGCLICK_SOUND,SMALLCLICK_SOUND);
  ButtonManager->set_radio(); //radio buttons
  //add buttons
  POINT point;
  point.x=209; point.y=130;
  ButtonManager->addbutton(point);
  point.x=209; point.y=210;
  ButtonManager->addbutton(point);
  point.x=209; point.y=291;
  ButtonManager->addbutton(point);
  point.x=209; point.y=372;
  ButtonManager->addbutton(point);
  //initialize image of radio button
  ButtonManager->buttondown(InputDevice,FALSE); //no sound
}


void CInputManager::SetupButtons(GamePhaseType phase){
//set up menu buttons
  switch(phase){
    case MENU_PHASE: SetupMainMenuButtons(); break;
    case DEVICEMENU_PHASE: SetupDeviceMenuButtons(); break;
  }
}
```

```
//keyboard handlers

void CInputManager::IntroKeyboard(WPARAM keystroke){
//keyboard handler for intro
  endphase=TRUE; //any key ends the phase
}

BOOL CInputManager::MainMenuKeyboard(WPARAM keystroke){
//keyboard handler for menu
  BOOL result=FALSE;
  switch(keystroke){
    case VK_ESCAPE:
    case 'Q': //exit the game
      result=TRUE;
      break;
    case 'N': //play new game
      NextPhase=PLAYING_PHASE; endphase=TRUE;
      break;
    case 'D':
      NextPhase=DEVICEMENU_PHASE; endphase=TRUE;
    default: break; //do nothing
  }
  return result;
}

void CInputManager::DeviceMenuKeyboard(WPARAM keystroke){
//keyboard handler //for device menu
  switch(keystroke){
    case VK_ESCAPE:
    case 'D': //exit menu
      endphase=TRUE;
      break;
    case 'K': //play using keyboard
      InputDevice=KEYBOARD_INPUT; //set device
      ButtonManager->buttondown(KEYBOARD_INPUT);
      break;
    case 'M': //play using mouse
      InputDevice=MOUSE_INPUT; //set device
      ButtonManager->buttondown(MOUSE_INPUT);
      break;
    case 'J': //play using joystick
      if(JoystickManager.exists()){ //if joystick exists
        InputDevice=JOYSTICK_INPUT;
        ButtonManager->buttondown(JOYSTICK_INPUT);
      }
      break;
    default: break;
  }
}
```

```
void CInputManager::GameKeyboard(WPARAM keystroke){
//keyboard handler for game play
  switch(keystroke){
    case VK_ESCAPE: endphase=TRUE; break;
    case VK_F1: show_framerate=!show_framerate; break;
    case VK_UP: ObjectManager.accelerate(0,-1); break;
    case VK_DOWN: ObjectManager.accelerate(0,1); break;
    case VK_LEFT: ObjectManager.accelerate(-1,0); break;
    case VK_RIGHT: ObjectManager.accelerate(1,0); break;
    case VK_SPACE: ObjectManager.fire_gun(); break;
    default: break;
  }
}


BOOL CInputManager::is_function_key(WPARAM keystroke){
  return keystroke==VK_ESCAPE||
    (keystroke>=VK_F1&&keystroke<=VK_F12);
}


BOOL CInputManager::Keyboard(WPARAM keystroke,
  BOOL virtual_keystroke){ //keyboard handler
  BOOL result=FALSE;
  switch(GamePhase){
    case LOGO_PHASE:
    case TITLE_PHASE:
    case SUCCESS_PHASE:
      IntroKeyboard(keystroke);
      break;
    case MENU_PHASE:
      result=MainMenuKeyboard(keystroke);
      break;
    case DEVICEMENU_PHASE:
      DeviceMenuKeyboard(keystroke);
      break;
    case PLAYING_PHASE:
      if(InputDevice==KEYBOARD_INPUT||
      is_function_key(keystroke)||virtual_keystroke)
        GameKeyboard(keystroke);
      break;
  }
  return result;
}


//mouse left button down handlers

void CInputManager::MainMenuLMouseDown(POINT point){
//mouse down handler for menu
  if(ButtonManager->hit(point)>=0) //if a valid hit
    ButtonManager->buttondown(point); //animate a button down
}
```

```cpp
void CInputManager::DeviceMenuLMouseDown(POINT point){
//mouse down handler for device menu
  int hit=ButtonManager->hit(point);
  switch(hit){
    case 0: Keyboard('K'); break; //keyboard
    case 1: Keyboard('M'); break; //mouse
    case 2: Keyboard('J'); break; //joystick
    case 3:
      ButtonManager->buttondown(hit); //quit button down
      break;
    default: break;
  }
}

void CInputManager::GameLMouseDown(POINT point){
//mouse down handler for game
  Keyboard(VK_SPACE,TRUE);
}

void CInputManager::decode(LPARAM lparam,POINT &point){
//decode mouse click lparam to point
  point.x=LOWORD(lparam); point.y=HIWORD(lparam);
}

void CInputManager::LMouseDown(LPARAM lparam){
//main mouse left button down handler
  POINT point; //mouse location on screen
  decode(lparam,point); //decode mouse point
  switch(GamePhase){
    case MENU_PHASE:
      MainMenuLMouseDown(point);
      break;
    case DEVICEMENU_PHASE:
      DeviceMenuLMouseDown(point);
      break;
    case PLAYING_PHASE:
      if(InputDevice==MOUSE_INPUT)
        GameLMouseDown(point);
      break;
  }
}

//mouse left button up handlers

void CInputManager::IntroLMouseUp(POINT point){
//mouse left button up handler for intro
  endphase=TRUE;
}
```

```
BOOL CInputManager::MainMenuLMouseUp(POINT point){
//mouse left button up handler for menu
  int hit=ButtonManager->release(point); //get button hit
  BOOL result=FALSE;
  //take action depending on which button was hit
  switch(hit){ //depending on which button was hit
    case 0: Keyboard('N'); break; //new game
    case 1: Keyboard('S'); break; //saved game
    case 2: Keyboard('D'); break; //devices
    case 3: Keyboard('L'); break; //high score list
    case 4: Keyboard('H'); break; //help
    case 5: result=Keyboard(VK_ESCAPE); break; //quit
    default: break;
  }
  //animate button images
  if(hit>=0)ButtonManager->buttonup(hit); //hit
  else ButtonManager->allbuttonsup(); //nonhit
  return result;
}

void CInputManager::DeviceMenuLMouseUp(POINT point){
//mouse left button up handler for device menu
  int hit=ButtonManager->release(point);
  switch(hit){
    case 3: //quit button up
      ButtonManager->buttonup(hit); //show quit button up
      Keyboard(VK_ESCAPE);
      break;
  }
  if(hit<0)ButtonManager->allbuttonsup(); //no hit
}

BOOL CInputManager::LMouseUp(LPARAM lparam){
//main mouse left button up handler
  BOOL result=FALSE;
  POINT point; //mouse location on screen
  decode(lparam,point); //decode mouse point
  switch(GamePhase){
    case LOGO_PHASE:
    case TITLE_PHASE:
    case SUCCESS_PHASE:
      IntroLMouseUp(point);
      break;
    case MENU_PHASE:
      result=MainMenuLMouseUp(point);
      break;
    case DEVICEMENU_PHASE:
      DeviceMenuLMouseUp(point);
      break;
  }
```

```
    return result;
  }

  //mouse motion handler

  void CInputManager::set_plane_speed(POINT point,SIZE extent){
  //set plane speed based on point's position in extent
    int xmin,xmax,ymin,ymax; //plane speed limits
    ObjectManager.speed_limits(xmin,xmax,ymin,ymax); //get them
    //bands for speed assignment
    const int XBANDWIDTH=extent.cx/(xmax-xmin+1);
    const int YBANDWIDTH=extent.cy/(ymax-ymin+1);
    int xspeed,yspeed; //speed of plane
    xspeed=point.x/XBANDWIDTH+xmin; //horizontal speed
    yspeed=point.y/YBANDWIDTH+ymin; //vertical speed
    ObjectManager.set_speed(xspeed,yspeed); //pass to plane
  }

  void CInputManager::MouseMove(LPARAM lparam){
    if(InputDevice!=MOUSE_INPUT)return; //bail if not needed
    if(GamePhase!=PLAYING_PHASE)return; //bail if not playing
    POINT point; //mouse location on screen
    decode(lparam,point); //decode mouse point
    //set extent
    SIZE extent; //extent that mouse moves in
    extent.cx=SCREEN_WIDTH;
    extent.cy=SCREEN_HEIGHT;
    //set plane speed based on point and extent
    set_plane_speed(point,extent);
  }

  //joystick handlers

  void CInputManager::GameJoystick(){
  //joystick handler for game play
    if(InputDevice!=JOYSTICK_INPUT)return; //bail if unneeded
    //buttons
    if(JoystickManager.button_down(1)) //button 1...
      Keyboard(VK_SPACE,TRUE); //...fires bullets
    //stick
    if(GamePhase!=PLAYING_PHASE)return; //bail if not playing
    POINT point; //coordinates of joystick
    JoystickManager.position(point); //get coordinates
    SIZE extent; //extent that joystick indicator moves in
    extent.cx=100; extent.cy=100; //set extent
    set_plane_speed(point,extent); //set plane speed
  }

  void CInputManager::IntroJoystick(){
  //joystick handler for intro
```

```
      if(JoystickManager.button_down(1)) //click out
        Keyboard(VK_ESCAPE);
}

void CInputManager::Joystick(){ //main joystick handler
  JoystickManager.poll(); //poll joystick
  switch(GamePhase){ //call joystick handler for phase
    case PLAYING_PHASE: GameJoystick(); break;
    case LOGO_PHASE:
    case TITLE_PHASE:
    case SUCCESS_PHASE:
      IntroJoystick(); break;
    case DEVICEMENU_PHASE:
    case MENU_PHASE:
      break; //do nothing
  }
}
```

Main.cpp

```
//main.cpp

//Copyright Ian Parberry, 1999
//Last updated May 22, 2000

//Added different levels, more crows as level number
//increases. Displays success screen in between levels.
//Player can now be hit by crows. Player has health and
//lives, managed by a score manager. Added text showing
//the level number, number of varmints, health, lives, and
//score. F1 toggles a frame rate display in lower
//right-hand corner.

//system includes
#include <windows.h>
#include <windowsx.h>
#include <ddraw.h>
#include <stdio.h>

//system defines
#define WIN32_LEAN_AND_MEAN

//custom includes
#include "defines.h" //global definitions
#include "bmp.h" //bmp file reader
#include "timer.h" //game timer
#include "csprite.h" //for clipped sprite class
#include "objects.h" //for object class
#include "objman.h" //for object manager
#include "view.h" //for viewpoint class
```

```
#include "random.h" //for random number generator
#include "sound.h" //for sound manager
#include "input.h" //for input manager
#include "text.h" //for text sprite manager
#include "score.h" //for score manager

//defines
#define MAX_OBJECTS 32 //max number of objects in game

//globals

BOOL ActiveApp; //is this application active?

LPDIRECTDRAW lpDirectDrawObject=NULL; //DirectDraw object
LPDIRECTDRAWSURFACE lpPrimary=NULL; //primary surface
LPDIRECTDRAWPALETTE lpPrimaryPalette; //its palette
LPDIRECTDRAWSURFACE lpSecondary=NULL; //back buffer
LPDIRECTDRAWPALETTE lpSecondaryPalette; //its palette
LPDIRECTDRAWSURFACE lpBackground=NULL; //background image

CTimer Timer; //game timer

CBmpFileReader background; //background image
CBmpSpriteFileReader g_cSpriteImages; //sprite images
CBmpSpriteFileReader g_cFrgndImages; //foreground images
CBmpSpriteFileReader g_cTextImages; //text images

CObjectManager ObjectManager(MAX_OBJECTS); //object manager

CClippedSprite *g_pSprite[NUM_SPRITES]; //sprites

CViewPoint Viewpoint; //player viewpoint
CRandom Random; //random number generator

GamePhaseType GamePhase; //current phase
GamePhaseType NextPhase; //next phase of game
BOOL endphase=FALSE; //should we abort current phase?
int PhaseTime=0; //time in phase
int level=1; //current level

BOOL show_framerate=FALSE; //TRUE to show the frame rate
int framerate_timer=0; //timer for updating frame rate display
int framecount=0; //number of frames in this interval (so far)
int last_framecount=0; //number of frames in last full interval

CSoundManager* SoundManager; //sound manager
CInputManager InputManager; //device input manager
CTextManager *Text; //text manager
CScoreManager ScoreManager; //score manager
```

```
//helper functions
LPDIRECTDRAWPALETTE CreatePalette(LPDIRECTDRAWSURFACE surface);
BOOL InitDirectDraw(HWND hwnd);
HWND CreateDefaultWindow(char* name,HINSTANCE hInstance);

BOOL LoadPlaneSprite(){
  BOOL result=TRUE;
  result=result&&g_pSprite[PLANE_OBJECT]->
    load(&g_cSpriteImages,0,1,1);
  result=result&&g_pSprite[PLANE_OBJECT]->
    load(&g_cSpriteImages,1,123,1);
  result=result&&g_pSprite[PLANE_OBJECT]->
    load(&g_cSpriteImages,2,245,1);
  result=result&&g_pSprite[PLANE_OBJECT]->
    load(&g_cSpriteImages,3,367,1);
  result=result&&g_pSprite[PLANE_OBJECT]->
    load(&g_cSpriteImages,4,489,1);
  result=result&&g_pSprite[PLANE_OBJECT]->
    load(&g_cSpriteImages,5,17,74);
  return result;
} //LoadPlaneSprite

BOOL LoadDamagedPlaneSprite(){
  BOOL result=TRUE;
  result=result&&g_pSprite[DAMAGEDPLANE_OBJECT]->
    load(&g_cSpriteImages,0,387,288);
  result=result&&g_pSprite[DAMAGEDPLANE_OBJECT]->
    load(&g_cSpriteImages,1,509,288);
  return result;
} //LoadDamagedPlaneSprite

BOOL LoadExplodingPlaneSprite(){
  BOOL result=TRUE;
  result=result&&g_pSprite[EXPLODINGPLANE_OBJECT]->
    load(&g_cSpriteImages,0,139,74);
  result=result&&g_pSprite[EXPLODINGPLANE_OBJECT]->
    load(&g_cSpriteImages,1,261,74);
  result=result&&g_pSprite[EXPLODINGPLANE_OBJECT]->
    load(&g_cSpriteImages,2,383,74);
  result=result&&g_pSprite[EXPLODINGPLANE_OBJECT]->
    load(&g_cSpriteImages,3,505,74);
  return result;
} //LoadExplodingPlaneSprite

BOOL LoadDeadPlaneSprite(){
  return g_pSprite[DEADPLANE_OBJECT]->
    load(&g_cSpriteImages,0,120,237);
} //LoadDeadPlaneSprite

BOOL LoadCrowSprite(){
```

```
  BOOL result=TRUE;
  result=result&&g_pSprite[CROW_OBJECT]->
    load(&g_cSpriteImages,0,256,183); //frame 0
  result=result&&g_pSprite[CROW_OBJECT]->
    load(&g_cSpriteImages,1,320,183); //frame 1
  result=result&&g_pSprite[CROW_OBJECT]->
    load(&g_cSpriteImages,2,256,237); //frame 2
  result=result&&g_pSprite[CROW_OBJECT]->
    load(&g_cSpriteImages,3,323,237); //frame 3
  return result;
} //LoadCrowSprite

BOOL LoadFrgndSprites(){ //load foreground sprites
  BOOL result=TRUE;
  result=result&&g_pSprite[FARM_OBJECT]->
    load(&g_cFrgndImages,0,0,0); //load farm sprite
  result=result&&g_pSprite[FIELD_OBJECT]->
    load(&g_cFrgndImages,0,640,0); //load field sprite
  return result;
} //LoadFrgndSprites

BOOL LoadDeadCrowSprite(){ //load dead crow
  return g_pSprite[DEADCROW_OBJECT]->
    load(&g_cSpriteImages,0,453,230);
} //LoadDeadCrowSprite

BOOL LoadExplodingCrowSprite(){ //load exploding crow
  BOOL result=TRUE;
  result=result&&g_pSprite[EXPLODINGCROW_OBJECT]->
    load(&g_cSpriteImages,0,257,294);
  result=result&&g_pSprite[EXPLODINGCROW_OBJECT]->
    load(&g_cSpriteImages,1,321,294);
  result=result&&g_pSprite[EXPLODINGCROW_OBJECT]->
    load(&g_cSpriteImages,2,386,162);
  result=result&&g_pSprite[EXPLODINGCROW_OBJECT]->
    load(&g_cSpriteImages,3,453,162);
  result=result&&g_pSprite[EXPLODINGCROW_OBJECT]->
    load(&g_cSpriteImages,4,386,230);
  result=result&&g_pSprite[EXPLODINGCROW_OBJECT]->
    load(&g_cSpriteImages,5,453,230);
  return result;
} //LoadExplodingCrowSprite

BOOL LoadBulletSprite(){ //load bullet
  return g_pSprite[BULLET_OBJECT]->
    load(&g_cSpriteImages,0,5,123);
} //LoadBulletSprite

BOOL LoadTextSprites(){ //load text sprites
  return Text->load(&g_cTextImages,1,102);
```

```
    } //LoadTextSprites

BOOL LoadImages(){ //load graphics from files to surfaces
  //get the background image
  if(!background.load("bckgnd.bmp"))return FALSE; //read file
  background.draw(lpBackground); //draw to background surface
  //set palettes in all surfaces
  if(!background.setpalette(lpPrimaryPalette))return FALSE;
  if(!background.setpalette(lpSecondaryPalette))return FALSE;
  //load the text sprites
  if(!g_cTextImages.load("text.bmp"))return FALSE;//read file
  Text=new CTextManager(19,30); //text manager
  LoadTextSprites();
  //load the sprites...
  if(!g_cSpriteImages.load("sprites.bmp"))return FALSE;
  //...the plane
  g_pSprite[PLANE_OBJECT]=new CClippedSprite(6,121,72);
  if(!LoadPlaneSprite())return FALSE; //load plane images
  //...the damaged plane
  g_pSprite[DAMAGEDPLANE_OBJECT]=new CClippedSprite(2,121,72);
  LoadDamagedPlaneSprite();
  //...the exploding plane
  g_pSprite[EXPLODINGPLANE_OBJECT]=new CClippedSprite(4,121,72);
  LoadExplodingPlaneSprite();
  //...the dead plane
  g_pSprite[DEADPLANE_OBJECT]=new CClippedSprite(1,119,54);
  LoadDeadPlaneSprite();
  //...the crow
  g_pSprite[CROW_OBJECT]=new CClippedSprite(4,58,37);
  if(!LoadCrowSprite())return FALSE; //load crow images
  //..the dead crow
  g_pSprite[DEADCROW_OBJECT]=new CClippedSprite(1,62,53);
  LoadDeadCrowSprite(); //load dead crow images
  //...the exploding crow
  g_pSprite[EXPLODINGCROW_OBJECT]=new CClippedSprite(6,62,53);
  LoadExplodingCrowSprite(); //load exploding crow images
  //...the bullet
  g_pSprite[BULLET_OBJECT]=new CClippedSprite(1,5,3);
  LoadBulletSprite(); //load bullet images
  //...the foreground sprites
  if(!g_cFrgndImages.load("farm.bmp"))return FALSE;
  g_pSprite[FARM_OBJECT]=new CClippedSprite(1,640,162);
  g_pSprite[FIELD_OBJECT]=new CClippedSprite(1,640,162);
  if(!LoadFrgndSprites())return FALSE; //load foreground
  return TRUE;
} //LoadImages

void CreateObjects(){
  const int reserved=6; //reserved positions for nonvermin
  int crowcount=5+level*3; //number of crows per level
```

```
      int i;
      ObjectManager.create(FARM_OBJECT,0,SCREEN_HEIGHT-1,1,0);
      ObjectManager.create(FIELD_OBJECT,SCREEN_WIDTH,
        SCREEN_HEIGHT-1,1,0);
      //compute numbers of objects
      if(crowcount>MAX_OBJECTS-reserved)
        crowcount=MAX_OBJECTS-reserved;
      if(crowcount<0)crowcount=0;
      //create objects
      for(i=0; i<crowcount/2; i++)
        ObjectManager.create(CROW_OBJECT,
          Random.number(0,WORLD_WIDTH-1),
          Random.number(100,400),-1,0);
      ObjectManager.set_current(
        ObjectManager.create(PLANE_OBJECT,320,271,-1,0));
      for(i=0; i<crowcount-crowcount/2; i++)
        ObjectManager.create(CROW_OBJECT,
          Random.number(0,WORLD_WIDTH-1),
          Random.number(100,400),-1,0);
    } //CreateObjects

    BOOL RestoreSurfaces(){ //restore all surfaces
      BOOL result=TRUE;
      //primary and secondary surfaces
      if(FAILED(lpPrimary->Restore()))return FALSE;
      if(FAILED(lpSecondary->Restore()))return FALSE;
      //surfaces containing images
      if(SUCCEEDED(lpBackground->Restore())) //if background restored
        result=result&&background.draw(lpBackground); //redraw image
      else return FALSE;
      if(g_pSprite[PLANE_OBJECT]->Restore()) //if plane restored
        result=result&&LoadPlaneSprite(); //redraw image
      else return FALSE;
      if(g_pSprite[DAMAGEDPLANE_OBJECT]->Restore()) //if restored
        result=result&&LoadDamagedPlaneSprite(); //redraw image
      else return FALSE;
      if(g_pSprite[EXPLODINGPLANE_OBJECT]->Restore()) //if restored
        result=result&&LoadExplodingPlaneSprite(); //redraw image
      else return FALSE;
      if(g_pSprite[DEADPLANE_OBJECT]->Restore()) //if restored
        result=result&&LoadDeadPlaneSprite(); //redraw image
      else return FALSE;
      if(g_pSprite[CROW_OBJECT]->Restore()) //if crow restored
        result=result&&LoadCrowSprite(); //redraw image
      else return FALSE;
      if(g_pSprite[DEADCROW_OBJECT]->Restore()) //if restored
        result=result&&LoadDeadCrowSprite(); //redraw image
      else return FALSE;
      if(g_pSprite[EXPLODINGCROW_OBJECT]->Restore()) //if restored
        result=result&&LoadExplodingCrowSprite(); //redraw image
```

```
        else return FALSE;
      if(g_pSprite[BULLET_OBJECT]->Restore()) //if restored
        result=result&&LoadBulletSprite(); //redraw image
      else return FALSE;
      if(g_pSprite[FARM_OBJECT]->Restore()&& //if farm and ...
        g_pSprite[FIELD_OBJECT]->Restore()) //... field restored
        result=result&&LoadFrgndSprites(); //redraw image
      else return FALSE;
      //input manager has button sprites
      if(!InputManager.Restore())return FALSE;
      //text manager has text sprites
      if(Text->Restore())
        result=result&&LoadTextSprites();
      else return FALSE;
      return result;
  } //RestoreSurfaces

void LoadSounds(int level=0){ //load sounds for level
    const int copies=4; //copies of repeatable sounds
    switch(level){
      case 0: //intro sounds
        SoundManager->load("intro.wav");
        SoundManager->load("larc.wav");
        break;
      case 1: //game engine sounds
        SoundManager->load("caw.wav",copies);
        SoundManager->load("gun.wav",copies);
        SoundManager->load("boom.wav",copies);
        SoundManager->load("thump.wav",copies);
        SoundManager->load("putt0.wav");
        SoundManager->load("putt1.wav");
        SoundManager->load("putt2.wav");
        SoundManager->load("bgclk.wav",2);
        SoundManager->load("smclk.wav",2);
        SoundManager->load("success.wav");
        SoundManager->load("failed.wav");
        SoundManager->load("life.wav");
        SoundManager->load("stings.wav");
        SoundManager->load("smarts.wav");
        break;
    }
}

BOOL PageFlip(){ //return TRUE if page flip succeeds
    if(lpPrimary->Flip(NULL,DDFLIP_WAIT)==DDERR_SURFACELOST)
      return RestoreSurfaces();
    return TRUE;
} //PageFlip

int chars_in_number(int n){ //return number of chars
```

```
    if(n==0)return 1; //0 has one character
    int count=0; //count of number of characters
    n=abs(n); //positive numbers only
    while(n>0){n/=10; count++;} //tally number of chars
    return count;
  } //chars_in_number

  void draw_number(int n,int center,
      LPDIRECTDRAWSURFACE surface,BOOL middle=FALSE){
    const int HALF_CHAR_WIDTH=10;
    char buffer[64]; //for display on screen
    char buffer2[16]; //temp buffer
    int margin=7;
    int width=chars_in_number(n); //width of number in chars
    for(int i=0; i<center-width/2-1; i++)
      buffer[i]=' '; //shift right
    buffer[i]=0; //end of string
    sprintf(buffer2,"%d",n);
    strcat(buffer,buffer2); //n to buffer
    //adjust to center
    if(!(width&1))margin+=HALF_CHAR_WIDTH;
    if(middle)margin-=HALF_CHAR_WIDTH;
    //draw
    Text->jump(margin,75); //start of line
    Text->draw(buffer,surface); //print number
  }

  void draw_text_header(LPDIRECTDRAWSURFACE surface){
    const int margin=7;
    Text->jump(margin,40);
    Text->draw("level varmints score health lives",surface);
    draw_number(level,3,surface);
    draw_number(ObjectManager.enemies(),11,surface,TRUE);
    draw_number(ScoreManager.score(),18,surface);
    draw_number(ScoreManager.health(),25,surface,TRUE);
    draw_number(ScoreManager.lives(),31,surface);
  }

  BOOL ComposeFrame(){ //compose a frame of animation
    Viewpoint.draw_background(lpBackground,lpSecondary,
      ObjectManager.speed()); //draw scrolling background
    ObjectManager.animate(lpSecondary); //draw objects
    draw_text_header(lpSecondary); //draw text header
    if(show_framerate){ //if we need to show the frame count
      char buffer[4];
      framecount++; //count frame
      if(Timer.elapsed(framerate_timer,1000)){
        last_framecount=framecount; framecount=0;
      }
      Text->jump(580,470);
```

```
        sprintf(buffer,"%d",last_framecount);
        Text->draw(buffer,lpSecondary);
    }
    return TRUE;
} //ComposeFrame

void display_screen(char *filename){ //display bmp file
  CBmpFileReader image; //file reader
  image.load(filename); //load from file
  image.draw(lpSecondary); //draw to back buffer
  image.setpalette(lpPrimaryPalette); //may have custom palette
  PageFlip(); //display it
 //draw to back buffer again for button animation
  image.draw(lpSecondary);
} //display_screen

void change_phase(GamePhaseType new_phase){ //go to new phase
  switch(new_phase){
    case LOGO_PHASE:
      display_screen("larc.bmp");
      LoadSounds(); //load sounds for intro sequence
      SoundManager->play(LOGO_SOUND); //signature chord
      break;
    case TITLE_PHASE:
      display_screen("title.bmp");
      SoundManager->stop(); //silence previous phase
      SoundManager->play(TITLE_SOUND); //title sound
      break;
    case MENU_PHASE:
      //set up buttons for menu
      InputManager.SetupButtons(MENU_PHASE);
      //sound
      switch(GamePhase){ //depending on previous phase
        case TITLE_PHASE: //from intro phase
          SoundManager->stop(); //silence previous phase
          SoundManager->clear(); //clear out old sounds
          LoadSounds(1); //set up game sounds
          break;
        case PLAYING_PHASE: //from game engine
          SoundManager->stop(); //silence game engine
          if(ScoreManager.lives()<0)
            SoundManager->play(FAILED_SOUND);
          break;
        case DEVICEMENU_PHASE: //device menu, do nothing
          break;
      }
      //display background
      display_screen("menu.bmp"); //display main menu
      //mouse cursor
      switch(GamePhase){ //what phase did we come in from?
```

```
      case PLAYING_PHASE:
      case TITLE_PHASE:
        ShowCursor(TRUE); //activate the mouse cursor
        break;
    }
    break;
  case DEVICEMENU_PHASE:
    //display button background
    display_screen("dmenu.bmp");
    //set up the button manager
    InputManager.SetupButtons(DEVICEMENU_PHASE);
    break;
  case PLAYING_PHASE: //prepare the game engine
    //mouse cursor
    SetCursorPos(SCREEN_WIDTH-1,SCREEN_HEIGHT/2); //throttle
    //start sounds
    SoundManager->stop(); //silence previous phase
    switch(GamePhase){//depending on previous phase
      case MENU_PHASE:
        ShowCursor(FALSE); //deactivate the mouse cursor
        level=1; ScoreManager.reset(); //reset score
        break;
      case SUCCESS_PHASE:
        level++; //go to next level
        //add score for level completion
        ScoreManager.add_to_score(LEVEL_BONUS_SCORE);
        break;
    }
    //create objects in game engine
    ObjectManager.reset(); //clear object manager
    CreateObjects(); //create new objects
    //initialize graphics
    background.setpalette(lpPrimaryPalette); //game palette
    ComposeFrame(); PageFlip(); //prime animation pump
    break;
  case SUCCESS_PHASE: //successful completion of level
    SoundManager->stop(); //stop sounds from previous phase
    SoundManager->play(SUCCESS_SOUND); //jubilation
    display_screen("success.bmp"); //display success screen
    break;
  }
  //change to new phase
  GamePhase=new_phase; PhaseTime=Timer.time();
  endphase=FALSE;
} //change_phase

void Redraw(){ //redraw in response to surface loss
  switch(GamePhase){
    case LOGO_PHASE:
      display_screen("larc.bmp");
```

```
        break;
      case TITLE_PHASE:
        display_screen("title.bmp");
        break;
      case MENU_PHASE:
        display_screen("menu.bmp"); //display main menu
        break;
      case PLAYING_PHASE:
        //do nothing, next frame of animation will catch it
        break;
      case DEVICEMENU_PHASE:
        display_screen("dmenu.bmp");
        InputManager.SetupButtons(DEVICEMENU_PHASE);
        break;
      case SUCCESS_PHASE:
        display_screen("success.bmp"); //display success screen
        break;
  }
}

void ProcessFrame(){ //process a frame of animation
  const int LOGO_DISPLAY_TIME=8500; //duration of logo
  const int TITLE_DISPLAY_TIME=10000; //duration of title
  const int SUCCESS_DISPLAY_TIME=4500; //duration of success
  InputManager.Joystick(); //process joystick input
  //check for lost surfaces, e.g., alt+tab
  if(lpPrimary->IsLost()){
    RestoreSurfaces(); Redraw();
  }
  switch(GamePhase){ //what phase are we in?
    case LOGO_PHASE: //displaying logo screen
      Sleep(100); //surrender time to other processes
      if(endphase||Timer.elapsed(PhaseTime,LOGO_DISPLAY_TIME))
        change_phase(TITLE_PHASE); //go to title screen
      break;
    case TITLE_PHASE: //displaying title screen
      Sleep(100); //surrender time to other processes
      if(endphase||Timer.elapsed(PhaseTime,TITLE_DISPLAY_TIME))
        change_phase(MENU_PHASE); //go to menu
      break;
    case MENU_PHASE: //main menu
      Sleep(100); //surrender time to other processes
      if(endphase)change_phase(NextPhase); //change phase
      break;
    case DEVICEMENU_PHASE:
      if(endphase)change_phase(MENU_PHASE); //go to menu phase
      break;
    case PLAYING_PHASE: //game engine
      ComposeFrame(); //compose a frame in back surface
      PageFlip(); //flip video memory surfaces
```

```
        if(ObjectManager.won()) //completed level
          change_phase(SUCCESS_PHASE);
        else if(endphase) //quit, go to menu
          change_phase(MENU_PHASE);
        break;
      case SUCCESS_PHASE: //displaying title screen
        Sleep(100); //surrender time to other processes
        if(endphase|| //if end of phase
        Timer.elapsed(PhaseTime,SUCCESS_DISPLAY_TIME))
          change_phase(PLAYING_PHASE); //start playing
        break;
    }
  } //ProcessFrame

  //message handler (window procedure)
  long CALLBACK WindowProc(HWND hwnd,UINT message,
                           WPARAM wParam,LPARAM lParam){
    switch(message){
      case WM_ACTIVATEAPP: ActiveApp=wParam; break;
      case WM_CREATE: break;
      case WM_KEYDOWN: //keyboard hit
        if(InputManager.Keyboard(wParam))
          DestroyWindow(hwnd);
        break;
      case WM_LBUTTONDOWN: //left mouse button down
        InputManager.LMouseDown(lParam); //handle it
        break;
      case WM_LBUTTONUP: //left mouse button up
        if(InputManager.LMouseUp(lParam))
          DestroyWindow(hwnd);
        break;
      case WM_MOUSEMOVE: //mouse move
        InputManager.MouseMove(lParam);
        break;
      case WM_DESTROY: //end of game
        ObjectManager.reset(); //clear objects
        if(lpDirectDrawObject!=NULL){ //if DD object exists
          if(lpSecondary!=NULL) //if secondary surface exists
            lpSecondary->Release(); //release secondary surface
          if(lpPrimary!=NULL) //if primary surface exists
            lpPrimary->Release(); //release primary surface
          if(lpBackground!=NULL) //if background exists
            lpBackground->Release(); //release background
          for(int i=0; i<NUM_SPRITES; i++){ //for each sprite
            if(g_pSprite[i]) //if sprite exists
              g_pSprite[i]->Release(); //release sprite
            delete g_pSprite[i]; //delete sprite
          }
          InputManager.Release(); //button surfaces
          Text->Release(); //release text manager sprites
```

```
            lpDirectDrawObject->Release(); //release DD object
        }
        delete SoundManager; //reclaim sound manager memory
        delete Text; //reclaim text manager memory
        ShowCursor(TRUE); //show the mouse cursor
        PostQuitMessage(0); //and exit
        break;
      default: //default window procedure
        return DefWindowProc(hwnd,message,wParam,lParam);
    } //switch(message)
    return 0L;
} //WindowProc

int WINAPI WinMain(HINSTANCE hInstance,HINSTANCE hPrevInstance,
LPSTR lpCmdLine,int nCmdShow){
  MSG msg; //current message
  HWND hwnd; //handle to full-screen window
  hwnd=CreateDefaultWindow("directX demo 11",hInstance);
  if(!hwnd)return FALSE;
  //set up window
  ShowWindow(hwnd,nCmdShow); UpdateWindow(hwnd);
  SetFocus(hwnd); //allow input from keyboard
  ShowCursor(FALSE); //hide the cursor
  //init graphics
  for(int i=0; i<NUM_SPRITES; i++) //null out sprites
    g_pSprite[i]=NULL;
  BOOL OK=InitDirectDraw(hwnd);//initialize DirectDraw
  if(OK)OK=LoadImages(); //load images from disk
  if(!OK){ //bail out if initialization failed
    DestroyWindow(hwnd); return FALSE;
  }
  //start game timer
  Timer.start();
  //init sound
  SoundManager=new CSoundManager(hwnd);
  //set initial phase
  change_phase(LOGO_PHASE);
  //message loop
  while(TRUE)
    if(PeekMessage(&msg,NULL,0,0,PM_NOREMOVE)){
      if(!GetMessage(&msg,NULL,0,0))return msg.wParam;
      TranslateMessage(&msg); DispatchMessage(&msg);
    }
    else if(ActiveApp)ProcessFrame(); else WaitMessage();
} //WinMain
```

Objects.h

```
//objects.h: header file for CObject class
```

```
//Copyright Ian Parberry, 1999
//Last updated December 7, 1999

#ifndef __OBJECTS__
#define __OBJECTS__

#include "bsprite.h"
#include "bmp.h"

//object types
enum ObjectType{CROW_OBJECT=0,PLANE_OBJECT,
  DAMAGEDPLANE_OBJECT,EXPLODINGPLANE_OBJECT,
  DEADPLANE_OBJECT,FARM_OBJECT,FIELD_OBJECT,BULLET_OBJECT,
  EXPLODINGCROW_OBJECT,DEADCROW_OBJECT,NUM_SPRITES};
//note: NUM_SPRITES must be last

enum MortalityType{MORTAL,IMMORTAL,ONESHOT_MORTAL};
enum LocomotionType{FLYING_MOTION,FALLING_MOTION,NO_MOTION};

class CObject{ //class for a moving object
  friend class CObjectManager;
  protected:
    int m_nX,m_nY; //current location
    int m_nXspeed,m_nYspeed; //current speed
    int m_nLastXMoveTime; //last time moved horizontally
    int m_nLastYMoveTime; //last time moved vertically
    CBaseSprite *m_pSprite; //pointer to sprite
    int m_nWidth,m_nHeight; //width and height of sprite
    int m_nMinXSpeed,m_nMaxXSpeed; //min, max horizontal speeds
    int m_nMinYSpeed,m_nMaxYSpeed; //min, max vertical speeds
    int m_nCurrentFrame; //frame to be displayed
    int m_nFrameCount; //number of frames in animation
    int m_nLastFrameTime; //last time the frame was changed
    int m_nFrameInterval; //interval between frames
    BOOL m_bForwardAnimation; //is animation going forward?
    LocomotionType m_eLocomotion; //mode of travel
    ObjectType m_eObject; //what kind of object is this?
    MortalityType m_eMortality; //whether it dies or not
    int m_nBirthTime; //time of creation
    int m_nLifeTime; //time that object lives
    BOOL m_bVulnerable; //vulnerable to bullets
    BOOL m_bIntelligent; //TRUE if object is intelligent
  public:
    CObject(ObjectType object,int x,int y,
      int xspeed,int yspeed); //constructor
    ~CObject(); //destructor
    void draw(LPDIRECTDRAWSURFACE surface); //draw
    void accelerate(int xdelta,int ydelta=0); //change speed
    virtual void move(); //move depending on time and speed
    void set_speed(int xspeed,int yspeed); //set speed
```

```
};

#endif
```

Objects.cpp

```cpp
//objects.cpp

//Copyright Ian Parberry, 1999
//Last updated November 9, 1999

#include "objects.h"
#include "timer.h" //game timer
#include "csprite.h" //for clipped sprite class
#include "random.h" //for random number generator
#include "view.h" //for viewpoint class
#include "sound.h" //for sound manager
#include "score.h" //for score manager

extern CClippedSprite *g_pSprite[]; //sprites
extern CTimer Timer; //game timer
extern CRandom Random; //random number generator
extern CViewPoint Viewpoint; //player viewpoint
extern CSoundManager* SoundManager; //sound manager
extern CScoreManager ScoreManager; //score manager

CObject::CObject(ObjectType object,int x,int y,
                 int xspeed,int yspeed){ //constructor
  //defaults
  m_nCurrentFrame=0; m_nLastFrameTime=Timer.time();
  m_bForwardAnimation=TRUE; m_nFrameInterval=30;
  m_eMortality=IMMORTAL; m_eLocomotion=NO_MOTION;
  m_nLifeTime=1000; m_bVulnerable=FALSE;
  m_bIntelligent=FALSE;
  //common values
  m_eObject=object; //type of object
  m_nLastXMoveTime=m_nLastYMoveTime=Timer.time(); //time
  m_nX=x; m_nY=y; //location
  m_nXspeed=xspeed; m_nYspeed=yspeed; //speed
  m_pSprite=g_pSprite[object];
  m_nFrameCount=m_pSprite->frame_count();
  m_nHeight=m_pSprite->height();
  m_nWidth=m_pSprite->width();
  m_nBirthTime=Timer.time(); //time of creation
  //customized values
  switch(object){
    case PLANE_OBJECT:
      switch(abs(m_nXspeed)){ //depending on horizontal speed
        case 1:
          SoundManager->play(SLOWPUTT_SOUND,LOOP_SOUND);
```

```
      break;
    case 2:
      SoundManager->play(MEDIUMPUTT_SOUND,LOOP_SOUND);
      break;
    case 3:
      SoundManager->play(FASTPUTT_SOUND,LOOP_SOUND);
      break;
  }
  m_nMinXSpeed=-3; m_nMaxXSpeed=-1;
  m_nMinYSpeed=-4; m_nMaxYSpeed=4;
  m_nFrameInterval=250;
  m_eMortality=IMMORTAL;
  m_eLocomotion=FLYING_MOTION;
  m_bVulnerable=FALSE;
  break;
case EXPLODINGPLANE_OBJECT:
  m_nYspeed=0;
  m_nMinXSpeed=-3; m_nMaxXSpeed=-1;
  m_nMinYSpeed=-4; m_nMaxYSpeed=4;
  m_nFrameInterval=200;
  m_eMortality=ONESHOT_MORTAL; m_bVulnerable=FALSE;
  m_eLocomotion=FLYING_MOTION;
  break;
case DEADPLANE_OBJECT:
  SoundManager->play(SMARTS_SOUND);
  m_nYspeed=0;
  m_nMinXSpeed=-3; m_nMaxXSpeed=-1;
  m_nMinYSpeed=-4; m_nMaxYSpeed=4;
  m_nFrameInterval=3000;
  m_eMortality=ONESHOT_MORTAL; m_bVulnerable=FALSE;
  m_eLocomotion=FLYING_MOTION;
  break;
case CROW_OBJECT:
  m_nMinXSpeed=-2; m_nMaxXSpeed=-1;
  m_nMinYSpeed=-1; m_nMaxYSpeed=1;
  m_nCurrentFrame=Random.number(0,m_nFrameCount-1);
  m_nFrameInterval=250+Random.number(-30,30);
  m_eMortality=IMMORTAL;
  m_eLocomotion=FLYING_MOTION;
  m_bVulnerable=TRUE;
  break;
case FARM_OBJECT:
case FIELD_OBJECT:
  m_nFrameCount=1;
  m_eMortality=IMMORTAL;
  m_eLocomotion=NO_MOTION;
  m_bVulnerable=FALSE;
  break;
case BULLET_OBJECT:
  SoundManager->play(GUN_SOUND); //sound of gun firing
```

```
            m_nFrameCount=1;
            m_eMortality=MORTAL;
            m_eLocomotion=FLYING_MOTION;
            m_bVulnerable=FALSE;
            m_nLifeTime=500+Random.number(0,200);
            break;
        case DEADCROW_OBJECT:
            m_nCurrentFrame=0;
            m_eMortality=MORTAL;
            m_eLocomotion=FALLING_MOTION;
            m_bVulnerable=FALSE;
            m_nLifeTime=1000;
            break;
        case EXPLODINGCROW_OBJECT:
            SoundManager->play(BOOM_SOUND); //sound of explosion
            m_nCurrentFrame=0;
            m_nFrameInterval=100;
            m_eMortality=ONESHOT_MORTAL;
            m_eLocomotion=FLYING_MOTION;
            m_bVulnerable=FALSE;
            break;
    }
}

CObject::~CObject(){ //destructor
  if(m_eObject==PLANE_OBJECT){ //kill plane engine sounds
    SoundManager->stop(SLOWPUTT_SOUND);
    SoundManager->stop(MEDIUMPUTT_SOUND);
    SoundManager->stop(FASTPUTT_SOUND);
  }
}

void CObject::draw(LPDIRECTDRAWSURFACE surface){ //draw
  //draw the current frame
  m_pSprite->draw(m_nCurrentFrame,Viewpoint.screen(m_nX),
    m_nY,surface);
  //figure out which frame is next
  if(m_eMortality==ONESHOT_MORTAL){ //animation plays once
    if(Timer.elapsed(m_nLastFrameTime,m_nFrameInterval))
      ++m_nCurrentFrame;
  }
  else{ //repeating animation
    int t=m_nFrameInterval/(1+abs(m_nXspeed)); //frame interval
    if(m_nFrameCount>1&&Timer.elapsed(m_nLastFrameTime,t))
      if(m_bForwardAnimation){ //forward animation
        if(++m_nCurrentFrame>=m_nFrameCount){ //wrap
          m_nCurrentFrame=m_nFrameCount-2;
          m_bForwardAnimation=FALSE;
        }
      }
```

```
      else{ //backward animation
        if(--m_nCurrentFrame<0){ //wrap
          m_nCurrentFrame=1;
          m_bForwardAnimation=TRUE;
        }
      }
    }
  //draw damage to plane - paste on top of plane image
  if(m_eObject==PLANE_OBJECT){
    switch(ScoreManager.health()){ //depending on health
      case 1: //heavy damage
        g_pSprite[DAMAGEDPLANE_OBJECT]->
          draw(1,Viewpoint.screen(m_nX),m_nY,surface);
        break;
      case 2: //mild damage
        g_pSprite[DAMAGEDPLANE_OBJECT]->
          draw(0,Viewpoint.screen(m_nX),m_nY,surface);
        break;
      default: break;
    }
  }
}

void CObject::accelerate(int xdelta,int ydelta){
//change speed
  int old_xspeed=m_nXspeed; //old speed
  //horizontal
  m_nXspeed+=xdelta;
  if(m_nXspeed<m_nMinXSpeed)m_nXspeed=m_nMinXSpeed;
  if(m_nXspeed>m_nMaxXSpeed)m_nXspeed=m_nMaxXSpeed;
  //vertical
  m_nYspeed+=ydelta;
  if(m_nYspeed<m_nMinYSpeed)m_nYspeed=m_nMinYSpeed;
  if(m_nYspeed>m_nMaxYSpeed)m_nYspeed=m_nMaxYSpeed;
  //change plane sound
  if(m_eObject==PLANE_OBJECT&&old_xspeed!=m_nXspeed){
    //stop old sound (one of these will work)
    SoundManager->stop(SLOWPUTT_SOUND);
    SoundManager->stop(MEDIUMPUTT_SOUND);
    SoundManager->stop(FASTPUTT_SOUND);
    //start new sound
    SoundManager->
      play(SLOWPUTT_SOUND-1+abs(m_nXspeed),LOOP_SOUND);
  }
}

void CObject::move(){ //move object
  const int XSCALE=16; //to scale back horizontal motion
  const int YSCALE=32; //to scale back vertical motion
  const int YMARGIN=20; //vertical margin
```

```
        int xdelta,ydelta; //change in position
        int time=Timer.time(); //current time
        int tfactor; //time since last move
        switch(m_eLocomotion){
          case FLYING_MOTION:
            //horizontal motion
            tfactor=time-m_nLastXMoveTime; //time since last move
            xdelta=(m_nXspeed*tfactor)/XSCALE; //x distance moved
            m_nX+=xdelta; //x motion
            Viewpoint.normalize(m_nX); //normalize to world width
            if(xdelta||m_nXspeed==0) //record time of move
              m_nLastXMoveTime=time;
            //vertical motion
            tfactor=time-m_nLastYMoveTime; //time since last move
            ydelta=(m_nYspeed*tfactor)/YSCALE; //y distance moved
            m_nY+=ydelta; //y motion
            if(m_nY<YMARGIN)m_nY=YMARGIN;
            if(m_nY>=SCREEN_HEIGHT)m_nY=SCREEN_HEIGHT-1;
            if(ydelta||m_nYspeed==0) //record time of move
              m_nLastYMoveTime=time;
            break;
          case FALLING_MOTION:
            m_nXspeed=0;
            //time since born, for acceleration due to gravity
            tfactor=time-m_nBirthTime;
            //vertical motion
            ydelta=tfactor/YSCALE; m_nY+=ydelta;
            if(m_nY<YMARGIN)m_nY=YMARGIN;
            if(ydelta||m_nYspeed==0) //record time of move
              m_nLastYMoveTime=time;
            //kill objects that have fallen below the screen
            if(m_nY>SCREEN_HEIGHT){
              SoundManager->play(THUMP_SOUND); //object hitting ground
              m_nLifeTime=0; m_eMortality=MORTAL; //force cull
            }
            break;
          default: break;
        }
}

void CObject::set_speed(int xspeed,int yspeed){ //set speed
  accelerate(xspeed-m_nXspeed,yspeed-m_nYspeed);
}
```

Objman.h

```
//objman.h: header file for the object manager

//Copyright Ian Parberry, 1999
//Last updated December 7, 1999
```

```cpp
#ifndef __OBJMAN__
#define __OBJMAN__

#include <windows.h>
#include <windowsx.h>
#include <ddraw.h>

#include "objects.h"

class CObjectManager{
  private:
    CObject **m_pObjectList; //list of objects in game
    int m_nCount; //how many objects in list
    int m_nMaxCount; //maximum number of objects
    int m_nCurrentObject; //index of the current object
    int m_nLastGunFireTime; //time gun was last fired
    int m_nStartInvulnerableTime; //time level started
    //distance functions
    int distance(int x1,int y1,int x2,int y2); //in universe
    int distance(int first,int second); //between objects
    //collision detection
    void collision_detection(); //all collisions
    BOOL collision_detection(int index); //with this object
    //managing dead objects
    void cull(); //cull dead objects
    void kill(int index); //remove object from list
    void replace(int index); //replace by next in series
  public:
    CObjectManager(int max); //constructor
    ~CObjectManager(); //destructor
    void reset(); //reset to original conditions
    BOOL won(); //TRUE if all enemies dead
    int create(ObjectType object,int x,int y,
      int xspeed,int yspeed); //create new object
    int create(int index,ObjectType object,
      int x,int y,int xspeed,int yspeed); //create at index
    //animate all objects
    void animate(LPDIRECTDRAWSURFACE surface);
    //the following functions operate on the current object
    void accelerate(int xdelta,int ydelta=0); //change speed
    void set_current(int index); //set current object
    int speed(); //return magnitude of speed
    void fire_gun(); //fire the gun
    void set_speed(int xdelta,int ydelta); //of current object
    void speed_limits(int &xmin,int &xmax,
      int &ymin,int &ymax); //speed limits
    int enemies(); //number of enemies left
};
```

```
        #endif
```

Objman.cpp

```
//objman.cpp: object manager class
//Copyright Ian Parberry, 1999
//Last updated December 7, 1999

#include <math.h> //for sqrt

#include "objman.h"
#include "view.h" //for viewpoint class
#include "timer.h" //game timer
#include "ai.h" //for intelligent objects
#include "score.h" //for score manager

//time that plane is invulnerable at start of level
const int INITIAL_INVULNERABLE_TIME=3000;

extern CViewPoint Viewpoint; //player viewpoint
extern CTimer Timer; //game timer
extern CScoreManager ScoreManager; //score manager

CObjectManager::CObjectManager(int max){ //constructor
  m_nMaxCount=max; m_nCount=0; m_nCurrentObject=0;
  m_nStartInvulnerableTime=Timer.time(); //start invulnerable
  m_nLastGunFireTime=0;
  m_pObjectList=new CObject*[max]; //object list
  for(int i=0; i<m_nMaxCount; i++) //create objects
    m_pObjectList[i]=NULL;
}

CObjectManager::~CObjectManager(){ //destructor
  for(int i=0; i<m_nMaxCount; i++) //for each object
    delete m_pObjectList[i]; //delete it
  delete[]m_pObjectList; //delete object list
}

int CObjectManager::create(ObjectType object,int x,int y,
                            int xspeed,int yspeed){
//create object at first available index
  if(m_nCount<m_nMaxCount){ //if room, create object
    int i=0;//index into object list
    while(m_pObjectList[i]!=NULL)i++; //find first free slot
    return create(i,object,x,y,xspeed,yspeed); //create it there
  }
  else return -1;
}

int CObjectManager::create(int index,ObjectType object,
```

```
                                  int x,int y,int xspeed,int yspeed){
  //create object at given index
    if(m_nCount<m_nMaxCount&&m_pObjectList[index]==NULL){
      if(object==CROW_OBJECT)
        m_pObjectList[index]=
          new CIntelligentObject(object,x,y,xspeed,yspeed);
      else
        m_pObjectList[index]=new CObject(object,x,y,xspeed,yspeed);
      m_nCount++;
      return index;
    }
    else return -1;
}

void CObjectManager::animate(LPDIRECTDRAWSURFACE surface){
  //move objects
  for(int i=0; i<m_nMaxCount; i++) //for each object slot
    if(m_pObjectList[i]!=NULL){ //if there's an object there
      m_pObjectList[i]->move(); //move it
      if(m_pObjectList[i]->m_bIntelligent) //if intelligent
        //tell object about plane current position
        ((CIntelligentObject*)m_pObjectList[i])->plane(
          m_pObjectList[m_nCurrentObject]->m_nX,
          m_pObjectList[m_nCurrentObject]->m_nY,
          distance(i,m_nCurrentObject));
    }
  //move viewpoint with plane
  Viewpoint.set_position(
    m_pObjectList[m_nCurrentObject]->m_nX);
  //collision detection
  collision_detection();
  //cull old objects
  cull();
  //draw objects
  for(i=0; i<m_nMaxCount; i++) //for each object slot
    if(m_pObjectList[i]!=NULL) //if there's an object there
      m_pObjectList[i]->draw(surface); //draw it
}

void CObjectManager::accelerate(int xdelta,int ydelta){
  //change speed of current object
  CObject *plane= m_pObjectList[m_nCurrentObject];
  if(plane->m_eObject==PLANE_OBJECT) //if not dead or exploding
    plane->accelerate(xdelta,ydelta);
}

void CObjectManager::set_current(int index){
  //set current object
  if(index>=0&&index<m_nCount)m_nCurrentObject=index;
}
```

```
int CObjectManager::speed(){
  //return magnitude of current object speed
  return abs(m_pObjectList[m_nCurrentObject]->m_nXspeed);
}

int CObjectManager::distance(int x1,int y1,int x2,int y2){
//return distance in universe
  int x=abs(x1-x2),y=abs(y1-y2);//x and y distance
  //compensate for wrap-around world
  if(x>WORLD_WIDTH/2)x-=WORLD_WIDTH;
  //return result
  return (int)sqrt((double)x*x+(double)y*y);
}

int CObjectManager::distance(int first,int second){
//return distance between objects
  //bail if bad index
  if(first<0||first>=m_nMaxCount)return -1;
  if(second<0||second>=m_nMaxCount)return -1;
  //get coordinates of centers
  int x1,y1,x2,y2; //coordinates of objects
  x1=m_pObjectList[first]->m_nX;
  y1=m_pObjectList[first]->m_nY-
    m_pObjectList[first]->m_nHeight/2;
  x2=m_pObjectList[second]->m_nX;
  y2=m_pObjectList[second]->m_nY-
    m_pObjectList[second]->m_nHeight/2;
  //return distance between coordinates
  return distance(x1,y1,x2,y2);
}

void CObjectManager::kill(int index){ //remove object
  //add to score for killing it
  ScoreManager.add_to_score(m_pObjectList[index]->m_eObject);
  //housekeeping
  m_nCount--;
  delete m_pObjectList[index];
  m_pObjectList[index]=NULL;
}

void CObjectManager::fire_gun(){ //fire current object's gun
  CObject *plane= m_pObjectList[m_nCurrentObject];
  if(plane->m_eObject==PLANE_OBJECT) //if not dead or exploding
    if(Timer.elapsed(m_nLastGunFireTime,200))
      create(BULLET_OBJECT,plane->m_nX-60,plane->m_nY-50,-5,0);
}

void CObjectManager::cull(){ //cull old objects
  CObject *object;
```

```
      for(int i=0; i<m_nMaxCount; i++){ //for each object
        object=m_pObjectList[i]; //current object
        if(object!=NULL){
          //died of old age
          if(object->m_eMortality==MORTAL&& //if mortal and ...
          //...lived long enough...
          (Timer.time()-object->m_nBirthTime>object->m_nLifeTime))
            kill(i); //...then kill it
          else //one-shot animation
            //if object played one time only...
            if(object->m_eMortality==ONESHOT_MORTAL&&
            //...and played once already...
            object->m_nCurrentFrame>=object->m_nFrameCount)
              replace(i); //...then replace the object
        }
      }
    }

void CObjectManager::replace(int index){
//replace object by next in series
  CObject *object=m_pObjectList[index]; //current object
  ObjectType newtype;
  BOOL successor=TRUE; //assume it has a successor
  //decide on new object type
  switch(object->m_eObject){
    case CROW_OBJECT: newtype=EXPLODINGCROW_OBJECT; break;
    case EXPLODINGCROW_OBJECT: newtype=DEADCROW_OBJECT; break;
    case PLANE_OBJECT: newtype=EXPLODINGPLANE_OBJECT; break;
    case EXPLODINGPLANE_OBJECT:
      newtype=DEADPLANE_OBJECT; //you're dead
      ScoreManager.deduct_life(); //deduct a life from score
      break;
    case DEADPLANE_OBJECT: //you're done being dead
      newtype=PLANE_OBJECT; //reincarnate as a regular plane
      m_nStartInvulnerableTime=Timer.time(); //start invulnerable
      break;
    default: successor=FALSE; break; //has no successor
  }
  //replace old object with new one
  int x=object->m_nX,y=object->m_nY; //location
  int xspeed=object->m_nXspeed;
  int yspeed=object->m_nYspeed;
  kill(index); //kill old object
  if(successor) //if it has a successor
    create(index,newtype,x,y,xspeed,yspeed); //create new one
}

void CObjectManager::collision_detection(){
//check for all collisions
  for(int i=0; i<m_nMaxCount; i++) //for each object slot
```

```
    if(m_pObjectList[i]!=NULL) //if object exists
      switch(m_pObjectList[i]->m_eObject){ //depending on type
        case BULLET_OBJECT: //if it is a bullet
          if(collision_detection(i)) //if object hit something
            kill(i); //kill object doing the hitting
          break;
        case PLANE_OBJECT: //if it was the plane
          if(Timer.time()>=m_nStartInvulnerableTime+
          INITIAL_INVULNERABLE_TIME) //if plane is vulnerable
            if(collision_detection(i)){ //if plane hit something
              if(ScoreManager.health()<=1) //if health low
                replace(m_nCurrentObject); //explosion
              ScoreManager.collision(); //register collision
            }
          break;
      }
}

BOOL CObjectManager::collision_detection(int index){
//check whether object with this index collides
  int i=0; //index of object collided with
  BOOL finished=FALSE; //finished when collision detected
  while(i<m_nMaxCount&&!finished){
    if(m_pObjectList[i]!=NULL) //if i is a valid object index
      if(m_pObjectList[i]->m_bVulnerable&& //if vulnerable
      distance(index,i)<m_pObjectList[i]->m_nHeight/2+
      m_pObjectList[index]->m_nHeight/2){ //and close enough
        finished=TRUE; //hit found
        replace(i); //replace object that is hit
      }
    ++i; //next object
  }
  return finished;
}

void CObjectManager::reset(){ //reset to original conditions
  m_nCount=0; m_nCurrentObject=0; m_nLastGunFireTime=0;
  m_nStartInvulnerableTime=Timer.time(); //start invulnerable
  for(int i=0; i<m_nMaxCount; i++){
    delete m_pObjectList[i];
    m_pObjectList[i]=NULL;
  }
}

BOOL CObjectManager::won(){ //TRUE if enemies all dead
  int count=0; //how many enemies left
  for(int i=0; i<m_nMaxCount; i++)
    if(m_pObjectList[i]!=NULL)
      switch(m_pObjectList[i]->m_eObject){
        case CROW_OBJECT:
```

```
        case EXPLODINGCROW_OBJECT:
        case DEADCROW_OBJECT:
          count++;
          break;
      }
    return count<=0;
}

void CObjectManager::set_speed(int xdelta,int ydelta){
  CObject *plane=m_pObjectList[m_nCurrentObject];
  if(plane->m_eObject==PLANE_OBJECT)
    plane->set_speed(xdelta,ydelta);
}

void CObjectManager::speed_limits(int &xmin,int &xmax,
                                  int &ymin,int &ymax){
//return speed limits on current object
  CObject *plane=m_pObjectList[m_nCurrentObject];
  xmin=plane->m_nMinXSpeed; xmax=plane->m_nMaxXSpeed;
  ymin=plane->m_nMinYSpeed; ymax=plane->m_nMaxYSpeed;
}

int CObjectManager::enemies(){ //return number of enemies
  int count=0; //how many enemies left
  for(int i=0; i<m_nMaxCount; i++)
    if(m_pObjectList[i]!=NULL)
      switch(m_pObjectList[i]->m_eObject){
        case CROW_OBJECT:
        case EXPLODINGCROW_OBJECT:
        case DEADCROW_OBJECT:
          count++;
          break;
      }
  return count;
}
```

Score.h

```
//score.h: header file for score manager class

//Copyright Ian Parberry, 1999
//Last updated December 7, 1999

#ifndef __SCORE__
#define __SCORE__

#include "objects.h" //for object types

const int LEVEL_BONUS_SCORE=10; //points for level completion
```

```
class CScoreManager{
  private:
    int m_nScore; //points scored
    int m_nHealth; //how many times plane has been hit
    int m_nLives; //how many lives the player has
  public:
    CScoreManager(); //constructor
    void reset(); //reset to start conditions
    int score(); //return current points score
    int health(); //return plane health
    int lives(); //return number of lives
    void add_to_score(int delta); //add delta to score
    void add_to_score(ObjectType object); //for killing object
    void collision(); //collision, bad for health
    void deduct_life(); //lose a life if health bad
};

#endif
```

Score.cpp

```
//score.cpp: score manager class
//Copyright Ian Parberry, 1999
//Last updated December 7, 1999

#include <windows.h>
#include <windowsx.h>

#include "score.h"
#include "sound.h" //for sound manager

extern CSoundManager* SoundManager; //sound manager
extern BOOL endphase; //level ends when last life gone

const int START_LIVES=3; //initial number of lives
const int MAX_HEALTH=3; //maximum plane health
const int SCORE_PER_LIFE=100; //points to earn another life

CScoreManager::CScoreManager(){ //constructor
  reset();
}

void CScoreManager::reset(){ //reset to start conditions
  m_nScore=0; m_nHealth=MAX_HEALTH; m_nLives=START_LIVES;
}

void CScoreManager::add_to_score(int delta){
  //add delta to score
  int oldscore=m_nScore; //old score
  m_nScore+=delta; //add to score
```

```
      //compute new lives, if any
      int newlives= //new lives earned
        m_nScore/SCORE_PER_LIFE-oldscore/SCORE_PER_LIFE;
      if(newlives) //play sound if nonzero
        SoundManager->play(NEWLIFE_SOUND);
      m_nLives+=newlives; //add new lives to counter
    }

    void CScoreManager::add_to_score(ObjectType object){
      //add score for killing object
      const int CROW_SCORE=3; //score for killing crow
      switch(object){ //score depends on object
        case DEADCROW_OBJECT: add_to_score(CROW_SCORE); break;
        default: break; //default is nothing
      }
    }

    void CScoreManager::collision(){ //collision, bad for health
      if(--m_nHealth>0) //deduct from health
        SoundManager->play(STINGS_SOUND); //play sound
    }

    void CScoreManager::deduct_life(){ //lose a life
      if(m_nHealth<=0){ //if health bad
        m_nHealth=MAX_HEALTH; //make healthy
        if(--m_nLives<0) //deduct a life, if last
          endphase=TRUE; //end of game
      }
    }

    int CScoreManager::lives(){ //return number of lives
      return m_nLives;
    }

    int CScoreManager::score(){ //return health
      return m_nScore;
    }

    int CScoreManager::health(){ //return score
      return m_nHealth;
    }
```

Sndlist.h

```
//sndlist.h: list of sound definitions

//Copyright Ian Parberry, 1999
//Last updated December 7, 1999

#ifndef __SNDLIST__
```

```
#define __SNDLIST__

#define LOOP_SOUND TRUE

enum GameSoundType{ //sounds used in game engine
  CAW_SOUND=0, //sound a crow makes
  GUN_SOUND, //sound of gun firing
  BOOM_SOUND, //sound of explosion
  THUMP_SOUND, //sound of object hitting the ground
  //next 3 sounds must be consecutive and in this order
  SLOWPUTT_SOUND, //sound of slow engine
  MEDIUMPUTT_SOUND, //sound of medium engine
  FASTPUTT_SOUND, //sound of fast engine
  //mouse clicks
  BIGCLICK_SOUND, //loud click
  SMALLCLICK_SOUND, //soft click
  //more game sounds
  SUCCESS_SOUND, //completion of level
  FAILED_SOUND, //sound of failing
  NEWLIFE_SOUND, //sound of getting a new life
  STINGS_SOUND, //that stings (damage)
  SMARTS_SOUND, //that smarts (damage)
};

enum IntroSoundType{ //sounds used during the intro
  TITLE_SOUND=0, //sound used during title screen
  LOGO_SOUND, //signature chord
};

#endif
```

Text.h

```
//text.h: header file for text.cpp

//Copyright Ian Parberry, 9
//Last updated December 7, 1999

#ifndef __TEXT__
#define __TEXT__

#include "csprite.h" //for text sprites

enum chartype{CHAR_A=0,CHAR_B,CHAR_C,CHAR_D,CHAR_E,CHAR_F,
  CHAR_G,CHAR_H,CHAR_I,CHAR_J,CHAR_K,CHAR_L,CHAR_M,CHAR_N,
  CHAR_O,CHAR_P,CHAR_Q,CHAR_R,CHAR_S,CHAR_T,CHAR_U,CHAR_V,
  CHAR_W,CHAR_X,CHAR_Y,CHAR_Z,CHAR_0,CHAR_1,CHAR_2,CHAR_3,
  CHAR_4,CHAR_5,CHAR_6,CHAR_7,CHAR_8,CHAR_9,NUM_CHARS};
```

```
class CTextManager{ //fixed width font text sprite manager
  private:
    CClippedSprite *character[NUM_CHARS]; //char sprites
    int width,height; //width and height of chars
    int x,y; //current cursor location
    void draw(chartype c,LPDIRECTDRAWSURFACE surface);
  public:
    CTextManager(int wdth,int ht); //constructor
    ~CTextManager(); //destructor
    BOOL load(CBmpSpriteFileReader *file,
      int x,int y); //load sprites from file at (x,y)
    void jump(int xloc,int yloc); //move cursor to here
    void draw(char* string,
      LPDIRECTDRAWSURFACE surface); //draw string
    BOOL Restore(); //restore sprite surfaces
    void Release(); //release sprite surfaces
};

#endif
```

Text.cpp

```
//text.cpp: code for text manager

//Copyright Ian Parberry, 1999
//Last updated December 7, 1999

#include <string.h>

#include "text.h"
#include "bmp.h"

CTextManager::CTextManager(int wdth,int ht){ //constructor
  width=wdth; height=ht; x=y=0;
  for(int i=0; i<NUM_CHARS; i++)
    character[i]=new CClippedSprite(1,width,height);
}

CTextManager::~CTextManager(){ //destructor
  for(int i=0; i<NUM_CHARS; i++)delete character[i];
}

BOOL CTextManager::load(CBmpSpriteFileReader *bmp,
                        int x,int y){ //load sprites
  BOOL result=TRUE;
  int cx=x,cy=y; //location to read from
  //grab numbers, assume they are first
  for(int c=CHAR_0; c<=CHAR_9; c++){
    result=result&&character[c]->load(bmp,0,cx,cy);
    cx+=width+1;
```

```
  }
  //grab letters
  cx=x; cy=y+height+1; //assume letters below numbers
  for(c=CHAR_A; c<=CHAR_Z; c++){
    result=result&&character[c]->load(bmp,0,cx,cy);
    cx+=width+1;
  }
  return result;
}

void CTextManager::jump(int xloc,int yloc){ //jump to here
  x=xloc; y=yloc;
}

void CTextManager::draw(chartype c,
    LPDIRECTDRAWSURFACE surface){ //draw char to surface
  int cx=x+width/2,cy=y; //compute location
  if(c>=0&&c<NUM_CHARS)
    character[c]->draw(0,cx,cy,surface); //draw
  x+=width; //advance to next char
}

void CTextManager::draw(char* string,
    LPDIRECTDRAWSURFACE surface){ //draw string to surface
  for(int i=0; i<(int)strlen(string); i++){ //for each char
    char c=string[i]; //grab character
    if(c>='0'&&c<='9') //number
      draw((chartype)(CHAR_0+c-'0'),surface);
    else if(c>='A'&&c<='Z') //uppercase
      draw((chartype)(CHAR_A+c-'A'),surface);
    else if(c>='a'&&c<='z') //lowercase
      draw((chartype)(CHAR_A+c-'a'),surface);
    else if(c==' ')x+=width; //space
  }
}

BOOL CTextManager::Restore(){ //restore sprite surfaces
  BOOL result=TRUE;
  for(int c=0; c<NUM_CHARS; c++) //for each char sprite
    result=result&&character[c]->Restore(); //restore it
  return result;
}

void CTextManager::Release(){ //release sprite surfaces
  for(int c=0; c<NUM_CHARS; c++) //for each char sprite
    character[c]->Release(); //release it
}
```

Chapter 14

Here's what you'll learn:

- How to manage the high score list entry and display using a high score manager

- What the Windows registry is and how to use it

- How to store the high score list in the Windows registry

- How to protect against tampering with the high score list by the average user

The High Score List

In Demo 12, we learn how to use the Windows registry to store the *high score list* (see Figure 14.1), a list of the highest scores that have been made since the game was installed. To be of any use, a high score list should be difficult to get into. A moderately sophisticated user can potentially cheat by modifying the high score list using the registry editor `Regedit`, which comes in any standard Windows installation. To guard against tampering, we store two difficult-to-fake checksums with the high score list, and delete the entire list if it looks like it has been tampered with. We add code to display the high score list from the main menu, to add a player's name into the high score list if their score is high enough, and to read and write the high score list to the Windows registry.

While the high score list must be stored in a portion of the Windows registry that is common to all users, there are game settings that, rather than being global in nature like the high score list, are potentially different for each user. As an example, we store the user's current input device (keyboard, mouse, or joystick) in a different portion of the registry, so that each time a player fires up the game, it starts using his or her last-used device instead of the keyboard.

Figure 14.1
The high score list

Experiment with Demo 12

Take a moment now to run Demo 12.

◉ Play a game. When the game is over, type your name when you are invited into the high score list. From the main menu, view the high score list by clicking on the "High Score List" button.

◉ Exit the game. After reading the section below on the Windows registry, use `Regedit` to read the values in `HKEY_LOCAL_MACHINE\SOFTWARE\LARC\NedFarm`. Do you see your name there?

◉ Attempt to alter your high score with the registry editor. Do this by first selecting your score in the right pane of the registry editor, then selecting Modify from the Edit menu. Type in a new value, than hit Enter.

◉ Now run Demo 12 and look at the high score list again. What happened to your altered entry? It's gone! That'll teach you to hack.

◉ Play a game with the mouse, and then exit completely. Restart Demo 12 and start a new game. Notice that the device used the second time is the mouse, unlike Demo 11, which would have gone back to the keyboard.

The Windows Registry

The *Windows registry* is the place where Windows applications are supposed to keep their settings. Values stored in the registry are *persistent*, that is, they will still be there the next time your program is run. It is organized similarly to the Windows file system, except instead of folders we have *keys*, and instead of files we have *values*. Windows provides a handy app called the Registry Editor, `Regedit.exe`. It is difficult to find, being hidden away in the `Windows` folder on your main hard drive (typically `C:\Windows`). You can run it by selecting Run from the Start menu of your computer, typing "`regedit`" into the edit box, then hitting the OK button. Since I use it a lot, I prefer to put a shortcut to it on my desktop. The registry editor looks a little like the explorer (see Figure 14.2). Keys are shown in the left pane, and values are shown in the right pane.

The registry on every Windows installation is organized into six primary keys, which are shown under My Computer in the left pane of the registry editor (see Figure 14.2). The two primary keys that are most important for game developers are `HKEY_CURRENT_USER` (shown highlighted in the left pane of Figure 14.2) and `HKEY_LOCAL_MACHINE` (shown immediately beneath `HKEY_CURRENT_USER`). `HKEY_CURRENT_USER` is where we store settings that are related to an individual player, such as the device (for *Ned's Turkey Farm*, the keyboard, the mouse, or the joystick) used the last time he or she played. `HKEY_LOCAL_MACHINE` is where we store settings that are common to all players on this computer, such as the high score list.

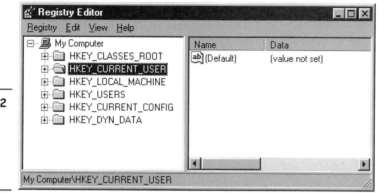

Figure 14.2
The Windows registry editor, Regedit

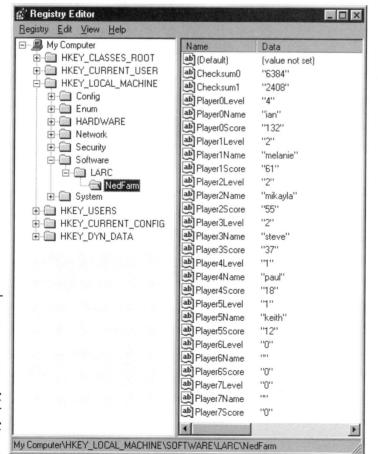

Figure 14.3
The registry editor showing the values in the key HKEY_LOCAL_MAC HINE\SOFT WARE\LARC \NedFarm

Beneath the primary keys in the registry are secondary keys. The two secondary keys of interest to us, which are the same on every Windows installation, are HKEY_LOCAL_MACHINE\Software and HKEY_CURRENT_USER\Software. (Windows 95 capitalizes "Software" as "SOFTWARE," but it doesn't matter how we capitalize it in the code.) Beneath each of these secondary keys are keys corresponding to software companies. These will be different on each computer, depending on what software has been installed. We will use LARC, the acronym of my lab at UNT, for this key. Beneath the company key, each piece of installed software from that company can have its own key. We will use NedFarm. So, for example, the high score list will be stored under the key (see Figure 14.3).

HKEY_LOCAL_MACHINE\SOFTWARE\LARC\NedFarm.

The player's device setting will be stored under (see Figure 14.4):

HKEY_CURRENT_USER\Software\LARC\NedFarm.

(Note that the registry editor contents on your computer will look different from that depicted in Figures 14.3 and 14.4; there will be more entries corresponding to whatever software is installed.)

Figure 14.4
The registry editor showing the values in the key HKEY_CURRENT_USER\Software\LARC\NedFarm

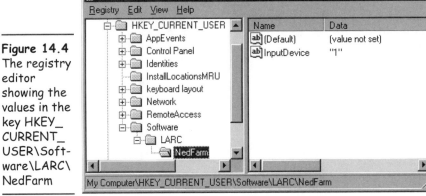

Changes to Defines.h and Sndlist.h

In `Defines.h`, we add new phase types for the high score phase (when the high score list is being displayed) and the new high score phase (when the player is entering his or her name for a new entry into the high score list). These are named `HIGHSCORE_PHASE` and `NEWHIGHSCORE_PHASE`, respectively, and are appended to the end of the enumerated type `GamePhaseType`.

```
enum GamePhaseType{
   LOGO_PHASE,TITLE_PHASE,MENU_PHASE,PLAYING_PHASE,
   DEVICEMENU_PHASE,SUCCESS_PHASE,HIGHSCORE_PHASE,
   NEWHIGHSCORE_PHASE
};
```

In `Sndlist.h`, we append the names of new sounds to the enumerated type `GameSoundType`. The first of these is `CONGRATS_SOUND`, which is a congratulatory sound played at the start of the new high score phase when the player is being invited to enter his or her name for a new entry into the high score list. The other three sounds are `TYPE_SPACE_SOUND`, `TYPE_RETURN_SOUND`, and `TYPE_CHAR_SOUND`, which are the sounds of a typewriter typing, respectively, a space, a carriage return, and an alphanumeric character. These will be played in response to the player's keystrokes as he or she types in his or her name.

```
CONGRATS_SOUND, //congratulations
TYPE_SPACE_SOUND, //typewriter typing a space
TYPE_RETURN_SOUND, //typewriter typing a return
TYPE_CHAR_SOUND, //typewriter typing a character
```

The High Score Manager

The high score manager is charged with maintaining the high score list and storing it in the Windows registry.

High Score Manager Overview

The header file for the high score manager is `Topscore.h`. It begins with the declaration of two constants, `MAX_TOPSCORES`, which is the maximum number of entries allowed in the high score list, and `MAX_TOPSCORE_NAMELENGTH`, which is the maximum number of characters allocated to each player's name in the high score list, including the null character at the end of the string.

```
#define MAX_TOPSCORES 8
#define MAX_TOPSCORE_NAMELENGTH 17
```

The high score manager `CHighScoreList` has seven private member variables. The first is a two-dimensional `char` array `m_pNames`, which will hold

MAX_TOPSCORES names. The name of entry i in the high score list will be held in the character string m_pNames[i].

```
char m_pNames[MAX_TOPSCORES][MAX_TOPSCORE_NAMELENGTH];
```

Next, we have two parallel arrays for the score and level. The score made by player m_pNames[i] in level number m_pTopLevel[i] will be m_pTopScore[i].

```
int m_pTopScore[MAX_TOPSCORES]; //top scores
int m_pTopLevel[MAX_TOPSCORES]; //top levels
```

The checksums m_nChecksum0 and m_nChecksum1 will be used to protect against interference with the high score list in the Windows registry by other programs such as Regedit. Our checksum method won't be foolproof, for any enterprising hacker with a symbolic disassembler will quickly be able to disable our code, but it will guard against casual attacks. (Note: If you ever wish to sue somebody for hacking your game, you will have a stronger case in court if you can show that you have made a reasonable effort to prevent hacking.)

```
int m_nChecksum0,m_nChecksum1; //checksums
```

Next, we have two private member variables for use when the player is typing his or her name for a new entry in the high score list. The character array m_szNamebuffer is a name buffer that will be used to store the name as it is typed in, and m_nNamesize will store the number of characters typed into it so far.

```
char m_szNamebuffer[MAX_TOPSCORE_NAMELENGTH]; //name buffer
int m_nNamesize; //size of name in name buffer
```

CHighScoreList has ten private member functions. There are two save functions, the first of which saves all high scores to the registry.

```
void save(); //save all high scores
```

The second save function has two parameters. The first parameter is RegistryKey, the handle to a registry key, which is the handle that we use to access values stored in a registry key. The second parameter is index, the index of a high score list entry to be saved.

```
void save(HKEY RegistryKey,int index); //save one high score
```

Similarly, there are two load functions to load high scores from the registry:

```
void load(); //load all high scores
void load(HKEY RegistryKey,int index); //load one high score
```

Function enumerate turns the high score list into a number to be used in calculating a checksum.

```
int enumerate(); //turn data into a number
```

Functions `checksum0` and `checksum1` compute different checksums:

```
int checksum0(); //calculate a checksum
int checksum1(); //calculate a checksum
```

The next two functions load and save the checksums between the registry and member variables `m_nChecksum0` and `m_nChecksum1`:

```
void load_checksums(HKEY RegistryKey); //load checksums
void save_checksums(HKEY RegistryKey); //save checksums
```

Function `checksums_ok` returns `TRUE` if the checksums in member variables `m_nChecksum0` and `m_nChecksum1` are consistent with the high score list stored in the other private member variables:

```
BOOL checksums_ok(); //TRUE if checksums are OK
```

`CHighScoreList` has seven public member functions, starting with a constructor.

```
CHighScoreList(); //constructor
```

Function `insert` inserts a new high score into the high score list. It has two parameters containing the `level` and the `score` to be recorded. The player's name is taken from the private member variable `m_szNamebuffer` which, it is assumed, has already been filled in by the player.

```
BOOL insert(int level,int score); //insert new high score
```

Function `draw` uses the text manager to draw the high score list to a `surface`. It assumes that the background has already been drawn there. We will later use a

Figure 14.5
The background for the high score list, hscore.bmp

background from a file named `Hscore.bmp` (see Figure 14.5). The job of the `draw` function is to make it look like Figure 14.1.

```
void draw(LPDIRECTDRAWSURFACE surface); //draw high score
```

Function `clear` deletes all data from the high score list:

```
void clear(); //clear all high scores
```

Function `made_the_grade` returns `TRUE` if `score` is high enough to get into the high score list, that is, it is greater than the smallest score in the list:

```
BOOL made_the_grade(int score); //TRUE if score gets on table
```

The last four `CHighScoreList` public member functions manipulate the player's name in the temporary buffer `m_szNamebuffer`. Function `append_to_current` appends a character `c` to the end of `m_szNamebuffer`, returning `FALSE` if it fails due to lack of room.

```
BOOL append_to_current(char c); //insert char at end
```

Function `delete_from_current` deletes the last character from `m_szNamebuffer`, returning `FALSE` if it was empty:

```
BOOL delete_from_current(); //delete char at end
```

Function `cancel_current` makes `m_szNamebuffer` empty:

```
void cancel_current(); //clear out the current name
```

The last `CHighScoreList` public member function is a reader function `current_name`, which returns a pointer to `m_szNamebuffer`:

```
char *current_name(); //return current name
```

High Score Manager Code

The code file for the high score manager is `Topscore.cpp`. It begins with the declaration of four 16-bit prime numbers. Prime numbers this small are relatively easy to compute and for the lazy, there are tables of small prime numbers all over the web. I found one quickly at

```
http://x1a-stxm98.nsls.bnl.gov/qt/primes.html
```

by typing "prime number table" into my favorite search engine. I chose 16-bit prime numbers because they can be multiplied in a 32-bit word. Cryptographically, 16-bit primes are very weak. If I were serious about this I would use 128-bit prime numbers, but then I would have to devote a chapter to a long arithmetic package and probabilistic prime number generators, which are fun but somewhat beyond the scope of this book.

```
const int PRIME0=16787; //a 16-bit prime number
const int PRIME1=15241; //a 16-bit prime number
```

```
const int PRIME2=16223; //a 16-bit prime number
const int PRIME3=15907; //a 16-bit prime number
```

The Constructor and the Clear Function

The CHighScoreList constructor initializes the high score manager:

```
CHighScoreList::CHighScoreList(){ //constructor
```

It clears the name buffer by setting the private member variable m_nNamesize to zero:

```
m_nNamesize=0;
```

It then clears each entry in the high score list by setting the first character of every name to the null character, and setting the score and level to zero:

```
for(int i=0; i<MAX_TOPSCORES; i++){
  m_pNames[i][0]=0; m_pTopScore[i]=m_pTopLevel[i]=0;
}
```

It sets both checksums to zero:

```
m_nChecksum0=m_nChecksum1=0; //checksums
```

Finally, it loads the high score list from the registry by calling the load member function:

```
load();
}
```

The CHighScoreList clear function clears the high score list and stores it to the registry:

```
void CHighScoreList::clear(){
```

The code to clear the high score list is the same as that used in the constructor:

```
for(int i=0; i<MAX_TOPSCORES; i++){
  m_pNames[i][0]=0; m_pTopScore[i]=m_pTopLevel[i]=0;
}
m_nChecksum0=m_nChecksum1=0; //checksums
```

It writes the cleared high score list to the registry by calling the save member function:

```
save();
}
```

The Insert Function

The CHighScoreList insert function makes a new entry in the high score list using the name in m_szNamebuffer and the level and score provided as parameters. It returns TRUE if the insertion succeeds, that is, score is high enough to get onto the existing high score list. The `insert` function assumes that the high score list is sorted in order of decreasing score and maintains this property by inserting the new score into the right place.

```
BOOL CHighScoreList::insert(int level,int score){
```

Two local variables `i` and `j` are used as indices into the high score list:

```
int i=0,j;
```

A local variable `result` is used for the return result:

```
BOOL result=FALSE;
```

We bail out if the score or the name is bad:

```
if(score<=0)return FALSE; //bail if no score
if(strlen(m_szNamebuffer)<=0)return FALSE; //bail if no name
```

A `while` loop increments `i` until we find a lower score in `m_pTopScore[i]`, or fall off the high score list:

```
while(i<MAX_TOPSCORES&&m_pTopScore[i]>=score)++i;
```

We check that we found a lower score:

```
if(i<MAX_TOPSCORES){ //new entry
```

If so, we record in `result` that the new `score` made it onto the high score list:

```
result=TRUE;
```

Next, we must move the entries below `i` down one place to make room for the new one. The last entry is discarded. We do this with a `for` loop that starts `j` at the last index in the high score list, and successively moves it up the array.

```
for(j=MAX_TOPSCORES-1; j>i; j--){
```

We move the score, level, and name down one place, overwriting the old values. The name string is moved by using the C standard library function `strcpy`.

```
m_pTopScore[j]=m_pTopScore[j-1]; //score
m_pTopLevel[j]=m_pTopLevel[j-1]; //level
strcpy(m_pNames[j],m_pNames[j-1]); //name
}
```

Now, the new high score can be put into the ith entry. This time I used `strncpy`, which you should always use instead of `strcpy` when there is doubt about whether the null character expected at the end of the string is actually there.

```
m_pTopLevel[i]=level; m_pTopScore[i]=score; //level, score
strncpy(m_pNames[i],m_szNamebuffer,
  MAX_TOPSCORE_NAMELENGTH-1); //name
```

Next, we compute the checksums using the private member functions checksum0 and checksum1, storing them in the private member variables m_nChecksum0 and m_nChecksum1, respectively:

```
m_nChecksum0=checksum0(); //compute checksum
m_nChecksum1=checksum1(); //compute checksum
```

Finally, we save the new high score list to the registry by calling the save member function:

```
save(); //save new high score list to registry
}
```

When everything is finished, we return result:

```
return result;
}
```

The Draw Function

The CHighScoreList draw function uses the text manager to draw the high score list to a DirectDraw surface:

```
void CHighScoreList::draw(LPDIRECTDRAWSURFACE surface){
```

It begins with the declaration of five constants. The first four are various margins, and the fifth is the line height in pixels.

```
const int topmargin=150; //margin at top
const int leftmargin=15; //margin at left
const int levelmargin=380; //left margin for level number
const int scoremargin=500; //left margin for score
const int vertskip=40; //line height
```

A local variable buffer is used as a temporary text buffer, and i will be used as an index into it:

```
char buffer[16]; //temporary text buffer
int i=0;
```

A while loop is used to increment i through the high score list. Unused entries at the end of the high score list have a score of zero (which is not a legitimate score for entry into the high score list), so we break out of the while loop early when a score of zero is detected.

```
while(i<MAX_TOPSCORES&&m_pTopScore[i]>0){ //for each score
```

A local variable y is set to the vertical coordinate of the current line of text, which is the top margin (topmargin) plus enough vertical space for i lines of text (i*vertskip):

```
int y=topmargin+i*vertskip;
```

We use the text manager to jump to the left side of the page and draw the name:

```
Text->jump(leftmargin,y); //start of line
Text->draw(m_pNames[i],surface); //print name
```

Then we draw the level:

```
Text->jump(levelmargin,y); //start of line
sprintf(buffer,"%d",m_pTopLevel[i]); //convert to string
Text->draw(buffer,surface); //print score
```

Then we draw the score:

```
Text->jump(scoremargin,y); //start of line
sprintf(buffer,"%d",m_pTopScore[i]); //convert to string
Text->draw(buffer,surface); //print score
```

We increment i and continue around the while loop. When the loop is over, we return.

```
    i++;
  }
}
```

Loading an Entry from the Registry

The first CHighScoreList load function loads the high score list entry with a given index from the registry key with handle RegistryKey, which it assumes has already been opened for reading:

```
void CHighScoreList::load(HKEY RegistryKey,int index){
```

We declare a local variable length for the length of a registry value:

```
unsigned long length; //length of entry
```

Next we declare a text buffer of size BUFSIZE:

```
const int BUFSIZE=32; //buffer size
char buffer[BUFSIZE]; //text buffer
```

A local variable type will be used to store type information from the API function that reads from the registry, although we won't actually use it in this application:

```
DWORD type; //type of registry entry
```

A character array id will be used to store the name of a value in the registry. We fill it with a name constructed from the index parameter; for example, if index is zero, id will contain the string "Player0Name" (see the right pane of Figure 14.6).

```
char id[16]; //player name (identifier)
sprintf(id,"Player%dName",index); //create id
```

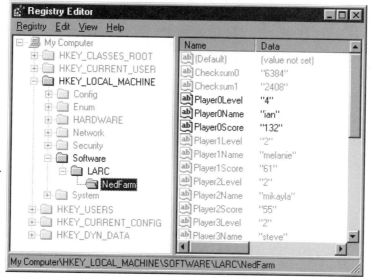

Figure 14.6
The values
for the
topmost high
score in the
registry

We set the local variable `length` to the length of the names in the high score list:

```
length=MAX_TOPSCORE_NAMELENGTH;
```

Now, we read a player name from the registry using the API function `RegQueryValueEx`. This function has six parameters. The first parameter is an open handle to a registry key, which was specified as parameter `RegistryKey`. The second parameter is the name of a value in that registry key which we constructed in the buffer `id`. The third parameter must be `NULL`. The fourth parameter is a pointer to a variable in which it will store type information; we will not use this information, being content to store everything as strings instead of using both strings and numbers.

```
RegQueryValueEx(RegistryKey,id,NULL,&type,
```

The fifth parameter is a pointer to where the contents of the registry value are to be written; we specify the start of the correct row of `m_pNames`. The sixth parameter is a pointer to a variable in which it will store the length of the string that it reads from the registry value.

```
(unsigned char *)(m_pNames[index]),&length);
```

We write a null character at the end of the player name to terminate the string, using the information placed in local variable `length` by the `RegQueryValueEx` function:

```
m_pNames[index][length]=0;
```

Next, we read the level from the registry. We begin by writing the name of the registry value into `id` (see Figure 14.6).

```
sprintf(id,"Player%dLevel",index);
```

We read the registry value into `buffer` this time:

```
length=BUFSIZE-1; buffer[0]=0;
RegQueryValueEx(RegistryKey,id,NULL,&type,
  (unsigned char *)buffer,&length);
```

If something of nonzero length was read, we parse it out of the buffer using the C standard library function `sscanf`:

```
if(length){
  buffer[length]=0;
  sscanf(buffer,"%d",&(m_pTopLevel[index]));
}
```

Otherwise, we use zero:

```
else m_pTopLevel[index]=0;
```

The level number is read from the registry similarly:

```
sprintf(id,"Player%dScore",index);
length=BUFSIZE-1; buffer[0]=0;
RegQueryValueEx(RegistryKey,id,NULL,&type,
  (unsigned char *)buffer,&length);
if(length){
  buffer[length]=0;
  sscanf(buffer,"%d",&(m_pTopScore[index]));
}
else m_pTopScore[index]=0;
}
```

Loading the High Score List from the Registry

The second `CHighScoreList load` function has no parameters. It loads the entire high score list from the registry. If the checksums do not match, it clears the high score list and saves it back to the registry to discourage tampering.

```
void CHighScoreList::load(){ //load from registry
```

A local variable `RegistryKey` will hold a handle to the *Ned's Turkey Farm* registry key:

```
HKEY RegistryKey;
```

We open the registry key using the Windows API `RegCreateKeyEx` function, which will open the registry key if it exists; if it doesn't exist, it will create it and then open it. The `RegCreateKeyEx` function has nine parameters, only four of which will actually be used. The first parameter is a predefined handle to the registry key HKEY_LOCAL_MACHINE.

```
int result=RegCreateKeyEx(HKEY_LOCAL_MACHINE,
```

The second parameter is a string containing the name of a subkey, which we set to SOFTWARE\LARC\NedFarm (notice the use of the double backslash in the code to get a single backslash character into the string). The third parameter must be zero, and the fourth parameter must be NULL. The fifth parameter is a set of options, which we will set to the default by using zero. The sixth parameter specifies the desired access rights, which we set to KEY_READ to get read access.

```
"SOFTWARE\\LARC\\NedFarm",0,NULL,0,KEY_READ,
```

The seventh parameter is a pointer to a security attributes structure, which we set to NULL because we don't need it. The eighth parameter is a pointer to a variable in which we want to place the registry handle which, in case you have forgotten it in this flurry of unused and unwanted parameters, is why we called this function in the first place. We won't use the last parameter, which the function uses to tell us whether or not the value actually existed, so we set it to NULL.

```
NULL,&RegistryKey,NULL);
```

RegCreateKeyEx will return ERROR_SUCCESS if it succeeds. If not, we bail out.

```
if(result!=ERROR_SUCCESS)return; //bail if failed
```

We use a for loop to load the individual registry entries using the other load function:

```
for(int i=0; i<MAX_TOPSCORES; i++)load(RegistryKey,i);
```

Next, we load the checksums and verify that they are OK. If not, we clear the high score list.

```
load_checksums(RegistryKey);
if(!checksums_ok())clear();
```

Finally, we close the registry key using the API function RegCloseKey. Don't forget to do this. You should be aware, however, that some versions of Windows will let you write to a registry key handle after you have closed it, which will cause major problems if another application has it open for writing at the same time.

```
RegCloseKey(RegistryKey);
}
```

The CHighScoreList load_checksums function loads the checksums from an open registry key handle RegistryKey:

```
void CHighScoreList::load_checksums(HKEY RegistryKey){
```

The local variables are similar to those used in the first `CHighScoreList load` function:

```
unsigned long length; //length of entry
const int BUFSIZE=32; //buffer size
char buffer[BUFSIZE]; //text buffer
DWORD type; //type of registry entry
```

We read the first checksum from registry value `Checksum0` into member variable `m_nChecksum0` using code that is similar to that used in the first `CHighScoreList load` function.

```
length=BUFSIZE-1; buffer[0]=0;
RegQueryValueEx(RegistryKey,"Checksum0",NULL,&type,
  (unsigned char *)buffer,&length);
if(length){
  buffer[length]=0;
  sscanf(buffer,"%d",&m_nChecksum0);
}
else m_nChecksum0=0;
```

Similarly, we read the second checksum from registry value `Checksum1` into member variable `m_nChecksum1`.

```
length=BUFSIZE-1; buffer[0]=0;
RegQueryValueEx(RegistryKey,"Checksum1",NULL,&type,
  (unsigned char *)buffer,&length);
if(length){
  buffer[length]=0;
  sscanf(buffer,"%d",&m_nChecksum1);
}
else m_nChecksum1=0;
}
```

Saving an Entry to the Registry

The first `CHighScoreList save` function saves the high score list entry with a given `index` to the registry key with handle `RegistryKey`, which it assumes has already been opened for writing:

```
void CHighScoreList::save(HKEY RegistryKey,int index){
```

The local variables `buffer` and `id` are the same as used in the first `CHighScoreList load` function:

```
const int BUFSIZE=32; //buffer size
char buffer[BUFSIZE]; //text buffer
char id[16]; //player name (identifier)
```

Once again, we use `sprintf` to create the registry value's name in `id`:

```
sprintf(id,"Player%dName",index);
```

We write the string m_pNames[index] into the registry using the Windows API RegSetValueEx function. RegSetValueEx has six parameters. The first parameter is a registry key handle, which was provided as a parameter. The second is a pointer to the string to be written, which in this case is id. The third parameter must be zero. The fourth parameter is a code that specifies the type of data pointed to by id, which is a null-terminated string, indicated by REG_SZ.

```
RegSetValueEx(RegistryKey,id,NULL,REG_SZ,
```

The fifth parameter is a pointer to the place that we want to save the data from, in this case the player name from the entry in the high score list given by the parameter index. The sixth parameter is the length in bytes of the data to be written to the registry, which in this case is the length of the string m_pNames[index] plus an extra byte for the null character at the end of the string.

```
(unsigned char *)m_pNames[index],strlen(m_pNames[index])+1);
```

Having saved the player name, we next save the level number m_pTopLevel[index]:

```
sprintf(id,"Player%dLevel",index);
sprintf(buffer,"%d",m_pTopLevel[index]);
RegSetValueEx(RegistryKey,id,NULL,REG_SZ,
  (unsigned char *)buffer,strlen(buffer)+1);
```

Finally, we save the score m_pTopScore[index] in the same manner:

```
sprintf(id,"Player%dScore",index);
sprintf(buffer,"%d",m_pTopScore[index]);
RegSetValueEx(RegistryKey,id,NULL,REG_SZ,
  (unsigned char *)buffer,strlen(buffer)+1);
}
```

Saving the High Score List to the Registry

The second CHighScoreList save function has no parameters. It saves the entire high score list to the registry.

```
void CHighScoreList::save(){ //save all data in registry
```

The local variable RegistryKey will hold a handle to the *Ned's Turkey Farm* registry key:

```
HKEY RegistryKey;
```

We open the registry key using the Windows API RegCreateKeyEx function. This time it is opened using the KEY_WRITE parameter instead of the KEY_READ parameter that was used in the second CHighScoreList load function. Again, we bail out if it fails.

```
int result=RegCreateKeyEx(HKEY_LOCAL_MACHINE,
```

```
"SOFTWARE\\LARC\\NedFarm",0,NULL,0,KEY_WRITE,
  NULL,&RegistryKey,NULL);
if(result!=ERROR_SUCCESS)return; //bail if failed
```

We use a `for` loop to save the individual registry entries. Then, we save the checksums.

```
for(int i=0; i<MAX_TOPSCORES; i++)save(RegistryKey,i);
save_checksums(RegistryKey);
```

Finally, we close the registry key handle and return:

```
RegCloseKey(RegistryKey);
}
```

If you've paid attention to all of the functions that load and save the high score list to the registry, then the `CHighScoreList save_checksums` function should contain no surprises for you:

```
void CHighScoreList::save_checksums(HKEY RegistryKey){
//save checksums to registry
  const int BUFSIZE=32; //buffer size
  char buffer[BUFSIZE]; //text buffer
  //checksum0
  sprintf(buffer,"%d",m_nChecksum0);
  RegSetValueEx(RegistryKey,"Checksum0",NULL,REG_SZ,
    (unsigned char *)buffer,strlen(buffer)+1);
  //checksum1
  sprintf(buffer,"%d",m_nChecksum1);
  RegSetValueEx(RegistryKey,"Checksum1",NULL,REG_SZ,
    (unsigned char *)buffer,strlen(buffer)+1);
}
```

The Made_the_grade Function

The `CHighScoreList made_the_grade` function returns `TRUE` if the score is high enough to make the high score list. We need only return `TRUE` if `score` is greater than the last score in the high score list, `m_pTopScore[MAX_TOP-SCORES-1]`. Notice that this works even if the high score list is not completely full, since the unused entries are filled with zero in the `CHighScoreList` constructor and `clear` function.

```
BOOL CHighScoreList::made_the_grade(int score){
//TRUE if entry fits in table
  return score>m_pTopScore[MAX_TOPSCORES-1];
}
```

The Checksums

`CHighScoreList` has four functions that assist in computing the checksums: `enumerate`, `checksum0`, `checksum1`, and `checksums_ok`. Each checksum turns the high score list into a 16-bit integer. Most checksums used in the industry simply take the exclusive-or of the integer or byte data. We will use a slightly more sophisticated technique that makes it difficult to determine from the registry data how to compute the checksum, even if your adversary knows the algorithm we are going to use. The only feasible way to figure it out (without the aid of this book) would be to disassemble *Ned's Turkey Farm* and extract the exact prime numbers that we have used from the code. Thus, although this method is of little use against a *real* hacker, it does guard against a casual attack.

Why use two checksums instead of one? To be sure, to be sure.

Function `enumerate` turns the high score list into a 16-bit integer by adding together all of the bytes in the names, and all of the scores and levels. It masks off the least significant 16 bits after each entry has been added into the sum.

```
int CHighScoreList::enumerate(){
```

It has three local variables: `result` for the return result, `i` to index the entry in the high score list, and `j` to index a character within an entry's name:

```
int result=0,i,j;
```

We declare a constant `mask` consisting of 16 high-order zeros and 16 low-order ones:

```
const int mask=0xFFFF; //mask for lower 16 bits
```

We loop through the entries of the high score list with a `for` loop on the index `i`:

```
for(i=0; i<MAX_TOPSCORES; i++){
```

Then we loop through the characters of the ith name with a `while` loop on the index `j`, terminating early when the null character at the end of the string is found. We add the jth character of the ith name into `result`.

```
j=0;
while(m_pNames[i][j]!=0){result+=m_pNames[i][j]; j++;}
```

When the `while` loop terminates, we add in the score and level, then mask off the least-significant 16 bits:

```
result+=m_pTopScore[i]+m_pTopLevel[i]; //score and level
result&=mask; //mask off lower 16 bits
}
```

When the `for` loop terminates, we return `result`:

```
return result;
}
```

The `CHighScoreList` `checksum0` and `checksum1` functions return a checksum by taking the result of `enumerate`, multiplying by a prime and taking the remainder modulo another prime. The functions are very similar, so let's look at `checksum0` in particular. (Warning: Abstract algebra ahead—skip the rest of this paragraph unless you got an "A" in advanced algebra in college.) It maps the integer returned by `enumerate` uniformly into the interval $[0, \text{PRIME1}-1]$ because the set of integers modulo a prime number forms a finite field under the operations of addition and multiplication, and any number coprime to the modulus (for example, `PRIME0`) is a multiplicative generator of that field. It is a reasonably secure thing to do because inversion in finite fields is not something that the average person can do in their head. If you wanted to make this process cryptographically secure, however, you should use the discrete logarithm function instead, which is widely believed to be intractable. (As mentioned already, you should use 128-bit checksums too.)

```
int CHighScoreList::checksum0(){ //compute a checksum
  return enumerate()*PRIME0%PRIME1;
}

int CHighScoreList::checksum1(){ //compute a checksum
  return enumerate()^PRIME2%PRIME3;
}
```

Function `checksums_ok` returns `TRUE` if the checksums in `m_nChecksum0` and `m_nChecksum1` are consistent with the checksums computed directly from the high score list:

```
BOOL CHighScoreList::checksums_ok(){ //TRUE if checksums are OK
  return m_nChecksum0==checksum0()&&m_nChecksum1==checksum1();
}
```

Entering the Player's Name

The remaining four `CHighScoreList` public member functions (`append_to_current`, `delete_from_current`, `cancel_current`, and `current_name`) deal with entering the player's name into the `CHighScoreList` private name buffer `m_szNamebuffer`. Function `append_to_current` has a character `c` as its parameter. It is used when the player types the letter `c` so that we can enter it at the end of the name we are accumulating in `m_szNamebuffer`.

```
BOOL CHighScoreList::append_to_current(char c){
```

The first thing we do is to check that there is space remaining in the name buffer. We check that `m_nNamesize` is less than `MAX_TOPSCORE_NAMELENGTH-1`, not `MAX_TOPSCORE_NAMELENGTH` because we need to leave space for the null character at the end of the string.

```
if(m_nNamesize<MAX_TOPSCORE_NAMELENGTH-1){ //if there is room
```

If there is room, we append the character to the end of the name buffer, then put a null character after it and return TRUE:

```
    m_szNamebuffer[m_nNamesize++]=c; //append character
    m_szNamebuffer[m_nNamesize]=0x00; //null at end
    return TRUE; //success
  }
```

Otherwise, there's no room so we return FALSE:

```
    else return FALSE; //no room
  }
```

The CHighScoreList delete_from_current function deletes the last character from the name buffer:

```
  BOOL CHighScoreList::delete_from_current(){
```

It first checks that the name buffer actually has something in it:

```
    if(m_nNamesize>0)
```

If it does, it decrements the counter and places a null character over the character that was in that place in the name buffer, effectively deleting it:

```
    m_szNamebuffer[--m_nNamesize]=0x00; //back off & put a null
```

Otherwise, the name buffer was empty, so we should return FALSE. The setting of m_nNamesize to zero is defensive coding; it should never need to happen.

```
    else{
      m_nNamesize=0; //fell off beginning of string
      return FALSE; //deletion didn't happen
    }
```

If we made it this far, we should return TRUE:

```
    return TRUE; //deletion actually happened
  }
```

The CHighScoreList cancel_current function clears the name buffer by setting the counter m_nNamesize to zero and placing a null character in the first place:

```
  void CHighScoreList::cancel_current(){ //clear the current name
    m_szNamebuffer[m_nNamesize=0]=0;
  }
```

The CHighScoreList current_name function is a simple reader function that returns a pointer to the name buffer:

```
  char* CHighScoreList::current_name(){ //return current name
    return m_szNamebuffer;
  }
```

Changes to the Input Manager

Changes to the input manager involve responding to keystrokes when the user types their name during the new high score phase, and saving the device used to play the game (keyboard, mouse, or joystick) in the registry.

Declarations

CInputManager has four new private member functions, listed in Input.h. Function letter returns TRUE if keystroke is a letter (either upper- or lowercase), and function number returns TRUE if keystroke is a digit.

```
BOOL letter(WPARAM keystroke); //keystroke is a letter
BOOL number(WPARAM keystroke); //keystroke is a digit
```

Functions init_input_device and set_input_device load and save the last used device from and to the registry, respectively:

```
void init_input_device(); //get last used device
void set_input_device(); //put last used device
```

Function NewhighscoreKeyboard is the keyboard handler for the new high score phase:

```
void NewhighscoreKeyboard(WPARAM keystroke); //keyboard handler
```

Storing the Device in the Registry

The first changes to the CInputManager code in Input.cpp involve loading and saving the input device to the registry. In the constructor, we replace the line of code that set private member variable InputDevice to KEYBOARD_INPUT with a line of code that calls the new private member function init_input_device. This function sets InputDevice using the information that *Ned's Turkey Farm* left in the registry the last time it was played.

```
init_input_device(); //current input device
```

The CInputManager init_input_device function loads the input device from the registry:

```
void CInputManager::init_input_device(){
```

Local variables declared in init_input_device include a handle to the registry key RegistryKey and a character buffer:

```
HKEY RegistryKey; //registry key
const int BUFSIZE=8; //buffer size
char buffer[BUFSIZE]; //text buffer
```

We open the registry key with a call to `RegCreateKeyEx`. The call is similar to the one we used in the `CHighScoreList load` function, except that here we open `HKEY_CURRENT_USER` instead of `HKEY_LOCAL_MACHINE`.

```
int result=RegCreateKeyEx(HKEY_CURRENT_USER,
  "SOFTWARE\\LARC\\NedFarm",0,NULL,0,KEY_READ,
  NULL,&RegistryKey,NULL);
```

A local variable `type` will store the type of the registry entry:

```
DWORD type; //type of registry entry
```

We check that the registry entry was opened or created successfully:

```
if(result==ERROR_SUCCESS){ //entry exists
```

If so, we create a local variable `length` for the length of the string loaded from the registry, and set the buffer to empty in case something goes wrong:

```
unsigned long length=BUFSIZE-1; buffer[0]=0;
```

We use the API function `RegQueryValueEx` to read value `InputDevice` from the registry key:

```
RegQueryValueEx(RegistryKey,"InputDevice",NULL,&type,
    (unsigned char *)buffer,&length); //get value into buffer
```

If something of nonzero length was put into `buffer`, we parse the number into the member variable `InputDevice` using `sscanf`:

```
if(length){ //success
  buffer[length]=0; sscanf(buffer,"%d",&InputDevice);
}
```

Otherwise, either the call to `RegQueryValueEx` failed, or the registry key did not exist and was created empty (which happens the first time Demo 12 is played), so we default to keyboard input:

```
else InputDevice=KEYBOARD_INPUT; //default to keyboard input
```

Finally, we close the registry key:

```
    RegCloseKey(RegistryKey);
  }
}
```

The `CInputManager set_input_device` function saves the input device to the registry:

```
void CInputManager::set_input_device(){
```

It begins with a local variable `RegistryKey` to store a handle to the registry key:

```
HKEY RegistryKey; //registry key
```

We open the registry key with a call to `RegCreateKeyEx`, this time opening with the `KEY_WRITE` parameter so we can write to the registry:

```
int result=RegCreateKeyEx(HKEY_CURRENT_USER,
  "SOFTWARE\\LARC\\NedFarm",0,NULL,0,KEY_WRITE,
  NULL,&RegistryKey,NULL);
```

We check that the registry entry was opened or created successfully:

```
if(result==ERROR_SUCCESS){ //entry exists
```

If so, we create a text buffer and print the input device there:

```
const int BUFSIZE=16; //buffer size
char buffer[BUFSIZE]; //text buffer
sprintf(buffer,"%d",InputDevice); //convert to string
```

Finally, we write the contents of the text buffer to the registry value `InputDevice`, and close the registry key:

```
RegSetValueEx(RegistryKey,"InputDevice",NULL,REG_SZ,
  (unsigned char *)buffer,strlen(buffer)+1); //set value
RegCloseKey(RegistryKey);
  }
}
```

The Keyboard Handler

The `CInputManager MainMenuKeyboard` function, the keyboard handler for the main menu, has a new `case` in its `switch` statement for the High Score List button, the keyboard equivalent for which is the "L" key. All it has to do is to signal the end of the phase and set the next phase to the high score phase.

```
case 'L': //see high score list
  NextPhase=HIGHSCORE_PHASE; endphase=TRUE;
  break;
```

The device menu keyboard handler has a new line of code to save the device setting to the registry when the player exits from the device menu. Notice that we only have to put this line of code in the device menu keyboard handler and not in the mouse handler because of our design decision (discussed in Chapter 11) to make all of the other device handlers call the keyboard handler to perform the actual work. The new line of code goes in the "exit" case (VK_ESCAPE and 'D') of the switch statement.

```
set_input_device(); //save new input device to registry
```

The `CInputManager letter` and `number` functions return `TRUE` if keystroke is a letter and a digit, respectively:

```
BOOL CInputManager::letter(WPARAM keystroke){
  return keystroke>='A'&&keystroke<='Z';
```

```
}

BOOL CInputManager::number(WPARAM keystroke){
  return keystroke>='0'&&keystroke<='9';
}
```

The `CInputManager` new high score list keyboard handler `Newhighscore-Keyboard` handles the process of the player typing in his or her name to the high score list:

```
void CInputManager::NewhighscoreKeyboard(WPARAM keystroke){
```

A series of `if` statements handles different kinds of characters. If the keystroke is a letter, we attempt to insert it into the name buffer held by the high score manager.

```
if(letter(keystroke)){ //enter a letter
  if(HighScoreList.append_to_current(keystroke-'A'+'a'))
```

If the insertion succeeds, we play a sound. The test prevents the sound from being played when the name buffer is full.

```
    SoundManager->play(TYPE_CHAR_SOUND);
}
```

Numeric characters are handled similarly:

```
else if(number(keystroke)){ //enter a numeric char
  if(HighScoreList.append_to_current(keystroke))
    SoundManager->play(TYPE_CHAR_SOUND);
}
```

A space character has its own sound:

```
else if(keystroke==VK_SPACE){ //enter a space
  if(HighScoreList.append_to_current(' '))
    SoundManager->play(TYPE_SPACE_SOUND);
}
```

The name is complete when the player hits the Enter key (whose virtual keycode is `VK_RETURN`), in which case we play a special sound and end the phase:

```
else if(keystroke==VK_RETURN){ //end of name
  SoundManager->play(TYPE_RETURN_SOUND); endphase=TRUE;
}
```

If the player hits the Delete key, we remove the last character from the name:

```
else if(keystroke==VK_DELETE){ //delete a char
  if(HighScoreList.delete_from_current())
    SoundManager->play(TYPE_SPACE_SOUND);
}
```

Finally, the player can abort the whole process (meaning that nothing goes into the high score list) by hitting the Escape key.

```
else if(keystroke==VK_ESCAPE){ //abort
  HighScoreList.cancel_current(); endphase=TRUE;
}
}
```

The `CInputManager` main keyboard handler `Keyboard` has a new `case` label added to the list of phases that call the `IntroKeyboard` function. (The same thing gets added to the `LMouseUp` and `Joystick` functions, too.)

```
case HIGHSCORE_PHASE:
```

It also has a new `case` for the new high score phase, which passes the keystroke to the `NewhighscoreKeyboard` member function to do the real work:

```
case NEWHIGHSCORE_PHASE:
  NewhighscoreKeyboard(keystroke);
  break;
```

Changes to Main.cpp

Changes to `Main.cpp` begin with the declaration of a pointer to a bmp file reader for the new high score background. This background is to be displayed while the player types in their name for a new entry into the high score list. Why does it get its own permanent file reader while other backgrounds, such as the menu screens, use a local variable in the `display_screen` function? The answer is that we will redraw the background to the new high score list in order to remove any deleted characters. It is a bit wasteful to redraw the whole screen, but there's not much else going on at the same time, so it's not really worth the trouble of writing custom code to redraw just the necessary rectangle.

```
CBmpFileReader *NewHighScoreBg; //new-high-score background
```

We also declare a high score list manager:

```
CHighScoreList HighScoreList; //high score list manager
```

The `LoadSounds` function has code added to `case 1` of the `switch` statement to load in new sounds:

```
SoundManager->load("congrats.wav");
SoundManager->load("twspace.wav",copies);
SoundManager->load("twret.wav",copies);
SoundManager->load("twchar.wav",copies);
```

Two New Display Functions

A new function `display_highscorelist` displays the high score list against a background drawn from the file with name `filename`:

```
void display_highscorelist(char *filename){ //display high scores
```

It calls the `display_screen` function to display the background:

```
display_screen(filename); //display background
```

It asks the high score manager to draw the text onto the secondary surface, then flips it to the screen:

```
HighScoreList.draw(lpSecondary); //draw high scores
PageFlip(); //flip to front surface
} //display_highscorelist
```

A new function `display_newhighscore` displays the new high score screen while the player types in their name. This function will be called repeatedly to animate the characters as the player types them.

```
void display_newhighscore(){ //display new high score entry page
```

The API function `Sleep` is used to slow down the animation, since there is really not much going on here. A frame rate of at most 20 frames per second is high enough.

```
Sleep(50); //slow down the animation
```

We draw the background from the bmp file reader pointer to by `NewHighScoreBg` to the secondary surface:

```
NewHighScoreBg->draw(lpSecondary); //draw background
```

Next, we jump to the correct place on the screen and draw the player name that has been partially typed in by the player, which we obtain from the high score manager `HighScoreList`. It will appear on a signpost near the bottom of the screen, as shown in Figure 14.7.

```
Text->jump(163,330);
Text->draw(HighScoreList.current_name(),lpSecondary);
```

Then, we flip it to the screen and return:

```
PageFlip(); //display it
} //display_newhighscore
```

Figure 14.7
The new high score screen from Newhsc.bmp

The Change_phase Function

The change_phase function has new code to deal with changing into and out of the two new phases, HIGHSCORE_PHASE and NEWHIGHSCORE_PHASE. When changing into MENU_PHASE, the secondary switch statement based on the previous phase needs a new case for coming out of NEWHIGHSCORE_PHASE, in which we delete the bmp file reader for the new high score background.

```
case NEWHIGHSCORE_PHASE:
  delete NewHighScoreBg; //delete background
  break;
}
```

We also add two new cases for the later switch statement for turning on the mouse cursor when entering MENU_PHASE. The switch statement in its entirety, including the two new cases, is now as follows.

```
switch(GamePhase){ //what phase did we come in from?
  case PLAYING_PHASE:
  case TITLE_PHASE:
  case HIGHSCORE_PHASE:
  case NEWHIGHSCORE_PHASE:
    ShowCursor(TRUE); //activate the mouse cursor
    break;
}
```

Two new cases are also added to the primary switch statement. The first is for entering HIGHSCORE_PHASE, in which we hide the mouse cursor and call the `display_highscorelist` function to display the high score list with a background from file `Hscore.bmp` (as shown in Figure 14.5).

```
case HIGHSCORE_PHASE: //display high score list
  ShowCursor(FALSE); //hide the cursor
  display_highscorelist("hscore.bmp"); //display high scores
  break;
```

The second new `case` is for entering `NEWHIGHSCORE_PHASE`:

```
case NEWHIGHSCORE_PHASE: //display high score list
```

We stop all currently playing sounds and play a congratulatory sound:

```
SoundManager->stop(); //stop sounds from previous phase
SoundManager->play(CONGRATS_SOUND); //play new sound
```

We create a new bmp file reader for the new high score background and load the background from `Newhsc.bmp` (as shown in Figure 14.7):

```
NewHighScoreBg=new CBmpFileReader; //background
NewHighScoreBg->load("newhsc.bmp"); //read from file
```

We then draw this background to the secondary surface, set the palette (which can be different from all of the other palettes to allow the artist to give it a different ambiance), and flip it to the screen:

```
NewHighScoreBg->draw(lpSecondary); //draw to back surface
NewHighScoreBg->setpalette(lpPrimaryPalette); //palette
PageFlip(); //display it
break;
```

The Redraw and ProcessFrame Functions

The `Redraw` function has two new `cases` for the new phases. The `case` for the `HIGHSCORE_PHASE` calls `display_highscorelist` to redisplay the high scores list with a background from `Hscore.bmp`.

```
case HIGHSCORE_PHASE:
  display_highscorelist("hscore.bmp"); //display high scores
  break;
```

The `case` for `NEWHIGHSCORE_PHASE` resets the palette and calls the `display_newhighscore` function:

```
case NEWHIGHSCORE_PHASE:
  NewHighScoreBg->setpalette(lpPrimaryPalette); //palette
  display_newhighscore();
  break;
```

Changes to function `ProcessFrame` begin with code that allows the successful player to add their name to the high score list at the end of the playing phase. We already have code that changes to SUCCESS_PHASE on the successful completion of a level.

```
if(ObjectManager.won()) //completed level
  change_phase(SUCCESS_PHASE);
```

We add an else clause to this if statement. In it, we check to see whether the phase ended for some other reason (such as escaping out of the game or being killed once too often):

```
else if(endphase){ //quit or died too often
```

If so, we then check that the player has lives remaining (dead players tell no tales) and has a score high enough to get into the high score list:

```
if(ScoreManager.lives()>=0&&
    HighScoreList.made_the_grade(ScoreManager.score()))
```

If so, then we change to NEWHIGHSCORE_PHASE:

```
change_phase(NEWHIGHSCORE_PHASE); //user enters name
```

If not, the player gets dumped back at the main menu:

```
else change_phase(MENU_PHASE); //quit, go to menu
}
```

ProcessFrame also has two new cases to allow it to process frames for the new phases. In HIGHSCORE_PHASE we check whether the phase has ended, and if so, go to MENU_PHASE.

```
case HIGHSCORE_PHASE: //displaying high scores
  Sleep(100); //surrender time to other processes
  if(endphase)change_phase(MENU_PHASE); //quit, go to menu
  break;
```

In NEWHIGHSCORE_PHASE, we display a frame of animation for the new high score entry, showing the characters appear and disappear as the player types and deletes them:

```
case NEWHIGHSCORE_PHASE:
  display_newhighscore(); //animate user typing in name
```

We check for the end of the phase, and when it comes, we direct the high score manager to insert the new high score into the high score list, then we change phases to the main menu:

```
if(endphase){ //insert new high score
  HighScoreList.insert(level,ScoreManager.score());
  change_phase(MENU_PHASE); //go to menu
}
break;
```

Demo 12 Files

Code Files

The following files in Demo 12 are used without change from Demo 11:

- Ai.h
- Ai.cpp
- Bmp.h
- Bmp.cpp
- Bsprite.h
- Bsprite.cpp
- Buttons.h
- Buttons.cpp
- Csprite.h
- Csprite.cpp
- Ddsetup.cpp
- Joystick.h
- Joystick.cpp
- Objects.h
- Objects.cpp
- Objman.h
- Objman.cpp
- Random.h
- Random.cpp
- Sbmp.h
- Sbmp.cpp
- Score.h
- Score.cpp
- Sound.h
- Sound.cpp
- Text.h
- Text.cpp
- Timer.h
- Timer.cpp

- View.h
- View.cpp

The following files in Demo 12 have been modified from Demo 11:

- Defines.h
- Input.h
- Input.cpp
- Main.cpp
- Sndlist.h

The following files are new in Demo 12:

- Topscore.h
- Topscore.cpp

Media Files

The following image files are new in Demo 12:

- Hscore.bmp
- Hewhsc.bmp

The following sound files are new in Demo 12:

- Congrats.wav
- Twchar.wav
- Twret.wav
- Twspace.wav

Required Libraries

- Ddraw.lib
- Dsound.lib
- Winmm.lib

Code Listings

Defines.h

```
//defines.h: essential defines
//Copyright Ian Parberry, 1999
//Last updated February 10, 2000

#ifndef __DEFINES_H__
#define __DEFINES_H__

#define SCREEN_WIDTH 640 //pixels wide
#define SCREEN_HEIGHT 480 //pixels high
#define COLORS 256 //number of colors
#define COLOR_DEPTH 8 //number of bits to store colors
#define TRANSPARENT_COLOR 255 //transparent palette position

enum GamePhaseType{
  LOGO_PHASE,TITLE_PHASE,MENU_PHASE,PLAYING_PHASE,
  DEVICEMENU_PHASE,SUCCESS_PHASE,HIGHSCORE_PHASE,
  NEWHIGHSCORE_PHASE
};

enum
InputDeviceType{KEYBOARD_INPUT=0,MOUSE_INPUT,JOYSTICK_INPUT};

#endif
```

Input.h

```
//input.h: header file for input class

//Copyright Ian Parberry, 1999
//Last updated March 17, 2000

#include <windows.h>
#include <windowsx.h>

#include "defines.h"
#include "buttons.h" //for button manager
#include "joystick.h" //for joystick manager


#ifndef __INPUT_H__
#define __INPUT_H__

class CInputManager{
  private:
    InputDeviceType InputDevice; //current input device
    CButtonManager *ButtonManager; //for managing menu buttons
```

```
    CJoystickManager JoystickManager; //joystick manager
    //helper functions
    BOOL is_function_key(WPARAM keystroke); //TRUE if fn key
    void decode(LPARAM lparam,POINT &point); //decode mouse click
    void set_plane_speed(POINT point,SIZE extent);
    //for text input
    BOOL letter(WPARAM keystroke); //keystroke is a letter
    BOOL number(WPARAM keystroke); //keystroke is a digit
    //setting of input device from registry
    void init_input_device(); //get last used device
    void set_input_device(); //put last used device
    //set up buttons for menus
    void SetupMainMenuButtons(); //main menu button manager
    void SetupDeviceMenuButtons(); //device menu button manager
    //keyboard handlers
    void IntroKeyboard(WPARAM keystroke); //keyboard handler
    BOOL MainMenuKeyboard(WPARAM keystroke); //keyboard handler
    void DeviceMenuKeyboard(WPARAM keystroke); //keyboard handler
    void NewhighscoreKeyboard(WPARAM keystroke); //keybd handler
    void GameKeyboard(WPARAM keystroke); //keyboard handler
    //left mouse button down handlers
    void MainMenuLMouseDown(POINT point); //mouse down handler
    void DeviceMenuLMouseDown(POINT point); //mouse down handler
    void GameLMouseDown(POINT point); //mouse down handler
    //left mouse button up handlers
    void IntroLMouseUp(POINT point); //mouse up handler
    BOOL MainMenuLMouseUp(POINT point); //mouse up handler
    void DeviceMenuLMouseUp(POINT point); //mouse up handler
    //joystick handlers
    void IntroJoystick(); //joystick handler
    void GameJoystick(); //joystick handler
  public:
    CInputManager(); //constructor
    ~CInputManager(); //destructor
    BOOL Restore(); //restore surfaces
    void Release(); //release surfaces
    void SetupButtons(GamePhaseType phase); //set up menu buttons
    BOOL Keyboard(WPARAM keystroke,
    BOOL virtual_keystroke=FALSE); //keyboard handler
    void LMouseDown(LPARAM lparam); //main mouse down handler
    BOOL LMouseUp(LPARAM lparam); //main mouse up handler
    void MouseMove(LPARAM lparam); //handle mouse motion
    void Joystick(); //main joystick handler
};

#endif
```

Input.cpp

```
//input.cpp: program file for input class

//Copyright Ian Parberry, 1999
//Last updated March 17, 2000

#include <stdio.h> //for sscanf, sprintf

#include "input.h"
#include "objman.h" //for object manager
#include "sound.h" //for sound manager
#include "topscore.h" //for high score list

extern BOOL show_framerate;

extern GamePhaseType GamePhase; //current phase
extern GamePhaseType NextPhase; //next phase of game
extern BOOL endphase; //should we abort current phase?
extern CObjectManager ObjectManager; //object manager
extern CSoundManager* SoundManager; //sound manager
extern CHighScoreList HighScoreList; //high score list manager

CInputManager::CInputManager(){ //constructor
  init_input_device(); //current input device
  ButtonManager=NULL; //for managing menu buttons
  JoystickManager.initialize(); //set up joystick
  JoystickManager.autorepeat(FALSE); //disable autorepeat
}

CInputManager::~CInputManager(){ //destructor
  delete ButtonManager;
}

BOOL CInputManager::Restore(){ //restore surfaces
  return ButtonManager->Restore();
}

void CInputManager::Release(){ //release surfaces
    ButtonManager->Release();
}

void CInputManager::SetupMainMenuButtons(){
//set up main menu button manager
  const int YDELTA=70; //y separation between buttons
  const int BUTTONCOUNT=6; //number of buttons
  SIZE size; //size of buttons
  size.cx=40; size.cy=40; //size of buttons
  POINT point; //top left corner of first button
  point.x=111; point.y=46; //first button location
```

```
    delete ButtonManager; //delete any old one
    ButtonManager=new //create new button manager
      CButtonManager(BUTTONCOUNT,size,point,YDELTA,
        "buttons.bmp");
  //set button sounds
    ButtonManager->
      setsounds(BIGCLICK_SOUND,SMALLCLICK_SOUND);
}

void CInputManager::SetupDeviceMenuButtons(){
//set up device menu button manager
  const int BUTTONCOUNT=4;
  delete ButtonManager; //if there is one already, delete it
  SIZE size; //size of buttons
  size.cx=40; size.cy=40; //size of buttons
  ButtonManager=new
    CButtonManager(BUTTONCOUNT,size,"buttons.bmp");
  ButtonManager->setsounds(BIGCLICK_SOUND,SMALLCLICK_SOUND);
  ButtonManager->set_radio(); //radio buttons
  //add buttons
  POINT point;
  point.x=209; point.y=130;
  ButtonManager->addbutton(point);
  point.x=209; point.y=210;
  ButtonManager->addbutton(point);
  point.x=209; point.y=291;
  ButtonManager->addbutton(point);
  point.x=209; point.y=372;
  ButtonManager->addbutton(point);
  //initialize image of radio button
  ButtonManager->buttondown(InputDevice,FALSE); //no sound
}

void CInputManager::SetupButtons(GamePhaseType phase){
//set up menu buttons
  switch(phase){
    case MENU_PHASE: SetupMainMenuButtons(); break;
    case DEVICEMENU_PHASE: SetupDeviceMenuButtons(); break;
  }
}

//registry access for current input device

void CInputManager::init_input_device(){
//get last used device from registry
  HKEY RegistryKey; //registry key
  const int BUFSIZE=8; //buffer size
  char buffer[BUFSIZE]; //text buffer
  int result=RegCreateKeyEx(HKEY_CURRENT_USER,
    "SOFTWARE\\LARC\\NedFarm",0,NULL,0,KEY_READ,
```

```
      NULL,&RegistryKey,NULL);
    DWORD type; //type of registry entry
    if(result==ERROR_SUCCESS){ //entry exists
      unsigned long length=BUFSIZE-1; buffer[0]=0;
      RegQueryValueEx(RegistryKey,"InputDevice",NULL,&type,
        (unsigned char *)buffer,&length); //get value into buffer
      if(length){ //success
        buffer[length]=0; sscanf(buffer,"%d",&InputDevice);
      }
      else InputDevice=KEYBOARD_INPUT; //default to keyboard input
      RegCloseKey(RegistryKey);
    }
}

void CInputManager::set_input_device(){
//save last used device to registry
  HKEY RegistryKey; //registry key
  int result=RegCreateKeyEx(HKEY_CURRENT_USER,
    "SOFTWARE\\LARC\\NedFarm",0,NULL,0,KEY_WRITE,
    NULL,&RegistryKey,NULL);
  if(result==ERROR_SUCCESS){ //entry exists
    const int BUFSIZE=16; //buffer size
    char buffer[BUFSIZE]; //text buffer
    sprintf(buffer,"%d",InputDevice); //convert to string
    RegSetValueEx(RegistryKey,"InputDevice",NULL,REG_SZ,
      (unsigned char *)buffer,strlen(buffer)+1); //set value
    RegCloseKey(RegistryKey);
  }
}

//keyboard handlers

void CInputManager::IntroKeyboard(WPARAM keystroke){
//keyboard handler for intro
  endphase=TRUE; //any key ends the phase
}

BOOL CInputManager::MainMenuKeyboard(WPARAM keystroke){
//keyboard handler for menu
  BOOL result=FALSE;
  switch(keystroke){
    case VK_ESCAPE:
    case 'Q': //exit the game
      result=TRUE;
      break;
    case 'N': //play new game
      NextPhase=PLAYING_PHASE; endphase=TRUE;
      break;
    case 'D':
      NextPhase=DEVICEMENU_PHASE; endphase=TRUE;
```

```
        break;
      case 'L': //see high score list
        NextPhase=HIGHSCORE_PHASE; endphase=TRUE;
        break;
      default: break; //do nothing
    }
    return result;
}

void CInputManager::DeviceMenuKeyboard(WPARAM keystroke){
//keyboard handler //for device menu
  switch(keystroke){
    case VK_ESCAPE:
    case 'D': //exit menu
      set_input_device(); //save new input device to registry
      endphase=TRUE;
      break;
    case 'K': //play using keyboard
      InputDevice=KEYBOARD_INPUT; //set device
      ButtonManager->buttondown(KEYBOARD_INPUT);
      break;
    case 'M': //play using mouse
      InputDevice=MOUSE_INPUT; //set device
      ButtonManager->buttondown(MOUSE_INPUT);
      break;
    case 'J': //play using joystick
      if(JoystickManager.exists()){ //if joystick exists
        InputDevice=JOYSTICK_INPUT;
        ButtonManager->buttondown(JOYSTICK_INPUT);
      }
      break;
    default: break;
  }
}

BOOL CInputManager::letter(WPARAM keystroke){
  return keystroke>='A'&&keystroke<='Z';
}

BOOL CInputManager::number(WPARAM keystroke){
  return keystroke>='0'&&keystroke<='9';
}

void CInputManager::NewhighscoreKeyboard(WPARAM keystroke){
  if(letter(keystroke)){ //enter a letter
    if(HighScoreList.append_to_current(keystroke-'A'+'a'))
      SoundManager->play(TYPE_CHAR_SOUND);
  }
  else if(number(keystroke)){ //enter a numeric char
    if(HighScoreList.append_to_current(keystroke))
```

```
          SoundManager->play(TYPE_CHAR_SOUND);
     }
   else if(keystroke==VK_SPACE){ //enter a space
     if(HighScoreList.append_to_current(' '))
       SoundManager->play(TYPE_SPACE_SOUND);
   }
   else if(keystroke==VK_RETURN){ //end of name
     SoundManager->play(TYPE_RETURN_SOUND); endphase=TRUE;
   }
   else if(keystroke==VK_DELETE){ //delete a char
     if(HighScoreList.delete_from_current())
       SoundManager->play(TYPE_SPACE_SOUND);
   }
   else if(keystroke==VK_ESCAPE){ //abort
     HighScoreList.cancel_current(); endphase=TRUE;
   }
}


void CInputManager::GameKeyboard(WPARAM keystroke){
//keyboard handler for game play
  switch(keystroke){
    case VK_ESCAPE: endphase=TRUE; break;
    case VK_F1: show_framerate=!show_framerate; break;
    case VK_UP: ObjectManager.accelerate(0,-1); break;
    case VK_DOWN: ObjectManager.accelerate(0,1); break;
    case VK_LEFT: ObjectManager.accelerate(-1,0); break;
    case VK_RIGHT: ObjectManager.accelerate(1,0); break;
    case VK_SPACE: ObjectManager.fire_gun(); break;
    default: break;
  }
}

BOOL CInputManager::is_function_key(WPARAM keystroke){
  return keystroke==VK_ESCAPE||
    (keystroke>=VK_F1&&keystroke<=VK_F12);
}

BOOL CInputManager::Keyboard(WPARAM keystroke,
  BOOL virtual_keystroke){ //keyboard handler
  BOOL result=FALSE;
  switch(GamePhase){
    case LOGO_PHASE:
    case TITLE_PHASE:
    case HIGHSCORE_PHASE:
    case SUCCESS_PHASE:
      IntroKeyboard(keystroke);
      break;
    case NEWHIGHSCORE_PHASE:
      NewhighscoreKeyboard(keystroke);
```

```
        break;
      case MENU_PHASE:
        result=MainMenuKeyboard(keystroke);
        break;
      case DEVICEMENU_PHASE:
        DeviceMenuKeyboard(keystroke);
        break;
      case PLAYING_PHASE:
        if(InputDevice==KEYBOARD_INPUT||
        is_function_key(keystroke)||virtual_keystroke)
          GameKeyboard(keystroke);
        break;
    }
    return result;
}


//mouse left button down handlers

void CInputManager::MainMenuLMouseDown(POINT point){
//mouse down handler for menu
  if(ButtonManager->hit(point)>=0) //if a valid hit
    ButtonManager->buttondown(point); //animate a button down
}

void CInputManager::DeviceMenuLMouseDown(POINT point){
//mouse down handler for device menu
  int hit=ButtonManager->hit(point);
  switch(hit){
    case 0: Keyboard('K'); break; //keyboard
    case 1: Keyboard('M'); break; //mouse
    case 2: Keyboard('J'); break; //joystick
    case 3:
      ButtonManager->buttondown(hit); //quit button down
      break;
    default: break;
  }
}

void CInputManager::GameLMouseDown(POINT point){
//mouse down handler for game
  Keyboard(VK_SPACE,TRUE);
}

void CInputManager::decode(LPARAM lparam,POINT &point){
//decode mouse click lparam to point
  point.x=LOWORD(lparam); point.y=HIWORD(lparam);
}

void CInputManager::LMouseDown(LPARAM lparam){
//main mouse left button down handler
```

```
      POINT point; //mouse location on screen
      decode(lparam,point); //decode mouse point
      switch(GamePhase){
        case MENU_PHASE:
          MainMenuLMouseDown(point);
          break;
        case DEVICEMENU_PHASE:
          DeviceMenuLMouseDown(point);
          break;
        case PLAYING_PHASE:
          if(InputDevice==MOUSE_INPUT)
            GameLMouseDown(point);
          break;
      }
    }


    //mouse left button up handlers

    void CInputManager::IntroLMouseUp(POINT point){
    //mouse left button up handler for intro
      endphase=TRUE;
    }


    BOOL CInputManager::MainMenuLMouseUp(POINT point){
    //mouse left button up handler for menu
      int hit=ButtonManager->release(point); //get button hit
      BOOL result=FALSE;
      //take action depending on which button was hit
      switch(hit){ //depending on which button was hit
        case 0: Keyboard('N'); break; //new game
        case 1: Keyboard('S'); break; //saved game
        case 2: Keyboard('D'); break; //devices
        case 3: Keyboard('L'); break; //high score list
        case 4: Keyboard('H'); break; //help
        case 5: result=Keyboard(VK_ESCAPE); break; //quit
        default: break;
      }
      //animate button images
      if(hit>=0)ButtonManager->buttonup(hit); //hit
      else ButtonManager->allbuttonsup(); //nonhit
      return result;
    }

    void CInputManager::DeviceMenuLMouseUp(POINT point){
    //mouse left button up handler for device menu
      int hit=ButtonManager->release(point);
      switch(hit){
        case 3: //quit button up
          ButtonManager->buttonup(hit); //show quit button up
          Keyboard(VK_ESCAPE);
```

```
        break;
    }
    if(hit<0)ButtonManager->allbuttonsup(); //no hit
}

BOOL CInputManager::LMouseUp(LPARAM lparam){
//main mouse left button up handler
    BOOL result=FALSE;
    POINT point; //mouse location on screen
    decode(lparam,point); //decode mouse point
    switch(GamePhase){
        case LOGO_PHASE:
        case TITLE_PHASE:
        case SUCCESS_PHASE:
        case HIGHSCORE_PHASE:
            IntroLMouseUp(point);
            break;
        case MENU_PHASE:
            result=MainMenuLMouseUp(point);
            break;
        case DEVICEMENU_PHASE:
            DeviceMenuLMouseUp(point);
            break;
    }
    return result;
}

//mouse motion handler

void CInputManager::set_plane_speed(POINT point,SIZE extent){
//set plane speed based on point's position in extent
    int xmin,xmax,ymin,ymax; //plane speed limits
    ObjectManager.speed_limits(xmin,xmax,ymin,ymax); //get them
    //bands for speed assignment
    const int XBANDWIDTH=extent.cx/(xmax-xmin+1);
    const int YBANDWIDTH=extent.cy/(ymax-ymin+1);
    int xspeed,yspeed; //speed of plane
    xspeed=point.x/XBANDWIDTH+xmin; //horizontal speed
    yspeed=point.y/YBANDWIDTH+ymin; //vertical speed
    ObjectManager.set_speed(xspeed,yspeed); //pass to plane
}

void CInputManager::MouseMove(LPARAM lparam){
    if(InputDevice!=MOUSE_INPUT)return; //bail if not needed
    if(GamePhase!=PLAYING_PHASE)return; //bail if not playing
    POINT point; //mouse location on screen
    decode(lparam,point); //decode mouse point
    //set extent
    SIZE extent; //extent that mouse moves in
    extent.cx=SCREEN_WIDTH;
```

```
    extent.cy=SCREEN_HEIGHT;
    //set plane speed based on point and extent
    set_plane_speed(point,extent);
}

//joystick handlers

void CInputManager::GameJoystick(){
//joystick handler for game play
  if(InputDevice!=JOYSTICK_INPUT)return; //bail if unneeded
  //buttons
  if(JoystickManager.button_down(1)) //button 1...
    Keyboard(VK_SPACE,TRUE); //...fires bullets
  //stick
  if(GamePhase!=PLAYING_PHASE)return; //bail if not playing
  POINT point; //coordinates of joystick
  JoystickManager.position(point); //get coordinates
  SIZE extent; //extent that joystick indicator moves in
  extent.cx=100; extent.cy=100; //set extent
  set_plane_speed(point,extent); //set plane speed
}

void CInputManager::IntroJoystick(){
//joystick handler for intro
  if(JoystickManager.button_down(1)) //click out
    Keyboard(VK_ESCAPE);
}

void CInputManager::Joystick(){ //main joystick handler
  JoystickManager.poll(); //poll joystick
  switch(GamePhase){ //call joystick handler for phase
    case PLAYING_PHASE: GameJoystick(); break;
    case LOGO_PHASE:
    case TITLE_PHASE:
    case SUCCESS_PHASE:
    case HIGHSCORE_PHASE:
      IntroJoystick(); break;
    case DEVICEMENU_PHASE:
    case MENU_PHASE:
      break; //do nothing
  }
}
```

Main.cpp

```
//main.cpp

//Copyright Ian Parberry, 1999
//Last updated March 27, 2000

//High score list kept in registry.  Two checksums are used to
//detect tampering. If tampering is detected, the high score
//list is cleared.  Note new code to (1) display high score
//list, (2) enter new name into high score list, (3) manage
//high score list using registry entry HKEY_LOCAL_MACHINE.

//The current input device is stored in the registry under
//HKEY_CURRENT_USER so that the device menu always starts with
//the device used the last time the game was played.

//system includes
#include <windows.h>
#include <windowsx.h>
#include <ddraw.h>
#include <stdio.h>

//system defines
#define WIN32_LEAN_AND_MEAN

//custom includes
#include "defines.h" //global definitions
#include "bmp.h" //bmp file reader
#include "timer.h" //game timer
#include "csprite.h" //for clipped sprite class
#include "objects.h" //for object class
#include "objman.h" //for object manager
#include "view.h" //for viewpoint class
#include "random.h" //for random number generator
#include "sound.h" //for sound manager
#include "input.h" //for input manager
#include "text.h" //for text sprite manager
#include "score.h" //for score manager
#include "topscore.h" //high score list

//defines
#define MAX_OBJECTS 32 //max number of objects in game

//globals

BOOL ActiveApp; //is this application active?

LPDIRECTDRAW lpDirectDrawObject=NULL; //direct draw object
LPDIRECTDRAWSURFACE lpPrimary=NULL; //primary surface
```

```
LPDIRECTDRAWPALETTE lpPrimaryPalette; //its palette
LPDIRECTDRAWSURFACE lpSecondary=NULL; //back buffer
LPDIRECTDRAWPALETTE lpSecondaryPalette; //its palette
LPDIRECTDRAWSURFACE lpBackground=NULL; //background image

CTimer Timer; //game timer

CBmpFileReader background; //background image
CBmpFileReader *NewHighScoreBg; //new-high-score background
CBmpSpriteFileReader g_cSpriteImages; //sprite images
CBmpSpriteFileReader g_cFrgndImages; //foreground images
CBmpSpriteFileReader g_cTextImages; //text images

CObjectManager ObjectManager(MAX_OBJECTS); //object manager

CClippedSprite *g_pSprite[NUM_SPRITES]; //sprites

CViewPoint Viewpoint; //player viewpoint
CRandom Random; //random number generator

GamePhaseType GamePhase; //current phase
GamePhaseType NextPhase; //next phase of game
BOOL endphase=FALSE; //should we abort current phase?
int PhaseTime=0; //time in phase
int level=1; //current level

BOOL show_framerate=FALSE; //TRUE to show the frame rate
int framerate_timer=0; //timer for updating frame rate display
int framecount=0; //number of frames in this interval (so far)
int last_framecount=0; //number of frames in last full interval

CSoundManager* SoundManager; //sound manager
CInputManager InputManager; //device input manager
CTextManager *Text; //text manager
CScoreManager ScoreManager; //score manager
CHighScoreList HighScoreList; //high score list manager

//helper functions
LPDIRECTDRAWPALETTE CreatePalette(LPDIRECTDRAWSURFACE surface);
BOOL InitDirectDraw(HWND hwnd);
HWND CreateDefaultWindow(char* name,HINSTANCE hInstance);

BOOL LoadPlaneSprite(){
  BOOL result=TRUE;
  result=result&&g_pSprite[PLANE_OBJECT]->
    load(&g_cSpriteImages,0,1,1);
  result=result&&g_pSprite[PLANE_OBJECT]->
    load(&g_cSpriteImages,1,123,1);
  result=result&&g_pSprite[PLANE_OBJECT]->
    load(&g_cSpriteImages,2,245,1);
```

```
    result=result&&g_pSprite[PLANE_OBJECT]->
      load(&g_cSpriteImages,3,367,1);
    result=result&&g_pSprite[PLANE_OBJECT]->
      load(&g_cSpriteImages,4,489,1);
    result=result&&g_pSprite[PLANE_OBJECT]->
      load(&g_cSpriteImages,5,17,74);
    return result;
} //LoadPlaneSprite

BOOL LoadDamagedPlaneSprite(){
    BOOL result=TRUE;
    result=result&&g_pSprite[DAMAGEDPLANE_OBJECT]->
      load(&g_cSpriteImages,0,387,288);
    result=result&&g_pSprite[DAMAGEDPLANE_OBJECT]->
      load(&g_cSpriteImages,1,509,288);
    return result;
} //LoadDamagedPlaneSprite

BOOL LoadExplodingPlaneSprite(){
    BOOL result=TRUE;
    result=result&&g_pSprite[EXPLODINGPLANE_OBJECT]->
      load(&g_cSpriteImages,0,139,74);
    result=result&&g_pSprite[EXPLODINGPLANE_OBJECT]->
      load(&g_cSpriteImages,1,261,74);
    result=result&&g_pSprite[EXPLODINGPLANE_OBJECT]->
      load(&g_cSpriteImages,2,383,74);
    result=result&&g_pSprite[EXPLODINGPLANE_OBJECT]->
      load(&g_cSpriteImages,3,505,74);
    return result;
} //LoadExplodingPlaneSprite

BOOL LoadDeadPlaneSprite(){
    return g_pSprite[DEADPLANE_OBJECT]->
      load(&g_cSpriteImages,0,120,237);
} //LoadDeadPlaneSprite

BOOL LoadCrowSprite(){
    BOOL result=TRUE;
    result=result&&g_pSprite[CROW_OBJECT]->
      load(&g_cSpriteImages,0,256,183); //frame 0
    result=result&&g_pSprite[CROW_OBJECT]->
      load(&g_cSpriteImages,1,320,183); //frame 1
    result=result&&g_pSprite[CROW_OBJECT]->
      load(&g_cSpriteImages,2,256,237); //frame 2
    result=result&&g_pSprite[CROW_OBJECT]->
      load(&g_cSpriteImages,3,323,237); //frame 3
    return result;
} //LoadCrowSprite

BOOL LoadFrgndSprites(){ //load foreground sprites
```

```
    BOOL result=TRUE;
    result=result&&g_pSprite[FARM_OBJECT]->
      load(&g_cFrgndImages,0,0,0); //load farm sprite
    result=result&&g_pSprite[FIELD_OBJECT]->
      load(&g_cFrgndImages,0,640,0); //load field sprite
    return result;
} //LoadFrgndSprites

BOOL LoadDeadCrowSprite(){ //load dead crow
  return g_pSprite[DEADCROW_OBJECT]->
    load(&g_cSpriteImages,0,453,230);
} //LoadDeadCrowSprite

BOOL LoadExplodingCrowSprite(){ //load exploding crow
    BOOL result=TRUE;
    result=result&&g_pSprite[EXPLODINGCROW_OBJECT]->
      load(&g_cSpriteImages,0,257,294);
    result=result&&g_pSprite[EXPLODINGCROW_OBJECT]->
      load(&g_cSpriteImages,1,321,294);
    result=result&&g_pSprite[EXPLODINGCROW_OBJECT]->
      load(&g_cSpriteImages,2,386,162);
    result=result&&g_pSprite[EXPLODINGCROW_OBJECT]->
      load(&g_cSpriteImages,3,453,162);
    result=result&&g_pSprite[EXPLODINGCROW_OBJECT]->
      load(&g_cSpriteImages,4,386,230);
    result=result&&g_pSprite[EXPLODINGCROW_OBJECT]->
      load(&g_cSpriteImages,5,453,230);
    return result;
} //LoadExplodingCrowSprite

BOOL LoadBulletSprite(){ //load bullet
  return g_pSprite[BULLET_OBJECT]->
    load(&g_cSpriteImages,0,5,123);
} //LoadBulletSprite

BOOL LoadTextSprites(){ //load text sprites
  return Text->load(&g_cTextImages,1,102);
} //LoadTextSprites

BOOL LoadImages(){ //load graphics from files to surfaces
  //get the background image
  if(!background.load("bckgnd.bmp"))return FALSE; //read file
  background.draw(lpBackground); //draw to background surface
  //set palettes in all surfaces
  if(!background.setpalette(lpPrimaryPalette))return FALSE;
  if(!background.setpalette(lpSecondaryPalette))return FALSE;
  //load the text sprites
  if(!g_cTextImages.load("text.bmp"))return FALSE;//read file
  Text=new CTextManager(19,30); //text manager
  LoadTextSprites();
```

```
  //load the sprites...
  if(!g_cSpriteImages.load("sprites.bmp"))return FALSE;
  //...the plane
  g_pSprite[PLANE_OBJECT]=new CClippedSprite(6,121,72);
  if(!LoadPlaneSprite())return FALSE; //load plane images
  //...the damaged plane
  g_pSprite[DAMAGEDPLANE_OBJECT]=new CClippedSprite(2,121,72);
  LoadDamagedPlaneSprite();
  //...the exploding plane
  g_pSprite[EXPLODINGPLANE_OBJECT]=new CClippedSprite(4,121,72);
  LoadExplodingPlaneSprite();
  //...the dead plane
  g_pSprite[DEADPLANE_OBJECT]=new CClippedSprite(1,119,54);
  LoadDeadPlaneSprite();
  //...the crow
  g_pSprite[CROW_OBJECT]=new CClippedSprite(4,58,37);
  if(!LoadCrowSprite())return FALSE; //load crow images
  //..the dead crow
  g_pSprite[DEADCROW_OBJECT]=new CClippedSprite(1,62,53);
  LoadDeadCrowSprite(); //load dead crow images
  //...the exploding crow
  g_pSprite[EXPLODINGCROW_OBJECT]=new CClippedSprite(6,62,53);
  LoadExplodingCrowSprite(); //load exploding crow images
  //...the bullet
  g_pSprite[BULLET_OBJECT]=new CClippedSprite(1,5,3);
  LoadBulletSprite(); //load bullet images
  //...the foreground sprites
  if(!g_cFrgndImages.load("farm.bmp"))return FALSE;
  g_pSprite[FARM_OBJECT]=new CClippedSprite(1,640,162);
  g_pSprite[FIELD_OBJECT]=new CClippedSprite(1,640,162);
  if(!LoadFrgndSprites())return FALSE; //load foreground
  return TRUE;
} //LoadImages

void CreateObjects(){
  const int reserved=6; //reserved positions for nonvermin
  int crowcount=5+level*3; //number of crows per level
  int i;
  ObjectManager.create(FARM_OBJECT,0,SCREEN_HEIGHT-1,0,0);
  ObjectManager.create(FIELD_OBJECT,SCREEN_WIDTH,
    SCREEN_HEIGHT-1,0,0);
  //compute numbers of objects
  if(crowcount>MAX_OBJECTS-reserved)
    crowcount=MAX_OBJECTS-reserved;
  if(crowcount<0)crowcount=0;
  //create objects
  for(i=0; i<crowcount/2; i++)
    ObjectManager.create(CROW_OBJECT,
      Random.number(0,WORLD_WIDTH-1),
      Random.number(100,400),-1,0);
```

```
    ObjectManager.set_current(
      ObjectManager.create(PLANE_OBJECT,320,271,-1,0));
    for(i=0; i<crowcount-crowcount/2; i++)
      ObjectManager.create(CROW_OBJECT,
        Random.number(0,WORLD_WIDTH-1),
        Random.number(100,400),-1,0);
} //CreateObjects


BOOL RestoreSurfaces(){ //restore all surfaces
  BOOL result=TRUE;
  //primary and secondary surfaces
  if(FAILED(lpPrimary->Restore()))return FALSE;
  if(FAILED(lpSecondary->Restore()))return FALSE;
  //surfaces containing images
  if(SUCCEEDED(lpBackground->Restore())) //if background restored
    result=result&&background.draw(lpBackground); //redraw image
  else return FALSE;
  if(g_pSprite[PLANE_OBJECT]->Restore()) //if plane restored
    result=result&&LoadPlaneSprite(); //redraw image
  else return FALSE;
  if(g_pSprite[DAMAGEDPLANE_OBJECT]->Restore()) //if restored
    result=result&&LoadDamagedPlaneSprite(); //redraw image
  else return FALSE;
  if(g_pSprite[EXPLODINGPLANE_OBJECT]->Restore()) //if restored
    result=result&&LoadExplodingPlaneSprite(); //redraw image
  else return FALSE;
  if(g_pSprite[DEADPLANE_OBJECT]->Restore()) //if restored
    result=result&&LoadDeadPlaneSprite(); //redraw image
  else return FALSE;
  if(g_pSprite[CROW_OBJECT]->Restore()) //if crow restored
    result=result&&LoadCrowSprite(); //redraw image
  else return FALSE;
  if(g_pSprite[DEADCROW_OBJECT]->Restore()) //if restored
    result=result&&LoadDeadCrowSprite(); //redraw image
  else return FALSE;
  if(g_pSprite[EXPLODINGCROW_OBJECT]->Restore()) //if restored
    result=result&&LoadExplodingCrowSprite(); //redraw image
  else return FALSE;
  if(g_pSprite[BULLET_OBJECT]->Restore()) //if restored
    result=result&&LoadBulletSprite(); //redraw image
  else return FALSE;
  if(g_pSprite[FARM_OBJECT]->Restore()&& //if farm and ...
    g_pSprite[FIELD_OBJECT]->Restore()) //... field restored
    result=result&&LoadFrgndSprites(); //redraw image
  else return FALSE;
  //input manager has button sprites
  if(!InputManager.Restore())return FALSE;
  //text manager has text sprites
  if(Text->Restore())
```

```
      result=result&&LoadTextSprites();
    else return FALSE;
    return result;
} //RestoreSurfaces

void LoadSounds(int level=0){ //load sounds for level
  const int copies=4; //copies of repeatable sounds
  switch(level){
    case 0: //intro sounds
      SoundManager->load("intro.wav");
      SoundManager->load("larc.wav");
      break;
    case 1: //game engine sounds
      SoundManager->load("caw.wav",copies);
      SoundManager->load("gun.wav",copies);
      SoundManager->load("boom.wav",copies);
      SoundManager->load("thump.wav",copies);
      SoundManager->load("putt0.wav");
      SoundManager->load("putt1.wav");
      SoundManager->load("putt2.wav");
      SoundManager->load("bgclk.wav",2);
      SoundManager->load("smclk.wav",2);
      SoundManager->load("success.wav");
      SoundManager->load("failed.wav");
      SoundManager->load("life.wav");
      SoundManager->load("stings.wav");
      SoundManager->load("smarts.wav");
      SoundManager->load("congrats.wav");
      SoundManager->load("twspace.wav",copies);
      SoundManager->load("twret.wav",copies);
      SoundManager->load("twchar.wav",copies);
      break;
  }
}

BOOL PageFlip(){ //return TRUE if page flip succeeds
  if(lpPrimary->Flip(NULL,DDFLIP_WAIT)==DDERR_SURFACELOST)
    return RestoreSurfaces();
  return TRUE;
} //PageFlip

int chars_in_number(int n){ //return number of chars
  if(n==0)return 1; //0 has one character
  int count=0; //count of number of characters
  n=abs(n); //positive numbers only
  while(n>0){n/=10; count++;} //tally number of chars
  return count;
} //chars_in_number

void draw_number(int n,int center,
```

```
      LPDIRECTDRAWSURFACE surface,BOOL middle=FALSE){
   const int HALF_CHAR_WIDTH=10;
   char buffer[64]; //for display on screen
   char buffer2[16]; //temp buffer
   int margin=7;
   int width=chars_in_number(n); //width of number in chars
   for(int i=0; i<center-width/2-1; i++)
     buffer[i]=' '; //shift right
   buffer[i]=0; //end of string
   sprintf(buffer2,"%d",n);
   strcat(buffer,buffer2); //n to buffer
   //adjust to center
   if(!(width&1))margin+=HALF_CHAR_WIDTH;
   if(middle)margin-=HALF_CHAR_WIDTH;
   //draw
   Text->jump(margin,75); //start of line
   Text->draw(buffer,surface); //print number
}

void draw_text_header(LPDIRECTDRAWSURFACE surface){
  const int margin=7;
  Text->jump(margin,40);
  Text->draw("level varmints score health lives",surface);
  draw_number(level,3,surface);
  draw_number(ObjectManager.enemies(),11,surface,TRUE);
  draw_number(ScoreManager.score(),18,surface);
  draw_number(ScoreManager.health(),25,surface,TRUE);
  draw_number(ScoreManager.lives(),31,surface);
}

BOOL ComposeFrame(){ //compose a frame of animation
  Viewpoint.draw_background(lpBackground,lpSecondary,
    ObjectManager.speed()); //draw scrolling background
  ObjectManager.animate(lpSecondary); //draw objects
  draw_text_header(lpSecondary); //draw text header
  if(show_framerate){ //if we need to show the frame count
    char buffer[4];
    framecount++; //count frame
    if(Timer.elapsed(framerate_timer,1000)){
      last_framecount=framecount; framecount=0;
    }
    Text->jump(580,470);
    sprintf(buffer,"%d",last_framecount);
    Text->draw(buffer,lpSecondary);
  }
  return TRUE;
} //ComposeFrame

void display_screen(char *filename){ //display bmp file
  CBmpFileReader image; //file reader
```

```
    image.load(filename); //load from file
    image.draw(lpSecondary); //draw to back buffer
    image.setpalette(lpPrimaryPalette); //may have custom palette
    PageFlip(); //display it
  //draw to back buffer again for button animation
    image.draw(lpSecondary);
} //display_screen

void display_highscorelist(char *filename){ //display high scores
    display_screen(filename); //display background
    HighScoreList.draw(lpSecondary); //draw high scores
    PageFlip(); //flip to front surface
} //display_highscorelist

void display_newhighscore(){ //display new high score entry page
    Sleep(50); //slow down the animation
    NewHighScoreBg->draw(lpSecondary); //draw background
    //draw text
    Text->jump(163,330);
    Text->draw(HighScoreList.current_name(),lpSecondary);
    PageFlip(); //display it
} //display_newhighscore

void change_phase(GamePhaseType new_phase){ //go to new phase
    switch(new_phase){
        case LOGO_PHASE:
            display_screen("larc.bmp");
            LoadSounds(); //load sounds for intro sequence
            SoundManager->play(LOGO_SOUND); //signature chord
            break;
        case TITLE_PHASE:
            display_screen("title.bmp");
            SoundManager->stop(); //silence previous phase
            SoundManager->play(TITLE_SOUND); //title sound
            break;
        case MENU_PHASE:
            //set up buttons for menu
            InputManager.SetupButtons(MENU_PHASE);
            //sound
            switch(GamePhase){ //depending on previous phase
                case TITLE_PHASE: //from intro phase
                    SoundManager->stop(); //silence previous phase
                    SoundManager->clear(); //clear out old sounds
                    LoadSounds(1); //set up game sounds
                    break;
                case PLAYING_PHASE: //from game engine
                    SoundManager->stop(); //silence game engine
                    if(ScoreManager.lives()<0)
                        SoundManager->play(FAILED_SOUND);
                    break;
```

```
      case DEVICEMENU_PHASE: //device menu, do nothing
        break;
      case NEWHIGHSCORE_PHASE:
        delete NewHighScoreBg; //delete background
        break;
    }
    //display background
    display_screen("menu.bmp"); //display main menu
    //mouse cursor
    switch(GamePhase){ //what phase did we come in from?
      case PLAYING_PHASE:
      case TITLE_PHASE:
      case HIGHSCORE_PHASE:
      case NEWHIGHSCORE_PHASE:
        ShowCursor(TRUE); //activate the mouse cursor
        break;
    }
    break;
  case DEVICEMENU_PHASE:
    //display button background
    display_screen("dmenu.bmp");
    //set up the button manager
    InputManager.SetupButtons(DEVICEMENU_PHASE);
    break;
  case PLAYING_PHASE: //prepare the game engine
    //mouse cursor
    SetCursorPos(SCREEN_WIDTH-1,SCREEN_HEIGHT/2); //throttle
    //start sounds
    SoundManager->stop(); //silence previous phase
    switch(GamePhase){//depending on previous phase
      case MENU_PHASE:
        ShowCursor(FALSE); //deactivate the mouse cursor
        level=1; ScoreManager.reset(); //reset score
        break;
      case SUCCESS_PHASE:
        level++; //go to next level
        //add score for level completion
        ScoreManager.add_to_score(LEVEL_BONUS_SCORE);
        break;
    }
    //create objects in game engine
    ObjectManager.reset(); //clear object manager
    CreateObjects(); //create new objects
    //initialize graphics
    background.setpalette(lpPrimaryPalette); //game palette
    ComposeFrame(); PageFlip(); //prime animation pump
    break;
  case SUCCESS_PHASE: //successful completion of level
    SoundManager->stop(); //stop sounds from previous phase
    SoundManager->play(SUCCESS_SOUND); //jubilation
```

```
        display_screen("success.bmp"); //display success screen
        break;
      case HIGHSCORE_PHASE: //display high score list
        ShowCursor(FALSE); //hide the cursor
        display_highscorelist("hscore.bmp"); //display high scores
        break;
      case NEWHIGHSCORE_PHASE: //display high score list
        SoundManager->stop(); //stop sounds from previous phase
        SoundManager->play(CONGRATS_SOUND); //play new sound
        NewHighScoreBg=new CBmpFileReader; //background
        NewHighScoreBg->load("newhsc.bmp"); //read from file
        NewHighScoreBg->draw(lpSecondary); //draw to back surface
        NewHighScoreBg->setpalette(lpPrimaryPalette); //palette
        PageFlip(); //display it
        break;
  }
  //change to new phase
  GamePhase=new_phase; PhaseTime=Timer.time();
  endphase=FALSE;
} //change_phase

void Redraw(){ //redraw in response to surface loss
  switch(GamePhase){
    case LOGO_PHASE:
      display_screen("larc.bmp");
      break;
    case TITLE_PHASE:
      display_screen("title.bmp");
      break;
    case MENU_PHASE:
      display_screen("menu.bmp"); //display main menu
      break;
    case PLAYING_PHASE:
      //do nothing, next frame of animation will catch it
      break;
    case DEVICEMENU_PHASE:
      display_screen("dmenu.bmp");
      InputManager.SetupButtons(DEVICEMENU_PHASE);
      break;
    case SUCCESS_PHASE:
      display_screen("success.bmp"); //display success screen
      break;
    case HIGHSCORE_PHASE:
      display_highscorelist("hscore.bmp"); //display high scores
      break;
    case NEWHIGHSCORE_PHASE:
      NewHighScoreBg->setpalette(lpPrimaryPalette); //palette
      display_newhighscore();
      break;
  }
```

```
}

void ProcessFrame(){ //process a frame of animation
  const int LOGO_DISPLAY_TIME=8500; //duration of logo
  const int TITLE_DISPLAY_TIME=10000; //duration of title
  const int SUCCESS_DISPLAY_TIME=4500; //duration of success
  InputManager.Joystick(); //process joystick input
  //check for lost surfaces, eg alt+tab
  if(lpPrimary->IsLost()){
    RestoreSurfaces(); Redraw();
  }
  //phase-related processing
  switch(GamePhase){ //what phase are we in?
    case LOGO_PHASE: //displaying logo screen
      Sleep(100); //surrender time to other processes
      if(endphase||Timer.elapsed(PhaseTime,LOGO_DISPLAY_TIME))
        change_phase(TITLE_PHASE); //go to title screen
      break;
    case TITLE_PHASE: //displaying title screen
      Sleep(100); //surrender time to other processes
      if(endphase||Timer.elapsed(PhaseTime,TITLE_DISPLAY_TIME))
        change_phase(MENU_PHASE); //go to menu
      break;
    case MENU_PHASE: //main menu
      Sleep(100); //surrender time to other processes
      if(endphase)change_phase(NextPhase); //change phase
      break;
    case DEVICEMENU_PHASE:
      if(endphase)change_phase(MENU_PHASE); //go to menu phase
      break;
    case PLAYING_PHASE: //game engine
      ComposeFrame(); //compose a frame in back surface
      PageFlip(); //flip video memory surfaces
      if(ObjectManager.won()) //completed level
        change_phase(SUCCESS_PHASE);
      else if(endphase){ //quit or died too often
        if(ScoreManager.lives()>=0&&
            HighScoreList.made_the_grade(ScoreManager.score()))
          change_phase(NEWHIGHSCORE_PHASE); //user enters name
        else change_phase(MENU_PHASE); //quit, go to menu
      }
      break;
    case SUCCESS_PHASE: //displaying title screen
      Sleep(100); //surrender time to other processes
      if(endphase|| //if end of phase
      Timer.elapsed(PhaseTime,SUCCESS_DISPLAY_TIME))
        change_phase(PLAYING_PHASE); //start playing
      break;
    case HIGHSCORE_PHASE: //displaying high scores
      Sleep(100); //surrender time to other processes
```

```
      if(endphase)change_phase(MENU_PHASE); //quit, go to menu
      break;
    case NEWHIGHSCORE_PHASE:
      display_newhighscore(); //animate user typing in name
      if(endphase){ //insert new high score
        HighScoreList.insert(level,ScoreManager.score());
        change_phase(MENU_PHASE); //go to menu
      }
      break;
  }
} //ProcessFrame

//message handler (window procedure)
long CALLBACK WindowProc(HWND hwnd,UINT message,
                         WPARAM wParam,LPARAM lParam){
  switch(message){
    case WM_ACTIVATEAPP: ActiveApp=wParam; break;
    case WM_CREATE: break;
    case WM_KEYDOWN: //keyboard hit
      if(InputManager.Keyboard(wParam))
        DestroyWindow(hwnd);
      break;
    case WM_LBUTTONDOWN: //left mouse button down
      InputManager.LMouseDown(lParam); //handle it
      break;
    case WM_LBUTTONUP: //left mouse button up
      if(InputManager.LMouseUp(lParam))
        DestroyWindow(hwnd);
      break;
    case WM_MOUSEMOVE: //mouse move
      InputManager.MouseMove(lParam);
      break;
    case WM_DESTROY: //end of game
      ObjectManager.reset(); //clear objects
      if(lpDirectDrawObject!=NULL){ //if DD object exists
        if(lpSecondary!=NULL) //if secondary surface exists
          lpSecondary->Release(); //release secondary surface
        if(lpPrimary!=NULL) //if primary surface exists
          lpPrimary->Release(); //release primary surface
        if(lpBackground!=NULL) //if background exists
          lpBackground->Release(); //release background
        for(int i=0; i<NUM_SPRITES; i++){ //for each sprite
          if(g_pSprite[i]) //if sprite exists
            g_pSprite[i]->Release(); //release sprite
          delete g_pSprite[i]; //delete sprite
        }
        InputManager.Release(); //button surfaces
        Text->Release();  //release text manager sprites
        lpDirectDrawObject->Release(); //release DD object
      }
```

```
      delete SoundManager; //reclaim sound manager memory
      delete Text; //reclaim text manager memory
      ShowCursor(TRUE); //show the mouse cursor
      PostQuitMessage(0); //and exit
      break;
    default: //default window procedure
      return DefWindowProc(hwnd,message,wParam,lParam);
  } //switch(message)
  return 0L;
} //WindowProc

int WINAPI WinMain(HINSTANCE hInstance,HINSTANCE hPrevInstance,
LPSTR lpCmdLine,int nCmdShow){
  MSG msg; //current message
  HWND hwnd; //handle to fullscreen window
  hwnd=CreateDefaultWindow("directX demo 12",hInstance);
  if(!hwnd)return FALSE;
  //set up window
  ShowWindow(hwnd,nCmdShow); UpdateWindow(hwnd);
  SetFocus(hwnd); //allow input from keyboard
  ShowCursor(FALSE); //hide the cursor
  //init graphics
  for(int i=0; i<NUM_SPRITES; i++) //null out sprites
    g_pSprite[i]=NULL;
  BOOL OK=InitDirectDraw(hwnd);//initialize DirectDraw
  if(OK)OK=LoadImages(); //load images from disk
  if(!OK){ //bail out if initialization failed
    DestroyWindow(hwnd); return FALSE;
  }
  //start game timer
  Timer.start();
  //init sound
  SoundManager=new CSoundManager(hwnd);
  //set initial phase
  change_phase(LOGO_PHASE);
  //message loop
  while(TRUE)
    if(PeekMessage(&msg,NULL,0,0,PM_NOREMOVE)){
      if(!GetMessage(&msg,NULL,0,0))return msg.wParam;
      TranslateMessage(&msg); DispatchMessage(&msg);
    }
    else if(ActiveApp)ProcessFrame(); else WaitMessage();
} //WinMain
```

Sndlist.h

```
//sndlist.h: list of sound definitions

//Copyright Ian Parberry, 1999
//Last updated February 10, 2000

#ifndef __SNDLIST__
#define __SNDLIST__

#define LOOP_SOUND TRUE

enum GameSoundType{ //sounds used in game engine
  CAW_SOUND=0, //sound a crow makes
  GUN_SOUND, //sound of gun firing
  BOOM_SOUND, //sound of explosion
  THUMP_SOUND, //sound of object hitting the ground
  //next 3 sounds must be consecutive and in this order
  SLOWPUTT_SOUND, //sound of slow engine
  MEDIUMPUTT_SOUND, //sound of medium engine
  FASTPUTT_SOUND, //sound of fast engine
  //mouse clicks
  BIGCLICK_SOUND, //loud click
  SMALLCLICK_SOUND, //soft click
  //more game sounds
  SUCCESS_SOUND, //completion of level
  FAILED_SOUND, //sound of failing
  NEWLIFE_SOUND, //sound of getting a new life
  STINGS_SOUND, //that stings (damage)
  SMARTS_SOUND, //that smarts (damage)
  //sounds for high score list
  CONGRATS_SOUND, //congratulations
  TYPE_SPACE_SOUND, //typewriter typing a space
  TYPE_RETURN_SOUND, //typewriter typing a return
  TYPE_CHAR_SOUND, //typewriter typing a character
};

enum IntroSoundType{ //sounds used during the intro
  TITLE_SOUND=0, //sound used during title screen
  LOGO_SOUND, //signature chord
};

#endif
```

Topscore.h

```
//topscore.h: header file for topscore.cpp

//Copyright Ian Parberry, 2000
//Last updated February 10, 2000

#ifndef __TOPSCORE__
#define __TOPSCORE__

#include <ddraw.h>

#define MAX_TOPSCORES 8
#define MAX_TOPSCORE_NAMELENGTH 17

class CHighScoreList{
  private:
    char m_pNames[MAX_TOPSCORES][MAX_TOPSCORE_NAMELENGTH];
    int m_pTopScore[MAX_TOPSCORES]; //top scores
    int m_pTopLevel[MAX_TOPSCORES]; //top levels
    int m_nChecksum0,m_nChecksum1; //checksums
    char m_szNamebuffer[MAX_TOPSCORE_NAMELENGTH]; //name buffer
    int m_nNamesize; //size of name in namebuffer
    void save(); //save all high scores
    void save(HKEY RegistryKey,int index); //save one high score
    void load(); //load all high scores
    void load(HKEY RegistryKey,int index); //load one high score
    int enumerate(); //turn data into a number
    int checksum0(); //calculate a checksum
    int checksum1(); //calculate a checksum
    void load_checksums(HKEY RegistryKey); //load checksums
    void save_checksums(HKEY RegistryKey); //save checksums
    BOOL checksums_ok(); //TRUE if checksums are OK
  public:
    CHighScoreList(); //constructor
    BOOL insert(int level,int score); //insert new high score
    void draw(LPDIRECTDRAWSURFACE surface); //draw high score
    void clear(); //clear all high scores
    BOOL made_the_grade(int score); //TRUE if score gets on table
    //the following functions affect the current name
    BOOL append_to_current(char c); //insert char at end
    BOOL delete_from_current(); //delete char at end
    void cancel_current(); //clear out the current name
    char *current_name(); //return current name
};

#endif
```

Topscore.cpp

```cpp
//topscore.cpp: high score list

//Copyright Ian Parberry, 2000
//Last updated February 10, 2000

#include <windows.h>
#include <stdio.h>

#include "topscore.h"
#include "text.h" //for text sprite manager

const int PRIME0=16787; //a 16-bit prime number
const int PRIME1=15241; //a 16-bit prime number
const int PRIME2=16223; //a 16-bit prime number
const int PRIME3=15907; //a 16-bit prime number

extern CTextManager *Text; //text manager

CHighScoreList::CHighScoreList(){ //constructor
  m_nNamesize=0;
  //null out data
  for(int i=0; i<MAX_TOPSCORES; i++){
    m_pNames[i][0]=0; m_pTopScore[i]=m_pTopLevel[i]=0;
  }
  m_nChecksum0=m_nChecksum1=0; //checksums
  //read data from registry
  load();
}

void CHighScoreList::clear(){
  //null out data
  for(int i=0; i<MAX_TOPSCORES; i++){
    m_pNames[i][0]=0; m_pTopScore[i]=m_pTopLevel[i]=0;
  }
  m_nChecksum0=m_nChecksum1=0; //checksums
  //write data from registry
  save();
}

BOOL CHighScoreList::insert(int level,int score){
//insert new entry, return TRUE if entry actually fits
  int i=0,j;
  BOOL result=FALSE;
  //bail out of bad data
  if(score<=0)return FALSE; //bail if no score
  if(strlen(m_szNamebuffer)<=0)return FALSE; //bail if no name
  //search for place in table sorted on score
  while(i<MAX_TOPSCORES&&m_pTopScore[i]>=score)++i;
```

```cpp
    if(i<MAX_TOPSCORES){ //new entry
      result=TRUE;
      //move data down in table to make room
      for(j=MAX_TOPSCORES-1; j>i; j--){
        m_pTopScore[j]=m_pTopScore[j-1]; //score
        m_pTopLevel[j]=m_pTopLevel[j-1]; //level
        strcpy(m_pNames[j],m_pNames[j-1]); //name
      }
      //enter new data in place
      m_pTopLevel[i]=level; m_pTopScore[i]=score; //level, score
      strncpy(m_pNames[i],m_szNamebuffer,
        MAX_TOPSCORE_NAMELENGTH-1); //name
      //compute checksums and save to registry
      m_nChecksum0=checksum0(); //compute checksum
      m_nChecksum1=checksum1(); //compute checksum
      save(); //save new high score list to registry
    }
    return result;
}

void CHighScoreList::draw(LPDIRECTDRAWSURFACE surface){
//draw to surface
  const int topmargin=150; //margin at top
  const int leftmargin=15; //margin at left
  const int levelmargin=380; //left margin for level number
  const int scoremargin=500; //left margin for score
  const int vertskip=40; //line height
  char buffer[16]; //temporary text buffer
  int i=0;
  while(i<MAX_TOPSCORES&&m_pTopScore[i]>0){ //for each score
    int y=topmargin+i*vertskip;
    //name
    Text->jump(leftmargin,y); //start of line
    Text->draw(m_pNames[i],surface); //print name
    //level
    Text->jump(levelmargin,y); //start of line
    sprintf(buffer,"%d",m_pTopLevel[i]); //convert to string
    Text->draw(buffer,surface); //print score
    //score
    Text->jump(scoremargin,y); //start of line
    sprintf(buffer,"%d",m_pTopScore[i]); //convert to string
    Text->draw(buffer,surface); //print score
    i++;
  }
}

void CHighScoreList::load(HKEY RegistryKey,int index){
//load one entry from registry
  unsigned long length; //length of entry
  const int BUFSIZE=32; //buffer size
```

```
          char buffer[BUFSIZE]; //text buffer
          DWORD type; //type of registry entry
          char id[16]; //player name (identifier)
          sprintf(id,"Player%dName",index); //create id
          //get name
          length=MAX_TOPSCORE_NAMELENGTH;
          RegQueryValueEx(RegistryKey,id,NULL,&type,
            (unsigned char *)(m_pNames[index]),&length);
          m_pNames[index][length]=0;
          //get level
          sprintf(id,"Player%dLevel",index);
          length=BUFSIZE-1; buffer[0]=0;
          RegQueryValueEx(RegistryKey,id,NULL,&type,
            (unsigned char *)buffer,&length);
          if(length){
            buffer[length]=0;
            sscanf(buffer,"%d",&(m_pTopLevel[index]));
          }
          else m_pTopLevel[index]=0;
          //get level
          sprintf(id,"Player%dScore",index);
          length=BUFSIZE-1; buffer[0]=0;
          RegQueryValueEx(RegistryKey,id,NULL,&type,
            (unsigned char *)buffer,&length);
          if(length){
            buffer[length]=0;
            sscanf(buffer,"%d",&(m_pTopScore[index]));
          }
          else m_pTopScore[index]=0;
        }

        void CHighScoreList::load(){ //load from registry
          HKEY RegistryKey;
          //open registry
          int result=RegCreateKeyEx(HKEY_LOCAL_MACHINE,
              "SOFTWARE\\LARC\\NedFarm",0,NULL,0,KEY_READ,
              NULL,&RegistryKey,NULL);
          if(result!=ERROR_SUCCESS)return; //bail if failed
          //load high scores and checksums
          for(int i=0; i<MAX_TOPSCORES; i++)load(RegistryKey,i);
          load_checksums(RegistryKey);
          if(!checksums_ok())clear();
          //close and exit
          RegCloseKey(RegistryKey);
        }

        void CHighScoreList::load_checksums(HKEY RegistryKey){
        //load checksums from registry
          unsigned long length; //length of entry
          const int BUFSIZE=32; //buffer size
```

```
    char buffer[BUFSIZE]; //text buffer
    DWORD type; //type of registry entry
    //checksum0
    length=BUFSIZE-1; buffer[0]=0;
    RegQueryValueEx(RegistryKey,"Checksum0",NULL,&type,
      (unsigned char *)buffer,&length);
    if(length){
      buffer[length]=0;
      sscanf(buffer,"%d",&m_nChecksum0);
    }
    else m_nChecksum0=0;
    //checksum1
    length=BUFSIZE-1; buffer[0]=0;
    RegQueryValueEx(RegistryKey,"Checksum1",NULL,&type,
      (unsigned char *)buffer,&length);
    if(length){
      buffer[length]=0;
      sscanf(buffer,"%d",&m_nChecksum1);
    }
    else m_nChecksum1=0;
}

void CHighScoreList::save(HKEY RegistryKey,int index){
//save one entry in registry
    const int BUFSIZE=32; //buffer size
    char buffer[BUFSIZE]; //text buffer
    char id[16]; //player name (identifier)
    //put name
    sprintf(id,"Player%dName",index);
    RegSetValueEx(RegistryKey,id,NULL,REG_SZ,
      (unsigned char *)m_pNames[index],strlen(m_pNames[index])+1);
    //put level
    sprintf(id,"Player%dLevel",index);
    sprintf(buffer,"%d",m_pTopLevel[index]);
    RegSetValueEx(RegistryKey,id,NULL,REG_SZ,
      (unsigned char *)buffer,strlen(buffer)+1);
    //put score
    sprintf(id,"Player%dScore",index);
    sprintf(buffer,"%d",m_pTopScore[index]);
    RegSetValueEx(RegistryKey,id,NULL,REG_SZ,
      (unsigned char *)buffer,strlen(buffer)+1);
}

void CHighScoreList::save(){ //save all data in registry
    HKEY RegistryKey;
    //open registry
    int result=RegCreateKeyEx(HKEY_LOCAL_MACHINE,
      "SOFTWARE\\LARC\\NedFarm",0,NULL,0,KEY_WRITE,
      NULL,&RegistryKey,NULL);
    if(result!=ERROR_SUCCESS)return; //bail if failed
```

```
  //save high scores and checksums
  for(int i=0; i<MAX_TOPSCORES; i++)save(RegistryKey,i);
  save_checksums(RegistryKey);
  //close and exit
  RegCloseKey(RegistryKey);
}

void CHighScoreList::save_checksums(HKEY RegistryKey){
//save checksums to registry
  const int BUFSIZE=32; //buffer size
  char buffer[BUFSIZE]; //text buffer
  //checksum0
  sprintf(buffer,"%d",m_nChecksum0);
  RegSetValueEx(RegistryKey,"Checksum0",NULL,REG_SZ,
    (unsigned char *)buffer,strlen(buffer)+1);
  //checksum1
  sprintf(buffer,"%d",m_nChecksum1);
  RegSetValueEx(RegistryKey,"Checksum1",NULL,REG_SZ,
    (unsigned char *)buffer,strlen(buffer)+1);
}

BOOL CHighScoreList::made_the_grade(int score){
//TRUE if entry fits in table
  return score>m_pTopScore[MAX_TOPSCORES-1];
}

int CHighScoreList::enumerate(){
//turn high score table into a number
  int result=0,i,j;
  const int mask=0xFFFF; //mask for lower 16 bits
  for(i=0; i<MAX_TOPSCORES; i++){
    j=0;
    while(m_pNames[i][j]!=0){result+=m_pNames[i][j]; j++;}
    result+=m_pTopScore[i]+m_pTopLevel[i]; //score and level
    result&=mask; //mask off lower 16 bits
  }
  return result;
}

int CHighScoreList::checksum0(){ //compute a checksum
  return enumerate()*PRIME0%PRIME1;
}

int CHighScoreList::checksum1(){ //compute a checksum
  return enumerate()*PRIME2%PRIME3;
}

BOOL CHighScoreList::checksums_ok(){ //TRUE if checksums are OK
  return m_nChecksum0==checksum0()&&m_nChecksum1==checksum1();
}
```

```
BOOL CHighScoreList::append_to_current(char c){
//insert char at end of current name
  if(m_nNamesize<MAX_TOPSCORE_NAMELENGTH-1){ //if there is room
    m_szNamebuffer[m_nNamesize++]=c; //append character
    m_szNamebuffer[m_nNamesize]=0x00; //null at end
    return TRUE; //success
  }
  else return FALSE; //no room
}

BOOL CHighScoreList::delete_from_current(){
//delete char at end of current name
  if(m_nNamesize>0)
    m_szNamebuffer[--m_nNamesize]=0x00; //back off & put a null
  else{
    m_nNamesize=0; //fell off beginning of string
    return FALSE; //deletion didn't happen
  }
  return TRUE; //deletion actually happened
}

void CHighScoreList::cancel_current(){ //clear the current name
  m_szNamebuffer[m_nNamesize=0]=0;
}

char* CHighScoreList::current_name(){ //return current name
  return m_szNamebuffer;
}
```

Chapter 15

Here's what you'll learn:

- How to pause the game timer

- How to pause the sounds in DirectSound

- How to use the ability to pause in other ways, such as breaking out the device menu and dealing with Alt+Tab

- How to add help and a credits screen

Pausing the Game

In Demo 13, we learn how to pause the game when the player hits the F1 key so that he or she can go take care of something in Real Life without having to quit the game. We need to give the player some indication of when the game is paused so that he or she doesn't assume that the game is frozen due to a bug. We will opt for something simple and display the word "Paused" in big bright letters on the screen (see Figure 15.1). Sounds will be paused too, within the limits allowed by DirectX. This means that, for example, if the game is paused in the middle of an explosion, the explosion sound will continue from the middle when the game is unpaused.

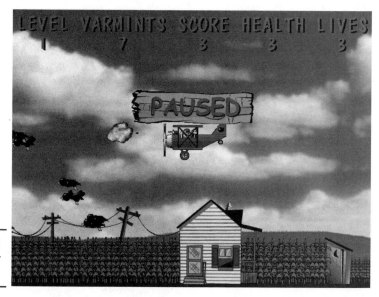

Figure 15.1
Screen shot
of Demo 13

Less obviously, the timer must be paused too. Recall from Chapter 5 that objects move a distance that is proportional to their speed multiplied by the amount of time since their last move. If the last move was an hour ago when the player paused the game to go watch TV, the crows will move an hour's worth of distance at warp speed when the game is unpaused! Obviously, we want to pause the timer so that this does not happen.

The Help button on the main menu screen will now display a series of help files created by the artist (see Figure 15.2). The player can page through by hitting any key on the keyboard, the left mouse button, or joystick button 1. Now that we can pause the game, we can also allow the user to break out of the game engine to access the device menu (F2), high score list (F3), and help (F4), continuing play afterward without going through the main menu screen. The frame rate key has been moved to function key F5 now.

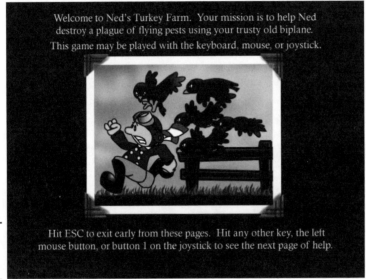

Figure 15.2
The first
page of help

One more small thing that we've added to the game is a credits screen that appears in the intro sequence after the title screen (see Figure 15.3). The credits screen lists all of the people who have worked on the game. It has its own sound, and like the other phases in the intro sequence, the user can click out of it early using the keyboard, mouse, or joystick. A credits screen is a Good Idea. It's the *only* place that your name will appear in the game. There are very few game developers whose name carries enough cachet for the publisher to allow it to appear on the box art or CD cover for their game. The credits screen is all yours though, so use it to advantage.

Figure 15.3
The credits
screen

CREDITS

Producer .... Ian Parberry
Programmer .... Ian Parberry
Artist .... Keith Smiley
Voices .... Steve and Mikayla Wilson

Experiment with Demo 13

Take a moment now to run Demo 13.

- Notice the credits screen in the intro sequence.

- Start a game. Pause and unpause it by hitting the F1 key. Notice that the action freezes and starts again from where it left off.

- Pause the game in the middle of a crow explosion. Notice that when you restart it, the explosion animation continues, and the sound continues from approximately where it left off.

- Use the device menu (F2) to change the device that you are playing with in the middle of a game.

- Access the high score list (F3) and the help screens (F4) from the middle of a game.

- Finally, hit Alt+Tab in the middle of a game. Notice that when you re-enter the game, it comes up paused. Why is this a good idea?

The Pausable Timer

The game timer class CGameTimer is derived from our timer class CTimer first met in Demo 2, and adds to it the ability to pause the timer. Recall that CTimer uses the API function timeGetTime, which returns the number of milliseconds since Windows was started. This means that the timer continues to tick even when the game is paused. What we need to do in CGameTimer is to keep track of the total time that the timer has been paused, and subtract that from the time reported by CTimer.

Pausable Timer Overview

The header file for the pausable game timer is Gtimer.h. CGameTimer has three private member variables: m_nPauseTime, which records the total amount of time spent paused, not including the current period spent paused (if the timer is currently paused); m_nCurrentPauseStart, which records the last time the timer was paused; and m_bPaused, which is TRUE when the timer is currently paused. In addition to a constructor, it has overrides for the CTimer functions start() and time(), and two new functions pause() and unpause().

```
class CGameTimer: public CTimer{ //game timer class
  private:
    int m_nPauseTime; //amount of time spent paused
    int m_nCurrentPauseStart; //last time timer was paused
    BOOL m_bPaused; //TRUE if currently paused
  public:
    CGameTimer(); //constructor
    void start(); //start the timer
    int time(); //return the time
    void pause(); //pause the timer
    void unpause(); //unpause the timer
};
```

Pausable Timer Code

The code file for the pausable game timer is Gtimer.cpp. It begins with the CGameTimer constructor, which calls the CTimer constructor and sets some sensible default values to the CGameTimer member variables.

```
CGameTimer::CGameTimer():CTimer(){ //constructor
  m_nPauseTime=m_nCurrentPauseStart=0; m_bPaused=TRUE;
}
```

The CGameTimer start function sets m_bPaused to FALSE to indicate that the timer is not initially paused and then calls the CTimer start function to start the timer:

```
void CGameTimer::start(){ //start the timer
  m_bPaused=FALSE; CTimer::start();
}
```

The CGameTimer time function returns the current time by first querying timeGetTime. It subtracts off the time previously spent paused, which is stored in the member variable m_nPauseTime. If the timer is currently paused (that is, if m_bPaused is TRUE), it then subtracts off the time currently spent paused, that is, the amount of time since m_nCurrentPauseStart (that is, current_time-m_nCurrentPauseStart). Finally, as in the CTimer time function, it subtracts the CTimer member variable m_nStartTime so that the time reported is the number of milliseconds since the timer was started, not counting time spent paused.

```
int CGameTimer::time(){ //return the time
  int current_time=timeGetTime();
  int result=current_time-m_nPauseTime;
  if(m_bPaused)result-=current_time-m_nCurrentPauseStart;
  return result-m_nStartTime;
}
```

The pause function simply needs to set m_bPaused to TRUE and record the time in m_nCurrentPauseStart:

```
void CGameTimer::pause(){ //pause the timer
  m_bPaused=TRUE; m_nCurrentPauseStart=timeGetTime();
}
```

The unpause function sets m_bPaused to FALSE and adds the current pause time to the accumulated pause time in m_nPauseTime:

```
void CGameTimer::unpause(){ //unpause the timer
  m_bPaused=FALSE;
  m_nPauseTime+=timeGetTime()-m_nCurrentPauseStart;
}
```

To use CGameTimer we need to change all of the includes of Timer.h to Gtimer.h, and all of the externs of CTimer Timer to CGameTimer Timer in the following files: Ai.cpp, Input.cpp, Joystick.cpp, Objects.cpp, Objman.cpp, and View.cpp. In Main.cpp we need to change the include and change the declaration of CTimer Timer to CGameTimer Timer.

The Pausable Sound Manager

The game sound manager class CGameSoundManager is derived from our sound manager class CSoundManager first met in Demo 8 (Chapter 10), and adds to it the ability to pause the sounds. Fortunately, DirectSound provides most of the functionality that we need. Our main job is to remember which sounds were looping and which were not so that they can be restarted the same way when they are unpaused.

Changes to the Sound Manager

Some changes need to be made to the class CSoundManager to enable CGameSoundManager to access some of the base class private member variables. Specifically, the following CSoundManager private member variables need to be made protected instead of private in Sound.h.

```
int m_nCount; //number of sounds loaded
LPLPDIRECTSOUNDBUFFER m_lpBuffer[MAX_SOUNDS]; //sound buffers
int m_nCopyCount[MAX_SOUNDS]; //num copies of each sound
BOOL m_bOperational; //DirectSound initialized correctly
```

Furthermore, the following CSoundManager member functions need to be made virtual so that the CGameSoundManager versions will override them at run time:

```
virtual BOOL CreateBuffer(int index,int length,int copies);
virtual void clear(); //clear all sounds
```

Pausable Sound Manager Overview

The header file for the pausable sound manager is Psound.h. The pausable sound manager class CGameSoundManager is derived from the sounds manager class CSoundManager.

```
class CGameSoundManager:public CSoundManager {
```

CGameSoundManager has two two-dimensional private member arrays, m_bPausedPlaying and m_bPausedLooping. We will use them as follows: m_bPausedPlaying[i][j] will be set to TRUE if copy j of sound i was paused while *playing*, and m_ bPausedLooping[i][j] will be set to TRUE if copy j of sound i was paused while *looping*. At declaration time we don't know how many copies of each sound there will be. Since there can potentially be a different number of copies for each sound, we will declare them both to be of type BOOL*[MAX_SOUNDS], and we will create enough space for a BOOL for each copy at run time.

```
BOOL *m_bPausedPlaying[MAX_SOUNDS]; //paused while playing
BOOL *m_bPausedLooping[MAX_SOUNDS]; //paused while looping
```

CGameSoundManager also has an override function for the CSoundManager private member function CreateBuffer:

```
BOOL CreateBuffer(int index,int length,int copies);
```

CGameSoundManager has six public member functions, beginning with a constructor:

```
CGameSoundManager(HWND hwnd); //constructor
```

The CGameSoundManager clear function is an override for the CSoundManager clear function:

```
void clear(); //clear all sounds
```

There are two pause functions. The first of these pauses all copies of a sound with a given index.

```
void pause(int index); //pause sound
```

The second version of pause pauses all copies of all sounds:

```
void pause(void); //pause all sounds
```

Similarly, there are two versions of unpause:

```
void unpause(int index); //unpause sound
void unpause(void); //unpause all sounds
```

Pausable Sound Manager Code

The code file for the pausable sound manager is Psound.cpp. It begins with the CGameSoundManager constructor, which calls the CSoundManager constructor and initializes the m_bPausedPlaying and m_bPausedLooping arrays to NULL.

```
CGameSoundManager::CGameSoundManager(HWND hwnd):
CSoundManager(hwnd){ //constructor
  for(int i=0; i<MAX_SOUNDS; i++)
    m_bPausedPlaying[i]=m_bPausedLooping[i]=NULL;
}
```

The CGameSoundManager clear() function, which resets all aspects of the sound manager, calls the CSoundManager clear() function, then deletes the space created for the m_bPausedPlaying and m_bPausedLooping arrays (one BOOL for each copy of each sound):

```
void CGameSoundManager::clear(){ //clear all sounds
  CSoundManager::clear();
  for(int i=0; i<m_nCount; i++){ //for each sound
```

```
      delete[]m_bPausedPlaying[i];
      delete[]m_bPausedLooping[i];
   }
}
```

The CGameSoundManager CreateBuffer function allocates space for the
m_bPausedPlaying and m_bPausedLooping arrays (one BOOL for each copy
of the sound), and initializes their values to FALSE for each copy. It then calls the
CSoundManager CreateBuffer function to create the sound buffers.

```
BOOL CGameSoundManager::CreateBuffer(int index,int length,
                                     int copies){
  //create and initialize pause flags
  m_bPausedPlaying[index]=new BOOL[copies];
  m_bPausedLooping[index]=new BOOL[copies];
  for(int i=0; i<copies; i++) //initialize them
    m_bPausedPlaying[index][i]=m_bPausedLooping[index][i]=FALSE;
  //create sound buffers
  return CSoundManager::CreateBuffer(index,length,copies);
}
```

Pausing and Unpausing

The parameterless versions of the CGameSoundManager pause and unpause
functions simply call the other versions for every sound; they do the real work
here:

```
void CGameSoundManager::pause(void){ //pause all sounds
  if(!m_bOperational)return; //bail if not initialized correctly
  for(int i=0; i<m_nCount; i++)pause(i); //pause them all
}

void CGameSoundManager::unpause(void){ //unpause all sounds
  if(!m_bOperational)return; //bail if not initialized correctly
  for(int i=0; i<m_nCount; i++)unpause(i); //unpause them all
}
```

The other CGameSoundManager pause function pauses all copies of the sound
with the given index. Actually, pausing the sound is almost no work at all, since
DirectSound will take care of it for you. We simply need to call the DirectSound
Stop member function of each sound buffer.

```
for(int i=0; i<m_nCopyCount[index]; i++){ //for each copy
  //stop sound copy (stays at same place in sound)
  m_lpBuffer[index][i]->Stop(); //stop playing
}
```

Unpausing is also relatively easy; calling the DirectSound Play member function
of each sound buffer will resume playing it from the place where it was stopped.
However, we must determine which copies of the sound were playing at the time

they were paused, and ask DirectSound to restart only those that were. Furthermore, for each copy that was playing, we must also specify to DirectSound whether it is to be played once or played looping. To facilitate this, the CGameSoundManager pause function will query DirectSound as to the status of each copy, specifically, which copies of the sound are currently looping, which are currently playing once, and which are currently silent. The information for copy i will be stored in the array entries m_bPausedPlaying[index][i] and m_bPausedLooping[index][i], from where they will be read and acted upon by unpause.

The status of copy i of the sound can be found by calling the DirectSound function m_lpBuffer[index][i]->GetStatus(&dwStatus), which will put the status information into DWORD dwStatus. If the copy is playing, dwStatus&DSBSTATUS_PLAYING will be TRUE, and if is looping, both that and dwStatus&DSBSTATUS_LOOPING will be TRUE. Therefore, we must check for looping first, then playing.

```
if(dwStatus&DSBSTATUS_LOOPING){ //looping
  m_bPausedLooping[index][i]=TRUE;
  m_bPausedPlaying[index][i]=FALSE;
}
else if(dwStatus&DSBSTATUS_PLAYING){ //playing not looping
  m_bPausedLooping[index][i]=FALSE;
  m_bPausedPlaying[index][i]=TRUE;
}
```

Otherwise, the copy of the sound is not playing, so we set both flags to FALSE:

```
else{ //not playing
  m_bPausedLooping[index][i]=FALSE;
  m_bPausedPlaying[index][i]=FALSE;
}
```

The GetStatus call may also fail (if it succeeds, it returns DS_OK), in which case we act prudently and assume that the sound buffer is unavailable, so we also set both flags to FALSE as above. Putting all this together, we get the following function.

```
void CGameSoundManager::pause(int index){ //pause sound
  if(!m_bOperational)return; //bail if not initialized correctly
  if(index<0||index>=m_nCount)return; //bail if bad index
  DWORD dwStatus=0; //to save status of sound copy
  for(int i=0; i<m_nCopyCount[index]; i++){ //for each copy
    //record status for later unpausing
    if(SUCCEEDED(m_lpBuffer[index][i]->GetStatus(&dwStatus))){
      if(dwStatus&DSBSTATUS_LOOPING){ //looping
        m_bPausedLooping[index][i]=TRUE;
        m_bPausedPlaying[index][i]=FALSE;
      }
```

```
      else if(dwStatus&DSBSTATUS_PLAYING){ //playing not looping
        m_bPausedLooping[index][i]=FALSE;
        m_bPausedPlaying[index][i]=TRUE;
      }
      else{ //not playing
        m_bPausedLooping[index][i]=FALSE;
        m_bPausedPlaying[index][i]=FALSE;
      }
    }
    else{ //if data is invalid, assume not in use
      m_bPausedLooping[index][i]=FALSE;
      m_bPausedPlaying[index][i]=FALSE;
    }
    //stop sound copy (stays at same place in sound)
    m_lpBuffer[index][i]->Stop(); //stop playing
  }
}
```

The CGameSoundManager unpause function replays copy i of the sound based on the values of m_bPausedPlaying[index][i] (TRUE means play it once) and m_bPausedLooping[index][i] (TRUE means play it looping). If both values are FALSE the copy is not played at all.

```
void CGameSoundManager::unpause(int index){ //unpause sound
  if(!m_bOperational)return; //bail if not initialized correctly
  if(index<0||index>=m_nCount)return; //bail if bad index
  for(int i=0; i<m_nCopyCount[index]; i++) //for each copy
    if(m_bPausedPlaying[index][i]) //was paused while playing
      m_lpBuffer[index][i]->Play(0,0,0); //restart playing
    else if(m_bPausedLooping[index][i]) //was paused looping
      m_lpBuffer[index][i]->Play(0,0,DSBPLAY_LOOPING); //so loop
}
```

Declaring the Sound Manager

Since the sound manager is created at run time, it is easier for us to substitute CGameSoundManager for CSoundManager than it was for us to substitute CGameTimer for CTimer. Aside from the code in Main.cpp, the input manager will be the only class that needs to use the new features that CGameSound-Manager provides, and so we need only change the #include in Main.cpp and Input.cpp. In the rest of the code we will take advantage of the fact that in C++ a pointer to a base type object can also point to a class derived from that base type, so the CSoundManager* SoundManager pointer can also point to a CGameSoundManager object without further changes to the code being necessary. Of course, in Main.cpp we need to change the line of code that creates the sound manager in WinMain to:

```
SoundManager=new CGameSoundManager(hwnd);
```

Pause Management

Now that we have the two main tools that we need—a pausable timer and a pausable sound manager—we are ready to discuss how to manage the whole pause process. The input manager will be given responsibility for handling the pause process because (with one exception) the game will be paused in response to a keystroke message from the player.

We start by declaring a global Boolean variable `GamePaused` in `Main.cpp`, which will be set to `TRUE` when the game is paused and `FALSE` otherwise.

```
BOOL GamePaused=FALSE; //TRUE if game paused
```

Changes to the Input Manager

With this in place, we enforce the rule that no input is processed while the game is paused (except `PAUSED_KEY`, which unpauses the game) by inserting the following bail-out code at the start of the `CInputManager` `GameKeyboard` function:

```
if(GamePaused&&keystroke!=PAUSED_KEY)return;
```

The pause key `PAUSED_KEY` is defined at the top of `Input.cpp`:

```
const WPARAM PAUSED_KEY=VK_F1; //pause key
```

Functions `GameJoystick` and `GameLMouseDown` are protected by inserting the following code at the top of each function:

```
if(GamePaused)return; //bail if game is paused
```

`CInputManager` has two new member functions to manage the pause process; we'll make them both public although only one of them really needs to be.

```
void pause(); //pause the game
void unpause(); //unpause the game
```

The `CInputManager pause()` member function sets `GamePaused` to `TRUE` and pauses the timer and the sound manager. Notice the typecast on the `SoundManager` pointer; this is because `SoundManager` was declared in `Main.cpp` to be of type `CSoundManager*`, not `CGameSoundManager*`. It is fine to have `SoundManager` point to a `CGameSoundManager` object at run time, but the compiler will object to an uncast `SoundManager->pause()` statement because, for all it knows, `SoundManager` can point to a base class `CSoundManager` object, which does not have a `pause()` member function.

```
void CInputManager::pause(){ //unpause the game
  GamePaused=TRUE;
  Timer.pause(); //pause the timer
  ((CGameSoundManager*)SoundManager)->pause(); //and the sound
}
```

The `CInputManager unpause()` member function does the opposite, setting `GamePaused` to `FALSE` and unpausing the timer and the sound manager:

```
void CInputManager::unpause(){ //unpause the game
  GamePaused=FALSE;
  Timer.unpause(); //unpause the timer
  ((CGameSoundManager*)SoundManager)->unpause(); //and the sound
}
```

Next, the new code is hooked up by inserting a new `case` to the main `switch` statement in the `CInputManager GameKeyboard` function. When `PAUSED_KEY` is hit, the game is paused if it is unpaused, and unpaused if it is paused (that makes sense, doesn't it?).

```
case PAUSED_KEY:
  if(GamePaused)unpause(); else pause();
break;
```

Changes to Main.cpp

There's one more thing to take care of, however: The game needs to be forcibly paused when the player's attention goes to some other process on his or her computer (for example, by pressing Alt+Tab). This can be done by adding code to the `WM_ACTIVEAPP case` in the `switch` statement in our windows message handler `WindowProc` in `Main.cpp`. Of course, this is only relevant when the game phase is `PLAYING_PHASE` and the game is not already paused.

```
case WM_ACTIVATEAPP:
  ActiveApp=wParam;
  //pause if swapped out while playing
  if(!ActiveApp&&GamePhase==PLAYING_PHASE&&!GamePaused)
    InputManager.pause();
  break;
```

To prevent the player from accidentally thinking that the game has frozen (apps don't do that often under Windows, do they?), we should at least display a sprite on the screen to let them know that the game is paused. In `Main.cpp` we declare a pointer to a `CClippedSprite` for this purpose. (Until further notice, the changes referred to in this section will take place in `Main.cpp`.)

```
CClippedSprite *PausedSprite; //display word "Paused"
```

This sprite can be loaded using the `LoadPausedSprite` function, which reads the image from position (`399,403`) in the bmp sprite file reader `g_cSpriteImages`:

```
BOOL LoadPausedSprite(){
  return PausedSprite->load(&g_cSpriteImages,0,399,403);
} //LoadPausedSprite
```

It is created and loaded by adding the following two lines of code to function `LoadImages`. Note that `PausedSprite` has a single frame and is `220x64` pixels in size.

```
PausedSprite=new CClippedSprite(1,220,64);
LoadPausedSprite();
```

Remembering that every new surface has to be restored, we add the following two lines of code to `RestoreSurfaces()`:

```
if(PausedSprite->Restore()) //if restored
    result=result&&LoadPausedSprite(); //redraw image
```

`PausedSprite` is actually drawn by one line of code added to the end of function `ComposeFrame()`. It should go at the end of the function so that the sprite is drawn on top of everything. Position `(320,200)` on the screen seems like a good place to draw it.

```
if(GamePaused) PausedSprite->draw(0,320,200,lpSecondary);
```

Finally, the surfaces in `PausedSprite` need to be released at the end of the game, and `PausedSprite` itself needs to be deleted. The following two statements are added to the `WM_DESTROY` case in the windows message handler `WindowProc`.

```
PausedSprite->Release(); delete PausedSprite;
```

Phase Management

Demo 13 has two new phases, designated `CREDITS_PHASE`, and `HELP_PHASE`, which we need to add to the enumerated type `GamePhaseType` in `Defines.h`. The credits phase has a sound sample that we play on entry to the phase, and the help phase has a sound sample that we play when flipping from one page of help to the next. We add the following constants to the enumerated types in `Sndlist.h`. At the end of `GameSoundType` we append:

```
PAGETURN_SOUND, //sound of page being turned
```

And at the end of `IntroSoundType` we append:

```
CREDITS_SOUND, //played during credits
```

The sounds get loaded in function `LoadSounds` by adding the following two lines of code at the end of `case 0` and `case 1`, respectively, in the main `switch` statement:

```
SoundManager->load("credits.wav");
SoundManager->load("pageturn.wav",2);
```

The modified flow of control between the different phases of our game is shown in Figure 15.4. The credits phase fits in sequentially between the title phase and the menu phase. The help phase is, of course, accessible from the fourth button on the menu screen displayed in the menu phase. In addition, the device menu phase, the high score phase, and the help phase are also accessible from the playing phase via the function keys.

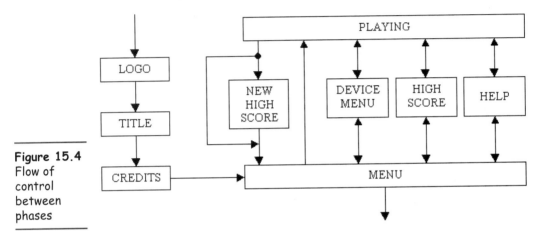

Figure 15.4
Flow of control between phases

The Credits Phase

Let's look at the credits phase first. The following code needs to be added to the switch statement in function change_phase in Main.cpp to display the credits screen and play the credits sound on entering the credits phase.

```
case CREDITS_PHASE:
  display_screen("credits.bmp");
  SoundManager->stop(); //silence previous phase
  SoundManager->play(CREDITS_SOUND); //credits sound
  break;
```

In that same switch statement, the MENU_PHASE case has two switch statements, both of which test the previous phase, which used to be TITLE_PHASE and now should be changed to CREDITS_PHASE.

Function Redraw, which is used to redraw the screen in response to surface loss, needs the following new case to redraw the credits screen:

```
case CREDITS_PHASE:
  display_screen("credits.bmp");
  break;
```

The code for the credits phase is completed with the addition of some code to function ProcessFrame in Main.cpp, whose job is to process a frame of animation during each phase, which in this case means simply to wait for the phase to end. We declare how long the phase should last.

```
const int CREDITS_DISPLAY_TIME=8000; //duration of credits
```

Then, in the `switch` statement we change the last line of code in the `case` `TITLE_PHASE` to:

```
change_phase(CREDITS_PHASE); //go to credits
```

instead of changing to `MENU_PHASE`.

Finally, we add a new `case` for the credits phase to the `switch` statement in function `ProcessFrame` in `Main.cpp`. This looks a lot like the corresponding code for the other intro phases: It simply waits for the phase to end either from having the global variable `endphase` set to `TRUE` from the input manager or from having the appropriate amount of time go by. Then it changes to the next phase, which in this case is the menu phase.

```
case CREDITS_PHASE: //displaying title screen
  Sleep(100); //surrender time to other processes
  if(endphase||Timer.elapsed(PhaseTime,CREDITS_DISPLAY_TIME))
    change_phase(MENU_PHASE); //go to menu
  break;
```

The Help Phase

When the Help button is clicked on the main menu, we want to start out displaying the first page of help, flipping to the next one every time the user hits a key (except for Esc) or clicks on the mouse or the joystick. After all pages of help have been displayed (or when the player hits Esc), we return to the main menu. The following global variables enable us to keep track of what's going on: `HelpPage` records the page of help currently being displayed, `FlipHelpPage` is set to `TRUE` when the player asks to see the next help page, and `NUMHELPPAGES` is a constant that is set to the number of help pages, in this case six—so `HelpPage` will be an integer between zero and `NUMHELPPAGES-1`, inclusive.

```
int HelpPage; //current page of help to be displayed
BOOL FlipHelpPage; //whether to flip help page
const int NUMHELPPAGES=6; //number of help pages
```

We begin coding for the help phase by adding a `case` for the help phase to the `switch` statement in function `change_phase` to take care of entry to the help phase by displaying the first page of help and initializing `HelpPage` and `FlipHelpPage`. We hide the mouse cursor while the help pages are being shown (to remove the temptation to click on anything, since our help system is primitive in the sense that it has no hyperlinks or buttons). We can look ahead at this point and realize that the cursor will only be showing if we enter the help phase from the menu phase and only bother hiding the cursor if it is showing.

```
case HELP_PHASE: //display first help page
  if(GamePhase==MENU_PHASE)ShowCursor(FALSE);
  display_screen("help000.bmp"); //show first page
  HelpPage=0; FlipHelpPage=FALSE; //reset to first page
  break;
```

In general we will want to be able to display an arbitrary help page, so we'll write a function display_helpscreen that reads the global variable HelpPage and displays the corresponding page of help using our display_screen function. Notice that it assumes that there are at most ten pages of help; I'm sure you can figure out how to modify it if there are more. Note that it simplifies coding if you start your game design with a three-digit number built into the filenames for your help files; even if there are only nine help files in the initial design, later design changes may make it necessary to add more.

```
void display_helpscreen(){
  //construct help file name
  char filename[16];
  strcpy(filename,"help000.bmp");
  filename[6]='0'+HelpPage;
  //display the help file
  display_screen(filename);
}
```

Function Redraw, which is used to redraw the screen in response to surface loss, needs the following new case to redraw the appropriate help screen using display_helpscreen:

```
case HELP_PHASE:
  display_helpscreen();
  break;
```

Now we move to function ProcessFrame in Main.cpp and add a new case to its switch statement. In addition to waiting for the end of the phase, we wait for the input manager to set the global variable FlipHelpPage to TRUE, and respond by incrementing the global variable HelpPage and displaying the next help page, exiting the phase by setting endphase to TRUE if there is no next help page.

```
case HELP_PHASE: //display help
  if(FlipHelpPage){ //turn the page
    FlipHelpPage=FALSE; //don't do it again
    if(++HelpPage>=NUMHELPPAGES)endphase=TRUE; //last page
    else{ //next page
      SoundManager->play(PAGETURN_SOUND); //page flip sound
      display_helpscreen(); //display help screen
```

```
      }
    }
```

At the end of this `case` we check whether `endphase` is `TRUE`, and if so, we move to the next phase. For now we can assume that the next phase is the menu phase, but rather than go into this now we can return to it later when we address accessing the help pages from the playing phase.

The input manager gets three new private member functions for handling input during the help phase:

```
void HelpKeyboard(WPARAM keystroke); //keyboard handler
void HelpLMouseUp(POINT point); //mouse up handler
void HelpJoystick(); //joystick handler
```

The keyboard manager exits from the help phase if the Esc button is pressed, and flips to the next help page for any other key:

```
void CInputManager::HelpKeyboard(WPARAM keystroke){
//help keyboard handler
  switch(keystroke){
    case VK_ESCAPE: endphase=TRUE; break;
    default: FlipHelpPage=TRUE; break;
  }
}
```

When the mouse left button up is detected, we flip to the next page of help. Notice that again the action is deferred to the keyboard manager so that input action takes place in only once place in the code.

```
void CInputManager::HelpLMouseUp(POINT point){
//mouse left button up handler for help
  Keyboard(VK_SPACE);
}
```

Similarly for joystick button 1:

```
void CInputManager::HelpJoystick(){
//joystick handler for help
  if(JoystickManager.button_down(1))
    Keyboard(VK_SPACE); //next page
}
```

Calls to these functions are added to the `switch` statements in the public `CInputManager` input handlers `Keyboard`, `LMouseUp`, and `Joystick` in the usual way. The help code is then activated from `Keyboard` by inserting the following code into the `switch` statement.

```
case 'H': //help
  NextPhase=HELP_PHASE; endphase=TRUE;
  break;
```

We already have code in the `CInputManager MainMenuLMouseUp` function to handle clicking on the Help button in the main menu; it just passes a fake "H" key event to the keyboard handler.

Breaking out of Gameplay

The last new feature that we need to cover is the ability to break out of gameplay to access the help pages, high score list, and device menu. Up until now, we could only enter these phases from the menu phase. Now we can also enter from the playing phase, so we need to make sure that entry to these phases is done correctly from either source. Fortunately, all that needs to be done is to show the cursor when entering the device menu phase from the playing phase, and to hide the cursor when entering the high score phase from menu phase (since the cursor is hidden during the playing phase and showing during the menu phase). We simply insert the appropriate conditional in front of the calls to `ShowCursor` in function `change_phase`. For case `DEVICEMENU_PHASE` we use:

```
if(GamePhase==PLAYING_PHASE)ShowCursor(TRUE);
```

and for case `HIGHSCORE_PHASE` we use:

```
if(GamePhase==MENU_PHASE)ShowCursor(FALSE); //hide cursor
```

To handle the changes that come from the new ways to enter the playing phase, we go to the `PLAYING_PHASE` case in the main `switch` statement in function `change_phase`. There is already a `switch` statement within this `case` to handle entry from the menu phase or the success phase. We simply add these new `cases` there to handle the new entry options; all they need to do is handle the mouse cursor and unpause the game.

```
case DEVICEMENU_PHASE:
  ShowCursor(FALSE);
  InputManager.unpause();
  break;
case HIGHSCORE_PHASE:
case HELP_PHASE:
  InputManager.unpause();
  break;
```

Finally, we add code to the `CInputManager GameKeyboard` function to pause the game and go to the appropriate phase in response to the various function keys:

```
case VK_F2: //device menu
  endphase=TRUE; NextPhase=DEVICEMENU_PHASE; pause();
  break;
case VK_F3: //high score list
  endphase=TRUE; NextPhase=HIGHSCORE_PHASE; pause();
  break;
case VK_F4: //help
```

```
            endphase=TRUE; NextPhase=HELP_PHASE; pause();
            break;
        case VK_F5: show_framerate=!show_framerate; break;
```

Demo 13 Files

Code Files

The following files in Demo 13 are used without change from Demo 12:

- Ai.h
- Bmp.h
- Bmp.cpp
- Bsprite.h
- Bsprite.cpp
- Buttons.h
- Buttons.cpp
- Csprite.h
- Csprite.cpp
- Ddsetup.cpp
- Joystick.h
- Objects.h
- Objman.h
- Random.h
- Random.cpp
- Sbmp.h
- Sbmp.cpp
- Score.h
- Score.cpp
- Text.h
- Text.cpp
- Timer.h
- Timer.cpp
- Topscore.h
- Topscore.cpp
- View.h

The following files in Demo 13 have been modified from Demo 12:

- Ai.cpp (changes minimal; not listed)
- Defines.h
- Input.h
- Input.cpp
- Joystick.cpp (changes minimal; not listed)
- Main.cpp
- Objects.cpp (changes minimal; not listed)
- Objman.cpp (changes minimal; not listed)
- Sndlist.h
- Sound.h
- Sound.cpp (changes minimal; not listed)
- View.cpp (changes minimal; not listed)

The following files are new in Demo 13:

- Gtimer.h
- Gtimer.cpp
- Psound.h
- Psound.cpp

Media Files

The following image files are new in Demo 13:

- Credits.bmp
- Farm.bmp
- Help000.bmp
- Help001.bmp
- Help002.bmp
- Help003.bmp
- Help004.bmp
- Help005.bmp

The following sound files are new in Demo 13:

- Credits.wav
- Pageturn.wav

Required Libraries

- Ddraw.lib
- Dsound.lib
- Winmm.lib

Code Listings

Defines.h

```
//defines.h: essential defines
//Copyright Ian Parberry, 1999
//Last updated March 14, 2000

#ifndef __DEFINES_H__
#define __DEFINES_H__

#define SCREEN_WIDTH 640 //pixels wide
#define SCREEN_HEIGHT 480 //pixels high
#define COLORS 256 //number of colors
#define COLOR_DEPTH 8 //number of bits to store colors
#define TRANSPARENT_COLOR 255 //transparent palette position

enum GamePhaseType{
  LOGO_PHASE,TITLE_PHASE,CREDITS_PHASE,MENU_PHASE,PLAYING_PHASE,
  DEVICEMENU_PHASE,SUCCESS_PHASE,HIGHSCORE_PHASE,
  NEWHIGHSCORE_PHASE,HELP_PHASE
};

enum
InputDeviceType{KEYBOARD_INPUT=0,MOUSE_INPUT,JOYSTICK_INPUT};

#endif
```

Gtimer.h

```
//gtimer.h, header file for gtimer.cpp
//Copyright Ian Parberry, 2000
//Last updated April 4, 2000

#ifndef __gtimer_h__
#define __gtimer_h__

//system includes
#include <windows.h> //needed for BOOL

#include "timer.h" //for base timer class
```

```
class CGameTimer: public CTimer{ //game timer class
  private:
    int m_nPauseTime; //amount of time spent paused
    int m_nCurrentPauseStart; //last time timer was paused
    BOOL m_bPaused; //TRUE if currently paused
  public:
    CGameTimer(); //constructor
    void start(); //start the timer
    int time(); //return the time
    void pause(); //pause the timer
    void unpause(); //unpause the timer
};

#endif
```

Gtimer.cpp

```
//gtimer.cpp, the game timer class
//Copyright Ian Parberry, 2000
//Last updated March 14, 2000

#include "gtimer.h"

CGameTimer::CGameTimer():CTimer(){ //constructor
  m_nPauseTime=m_nCurrentPauseStart=0; m_bPaused=TRUE;
}

void CGameTimer::start(){ //start the timer
  m_bPaused=FALSE; CTimer::start();
}

void CGameTimer::pause(){ //pause the timer
  m_bPaused=TRUE; m_nCurrentPauseStart=timeGetTime();
}

void CGameTimer::unpause(){ //unpause the timer
  m_bPaused=FALSE;
  m_nPauseTime+=timeGetTime()-m_nCurrentPauseStart;
}

int CGameTimer::time(){ //return the time
  int current_time=timeGetTime();
  int result=current_time-m_nPauseTime;
  if(m_bPaused)result-=current_time-m_nCurrentPauseStart;
  return result-m_nStartTime;
}
```

Input.h

```
//input.h: header file for input class

//Copyright Ian Parberry, 1999
//Last updated March 15, 2000

#include <windows.h>
#include <windowsx.h>

#include "defines.h"
#include "buttons.h" //for button manager
#include "joystick.h" //for joystick manager


#ifndef __INPUT_H__
#define __INPUT_H__

class CInputManager{
  private:
    InputDeviceType InputDevice; //current input device
    CButtonManager *ButtonManager; //for managing menu buttons
    CJoystickManager JoystickManager; //joystick manager
    //helper functions
    BOOL is_function_key(WPARAM keystroke); //TRUE if fn key
    void decode(LPARAM lparam,POINT &point); //decode mouse click
    void set_plane_speed(POINT point,SIZE extent);
    //for text input
    BOOL letter(WPARAM keystroke); //keystroke is a letter
    BOOL number(WPARAM keystroke); //keystroke is a digit
    //setting of input device from registry
    void init_input_device(); //get last used device
    void set_input_device(); //put last used device
    //set up buttons for menus
    void SetupMainMenuButtons(); //main menu button manager
    void SetupDeviceMenuButtons(); //device menu button manager
    //keyboard handlers
    void IntroKeyboard(WPARAM keystroke); //keyboard handler
    BOOL MainMenuKeyboard(WPARAM keystroke); //keyboard handler
    void DeviceMenuKeyboard(WPARAM keystroke); //keyboard handler
    void NewhighscoreKeyboard(WPARAM keystroke); //keybd handler
    void GameKeyboard(WPARAM keystroke); //keyboard handler
    void HelpKeyboard(WPARAM keystroke); //keyboard handler
    //left mouse button down handlers
    void MainMenuLMouseDown(POINT point); //mouse down handler
    void DeviceMenuLMouseDown(POINT point); //mouse down handler
    void GameLMouseDown(POINT point); //mouse down handler
    //left mouse button up handlers
    void IntroLMouseUp(POINT point); //mouse up handler
    BOOL MainMenuLMouseUp(POINT point); //mouse up handler
```

```
          void DeviceMenuLMouseUp(POINT point); //mouse up handler
          void HelpLMouseUp(POINT point); //mouse up handler
          //joystick handlers
          void IntroJoystick(); //joystick handler
          void GameJoystick(); //joystick handler
          void HelpJoystick(); //joystick handler
        public:
          CInputManager(); //constructor
          ~CInputManager(); //destructor
          BOOL Restore(); //restore surfaces
          void Release(); //release surfaces
          void SetupButtons(GamePhaseType phase); //set up menu buttons
          BOOL Keyboard(WPARAM keystroke,
            BOOL virtual_keystroke=FALSE); //keyboard handler
          void LMouseDown(LPARAM lparam); //main mouse down handler
          BOOL LMouseUp(LPARAM lparam); //main mouse up handler
          void MouseMove(LPARAM lparam); //handle mouse motion
          void Joystick(); //main joystick handler
          void pause(); //pause the game
          void unpause(); //unpause the game
        };

        #endif
```

Input.cpp

```
        //input.cpp: program file for input class

        //Copyright Ian Parberry, 1999
        //Last updated March 15, 2000

        #include <stdio.h> //for sscanf, sprintf

        #include "input.h"
        #include "objman.h" //for object manager
        #include "psound.h" //for sound manager
        #include "topscore.h" //for high score list
        #include "gtimer.h" //game timer

        extern BOOL show_framerate;

        extern GamePhaseType GamePhase; //current phase
        extern GamePhaseType NextPhase; //next phase of game
        extern BOOL endphase; //should we abort current phase?
        extern CObjectManager ObjectManager; //object manager
        extern CSoundManager* SoundManager; //sound manager
        extern CHighScoreList HighScoreList; //high score list manager
        extern CGameTimer Timer; //game timer

        extern BOOL GamePaused; //TRUE if game is paused
```

```
extern BOOL FlipHelpPage; //whether to flip help page

const WPARAM PAUSED_KEY=VK_F1; //pause key

CInputManager::CInputManager(){ //constructor
  init_input_device(); //current input device
  ButtonManager=NULL; //for managing menu buttons
  JoystickManager.initialize(); //set up joystick
  JoystickManager.autorepeat(FALSE); //disable autorepeat
}

CInputManager::~CInputManager(){ //destructor
  delete ButtonManager;
}

BOOL CInputManager::Restore(){ //restore surfaces
  return ButtonManager->Restore();
}

void CInputManager::Release(){ //release surfaces
    ButtonManager->Release();
}

void CInputManager::SetupMainMenuButtons(){
//set up main menu button manager
  const int YDELTA=70; //y separation between buttons
  const int BUTTONCOUNT=6; //number of buttons
  SIZE size; //size of buttons
  size.cx=40; size.cy=40; //size of buttons
  POINT point; //top left corner of first button
  point.x=111; point.y=46; //first button location
  delete ButtonManager; //delete any old one
  ButtonManager=new //create new button manager
    CButtonManager(BUTTONCOUNT,size,point,YDELTA,
      "buttons.bmp");
 //set button sounds
  ButtonManager->
    setsounds(BIGCLICK_SOUND,SMALLCLICK_SOUND);
}

void CInputManager::SetupDeviceMenuButtons(){
//set up device menu button manager
  const int BUTTONCOUNT=4;
  delete ButtonManager; //if there is one already, delete it
  SIZE size; //size of buttons
  size.cx=40; size.cy=40; //size of buttons
  ButtonManager=new
    CButtonManager(BUTTONCOUNT,size,"buttons.bmp");
  ButtonManager->setsounds(BIGCLICK_SOUND,SMALLCLICK_SOUND);
  ButtonManager->set_radio(); //radio buttons
```

```
  //add buttons
  POINT point;
  point.x=209; point.y=130;
  ButtonManager->addbutton(point);
  point.x=209; point.y=210;
  ButtonManager->addbutton(point);
  point.x=209; point.y=291;
  ButtonManager->addbutton(point);
  point.x=209; point.y=372;
  ButtonManager->addbutton(point);
  //initialize image of radio button
  ButtonManager->buttondown(InputDevice,FALSE); //no sound
}

void CInputManager::SetupButtons(GamePhaseType phase){
//set up menu buttons
  switch(phase){
    case MENU_PHASE: SetupMainMenuButtons(); break;
    case DEVICEMENU_PHASE: SetupDeviceMenuButtons(); break;
  }
}

//registry access for current input device

void CInputManager::init_input_device(){
//get last used device from registry
  HKEY RegistryKey; //registry key
  const int BUFSIZE=8; //buffer size
  char buffer[BUFSIZE]; //text buffer
  int result=RegCreateKeyEx(HKEY_CURRENT_USER,
    "SOFTWARE\\LARC\\NedFarm",0,NULL,0,KEY_READ,
    NULL,&RegistryKey,NULL);
  DWORD type; //type of registry entry
  if(result==ERROR_SUCCESS){ //entry exists
    unsigned long length=BUFSIZE-1; buffer[0]=0;
    RegQueryValueEx(RegistryKey,"InputDevice",NULL,&type,
       (unsigned char *)buffer,&length); //get value into buffer
    if(length){ //success
      buffer[length]=0; sscanf(buffer,"%d",&InputDevice);
    }
    else InputDevice=KEYBOARD_INPUT; //default to keyboard input
    RegCloseKey(RegistryKey);
  }
}

void CInputManager::set_input_device(){
//save last used device to registry
  HKEY RegistryKey; //registry key
  int result=RegCreateKeyEx(HKEY_CURRENT_USER,
    "SOFTWARE\\LARC\\NedFarm",0,NULL,0,KEY_WRITE,
```

```
    NULL,&RegistryKey,NULL);
  if(result==ERROR_SUCCESS){ //entry exists
    const int BUFSIZE=16; //buffer size
    char buffer[BUFSIZE]; //text buffer
    sprintf(buffer,"%d",InputDevice); //convert to string
    RegSetValueEx(RegistryKey,"InputDevice",NULL,REG_SZ,
      (unsigned char *)buffer,strlen(buffer)+1); //set value
    RegCloseKey(RegistryKey);
  }
}


//keyboard handlers

void CInputManager::IntroKeyboard(WPARAM keystroke){
//keyboard handler for intro
  endphase=TRUE; //any key ends the phase
}

BOOL CInputManager::MainMenuKeyboard(WPARAM keystroke){
//keyboard handler for menu
  BOOL result=FALSE;
  switch(keystroke){
    case VK_ESCAPE:
    case 'Q': //exit the game
      result=TRUE;
      break;
    case 'N': //play new game
      NextPhase=PLAYING_PHASE; endphase=TRUE;
      break;
    case 'D':
      NextPhase=DEVICEMENU_PHASE; endphase=TRUE;
      break;
    case 'L': //see high score list
      NextPhase=HIGHSCORE_PHASE; endphase=TRUE;
      break;
    case 'H': //help
      NextPhase=HELP_PHASE; endphase=TRUE;
      break;
    default: break; //do nothing
  }
  return result;
}

void CInputManager::DeviceMenuKeyboard(WPARAM keystroke){
//keyboard handler //for device menu
  switch(keystroke){
    case VK_ESCAPE:
    case 'D': //exit menu
      set_input_device(); //save new input device to registry
      endphase=TRUE;
```

```
      break;
    case 'K': //play using keyboard
      InputDevice=KEYBOARD_INPUT; //set device
      ButtonManager->buttondown(KEYBOARD_INPUT);
      break;
    case 'M': //play using mouse
      InputDevice=MOUSE_INPUT; //set device
      ButtonManager->buttondown(MOUSE_INPUT);
      break;
    case 'J': //play using joystick
      if(JoystickManager.exists()){ //if joystick exists
        InputDevice=JOYSTICK_INPUT;
        ButtonManager->buttondown(JOYSTICK_INPUT);
      }
      break;
    default: break;
  }
}

BOOL CInputManager::letter(WPARAM keystroke){
  return keystroke>='A'&&keystroke<='Z';
}

BOOL CInputManager::number(WPARAM keystroke){
  return keystroke>='0'&&keystroke<='9';
}

void CInputManager::NewhighscoreKeyboard(WPARAM keystroke){
  if(letter(keystroke)){ //enter a letter
    if(HighScoreList.append_to_current(keystroke-'A'+'a'))
      SoundManager->play(TYPE_CHAR_SOUND);
  }
  else if(number(keystroke)){ //enter a numeric char
    if(HighScoreList.append_to_current(keystroke))
      SoundManager->play(TYPE_CHAR_SOUND);
  }
  else if(keystroke==VK_SPACE){ //enter a space
    if(HighScoreList.append_to_current(' '))
      SoundManager->play(TYPE_SPACE_SOUND);
  }
  else if(keystroke==VK_RETURN){ //end of name
    SoundManager->play(TYPE_RETURN_SOUND); endphase=TRUE;
  }
  else if(keystroke==VK_DELETE){ //delete a char
    if(HighScoreList.delete_from_current())
      SoundManager->play(TYPE_SPACE_SOUND);
  }
  else if(keystroke==VK_ESCAPE){ //abort
    HighScoreList.cancel_current(); endphase=TRUE;
  }
```

```
}


void CInputManager::GameKeyboard(WPARAM keystroke){
//keyboard handler for game play
  //bail if game is paused unless end pause key pressed
  if(GamePaused&&keystroke!=PAUSED_KEY)return;
  //process keystroke
  switch(keystroke){
    //function keys
    case VK_ESCAPE: endphase=TRUE; break;
    case PAUSED_KEY:
      if(GamePaused)unpause(); else pause();
    break;
    case VK_F2: //device menu
      endphase=TRUE; NextPhase=DEVICEMENU_PHASE; pause();
      break;
    case VK_F3: //high score list
      endphase=TRUE; NextPhase=HIGHSCORE_PHASE; pause();
      break;
    case VK_F4: //help
      endphase=TRUE; NextPhase=HELP_PHASE; pause();
      break;
    case VK_F5: show_framerate=!show_framerate; break;
    //regular keys
    case VK_UP: ObjectManager.accelerate(0,-1); break;
    case VK_DOWN: ObjectManager.accelerate(0,1); break;
    case VK_LEFT: ObjectManager.accelerate(-1,0); break;
    case VK_RIGHT: ObjectManager.accelerate(1,0); break;
    case VK_SPACE: ObjectManager.fire_gun(); break;
    default: break;
  }
}

void CInputManager::HelpKeyboard(WPARAM keystroke){
//help keyboard handler
  switch(keystroke){
    case VK_ESCAPE: endphase=TRUE; break;
    default: FlipHelpPage=TRUE; break;
  }
}

BOOL CInputManager::is_function_key(WPARAM keystroke){
  return keystroke==VK_ESCAPE||
    (keystroke>=VK_F1&&keystroke<=VK_F12);
}

BOOL CInputManager::Keyboard(WPARAM keystroke,
  BOOL virtual_keystroke){ //keyboard handler
  BOOL result=FALSE;
```

```
switch(GamePhase){
  case LOGO_PHASE:
  case TITLE_PHASE:
  case CREDITS_PHASE:
  case HIGHSCORE_PHASE:
  case SUCCESS_PHASE:
    IntroKeyboard(keystroke);
    break;
  case NEWHIGHSCORE_PHASE:
    NewhighscoreKeyboard(keystroke);
    break;
  case MENU_PHASE:
    result=MainMenuKeyboard(keystroke);
    break;
  case DEVICEMENU_PHASE:
    DeviceMenuKeyboard(keystroke);
    break;
  case HELP_PHASE: HelpKeyboard(keystroke); break;
  case PLAYING_PHASE:
    if(InputDevice==KEYBOARD_INPUT||
    is_function_key(keystroke)||virtual_keystroke)
      GameKeyboard(keystroke);
    break;
  }
  return result;
}

//mouse left button down handlers

void CInputManager::MainMenuLMouseDown(POINT point){
//mouse down handler for menu
  if(ButtonManager->hit(point)>=0) //if a valid hit
    ButtonManager->buttondown(point); //animate a button down
}

void CInputManager::DeviceMenuLMouseDown(POINT point){
//mouse down handler for device menu
  int hit=ButtonManager->hit(point);
  switch(hit){
    case 0: Keyboard('K'); break; //keyboard
    case 1: Keyboard('M'); break; //mouse
    case 2: Keyboard('J'); break; //joystick
    case 3:
      ButtonManager->buttondown(hit); //quit button down
      break;
    default: break;
  }
}

void CInputManager::GameLMouseDown(POINT point){
```

```
//mouse down handler for game
  Keyboard(VK_SPACE,TRUE);
}

void CInputManager::decode(LPARAM lparam,POINT &point){
//decode mouse click lparam to point
  point.x=LOWORD(lparam); point.y=HIWORD(lparam);
}

void CInputManager::LMouseDown(LPARAM lparam){
//main mouse left button down handler
  POINT point; //mouse location on screen
  decode(lparam,point); //decode mouse point
  switch(GamePhase){
    case MENU_PHASE:
      MainMenuLMouseDown(point);
      break;
    case DEVICEMENU_PHASE:
      DeviceMenuLMouseDown(point);
      break;
    case PLAYING_PHASE:
      if(InputDevice==MOUSE_INPUT)
        GameLMouseDown(point);
      break;
  }
}

//mouse left button up handlers

void CInputManager::IntroLMouseUp(POINT point){
//mouse left button up handler for intro
  endphase=TRUE;
}

BOOL CInputManager::MainMenuLMouseUp(POINT point){
//mouse left button up handler for menu
  int hit=ButtonManager->release(point); //get button hit
  BOOL result=FALSE;
  //take action depending on which button was hit
  switch(hit){ //depending on which button was hit
    case 0: Keyboard('N'); break; //new game
    case 1: Keyboard('S'); break; //saved game
    case 2: Keyboard('D'); break; //devices
    case 3: Keyboard('L'); break; //high score list
    case 4: Keyboard('H'); break; //help
    case 5: result=Keyboard(VK_ESCAPE); break; //quit
    default: break;
  }
  //animate button images
  if(hit>=0)ButtonManager->buttonup(hit); //hit
```

```
    else ButtonManager->allbuttonsup(); //nonhit
    return result;
}

void CInputManager::DeviceMenuLMouseUp(POINT point){
//mouse left button up handler for device menu
  int hit=ButtonManager->release(point);
  switch(hit){
    case 3: //quit button up
      ButtonManager->buttonup(hit); //show quit button up
      Keyboard(VK_ESCAPE);
      break;
  }
  if(hit<0)ButtonManager->allbuttonsup(); //no hit
}

void CInputManager::HelpLMouseUp(POINT point){
//mouse left button up handler for help
  Keyboard(VK_SPACE);
}

BOOL CInputManager::LMouseUp(LPARAM lparam){
//main mouse left button up handler
  BOOL result=FALSE;
  POINT point; //mouse location on screen
  decode(lparam,point); //decode mouse point
  switch(GamePhase){
    case LOGO_PHASE:
    case TITLE_PHASE:
    case CREDITS_PHASE:
    case SUCCESS_PHASE:
    case HIGHSCORE_PHASE:
      IntroLMouseUp(point);
      break;
    case MENU_PHASE:
      result=MainMenuLMouseUp(point);
      break;
    case DEVICEMENU_PHASE:
      DeviceMenuLMouseUp(point);
      break;
    case HELP_PHASE:
      HelpLMouseUp(point);
      break;
  }
  return result;
}

//mouse motion handler

void CInputManager::set_plane_speed(POINT point,SIZE extent){
```

```
    //set plane speed based on point's position in extent
      int xmin,xmax,ymin,ymax; //plane speed limits
      ObjectManager.speed_limits(xmin,xmax,ymin,ymax); //get them
      //bands for speed assignment
      const int XBANDWIDTH=extent.cx/(xmax-xmin+1);
      const int YBANDWIDTH=extent.cy/(ymax-ymin+1);
      int xspeed,yspeed; //speed of plane
      xspeed=point.x/XBANDWIDTH+xmin; //horizontal speed
      yspeed=point.y/YBANDWIDTH+ymin; //vertical speed
      ObjectManager.set_speed(xspeed,yspeed); //pass to plane
    }

    void CInputManager::MouseMove(LPARAM lparam){
      if(InputDevice!=MOUSE_INPUT)return; //bail if not needed
      if(GamePhase!=PLAYING_PHASE)return; //bail if not playing
      if(GamePaused)return; //bail if game is paused
      POINT point; //mouse location on screen
      decode(lparam,point); //decode mouse point
      //set extent
      SIZE extent; //extent that mouse moves in
      extent.cx=SCREEN_WIDTH;
      extent.cy=SCREEN_HEIGHT;
      //set plane speed based on point and extent
      set_plane_speed(point,extent);
    }

    //joystick handlers

    void CInputManager::GameJoystick(){
    //joystick handler for game play
      if(InputDevice!=JOYSTICK_INPUT)return; //bail if unneeded
      if(GamePaused)return; //bail if game is paused
      //buttons
      if(JoystickManager.button_down(1)) //button 1...
        Keyboard(VK_SPACE,TRUE); //...fires bullets
      //stick
      if(GamePhase!=PLAYING_PHASE)return; //bail if not playing
      POINT point; //coordinates of joystick
      JoystickManager.position(point); //get coordinates
      SIZE extent; //extent that joystick indicator moves in
      extent.cx=100; extent.cy=100; //set extent
      set_plane_speed(point,extent); //set plane speed
    }

    void CInputManager::IntroJoystick(){
    //joystick handler for intro
      if(JoystickManager.button_down(1)) //click out
        Keyboard(VK_ESCAPE);
    }
```

```
void CInputManager::HelpJoystick(){
//joystick handler for help
  if(JoystickManager.button_down(1))
    Keyboard(VK_SPACE); //next page
}

void CInputManager::Joystick(){ //main joystick handler
  JoystickManager.poll(); //poll joystick
  switch(GamePhase){ //call joystick handler for phase
    case PLAYING_PHASE: GameJoystick(); break;
    case LOGO_PHASE:
    case TITLE_PHASE:
    case CREDITS_PHASE:
    case SUCCESS_PHASE:
    case HIGHSCORE_PHASE:
      IntroJoystick(); break;
    case DEVICEMENU_PHASE:
    case MENU_PHASE:
      break; //do nothing
    case HELP_PHASE: HelpJoystick(); break;
  }
}

void CInputManager::unpause(){ //unpause the game
  GamePaused=FALSE;
  Timer.unpause(); //unpause the timer
  ((CGameSoundManager*)SoundManager)->unpause(); //and the sound
}

void CInputManager::pause(){ //unpause the game
  GamePaused=TRUE;
  Timer.pause(); //pause the timer
  ((CGameSoundManager*)SoundManager)->pause(); //and the sound
}
```

Main.cpp

```
//main.cpp

//Copyright Ian Parberry, 2000
//Last updated May 20, 2000

//Interrupting the game engine.  Pause key is F1.  When paused,
//the screen is frozen and the word "paused" is displayed on
//the screen.  Note that sounds are (approximately) paused too.
//Note also the use of the pause in the timer to make sure that
//objects don't move too far when the game is unpaused.

//The help button in the main menu now displays the help files.
```

```
//Can also break out of the game engine to see the device menu
//(F2), high score list (F3), help (F4). Frame rate is F5 now.

//system includes
#include <windows.h>
#include <windowsx.h>
#include <ddraw.h>
#include <stdio.h>

//system defines
#define WIN32_LEAN_AND_MEAN

//custom includes
#include "defines.h" //global definitions
#include "bmp.h" //bmp file reader
#include "gtimer.h" //game timer
#include "csprite.h" //for clipped sprite class
#include "objects.h" //for object class
#include "objman.h" //for object manager
#include "view.h" //for viewpoint class
#include "random.h" //for random number generator
#include "psound.h" //for sound manager
#include "input.h" //for input manager
#include "text.h" //for text sprite manager
#include "score.h" //for score manager
#include "topscore.h" //high score list

//defines
#define MAX_OBJECTS 32 //max number of objects in game

//globals

BOOL ActiveApp; //is this application active?

LPDIRECTDRAW lpDirectDrawObject=NULL; //direct draw object
LPDIRECTDRAWSURFACE lpPrimary=NULL; //primary surface
LPDIRECTDRAWPALETTE lpPrimaryPalette; //its palette
LPDIRECTDRAWSURFACE lpSecondary=NULL; //back buffer
LPDIRECTDRAWPALETTE lpSecondaryPalette; //its palette
LPDIRECTDRAWSURFACE lpBackground=NULL; //background image

CGameTimer Timer; //game timer

CBmpFileReader background; //background image
CBmpFileReader *NewHighScoreBg; //new-high-score background
CBmpSpriteFileReader g_cSpriteImages; //sprite images
CBmpSpriteFileReader g_cFrgndImages; //foreground images
CBmpSpriteFileReader g_cTextImages; //text images

CObjectManager ObjectManager(MAX_OBJECTS); //object manager
```

```
CClippedSprite *g_pSprite[NUM_SPRITES]; //sprites

CViewPoint Viewpoint; //player viewpoint
CRandom Random; //random number generator

GamePhaseType GamePhase; //current phase
GamePhaseType NextPhase; //next phase of game
BOOL endphase=FALSE; //should we abort current phase?
int PhaseTime=0; //time in phase
int level=1; //current level

BOOL show_framerate=FALSE; //TRUE to show the frame rate
int framerate_timer=0; //timer for updating frame rate display
int framecount=0; //number of frames in this interval (so far)
int last_framecount=0; //number of frames in last full interval

CSoundManager* SoundManager; //sound manager
CInputManager InputManager; //device input manager
CTextManager *Text; //text manager
CScoreManager ScoreManager; //score manager
CHighScoreList HighScoreList; //high score list manager

int HelpPage; //current page of help to be displayed
BOOL FlipHelpPage; //whether to flip help page
const int NUMHELPPAGES=6; //number of help pages
CClippedSprite *PausedSprite; //display word "Paused"
BOOL GamePaused=FALSE; //TRUE if game paused

//helper functions
LPDIRECTDRAWPALETTE CreatePalette(LPDIRECTDRAWSURFACE surface);
BOOL InitDirectDraw(HWND hwnd);
HWND CreateDefaultWindow(char* name,HINSTANCE hInstance);

BOOL LoadPlaneSprite(){
  BOOL result=TRUE;
  result=result&&g_pSprite[PLANE_OBJECT]->
    load(&g_cSpriteImages,0,1,1);
  result=result&&g_pSprite[PLANE_OBJECT]->
    load(&g_cSpriteImages,1,123,1);
  result=result&&g_pSprite[PLANE_OBJECT]->
    load(&g_cSpriteImages,2,245,1);
  result=result&&g_pSprite[PLANE_OBJECT]->
    load(&g_cSpriteImages,3,367,1);
  result=result&&g_pSprite[PLANE_OBJECT]->
    load(&g_cSpriteImages,4,489,1);
  result=result&&g_pSprite[PLANE_OBJECT]->
    load(&g_cSpriteImages,5,17,74);
  return result;
} //LoadPlaneSprite
```

```
BOOL LoadDamagedPlaneSprite(){
  BOOL result=TRUE;
  result=result&&g_pSprite[DAMAGEDPLANE_OBJECT]->
    load(&g_cSpriteImages,0,387,288);
  result=result&&g_pSprite[DAMAGEDPLANE_OBJECT]->
    load(&g_cSpriteImages,1,509,288);
  return result;
} //LoadDamagedPlaneSprite

BOOL LoadExplodingPlaneSprite(){
  BOOL result=TRUE;
  result=result&&g_pSprite[EXPLODINGPLANE_OBJECT]->
    load(&g_cSpriteImages,0,139,74);
  result=result&&g_pSprite[EXPLODINGPLANE_OBJECT]->
    load(&g_cSpriteImages,1,261,74);
  result=result&&g_pSprite[EXPLODINGPLANE_OBJECT]->
    load(&g_cSpriteImages,2,383,74);
  result=result&&g_pSprite[EXPLODINGPLANE_OBJECT]->
    load(&g_cSpriteImages,3,505,74);
  return result;
} //LoadExplodingPlaneSprite

BOOL LoadDeadPlaneSprite(){
  return g_pSprite[DEADPLANE_OBJECT]->
    load(&g_cSpriteImages,0,120,237);
} //LoadDeadPlaneSprite

BOOL LoadCrowSprite(){
  BOOL result=TRUE;
  result=result&&g_pSprite[CROW_OBJECT]->
    load(&g_cSpriteImages,0,256,183); //frame 0
  result=result&&g_pSprite[CROW_OBJECT]->
    load(&g_cSpriteImages,1,320,183); //frame 1
  result=result&&g_pSprite[CROW_OBJECT]->
    load(&g_cSpriteImages,2,256,237); //frame 2
  result=result&&g_pSprite[CROW_OBJECT]->
    load(&g_cSpriteImages,3,323,237); //frame 3
  return result;
} //LoadCrowSprite

BOOL LoadFrgndSprites(){ //load foreground sprites
  BOOL result=TRUE;
  result=result&&g_pSprite[FARM_OBJECT]->
    load(&g_cFrgndImages,0,0,0); //load farm sprite
  result=result&&g_pSprite[FIELD_OBJECT]->
    load(&g_cFrgndImages,0,640,0); //load field sprite
  return result;
} //LoadFrgndSprites
```

```
BOOL LoadDeadCrowSprite(){ //load dead crow
  return g_pSprite[DEADCROW_OBJECT]->
    load(&g_cSpriteImages,0,453,230);
} //LoadDeadCrowSprite

BOOL LoadExplodingCrowSprite(){ //load exploding crow
  BOOL result=TRUE;
  result=result&&g_pSprite[EXPLODINGCROW_OBJECT]->
    load(&g_cSpriteImages,0,257,294);
  result=result&&g_pSprite[EXPLODINGCROW_OBJECT]->
    load(&g_cSpriteImages,1,321,294);
  result=result&&g_pSprite[EXPLODINGCROW_OBJECT]->
    load(&g_cSpriteImages,2,386,162);
  result=result&&g_pSprite[EXPLODINGCROW_OBJECT]->
    load(&g_cSpriteImages,3,453,162);
  result=result&&g_pSprite[EXPLODINGCROW_OBJECT]->
    load(&g_cSpriteImages,4,386,230);
  result=result&&g_pSprite[EXPLODINGCROW_OBJECT]->
    load(&g_cSpriteImages,5,453,230);
  return result;
} //LoadExplodingCrowSprite

BOOL LoadBulletSprite(){ //load bullet
  return g_pSprite[BULLET_OBJECT]->
    load(&g_cSpriteImages,0,5,123);
} //LoadBulletSprite

BOOL LoadTextSprites(){ //load text sprites
  return Text->load(&g_cTextImages,1,102);
} //LoadTextSprites

BOOL LoadPausedSprite(){
  return PausedSprite->load(&g_cSpriteImages,0,399,403);
} //LoadPausedSprite

BOOL LoadImages(){ //load graphics from files to surfaces
  //get the background image
  if(!background.load("bckgnd.bmp"))return FALSE; //read file
  background.draw(lpBackground); //draw to background surface
  //set palettes in all surfaces
  if(!background.setpalette(lpPrimaryPalette))return FALSE;
  if(!background.setpalette(lpSecondaryPalette))return FALSE;
  //load the text sprites
  if(!g_cTextImages.load("text.bmp"))return FALSE;//read
  Text=new CTextManager(19,30); //text manager
  LoadTextSprites();
  //load the sprites...
  if(!g_cSpriteImages.load("sprites.bmp"))return FALSE;
  //...the plane
  g_pSprite[PLANE_OBJECT]=new CClippedSprite(6,121,72);
```

```
    if(!LoadPlaneSprite())return FALSE; //load plane images
    //...the damaged plane
    g_pSprite[DAMAGEDPLANE_OBJECT]=new CClippedSprite(2,121,72);
    LoadDamagedPlaneSprite();
    //...the exploding plane
    g_pSprite[EXPLODINGPLANE_OBJECT]=new CClippedSprite(4,121,72);
    LoadExplodingPlaneSprite();
    //...the dead plane
    g_pSprite[DEADPLANE_OBJECT]=new CClippedSprite(1,119,54);
    LoadDeadPlaneSprite();
    //...the crow
    g_pSprite[CROW_OBJECT]=new CClippedSprite(4,58,37);
    if(!LoadCrowSprite())return FALSE; //load crow images
    //..the dead crow
    g_pSprite[DEADCROW_OBJECT]=new CClippedSprite(1,62,53);
    LoadDeadCrowSprite(); //load dead crow images
    //...the exploding crow
    g_pSprite[EXPLODINGCROW_OBJECT]=new CClippedSprite(6,62,53);
    LoadExplodingCrowSprite(); //load exploding crow images
    //...the bullet
    g_pSprite[BULLET_OBJECT]=new CClippedSprite(1,5,3);
    LoadBulletSprite(); //load bullet images
    //...the paused sprite
    PausedSprite=new CClippedSprite(1,220,64);
    LoadPausedSprite();
    //...the foreground sprites
    if(!g_cFrgndImages.load("farm.bmp"))return FALSE;
    g_pSprite[FARM_OBJECT]=new CClippedSprite(1,640,162);
    g_pSprite[FIELD_OBJECT]=new CClippedSprite(1,640,162);
    if(!LoadFrgndSprites())return FALSE; //load foreground
    return TRUE;
} //LoadImages

void CreateObjects(){
    const int reserved=6; //reserved positions for nonvermin
    int crowcount=5+level*3; //number of crows per level
    int i;
    ObjectManager.create(FARM_OBJECT,0,SCREEN_HEIGHT-1,0,0);
    ObjectManager.create(FIELD_OBJECT,SCREEN_WIDTH,
        SCREEN_HEIGHT-1,0,0);
    //compute numbers of objects
    if(crowcount>MAX_OBJECTS-reserved)
        crowcount=MAX_OBJECTS-reserved;
    if(crowcount<0)crowcount=0;
    //create objects
    for(i=0; i<crowcount/2; i++)
        ObjectManager.create(CROW_OBJECT,
            Random.number(0,WORLD_WIDTH-1),
            Random.number(100,400),-1,0);
    ObjectManager.set_current(
```

```
        ObjectManager.create(PLANE_OBJECT,320,271,-1,0));
     for(i=0; i<crowcount-crowcount/2; i++)
        ObjectManager.create(CROW_OBJECT,
          Random.number(0,WORLD_WIDTH-1),
          Random.number(100,400),-1,0);
} //CreateObjects

BOOL RestoreSurfaces(){ //restore all surfaces
  BOOL result=TRUE;
  //primary and secondary surfaces
  if(FAILED(lpPrimary->Restore()))return FALSE;
  if(FAILED(lpSecondary->Restore()))return FALSE;
  //surfaces containing images
  if(SUCCEEDED(lpBackground->Restore())) //if background restored
    result=result&&background.draw(lpBackground); //redraw image
  else return FALSE;
  if(g_pSprite[PLANE_OBJECT]->Restore()) //if plane restored
    result=result&&LoadPlaneSprite(); //redraw image
  else return FALSE;
  if(g_pSprite[DAMAGEDPLANE_OBJECT]->Restore()) //if restored
    result=result&&LoadDamagedPlaneSprite(); //redraw image
  else return FALSE;
  if(g_pSprite[EXPLODINGPLANE_OBJECT]->Restore()) //if restored
    result=result&&LoadExplodingPlaneSprite(); //redraw image
  else return FALSE;
  if(g_pSprite[DEADPLANE_OBJECT]->Restore()) //if restored
    result=result&&LoadDeadPlaneSprite(); //redraw image
  else return FALSE;
  if(g_pSprite[CROW_OBJECT]->Restore()) //if crow restored
    result=result&&LoadCrowSprite(); //redraw image
  else return FALSE;
  if(g_pSprite[DEADCROW_OBJECT]->Restore()) //if restored
    result=result&&LoadDeadCrowSprite(); //redraw image
  else return FALSE;
  if(g_pSprite[EXPLODINGCROW_OBJECT]->Restore()) //if restored
    result=result&&LoadExplodingCrowSprite(); //redraw image
  else return FALSE;
  if(g_pSprite[BULLET_OBJECT]->Restore()) //if restored
    result=result&&LoadBulletSprite(); //redraw image
  else return FALSE;
  if(PausedSprite->Restore()) //if restored
    result=result&&LoadPausedSprite(); //redraw image
  else return FALSE;
  if(g_pSprite[FARM_OBJECT]->Restore()&& //if farm and ...
    g_pSprite[FIELD_OBJECT]->Restore()) //... field restored
    result=result&&LoadFrgndSprites(); //redraw image
  else return FALSE;
  //input manager has button sprites
  if(!InputManager.Restore())return FALSE;
  //text manager has text sprites
```

```cpp
    if(Text->Restore())
      result=result&&LoadTextSprites();
    else return FALSE;
    return result;
} //RestoreSurfaces

void LoadSounds(int level=0){ //load sounds for level
  const int copies=4; //copies of repeatable sounds
  switch(level){
    case 0: //intro sounds
      SoundManager->load("intro.wav");
      SoundManager->load("larc.wav");
      SoundManager->load("credits.wav");
      break;
    case 1: //game engine sounds
      SoundManager->load("caw.wav",copies);
      SoundManager->load("gun.wav",copies);
      SoundManager->load("boom.wav",copies);
      SoundManager->load("thump.wav",copies);
      SoundManager->load("putt0.wav");
      SoundManager->load("putt1.wav");
      SoundManager->load("putt2.wav");
      SoundManager->load("bgclk.wav",2);
      SoundManager->load("smclk.wav",2);
      SoundManager->load("success.wav");
      SoundManager->load("failed.wav");
      SoundManager->load("life.wav");
      SoundManager->load("stings.wav");
      SoundManager->load("smarts.wav");
      SoundManager->load("congrats.wav");
      SoundManager->load("twspace.wav",copies);
      SoundManager->load("twret.wav",copies);
      SoundManager->load("twchar.wav",copies);
      SoundManager->load("pageturn.wav",2);
      break;
  }
}

BOOL PageFlip(){ //return TRUE if page flip succeeds
  if(lpPrimary->Flip(NULL,DDFLIP_WAIT)==DDERR_SURFACELOST)
    return RestoreSurfaces();
  return TRUE;
} //PageFlip

int chars_in_number(int n){ //return number of chars
  if(n==0)return 1; //0 has one character
  int count=0; //count of number of characters
  n=abs(n); //positive numbers only
  while(n>0){n/=10; count++;} //tally number of chars
  return count;
```

```
} //chars_in_number

void draw_number(int n,int center,
    LPDIRECTDRAWSURFACE surface,BOOL middle=FALSE){
  const int HALF_CHAR_WIDTH=10;
  char buffer[64]; //for display on screen
  char buffer2[16]; //temp buffer
  int margin=7;
  int width=chars_in_number(n); //width of number in chars
  for(int i=0; i<center-width/2-1; i++)
    buffer[i]=' '; //shift right
  buffer[i]=0; //end of string
  sprintf(buffer2,"%d",n);
  strcat(buffer,buffer2); //n to buffer
  //adjust to center
  if(!(width&1))margin+=HALF_CHAR_WIDTH;
  if(middle)margin-=HALF_CHAR_WIDTH;
  //draw
  Text->jump(margin,75); //start of line
  Text->draw(buffer,surface); //print number
}

void draw_text_header(LPDIRECTDRAWSURFACE surface){
  const int margin=7;
  Text->jump(margin,40);
  Text->draw("level varmints score health lives",surface);
  draw_number(level,3,surface);
  draw_number(ObjectManager.enemies(),11,surface,TRUE);
  draw_number(ScoreManager.score(),18,surface);
  draw_number(ScoreManager.health(),25,surface,TRUE);
  draw_number(ScoreManager.lives(),31,surface);
}

BOOL ComposeFrame(){ //compose a frame of animation
  Viewpoint.draw_background(lpBackground,lpSecondary,
    ObjectManager.speed()); //draw scrolling background
  ObjectManager.animate(lpSecondary); //draw objects
  draw_text_header(lpSecondary); //draw text header
  if(show_framerate){ //if we need to show the frame count
    char buffer[4];
    if(!GamePaused)framecount++; //count frame
    if(Timer.elapsed(framerate_timer,1000)){
      last_framecount=framecount; framecount=0;
    }
    Text->jump(580,470);
    sprintf(buffer,"%d",last_framecount);
    Text->draw(buffer,lpSecondary);
  }
  //display word "paused" if game is paused
  if(GamePaused)PausedSprite->draw(0,320,200,lpSecondary);
```

```
      return TRUE;
    } //ComposeFrame

void display_screen(char *filename){ //display bmp file
  CBmpFileReader image; //file reader
  image.load(filename); //load from file
  image.draw(lpSecondary); //draw to back buffer
  image.setpalette(lpPrimaryPalette); //may have custom palette
  PageFlip(); //display it
 //draw to back buffer again for button animation
  image.draw(lpSecondary);
} //display_screen

void display_highscorelist(char *filename){ //display high scores
  display_screen(filename); //display background
  HighScoreList.draw(lpSecondary); //draw high scores
  PageFlip(); //flip to front surface
} //display_highscorelist

void display_newhighscore(){ //display new high score entry page
  Sleep(50); //slow down the animation
  NewHighScoreBg->draw(lpSecondary); //draw background
  //draw text
  Text->jump(163,330);
  Text->draw(HighScoreList.current_name(),lpSecondary);
  PageFlip(); //display it
} //display_newhighscore

void change_phase(GamePhaseType new_phase){ //go to new phase
  switch(new_phase){
    case LOGO_PHASE:
      display_screen("larc.bmp");
      LoadSounds(); //load sounds for intro sequence
      SoundManager->play(LOGO_SOUND); //signature chord
      break;
    case TITLE_PHASE:
      display_screen("title.bmp");
      SoundManager->stop(); //silence previous phase
      SoundManager->play(TITLE_SOUND); //title sound
      break;
    case CREDITS_PHASE:
      display_screen("credits.bmp");
      SoundManager->stop(); //silence previous phase
      SoundManager->play(CREDITS_SOUND); //credits sound
      break;
    case MENU_PHASE:
      //set up buttons for menu
      InputManager.SetupButtons(MENU_PHASE);
      //sound
      switch(GamePhase){ //depending on previous phase
```

```
      case CREDITS_PHASE: //from intro phase
        SoundManager->stop(); //silence previous phase
        SoundManager->clear(); //clear out old sounds
        LoadSounds(1); //set up game sounds
        break;
      case PLAYING_PHASE: //from game engine
        SoundManager->stop(); //silence game engine
        if(ScoreManager.lives()<0)
          SoundManager->play(FAILED_SOUND);
        break;
      case DEVICEMENU_PHASE: //device menu, do nothing
        break;
      case NEWHIGHSCORE_PHASE:
        delete NewHighScoreBg; //delete background
        break;
    }
    //display background
    display_screen("menu.bmp"); //display main menu
    //mouse cursor
    switch(GamePhase){ //what phase did we come in from?
      case PLAYING_PHASE:
      case CREDITS_PHASE:
      case HIGHSCORE_PHASE:
      case NEWHIGHSCORE_PHASE:
      case HELP_PHASE:
        ShowCursor(TRUE); //activate the mouse cursor
        break;
    }
    break;
  case DEVICEMENU_PHASE:
    //display button background
    display_screen("dmenu.bmp");
    //set up the button manager
    InputManager.SetupButtons(DEVICEMENU_PHASE);
    if(GamePhase==PLAYING_PHASE)ShowCursor(TRUE);
    break;
  case HELP_PHASE: //display first help page
    if(GamePhase==MENU_PHASE)ShowCursor(FALSE);
    display_screen("help000.bmp"); //show first page
    HelpPage=0; FlipHelpPage=FALSE; //reset to first page
    break;
  case PLAYING_PHASE: //prepare the game engine
    //mouse cursor
    SetCursorPos(SCREEN_WIDTH-1,SCREEN_HEIGHT/2); //throttle
    switch(GamePhase){//depending on previous phase
      case MENU_PHASE:
        SoundManager->stop(); //silence previous phase
        ShowCursor(FALSE); //deactivate the mouse cursor
        level=1; ScoreManager.reset(); //reset score
        //create objects in game engine
```

```
        ObjectManager.reset(); //clear object manager
        CreateObjects(); //create new objects
        break;
      case SUCCESS_PHASE:
        SoundManager->stop(); //silence previous phase
        level++; //go to next level
        //add score for level completion
        ScoreManager.add_to_score(LEVEL_BONUS_SCORE);
        //create objects in game engine
        ObjectManager.reset(); //clear object manager
        CreateObjects(); //create new objects
        break;
      case DEVICEMENU_PHASE:
        ShowCursor(FALSE);
        InputManager.unpause();
        break;
      case HIGHSCORE_PHASE:
      case HELP_PHASE:
        InputManager.unpause();
        break;
    }
    //initialize graphics
    background.setpalette(lpPrimaryPalette); //game palette
    ComposeFrame(); PageFlip(); //prime animation pump
    break;
  case SUCCESS_PHASE: //successful completion of level
    SoundManager->stop(); //stop sounds from previous phase
    SoundManager->play(SUCCESS_SOUND); //jubilation
    display_screen("success.bmp"); //display success screen
    break;
  case HIGHSCORE_PHASE: //display high score list
    if(GamePhase==MENU_PHASE)ShowCursor(FALSE); //hide cursor
    display_highscorelist("hscore.bmp"); //display high scores
    break;
  case NEWHIGHSCORE_PHASE: //display high score list
    SoundManager->stop(); //stop sounds from previous phase
    SoundManager->play(CONGRATS_SOUND); //play new sound
    NewHighScoreBg=new CBmpFileReader; //background
    NewHighScoreBg->load("newhsc.bmp"); //read from file
    NewHighScoreBg->draw(lpSecondary); //draw to back surface
    NewHighScoreBg->setpalette(lpPrimaryPalette); //palette
    PageFlip(); //display it
    break;
  }
  //change to new phase
  GamePhase=new_phase; PhaseTime=Timer.time();
  endphase=FALSE;
} //change_phase

void display_helpscreen(){
```

```cpp
  //construct help file name
  char filename[16];
  strcpy(filename,"help000.bmp");
  filename[6]='0'+HelpPage;
  //display the help file
  display_screen(filename);
}

void Redraw(){ //redraw in response to surface loss
  switch(GamePhase){
    case LOGO_PHASE:
      display_screen("larc.bmp");
      break;
    case TITLE_PHASE:
      display_screen("title.bmp");
      break;
    case CREDITS_PHASE:
      display_screen("credits.bmp");
      break;
    case MENU_PHASE:
      display_screen("menu.bmp"); //display main menu
      break;
    case PLAYING_PHASE:
      //do nothing, next frame of animation will catch it
      break;
    case DEVICEMENU_PHASE:
      display_screen("dmenu.bmp");
      InputManager.SetupButtons(DEVICEMENU_PHASE);
      break;
    case SUCCESS_PHASE:
      display_screen("success.bmp"); //display success screen
      break;
    case HIGHSCORE_PHASE:
      display_highscorelist("hscore.bmp"); //display high scores
      break;
    case NEWHIGHSCORE_PHASE:
      NewHighScoreBg->setpalette(lpPrimaryPalette); //palette
      display_newhighscore();
      break;
    case HELP_PHASE:
      display_helpscreen();
      break;
  }
}

void ProcessFrame(){ //process a frame of animation
  const int LOGO_DISPLAY_TIME=8500; //duration of logo
  const int TITLE_DISPLAY_TIME=10000; //duration of title
  const int CREDITS_DISPLAY_TIME=8000; //duration of credits
  const int SUCCESS_DISPLAY_TIME=4500; //duration of success
```

```
InputManager.Joystick(); //process joystick input
//check for lost surfaces, eg alt+tab
if(lpPrimary->IsLost()){
  RestoreSurfaces(); Redraw();
}
//phase-related processing
switch(GamePhase){ //what phase are we in?
  case LOGO_PHASE: //displaying logo screen
    Sleep(100); //surrender time to other processes
    if(endphase||Timer.elapsed(PhaseTime,LOGO_DISPLAY_TIME))
      change_phase(TITLE_PHASE); //go to title screen
    break;
  case TITLE_PHASE: //displaying title screen
    Sleep(100); //surrender time to other processes
    if(endphase||Timer.elapsed(PhaseTime,TITLE_DISPLAY_TIME))
      change_phase(CREDITS_PHASE); //go to credits
    break;
  case CREDITS_PHASE: //displaying title screen
    Sleep(100); //surrender time to other processes
    if(endphase||Timer.elapsed(PhaseTime,CREDITS_DISPLAY_TIME))
      change_phase(MENU_PHASE); //go to menu
    break;
  case MENU_PHASE: //main menu
    Sleep(100); //surrender time to other processes
    if(endphase)change_phase(NextPhase); //change phase
    break;
  case DEVICEMENU_PHASE:
    if(endphase)
      if(GamePaused)change_phase(PLAYING_PHASE); //resume
      else change_phase(MENU_PHASE); //go to menu phase
    break;
  case PLAYING_PHASE: //game engine
    if(GamePaused)Sleep(100); //be nice if paused
    ComposeFrame(); //compose a frame in back surface
    PageFlip(); //flip video memory surfaces
    if(ObjectManager.won()) //completed level
      change_phase(SUCCESS_PHASE);
    else if(endphase){ //stop playing
      //mouse to screen center
      SetCursorPos(SCREEN_WIDTH/2,SCREEN_HEIGHT/2);
      if(GamePaused)change_phase(NextPhase); //in a menu
      else{ //quit or died, check for new high score
        if(ScoreManager.lives()>=0&&
      HighScoreList.made_the_grade(ScoreManager.score()))
          change_phase(NEWHIGHSCORE_PHASE); //user enters name
        else change_phase(MENU_PHASE); //quit, go to menu
      }
    }
    break;
  case SUCCESS_PHASE: //displaying title screen
```

```
      Sleep(100); //surrender time to other processes
      if(endphase|| //if end of phase
      Timer.elapsed(PhaseTime,SUCCESS_DISPLAY_TIME))
        change_phase(PLAYING_PHASE); //start playing
      break;
    case HIGHSCORE_PHASE: //displaying high scores
      Sleep(100); //surrender time to other processes
      if(endphase)
        if(GamePaused)change_phase(PLAYING_PHASE); //back to game
        else change_phase(MENU_PHASE); //quit, go to menu
      break;
    case NEWHIGHSCORE_PHASE:
      display_newhighscore(); //animate user typing in name
      if(endphase){ //insert new high score
        HighScoreList.insert(level,ScoreManager.score());
        change_phase(MENU_PHASE); //go to menu
      }
      break;
    case HELP_PHASE: //display help
      if(FlipHelpPage){ //turn the page
        FlipHelpPage=FALSE; //don't do it again
        if(++HelpPage>=NUMHELPPAGES)endphase=TRUE; //last page
        else{ //next page
          SoundManager->play(PAGETURN_SOUND); //page flip sound
          display_helpscreen(); //display help screen
        }
      }
      if(endphase) //clicked out
        if(GamePaused)change_phase(PLAYING_PHASE); //back to game
        else change_phase(MENU_PHASE); //quit, go to menu
      break;
  }
} //ProcessFrame

//message handler (window procedure)
long CALLBACK WindowProc(HWND hwnd,UINT message,
                         WPARAM wParam,LPARAM lParam){
  switch(message){
    case WM_ACTIVATEAPP:
      ActiveApp=wParam;
      //pause if swapped out while playing
      if(!ActiveApp&&GamePhase==PLAYING_PHASE&&!GamePaused)
        InputManager.pause();
      break;
    case WM_CREATE: break;
    case WM_KEYDOWN: //keyboard hit
      if(InputManager.Keyboard(wParam))
        DestroyWindow(hwnd);
      break;
    case WM_LBUTTONDOWN: //left mouse button down
```

```
        InputManager.LMouseDown(lParam); //handle it
        break;
      case WM_LBUTTONUP: //left mouse button up
        if(InputManager.LMouseUp(lParam))
          DestroyWindow(hwnd);
        break;
      case WM_MOUSEMOVE: //mouse move
        InputManager.MouseMove(lParam);
        break;
      case WM_DESTROY: //end of game
        ObjectManager.reset(); //clear objects
        if(lpDirectDrawObject!=NULL){ //if DD object exists
          if(lpSecondary!=NULL) //if secondary surface exists
            lpSecondary->Release(); //release secondary surface
          if(lpPrimary!=NULL) //if primary surface exists
            lpPrimary->Release(); //release primary surface
          if(lpBackground!=NULL) //if background exists
            lpBackground->Release(); //release background
          for(int i=0; i<NUM_SPRITES; i++){ //for each sprite
            if(g_pSprite[i]) //if sprite exists
              g_pSprite[i]->Release(); //release sprite
            delete g_pSprite[i]; //delete sprite
          }
          InputManager.Release(); //button surfaces
          Text->Release();  //release text manager sprites
          PausedSprite->Release(); delete PausedSprite;
          lpDirectDrawObject->Release(); //release DD object
        }
        delete SoundManager; //reclaim sound manager memory
        delete Text; //reclaim text manager memory
        ShowCursor(TRUE); //show the mouse cursor
        PostQuitMessage(0); //and exit
        break;
      default: //default window procedure
        return DefWindowProc(hwnd,message,wParam,lParam);
    } //switch(message)
    return 0L;
} //WindowProc

int WINAPI WinMain(HINSTANCE hInstance,HINSTANCE hPrevInstance,
LPSTR lpCmdLine,int nCmdShow){
  MSG msg; //current message
  HWND hwnd; //handle to fullscreen window
  hwnd=CreateDefaultWindow("directX demo 13",hInstance);
  if(!hwnd)return FALSE;
  //set up window
  ShowWindow(hwnd,nCmdShow); UpdateWindow(hwnd);
  SetFocus(hwnd); //allow input from keyboard
  ShowCursor(FALSE); //hide the cursor
  //init graphics
```

```
      for(int i=0; i<NUM_SPRITES; i++) //null out sprites
        g_pSprite[i]=NULL;
      BOOL OK=InitDirectDraw(hwnd);//initialize DirectDraw
      if(OK)OK=LoadImages(); //load images from disk
      if(!OK){ //bail out if initialization failed
        DestroyWindow(hwnd); return FALSE;
      }
      //start game timer
      Timer.start();
      //init sound
      SoundManager=new CGameSoundManager(hwnd);
      //set initial phase
      change_phase(LOGO_PHASE);
      //message loop
      while(TRUE)
        if(PeekMessage(&msg,NULL,0,0,PM_NOREMOVE)){
          if(!GetMessage(&msg,NULL,0,0))return msg.wParam;
          TranslateMessage(&msg); DispatchMessage(&msg);
        }
        else if(ActiveApp)ProcessFrame(); else WaitMessage();
    } //WinMain
```

Psound.h

```
//psound.h: header class for psound.cpp
//CGameSoundManager extends CSoundManager by allowing pause
//Copyright Ian Parberry, 2000
//Last updated March 14, 2000

#ifndef __PSOUND__
#define __PSOUND__

#include "sound.h" //simple sound manager

class CGameSoundManager:public CSoundManager{
  //game sound manager - can be paused
  private:
    BOOL *m_bPausedPlaying[MAX_SOUNDS]; //paused while playing
    BOOL *m_bPausedLooping[MAX_SOUNDS]; //paused while looping
    BOOL CreateBuffer(int index,int length,int copies);
  public:
    CGameSoundManager(HWND hwnd); //constructor
    void clear(); //clear all sounds
    void pause(int index); //pause sound
    void pause(void); //pause all sounds
    void unpause(int index); //unpause sound
    void unpause(void); //unpause all sounds
};

#endif
```

Psound.cpp

```
//psound.cpp: pausable sound manager

//Copyright Ian Parberry, 2000
//Last updated March 14, 2000

#include "psound.h"

CGameSoundManager::CGameSoundManager(HWND hwnd):
CSoundManager(hwnd){ //constructor
  for(int i=0; i<MAX_SOUNDS; i++)
    m_bPausedPlaying[i]=m_bPausedLooping[i]=NULL;
}

void CGameSoundManager::clear(){ //clear all sounds
  CSoundManager::clear();
  for(int i=0; i<m_nCount; i++){ //for each sound
    delete[]m_bPausedPlaying[i];
    delete[]m_bPausedLooping[i];
  }
}

BOOL CGameSoundManager::CreateBuffer(int index,int length,
                                     int copies){
  //create and initialize pause flags
  m_bPausedPlaying[index]=new BOOL[copies];
  m_bPausedLooping[index]=new BOOL[copies];
  for(int i=0; i<copies; i++) //initialize them
    m_bPausedPlaying[index][i]=m_bPausedLooping[index][i]=FALSE;
  //create sound buffers
  return CSoundManager::CreateBuffer(index,length,copies);
}

void CGameSoundManager::pause(int index){ //pause sound
  if(!m_bOperational)return; //bail if not initialized correctly
  if(index<0||index>=m_nCount)return; //bail if bad index
  DWORD dwStatus=0; //to save status of sound copy
  for(int i=0; i<m_nCopyCount[index]; i++){ //for each copy
    //record status for later unpausing
    if(SUCCEEDED(m_lpBuffer[index][i]->GetStatus(&dwStatus))){
      if(dwStatus&DSBSTATUS_LOOPING){ //looping
        m_bPausedLooping[index][i]=TRUE;
        m_bPausedPlaying[index][i]=FALSE;
      }
      else if(dwStatus&DSBSTATUS_PLAYING){ //playing not looping
        m_bPausedLooping[index][i]=FALSE;
        m_bPausedPlaying[index][i]=TRUE;
      }
      else{ //not playing
```

```
            m_bPausedLooping[index][i]=FALSE;
            m_bPausedPlaying[index][i]=FALSE;
        }
    }
    else{ //if data is invalid, assume not in use
      m_bPausedLooping[index][i]=FALSE;
      m_bPausedPlaying[index][i]=FALSE;
    }
    //stop sound copy (stays at same place in sound)
    m_lpBuffer[index][i]->Stop(); //stop playing
  }
}

void CGameSoundManager::pause(void){ //pause all sounds
  if(!m_bOperational)return; //bail if not initialized correctly
  for(int i=0; i<m_nCount; i++)pause(i); //pause them all
}

void CGameSoundManager::unpause(int index){ //unpause sound
  if(!m_bOperational)return; //bail if not initialized correctly
  if(index<0||index>=m_nCount)return; //bail if bad index
  for(int i=0; i<m_nCopyCount[index]; i++) //for each copy
    if(m_bPausedPlaying[index][i]) //was paused while playing
      m_lpBuffer[index][i]->Play(0,0,0); //restart playing
    else if(m_bPausedLooping[index][i]) //was paused looping
      m_lpBuffer[index][i]->Play(0,0,DSBPLAY_LOOPING); //so loop
}

void CGameSoundManager::unpause(void){ //unpause all sounds
  if(!m_bOperational)return; //bail if not initialized correctly
  for(int i=0; i<m_nCount; i++)unpause(i); //unpause them all
}
```

Sndlist.h

```
//sndlist.h: list of sound definitions

//Copyright Ian Parberry, 1999
//Last updated March 14, 2000

#ifndef __SNDLIST__
#define __SNDLIST__

#define LOOP_SOUND TRUE

enum GameSoundType{ //sounds used in game engine
  CAW_SOUND=0, //sound a crow makes
  GUN_SOUND, //sound of gun firing
  BOOM_SOUND, //sound of explosion
  THUMP_SOUND, //sound of object hitting the ground
```

```
    //next 3 sounds must be consecutive and in this order
    SLOWPUTT_SOUND, //sound of slow engine
    MEDIUMPUTT_SOUND, //sound of medium engine
    FASTPUTT_SOUND, //sound of fast engine
    //mouse clicks
    BIGCLICK_SOUND, //loud click
    SMALLCLICK_SOUND, //soft click
    //more game sounds
    SUCCESS_SOUND, //completion of level
    FAILED_SOUND, //sound of failing
    NEWLIFE_SOUND, //sound of getting a new life
    STINGS_SOUND, //that stings (damage)
    SMARTS_SOUND, //that smarts (damage)
    //sounds for high score list
    CONGRATS_SOUND, //congratulations
    TYPE_SPACE_SOUND, //typewriter typing a space
    TYPE_RETURN_SOUND, //typewriter typing a return
    TYPE_CHAR_SOUND, //typewriter typing a character
    PAGETURN_SOUND, //sound of page being turned
};

enum IntroSoundType{ //sounds used during the intro
    TITLE_SOUND=0, //sound used during title screen
    LOGO_SOUND, //signature chord
    CREDITS_SOUND, //played during credits
};

#endif
```

Sound.h

```
//sound.h: header class for sound.cpp
//CSoundManager allows you to play multiple copies of each
//sound simultaneously

//Copyright Ian Parberry, 1999
//Last updated November 2, 1999

#ifndef __SOUND__
#define __SOUND__

#include <dsound.h> //DirectSound
#include "sndlist.h" //list of sound names

#define MAX_SOUNDS 64 //maximum number of different sounds

#define DS_NUMCHANNELS 8 //number of channels
#define DS_CHANSPERSAMPLE 1 //mono sound
#define DS_BITSPERSAMPLE 8 //8-bit sound
#define DS_SAMPLERATE 22050 //22KHz sampling
```

```
class CSoundManager{ //sound manager
  protected:
    int m_nCount; //number of sounds loaded
    LPLPDIRECTSOUNDBUFFER m_lpBuffer[MAX_SOUNDS]; //sound buffers
    int m_nCopyCount[MAX_SOUNDS]; //num copies of each sound
    BOOL m_bOperational; //DirectSound initialized correctly
    virtual BOOL CreateBuffer(int index,int length,int copies);
  private:
    LPDIRECTSOUND m_lpDirectSound; //directSound object
    BOOL LoadBuffer(int index,BYTE *buffer,int length);
    int LoadSound(char *filename,BYTE **sound); //load from file
    BOOL CopyBuffer(int index,int copies); //copy sound
  public:
    CSoundManager(HWND hwnd); //constructor
    ~CSoundManager(); //destructor
    virtual void clear(); //clear all sounds
    void load(char *filename,int copies=1); //load from file
    void play(int index,BOOL looping=FALSE); //play sound
    void stop(int index); //stop playing sound
    void stop(void); //stop playing all sounds
};

#endif
```

Postscript

It's almost 9 P.M. in Denton, Texas. I've been teaching game programming for almost three hours into the evening of a long, long day. The students filter out of the classroom in small groups; some are elated, some subdued, some simply stunned. Tired, I wait for the last one to leave so I can go home and write code. He is very young, unsure of himself. Hesitatingly, he approaches me at the front of the classroom, unwilling to meet my eyes directly. Looking around quickly to make sure we are alone, he haltingly addresses me.

"Ummm, you know, the code you showed us tonight, the overall design... I've been thinking..." Red-faced, he searches for the right words and stumbles on.

"I wouldn't do it that way at all. If you do it *this* way it's much better... "

At the end of his explanation he meets my eyes, his shyness overcome for a moment by the need to show that his way of coding is not just *better*; it's elegant, it's logical, it makes everything fall into place. But he's still not completely sure I won't slap him down for Daring to Criticize The Professor.

But I smile. "Grasshopper," I say, "now it is time for you to leave."

For a moment he is taken aback, but then he smiles as he recognizes the mangled quote from a 1970s-era TV program that he has seen only in reruns.

So, Grasshopper, is it time for *you* to leave?

Index

559

I don't have time for learning curves.

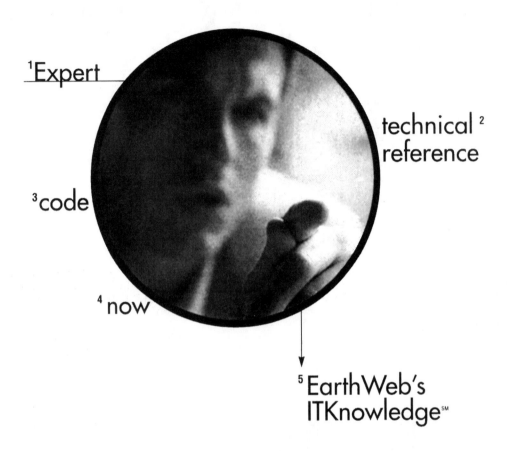

[1]Expert

technical [2]
reference

[3]code

[4] now

[5] EarthWeb's
ITKnowledge℠

They rely on you to be the **❶** expert on tough development challenges. There's no time for learning curves, so you go online for **❷** technical references from the experts who wrote the books. Find answers fast simply by clicking on our search engine. Access hundreds of online books, tutorials and even source **❸** code samples **❹** now. Go to **❺** EarthWeb's ITKnowledge, get immediate answers, and get down to it.

Get your FREE ITKnowledge trial subscription today at itkgo.com.
Use code number 026.

EARTHWEB
Go further *faster*

About the CD

The companion CD-ROM contains the example game *Ned's Turkey Farm*, in addition to the DirectX 7.0a SDK and an electronic version of this book in pdf format.

To load the game files, simply insert the CD into your CD drive. It should autorun. If it doesn't, open the CD drive with Explorer, double-click the Setup.exe icon, and follow the instructions.

To load the DirectX 7.0a SDK, be sure to check the DirectX checkbox in the final dialog box of the *Ned's Turkey Farm* setup.

For more information about the CD files, see Chapter 1.

Warning: Opening the CD package makes this book non-returnable.